Adobe® Premiere® Pro
CS3 Bible

Adobe® Premiere® Pro CS3 Bible

Adele Droblas
Seth Greenberg

1807
WILEY
2007

Wiley Publishing, Inc.

Adobe® Premiere® Pro CS3 Bible

Published by
Wiley Publishing, Inc.
10475 Crosspoint Boulevard
Indianapolis, IN 46256
www.wiley.com

Copyright © 2008 by Wiley Publishing, Inc., Indianapolis, Indiana

Published simultaneously in Canada

ISBN: 978-0-470-13064-3

Manufactured in the United States of America

10 9 8 7 6 5 4 3 2 1

For general information on our other products and services or to obtain technical support, please contact our Customer Care Department within the U.S. at (800) 762-2974, outside the U.S. at (317) 572-3993 or fax (317) 572-4002.

Library of Congress Control Number: 2007936466

About the Authors

Adele Droblas is an artist. For more information about Adele, go to www.BonitaVida.com.

Seth Greenberg is a computer consultant, programmer, and author. He has worked as an interactive project manager, television producer, and scriptwriter.

To our family and to Angelique and Laurence,
The stars of our videos,
Who make every day and every night shine.

Credits

Acquisitions Editor
Kim Spilker

Project Editor
Chris Wolfgang

Technical Editor
Alan Hamill

Copy Editor
Marylouise Wiack

Editorial Manager
Robyn Siesky

Business Manager
Amy Knies

Vice President and Executive Group Publisher
Richard Swadley

Vice President and Executive Publisher
Bob Ipsen

Vice President and Publisher
Barry Pruett

Project Coordinator
Kristie Rees

Graphics and Production Specialists
Stacie Brooks
Carrie A. Cesavice
Joyce Haughey
Jennifer Mayberry
Ronald Terry

Quality Control Technicians
Cynthia Fields
John Greenough

Media Development Project Supervisor
Laura Moss-Hollister

Media Development Specialist
Josh Frank

Proofreading and Indexing
Ty Koontz
Christine Sabooni

Preface

As you read these words, a revolution in desktop video is taking place. A main cause of this is the ever-growing popularity of the digital video camera, which digitizes high-quality video directly in the camera. After the signal is digitized, it can transfer directly over a cable to a personal computer. After your computer gets hold of the video, you need Adobe Premiere Pro CS3 to help you creatively shape it into a compelling desktop video production.

Adobe Premiere Pro CS3 combines power and ease of use to provide a complete authoring environment for producing desktop digital video productions. By using Premiere Pro CS3, you can capture video directly from your camcorder into Premiere Pro CS3's capture window. After you've captured or imported video and sound, you can assemble your clips into a production by simply clicking and dragging a video clip from one window to another. Placing clips and reassembling them is almost as easy as snapping together the cars in a child's toy train set. Creating transitions that dissolve one scene into another or wipe one scene away to reveal another is simply a matter of dragging an icon representing the transition between the two clips. To fine-tune your work, Premiere Pro CS3 provides numerous digital-editing tools. After you've finished editing, you can output your digital movie with settings for the Web, videotape, or DVD. If you've ever tried creating a video production by using traditional videotape hardware, Adobe Premiere Pro CS3 can revolutionize the way you work.

Acknowledgments

Thanks to Adobe Systems for creating products that allow us to express our creative visions. Thanks in particular to these people at Adobe Systems: Jason Levine, Bruce Bowman, Steve Kilisky, Vishal Khandpur, Wendy Kuramoto, Charat Maheshwari, Vinay Krishan Sharma, Silas Lepcha, Kevin Coleman, Jill Devlin, Peter Green, Ron Day, Philip Guindi, Michael Natkin, Chris Prosser, Mike Hogan, Mike Downey, Mally Gardiner, and Richard Galvan.

Thanks to everyone at Wiley Publishing, Inc., especially to acquisitions editor Kimberly Spilker who helped get *Adobe Premiere Pro CS3 Bible* off the ground. Thanks also to project editor Chris Wolfgang for keeping the editorial process well organized and flowing smoothly. Thanks to copy editor Marylouise Wiack for doing such a careful and meticulous job. Thanks, too, to Kristie Rees, the production coordinator, and the graphics department for their help with the book. For their help in putting the DVD together, we thank Laura Moss-Hollister and Josh Frank. Thanks especially to Alan Hamill for his job in tech editing *Adobe Premiere Pro CS3 Bible*.

Thanks to Julie Hill from Artbeats, and Jimmy and Lorrie from FilmDisc for supplying us with digital stock video clips for use on the DVD that accompanies the book. Thanks to Brian Dickman from Smartsound for supplying us with digital stock sound clips for use on the DVD of this book.

Thanks to all the people (family; friends, especially our musician and computer friends; the children of today, who are the future; and to all those we have met who radiate peace and happiness) who have touched our lives and inspired us to want to capture those wonderful moments that life has to offer. Hopefully, *Adobe Premiere Pro CS3 Bible* will help capture those special moments in your life and allow you to share them with friends and loved ones.

We hope you enjoy *Adobe Premiere Pro CS3 Bible*.

Contents at a Glance

Contents

Contents

Contents

Contents

Contents

Contents

Contents

Contents

Who Should Read This Book

Adobe Premiere Pro CS3 Bible is for video producers, video editors, filmmakers, multimedia producers, Web designers, graphic designers, artists — anyone interested in using a computer to create desktop video productions or to output desktop video to videotape, DVD, or the Web. As you read through *Adobe Premiere Pro CS3 Bible,* you can quickly see that it is more than just a reference to virtually all the features in Adobe Premiere Pro. The book is filled with short tutorial exercises that help you understand concepts and put into practice the key Premiere Pro features covered in a chapter. This book will prove indispensable as you learn to use Adobe Premiere Pro CS3 (and a useful reference book after you've mastered Premiere Pro CS3's key features). So don't wait another moment — start reading and learning what you can do with your creative visions.

How This Book Is Organized

If you read *Adobe Premiere Pro CS3 Bible*'s chapters in order, you'll gradually become an expert at using Adobe Premiere Pro. However, we expect that most readers will jump in and out of chapters as needed or as their interest moves from subject to subject. Throughout the book, we've included numerous step-by-step tutorials to guide you through the process of creating video sequences by using many Adobe Premiere Pro features. As you work, many clips on the DVD can aid you in quickly and efficiently creating short examples that illustrate and help explain chapter topics.

 **For updated information on Adobe Premiere Pro, be sure to visit Adobe's Web site at www.adobe.com.**

Adobe Premiere Pro CS3 Bible is divided into seven main parts, each described in the following sections.

Part I: Getting Started with Premiere Pro

Part I provides an introduction to as well as an overview of Adobe Premiere Pro. The Quick Start chapter just before Part I is a get-started tutorial that introduces you to the basics of creating a desktop video production using Adobe Premiere Pro. Chapter 1 provides an overview of the Premiere Pro interface, menus, palettes, and tools. Chapter 2 takes a look at how to customize Premiere Pro so that you can save time when creating projects. Chapter 3 introduces you to Premiere Pro's basic project settings. Chapter 4 shows you how to capture video directly into Premiere Pro from a digital video camcorder or an analog camcorder.

Part II: Editing with Premiere Pro

Part II provides a thorough look at the basics of putting together a digital video production. Chapter 5 shows you how to use Premiere Pro's Timeline and sequences to assemble a video production. It also reviews many features to ease production project management. Chapter 6 provides the basics of editing using the Timeline panel and Source Monitor. Chapters 7 and 8 provide a look at Premiere Pro's audio features. Chapter 9 rounds out this part with a discussion of how to use transitions to smooth changes from one clip to another.

Part III: Working with Type and Graphics

Part III is dedicated to type and graphics, showing you how to use the Title Designer panel and titling tools. You learn how to create titles with styles, templates, and logos; how to create rolling and scrolling credits; and how to create titles with drop shadows. You also learn how to create graphics using the Title using Adobe Illustrator and Adobe Photoshop. Chapters 10 and 11 cover creating type and graphic effects.

Part IV: Advanced Techniques and Special Effects

Part IV covers advanced editing techniques and special effects. Chapter 12 covers sophisticated editing features in Premiere Pro, such as three-point and four-point edits. It also provides a discussion on how to use Premiere Pro's Rolling Edit and Ripple Edit tools, as well as its Slip and Slide editing tools. Chapter 12 also covers precise frame-by-frame editing with the Trim panel. Chapter 13 reviews the video effects in the Effects panel, and Chapter 14 covers the program's transparency effects (found in the Keying bin of the Effects panel). Chapter 15 provides you with information on how to create color mattes and backgrounds using Premiere Pro, Photoshop, and Illustrator. If you want to create motion effects in Premiere Pro, check out Chapter 16, which provides a thorough look at Motion effects. Chapter 17 shows you how to enhance your video using Premiere Pro's color correction tools.

Part V: Outputting Digital Video

After you've learned how to create a digital video production in Premiere Pro, your next concern is how to output your work in the best possible manner. This part covers all the bases. Chapter 18 reviews Premiere Pro's settings for exporting QuickTime, AVI, and MPEG movies. It also shows you how to use Premiere Pro's DVD markers as the basis for interactive buttons in DVD templates. Chapters 19 and 20 describe how to obtain the best possible quality when outputting a movie to the Web. Chapter 21 provides a discussion of outputting to videotape, while Chapter 22 covers outputting video to Flash and the Web. Chapter 23 covers outputting to CD as well as using Premiere Pro with Macromedia Director.

Part VI: Premiere Pro and Beyond

The chapters in this section provide a look at using Premiere Pro with different software packages, such as Adobe Audition, Adobe Soundbooth, Adobe Encore, Adobe Photoshop, Adobe Illustrator, and Adobe After Effects. Chapter 24 reviews using Adobe Audition. Chapter 25 reviews the use of Adobe Soundbooth. Chapters 26 and 27 take you on a tour of how to create a DVD with Adobe Encore. Chapter 28 shows you how to create alpha channels in Photoshop that can be used in Premiere Pro; it also shows you how to edit Premiere Pro frames in Photoshop and export them back into Premiere Pro. Chapter 29 shows how to create graphics and text using Adobe Illustrator. These graphics and texts are then imported and used in Adobe Premiere Pro, often as masks. Chapters 30, 31, and 32 deal with working with Adobe After Effects. Chapter 30 provides a look at how to trim clips using Adobe After Effects. In Chapter 31, you learn how to create and animate masks using After Effects Bezier masks. In Chapter 32, you learn how to use After Effects to animate Photoshop and Illustrator files, how to use After Effects' powerful motion paths to animate objects, animating type and how to create composite video clips.

Part VII: Appendixes

Adobe Premiere Pro CS3 Bible appendixes provide a hardware overview geared to non-technical users, as well as a resource guide. Appendix A is a guide to the *Adobe Premiere Pro CS3 Bible* DVD. Appendix C provides a look at computer systems and IEEE 1394/FireWire ports, and it also provides a short guide to DV camcorders and audio. Appendix B provides a Web guide for digital video and sound equipment as well as the Web addresses for magazines and publishers specializing in video, audio, and lighting.

Things to Note

Adobe Premiere Pro CS3 Bible runs on Windows XP Professional and XP Home Edition with Service Pack 2 or Windows Vista. The program also runs on a Macintosh with Mac OS X 10.4.9. The program's target user is the video professional.

Key combinations

Here are some conventions in this book that you should note. To save your file, press Ctrl+S (Windows), ⌘+S (Mac OS). When keyboard instructions call for pressing several keys simultaneously, the keys are separated by a plus sign. For example, to deselect all clips in the Timeline, press Ctrl+Shift+A (Windows), ⌘+Shift+S (Mac OS).

Mouse instructions

When the text specifies to click an item, move the mouse pointer over the item and click once. Windows users always click the left mouse button unless otherwise instructed. If the text specifies that you double-click, click the mouse twice without moving it. Typically in Premiere Pro, a Windows command to right-click the mouse is substituted by ⌘+Click on the Mac.

Menu commands

When the text specifies steps for executing a menu command, the menu and the command are separated by an arrow symbol, such as File⇨Import. When submenus are specified, you often see an arrow separating each menu command. For example, to export a project from Premiere Pro, you'll see the instructions written as File⇨Export⇨Movie.

Quick Start

Premiere Pro Quick Start

Welcome to the world of Adobe Premiere Pro and digital video. For both experts and beginners alike, Premiere Pro packs the power you need to create sophisticated digital video productions. You can create digital movies, documentaries, sales presentations, and music videos directly from your desktop computer or laptop. Your digital video production can be output to videotape, to the Web, or to DVD, or you can integrate it into projects in other programs, such as Adobe After Effects, Adobe Encore, and Adobe Flash.

This chapter introduces you to the basics of Premiere Pro, by helping you understand what it is and what you can do with it. This chapter also provides a simple Quick Start project to acquaint you with the Premiere Pro production process. You'll see how easy it is to load digital video clips and graphics into a Premiere Pro project and edit them into a short presentation. After you finish editing the project, you'll export the movie as either a QuickTime or Windows Media file for use in other programs.

IN THIS CHAPTER

What you can do with Premiere Pro

Understanding how Premiere Pro works

Create your first video production

What You Can Do with Premiere Pro

Whether you need to create a simple video clip for the Web, a sophisticated documentary, a rock video, or a video of an artistic event or wedding, Premiere Pro has the tools you need to create a dynamic video production. In fact, the best way to think about Premiere Pro is to visualize it as a complete production facility. You would need a room full of videotape and special effects equipment to do everything that Premiere Pro can do.

1

Here's a short list of some of the production tasks that you can accomplish with Premiere Pro:

- Edit digital video clips into a complete digital video production.
- Capture video from a camcorder or videotape recorder.
- Capture audio from a microphone or audio playback device.
- Load stock digital graphics, video, and audio clips.
- Create titles and animated title effects, such as scrolling or rolling titles.
- Integrate files from different sources into your production. Premiere Pro can import not only digital video and audio files, but also Adobe Photoshop, Adobe Illustrator, JPEG, and TIFF graphics.
- Create special effects, such as distortions, blurring, and pinching.
- Create motion effects in which logos or graphics fly or bounce across the screen.
- Create transparency effects. You can superimpose titles over backgrounds or use color, such as blue or green, to mask the background from one image so that you can superimpose a new background.
- Edit sound. Premiere Pro enables you to cut and assemble audio clips as well as create sophisticated audio effects, such as cross fades and pans.
- Create transitions. Premiere Pro can create simple dissolves from one scene to another, as well as a host of sophisticated transition effects, such as page curls and curtain wipes.
- Output files in a variety of digital formats. Premiere Pro can output QuickTime, Windows Media, Video for Windows, MPEG, and Flash video files. You can import these files into other multimedia applications, as well as view them on the Web.
- Output files to videotape and DVD.

Understanding How Premiere Pro Works

To understand the Premiere Pro production process, you need a basic understanding of the steps involved in creating a conventional videotape production in which the production footage is *not* digitized. In traditional, or *linear*, video production, all production elements are transferred to videotape. During the editing process, the final production is electronically edited onto one final or *program* videotape. Even though computers are used while editing, the linear or analog nature of videotape makes the process very time-consuming; during the actual editing session, videotape must be loaded and unloaded from tape or cassette machines. Time is wasted as producers simply wait for videotape machines to reach the correct editing point. The production is usually assembled sequentially. If you want to go back to a previous scene and replace it with one that is shorter or longer, all subsequent scenes must be rerecorded to the program reel.

Nonlinear editing programs (often abbreviated as NLE) such as Premiere Pro have revolutionized the entire process of video editing. Digital video and Premiere Pro eliminate many of the time-consuming production chores of traditional editing. When using Premiere Pro, you don't need to hunt for tapes or load and remove them from tape machines. When producers use Premiere Pro, all production elements are digitized to disk. Icons in Premiere Pro's Project panel represent each element in a production, whether it is a video clip, a sound clip, or a still image. The final production is represented by icons in a panel called the *Timeline*. The focal points of the Timeline are its video and audio tracks, which appear as parallel bars that stretch from left to right across the screen. When you need to use a video clip, sound clip, or still image, you can simply select it in the Project panel and drag it to a track in the Timeline. You can place the items of your production sequentially or drag them to different tracks. As you work, you can access any portion of your production by clicking with the mouse in the desired portion of the Timeline. You can also click and drag the beginning or end of a clip to shorten or extend its duration.

To fine-tune your edits, you can view and edit the clips, frame by frame, in Premiere Pro's Source and Program Monitors. You can also set in and out points in the Source Monitor panel. Setting an *in point* specifies where a clip starts playing, and setting an *out point* specifies where a clip stops playing. Because all clips are digitized (and no videotape is involved), Premiere Pro can quickly adjust the final production as you edit.

This list summarizes some of the digital-editing magic that you can perform in Premiere Pro by simply dragging clips in the Timeline:

- **Rolling edit:** As you click and drag a clip edge to the right in the Timeline, Premiere Pro automatically subtracts from the frames in the next clip. If you click and drag left to remove frames, Premiere Pro automatically adds back frames from the next clip in the Timeline.

- **Ripple edit:** As you click and drag a clip edge left or right, you add or subtract frames to the clip. Premiere Pro automatically adds to or subtracts from the entire program's duration.

- **Slip edit:** Dragging a clip between two other clips to the left or right automatically changes both in and out points of the clip without changing the program duration.

- **Slide edit:** Dragging a clip between two other clips to the left or right keeps the clip's duration intact but changes the in or out points of the preceding or succeeding clip.

CROSS-REF Chapters 6 and 12 provide in-depth discussions of Premiere Pro editing techniques.

As you work, you can easily preview edits, special effects, and transitions. Changing edits and effects is often a simple matter of changing in and out points. There's no hunting down the right videotape or waiting for the production to be reassembled on tape. When all of your editing is completed, you can export the file to videotape or create a new digital file in one of several formats. You can export it as many times as you want, in many different file formats at different frame sizes and frame rates. Furthermore, if you want to add more special effects to your Premiere Pro projects, you can easily import them into Adobe After Effects. You can also integrate your Premiere Pro movie into a Web page or import it into Adobe Encore to create a DVD production.

CROSS-REF After Effects is covered in Chapters 31 and 32. Encore is covered in Chapters 26 and 27.

Create Your First Video Production

The following sections provide a Quick Start editing session that leads you step-by-step through the process of creating a very short video production in Premiere Pro. As you work through the tutorial, you learn how to place clips in the Timeline, edit clips in the Source Monitor, apply transitions, and fade video and audio.

In this project, you create a simple video sequence called Escape from the City. Figure QS.1 shows frames of the production in Premiere Pro's Timeline panel.

FIGURE QS.1

Scenes from the Escape from the City project

The clips used to create the project are from Artbeats (www.artbeats.com), FilmDisc (www.filmdisc.com), and SmartSound (www.smartsound.com). The production begins with a title created in Premiere Pro's Title Designer, viewed over an opening scene of city traffic. After a few seconds, a clock with its hands spinning is superimposed over the traffic. The traffic and clock dissolve to an airport where a man is seen boarding a jet. The project ends with a fade to black.

NOTE You can download a free copy of Quicktracks for Premiere Pro from SmartSound's Web site. Quicktracks is a plug-in that resides in Premiere Pro and allows you to search for music and then customize it to fit the duration of a project. Quicktracks also comes with ten royalty-free music scores.

ON the DVD Many of the projects in this book use footage from Artbeats, FilmDisc, and SmartSound. These companies sell royalty-free footage for use in multimedia production. The DVD contains Artbeats, FilmDisc, and SmartSound folders. In this chapter, the clock footage (bc0104) and the traffic footage (cm0105) can be found in the FilmDisc folder. The airport scene (bg113) can be found in the Artbeats folder. The sound clip, The Great Escape, is in the SmartSound folder.

TIP For best performance, copy the files you need for each chapter to your hard drive. You might also want to place footage for each chapter in separate folders. You can then load the contents of the folder into Premiere Pro using the File ⇨ Import Folder command. When you use this command, Premiere Pro creates a bin (folder) in the Project panel and places the clips from the folder in the bin.

Starting a Premiere Pro project

A Premiere Pro digital video production is called a *project* instead of a video production. The reason for this is that Premiere Pro not only enables you to create the production, but it also enables you to manage production assets as well as create and store titles, transitions, and effects. Thus, the file you work in is much more than just a production — it's truly a project.

Your first step in creating a digital video production in Premiere Pro is to create a new project. Follow these steps:

1. **To launch Premiere Pro, double-click the Adobe Premiere Pro icon (Windows users may also be able to click it in the Windows Start menu).** When you launch Premiere Pro, the program automatically assumes that you want to create a new project or open one that was previously created.

2. **To create a new project, click the New Project icon.** If Premiere Pro is already loaded, you can create a new project by choosing File ⇨ New Project.

Specifying project settings

Before you can start importing files and editing, you must specify video and audio settings for the project. The New Project dialog box, shown in Figure QS.2, appears whenever you create a new project. This dialog box enables you to quickly choose predetermined video and audio settings. The most important project settings determine the frame rate (frames per second) and the frame size (viewing area) of your project, as well as how the digital video is compressed. (As a general rule, choose project settings that match your source footage.)

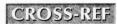 For a detailed description of project settings, see Chapter 3.

FIGURE QS.2

Use the New Project dialog box to quickly choose project settings.

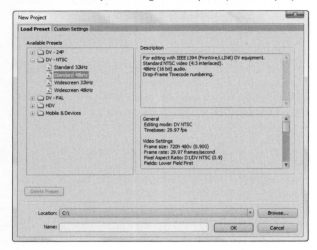

Follow these steps to specify the settings for the Quick Start project:

1. **To work with the tutorial footage, choose the DV - NTSC Standard 48 kHz preset.** After you click this preset, Premiere Pro displays information about the project settings.

   Notice that the frame size is 720 x 480 pixels. Also note that under Video Settings, the display shows a pixel aspect ratio of D1/DV NTSC (0.9). This indicates that you are creating a project for footage with non-square pixels. Because the tutorial footage uses non-square pixels, it is the correct choice for this project.

 To learn more about pixel aspect ratio and choosing project settings, see Chapter 3.

TIP If you are creating projects for the Web or for multimedia application, you often export your project at a smaller frame size, slower frame rate, and lower-resolution audio than your original project settings. Typically, you export your project after you have edited it using project settings that match your source footage.

2. **Select a location to store your file.** If you want to change the default file location, click Browse and use the mouse to navigate to the folder where you want to store your project.

3. **Enter a name, such as Escape, in the Name field.**

4. **To open your new project, click OK.**

Setting a workspace

Before you start editing, you may want to set your workspace so that you can view the most important Premiere Pro panels that are used in editing. You can easily do this by selecting an editing workspace. Choose Window ➪ Workspace ➪ Editing. This opens the Project, Source Monitor, Program Monitor, and Timeline panels, as well as the Info and History panels. In this tutorial, you use the Project panel as your home for source footage. You edit your clips in the Timeline and Source Monitor panels, and you view the edited project in the Program Monitor.

 If you change the size and location of the panels on-screen, you can return them to their original settings by choosing Window ➪ Workspace ➪ Reset Current Workspace.

Importing production elements

You can place and edit video, audio, and still images in your Premiere Pro projects as long as they are in a digital format. Table QS.1 lists the major file formats that you can import into Premiere Pro. All media footage, or *clips*, must first be saved to disk. Even if your video is stored on a digital camcorder, it still must be transferred to disk. Premiere Pro can capture the digital video clips and automatically store them in your projects. Analog media such as motion picture film and videotape must first be digitized before Premiere Pro can use it. In this case, Premiere Pro, in conjunction with a capture board, can capture your clips directly into a project.

 For more information about capturing video and audio, see Chapter 4.

TABLE QS.1

Supported Files in Premiere Pro

Media	File Formats
Video	Video for Windows (AVI Type 2), QuickTime (MOV) (Apple's QuickTime must also be installed), MPEG-1, MPEG-2, and Windows Media (WMV, WMA)
Audio	AIFF, WAV, AVI, MOV, and MP3
Still Images and Sequences	TIFF, JPEG, BMP, PNG, EPS, GIF, Filmstrip, Illustrator, and Photoshop

After the Premiere Pro panels open, you're ready to import the various graphic and sound elements that will comprise your digital video production. All the items that you import appear in a list in the Project panel. An icon represents each item. Next to the icon, Premiere Pro displays whether the item is a video clip, an audio clip, or a graphic.

When importing files into Premiere Pro, you can choose whether to import one file, multiple files (by pressing and holding Ctrl/⌘ as you click the file), or an entire folder. If desired, you can even import one project into another, using the File ➪ Import ➪ Project command. Follow these steps to load the production elements for the Escape from the City project:

1. Choose File ⇨ Import.

2. Load the following files from the Artbeats, FilmDisc, and SmartSound folders:

    ▪ **bc0104 and cm0105:** FilmDisc folder

    ▪ **BG113:** Artbeats folder

    ▪ **The Great Escape:** SmartSound folder

3. **Rename each clip.** Because the names of imported clips may not clearly describe their footage, you can rename them in the Project panel. To rename a clip, click it in the Project panel and choose Clip ⇨ Rename. (As a shortcut, you can also right-click/control-click the clip and choose Rename from the drop-down menu that appears.) Here are the filenames and the new names to use:

    ▪ Name the bc0104 clip **Clock**.

    ▪ Name the BG113 clip **Airport**.

    ▪ Name the cm0105 clip **Traffic**.

Figure QS.3 shows the Project panel with all of the clips needed to create the Escape from the City project. You will create the Intro title later in this chapter.

 Once a clip is on the Timeline, you can right-click/Ctrl-click the clip and rename it in the Timeline. This does not rename the clip in the Project panel.

FIGURE QS.3

The Project panel with the items needed to create the Escape from the City project

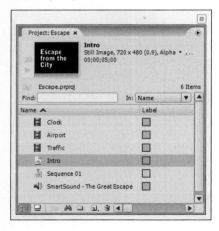

The Escape project requires the following files:

■ A video clip of city traffic (Traffic)

■ A video clip of a clock (Clock)

- A video clip of man boarding a small jet (Airport)
- A sound clip of background music (The Great Escape)

 Creating titles in Premiere Pro is discussed in Chapter 10.

Viewing clips in the Project panel

Before you begin assembling your production, you may want to view a clip or graphic, or listen to an audio track. You can see a thumbnail preview of any of the clips in the Project panel by clicking the clip. The preview appears in the upper-left corner of the Project panel. A Play button (small triangle) appears to the left of the thumbnail preview area. Click the Play button to see a preview of a video clip or to hear an audio clip. If you prefer, you can click and drag the tiny slider below the thumbnail preview to view the clip.

NOTE   Double-clicking the clip in the Project panel opens the clip in the Source Monitor. You can preview the clip there by clicking the Source Monitor's Play button.

Assembling production elements

After you import all of your production elements, you need to place them in a sequence in the Timeline panel so that you can start editing your project. A sequence is a sequential assembly of video, audio, effects, and transitions that comprise part of your production.

NOTE   If you are working on long projects in Premiere Pro, you may want to break your work into multiple sequences. After you edit the sequences, you can drag them into another Timeline panel, where they appear as nested sequences. Using nested sequences is discussed in Chapter 5.

Placing clips in the Timeline

To move a clip or graphic from the Project panel to the Timeline panel, you can simply click it in the Project panel and then drag the item to a track in the Timeline. The item then appears in the Timeline as an icon. The duration of the clip or graphic is represented by the length of the clip in the Timeline.

NOTE   You can place clips directly in the Timeline by opening them in the Source Monitor panel and clicking the Insert or Overlay button. This technique is discussed in Chapter 6.

Selecting clips in the Timeline

You'll spend a great deal of time positioning clips in the Timeline while editing your production. Premiere Pro's Selection and Range Select tools help you assemble your program's clips in the order you want. Here's how to select and move clips:

 - **Single clip:** Click the Selection tool (the arrow icon in the upper-left corner of the Timeline). Then click in the middle of the clip in the Timeline. (To quickly activate the Selection tool, press V on your keyboard.) With the clip selected, click and drag it to the desired location.

■ **Entire track:** Click the Track Select tool (the dashed-line rectangular icon in the Toolbox located to the right or below the Selection tool) on a clip. The Track Select tool selects the entire track from the point where you click.

Figure QS.4 displays the Timeline panel for the Escape from the City project. The title appears in the Video 2 track. It is placed here in this example so that you can create a transparency effect in which the title text fades in over the background video in the Video 1 track. The Traffic video clip appears in the Video 1 track, as does the next clip (the Airport clip). This example creates a super-imposition effect showing the spinning hands of the clock over the traffic. Later, you'll see how to lower opacity in a clip to create this effect. Between the Traffic and Airport clips is a transition (a dissolve created by dragging this effect from the Video Effects panel). The short project ends by fading out the Airport clip and the sound clip.

FIGURE QS.4
_____

The Timeline panel with the clips for the Escape from the City project

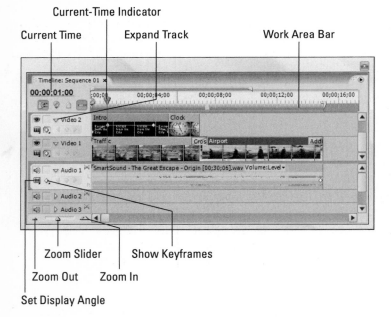

Trying out the Timeline panel

As mentioned earlier, the Timeline provides a graphical overview of your project. Before continuing, try changing zoom settings, clicking and dragging the current-time indicator, and expanding a video track. Doing so helps to familiarize you with the Timeline controls you'll be working with in this chapter.

Changing the zoom level

Most Premiere Pro users create their video projects at 29.97 frames per second. Viewing all of these frames on the Timeline quickly consumes valuable screen space. As you work, you may want to zoom in and out between close-up and bird's-eye views of your work. When you zoom in, you see fewer frames, which may make fine-tuning your project easier, particularly because the space expands between time intervals in the Timeline. When you want to see an overview of your entire project, you can zoom out.

To zoom in and out, click the Timeline Zoom slider in the lower-left corner of the Timeline. Figure QS.4 shows the Timeline Zoom slider, as well as the Zoom In and Zoom Out buttons. Clicking and dragging left (zooming out) shows more footage in the Timeline; clicking and dragging right (zooming in) shows less footage. For example, if you zoom out, a one-minute clip takes up less space in the Timeline, which means you can see many different clips in addition to your one-minute clip. If you zoom in, a one-minute clip occupies more space in the Timeline, which means that it may be the only clip visible.

Moving the current-time indicator

The current-time indicator (sometimes referred to as CTI) is the blue triangular icon at the top of the ruler area in the Timeline. If you click and drag the current-time indicator, you move the red edit line. The edit line shows you the current editing position in the Program Monitor. Try clicking and dragging the current-time indicator. Notice that as you drag, the blue current time readout changes, showing your current position in the Timeline. In Figure QS.4, the edit line is at the beginning of the 2-second mark, after the title fades in. If you want to quickly jump to an area in the Timeline, just click in the ruler area. If you want to slowly move through the Timeline one frame at a time, select the Timeline and then press the right- or left-arrow keys.

Expanding tracks

By default, you see three video tracks in the Timeline. If you expand a track, you can see video frames in the track and video effects. Later, you'll change the display style to show frames in the video tracks and volume in the audio tracks. The small diamond icons in the audio and video tracks in Figure QS.4 are keyframes, which indicate a change in volume or opacity. By default, the Video 1 track and Audio 1 track are expanded. In this project, you also use the Video 2 track. Try expanding it now by clicking the right-pointing triangle to the left of the Video 2 track.

Creating the title

If you are creating a Premiere Pro project, you'll probably create your titles after you start editing. However, to keep this Quick Start tutorial easy to follow, you're going to build the project sequentially, and start by creating a title and adding it to the Timeline.

Premiere Pro automatically includes an *alpha channel* in the title, which allows the background video to appear where the black areas occur in the alpha channel. In this section you'll create the title and place it in the Video 2 track. This enables the background video to show through as the title fades in.

CROSS-REF You can edit a title in the Title Designer by double-clicking it in the Project panel. See Chapter 10 to learn more about the Title Designer.

Follow these steps to create the title:

1. **Choose File ➪ New ➪ Title.**

2. **In the New Title dialog box, name the title Intro.** Click OK. This opens the Title panel, as shown in Figure QS.5.

3. **In the Title panel, click and enter the words Escape from the City, as shown in Figure QS.5.** Press the Enter/Return key to create carriage returns.

4. **Use the Selection tool (arrow icon) to position the title within the frame, as shown in Figure QS.5.**

5. **If you want to change the type style, click the Selection tool.** Click any of the styles in the Title Styles panel beneath the Title panel.

6. **Close the Title panel.** The title is automatically added to the Project panel. By default, Premiere Pro makes the title 5 seconds long.

FIGURE QS.5

Use the Title panel to create and format production titles.

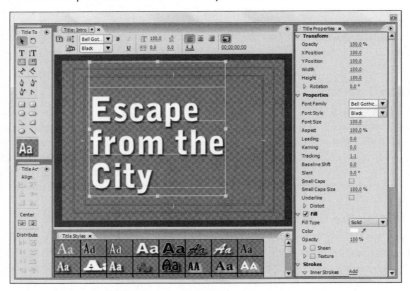

Now follow these steps to add the title to the Timeline:

1. **Click the Intro title in the Project panel and drag it into the Video 2 track.**

2. **If you would like to see more of the title in the Timeline, zoom in by clicking and dragging the Zoom slider to the right.**

3. **Expand the Video 2 track by clicking the triangle to the left of the words** *Video 2.* This allows you to access the Set Display Style drop-down menu.

4. **View the footage as individual frames in the Timeline.** In the Video 2 track, click the Set Display Style drop-down menu and choose Show Frames. (This drop-down menu is a tiny frame icon directly below the eye icon in the track.)

Fading in the title

You can now fade in the titles. In Figure QS.6, the first diagonal line segment in the track represents the fade-in effect. The diagonal line indicates that the title fades in gradually over the first second. In this section, you create the fade-in effect by changing the opacity of the title clip in the Effect Controls panel. Figure QS.6 shows the Effect Controls panel and the Opacity slider. The diamonds in the Effect Controls panel timeline display are called *keyframes*. When you make opacity setting changes over time, Premiere Pro creates keyframes; it gradually changes the opacity between the keyframes.

FIGURE QS.6

Changing opacity creates a fade-in effect.

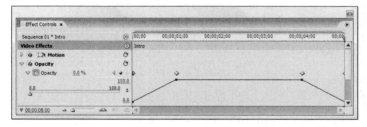

Follow these steps to change opacity:

1. **Select the Intro title in the Timeline by clicking it.**

2. **Open the Effect Controls panel by choosing Window ⇨ Effect Controls.**

3. **Expand the Effect Controls panel, so that you can see the panel's Timeline and Zoom slider, by clicking the Show/Hide Timeline view icon (the chevron to the right of the Sequence and Title name).** Before continuing, note that the Effect Controls panel includes a Zoom slider in the lower-left corner and a current-time indicator. Both elements function exactly as they do in the Timeline panel.

4. Set the current-time indicator to 00;00;00 in the Effect Controls or Timeline panel.

5. Expand the Opacity effect by clicking the right-pointing triangle button (to the left of the word *Opacity*). The Opacity control expands. You can easily change opacity by clicking and dragging the Opacity slider. To view the slider, click the right-pointing arrow to the left of the stopwatch icon in the Opacity section.

6. If the Stopwatch icon to the left of the word Opacity isn't darkened (selected), click it. This is the Toggle Animation button, and it allows Premiere Pro to create keyframes and interpolate between changes in opacity, which results in a gradual change in opacity.

7. Lower the opacity to zero. To lower opacity, click and drag the Opacity slider left until the display reads 0 percent, as shown in Figure QS.6.

8. Now drag the current-time indicator in the Effect Controls panel to the 1-second mark. As you click and drag, you see the time display change in the lower-left corner. Stop when you reach 1 second.

TIP   You can also move the current-time indicator by clicking and dragging left or right over the time readout in the Effect Controls panel.

9. Raise the opacity back to 100 percent by clicking and dragging the Opacity slider to the right. As you drag, the percentage increases. The changes in opacity create two keyframes, one at the start of the clip and another 1 second later. Between the two keyframes, Premiere Pro adjusts opacity to gradually increase from 0 to 100 percent.

10. Create a fade-out that starts at the 4-second mark. Click and drag the current-time indicator to the 4-second mark, and then click the Add/Remove Keyframe button.

11. Drag the current time indicator slider to the end of the Effect Controls Timeline, to the 4-second, or 29-frame, mark. Click and drag the Opacity slider to 0 percent. After you make the change, Premiere Pro adds another keyframe. When you're finished, the Effect Controls panel should resemble Figure QS.6.

If you'd like to practice creating opacity keyframes in the Effect Controls panel, fade in the opacity of the Traffic clip, using the same technique used to fade in the intro title.

NOTE   You can also change video opacity directly in the Timeline with the Pen or Selection tool. Ctrl/⌘-clicking the Opacity graph line in the Timeline creates keyframes. After you create keyframes, you can adjust opacity by clicking and dragging with the Pen or Selection tool.

TIP   If you need to delete a keyframe, right-click/control-click it in the Effect Controls panel and then choose Clear in the drop-down menu.

Trimming clips in the Timeline panel

You can edit video and audio clips in several ways. You can start simply, editing the first clip by clicking and dragging its out point in the Timeline. Before editing a clip, you may want to play it in the Source Monitor panel. To play any clip, double-click it in the Project panel. When the clip appears in the Source Monitor panel, click the Play button to view the clip, as shown in Figure QS.7.

Follow these steps to add the first video clip (the Traffic clip) to the Timeline and edit it (the clip is about 12 seconds long, but you only need the first 7 seconds):

1. **Drag the Traffic clip from the Source Monitor into the Video 1 track.** Position the clip at the beginning of the Timeline.

2. **Move the current-time indicator to the 7-second mark in the timeline panel.** You'll use the current-time indicator's position (the edit line) as a visual guide for shortening the clip.

FIGURE QS.7
_____

You can click the Source Monitor panel's Play button to play a clip.

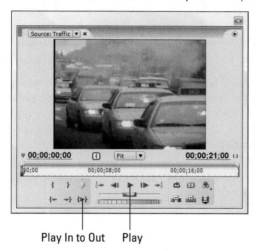

Play In to Out   Play

---

3. **Position the mouse pointer at the end of the Traffic clip.** The cursor changes to a bracket.

4. **Click and drag to the left to shorten the clip.** Make the clip about 7 seconds long so that it ends on the 7-second mark (00;00;07;00) on the Timeline. To do this precisely, try dragging the current-time indicator to the 7-second mark first (the position of the current-time indicator is displayed in the left side of the Program Monitor) and then adjust the clip by clicking and dragging the right edge of the clip to the left so that it snaps on the edit line. As you drag to the left, notice that the clip's duration displays in the Program Monitor.

TIP If you become lost in the Timeline and inadvertently move out of the edited area, zoom out so that you can see the clips that you've placed in the Timeline. Move the current-time indicator into the edited area, and then zoom in.

Previewing in the Program Monitor

As you work, you may notice the red line that appears just below the ruler area of the Timeline. The red color indicates that Premiere Pro hasn't *rendered* the video. When Premiere Pro renders, it creates and shows preview files that display with effects. Although you can view many effects by simply playing them, to ensure that all effects are rendered, you need to press Enter or choose Sequence ➪ Render Work Area. When Premiere Pro renders, it also restarts the project from the beginning of the Timeline and plays back the clip. Press Enter now and watch the titles fade in. As the program plays, you see the clip fade in and the Traffic clip superimposed beneath the opening title. The Traffic clip appears only in the black area of the Title clip.

If you don't render your video, you can still start and stop playing it from the current time indicator by pressing the Spacebar. The Program Monitor plays the program that is being edited in the current sequence in the Timeline panel.

> **TIP**   You can play your video without rendering it by clicking the Enable or Disable Previews button on the Timeline, and then clicking Play or pressing the Spacebar.

> **TIP**   If you want to play your production in the Program Monitor from the current-time indicator position, press the Spacebar or click the Play/Stop toggle button in the Program Monitor. To stop playback using the keyboard, press the Spacebar again.

Editing in the Source Monitor

The Source Monitor panel provides precise controls for editing clips. Using the Source Monitor, you can easily navigate to specific frames and then mark in and out points. After you set the in and out points, you can drag the clip directly to the Timeline.

A Note about Rendering and Playback Quality

As Premiere Pro plays your program in the Program Monitor, it attempts to adjust the output to deliver the highest quality possible, by attempting to play back at the project's full frame rate. If a portion of your program cannot display properly, a red preview bar appears on-screen. This indicates that the area must be rendered to disk. After rendering, Premiere Pro uses the rendered disk file to properly display the effect. If you want to render your entire project, press Enter. If you want to render only a portion of your project, first adjust the work area bar so that it encompasses only the area that you want to render, and then press Enter. If you want to lower the processing requirements so that you can see effects at a lower-quality setting without rendering, you can change to Draft Quality in the Monitor drop-down menu.

You should also note that despite the quality setting in the Program Monitor panel, playback quality in the Program Monitor is not as high as that of exported video. When Premiere Pro processes video in the Program Monitor panel, it uses *bilinear pixel resampling*. When Premiere Pro exports video, it uses *cubic resampling*, a higher-quality method that also produces higher-quality sound.

In the following steps, you learn to set the in and out points in the Source Monitor panel. To learn about the different ways to edit a video clip, see Chapters 6 and 12. In this section, you edit the Clock clip down to 2.5 seconds in the Source Monitor panel and then drag it to the Video 2 track. Later, you'll create a transparency effect showing the clock's hands spinning over the traffic.

 You can also click the Insert button or Overlay button in the Source Monitor panel to place a clip in the Timeline. This technique is described in Chapter 6.

 By default, Premiere Pro automatically snaps two adjacent clips together. You can also turn snap on or off by clicking the Snap button (magnet icon) in the Timeline panel.

1. **Double-click the Clock clip in the Project panel.** This opens the clip in the Source Monitor, shown in Figure QS.8. As discussed earlier, the Source Monitor displays source clips, and the Program Monitor displays the edited sequence in the Timeline panel. If the current-time indicator is on the Traffic clip, you see it in the Program Monitor.

FIGURE QS.8

You can edit clips in the Source Monitor panel.

Time Display   Step Backward   Step Forward

Go to In Point   Set Out Point   Shuttle

Set In Point   Go to Out Point   Jog

Current-Time Indicator

2. **Play the clip by clicking the Play button in the Source Monitor.** The scene shows the clock handles spinning around. Before you edit the clip's in and out points, you need to go to the precise frame that you want to edit.

3. **Before editing the clip, jump back to its first frame by clicking the Go to In Point button.**

4. **Now you want to be able to move slowly through the clip to set the in point.** Use one of the following techniques:

   ▪ **Click the current-time indicator in the Source Monitor and drag.** As you drag, you move, or scrub, through the clip frame by frame.

   ▪ **Click and drag in the jog tread at the bottom of the Source Monitor panel.** As you click and drag, you move through the clip frame by frame.

   ▪ **Click and hold down the shuttle control to move in slow or fast motion.** Speed is controlled by how far left or right you move the shuttle. Moving the shuttle to the right moves forward through the clip, while moving the shuttle to the left moves backward.

   ▪ **Click the Step Backward or Step Forward button to move backward or forward one frame at a time.**

5. **Click and drag the jog tread to the right, or drag the current-time indicator in the Source Monitor to the right, about 15 frames into the clip.**

6. **Click the Set In Point button (refer to Figure QS.8).**

7. **Position the current-time indicator in the Source Monitor panel at 00;00;03;00, by either clicking and dragging or typing this precise location into the Time display.**

8. **Click the Set Out Point button (refer to Figure QS.8).**

 To clear an in or out point, press Alt/Opt while clicking the Set In Point or Set Out Point button.

9. **Drag the clip to the Timeline so that it snaps to the Intro clip.**

Note that the Clock clip extends beyond the Traffic clip. This is done intentionally to extend the superimposition effect that you will create in the next section.

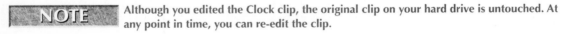 Although you edited the Clock clip, the original clip on your hard drive is untouched. At any point in time, you can re-edit the clip.

Creating a superimposition effect

As mentioned earlier, you placed the clock in Video track 2 so that you could create a superimposition effect showing the clock hands spinning over traffic. To do this, you need to reduce the opacity of the Clock clip. Because you can do this quite easily with the mouse, you'll change opacity in the Timeline rather than in the Effect Controls panel:

1. **Drag the current time indicator over any portion of the Clock clip.** The clock appears in the Program Monitor panel.

2. **Click the Keyframe drop-down menu for the Video 2 track.** Choose Show Opacity Handles.

3. **Drag down the yellow Opacity graph line in the Clock clip in the Timeline panel.** As you drag, you should see a readout displaying the opacity percentage. View the Program Monitor and decide how you want the effect to look as you lower the opacity. This example sets the opacity to 50 percent.

4. **To view the effect, press Enter to render the project.**

Editing the Airport clip

In the following steps, you edit the Airport clip in the Source Monitor panel and add it to the program. You'll make the Airport clip about 8 seconds long:

1. **Double-click the Airport clip in the Project panel.** This opens the clip in the Source Monitor.

2. **Set the in point.** Click and drag the current-time indicator in the Source Monitor (in the area below the Monitor preview and above the Play button) to choose a frame at about one second (30 frames into the clip). Click the Set In Point button.

3. **Set the out point.** Click and drag the Source Monitor current-time indicator to find a point about 9 seconds into the clip. Watch the time display at the bottom-right corner of the panel to select the frame. When you find the frame you want, click the Set Out Point button.

4. **After you set the in and out points, drag the clip directly from the Source Monitor or the Project panel to the Timeline so that it touches the end of the Traffic clip.**

Creating a transition

Preview your production in the Program Monitor. To start the preview from the beginning of the Timeline, click the Play In to Out button in the Program Monitor. As you watch the preview, notice that the cut from the Traffic clip to the Airport clip is quite abrupt. To smooth the flow of the production, you can add a *transition* between the two clips.

CROSS-REF For more information on using transitions, see Chapter 9.

Follow these steps to add a Cross Dissolve transition to your project:

1. **If the Effects panel is not open, choose Window ⇨ Effects.**

2. **In the Effects panel, open the Video Transitions bin by clicking its triangle icon.**

3. **Open the Dissolve bin by clicking its triangle icon.**

NOTE Folders with effects and clips are referred to as *bins* in Premiere Pro.

4. **To add the transition to your project, click and drag the Cross Dissolve transition over end of the Traffic clip and the beginning of the Airport clip in the Timeline.** Release the mouse.

5. **To open the Cross Dissolve controls, double-click the Cross Dissolve icon in the Timeline.** This opens the transition in the Effect Controls panel.

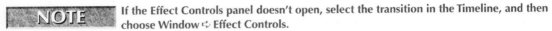 If the Effect Controls panel doesn't open, select the transition in the Timeline, and then choose Window ✏ Effect Controls.

6. **Adjust the position and length of the transition (optional).** You can adjust the position and the duration of the transition by clicking and dragging the mouse on the transition icon in the Effect Controls panel. However, the fastest technique is to enter a value in the Duration readout and change settings in the Alignment drop-down menu. For example, you could set the Duration to 15 frames by changing the time readout to 00;00;00;15. Make sure that Center at Cut is chosen in the Alignment drop-down menu, as shown in Figure QS.9. Center at Cut ensures that half of the transition occurs at the end of the Traffic clip, and half occurs at the beginning of the Airport clip.

FIGURE QS.9

The Cross Dissolve transition in the Effect Controls panel

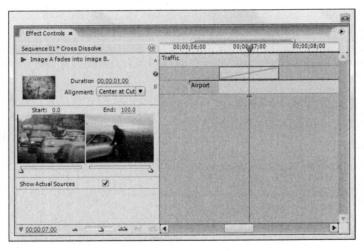

7. **View a thumbnail preview.** Preview the final transition by clicking the Play Transition button in the Effect Controls panel. To see a preview of the effect with the footage, select the Show Actual Sources check box.

Previewing the transition

To render the project from the beginning, press Enter.

Adding a fade-out

You can end the video of your production with a simple fade to black, courtesy of the Transitions bin in the Video Effects panel:

1. **Click the Effects panel tab to display the panel contents.** If the Effects panel is not open, choose Window ⇨ Effects.

2. **In the Effects panel, open the Video Transitions bin by clicking its triangle icon.**

3. **Open the Dissolve bin by clicking its triangle icon.**

4. **Click and drag the Dip to Black transition over the right end of the Airport clip.**

Adding and fading in the audio track

Now that the majority of the editing is complete, it's time to add the audio track. Fortunately, Premiere Pro treats audio much the same as it does video. In this section, you drag the music track to the Timeline and then use the Pen tool to create a fade-out using keyframes in an audio track:

1. **Listen to SmartSound's The Great Escape music clip by double-clicking it in the Project panel.** After the clip opens in the Source Monitor panel, click the Play button.

2. **Drag the Background Music clip from the Project panel to the Audio 1 track in the Timeline.** Line up the beginning of the audio track with the beginning of the video track.

3. **Shorten the audio track so that it ends simultaneously with the video.** To do this, click and drag the right end of the track so that it ends at the 15-second mark.

4. **If the Audio 1 track is not expanded, expand it by clicking the triangle icon at the far-left side of the track.**

5. **Click the audio track's Show Keyframes drop-down menu, and choose Show Clip Volume.**

6. **Activate the Pen tool in the Tool panel.**

7. **Use the Pen tool to create a keyframe toward the end of the audio.** About 14 seconds into the project, Ctrl-click/⌘-click with the Pen tool to create a keyframe.

8. **Create a keyframe at the very end of the audio clip by Ctrl-clicking/⌘-clicking again.** Then drag the final keyframe down to create the fade-out.

9. **Press Enter to preview your entire project and hear the fade-out.**

> **NOTE** Audio fade-ins can also be created using the Crossfade audio transition. You can also fade audio in and out using the Volume effect in the Effect Controls panel. See Chapter 8 to learn more about audio effects. Also keep in mind that Premiere Pro allows you to change the volume of the entire audio track as well as individual clips.

Fine-tuning the project

This project is an introduction to basic editing in Premiere Pro. Feel free to enhance, change, and re-edit as you desire. You can also create pure black video and place it in a video track. To create black video, choose File ⇨ New ⇨ Black Video. This command places the black video clip into the Project panel. From there, you can drag it into the Timeline. If you want to fade in or out to the black video, place it in the Video 2 track.

Exporting your first movie

When you finish editing your movie, you can export it as a new file in a variety of formats. Premiere Pro enables you to export movies in video formats such as QuickTime, RealVideo, and Advanced Windows Media, as well as formats for DVD. As mentioned earlier, if your video's final destination is the Web or a multimedia application, you can change frame size and frame rate, and lower audio resolution when exporting.

Here is a summary of Premiere Pro's export commands:

- If you want to export your file in a format for Web or DVD use, select the Timeline panel and choose File ⇨ Export ⇨ Adobe Media Encoder. The Media Encoder allows you to create MPEG-2, Windows Media, RealVideo, and QuickTime streaming files.

- If you want to export your movie as an AVI, QuickTime, or animated GIF file, select the Timeline panel and choose File ⇨ Export ⇨ Movie.

- If you want to export your movie to videotape, select the Timeline panel and choose File ⇨ Export to Tape. Note that a recording device must be connected for this command to work.

- If you want to embed your movie in an Adobe Acrobat PDF file for workgroup review, select the Timeline panel and choose File ⇨ Export ⇨ Adobe Clip Notes.

- If you want to burn a DVD directly from Premiere Pro, choose Window ⇨ Export to Encore. To burn the DVD without creating menus in Encore, choose the Direct Burn Without Menus option.

Exporting a Windows Media file

Windows Media files are commonly used on the Web and can be imported into multimedia programs such as Macromedia Director. To export your movie in Windows Media format, follow these steps:

1. **Select the Timeline panel that contains the project you want to export.**

2. **Choose File ⇨ Export ⇨ Adobe Media Encoder.** The Export Settings dialog box appears.

3. **In the Format drop-down menu, choose Windows Media (if it isn't already selected), as shown in Figure QS.10.**

4. **Choose a preset in the Preset drop-down menu.** For example, if you have a streaming media server and you want to export your file for multiple Web audiences, including those with higher-speed Internet connections, you can choose the NTSC Source to Streaming choice in the Preset drop-down menu. When you select the preset, the Summary area in the Export Settings dialog box displays frame height, frame rate, and other exporting details for the slowest video stream. The NTSC streaming preset includes different streams at different frame rates, and different frame sizes for different Web connections, from 56 Kbps modem to Corporate LAN or cable modem DSL/384 Kbps. To continue with the export, click OK.

5. **In the Save File dialog box, select a destination folder in which to store the finished Windows Media file, and enter a filename.**

6. **To start the export, click Save.**

 For an in-depth review of the Adobe Media Encoder, see Chapter 20.

FIGURE QS.10

Use the Adobe Media Encoder's Export Settings dialog box to create a Windows Media file for the Web.

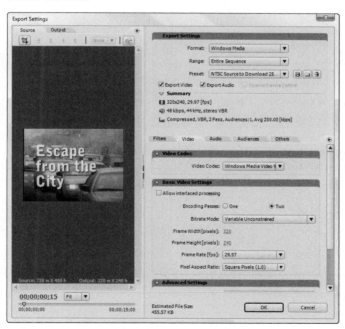

Exporting a QuickTime movie

Apple's QuickTime format is widely used on the Web and in most multimedia applications. Depending on the final destination of your project, you may want to change the frame size and frame rate of your video before exporting. For example, if you export a file to a multimedia project, you may want to reduce the DV frame size from 720 x 480 pixels to a smaller size that fits comfortably into your production. Follow these steps for exporting your project as a QuickTime movie:

1. **Select the Timeline panel.**

2. **Choose File ➪ Export ➪ Movie.** The Export Movie dialog box appears.

3. **Click the Settings button.** The Export Movie Settings dialog box appears, where you can view export settings.

4. **Choose QuickTime from the File Type drop-down menu, as shown in Figure QS.11.**

5. **To switch the frame size and frame rate, choose Video from the list box in the upper-left corner of the Export Movie Settings dialog box.** The Video Settings dialog box appears. These settings are covered in detail in Chapter 3.

6. **If you are creating a multimedia project that will play on a computer, select Sorenson as the compressor.** You can change the frame size to 320 x 240 pixels and change the frame rate, if desired. If you are outputting the file for CD-ROM, you probably want to change the data rate. Doing so slows the data rate to prevent frames from being dropped during playback. See Chapter 18 for more details.

7. **After you make your changes, click OK.** Premiere Pro returns you to the Export Movie dialog box.

8. **In the Export Movie dialog box, type a name for your file.**

9. **Click Save.** Premiere Pro builds the export file and then opens it in the Program Monitor for viewing.

FIGURE QS.11

Choose QuickTime in the File Type drop-down menu.

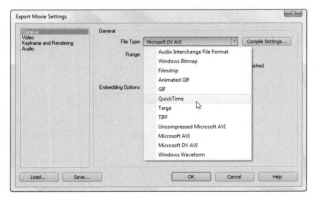

Summary

This chapter gave you an opportunity to experiment with the basic concepts of editing in Premiere Pro. You learned how to do the following:

- Create a project by choosing File ⇨ New Project.
- Add clips to the Timeline by dragging them from the Project or Source Monitor panel.
- Edit clips in the Source Monitor panel by clicking the Set In and Set Out Point buttons.
- Change clip opacity by selecting the clip and adjusting the Opacity effect in the Effect Controls panel.
- Create a transition by dragging a transition from the Effects panel.
- Preview your production in the Program Monitor panel.
- Fade audio in and out by creating keyframes in the Timeline.
- Export in different video formats using the Adobe Media Encoder.

Part I

Getting Started with Premiere Pro

Chapter 1

Premiere Pro Basics

The Adobe Premiere Pro user interface is a combination of a video-editing studio and an electronic image-editing studio. If you're familiar with film, video editing, or audio editing, you should feel right at home working within Premiere Pro's Project, Monitor, and Audio windows. If you have worked with such programs as Adobe After Effects, Macromedia Flash, or Macromedia Director, then Premiere Pro's Timeline, digital tools, and panels should also be familiar to you. If you're completely new to video editing and computers, don't worry; Premiere Pro panels, windows, and menus are efficiently designed to get you up and running quickly.

To help get you started, this chapter provides an overview of Premiere Pro windows and menus. Consider it a thorough introduction to the program's workspace and a handy reference for planning and producing your own digital video productions.

IN THIS CHAPTER

Premiere Pro's panels

Premiere Pro's menus

Premiere Pro's Panels

After you first launch Premiere Pro, several panels automatically appear onscreen, each vying for your attention. Why do you need more than one panel opened at once? A video production is a multifaceted undertaking. In one production, you may need to capture video, edit video, and create titles, transitions, and special effects. Premiere Pro windows help keep these tasks separated and organized for you.

You can access any Premiere Pro panel by clicking its name in the Windows menu. For example, if you want to open the Timeline, Monitor, Audio Mixer, History, Info, or Tools panel, you can choose the Window menu and then click the desired panel name. If the panel is already open, a check box appears by its name. If the panel isn't open, it opens in a window when you choose it in the Windows menu. If you have more than one video sequence on the screen, you see them listed in the Window ➪ Timelines submenu.

This section provides an overview of the panels that enable you to create the various elements of your digital video project.

Manipulating Premiere Pro panels

You can work more efficiently if you know how to group and dock Premiere Pro's panels. Grouping and docking panels helps to ensure that you're making the best use of available screen real estate.

All of Premiere Pro's video-editing tools reside in panels that you can group or dock together in virtually any combination. When panels are docked, they are attached to each other, so resizing one panel resizes another. Figure 1.1 shows the Program Monitor being resized. Notice in the second frame of Figure 1.1 that enlarging the Program Monitor reduces the size of the Source Monitor panel.

ON the DVD   The images in Figure 1.1 are from the Premiere Pro CS3 QuickStart chapter. The Clock image (bc0104.mov) is in the FilmDisc folder. The Airport image (BG113.mov) is in the Artbeats folder.

FIGURE 1.1

Resizing panels

Figure 1.1 shows the Project panel grouped with the Effects and Audio Mixer tabs peeking out from behind in the same panel group. You can easily add or remove a panel from a group by clicking the indented dots at the left-hand corners of the tabs and dragging the panel tab.

If you want a panel to appear as a standard window that floats above other panels, you can drag the panel out from behind the others. As you read through the following sections that explain how to resize, group, and separate panels, try adjusting a few panels.

Resizing docked panels

Windows that are grouped together are referred to as *panels*. To resize a panel, move the cursor over the dividing line between panels. When the cursor changes to two arrows, as shown in Figure 1.1, you can drag left or right on the vertical border between panels, or up and down on the horizontal border between panels. If you want to resize the panel both horizontally and vertically, position the mouse cursor over a panel corner. When the mouse pointer changes to four arrows, click and drag the corner.

Docking and grouping panels

If you want to dock one panel with another one (the target panel), click and drag it over to the top, bottom, left, or right portion of the target panel. Before releasing the mouse, wait for the dim preview of the docked panel to appear. If you are satisfied with the results, release the mouse; otherwise, press Esc.

If you want to place one panel into another panel — or group the panels — click and drag the panel's tab. Drag it into the target panel, and then release the mouse. The panel's tab now appears on the far right of all existing tabs.

Creating floating windows

To separate a panel so that it floats on the screen independently like a standard window, choose Undock panel in the panel's menu. Alternatively, press Ctrl/⌘ while clicking the panel's tab. Release the mouse to create the new floating window, and then release Ctrl/⌘. Alternatively, you can click and drag the panel outside of Premiere Pro — provided you have the screen space. Once you create a new floating window, you can create a panel group by clicking and dragging other panels to it.

Closing and saving workspaces

Premiere Pro's primary panels sometimes open automatically onscreen. If you want to close one of them, simply click its Close window (X) icon.

If you have organized your windows and panels in specific positions at specific sizes, you can save this configuration by choosing Window ➪ Workspace ➪ New Workspace. After you name your workspace and save it, the name of the workspace appears in the Window ➪ Workspace submenu. Whenever you want to use that workspace, simply click its name.

The Project panel

If you've ever worked on a project with many video and audio clips as well as other production elements, you can appreciate Premiere Pro's Project panel, shown in Figure 1.2. The Project panel provides an overview of your production elements (often called *assets*), and even enables you to preview a clip by clicking its Play button.

As you work, Premiere Pro automatically loads items into the Project panel. When you import a file, the video and audio clips are automatically loaded into the Project panel. If you import a folder of clips, Premiere Pro creates a new bin (or folder) for the clips, using the folder name as the bin name. When you capture sound or video, you can quickly add the captured media to a Project panel bin before closing the clip. Later, you can create your own bins by clicking the Bin button, at which point you can drag production elements from one bin to another.

FIGURE 1.2

Premiere Pro's Project panel stores production elements.

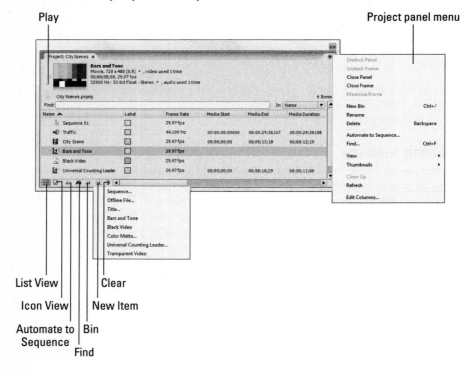

The New Item button (shown in Figure 1.2) enables you to quickly create a new title or other production element, such as a transparent video clip (often used with Premiere Pro's Timecode video effect to overlay timecode over other clips), color matte (covered in Chapter 15), or bars and tone (used to calibrate color and sound when editing). The New Item button also allows you to add new sequences, offline files, black video, and universal counting leaders. If you click the Icon button, all production elements appear as icons onscreen rather than in list format. Clicking the List button returns the display of the Project panel to List view. If you want to quickly add Project panel elements to the Timeline, you can simply select them and then click the Automate to Sequence button.

If you expand the Project panel by clicking and dragging the panel border, you see that Premiere Pro lists the start and stop times as well as the in and out points and the duration of each clip. If you click the Project panel's menu, you can choose to add or remove columns from the Project panel. You can also rearrange the column order by dragging them.

In the Project panel, production assets are grouped according to the current sort order. You can change the order of production elements so that they are arranged by any of the column headings. To sort by one of the column categories, simply click the category. The first time you click it, production items are sorted in ascending order. To sort in descending order, click the column heading again. The sort order is represented by a small triangle. When the arrow points up, the sort order is ascending. When it points down, the sort order is descending.

> **TIP** To find a production item in the Project panel, simply click in the Project panel's Find field and type what you're looking for. Next, choose the category that you are searching for (such as Name, Scene, Shot/Take) in the In drop-down menu. After the item or items are found, you can return the Project panel view back to normal by clicking the X that appears in the Find field.

> **TIP** To play a clip in the thumbnail monitor in the Project panel, click the clip and then click the Play button — the small triangle next to the thumbnail monitor.

To preserve space and hide the Project window's thumbnail monitor, choose View ⇨ Preview Area in the Project Panel Menu. This toggles the monitor display off and on.

To keep your production assets well organized, you can create bins to store similar elements. For example, you can create a bin for all sound files or a bin for all interview clips. If the bin gets full, you can see more elements at one time by switching from the default Thumbnail view to List view, which lists each item but doesn't show a thumbnail image.

Using FlexBins

If you create several bins, you can easily manage them by using Premiere Pro's *FlexBin* feature. This allows you to open up different bins in separate windows, or as tabs. To open a bin as a separate window, simply double-click it. Once the bin opens in a separate window, it can function like any other panel. This means you can dock it or embed it within other panel groups. To change the default preferences for how flex bins open, choose Edit ⇨ Preferences ⇨ General. On a Mac, choose Premiere Pro ⇨ Preferences ⇨ General.

If you don't want to change preferences for FlexBin operations, you can use the following keyboard commands to open up bins:

- **Ctrl/⌘+Double-click:** Opens the bin in the project panel, with no other bins displayed. (To close the bin click the tiny folder icon beneath thumbnail monitor display in the Project panel.)

- **Alt/Option+Double-click:** Creates a tab for the bin in the parent bin. Clicking the tab displays the contents of the child bin.

> **TIP**   You can change the speed and duration of a clip by right-clicking the clip in the Project panel and choosing Speed/Duration. You can also quickly place the clip in the Source Monitor by right-clicking the clip and choosing Open in Source Monitor.

The Timeline panel

The Timeline panel, shown in Figure 1.3, is the foundation of your video production. It provides a graphic and temporal overview of the video sequences, effects, titles, and transitions that comprise your project. The Timeline is not just for viewing — it is also interactive. Using your mouse, you can build your production by dragging video and audio clips, graphics, and titles from the Project panel to the Timeline. By clicking and dragging the current-time indicator (the blue triangle), you can jump to any part of your production. As you click and drag, the time display at the top-left corner of the Timeline indicates the position of the current frame.

Using Premiere Pro tools, you can arrange, cut, and extend clips. By clicking and dragging the work area markers at either end of the work area bar — edges of the light-gray bar at the top of the Timeline — you can specify the portion of the Timeline that Premiere Pro previews or exports. The thin, colored bar beneath the work area bar indicates whether a preview file for the project exists. A red bar indicates no preview, and a green bar indicates that a video preview has been created. If an audio preview exists, a thinner, light-green bar appears. (To create the Preview file, choose Sequence ⇨ Render Work Area or press Enter to render the work area.)

> **TIP**   Rendering the work area helps ensure that your project plays back at the project frame rate. If you create video and audio effects, the Preview file stores the rendered effects. Thus, the next time you play back the effect, Premiere Pro does not have to process the effect again.

Undoubtedly, the most useful visual metaphor in the Timeline window is its representation of video and audio tracks as parallel bars. Premiere Pro provides multiple, parallel tracks so that you can both preview and conceptualize a production in real time. For example, parallel video and audio tracks enable you to view video as audio plays. The Timeline also includes icons for hiding or viewing tracks. Clicking the video Toggle Track Output button (Eye icon) hides a track while you preview your production; clicking it again makes the track visible. Clicking the audio Toggle Track Output button (Speaker icon) turns audio tracks on and off. Beneath the Eye icon is another icon that sets the display mode for clips in the track. Clicking the Set Display Style icon allows you to choose whether you want to see frames from the actual clip in the Timeline or only the name of the clip.

At the bottom-left corner of the window, the Time Zoom Level slider enables you to change the Timeline's time intervals. For example, zooming out shows your project over less Timeline space, and zooming in shows your work over a greater area of the Timeline. Thus, if you are viewing frames in the Timeline, zooming in reveals more frames. You can also zoom in and out by clicking the edges of the Viewing Area bar at the top of the Timeline. To learn more about the many features of the Timeline panel, see Chapter 6.

FIGURE 1.3

The Timeline panel provides an overview of your project and enables you to edit clips.

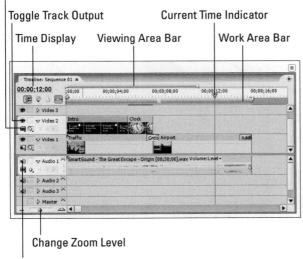

The Monitor panels

The Monitor panels, shown in Figure 1.4, are primarily used to preview your production as you create it. When previewing your work, click the Play button to play it in the Source or Program Monitor. As you work, you can also click and drag in the *tread area* (serrated lines just below the clip) to *jog*, or slowly scroll, through your footage. Below the tread area is a triangular icon called the *shuttle slider*. You can click and drag the shuttle slider to jump to a specific clip area. As you click, the time display in the Monitor panel indicates your position in the clip. The Monitor panels can also be used to set in and out points. As discussed in The Premiere Pro QuickStart chapter, the in and out points determine which part of a clip appears in your project.

ON the DVD   The images in Figure 1.4 are from the SP123.mov file in the Artbeats folder on the Premiere Pro Bible CS3 DVD.

Premiere Pro provides five different monitor panels: the Source Monitor, the Program Monitor, the Trim Monitor, the Reference Monitor, and the Multi-Camera monitor. You can access the Trim, Reference, and Multi-Camera monitors from the Program Monitor's panel menu.

Premiere Pro provides five different monitor panels: the Source Monitor, the Program Monitor, the Trim Monitor, the Reference Monitor, and the Multi-Camera monitor. You can access the Trim, Reference, and Multi-Camera monitors from the Program Monitor's panel menu.

- **Source Monitor:** The Source Monitor shows source footage that has not yet been placed on the video sequence in the Timeline. You can use the Source Monitor to set in and out points of clips and then insert or overlay them into your production. The Source Monitor can also display audio waveforms of audio clips. (To display the audio waveform, set the Take Audio/Video button to audio or double-click unlinked audio. See Chapter 7 for more details.)

- **Program Monitor:** The Program Monitor displays your video program: the clips, graphics, effects, and transitions that you have assembled in a video sequence in the Timeline window. You can also use the Lift and Extract buttons in the Program Monitor to remove footage. To play a sequence in the Program Monitor, you can either click the window's Play button or press the Spacebar.

- **Trim Monitor:** The Trim Monitor allows you to precisely fine-tune edits. You can access the Trim Monitor from the Program Monitor, either by clicking Trim in the Program Monitor panel menu or by clicking the Trim button.

  In the Trim panel, the left and right sides of an edit are shown on either side of the window. To edit, you can click and drag between the two monitor views of the edit to add or subtract frames from either side of the edit (see Figure 1.4). You can also click and drag in the left or right monitor to edit only the left or right side of the edit. You can also choose to edit one frame or five frames at a time by simply clicking a button. Using the Trim Monitor is covered in Chapter 12.

- **Reference Monitor:** In many respects, the Reference Monitor is a second Program Monitor. Many Premiere Pro editors use it when making color and tonal adjustments because it allows them to view video scopes (which display hue and saturation levels) in the Reference Monitor while simultaneously viewing the actual footage in the Program Monitor. The Reference Monitor can be *ganged*, or set to play in sync, with the Program Monitor, or it can be unganged. Using the Reference Monitor is discussed in Chapter 17.

- **Multi-Camera Monitor:** The Multi-Camera Monitor allows you to view four different clips simultaneously in one monitor. As footage plays in the monitor, you can use the mouse or keyboard to select a scene to insert into your program sequence. The Multi-Camera Monitor is most helpful when editing event footage shot simultaneously from different cameras. See Chapter 12 to learn more about using the Multi-Camera Monitor.

FIGURE 1.4

The Source, Program, and Trim Monitors

Play/Stop Step Forward

Step Backward   Take Audio/Video

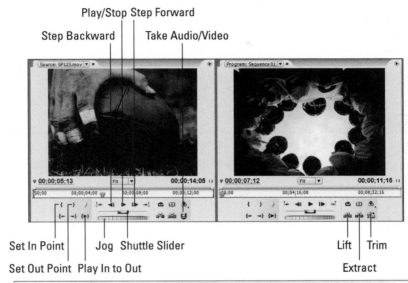

Set In Point   Jog Shuttle Slider   Lift Trim

Set Out Point Play In to Out   Extract

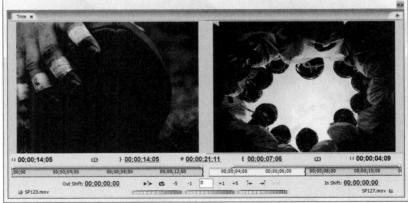

The Audio Mixer panel

The Audio Mixer panel, shown in Figure 1.5, enables you to mix different audio tracks, create audio effects, and record narration. The Audio Mixer's ability to work in real time gives you the advantage of mixing the audio tracks and applying audio effects while viewing the accompanying video.

You can raise and lower audio levels for tracks by clicking and dragging the volume fader controls with the mouse. The round, knob-like controls enable you to pan or balance audio. You can change the settings by clicking and dragging the knob icon. The buttons below the balance controls let you play all tracks, select the tracks that you want to hear, or select the tracks that you want to mute.

The familiar controls at the bottom of the Audio Mixer window enable you to start and stop recording while the audio runs. Chapter 4 covers how to record audio using the Audio Mixer. Chapter 8 provides an in-depth discussion of how to mix and apply effects using the Audio Mixer.

Use the Audio Mixer to mix audio and create audio effects.

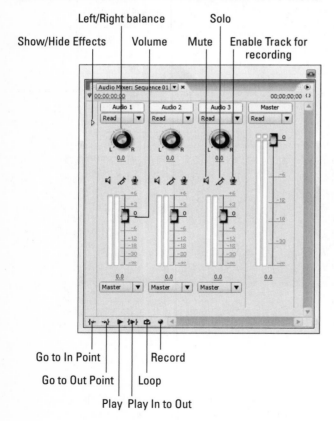

Left/Right balance

Solo

Show/Hide Effects   Volume   Mute   Enable Track for recording

Go to In Point

Go to Out Point

Play   Play In to Out

Loop

Record

The Effects panel

The Effects panel allows you to quickly apply a variety of useful audio effects, video effects, and transitions. For example, the Video Effects bin (folder) includes effects that correct color, change an image's contrast, and distort and blur images. As shown in Figure 1.6, the effects are organized into bins. For example, the Distort bin contains effects that distort clips by bending or pinching them.

Applying an effect is simple: Just click and drag the effect over a clip in the Timeline. You can then edit the effect using controls in the Effect Controls panel.

 The Effects panel allows you to create your own bins and move effects into them so that you can quickly access the effects you want to use in each project.

Premiere Pro's Video Transitions bin, which also appears in the Effects panel, features more than 70 transitional effects. Some transitions, such as the Dissolve group, can provide a smooth transition from one video clip to another. Other transitions, such as Page Peel, can be used as a special effect to dramatically jump from one scene to another.

FIGURE 1.6

Use the Effects panel to apply transitions and special effects.

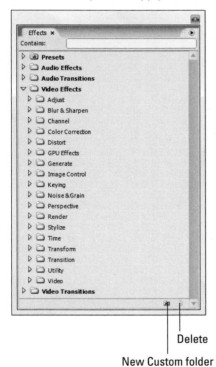

Delete

New Custom folder

If you are using the same transitions throughout a production, you can create a bin, name it, and keep the transitions in the custom bin for quick access.

CROSS-REF See Chapter 9 for more information on creating transitions; see Chapter 13 for more information on using video effects.

The Effect Controls panel

The Effect Controls panel, shown in Figure 1.7, allows you to quickly create and control audio and video effects and transitions. For example, you can add an effect to a clip by selecting it in the Effects panel and then dragging the effect over the clip in the Timeline or directly into the Effect Controls panel. As shown in Figure 1.7, the Effect Controls panel includes its own version of the Timeline as well as a slider control for zooming into the Timeline. By clicking and dragging the Timeline and changing effect settings, you can change effects over time. As you change settings, you create keyframes (indicated by diamond icons) in the Effect Controls panel and in the Timeline.

If you create multiple effects for one clip, you can see the settings for the different effects by selecting the clip and opening the Effect Controls panel.

FIGURE 1.7

The Effect Controls panel enables you to quickly display and edit video and audio effects.

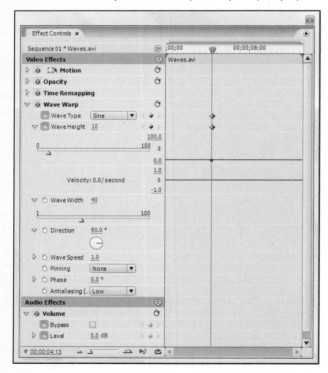

The Tools panel

The tools in Premiere Pro's Tools panel, shown in Figure 1.8, are primarily used to edit clips in the Timeline. You can activate each tool by clicking it in the Tools panel. Here is a brief summary of the tools:

- The Selection tool is often used for selecting and moving clips on the Timeline.

- The Track Select tool selects all items on a track. Pressing Shift while clicking the Track Select tool selects multiple tracks.

- The Ripple Edit, Rolling Edit, Slip, and Slide tools, covered in Chapter 12, are used to adjust edits on the Timeline.

- The Razor tool allows you to cut a clip simply by clicking it. Pressing Shift while clicking the Razor tool cuts footage in multiple tracks.

- The Rate Stretch tool allows you to change the speed of a clip by clicking and dragging a clip edge with the tool.

- The Pen tool allows you to create keyframes on the Timeline when adjusting video and audio effects. Audio effects are covered in Chapter 7. Video effects are covered in Chapter 13.

- The Hand tool enables you to scroll through different parts of the Timeline without changing the Zoom level.

- The Zoom tool provides yet another means of zooming in and out in the Timeline. With the Zoom tool activated, you can click to zoom in and Ctrl/⌘-click to zoom out.

FIGURE 1.8

Premiere Pro's Tools panel

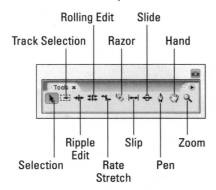

The History panel

Premiere Pro's History panel, shown in Figure 1.9, lets you perform virtually unlimited Undo operations.

FIGURE 1.9

The History panel provides virtually unlimited Undo operations.

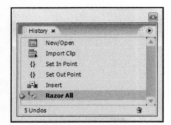

As you work, the History panel records your production steps. To return to a previous version of your project, just click that history state in the History panel. After you click and begin working again, you rewrite history — all past steps following the state you returned to are removed from the panel as new ones appear. If you want to clear all history from the panel, choose Clear in the panel menu (opened by clicking the right triangle icon). To delete a history state, select it and then click the Delete button (trashcan icon) in the panel.

 **If you click a history state in the History panel to undo an action and then begin to work, all steps after the one you clicked are removed from your project.**

The Info panel

The Info panel provides important information about clips and transitions, and even about gaps in the Timeline. To see the Info panel in action, click a clip, transition, or empty gap in the Timeline. The Info window shows the size, duration, and starting and ending points of the clip or gap, as shown in Figure 1.10.

The Info panel can be very useful when editing because the panel displays starting and ending points of the clips as you edit them in the Timeline panel.

The Event panel

The Event panel lists errors that may occur when using third-party video and audio plug-ins. Selecting the error message in the Event panel, and then clicking Details, provides more information about the specific error.

FIGURE 1.10

FIGURE 1.10

The Info panel displays information about clips and transitions.

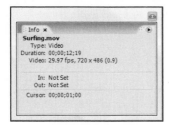

The Title Designer

Premiere Pro's Title Designer allows you to quickly create titles for video projects. You can also use the Title Designer to create animated title effects. To aid title placement, the Title Designer can display video behind the titles you are creating. Tools and other options for creating titles can be opened onscreen from the Title Designer's menu, or by choosing Window ⇨ Title Tools, Title Styles, Title Actions, or Title properties. In Figure 1.11, the Title tools are in the upper-left corner, displayed vertically; the Title Actions are below the Title tools, and also display vertically. To create a title with the Title Designer, choose File ⇨ New ⇨ Title. If you wish to edit a title that is already on the Timeline, double-click the title and it opens in the Title Designer.

FIGURE 1.11

The Title Designer with tools and options for editing titles

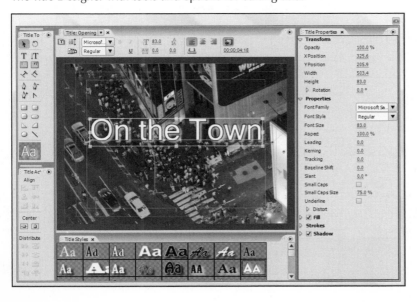

Premiere Pro's Menus

Premiere Pro features nine main menus: File, Edit, Project, Clip, Sequence, Marker, Title, Window, and Help. The following sections provide an overview of the different menus and include tables that summarize each menu's commands.

The File menu

The File menu consists of standard Windows commands such as New, Open, Close, Save, Save As, Revert, and Quit. The menu also includes commands for loading movie clips and folders full of files. You can use the File ➪ New ➪ Sequence command to add Timelines to a project. Table 1.1 summarizes the File menu commands.

TABLE 1.1

File Menu Commands

Command	Shortcut	Description
New ➪ Project	Ctrl/⌘+Alt+N	Creates a new file for a new digital video production
New ➪ Sequence	Ctrl/⌘+N	Adds a new sequence to the current project
New ➪ Bin	Ctrl/⌘+/	Creates a new bin in the Project panel
New ➪ Offline File		Creates a new file entry in the Project panel that can be used for footage to be captured
New ➪ Title	F9	Opens the Title Designer for creating text and graphic titles
New ➪ Photoshop File		Creates a new, blank Photoshop file using project dimensions
New ➪ Bars and Tone		Adds color bars and a sound tone to the bin in the Project panel
New ➪ Black Video		Adds a pure-black video clip to the bin in the Project panel
New ➪ Color Matte		Creates a new color matte in the Project panel
New ➪ Universal Counting Leader		Automatically creates a countdown clip
New ➪ Transparent Video		Creates a transparent video that can be placed in a track, and used to display a timecode
Open Project	Ctrl/⌘+O	Opens a Premiere Pro project file
Open Recent Project		Opens a recently used Premiere Pro movie
Browse	Ctrl/⌘+Alt/Option+O	Opens Adobe Bridge
Close	Ctrl/⌘+W	Closes the Project panel

Command	Shortcut	Description
Save	Ctrl/⌘+S	Saves a project file to disk
Save As	Ctrl/⌘+Shift+S	Saves a project file under a new name, or saves it to a different disk location; this command leaves the user in the newly created file.
Save a Copy	Ctrl/⌘+Alt/ Option+Shift	Creates a copy of the project on disk, but the user remains in the current project
Revert		Reverts a project to the previously saved version
Capture		Captures clips from videotape
Batch Capture		Automatically captures multiple clips from the same tape; this command requires device control.
Adobe Dynamic Link ⇨New After Effects Composition		Allows you to create a new Adobe After Effects Composition linked to a Premiere Pro project
Adobe Dynamic Link ⇨ Import After Effects Composition		Creates a link and imports the file from Adobe After Effects
Import	Ctrl/⌘+I	Imports a video clip, audio clip, or graphic
Import Recent File		Imports recently used files into Premiere Pro
Import Clip Notes Comments		Imports clip comments from Adobe Acrobat
Export ⇨ Movie		Exports a movie to disk according to the settings in the Export Movie dialog box
Export ⇨ Frame		Exports a frame to be used as a still image
Export ⇨ Audio		Exports Timeline audio to disk according to the settings in the Audio Settings dialog box
Export ⇨ Title		Exports a title from the Project panel
Export ⇨ Export to Tape		Exports a Timeline to videotape
Export ⇨ Export to DVD		Burns a DVD from the Timeline
Export ⇨ Export to EDL		Exports the Edit Decision List
Export ⇨ Adobe Media Encoder		Exports in different formats: MPEG1, MPEG2, Real Media, QuickTime, Windows Media
Get Properties for ⇨ File		Provides size, resolution, and other digital information about a file
Get Properties for ⇨ Selection		Provides size, resolution, and other digital information about a selection in the Project panel

continued

TABLE 1.1	*(continued)*	
Command	**Shortcut**	**Description**
Reveal in Bridge		Opens information about a file in Adobe Bridge
Interpret Footage		Changes the frame rate and pixel aspect ratio of a selected item in the Project window; this command also inverts and ignores the alpha channel
Timecode		Sets the timecode starting point of a selected clip in the Project panel
Exit	Ctrl/⌘+Q	Quits Premiere Pro

The Edit menu

Premiere Pro's Edit menu consists of standard editing commands, such as Copy, Cut, and Paste, which you can use throughout the program. The Edit menu also provides special paste functions for editing, as well as preferences for Premiere Pro's default settings. Table 1.2 describes the Edit menu commands.

TABLE 1.2

Edit Menu Commands

Command	Shortcut	Description
Undo	Ctrl/⌘+Z	Undoes the last action
Redo	Ctrl/⌘+Shift+Z	Repeats the last action
Cut Clipboard	Ctrl/⌘+X	Cuts a selected item from the screen, placing it into the
Copy	Ctrl/⌘+C	Copies a selected item into the Clipboard
Paste paste area	Ctrl/⌘+V	Changes the out point of a pasted clip so that it fits in the
Paste Insert	Ctrl/⌘+Shift+V	Pastes and inserts a clip
Paste Attributes	Ctrl/⌘+Alt+V	Pastes attributes of one clip to another
Clear	Backspace	Cuts an item from the screen without saving it in the Clipboard
Ripple Delete	Ctrl/⌘+Shift+Delete	Deletes selected clips without leaving a gap in the Timeline
Duplicate	Ctrl/⌘+Shift+/	Copies a selected element in the Project panel
Select All	Ctrl/⌘+A	Selects all elements in the Project panel
Deselect All	Ctrl/⌘+Shift+A	Deselects all elements in the Project panel

Command	Shortcut	Description
Find	Ctrl/⌘+F	Finds elements in the Project panel (the Project must be opened)
Label		Allows a choice of label colors in the Project panel
Edit Original	Ctrl/⌘+E	Loads a selected clip or graphic from disk in its original application
Edit in Adobe Soundbooth		Opens an audio file for editing in Adobe Soundbooth
Edit in Adobe Photoshop		Opens a graphic file for editing in Adobe Photoshop
Keyboard Customization		Assigns keyboard shortcuts
Preferences		Allows you to access a variety of setup preferences

The Project menu

The Project menu provides commands that change attributes for the entire project. The most important commands enable you to set compression, frame size, and frame rate. Table 1.3 describes the Project menu commands.

TABLE 1.3

Project Menu Commands

Command	Description
Project Settings ⇨ General	Sets the video movie, timebase, and time display; displays video and audio settings
Project Settings ⇨ Capture	Provides settings for capturing audio and video
Project Settings ⇨ Video Rendering	Sets options for rendering video
Project Settings ⇨ Default Sequence	Sets Timeline defaults for video and audio tracks
Link Media	Replaces an offline file in the Project panel with a captured file on disk
Make Offline	Makes a clip offline, so that it is unavailable in a project
Automate to Sequence	Sequentially places the contents of Project panel files into the Timeline
Import Batch List	Imports a Batch list into the Project panel

continued

TABLE 1.3   *(continued)*

Command	Description
Export Batch List	Exports a Batch list from the Project panel as text
Project Manager	Opens the Project Manager; this command allows the creation of a trimmed version of a project
Remove Unused	Removes unused assets from the Project panel
Export Project as AAF	Exports a project in Advanced Authoring Format for use in other applications

The Clip menu

The Clip menu provides options that change a clip's motion and transparency settings. It also includes features that help you edit clips in the Timeline. Table 1.4 describes the Clip menu commands.

TABLE 1.4

Clip Menu Commands

Command	Shortcut	Description
Rename		Renames the selected clip
Make Subclip		Creates a subclip from a clip that was edited in the Source Monitor
Edit Subclip		Allows editing of in and out points of a subclip
Capture Settings ⇨ Set Capture Settings		Sets capture settings for offline files
Capture Settings ⇨ Clear Capture Settings		Clears capture settings for offline files
Insert		Automatically inserts a clip into the Timeline at the current-time indicator
Overlay		Drops a clip into the area of the current-time indicator position, overlaying any existing footage
Replace with Clip ⇨ From Source Monitor		Replaces selected clip in Timeline with clip from Source monitor
Replace with Clip ⇨ From Source Monitor, Match Frame		Replaces selected clip in Timeline with clip from Source monitor and matches frame

Command	Shortcut	Description
Replace with Clip ⇨From Bin		Replaces selected clip in Timeline with clip from Project panel bin
Enable		Allows clips in the Timeline to be enabled or disabled. Disabled clips are not viewed in the Program Monitor and are not exported
Link/Unlink		Unlinks audio from a video clip, and links audio to video
Group	Ctrl/⌘+G	Places Timeline clips in a group so they can be manipulated together
UnGroup	Ctrl/⌘+Shift+G	Ungroups clips
Synchronize		Lines up a clip on the Timeline according to the clip's start, end, or timecode
Multicamera ⇨ Camera 1,2,3, or 4		Replaces footage created in a multicamera edit with footage from a different camera
Video Options ⇨ Frame Hold		Specifies settings for making a still frame from a clip
Video options ⇨ Field Options		Sets interlace options; also sets reverse field dominance
Video options ⇨ Frame Blend		Smoothes the motion of clips whose speed or frame rate has been changed
Video options ⇨ Scale to Frame Size		Scales a clip or graphic to the project size
Audio Options ⇨ Audio Gain		Allows a change of audio level
Audio Options ⇨ Source Channel Mappings		Allows mapping of a mono audio clip as stereo
Audio Options ⇨ Render and Replace		Replaces a selected audio clip with a new clip and maintains effects
Audio Options ⇨ Extract Audio		Creates a new audio clip from a selected clip
Speed/Duration		Allows changing speed and/or duration

The Sequence menu

The Sequence menu enables you to preview the clips in the Timeline window and to change the number of video and audio tracks that appear in the Timeline window. Table 1.5 describes the Sequence menu commands.

TABLE 1.5

Sequence Menu Commands

Command	Shortcut*	Description
Render Work Area	Enter	Creates a preview of the work area; stores the preview file on disk
Delete Render Files		Removes render files from disk
Razor at Current-time Indicator	Ctrl/⌘+K	Cuts a project at the current-time indicator in the Timeline
Lift	;	Removes frames from in to out points set in the Program Monitor and leaves a gap in the Timeline
Extract	'	Removes frames from a sequence from in to out points set in the Program Monitor without leaving a gap in the Timeline
Apply Video Transition	Ctrl/⌘+D	Applies a default video transition between two clips at the current-time indicator
Apply Audio Transition	Ctrl/⌘+Shift+D	Applies a default audio transition between two clips at the current-time indicator
Zoom In	=	Zooms into the Timeline
Zoom Out	-	Zooms back from the Timeline
Snap	S	Turns on/off snap to edges for clips
Add Tracks		Adds tracks to the Timeline
Delete Tracks		Deletes tracks from the Timeline

The Marker menu

Premiere Pro's Edit menu provides commands for creating and editing clip and sequence markers. Markers are designated by pentagon-like shapes just below the Timeline ruler or within a clip in a Timeline. You can use markers to quickly jump to a specific area of the Timeline or to a specific frame in a clip. Table 1.6 summarizes the Marker menu.

TABLE 1.6

Marker Menu Commands

Command	Description
Set Clip Marker	Sets a clip marker for a clip in the Source Monitor at a point specified in the submenu
Go to Clip Marker	Goes to a clip marker at a point specified in the submenu
Clear Clip Marker	Clears a selected clip marker

Command	Description
Set Sequence Marker	Sets a sequence marker specified in the submenu
Go to Sequence Marker	Goes to a sequence marker specified in the submenu
Clear Sequence Marker	Clears a sequence marker specified in the submenu
Set Encore Chapter Marker	Creates an Encore chapter marker at the current-time indicator position
Go to Encore Chapter Marker	Sends the current-time indicator to an Encore chapter marker
Clear Encore Chapter Marker	Removes an Encore chapter marker
Edit Encore Chapter Marker	Allows editing of an Encore chapter marker
Edit Sequence Marker	Allows editing of Timeline markers

The Title menu

Most of Premiere Pro's Title menu is activated after you create a new title in Premiere Pro's Title Designer. The commands in the Title menu alter text and graphics created in the Title Designer. Table 1.7 summarizes the Title menu commands.

TABLE 1.7

Title Menu Commands

Command	Shortcut	Description
New Title ⇨ Default Still		Creates a new title screen with options for creating still titles
New Title ⇨ Default Roll		Creates a new title screen with options for creating rolling titles
New Title ⇨ Default Crawl		Creates a new title screen with options for creating crawling titles
New Title ⇨ Based on Current Title		Creates a new title screen from current titles
New Title ⇨ Based on Template		Creates a new title screen from a template
Font		Provides a choice of fonts
Size		Provides a choice of sizes
Type Alignment		Allows left, center, or right alignment
Orientation		Controls horizontal and vertical orientation of objects
Word Wrap		Turns word wrap on and off
Tab Stops		Sets tabs in a text box

continued

51

TABLE 1.7	*(continued)*	
Command	**Shortcut**	**Description**
Templates	Ctrl/⌘+J	Allows the use and creation of templates for titles
Roll/Crawl Options		Allows the creation and control of animated titles
Logo		Allows graphics to be imported into a title
Transform		Provides visual transformation commands: Position, Scale, Rotation, and Opacity
Select		Provides commands for selecting stacked objects
Arrange		Sends stacked objects forward and backward
Position		Positions a selected item onscreen
Align Objects		Aligns deselected objects
Distribute Objects		Distributes or spreads out selected objects onscreen
View		Allows viewing of title and action-safe areas, text baselines, tab markers, and video

The Window menu

The Window menu enables you to open Premiere Pro panels. Most of the commands work identically to each other. When you choose the name of the panel that you want to open in the menu, that panel opens. (Open panels display with a check mark in front of them.)

Premiere Pro's panels include the following: Effects, Effect Controls, Events, History, Info, Tools, Title Tools, Title Styles, Title Actions, Title Properties, Audio Master Meters, Audio Mixer, DVD Layout, Multi-Camera Monitor, Project, Program Monitor (choose sequence in submenu), Reference Monitor Project, Source Monitor, Timelines (choose sequence in submenu), Title Designer and VST Editor (for third-party audio effects).

You can open panels that are specific to different types of editing work by choosing Window ➪ Workspace ➪ Editing, Window ➪ Workspace ➪ Effects, Window ➪ Workspace ➪ Audio, or Window ➪ Workspace ➪ Color Correction.

You can also save your viewing setup by choosing Window ➪ Workspace ➪ New Workspace Workspace. Later, you can delete the workspace by choosing Window ➪ Workspace ➪ Delete. To reset the current workspace to its original settings choose Window ➪ Workspace ➪ Reset Current Workspace.

The Help menu

Premiere Pro's Help menu provides formatted documents that are viewable in the Adobe Help Center. Choose Help ➪ Adobe Premiere Pro Help to load the main Help screen. From this screen, you can choose to view help about different Adobe applications and search for a topic to learn about it. Figure 1.12 shows the Help screen after choosing help for Premiere Pro. If you click Index, the alphabet appears. Clicking a letter loads the index listings for terms that begin with that letter. If you click the Search button, you can search for help by entering a word or words to search for. For example, if you type the word *edit* and click Search, a long list of topics related to the word *edit* appears. Clicking one of the edit topics brings you to the Help page for that item. To work efficiently when searching, put quotes around search phrases. For example, searching for *"timecode effect"* produces one listing related to the Timecode effect. If you type *timecode effect* without quotes, the search responds with a long list containing all content with the words *timecode* or *effect*.

FIGURE 1.12

Premiere Pro's online help allows you to search for help topics.

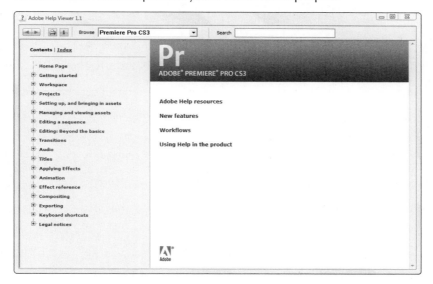

Other Help menu commands access information from the Web. You can choose Help ⇨ Online Support to access Adobe's Web site. To register your version of Premiere Pro online, you can choose Help ⇨ Registration.

Summary

Premiere Pro's panels and menus provide you with an efficient interface and powerful tools to create digital video productions. This chapter covered the following topics:

- The Project panel displays production elements.
- The Timeline panel provides a visual display of your project. You can edit audio and video directly in the Timeline.

- You can use the Effect Controls panel to create video and audio effects and audio transitions.
- The Monitor panels allow you to edit and preview your production.
- The Audio Mixer enables you to mix audio and create audio effects.

Chapter 2

Customizing Premiere Pro

After you become familiar with Premiere Pro, you are certain to appreciate its many timesaving features. As you edit and fine-tune your work, you'll undoubtedly want to save as much time as possible. Fortunately, Premiere Pro provides numerous utilities for keyboard and program customization. This chapter takes a look at how you can create your own keyboard shortcuts to customize Premiere Pro to respond to your every touch. The chapter also provides an overview of Premiere Pro's default settings, which you can also customize to help you work more efficiently. For example, you can create custom tabs in the project panel, and specify both the default frame-length of graphic and still images and the preroll time needed when capturing video with an external device such as a camcorder or VCR.

IN THIS CHAPTER

Creating keyboard shortcuts

Setting program preferences

Creating Keyboard Shortcuts

Keyboard shortcuts can help take the drudgery out of repetitive tasks and speed up your production work. Fortunately, Premiere Pro provides keyboard shortcuts for activating its tools, opening all of its panels, and accessing most of its menu commands. These commands are preset but can easily be altered. If a keyboard command does not exist for a Premiere Pro operation, you can create your own.

To change keyboard shortcuts, open the Keyboard Customization dialog box by choosing Edit ⇨ Keyboard Customization. The Keyboard Customization dialog box, shown in Figure 2.1, is divided into three sections: Application, Panels, and Tools.

The Keyboard Customization dialog box allows you to customize keyboard commands.

Changing Application keyboard preferences

To change Application keyboard commands, choose Application in the drop-down menu below the Set drop-down menu. To change or create a keyboard setting, click the triangle to open the menu heading that contains the command. The following steps show you how to create a keyboard shortcut for the Revert command, which allows you to immediately return to the previously saved version of your work. Use these steps as a guide for changing or creating your own keyboard commands:

1. **Click the triangle icon to open the File menu commands**.

2. **Click in the Shortcut column of the Revert command line, as shown in Figure 2.2.** The Revert command line is activated.

3. **To create the keyboard command, simply press a function key or a modifier key combination.** Use any unassigned shortcut, such as Ctrl/⌘+Shift+R or Alt/Opt+Shift+R.

4. **To create the new keyboard command, click OK.**

If you want to save your keyboard command in a new keyboard command set, click Save As. Then name it in the Name Key Set dialog box, shown in Figure 2.5. If you make a mistake or want to cancel the command, simply click Clear in the Keyboard Customization dialog box.

FIGURE 2.2

Creating a keyboard shortcut for the Revert command

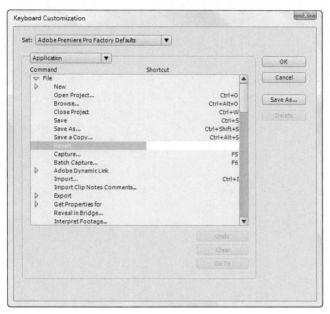

Changing Premiere Pro Panels keyboard commands

Premiere Pro's keyboard customization of its panel commands is quite extensive. To access the Panels keyboard commands, choose Panels from the drop-down menu in the Keyboard Customization dialog box. The keyboard commands found here provide shortcuts for many commands that would normally require one click or clicking and dragging the mouse. Thus, even if you are not going to create or change existing keyboard commands, it is worth taking the time to examine the Panels keyboard commands to see the many timesaving shortcuts that Premiere Pro offers. For example, Figure 2.3 shows the keyboard shortcuts for Timeline operations. Notice that you can use a few simple keystrokes to nudge a clip left or right one or five frames. If you want to change a keyboard command, follow the same procedures described in the preceding section: Click in the shortcut column of the command line and press the command keys that you want to use for the shortcut.

FIGURE 2.3

Keyboard shortcuts for Timeline commands

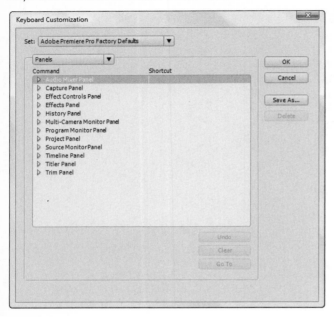

Changing Tools keyboard preferences

Premiere Pro provides keyboard shortcuts for each of its tools. To access the Tools keyboard short-cuts, shown in Figure 2.4, choose Tools from the drop-down menu in the Keyboard Customization dialog box. To change a keyboard command in the Tools section of the dialog box, simply click in the shortcut column in a tool's row and enter your keystroke shortcut on the keyboard.

Saving and loading custom commands

When you change keyboard commands, Premiere Pro automatically adds a new custom set to the Set drop-down menu. This prevents you from overwriting Premiere Pro's factory default settings. If you want to provide a name for the custom set or create multiple custom sets, click Save As in the Keyboard Customization dialog box. This opens the Name Key Set dialog box, shown in Figure 2.5, where you can enter a name. After you save the name, it appears in the Set drop-down menu, along with Adobe's factory default settings. If you want to delete the custom set, select it from the drop-down menu and click Delete.

FIGURE 2.4

Keyboard shortcuts for tools

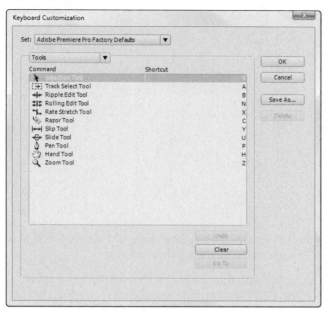

FIGURE 2.5

Name a custom setting in the Name Key Set dialog box.

Setting Program Preferences

Premiere Pro's Program preferences control a variety of default settings that load each time you open a project. You can change these preference settings in the current project, but the changes aren't activated until you create or open a new project. You can change the defaults for capture devices and the duration of transitions and still images, as well as the label colors in the Project menus. This section provides an overview of the many default settings that Premiere Pro offers. You access each of the settings by choosing Edit ⇨ Preferences and then selecting a choice from the Preferences submenu, shown in Figure 2.6. This section provides a review of the different sections of Premiere Pro's Preferences dialog box.

FIGURE 2.6

Use the Preferences submenu to change default settings.

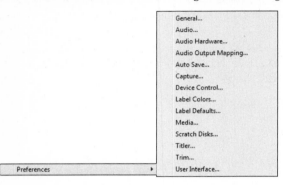

General

The General preferences, shown in Figure 2.7, provide settings for a variety of Premiere Pro default preferences. The commands to control Timeline and clip settings are as follows:

- **Preroll and Postroll:** These settings control the footage that Premiere Pro plays before and after the current-time indicator (CTI) location when you click Play Around. (To Play Around in the Source or Program Monitor, Alt-click the Play In to Out button.) If you click Play Around in the Source, Program, or Multi-Camera Monitor, the CTI backs up to the preroll position and plays to the postroll position. Set the time in seconds in the Preroll and Postroll fields.

- **Video Transition Default Duration:** This setting controls the duration of transitions when you first apply them. By default, this field is set to 30 frames — approximately 1 second.

- **Audio Transition Default Duration:** This setting controls the duration of audio transitions when you first apply them. The default setting is 1 second.

- **Still Image Default Duration:** This setting controls the duration of still images when you first place them on the Timeline. The default setting is 150 frames (5 seconds at 30 frames per second).

- **Timeline Playback Auto-Scrolling:** This setting allows you to choose whether the Timeline panel scrolls during playback. Auto-scrolling allows you to stop at a specific point in the Timeline when interrupting playback, and it can provide a sense of how your Timeline edits are reflected during playback. You can set the Timeline to scroll during playback on a page-by-page basis, to scroll smoothly (with the CTI in the middle of the visible area of the Timeline), or to not scroll at all.

- **Play work area after rendering previews:** By default, Premiere Pro plays the work area after rendering. Deselect this option if you do not want playback after rendering previews.

■ **Default scale to frame size:** By default, Premiere Pro does not shrink or enlarge footage that does not match the project frame size. Select this option if you want Premiere Pro to scale imported footage automatically. Note that if you choose to have Premiere Pro scale to frame size, imported images that are not created at your project frame size may appear distorted.

■ **Bins:** The Bins section allows you to manage footage in the Project panel. Click in the drop-down menu to choose whether you want to open bins (represented by folder icons) by double-clicking, by clicking a tab, or by using keyboard commands.

FIGURE 2.7

The General section in the Preferences dialog box

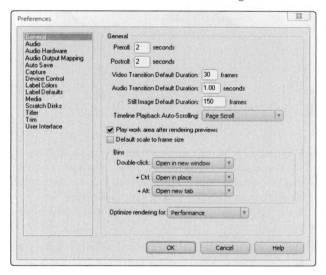

Audio

Premiere Pro's Audio preferences, shown in Figure 2.8, control settings for Premiere Pro's Audio mixer:

■ **Automatch Time:** Use this setting in conjunction with the Touch option in the Audio Mixer. When you choose Touch in the Audio Mixer panel, Premiere Pro returns to the previous values used before changes were made — but only after a specific number of seconds. For example, if you changed audio levels for Track 1 during a mix, then after making the change, the level would revert back to its previous setting — to those just before the changes were recorded. The Automatch setting controls the time interval before Premiere Pro returns to the previous values before audio changes were made.

CROSS-REF For more information about using the Audio Mixer, see Chapter 8.

◦ FIGURE 2.8

The Audio section in the Preferences dialog box provides options relating to audio editing.

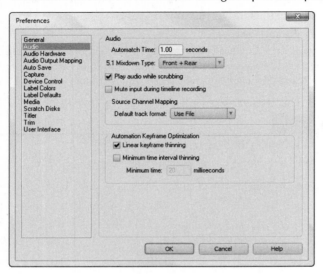

- **5.1 Mixdown Type:** These settings control 5.1 surround-sound track mixes. A 5.1 track is composed of these essential channels: left, center, and right channels (the first three of five main channels), with left- and right-rear channels (two more channels make five), plus a low-frequency channel (LFE). The 5.1 Mixdown Type drop-down menu allows you to change settings for the channels used when mixing, which reduces the number of audio channels.

- **Play audio while scrubbing:** This setting controls whether audio plays while scrubbing in the Timeline or monitor panels.

- **Mute input during timeline recording:** This setting turns off audio while recording using the Audio Mixer. Selecting this option can prevent audio feedback when speakers are connected to your computer.

- **Automation Keyframe Optimization:** This setting helps to prevent the Audio Mixer from creating too many keyframes, which can result in performance degradation. The choices are:

  - **Linear keyframe thinning:** This setting attempts to create keyframes only at the endpoints of a straight line. For example, a diagonal line indicating a change in volume would have one keyframe at either endpoint.

  - **Minimum time interval thinning:** Use this setting to control the minimum time between keyframes. For example, if you set the interval time to 20 milliseconds, then keyframes are created only after an interval of 20 milliseconds.

Audio Hardware

The Audio Hardware preferences, shown by the DirectSound Full Duplex Setup dialog box in Figure 2.9, provide details and options about installed audio hardware. Figure 2.9 shows Audio Stream Input/Output (ASIO) cards for audio input and output ports. The options that appear are based on the specific hardware that is installed in your computer.

FIGURE 2.9

The DirectSound Full Duplex Setup dialog box provides settings for audio hardware.

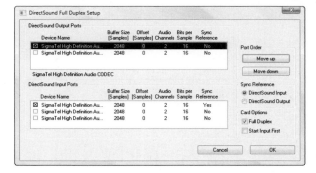

Audio Output Mapping

Audio Output Mapping provides a display of speaker output for Stereo and 5.1 surround sounds. Darkened speakers in the stereo display and black dots in the 5.1 display indicate how the audio is mapped out to sound devices.

Auto Save

If you're worried about forgetting to save your projects as you work, don't worry too much: Premiere Pro's Auto Save preference is turned on by default. When this option is activated, Premiere Pro saves your project every 20 minutes and creates five different versions of your work. In the Auto Save section, shown in Figure 2.10, you can change the time interval for saving. You can also change the number of different versions that Premiere Pro saves.

NOTE   Don't worry about consuming massive amounts of hard drive space with Auto Save. When Premiere Pro saves, it only saves references to the media files. It doesn't resave the files each time it creates a new version of your work.

Premiere Pro's Auto Save default preferences ensure that it automatically saves multiple versions of your work.

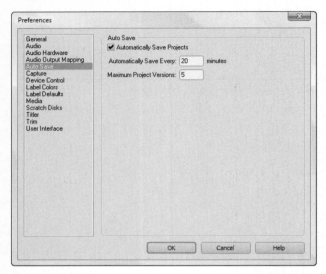

Capture

Premiere Pro's default Capture settings provide options for video and audio capture. The Capture preferences are self-explanatory. You can choose to abort the capture when frames are dropped. You can also choose to view a report on-screen about the capture process and dropped frames. The Generate batch log file option saves a log file to your hard drive, listing the results of an unsuccessful batch capture.

Device Control

The Device Control preferences section, shown in Figure 2.11, lets you choose a current capture device such as a camcorder or VCR. The Preroll setting allows you to set the interval between the times the tape rolls and capture begins. This lets the camcorder or VCR get up to speed before capture. The Timecode Offset option allows you to specify an interval in quarter-frames that provides an offset between the timecode of the captured material and the actual tape. This option allows you to attempt to set the timecode of the captured video so that it matches frames on the videotape.

Clicking the Options button in the dialog box opens the DV Device Control Options dialog box, where you can choose the brand of your capture device, set the timecode format, and check to see whether the device is online or offline.

 For more information about capturing video and the DV Device Control Options dialog box, see Chapter 4.

FIGURE 2.11

Premiere Pro's Device Control preferences allow you to choose preroll time and a capture device.

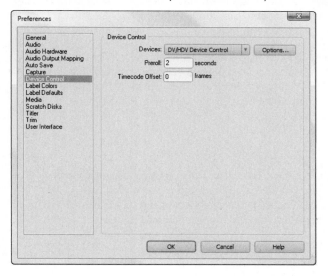

Label Colors and Label Defaults

The Label Colors default setting allows you to change colors of the labels that appear in the Project panel. For example, you can assign specific colors to different media types in the Project panel. To change colors, click the colored label swatch. This opens Premiere Pro's Color Settings dialog box. Here you can change colors by clicking and dragging the vertical slider and by clicking in the rectangular colored box. You can also change colors by entering numbers into the numeric fields. After you change colors, you can edit the color names in the Label Colors section of the Preferences dialog box.

In the Label Defaults preference section, you can change label colors assigned to assets such as Video, Audio, Bins, and Sequences labels that appear in the Project panel. If you don't like the choices that Adobe made when assigning label colors to different media types, you can change color assignments. For example, to change the Label color of video, click the drop-down menu in the Video line and choose a different color.

Media

Premiere Pro's Media preferences allow you to set the location of its Media Cache database, which keeps track of cached media that is used in your production. A computer uses a cache to quickly access data that has been recently used. Cached data files in Premiere Pro can be recognized as follows: .pek (Peak audio files), .cfa (conformed audio files), and MPEG video index files. Clicking the Clean button removes these unnecessary cache files from your computer. After you click Clean, Premiere Pro surveys original files, compares them to cached files, and removes files that are no longer needed.

The Media preferences also set timecode to be displayed using the frame rate of the source footage. If you deselect this option, the project frame rate is used instead. (The project frame rate is set in the Timebase field in the Custom Settings tab when you create a new project.) The In/Out points show media offset option provides a display of the clip's in and out points in relation to the clip's timecode.

Scratch Disks

The Scratch Disks section allows you to set the default disks for a variety of files that Premiere Pro uses while you edit. These include Captured Video, Captured Audio, Video Previews, Audio Previews, Proxies, Media Cache, and DVD Encoding. To set a specific disk and folder, click the Browse button and navigate to the storage device and folder that you want to use.

Titler and Trim

The Titler and Trim preferences provide a variety of default settings for clips.

The Titler preferences control the display of the style swatches and fonts browser that appear in the Adobe Title Designer (choose File ➪ New ➪ Title to open the Title Designer).

The Trim preferences allow you to change the Large Trim offset that appears in the Monitor panel when the Program monitor panel is in Trim view. By default, the Large Trim offset is set to 5 frames. When you click the Trim offset button, five frames are trimmed from an edits in or out point. If you change the value in the Large Trim offset field in the Trim section, the next time you create a project, that value appears as a button in the Monitor panel. The Audio Trim units controls how many audio units are trimmed.

CROSS-REF See Chapter 12 for a discussion on how to edit in Trim view in the Monitor panel.

User Interface

The User Interface Brightness preference controls the brightness of Premiere Pro's panels. Click and drag the slider to the left to create a dark-gray background; click and drag to the right to lighten the panel background.

Summary

Premiere Pro provides many options for customizing its commands and features. You can use these options to help streamline your workflow:

- Use the Edit ➪ Keyboard Customization command to customize keyboard commands for the tools and other panels.

- To edit default settings in Premiere Pro, choose Edit ➪ Preferences.

Chapter 3

Working with
Project Settings

IN THIS CHAPTER

What is digital video?

Understanding project settings

When you first begin creating projects in Premiere Pro, digital video terminology and the numerous settings for video, compression, capturing, and exporting can seem overwhelming. If you're just getting started with Premiere Pro and are primarily interested in learning the basics of the program, you needn't worry too much about understanding all of the options in all of the project-settings dialog boxes. However, if you don't understand such terms as *frame rate*, *frame size*, and *pixel aspect ratio* — terms used in Premiere Pro's project-settings dialog boxes — you're likely to be frustrated when you attempt to output your production.

This chapter provides an overview of key digital video concepts. It also provides a guide to the different dialog boxes in which you designate the startup settings for Premiere Pro projects. For the most part, these are settings that Premiere Pro uses while you are editing in Premiere Pro. Settings for capturing video are covered in Chapter 4. Project settings for exporting video are covered later in Part V of this book.

What Is Digital Video?

In the past few years, the term *digital video* has taken on a variety of new meanings. To the consumer, digital video may simply mean shooting video with the latest video camera from Canon, JVC, Panasonic, or Sony. A digital video camera is named as such because the picture information is stored as a digital signal. The camera translates the picture data into digital signals and saves it on tape in much the same way that your computer saves data to a hard drive.

Some video-recording systems store information in an analog format on tape. In analog format, information is recorded as a continuously modulated signal rather than as individual bits of data.

In Premiere Pro, a digital video *project* usually contains video, still images, and audio that has been *digitized*, or converted from analog to digital format. Video and audio information stored in digital format from digital video cameras can be transferred directly to a computer through an IEEE 1394 port. (Although Apple Computer's trade name for the IEEE port is *FireWire* and Sony's is *i.Link*, the specifications are identical.) Because the data is already digitized, the IEEE 1394 port provides a fast means of transferring the data. However, using video footage shot on an analog video camera or recorded on an analog video deck requires the additional step of first digitizing the footage. Analog-to-digital capture boards that can be installed in PCs generally handle this process. These boards digitize both audio and video. Professional video, broadcast, and postproduction facilities may also use a serial data transport interface (SDTI or SDI) to transfer compressed and uncompressed data.

Visual media, such as photographs and slides, also need to be converted to a digital format before Premiere Pro can use them. Scanners digitize slides and still photos, but you can also digitize slides and photos by photographing them with a digital still camera. Once digitized and saved to the computer's hard drive, you can load these images directly into Premiere Pro. After you have fine-tuned your project, the last step of the digital video production process is to output it to your hard drive, to a DVD, or to videotape.

NOTE The abbreviation DV refers to a distinct digital video format used in consumer and "pro-sumer" camcorders. DV (also known as DV25) utilizes a specific frame size and frame rate, which are discussed in the section "Digital video essentials," later in this chapter.

Digital video provides numerous advantages over traditional analog video. In digital video, you can freely duplicate video and audio without losing quality. However, with analog video, you "go down a generation" each time you copy a clip on videotape, thus losing a little quality.

One major advantage of digital video is that it enables you to edit video in a *nonlinear* fashion. Traditional video editing requires the editor to assemble a videotape production piece by piece from start to finish, in a *linear* manner. In linear editing, each video clip is recorded after the previous clip onto a *program* reel. One problem with a linear system is the time it takes to re-edit a segment or to insert a segment that is not the same duration as the original segment to be replaced. If you need to re-edit a clip in the middle of a production, the entire program needs to be reassembled. The process is similar to creating a necklace with a string of beads. If you want to add beads to the middle of the necklace, you need to pull out all of the beads, insert the new ones, and put the old beads back in the necklace, all the while being careful to keep everything in the same order.

In a nonlinear video system, you can freely insert, remove, and rearrange footage. If you reconsider the bead necklace analogy, nonlinear editing enables you to magically pop the beads on the necklace wherever you want, as if the string didn't exist. Because the image is made up of digital pixels that can be transformed and replaced, digital video enables you to create numerous transitions and effects that are not possible on a purely analog system. To return to the necklace analogy, a digital system lets you not only insert and replace beads freely, but it also allows you to change their color and shape at will.

Digital video essentials

Before you begin creating a digital video project, it's important to understand some basic terminology. Terms such as *frame rate, compression,* and *frame size* abundantly populate Premiere Pro's dialog boxes. Understanding these terms helps you make the right decisions as you create new projects and export them to videotape, to your hard drive, to the Web, or to DVD.

Video frame rates

If you take a strip of motion picture film in your hand and hold it up to the light, you can see the individual picture frames that comprise the production. If you look closely, you can see how motion is created: Each frame of a moving image is slightly different than the previous frame. A change in the visual information in each frame creates the illusion of motion.

If you hold up a piece of videotape to light, you won't see any frames. However, the video camera does electronically store the picture data as individual video frames. The standard DV NTSC (North American and Japanese standard) frame rate in video is 29.97 frames per second; in Europe, the standard frame rate is 25 frames per second. Europe uses the Phase Alternate Line (PAL) system. The standard frame rate of film is 24 frames per second. Newer high-definition video camcorders can also record at 24 frames per second (23.976 to be exact).

Frame rate is extremely important in Premiere Pro because it helps determine the smoothness of the motion in your project. Typically, the frame rate of your project matches the frame rate of your video footage. For example, if you capture video directly into Premiere Pro using DV equipment, the capture rate is set to 29.97 frames per second, which matches Premiere Pro's DV project setting frame rate. Although you want the project frame rate to be the same rate as the source footage, you may want to export at a lower frame rate if you are preparing the project for the Web. By exporting at a lower frame rate, you enable the production to quickly download to a Web browser. Exporting to the Web is covered in Chapter 20.

Interlaced and progressive scanning

Filmmakers who are new to video may wonder why all camcorders don't record and play back at the film rate of 24 frames per second. The answer is rooted in the basics of early television display technology. Video engineers devised a scanning technique of creating images by shooting electron beams one line at a time across the internal phosphor screen of the video display. To prevent the top lines from fading as the scan reached the bottom, engineers divided the video frame into two sets of scanned lines: the even lines and the odd lines. Each scan (called a video field) darts down the screen at one-sixtieth of a second. During the first scan, the odd lines of the video screen are drawn from right to left (lines 1, 3, 5, and so on). During the second pass, the even lines are scanned. The scan is so fast that your eye isn't supposed to see the flicker. This process is known as *interlacing.* Because each field displays at a sixtieth of a second, one video frame appears each thirtieth of a second; thus, the video frame rate is 30 frames per second. Video recording equipment was designed around this process of creating interlaced fields at a sixtieth of a second.

> **NOTE**   To provide a more film-like look, video camera manufacturers have released cameras that can record video at 24 (23.97) frames per second. Premiere Pro includes settings for these cameras.

Many newer video cameras can render a complete video frame in one pass. Thus, there is no need for interlacing. Each video frame is drawn progressively from line 1 to line 2 to line 3, and so on. This process is known as *progressive scan*. Some video cameras that record using progressive scan can record at 24 frames per second and deliver a higher-quality image than interlaced video. Premiere Pro has presets for progressive scan equipment. The future undoubtedly will see more video shot on progressive scan equipment. Once progressive scan video is edited in Premiere Pro, producers can export to programs like Adobe Encore DVD, where they can create progressive scan DVDs.

Frame size

The frame size of a digital video production determines the width and height of your Premiere Pro project. In Premiere Pro, frame size is measured in *pixels*. A pixel is the smallest picture element that displays on a computer monitor. If you are working on a project that uses DV footage, you typically are using the DV standard frame size of 720 x 480 pixels. HDV video camcorders (Sony and JVC) can record at 1280 x 720 and 1440 x 1080. More expensive high-definition (HD) equipment can shoot at 1920 x 1080.

> **NOTE**   High-definition video camcorders can record either interlaced or progressive video; some can record both. In video specifications, *720 p* indicates progressive video at a frame size of 1280 x 720. High-definition formats of 1920 x 1080 can be either progressive or interlaced. In video specifications, *1080 60i* designates interlaced video at a frame height of 1080 pixels. The number 60 refers to the number of fields per second, thus indicating a recording rate of 30 frames per second.

To view a white paper on high-definition cameras and tape formats, go to www.adobe.com/products/premiere/pdfs/hdprimer.pdf.

> **NOTE**   In Premiere Pro you can also work in a project that has a frame size that is different from the frame size of the original video. For example, even if you are using DV footage (720 x 480 pixels), you can create a project with settings for a video iPod or cell phone. The editing frame size for the project will be 640 x 480 pixels, but it will be output at the QVGA (Quarter Video Graphics Array) frame size of 240 x 480 pixels. You can also create a Custom frame size to edit in other frame sizes.

Non-square pixels and pixel aspect ratio

Before the advent of DV, the standard frame size used in most desktop computer video systems was 640 x 480 pixels. Computer images are composed of square pixels, and so the frame size of 640 x 480 and 320 x 240 (for multimedia) conformed nicely to the aspect ratio (width to height) of television, which is 4:3 (for every four square horizontal pixels, there are three square vertical pixels).

But when you're working with a DV frame size of 720 x 480 or 720 x 486, the math isn't so clean. The problem is this: If you create a 720 x 480 frame size, the aspect ratio is 3:2, and not the television standard of 4:3. How do you squeeze 720 x 480 pixels into a 4:3 ratio? The answer is to use rectangular pixels, essentially non-square pixels that are taller than they are wide. (In PAL DV systems — 720 x 576 — the pixels are horizontally longer than they are wide.)

If the concept of square versus non-square pixels seems a bit confusing, remember that 640 x 480 provides a 4:3 aspect ratio. One way of viewing the problem presented by a 720 x 480 frame size is to ask how the width of 720 is converted down to 640. A little high school math comes in handy here: 720 times what number equals 640? The answer is .90 — 640 is 90 percent of 720. Thus, if each square pixel is kind enough to shave its width to 9/10 of its former self, then you can translate 720 x 480 into a 4:3 aspect ratio. If you're working with DV, you may frequently see the number 0.9 (short for 0.9:1). This is called the *pixel aspect ratio*.

When you create a DV project in Premiere Pro, you see that the DV pixel aspect ratio is set to 0.9 instead of 1 (for square pixels). Furthermore, if you import footage with a frame size of 720 x 480 into Premiere Pro, the pixel aspect ratio is automatically set to 0.9.

> **TIP** You can calculate the pixel aspect ratio for an image by using this formula: frame height / frame width × aspect ratio width / aspect ratio height. Thus, for a 4:3 aspect ratio 480 / 640 × 4 / 3 = 1. For .720 / 480; to be more precise we use 704 / 480 × 4 / 3 = .9. For PAL systems, the calculation would be 576 / 704 × 4 / 3 = 1.067. Note that 704 pixels is used instead of 720, because 704 is the actual active picture area

When you create a DV project in Premiere Pro, the pixel aspect ratio is chosen automatically. Premiere Pro also adjusts the computer display so that images created from non-square pixel footages are not distorted when you view them on your square-pixel computer display. Nonetheless, it's helpful to understand the concept of square versus non-square pixels because you may need to export a DV project to the Web, a multimedia application, cell phone, or iPod (all of which display square pixels because they are viewed on progressive scanning displays). You might also need to work in a project with source material created from both square and non-square pixels. For example, if you import footage digitized with an analog video board (which digitizes using square pixels) or import images created in a computer graphics program that uses square pixels into a DV project with DV footage, you have two flavors of pixels in your video stew. To prevent distortion, you may need to use Premiere Pro's Interpret Footage command to properly set frame sizes of imported graphics and footage. (For more information, see the sidebar "Preventing Display Distortion.")

RGB color and bit depth

A color image on the computer screen is created from the combination of red, green, and blue color phosphors. The combination of different amounts of red, green, and blue light enables you to display millions of different colors. In digital imaging programs, such as Premiere Pro and Photoshop, the red, green, and blue color components are often called *channels*. Each channel can provide 256 colors (2^8, often referred to as 8-bit color because 8 bits are in a byte), and the combination of 256 red colors × 256 green colors × 256 blue colors results in over 17.6 million colors. Thus, when creating projects in Premiere Pro, you see most color depth options set to millions of colors. A color depth of millions of colors is often called *24-bit color* (2^{24}). Some new high-definition cameras can record at 10 bits per pixel, providing 1024 colors for each red, green, and blue pixel. That's quite a bit more than 256 for each red, green, and blue color channel. Nevertheless, most video is sampled down to 8 bits per pixel, and so 10-bit color may not offer a great production advantage over 8-bit color.

Preventing Display Distortion

When nonsquare pixels that haven't been altered are viewed on a computer monitor (which displays square pixels), images may appear distorted. The distortion does not appear when the footage is viewed on a video monitor instead of on a computer display. Fortunately, Premiere Pro adjusts nonsquare pixel footage on a computer display and, thus, does not distort nonsquare footage when it imports the footage into a DV project. Furthermore, if you export a project for the Web using Premiere Pro's Adobe Media Encoder (covered in Chapter 18), you can adjust the pixel aspect ratio to prevent distortion. However, if you create a graphic at 720 x 480 (or 720 x 486) in a square-pixel program such as Photoshop 7 and then import it into an NTSC DV project, the graphic may appear distorted in Premiere Pro. The figure shows an image of a circle in a square created at 720 x 480 in Photoshop. Notice that the image appears distorted in Premiere Pro's Source monitor panel. The graphic is distorted because Premiere Pro automatically converts it to a nonsquare 0.9 pixel aspect ratio.

If you create a graphic at 720 x 576 in a square-pixel program and import it into a PAL DV project, Premiere Pro also converts it to a nonsquare pixel aspect ratio. Distortion can occur because Premiere Pro interprets any digital source file created at a DV frame size as nonsquare pixel data. (This file import rule is specified in a text file called "Interpretation Rules.txt." The file, which includes instructions on how to edit the interpretation rules, is found in Premiere Pro's Plug-ins folder [in the en_US folder] and can be edited so that Premiere Pro interprets graphic and video files differently.)

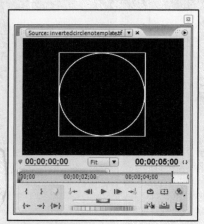

A distorted graphic created with square pixels imported into a DV project.

Fortunately, if you are creating graphics in Photoshop CS2 or greater, you can avoid distorted graphics. Photoshop versions CS2 and greater allow you to preview graphics on video monitor and feature video presets, such as a 720 x 480 DV setting that provides a pixel aspect ratio in a file to 0.9. If you use this preset, you can preview graphics before importing them into a DV project. If a Photoshop CS version is installed on the same computer as Premiere Pro, you can create a Photoshop file in

Premiere Pro by choosing File ⇨ New ⇨ Photoshop File. The file is configured to match the pixel aspect ratio of your Premiere Pro project. If you are using Photoshop CS or greater, you can even set the pixel aspect ratio of an image to match the pixel aspect ratio of your Premiere project. First choose Image ⇨ Image Size to set the frame size to match that of your Premiere project. Next choose Image ⇨ Pixel Aspect Ratio and choose the pixel aspect ratio that matches your project.

However, If you are not using a version of Photoshop CS, you should create full-screen graphics for DV projects at 720 x 534 (DV/DVD), or 720 x 540 and 768 x 576 for PAL. For widescreen projects, choose 864 x 480 (DV/DVD) or 1024 x 576 (PAL). After creating your graphics, import them into Premiere Pro by selecting them in the Project panel and then choosing Clip ⇨ Video Options ⇨ Scale to Frame Size. This squeezes graphics to fit into your DV project without distortion.

If you do create a graphic file at 720 x 480 in a square-pixel program and import it into a Premiere Pro DV project, you may notice distortion because Premiere Pro displays the file as though it were created with non-square pixels. Fortunately, you can "fix" the image in Premiere Pro using its Interpret Footage command. Note that, if you use this technique, Premiere Pro must interpolate (adding about 10 percent more pixels to the image), which may make it appear less sharp.

Here's how to convert your graphics back to square pixels using Premiere Pro's Interpret Footage command to correct distorted images:

1. **Select the graphic image in the Project window.** Note that the Project window indicates that the pixel aspect ratio is not set to 1.0.

2. **To change the pixel aspect ratio back to square pixels, choose File ⇨ Interpret Footage.**

3. **In the Pixel Aspect Ratio section of the Interpret Footage dialog box, click Conform to.** Then choose Square Pixels (1.0) in the drop-down menu. Click OK.

   After you click OK, the listing in the Project window indicates that the image has been converted to square pixels.

NOTE Although television uses a monitor very much like a computer display, it does not use RGB color. Instead, television uses a color system called YCbCr. The Y stands for *luminance*, which controls brightness levels. Both C channels are chroma (hue and saturation) channels. YCbCr was created when television was transitioning between black-and-white and color systems to enable viewers with black-and-white systems as well as those with color systems to view the TV signal. YCbCr is a form of the YUV color system, which also uses luminance and two chroma channels. The two terms are often used synonymously

Compression

Larger frame sizes with 24-bit color, and 24 to 30 frames per second produce a high-quality Premiere Pro digital video project. Unfortunately, a full-frame, 24-bit color, 30-frames-per-second video production requires vast amounts of storage space. You can easily calculate how much hard drive space a full-frame production would require. Start by multiplying the frame dimensions. Assume that you are creating a project at 720 x 480 pixels. Each pixel needs to be capable of displaying red, green, and blue elements of color, so multiply 720 × 480 × 3. Each frame is more than 1MB. Thus, one second of video at 30 frames per second is more than 30MB. (This doesn't even include sound.) A five-minute uncompressed production consumes more than 8GB of storage space. Obviously, uncompressed HD formats would consume even more space.

To store more data in less space with a minimum loss of quality, software engineers have created a variety of video compression schemes. The two primary compression schemes are *spatial* and *temporal*. Here's a brief description of each:

- **Spatial compression (also known as intra-frame):** In spatial compression, computer software analyzes the pixels in an image and then saves a pattern that simulates the entire image. The compression is handled within individual frames without processing other frames (that's why this compression scheme is also called *intra-frame compression*). DV camcorders primarily use intra-frame compression. Because all of the compression information for the frame is within one frame, the CPU works less when editing in programs like Premiere Pro.

- **Temporal compression (inter-frame compression):** Temporal compression works by analyzing the pixels in video frames for screen areas that don't change. Rather than creating many frames with the same image, temporal compression works by creating one keyframe for image areas that don't change. The system calculates the differences between frames to create the compression.

    For example, in a video that consists of frames of a flower that sometimes blows in the wind, the computer needs to store only one frame for the flower and record more frames only when the flower moves. Without temporal compression, different frames would need to be saved to disk for each second of video, whether or not the image on-screen changes.

MPEG-2 (named after the Motion Picture Engineering Group, which oversees the creation of different MPEG file formats) uses inter-frame compression. In this compression scheme, Groups of Pictures (GOP) are analyzed and compressed into one frame. For example, in MPEG-2, as many as 15 frames may be grouped together (12 frames in PAL). The GOP consists of I frames, P frames, and B frames. An *I frame* is a keyframe of the entire frame data, and a *P frame* is a predictive frame that can be a small percentage of the size of the I frame. A *B frame* is a frame that can use a portion of the I frame and the P frame. Because compression data is stretched over several frames, the CPU is taxed to pull all the pieces together when you edit. That is why many desktop editing systems do not edit using MPEG-2 source material.

When you work with compression in Premiere Pro, you don't have to choose spatial or temporal compression. Instead, depending upon your project settings, you choose compression settings by specifying an editing compression format or *CODEC*. CODEC stands for compression and decompression. For example, if you are using DV, you are using a DV codec. When you work with Premiere Pro, you're not actually looking at the compressed video, you are viewing the video after the CODEC has decompressed. When you've completed your project, you can export it using another compression format.

NOTE A DV camera compresses video before it is transferred to your computer. The standard compression ratio used is 5:1, which makes the transferred video signal five times smaller than the original video signal. The DV video data rate is 25 Mb/s (megabits per second; thus 25 million bits per second); DV camcorders primarily use intra-frame compression. DV50 formats such as DVCPro and DVCam have a 50-megabit per second data rate.

QuickTime, Video for Windows, and MPEG

In order for your computer to use a video compression system, software, and sometimes hardware must be installed. Both PCs and Macs usually have video compression software built into their operating systems. QuickTime is the digital video compression system that automatically installs with the Macintosh operating system; Video for Windows (AVI) is the digital video compression system that automatically installs in the Windows operating system. Both QuickTime and AVI use a variety of CODECs. However, QuickTime can also be installed on PCs. Because QuickTime is a cross-platform system, it is one of the more popular digital video systems for CD-ROM and Web digital video.

When you export a movie from Premiere Pro, you can access the QuickTime (if it is installed on your PC) or AVI compression settings, which enables you to choose from a list of QuickTime or AVI CODECs (the QuickTime and AVI categories both include DV CODECS). If you have a capture board installed in your computer, the capture board typically provides a set of CODECs from which to choose.

You can import both QuickTime and AVI video clips into Premiere Pro as well as integrate both into a Premiere Pro project. Premiere Pro supports the following file formats: Type 2 AVI, MOV (QuickTime), Open DML, and WMV (Windows Media). Premiere Pro also supports MPEG (including MPG and MPE). However, because MPEG-2 uses inter-frame compression, the CPU is heavily taxed when using MPEG-2 source files.

You can export your file in a variety of compression formats. You can also use the Adobe Media Encoder to export in Flash Video, Windows Media, QuickTime, Real, or MPEG-1 (sometimes used in multimedia and for Web purposes), as well as MPEG-2 format. Outputting in MPEG formats is covered in Chapter 18. MPEG-2 compression is used to create DVDs, which can provide up to two hours of video with eight tracks of audio. MPEG-1 compression, which can be used on the Web or on CD-ROMs, provides VHS-quality video. The newest MPEG standard, MPEG-4 (available in QuickTime 6), provides even better compression than MPEG-2.

Digital format overview

If you haven't dealt extensively with the concepts of video formats, frame sizes, and aspect ratios, you may find it helpful to see these formats organized in a table. Table 3.1 provides an overview of DV formats for NTSC and PAL. As you view the table, you can see the difference between standard and widescreen DV formats, as well as the difference in frame size between HDV and standard-definition DV. HDV has five times as much picture information as standard DV. HDV camcorders are also substantially cheaper than HD cameras. The format is called HDV because it uses the horizontal line resolution of high definition but is compressed to fit on mini-DV tapes. Most video reviewers have praised the high quality of HDV footage. But the advantage of HDV will be most important when a high-definition DVD format becomes standardized. Because the current standard DVD frame size matches the DV frame size (not the HD frame size), DVD viewers aren't yet getting the full benefit of viewing material shot on HD or HDV systems (at least at the time of this book's publication).

TABLE 3.1

Digital Video Specs

Format	Frame Size	Aspect Ratio/Pixel Aspect Ratio	Frames per Second*
D1** / DV NTSC	720 x 486 / 720 x 480	4:3 / 0.9	29.97
DV NTSC (Widescreen)	720 x 480	16:9 / 1.2	29.97
D1 / DV (PAL)	720 x 576	4:3 / 1.067	25
DV Widescreen (PAL)	720 x 576	16:9 / 1.422	25
HDV 720	1280 x 720	16:9 / 1	29.97
HDV 1080	1440 x 1080	16:9 / 1.33	25 / 29.97
HD 1080	1920 x 1080	16:9 / 1	25 / 29.97 / 23.97
HD 720	1280 x 720	16:9 / 1	59.94

* Note that frames per second for HD and HDV video depends upon the manufacturer and whether the video is interlaced or progressive.

** D1 is an expensive, broadcast-quality, uncompressed digital format that was introduced in 1986 by Sony.

Understanding Project Settings

After you gain a basic understanding of frame rate, frame size, and compression, you can better choose settings when you create a project in Premiere Pro. If you choose your project settings carefully, you can produce better quality video and audio. Figure 3.1 shows Premiere Pro's New Project dialog box, which appears when you create a new project in Premiere Pro.

The New Project dialog box appears when you click New Project after starting Premiere Pro, or when you choose File ⇨ New Project. The creators of Premiere Pro have streamlined the process of choosing project settings. To get started, you can simply click one of the available presets. Notice that Premiere Pro provides DV (Digital Video) format presets for NTSC television and the PAL standards. If you are working with HDV or HD, you can also choose presets.

How do you decide which preset to choose? If you are working on a DV project and your video is not going to be in a widescreen format (16:9 aspect ratio), you can choose the Standard 48 kHz option. The sound quality is indicated by 48 kHz, which should match the sound quality of your source footage. The 24 P Preset folder is for use with footage shot at 24 frames per second, and progressively scanned at a frame size of 720 x 480 (Panasonic and Canon make cameras that shoot in this mode). If you have a third-party video capture board, you may see other presets that were specifically created to work with your capture board.

The New Project dialog box includes project presets.

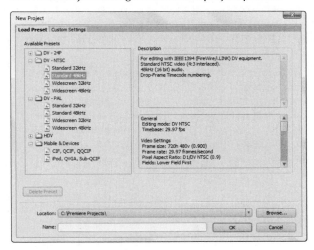

Clicking one of the presets displays its settings for Compression, Frame Size, Pixel Aspect Ratio (discussed later in this chapter), Frame Rate, and Bit Depth, as well as for audio settings. If you are working with DV footage, you probably do not need to change the default settings. If you need to alter the presets, click the Custom Settings tab. This opens the General section of the New Project dialog box.

TIP If you create a custom preset in the Custom Tab of the New Project dialog box, you can save it for use in other projects by clicking Save Preset. Saved presets can be loaded from a folder called Custom that appears in the Load Preset tab in the New Project dialog box.

Video and audio project settings are divided into four categories: General, Capture, Video Rendering, and Default Sequence. The sections that follow describe the General, Video Rendering, and Default Sequence settings. All of these sections of the New Project dialog box are accessible when you first create a project. If you want to view project settings after creating a project, choose Project ⇨ Project Settings ⇨ General. However, note that after you create a project, most settings cannot be changed.

CROSS-REF You can find out more about audio settings in Chapter 7, and about capture settings in Chapter 4. See Chapter 19 for more information about exporting Premiere Pro projects.

Mobile and iPod Video Presets

Premiere Pro offers presets for mobile phone video and other mobile devices such as video iPods. Common Intermediate Format (CIF) and Quarter Common Intermediate Format (QCIF) are standards that were created for video teleconferencing. Premiere Pro's CIF editing presets are designed specifically for mobile devices that support the Third Generation Partnership Project (3GP2) format. The 3G mobile networks are Third Generation mobile networks that allow videoconference and the sending and receiving of full-motion video with audio. The 3GP2 format is the most used Third Generation format in the world. The two Third Generation video formats, 3GPP and 3GPP2, are based on MPEG-4.

Premiere Pro's CIF and QVGA (used in video iPods) presets are quite different from video recording settings. For example, the standard mobile phone screen is 176 x 220. You should use the CIF or QVGA presets if your source footage conforms to the mobile standards. When you export your CIF or QVGA projects, you need to choose the H.264 output format with the Adobe Media Encoder, which provides output specifications for QCIF and QVGA. If your source footage is not CIF or QVGA, you can still use the H.264 option when you create projects for mobile devices. The Mobile presets and frame sizes are summarized in Table 3.2.

TABLE 3.2

Mobile Handset Presets

Format	Editing and Export Frame Size	Aspect Ratio/Pixel Aspect Ratio	Frame Rate
CIF	352 x 480 Export at: 176 x 144 or 88 x 72	11:10 / 1	15
IPOD, QVGA, SubQCIF	640 x 480 Export at: 320 x 240 or 128 x 96	4:3 / 1	15

General settings

The General settings section of the New Project dialog box, shown in Figure 3.2, provides a summary of the individual project settings.

You can access this dialog box by choosing File ➪ New Project (or by clicking the New Project button) and then clicking the Custom Settings tab. To access this dialog box after creating a project, choose Project ➪ Project Settings ➪ General.

FIGURE 3.2

The General settings section of the Custom Settings tab in the New Project dialog box

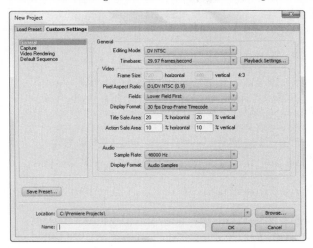

You can change the following settings:

- **Editing Mode:** The editing mode is determined by the chosen preset in the Load Preset tab of the New Project dialog box. The editing mode choice sets the Timeline playback method, as well as compression settings. When you choose a DV preset, the editing mode is automatically set to DV NTSC or DV PAL. If you don't pick a preset, you can choose a variety of editing modes from the Custom Settings tab. These choices are shown in Figure 3.3.

  If you are working with analog video that uses square pixels, you can change the editing mode to Desktop, which allows you to access frame size options that you can change to match the footage that you will be using.

FIGURE 3.3

The Custom video editing choices

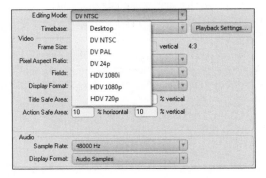

- **Timebase:** The timebase determines how Premiere Pro divides video frames each second when calculating editing precision. In most projects, the timebase should match the frame rate of captured footage. For DV projects, the timebase is set to 29.97 and cannot be changed. You should set the timebase to 25 for PAL projects, 24 for film projects, and 15 for mobile devices. The timebase setting also determines which choices are available in the Display Format field. Both the Timebase and the Display Format fields determine the positions of the ruler tick marks in the Timeline window.

NOTE   By default, Source footage timecode is displayed using the frame rate of the source footage, not the frame rate specified in the Timebase field. In previous versions of Premiere, Source footage timecode was displayed using the project frame rate. You can choose to have Source footage timecode displayed using the project frame rate by choosing Preferences ⬩ Media. In the Preferences dialog box, deselect Display Media Timecode in Source Frame Rate.

- **Frame Size:** The frame size of your project is its width and height in pixels. The first number represents the frame width, and the second number represents the frame height. If you choose a DV preset, the frame size is set to the DV defaults (720 x 480). If you are using the DV editing mode, you cannot change the project frame size. However, you can change the frame size if you create a project using the Desktop editing mode. If you are creating a project for the Web or CD-ROM, you can reduce its frame size when exporting your project (this is discussed in Part V of this book).

- **Pixel Aspect Ratio:** This setting should match the shape of the image pixels — the width-to-height ratio of one pixel in your image. For analog video and images that you have scanned or created in graphics programs, choose square pixels. The default setting for a D1/DV project is 0.9. The drop-down menu allows you to choose different settings, depending upon the editing mode choice. For example, if you pick DV NTSC, you can choose from 0.9 or 1.2 for widescreen footage. If you choose Desktop as the editing mode, you can freely choose pixel aspect ratio, although this format will most likely be used by those who need to work with square pixels.

  Choose the Anamorphic 2:1 format if the video was shot on film with an anamorphic lens. These lenses squeeze the images during shooting, but when projected, an anamorphic projection lens reverses the compression to create a widescreen effect.

TIP   If you need to change the frame rate or the pixel aspect ratio of an imported clip (because either one doesn't match your Project settings), select the clip in the Project panel and choose File ⬩ Interpret Footage. To change the frame rate, in the Interpret Footage dialog box, click Assume this frame rate. Then enter the new frame rate in the field. To change the pixel aspect ratio, click Conform to. Then choose from a list of pixel aspect ratios. After you click OK, the Project panel indicates the changes.

TIP   If you need to import widescreen footage with a 16:9 aspect ratio into a project that uses a 4:3 aspect ratio, you can scale or manipulate the widescreen footage using the Position and Scale options of the Motion video effect. See Chapter 16 for more information about using the Motion video effect.

■ **Fields:** Fields are relevant when working on a project that you will export to videotape. Each video frame is divided into two fields that appear for one-sixtieth of a second. In the PAL standard, each field displays every one-fiftieth of a second. Choose either the Upper or Lower setting in the fields section, depending upon which field your system expects. (See Chapter 21 for more information.)

■ **Display Format:** This setting determines the number of frames that Premiere Pro uses when it plays back from the Timeline, and whether drop frame or non–drop frame timecode is used. In Premiere Pro, time for video projects is displayed in the Timeline and other panels using Society of Motion Picture Television Engineers (SMPTE) video time readouts called *timecode*. In non–drop frame timecode, *colons* are used to separate hours, minutes, seconds, and frames. At 29.97 or 30 frames per second in non–drop frame timecode, the frame following 1:01:59:29 is 1:02:00:00.

In drop frame timecode, *semicolons* are used to separate hours, minutes, seconds, and frames. For example, the frame after 1;01;59;29 is 01;02;00;02. The visual frame display drops numbers each minute to compensate for the fact that the NTSC video frame rate is 29.97, and not 30 frames per second. Note that video frames are not dropped; only numbers in the timecode display are dropped.

If you are working on a film project at 24 frames per second, you can choose options for either 16mm or 35mm.

CROSS-REF The difference between drop frame and non–drop frame timecode is discussed in more detail in Chapter 4.

■ **Title Safe Area and Action Safe Area:** These two settings are important if your project will be viewed on a video monitor. The settings help you to compensate for monitor overscan, which can cause a TV monitor to cut off the edges of the pictures. The settings provide a warning border, showing the limits where titles and actions can safely be viewed. You can change the percentages for the title safe and action safe zones. To view the safe areas in the Monitor window, choose Safe Margins from the Monitor window menu. When the safe areas appear, as shown in Figure 3.4, make sure that all titles appear within the first boundary and all actions appear within the second boundary. The clip in Figure 3.4 is FilmDisc cm0105.

■ **Sample Rate:** The audio sample rate determines audio quality. Higher rates provide better-quality audio. It's best to keep this setting at the rate at which your audio was recorded. If you change this setting to another rate, then more processing is required, and quality may be adversely affected.

■ **Display Format:** When working with audio clips, you can change the Timeline or Program Monitor panel display to show audio units instead of video frames. The audio display format allows you to set audio units to be in milliseconds or audio samples. (Like a frame in video, an audio sample is the smallest increment that can be used in editing.)

CROSS-REF For more information about audio sample rates and audio display formats, see Chapter 7.

CAUTION Because DV projects use industry standard settings, you should not change settings for pixel aspect ratio, timebase, frame size, or fields.

FIGURE 3.4

Title safe (inner rectangle) and action safe (outer rectangle) areas, viewed in the Monitor window

Action Safe Area   Title Safe Area

If you are working with a DV, HD, or HDV editing mode, you can click the Playback Settings button, which opens the Playback Settings dialog box, as shown in Figure 3.5.

■ **RealTime Playback:** In this section, select how you want to view your project as you edit. You can select an online camcorder or VCR from the External Device drop-down menu as your playback output. If you will be exporting your project to videotape, then outputting to a video monitor or to your camcorder monitor (rather than to your computer display) provides the best preview of your project. If you only want to view the video on an external monitor, and don't want to display video on your computer during playback, deselect Desktop Video Display during playback.

■ **Aspect Ratio Conversion:** This allows you to choose whether your system's hardware or software controls pixel aspect ratio conversion.

■ **Export:** If you will be exporting to an external device such as a camcorder or VCR, choose it from the Export External Device drop-down menu.

■ **24p Conversion Method:** This section allows you to specify how Premiere Pro handles displaying 24 frames-per-second (fps) progressive video in a 30 fps video. To do this, Premiere Pro must generate a new frame to compensate for the difference between 24 frames per second and 30 frames per second. For example, for every 4 frames at 24 frames per second, Premiere Pro must make 5 frames. In order to understand the choices, first assume that the 4 frames of your 24 fps footage are labeled A, B, C, and D. The Repeat Frame (ABBCD) option simply repeats when needed to make the 5 frames.

The Interlaced Frame (2:3:3:2) option uses interlacing to create an extra frame. It taxes the computer's CPU more than the ABBCD choice, but it provides smoother playback. Here's how 2:3:3:2 works (we start with Frames A, B, C, and D and end up with Frames 1, 2, 3, 4, and 5):

- **New Frame 1:** From first field of **A** and second field of **A**
- **New Frame 2:** From first field of **B** and second field of **B**
- **New Frame 3:** From second field of **B** and first field of **C** (shares fields from **B** and **C**)
- **New Frame 4:** From first field of **C** and second field of **C**
- **New Frame 5:** From first field of **D** and second field of **D**

If you count the fields used, you get two As, three Bs, three Cs, and two Ds. Thus, the ratio 2:3:3:2.

 You can simulate a "telecine" video-on-film look with 24p footage by selecting it in the Project panel and choosing File ⇨ Interpret Footage. In the Frame Rate section, choose Remove 24P DV Pulldown.

- **Desktop Display Mode:** Choose the option that matches your graphics display. Select Compatible if your display does not support Direct 3D 9.0 acceleration. This provides the slowest performance. Select Standard if your display card supports Direct 3D 9.0 acceleration. This setting provides accelerated display video. Select Accelerated GPU Effects mode if have a new generation Direct 3D 9.0 card, which accelerates video playback and effects.

- **Disable video output when Premiere Pro is in the background:** Selecting this option disables output to a video monitor when Premiere Pro is not the active application.

NOTE Third-party software plug-ins may also allow different playback options.

FIGURE 3.5
_____

Use the DV Playback Settings dialog box to select playback options for DV camcorders and VCRs.

Video rendering

The Video Rendering section of the New Project dialog box, shown in Figure 3.6, specifies settings for playing back video. You can access the Video Rendering section by choosing File ⇨ New Project (or by clicking the New Project button), clicking the Custom Settings tab, and clicking Video Rendering. To access this dialog box after creating a project, choose Project ⇨ Project Settings ⇨ Video Rendering.

Maximum Bit Depth

The Maximum Bit Depth option instructs Premiere Pro to display video at the maximum bit depth available, based on project settings. The highest bit depth is 32 bits.

Previews

The Previews section of the Video Rendering settings specifies how video is previewed when you are using Premiere Pro. Most of the choices are determined by the project editing mode and cannot be changed. For example, for DV projects, you cannot change any options. If you choose the Desktop Editing Mode, you can pick a CODEC in the Compressor drop-down menu, and you can also choose an uncompressed 8-bit or 10-bit file format. If you choose an HD Editing Mode, you can choose a file format. If options are available in the Previews section, choose the combination of file format, compressor, and color depth that provide the best balance between playback quality, rendering time, and file size.

Choosing the Optimize Stills option instructs Premiere Pro to use fewer frames when rendering still images. For example, instead of creating 30 frames of video to render a one-second still image, Premiere Pro can optimize output by creating one frame that is one second long. If still images do not display cleanly when you select this option, deselect it and export your video again.

Default Sequence

The Default Sequence section of the New Project dialog box, shown in Figure 3.7, provides options for setting up Timeline defaults for new projects, including the number of video and audio tracks in the Timeline window. You can access Default Sequence settings when you create a new project by clicking File ⇨ New Project (or by clicking the New Project button), clicking the Custom Settings tab, and then clicking Default Sequence. To access this dialog box after creating a project, click Project ⇨ Project Settings ⇨ Default Sequence.

Changing settings in this dialog box section does not alter the current Timeline. However, if you create a new project or a new sequence (by choosing File ⇨ New Sequence), the next Timeline that is added to the project displays the new settings. Options in the dialog box allow you to change the number of video and audio tracks. You can also choose whether to create submix tracks and Dolby Digital tracks. The audio submix and Dolby 5.1 options are covered in Chapters 7 and 8.

FIGURE 3.6

The Video Rendering section of the New Project dialog box provides settings for video output.

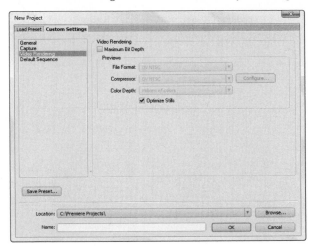

FIGURE 3.7

Use the Default Sequence section of the New Project dialog box to set Timeline defaults.

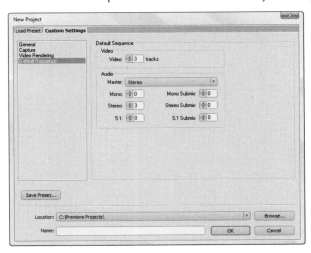

Summary

Premiere Pro provides a nonlinear system for creating desktop video projects. A nonlinear system lets you edit video quickly and efficiently. You can easily edit and insert clips without reassembling your entire project. When you create a new project, you need to specify project settings. This chapter covered the following topics:

- When creating a new project, the easiest way to pick project settings is to choose a preset from the New Project dialog box.

- If you are creating a DV project, you shouldn't need to change most DV presets.

- To change project settings in a new project, click the Custom Settings tab in the New Project dialog box.

- Use the Default Sequence section of the New Project or Project Settings dialog box to change the number of video and audio tracks in new projects.

Chapter 4

Capturing Video and Audio

The quality of video clips in a Premiere Pro project can often mean the difference between a production that attracts viewers and firmly holds their attention and one that sends them looking for other sources of information or entertainment. Undoubtedly, one of the primary factors in determining the quality of source material is how the video is captured. Fortunately, Premiere Pro provides extremely efficient and reliable capture options.

If you have a capture board or peripheral card that digitizes analog video, you may be able to access the capture board directly from Premiere Pro to digitize video. If you have an IEEE 1394 port, you may also be able to use Premiere Pro's Capture window to transfer clips directly from your DV camera. Depending upon the sophistication of your equipment and the quality requirements of your production, you may be able to capture all of your video source material by using Premiere Pro.

This chapter focuses on capturing video and audio using Premiere Pro. It leads you step-by-step through the process of using Premiere Pro's Capture window to capture videotape to your computer's hard drive. If your equipment enables device control, you can start and stop a camcorder or tape deck directly from Premiere Pro. You may also be able to set up a batch capture session in which Premiere Pro automatically uses a list of clips' in and out points to capture multiple clips during one session.

Getting Started

Before you start capturing video for a production, you should first realize that the quality of the final captured footage depends on the sophistication of your digitizing equipment and the speed of the hard drive that you are using to capture the material. Much of the equipment sold today can provide quality suitable for the Web or in-house corporate video. However, if your goal is to create very high quality video productions and transfer them to videotape, you should analyze your production needs and carefully assess exactly what hardware and software configuration best suits your needs.

Fortunately, Premiere Pro can capture audio and video using both low-end and high-end hardware. Capture hardware, whether low end or high end, usually falls into three categories:

- **FireWire/IEEE 1394:** Apple Computer created the IEEE 1394 port primarily as a way to quickly send digitized video from video devices to a computer. In Apple computers, the IEEE 1394 board is called a FireWire port. Several PC manufacturers, including Sony and Dell, sell computers with IEEE preinstalled (Sony calls its IEEE 1394 port an i.Link port). If you are shopping for an IEEE 1394 board, hardware should be OHCI (Open Host Controller Interface) compliant. OHCI is a standard interface that allows Windows to work with and recognize the card. If Windows has no problems recognizing the card, most DV software applications can use the card without problems.

  If your computer has an IEEE 1394 port, you can transfer digitized data directly from a DV camcorder to your computer. As mentioned in Chapter 4, DV and HDV camcorders actually digitize and compress the signal as you shoot. Thus, the IEEE 1394 port is a conduit between the already digitized data and Premiere Pro. If your equipment is Premiere Pro-compatible, you can use Premiere Pro's Capture window to start, stop, and preview the capture process. If you have an IEEE 1394 board in your computer, you may be able to start and stop a camcorder or tape deck from within Premiere Pro; this is called *device control*. With device control, you can control everything from Premiere Pro. You can cue up the video source material to specific tape locations, record timecode, and set up batch sessions, which enables you to record different sections of videotape automatically in one session.

NOTE To ensure high-quality capture, your hard drive should be able to sustain a data rate of 3.6 MB per second — the DV data rate.

- **Analog-to-digital capture cards:** These cards take an analog video signal and digitize it. Some computer manufacturers have sold models with these boards built directly into the computer. On the PC, most analog-to-digital capture boards are add-ins that must be installed in the computer. More expensive analog-to-digital capture boards permit device control, enabling you to start and stop a camcorder or tape deck as well as cue it up to the tape location that you want to record. If you are using an analog-to-digital capture card, you must realize that not all cards are designed with the same standards, and some may not be compatible with Premiere Pro. To check video card compatibility, see www.adobe.com/products/premiere/dvhdwrdb.html.

- **HD or SD Capture Card with SDI input:** If you are capturing HD footage, you need a Premiere Pro–compliant HD capture card installed in your system. The card must have a Serial Device Interface (SDI). Premiere Pro internally supports AJA's HD SDI card. For more information about AJA cards, visit the Windows section of www.aja.com. Premiere Pro also supports Standard Definition (SD) SDI cards.

Making the Right Connection

Before you begin the process of capturing video or audio, make sure that you read all relevant documentation supplied with the hardware. Many cards include plug-ins so that you can capture directly into Premiere Pro (rather than first capturing in another software application and then importing into Premiere Pro). This section provides a brief description of the connection requirements for analog-to-digital boards and IEEE 1394 ports:

- **The IEEE 1394/FireWire connection:** Making the connection from a DV or HDV camera to your computer's IEEE 1394 port is easy. Simply plug the IEEE 1394 cable into the DV In/Out jack of your camcorder, and plug the other end into the IEEE 1394 jack of your computer. Although this is a simple procedure, be sure to read all documentation. For example, the connection may not work unless you supply external power to your DV/HDV camera, and the transfer may not work on the DV/HDV camera's batteries alone.

NOTE IEEE 1394 cables for desktop and laptop computers are usually different and are not interchangeable. Furthermore, an IEEE 1394 cable that connects an external FireWire hard drive to a computer may be different from an IEEE 1394 cable that connects a computer to a camcorder. Before purchasing an IEEE 1394 cable, make sure it is the right cable for your computer.

- **Analog to digital:** Most analog-to-digital capture boards use Composite Video or S-Video systems. Some boards provide both Composite and S-Video. Hooking up a Composite system usually entails connecting a cable with three RCA jacks from the video and sound output jacks of your camcorder or tape deck to the video and sound input jacks of your computer's capture board. The S-Video connection provides video output from your camcorder to the capture board. Typically, this means simply connecting one cable from the camcorder or tape deck's S-Video output jack to the computer's S-Video input jack. Some S-Video cables also have an extra jack for sound.

- **Serial device control:** Premiere Pro allows you to control professional videotape recording equipment through your computer's serial communications (COM) port. (A computer's serial communications port is often used for modem communication and printing.) Serial control allows transport and timecode information to be sent over the computer's serial port. Using serial device control, you can capture playback and record video. Because serial control exports only timecode and transport signals, you need a hardware capture card to send the video and audio signals to tape. Premiere Pro supports the following standards: nine-pin serial port, Sony RS-422, Sony RS-232, Sony RS-232 UVW, Panasonic RS-422, Panasonic RS-232, and JVC-232.

Starting the Capture Process

Many settings in Premiere Pro depend upon the actual equipment you have installed in your computer. The dialog boxes that appear during the capture process depend upon the hardware and software installed in your computer. The dialog boxes that appear in this chapter may vary from what you see onscreen, but the general steps for capturing video and audio are very similar.

However, if you have a capture board that digitizes analog video, the setup process is different than if you have an IEEE 1394 port installed in your computer. The following sections describe how to set up Premiere Pro for both systems.

> **NOTE** To ensure that your capture session is successful, be sure to read all of your manufacturer's read-me files and documentation. It is important that you know exactly what is installed in your computer.

Reviewing capture settings

Before you begin the capture process, review Premiere Pro's project and default settings, as they affect the capture process. After the defaults are set, they remain saved when you relaunch the program. Defaults that affect capture include scratch disk settings and device control settings.

Setting scratch disk preferences

Whether you are capturing digital video or digitizing analog video, one of your first steps should be to ensure that Premiere Pro's capture *scratch disk* locations are set up properly. The scratch disk is the disk used to actually perform the capture. Make sure that the scratch disk is the fastest one connected to your computer and that the hard drive is the one with the most free space. In Premiere Pro, you can set different scratch disk locations for video and audio. To check scratch disk settings, choose Edit ➪ Preferences ➪ Scratch Disks. If you want to change settings for captured video or audio, click the appropriate Browse button and set a new capture path by navigating to a specified drive and folder with your mouse.

In the Capture Locations section, click the Browse button to choose the hard drive or drives that you want to use for capturing video and audio.

> **NOTE** During the capture process, Premiere Pro also creates a conformed high-quality audio file that Premiere Pro uses to quickly access audio. The Scratch Disk section of the Preferences dialog box (Edit ➪ Preferences) also allows you to set a scratch disk location for conformed audio.

Setting Capture preferences

Premiere's Pro's Capture preferences allow you to specify whether you want to stop the capture session if frames are dropped, report the dropped frames, or generate a batch log file if the capture is unsuccessful. The batch log file is a text file listing the clip information about the failed capture. To view Capture preferences, shown in Figure 4.1, choose File ➪ Preferences ➪ Capture. In the Capture section of the Preferences dialog box, choose the Use device control timecode option if you want to use the timecode created by an external device rather than the timecode of the source material.

Using device control default settings

If your system allows device control, you can start and stop recording and set in and out points using onscreen buttons in Premiere Pro. You can also perform batch capture operations in which Premiere Pro captures multiple clips automatically. To access the default settings for device control, choose Edit ➪ Preferences ➪ Device Control. As discussed in Chapter 2, the Device Control section of the Preferences dialog box, shown in Figure 4.2, allows you to set preroll and timecode settings, as well as choose your video and audio source device.

FIGURE 4.1

The Capture section of the Preferences dialog box

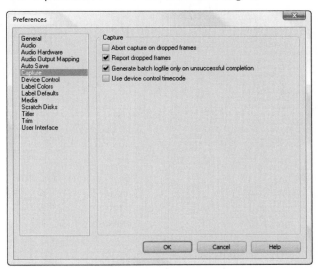

The Device Control section contains the following options:

- **Devices:** If you are using device control, use this drop-down menu to choose DV/HDV Device Control or a device control option provided by your board manufacturer. If you are not using device control, you can set this option to None. If you are using serial device control, choose the Serial Device Control option. For more information, see the section "Using Serial Device Control" later in this chapter.

- **Preroll:** Set a preroll time to enable your playback device to back up and get up to speed before the capture starts. Refer to camcorder and tape deck instructions for specific information.

- **Timecode Offset:** This setting allows you to alter the timecode recorded on the captured video so that it accurately matches the same frame on the source videotape.

- **Options:** Clicking the Options button opens up the DV/HDV Device Control Settings dialog box, shown in Figure 4.3. Here you can set your preferred video standard (NTSC or PAL), the device brand, device type (for example, Standard or HDV), and timecode format (Drop-Frame or Non-Drop-Frame). If your device is properly connected to your computer, turned on, and in VCR mode, the status readout should be *Online*. If you can't get your device online and you have an Internet connection, try clicking the Go Online for Device Info button, which takes you to an Adobe Web page with compatibility information.

FIGURE 4.2

You can set device control defaults in the Device Control section of the Preferences dialog box.

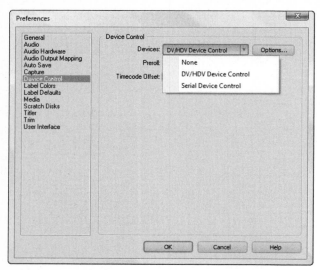

FIGURE 4.3

Choose your video source and check its status in the DV/HDV Device Control Settings dialog box.

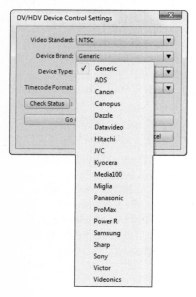

Drop-Frame versus Nondrop-Frame Timecode

In professional video systems, Society of Motion Picture and Television Engineers (SMPTE) timecode is *striped*, or recorded, on tape on a track separate from the video track. (In DV format the timecode is not the video data, not on a separate track.) Video producers use the timecode as a way to specify exact in and out points during edit sessions. When previewing footage, producers often create a *window dub* of the timecode so that the timecode appears in a window. This enables the producers to view the tape and the timecode at the same time. By default, Premiere Pro uses timecode to display times in this format: hour: minute: second: frame.

If you're new to video or Premiere Pro, this can take some getting used to. For example, the next readout after 01:01:59:29 is 01:02:00:00 (when using 30 frames per second). This timecode format is called *nondrop-frame*. However, professional video producers typically use a timecode format called *drop-frame*.

Drop-frame timecode is necessary because the NTSC professional video frame rate is 29.97 (not 30) frames per second. Over a long duration, the .03-frame difference between 30 frames and 29.97 frames begins to add up, resulting in inaccurate program times. To solve the problem, professional video producers created a timecode system that would actually visually drop frames in the code without dropping frames in the video. When SMPTE nondrop-frame is striped, two frames of every minute are skipped — except for the tenth minute. In drop-frame timecode, the frame after 01;01;59;29 is 01;02;00;02. Notice that semicolons are used to designate drop-frame from nondrop-frame.

If you are not creating video where exact time duration is important, you do not need to use drop-frame timecode; you can capture and use 30 frames per second instead of the 29.97 project setting. Keep in mind that nondrop-frame was created for NTSC video. Do not use it for PAL or SECAM, which use 25 frames per second.

Capture project settings

The Capture settings for a project determine how video and audio are captured. The Capture settings are determined by project presets. If you want to capture video from a DV camera or DV tape deck, the capture process is straightforward. Because DV cameras compress and digitize, very few settings need to change. However, to ensure the best quality capture, you must create a DV project before the capture session.

Review these general project setup steps before capturing:

1. **Create a new project by choosing File ⇨ New Project.** If you are capturing from a DV or HDV source, choose a DV or HDV project preset. If you are capturing from an analog card, you may need to choose a non-DV preset or one recommended by your card manufacturer.

Timecode Troubles

If you are using device control and are capturing a videotape with recorded timecode, you must ensure that the timecode is continuous — that no timecode is repeated. If you start and stop recording timecode while shooting, two or more frames on one tape may have the same timecode. For example, two different frames on the tape may have 01;02;00;02 as their recorded code. This creates a problem for Premiere Pro. When Premiere Pro captures video using device control and batch processing, it seeks out a specific frame of recorded timecode for the in point and captures until a frame of timecode is designated as the out point. If the same timecode appears on the tape at different points, Premiere Pro becomes confused and does not capture the correct sequence.

One solution to this problem is to stripe all tape with continuous timecode before shooting. Simply record black (with the lens cap on) while you record timecode on the entire tape. Use the same settings that you will use when shooting video, but don't record audio.

Alternatively, you can try a sort of rhythm method of shooting that prevents timecode numbers from being re-recorded. To do so, shoot an extra 5 to 10 seconds of video after the scene that you want recorded ends. When you start recording again, first rewind the tape so it begins at a location that already has timecode recorded on it. If you see the timecode starting again at 00;00;00, rewind until you reach a section of previously recorded timecode.

2. **Set Capture Project settings.** Open the Capture Project Settings dialog box by choosing Project ⇨ Project Settings ⇨ Capture. Click the setting in the Capture Format drop-down menu, shown in Figure 4.4, that matches your source footage: DV Capture, or HDV Capture. If you are using a third-party board, you may see settings for frame rate, frame size, compressor, format (or bit depth), and number of audio channels.

3. **Check connections.** Check all connections from your video equipment to your computer. Turn on your video and audio source. If you're using a camcorder, set it to VCR mode.

NOTE To prevent dropped frames during a capture session, your hard drive should be able to sustain a 3.6MB-per-second data rate. Also note that the system requirements for HDV and HD are different from those for DV. See Appendix C for details.

4. **If your equipment supports device control, check settings by choosing Edit ⇨ Preferences ⇨ Device Control.** If you are capturing using DV or HDV, choose DV or HDV Device Control in the Devices drop-down menu. If you are capturing using serial device control, choose Serial Device Control.

To set device control for a DV device, click Options. In the DV Device Control Options dialog box, choose your brand and device type. If your camcorder is already attached to your computer and is set to VCR mode, it should appear online (you can also check this later in the Capture window).

If you are capturing using serial device control, see the section "Capturing with Device Control," later in this chapter.

The Capture settings in the Project Settings dialog box

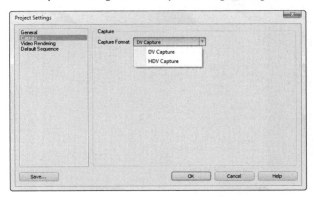

5. **Choose Project ⇨ Project Settings ⇨ Capture.** Choose the appropriate setting: Adobe HD or HDV. Users with third-party boards may be able to change frame size, frame rate, and audio settings.

> **TIP** Before beginning a capture session, make sure that no other programs besides Premiere Pro are running. Also, be sure that your hard drive is not fragmented. Windows XP Pro users can defragment and test for hard drive errors by right-clicking their hard drives and then clicking Properties. Next, click the Tools tab to access hard drive maintenance utilities.

Capture window settings

Before you start capturing, become familiar with the Capture window settings. These settings determine whether video and audio are captured together or separately. This window also allows you to change scratch disk and device control settings.

To open the Capture window, shown in Figure 4.5, choose File ⇨ Capture. To view capture settings, click the Settings tab. If the Settings tab isn't visible, click the Capture window menu and choose Expand Window (which changes to Collapse Window after the window is expanded, as shown in Figure 4.5). The following sections describe different areas of the Capture window: the Capture window menu and the Capture Settings, Capture Locations, and Device Control sections.

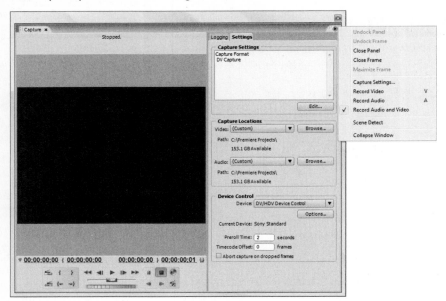

FIGURE 4.5

The Capture panel with the Settings tab selected

Capture panel menu

The following sections describe key areas of the Capture panel shown at the upper-right corner in Figure 4.5.

- **Capture Settings:** Clicking this menu item opens the Project Settings Capture dialog box, where you can check or change capture settings.

- **Record Audio and Record Video:** Here you can choose whether to capture audio only or video only. The default setting is Record Audio and Video.

- **Scene Detect:** This menu item turns on Premiere Pro's automatic scene detection, which is available with device control. When Scene Detect is on, Premiere Pro automatically breaks up the capture into different clips when Premiere Pro detects a change in the video timestamp, which occurs when the Pause button is pressed on a camcorder.

 **As of the writing of this book, Scene Detect was not implemented in Premiere Pro for HDV capture.**

- **Collapse Window:** This command removes the Settings and Logging tabs from the window. When the window is collapsed, the menu command changes to Expand Window.

Capture Settings

This section of the Capture window displays the selected capture settings from the Project Settings dialog box. Clicking the Settings tab opens the Capture Settings dialog box. As mentioned earlier, if you are capturing DV, you cannot change frame size or audio options because all capture settings conform to the IEEE 1394 standard. Premiere Pro users with a third-party board may see settings that allow them to change frame size, frame rate, and audio sample rates.

Capture Locations

This section displays the default settings for video and audio. You can change locations for video and audio by clicking either of the Browse buttons.

Device Control

This section displays defaults from the Device Control Preferences dialog box. You can change the defaults here as well, and click the Options button to choose your playback device and see whether it is online. In this section, you can also choose to abort the session if any frames are dropped during capture.

Capturing Video in the Capture Window

If your system does not allow device control, you can capture video by turning on your tape deck or camera and viewing the footage in the Capture window. By manually starting and stopping the camera or tape deck, you can preview the source material. Follow these steps to capture video without device control:

1. **Make sure that all cables are properly connected.**

2. **Choose File ⇨ Capture.** You can change the window size by clicking and dragging the lower-right edge of the window.

3. **If you want to capture only video or only audio, change the appropriate settings in the Capture window menu.** You can also change settings by clicking the Logging tab and choosing Video (only) or Audio (only) from the drop-down menu.

4. **Set the camera or tape deck to Play mode.** You should see and hear the source clip in the Capture window as the tape plays.

5. **Click the Record button in the Movie Capture window five to seven seconds before the section that should be recorded appears.** At the top of the capture screen, you see a display of the capture progress, including whether any frames were dropped during the recording.

6. **To stop recording, press Esc.** When the recording is paused, the Filename dialog box appears.

Where's My Audio?

If you've captured video and audio and don't hear the audio, you may need to wait until Premiere Pro finishes creating an audio conforming file for the captured segment. When an AVI video file is created, the audio is interleaved with the video. By creating a separate high-quality conforming audio file, Premiere Pro can access and process audio faster as you edit. The downside of a conforming file is that you must wait for it to be created, and it takes up extra hard drive space. However, the advantages of faster audio processing outweigh the disadvantages.

7. **Type a filename for the clip.** Optionally, you may type additional comments in the Comments box.

8. **Click OK to save the file.** The captured clip appears in the Project window.

9. **Press the Stop button on your playback device.**

TIP To view clip information about dropped frames, data rate, and file location, right-click the clip in the Project window and choose Properties from the drop-down menu that appears. Alternatively, select the clip and choose File ⇨ Get Properties for ⇨ Selection.

Capturing with Device Control

During the capture session, device control enables you to start and stop a camera or tape deck directly from Premiere Pro. If you have an IEEE 1394 connection and are capturing from a camcorder, chances are good that you can use device control. Otherwise, to work with device control, you need a capture board that supports device control as well as a frame-accurate tape deck (that is controlled by the board). If you do not have a DV board, you probably need a Premiere Pro–compatible plug-in to use device control. If device control is supported by your system, you may also be able to import the timecode and automatically generate a batch list to batch capture clips automatically.

The device control buttons provided at the bottom of the Capture window magically control your camcorder or VCR. The buttons are shown in Figure 4.6. Using these buttons, you can start and stop, as well as set in and out points for, the video.

NOTE Premiere Pro's Scene Detect button attempts to automatically break up sequences into separate files based upon the Time/Date stamp. It can be very helpful when capturing an entire tape as described in the section "Capturing a Tape with Scene Detection." You can activate scene detection by clicking Scene Detect in the device control area or by clicking Scene Detect in the Capture area of the Capture window.

TIP Clicking the Fast Forward button when the tape is either playing or paused allows you to fast forward while previewing the video. Clicking the Rewind button when the tape is either playing or paused allows you to rewind while previewing the video.

FIGURE 4.6

The Capture window device control buttons

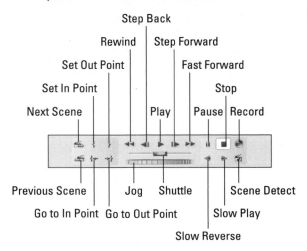

You may also want to review the default keyboard commands for the Capture window:

Eject	E
Fast Forward	F
Go to In Point	Q
Go to Out Point	W
Record	G
Rewind	R
Set Out Point	O
Set In Point	I

When you are ready to capture with device control, follow these steps:

1. **Choose File ⇨ Capture.**

2. **Check Capture settings by clicking the Settings tab.** In the Device Control area, make sure that the Device drop-down menu is set to Device Control. If you need to check the status of your playback device, click Options.

   You can change project settings by clicking the Edit button in the Capture Settings area. If you want to change the location of video or audio scratch disks, click the Browse buttons in the Capture Locations area.

3. **Click the Logging tab.** The Logging section of the Capture window includes buttons for automatically capturing from a clip's in point to its out point. It also includes a Scene Detect check box, another method of turning on Premiere Pro's Scene Detect option.

4. **Click the controls onscreen to move to the point from which you want to start capturing video.**

Click and drag the jog control area to the left to rewind one frame; click and drag to the right to advance one frame. Drag the shuttle control to change speed as you view the footage.

5. **Click either the Set In Point icon or the Set In button in the Timecode section of the Logging tab, shown in Figure 4.7.**

6. **Click the controls onscreen to move to the point at which you want to stop capturing video.**

7. **Click either the Set Out Point icon or the Set Out button in the Timecode section of the Logging tab.** At this point, you can review your in and out points by clicking the Go to In Point button or Go to Out Point button.

If scene detection is on, Premiere Pro may break a clip between specified in and out points.

FIGURE 4.7

Video captured in the Capture window

8. **If you want to add frames before the in point and after the out point of the captured clips, enter the number of frames in the Handles field in the Capture area.**

9. **To begin capturing, click the In/Out button in the Capture section of the Logging tab.** Premiere Pro starts the preroll. After the preroll, your video appears in the Capture window, as shown in Figure 4.7. Premiere Pro starts the capture session at the in point and ends it at the out point.

10. **When the Filename dialog box appears, type a name for the clip.** If a project is open onscreen, the clip automatically appears in the Project window.

 If you don't want to set in and out points for recording, you can just click the Play button and then click Record to capture the sequence that appears in the Capture window.

Capturing a Tape with Scene Detection

The bottom Capture section of the Logging tab in the Capture panel provides options for capturing an entire tape with scene detection. Follow these steps:

1. **Insert the tape that you want to capture into your playback device.**

2. **When prompted by Premiere Pro, name the tape.**

3. **If necessary, rewind the tape.**

4. **If you want Premiere Pro to automatically break up the tape into separate scenes, click the Scene Detection button.** If you want to add frames before the in point and after the out point of the captured clips, enter the number of frames in the Handles field.

5. **To start recording, click Tape in the Capture section.**

Using Serial Device Control

Serial device control allows you to precisely control videotape decks and camcorders through your computer's serial port. To use serial device control, choose serial device control as your Device Control preference and then calibrate for it. This section describes these steps. After you complete them, you can capture video using the steps discussed earlier in the section "Capturing with Device Control."

Setting up serial device control

Before you can capture or export video using serial device control, you must set up Premiere Pro's Serial Device Control preferences. Before you begin, read your equipment manuals, connect your recording equipment to your computer's COM port, and then follow these steps in Premiere Pro:

1. Open the Device Control Preferences dialog box by choosing Edit ➪ Preferences ➪ Device Control.

2. In the Device Control Preferences dialog box, choose Serial Device Control in the Control Device drop-down menu. This opens the Options dialog box for Serial Device Control

3. In the Options dialog box that appears, shown in Figure 4.8, choose from the following options:

    ▪ **Protocol:** In the Protocol drop-down menu, choose the serial protocol specified by your recording equipment manufacturer.

    ▪ **Port:** Choose your COM port from the Port drop-down menu.

    ▪ **Use VTRs internal Cue:** This option may be necessary if your equipment cannot properly cue to specific timecode numbers. (It should not be necessary if you are using high-end equipment.)

    ▪ **Use 19.2K Baud for RS-232:** This is a high-speed communication option that can improve editing accuracy. This option is available only for RS-232 mode equipment.

    ▪ **Time Source:** Choose the time source used by your source videotape. If you want your equipment to choose, select the LTC+VITC option. Otherwise, choose LTC (Longitudinal Timecode) or VITC (Vertical Interval Timecode).

    ▪ **Timebase:** In the Timebase drop-down menu, select the timebase that matches your source videotape.

FIGURE 4.8

Set serial device options in the Options dialog box.

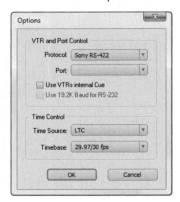

Calibrating for serial capture

To help ensure accuracy when capturing with serial control, you should compare captured time-code with the timecode on the original tape. Follow these steps to calibrate with serial control:

1. **Capture a clip using the steps described in the section "Capturing with Device Control."** Do not close the Capture panel.

2. **Compare the timecode of the clip (in the Source Monitor) with the timecode in the original tape.** If the two codes do not match, follow these steps:

   a. **Calculate the offset difference in frames.** If the captured clip in the Source Monitor is greater than the original source clip, the offset is positive. If the captured clip in the Source Monitor is less than the original source clip, the offset is negative.

   b. **Click the Settings tab in the Capture panel, and type the offset frame value in the Timecode Offset field.**

   c. **Repeat from step 1 until the captured timecode matches the source timecode.**

Performing a Batch Capture

If your capture board supports device control, you can set up a *batch capture list* that appears in the Project panel, as shown in Figure 4.9. The list appears as a series of offline clips with in and out points to be used when the File ➪ Batch Capture command is executed (in Figure 4.9, we dragged the Video In, Video Out, and Capture Settings columns to the left to make them visible). Note that the icon for the offline clips is different than the normal online icon in the Project panel. After creating the list, you can select the clips that you wish to capture and have Premiere Pro capture each of the clips automatically while you go off and take a coffee break. You can create a batch capture list manually or by using device control. If you create a batch list manually, you need to type the timecode in and out points for all clips. If you use device control, Premiere Pro enters the start and stop times after you click the Set In and Set Out buttons in the Timecode section of the Logging tab in the Capture window.

> **TIP** When Premiere Pro captures from a batch capture list, it automatically captures using the settings of the current project. Although you most likely want to batch capture clips using the frame size and other settings of the current project, you can select a clip to be captured in the Project panel and choose a capture setting for it by choosing Clip ➪ Capture Settings ➪ Set Capture Settings. This places an X in the clip's Capture Settings column in the Project panel. To clear capture settings for a clip, select the clip and choose Clip ➪ Capture Settings ➪ Clear Capture Settings.

> **NOTE** You can also right-click on an offline clip in the Project panel and choose Batch Capture in the drop-down menu that appears. This opens the Batch Capture dialog box where you can click Override Capture Settings, then choose another capture format.

FIGURE 4.9

A batch capture list in the Project panel

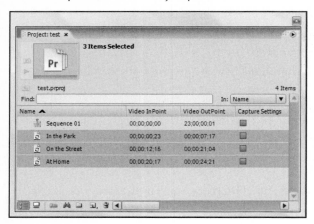

Creating a batch capture list manually

To create a batch capture list of clips that you specify manually, follow these steps:

1. **If you want the batch list to appear in a bin in the Project panel, open the bin or create one by clicking the folder button at the bottom of the panel.**

2. **To create the batch file listing, choose File ➪ New Offline File (or click the New Item icon and choose New Offline file).** The Offline File dialog box opens, as shown in Figure 4.10.

3. **Type an in point, an out point, and a filename for the clip.** Add other descriptive notes, such as a tape name.

4. **Click OK.** The clip's information is added to the Project panel.

5. **For each clip that you want captured, repeat steps 2 to 4.**

NOTE You can edit the in and out points of offline files by clicking in the Video In and Out Point column for the specific clip, and changing the timecode readouts.

6. **If you want to save the batch list to disk so that you can capture the clips at another time, or so that you can load the list into another computer application, choose Project ➪ Export Batch list.** You can reload the list later when you want to begin the capture session by choosing Project ➪ Import Batch List.

FIGURE 4.10

Use the Offline File dialog box to manually log clips.

Creating a batch capture list with device control

If you want to create a batch capture list but do not want to type the in and out points of all clips, you can use Premiere Pro's Capture window to do the job for you. Follow these steps:

1. **Open the Movie Capture panel by choosing File ⇨ Capture.**

2. **Click the Logging tab.** In the Clip Data section, enter a tape name and the clip name that you want to see in the Project panel. Add other comments as desired.

3. **Use the capture control icons to locate the portion of the tape that includes the section you want to capture.**

4. **Click the Set In button.** The in point appears in the Logging tab's In field.

5. **Use the capture control icons to locate the clip's out point.**

6. **Click the Set Out button.** The out point appears in the Out field.

7. **Click the Log Clip button and enter a filename for the clip (unless you want to use the default name provided).** If desired, type comments in the dialog box and then click OK.

8. For every clip you want to capture, repeat steps 3 through 7.

9. If you want to save the batch list to disk, so that you can capture the clips at another time or so that you can load the list into another computer application, choose Project ➪ Export Batch list. You can reload the list later when you want to begin the capture session by choosing Project ➪ Import Batch list.

10. Close the Movie Capture window.

Capturing using a batch list

After you create a batch list of clips that you want to capture, you can have Premiere Pro capture the clips automatically from a list in the Project panel. In order to complete the following steps, you need to create a batch list as described in the previous section.

 Batch lists can be automatically captured only by systems that support device control.

1. If your batch list of offline files is saved and not loaded into the Project panel, load the list by choosing Project ➪ Import Batch list. This loads the list of files into the Project panel.

2. To specify which clips you want captured, select the offline clips in the Project panel by clicking the first clip and then shift-clicking to extend the selection.

3. Choose File ➪ Batch Capture. This opens the Batch Capture dialog box where specify whether you want to capture with handles (set the number of frames you want captured before the in point and after the out point) and you can change capture settings by clicking Override Capture Settings, if desired; otherwise, click OK.

4. When the Insert Tape dialog box appears, make sure that the correct tape is in your camcorder or playback device and then click OK. The Capture window opens, and the capture process begins.

5. Check to see the capture status. When the batch process is over, an alert appears, indicating that the clips have been captured. In the Project panel, Premiere Pro changes the icons of the filenames to indicate that they are now linked to files on disk. To see the status of the captured clips, scroll right in the Project panel. You'll see check marks for captured clips in the Capture Settings column. The status for the clips should be *Online*, another indication that the clips are linked to disk files.

NOTE   If you have offline files in the Project panel and you want to link them to files that have already been captured, right-click the clip in the Project panel and choose Link Media. You then need to navigate with the mouse to the actual clip on your hard drive.

Changing a Clip's Timecode

High-end video cameras and mid-range DV cameras can record timecode to videotape (often called SMPTE timecode, for the Society of Motion Picture and Television Engineers). The timecode provides a frame-accurate readout of each videotape frame in hour:minute:second:frame format. Timecode is used by video producers to move to specific locations on tape and also to set in and out points. During an edit session, broadcast equipment uses the timecode to create frame-accurate edits of the source material on the final program tape.

When capturing with device control, Premiere Pro captures the timecode along with the video. However, for project management purposes you may want to reset the timecode. Follow these steps:

1. **Select the clip in the Project panel.** If you don't want the timecode to start at the beginning of the clip, double-click it to open it in the Source Monitor panel. Then move to the frame at which you want to begin the timecode.

2. **Choose File ➪ Timecode.**

3. **In the Timecode dialog box, shown in Figure 4.11, enter the starting timecode that you want to use.**

FIGURE 4.11

Use the Timecode dialog box to set the timecode for a clip.

4. **If you moved to a specific frame and want to start the timecode at that point, click the Set at Current Frame option.**

5. **Enter a tape name.**

6. **Click OK.**

TIP To help review footage, you can use the Timecode video effect to overlay timecode on footage. The Timecode video effect can be found in the Video bin in the Video Effects bin in the Effects panel.

Capturing Audio

You can capture audio independently of video using Premiere Pro's Audio Mixer panel. Using the Audio Mixer, you can record directly into Premiere Pro from an audio source such as a microphone or tape recorder. You can even record narration while viewing video in the Program monitor. When you capture audio, quality is based on the sample rate and bit depth set for your audio hardware. To view these settings, choose Edit ⇨ Preferences ⇨ Audio Hardware and click the ASIO (Audio Stream Input Output) button. Hardware details generally include information about audio sample rates and bit depth. The sample rate is the number of samples taken each second. The bit depth is the number of bits (8 bits are in a byte of data) per each sample of the actual digitized audio. The minimum bit depth of most audio codecs is 16.

To record using the Audio Mixer, follow these steps:

1. **Connect the tape recorder, microphone, or other audio source to the sound port or sound card of your computer.**

NOTE   If you want to create a new audio track for audio capture, choose Sequence ⇨ Add Track. In the Audio track section, enter 1 in the Add Audio Track field. If you are using a monophonic microphone, choose Mono in the Track Type drop-down menu and enter 0 in the Add Video Track and Add Submix Tracks fields.

2. **Open the Audio Mixer, shown in Figure 4.12, by choosing Window ⇨ Audio Mixer.** You can rename a track by right-clicking the track name and choosing Rename in the drop-down menu that appears.

FIGURE 4.12

Use the Audio Mixer panel to record analog audio directly into Premiere Pro.

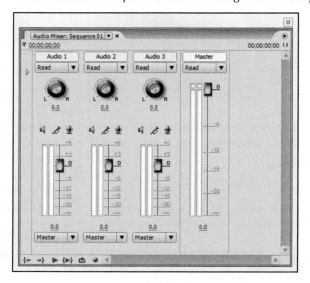

3. **If you have video on the Timeline and want to record narration for the video, move the Timeline about five seconds before you want the audio to begin.**

4. **To prepare for recording, click the Record Enable button (microphone) in the Audio Mixer panel in the track section for the track you are recording.** The Record Enable button turns red. If you are recording voice-over narration, you may want to click the Solo button for the track to mute output from other audio tracks.

5. **Click the Record button at the bottom of the Audio Mixer panel.** The Record button starts to blink.

6. **Test audio levels.** In the Audio Mixer panel menu, choose Meter Input(s) Only. When this option is selected, a check mark appears in the panel menu and a VU meter replaces the volume control to display hardware input for any track being recorded. Note that when Meter Input(s) Only is activated, you can still view track levels for those tracks that you aren't recording.

7. **Speak into the microphone.** As you speak, sound levels should be near 0 dB without entering the red zone.

8. **If necessary, adjust levels for your microphone or your recording input device.** For example, in most systems with a microphone directly connected to a computer, you can change recording levels in the Audio tab of the Sounds and Audio Properties control panel. (Click the Start menu, and then choose Control Panel to access the Sounds and Audio Properties control panel.)

9. **To start recording, click the Play button at the bottom of the Audio Mixer panel.**

10. **Play the tape recorder or begin speaking into the microphone to record the narration.**

11. **When the narration or audio is complete, click the Record button to stop recording in the Audio Mixer panel.**

CROSS-REF Chapter 8 covers mixing audio using the Audio Mixer panel.

Introduction to OnLocation

Adobe OnLocation is an application that captures video and audio directly to your computer's hard drive. It also provides a suite of video and audio analytical tools that can help improve the quality of the captured audio and video. Why use OnLocation? Although Premiere Pro's Capture window provides an efficient means of logging and capturing footage, it offers little help in judging the quality of your video before or during capture.

Depending upon how you shoot your video, OnLocation may help to ensure the highest-quality footage your equipment can provide. You can use its analytical tools to analyze video and audio signals before and during shooting. Apart from video tools, OnLocation also provides other notable features: OnLocation can pause during recording without creating another clip. It includes a frame-grabbing utility and can perform stop motion and time-lapse recording. OnLocation also provides split-screen and onion-skinning options that can help ensure continuity by allowing you to compare the quality and lighting of one clip with another.

In many respects, working with OnLocation is like having a rack of video and audio diagnostic tools that a location crew would bring to a shoot. A technical discussion of all of its tools is beyond the scope of its book; however, this introduction should provide you with the basics of using the program.

 OnLocation is a separate Windows application packaged with Premiere Pro. Mac users can run it with Boot Camp and Windows, which must be purchased separately.

 If your computer monitor is set to a resolution higher than 1024 x 768 pixels, the OnLocation window is resizable and its menus appear onscreen. At a lower resolution, you cannot see the OnLocation menus. You need to right-click to access OnLocation menus. To switch to another computer application, press Alt+Tab.

Component review

The best way to become familiar with OnLocation is to learn about the analytical components that appear onscreen when you launch the program. Among the analytical components OnLocation provides are a field monitor, vectorscope, digital video recorder, waveform monitor, and audio frequency analyzer. You can click and drag to rearrange these components, and remove them from and add them to the screen. To remove a component, you simply click its Power button; to add a component to the screen, right-click onscreen and choose the component from the drop-down menu that appears.

Controls for most components can be turned on and off by clicking the mouse, and adjustments are made by clicking and dragging. Here is a brief review of the OnLocation components.

Field Monitor

This component, shown in Figure 4.13, displays the video image as it will appear after being compressed during recording. Because the Field Monitor displays an image with the effects of compression, the brightness, saturation, hue, and resolution provide a more accurate display than a camera's viewfinder. The Field Monitor includes options such as underscan, overscan, video safe area, and letter-box mask. It also includes a Zebra option to alert you when brightness levels are too high.

For best results when capturing video, you should use color bars to calibrate the Field Monitor. When you calibrate, you adjust the screen display to better reflect the video being recorded to tape (calibrating the monitor does not affect or change the recording). You calibrate using the Field Monitor's Brightness, Chroma Phase, and Contrast controls. After calibration you shouldn't need to adjust these controls during recording. Instructions on calibrating to color bars are provided in the OnLocation help.

 To access all of the Field Monitor's options, click the Menu control in the lower-left corner of the Field Monitor window.

FIGURE 4.13

The Field Monitor displays video during the capture session.

Digital Video Recorder

You can use the Digital Video Recorder (DVR) to record and play back video. Shown in Figure 4.14, the DVR includes record and playback buttons. *Trays* display information about the recorded clips. You can click a tray, and then click Play to play back a clip. You can use the following keyboard commands with the DVR:

Record	F2
Stop Recording	F4
Play Clip	Spacebar or F5
Pause Recording or Playback	Spacebar or F7
Jump to Beginning of Clip	Home key
Jump to End of Clip	End key
Stop Playback and Return to Live Camera	F7
Stop Motion Recording	F3
Time-lapse Recording	Ctrl +F3

Use the Digital Video Recorder to record and play back video.

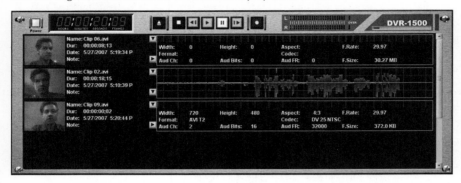

Waveform Monitor

This component, shown in Figure 4.15, provides a waveform representation of video signal intensity. (Y represents luminance, and C represents chrominance.) In the YC Waveform, the horizontal axis represents the actual video clip, while the vertical axis charts signal intensity measured in IRE (for Institute of Radio Engineers).

The green waveform pattern in the scope represents video luminance. The waveform for brighter video appears at the top of the chart; the waveform for darker video appears at the bottom of the chart. OnLocation features a YUV and an RGB waveform. The waveforms display brightness on a scale of 1 to 100 IRE.

The Waveform Monitor provides a waveform representation of video signal intensity.

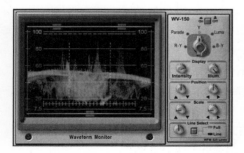

Vectorscope

This component provides a visual representation of color in a video signal. The Vectorscope, shown in Figure 4.16, displays hues along a color wheel with Red, Magenta, Blue, Cyan, Green, and Yellow (R, Mg, B, Cy, G, Yl) markers. Thus, the angle of the readout indicates hue properties. Readings toward the outer edges of the Vectorscope indicate highly saturated colors. Moderately saturated colors appear between the center of the circle and its outer edges. Black-and-white portions of the video appear at the center.

The outside circle represents the limit of safe broadcast colors. Thus, the signal should not extend beyond this circle.

FIGURE 4.16

The Vectorscope displays a graphical representation of a clip's color signal.

Spectra 60

This component allows you to analyze the chroma and luminance values of a specific pixel in an image. To choose a specific pixel, click the Lock button, and then click in the image.

Audio Spectrum Analyzer

This component provides a graphical representation of audio frequency, as shown in Figure 4.17. You can use it to help set audio levels and choose the best location for a microphone.

FIGURE 4.17

The Audio Spectrum Analyzer provides a graphical representation of audio frequency.

DV Grabber

This component saves the current video frame as a still image in JPG, BMP, or PNG format. Simply click the Grab button to capture the current frame displayed in the Field Monitor.

Shot Clock

This component can be used as a production clock, to time a production, and to count down. You can slave the clock to your video camera by setting the Shot Clock Slave option in the Field Monitor's menu (click the Menu button in the lower-left corner of the Field Monitor).

Automatic Quality Monitor

The DV-QM helps to monitor audio and video levels by allowing you to establish clipping thresholds. When the audio or video level surpasses the threshold, the word *Over* appears in the DV-QM. The DV-QM includes an Audio Pop slider that alerts you to "popping" sounds that don't exceed audio levels but may hinder audio quality.

SureShot

This is a utility that helps you check framing, focus, exposure, and white balance. To use SureShot, shown in Figure 4.18, print out the SureShot cards from one of the SureShot PDF files included with OnLocation. Follow the instructions in the SureShot documentation.

FIGURE 4.18

The SureShot utility checks framing, focus, and exposure.

Recording with OnLocation

Recording with OnLocation is quite easy. However, as discussed earlier, for best results, you should calibrate your monitor with Color Bars and use SureShot to check your camera. Use the OnLocation components to prepare and test video signals and audio levels. Here are the fundamental steps to capture video:

1. **Create a new project by choosing File ➪ New Project.** Name your project. Click Browse Folders if you want to select a disk location for your project. Then click Save.

2. **Connect your camera to a laptop or workstation.** Note that Adobe recommends that you use a dedicated 7,200 RPM hard drive for DV and HDV capture.

3. **Set your camera or camcorder in Preview mode**. This should send the video signal to your computer.

4. **Select your camera in the OnLocation Devices menu.** If you can't view OnLocation menus onscreen, right-click the screen and choose your camera from the Devices menu. You should see the image from your camera in OnLocation's Field Monitor.

5. **To start recording, click the Record key or press F2.**

6. **To stop recording, click Stop or press F4.**

Each clip you record appears in the DVR. If you want to play back one of the clips, select it, and then click the Play button. If you want to remove a clip from the DVR so you can import it into Premiere, click Eject.

Clip management with OnLocation

OnLocation stores video clips within specially named folders in the project location. The folders are Clips in Use, Ejected Clips, Garbage Clips, and Grabbed Stills. You should not delete, rename, or move clips in these folders. Otherwise, OnLocation may lose track of the clip.

 You can add a clip to the Digital Video Recorder by clicking and dragging it from any folder into the DVR.

Here is a description of the different folders and how they are used:

- **Clips in Use:** Clips you see listed in the Digital Video Recorder are stored in the Clips in Use folder. On the DVR, you can click and drag to rearrange these clips onscreen, and you can click in the Name field and rename the clip.

- **Ejected Clips:** These are clips you want to use, but that you have removed from the DVR display. When you want to remove a clip, select it and click the onscreen Eject button or press Delete. You can then import the clips into Premiere Pro from the Ejected Clips folder.

- **Garbage Clips:** These are clips that you probably will not use. To move a clip into the Garbage Clips folder, select it in the DVR and press Ctrl while clicking Eject (or press Ctrl+Delete). When you quit OnLocation or change projects, OnLocation asks whether you want to delete the clips in the Garbage Clips folder. Be aware that clips deleted from the Garbage Clips folder are permanently deleted; they are not placed in the Windows Recycle Bin.

Summary

Premiere Pro enables you to capture video and audio directly from a video camera or videotape recorder. You can also capture audio from a tape recorder or other sound device. This chapter covered these topics:

- Before starting a capture session, you should read all documentation related to your capture hardware.

- You need to set up cables properly before the capture session.

- You can set up default settings for capturing video by choosing Edit ➪ Preferences ➪ Capture and Edit Preferences ➪ Device Control.

- If you are capturing video, you should create a project before the capture session, using the settings recommended by your computer or board manufacturer.

- If your equipment allows device control, you can set up a batch capture session.

- To capture analog audio, you can use Premiere Pro's Audio Mixer.

- You can capture audio and video directly to your hard drive using Adobe OnLocation.

- OnLocation provides a suite of analytical tools to help ensure high-quality audio and video capture.

Part II

Editing with Premiere Pro

Chapter 5

Timeline, Sequences, and Clip Management

Undoubtedly, the Timeline is Premiere Pro's most versatile panel. The Timeline not only provides a graphical overview of clips, transitions, and effects, but it also provides a practical framework for managing projects. Using the Timeline, you can edit and assemble digital footage and control transparency and audio volume. You can also add keyframes to both audio and video effects. With all of this power packed into one Timeline, you'll want to take full advantage of all that it has to offer. If you do, you're sure to be working as efficiently as possible in Premiere Pro.

To get you started, this chapter provides a thorough review of Timeline panel features and options. It shows you how to navigate through footage in the Timeline, add tracks, lock tracks, and change viewing modes. This chapter also includes a section on how to use *sequences*. In Premiere Pro, a sequence is the assembled footage that is placed in the Timeline panel. As you'll soon see, Premiere Pro allows you to create multiple sequences in a Timeline panel, separate sequences into different Timeline panels, and drag one sequence into another to create a "nested" sequence.

After covering the Timeline panel, this chapter concludes with a look at a variety of features for managing Premiere Pro projects, including trimming projects, using subclips, and using Adobe Bridge.

Touring the Timeline

At first glance, trying to decipher all of the Timeline buttons, icons, sliders, and controls may seem like an overwhelming task. But after you start using the Timeline, you'll gradually learn what each feature does and how to use it.

To make the process of exploring the Timeline easier, this section is organized according to three specific Timeline elements: the ruler area and icons that control the ruler, the video tracks, and the audio tracks. Before you get started, you may want to place a video and audio clip from the *Adobe Premiere Pro CS3 Bible* DVD into the Timeline panel. This allows you to experiment with the different viewing options discussed in this section. To load a video or audio clip from the ArtBeats, FilmDisc, or SmartSound folders on the DVD, choose File ⇨ Import. After the clip appears in the Project panel, click and drag the video footage to the Video 1 track. Click and drag the audio file into the Audio 1 track.

 If the Timeline panel is not visible onscreen, you can open it by double-clicking its Sequence icon in the Project panel.

Timeline ruler options

The Timeline ruler icons and controls determine how footage is viewed and what areas are rendered and exported by Premiere Pro. Figure 5.1 provides a look at the Timeline ruler icons and controls.

FIGURE 5.1

Timeline ruler options

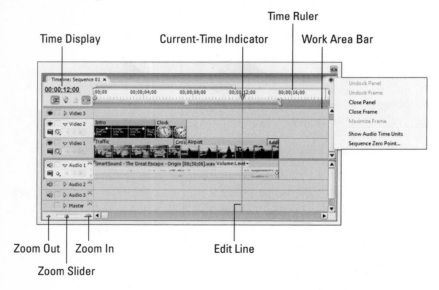

The Timeline ruler contains the following controls:

- **Time ruler:** The Time ruler is a visual display of time intervals divided into frames per second, which corresponds to your project frame rate. The actual number of tick marks between numbers that appear on the ruler is controlled by the current zoom level, which you can adjust by dragging the viewing area bar or zoom slider.

> **TIP** By default, the Timeline ruler displays time intervals in frames per second. If you are editing audio, you can change the ruler to display audio units in milliseconds or audio samples. To switch to audio units, choose Audio units in the Timeline menu (refer to Figure 5.1). Choose either milliseconds or audio samples in the Audio section of the Project Settings dialog box (Project ↔ Project Settings ↔ General).

- **Current-time indicator:** The current-time indicator (CTI) is the blue triangular icon that appears in the ruler. You can click and drag the CTI to gradually move through your footage. You can click in the Ruler area to move the CTI to a specific frame, or you can type a time entry in the Time display and press Enter to move to that position. You can also click and drag left or right in the Time display to move the CTI left or right along the ruler.

- **Time display:** As you move the CTI through the Timeline, the Time display indicates the position of the current frame. You can quickly jump to a specific frame by clicking the Time display and entering a time. When you type, you do not need to enter semicolons or colons. For example, you can move to frame 02:15:00 by clicking in the Frame read-out area, typing **215**, and pressing Enter. If you set a project's Display Format to be drop-frame, then the time displays with semicolons. If you set a project's Display Format to be non-drop-frame, then the time displays with colons. To view or change the Display Format for a project, choose Project ↔ Project Settings ↔ General.

- **Viewing area bar:** Clicking and dragging the viewing area bar changes the zoom level in the Timeline. The zoom level determines ruler increments and the length of footage that appears in the Timeline panel. You can click and drag either end of the viewing area bar to change the zoom level. Clicking and dragging the right viewing endpoint of the viewing area bar to the left displays fewer frames on the Timeline. Consequently, this increases the distance on the ruler between tick marks as shorter time intervals are displayed. Dragging right shows more footage and decreases the time intervals on the Timeline. To summarize: To zoom in, click and drag left on the viewing area bar; to zoom out, click and drag right. As you click and drag, notice that the zoom slider in the lower-left corner changes accordingly. Figure 5.2 shows the Timeline footage zoomed in. Note the difference between the zoomed-out view in Figure 5.1 and the zoomed-in view in Figure 5.2.

- **Work area bar:** Beneath the Timeline ruler is Premiere Pro's work area bar, which you can use to designate a work area for exporting or rendering. You can click and drag either endpoint of the work area bar or drag the entire bar from left to right. Why would you change the work area bar? When you render your project, Premiere Pro renders only the area defined by the work area bar. Thus, you don't need to wait for the entire project to be rendered when you want to see how a complex effect will look. Furthermore, when you export your file, you can choose to export only the work area section of the selected sequence in the Timeline.

FIGURE 5.2

Timeline zoomed-in view

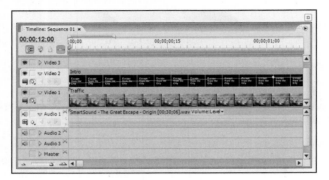

> **TIP** You can quickly adjust the width and position of the work area bar by resetting its end-
> points with keyboard shortcuts. To set the left endpoint, move the CTI to a specific
> frame and press Alt/Option+[. To set the right endpoint, move the CTI to a specific frame and press
> Alt/Option+]. You can also expand or contract the work area bar to encompass the footage in the
> current sequence or the width of the Timeline window (whichever is shorter), by double-clicking the
> work area bar.

- **Preview indicator:** The preview indicator displays which portion of your program has
  been rendered. After footage is rendered, transitions and effects appear at their highest
  quality (if you set Highest Quality or Automatic Quality as the display choice in the
  Source Monitor or Program Monitor panel menu). As Premiere Pro renders a sequence, it
  saves the rendered work file to your hard disk. Green areas in the Preview indicator area
  indicate footage that has been rendered. Red indicates non-rendered footage. To render
  the work area, press Enter or choose Sequence ➪ Render Work Area.

- **Enable or Disable Previews:** The tiny bar to the left of the time rule determines whether
  Premiere Pro previews effects during playback. When previews are enabled the colored
  Preview indicator is visible and Premiere Pro attempts to preview effects in real time; but
  this can cause a loss of quality. When Previews are disabled, the colored Preview indicator
  disappears, and video and audio can be rendered quickly, without affecting playback
  quality while editing

- **Zoom slider:** Clicking and dragging the zoom slider serves the same purpose as clicking
  and dragging the viewing area bar. Clicking and dragging left zooms out (you can also
  click the Zoom Out button). As you zoom out, more tick marks display on the Timeline,
  allowing you to see more of your footage within the boundaries of the Timeline panel.
  Clicking and dragging right to zoom in increases the distance between tick marks and
  shows less of your footage in the Timeline panel.

- **Set Unnumbered Marker button:** Sequence markers allow you to set points on the Timeline to which you can quickly jump. Sequence markers can also help you divide up your work in the Timeline as you edit. You can also use markers as chapter headings when you export Premiere Pro projects to Encore DVD. To set an unnumbered marker, drag the CTI to the frame where you want the marker to appear, and then click the Set Unnumbered Marker button (the pentagon icon to the right of the DVD icon).

 **If you'd like to write a comment about the marker area, double-click the marker icon. This opens the marker's dialog box, where you can enter text into the comments field.**

- **Encore Chapter marker:** If you're creating DVD projects with Encore DVD, you can set an Encore Chapter marker for chapter points that will appear when you import your footage into Encore DVD. To set an Encore DVD marker, drag the CTI to the frame where you want the marker to appear, and click the DVD Marker button (to the right of the magnet icon). For more information about using DVD markers, see Chapter 18.

Timeline track icons and options

The most important areas of the Timeline are its video and audio tracks, which provide a visual representation of your video and audio footage, transitions, and effects. Using Timeline track options, you can add and delete tracks and control how tracks display. You can control whether specific tracks are output when you export your project. You can also lock tracks and specify whether to view video frames in video tracks.

The following is a review of the icons and track options shown in Figure 5.3:

- **Snap:** The Snap icon toggles Premiere Pro's Snap to Edges command. When Snap is on, frames from one sequence snap to touch frames from the next sequence. This magnetic effect helps to ensure that no gaps appear in your production. To enable Snap, you can click the Snap icon, choose Sequence ➪ Snap, or press S on your keyboard. When Snap is on, the magnet in the upper-left corner of the Timeline appears to be pressed down.

- **Target:** When you insert footage using the Source monitor or edit footage with the Program, or Trim monitors, Premiere Pro alters the footage in the current target track in the Timeline. To specify a target track, simply click in the far-left area of the track. The left edge of the target track changes to display rounded edges, and also changes to a light shade of gray, as shown in Track 1 in Figure 5.3.

- **Collapse/Expand:** To view all of the options that are available for a track, click the Collapse/Expand Track button. If you are not placing footage in a track, you might as well leave the track in its unexpanded mode so that it doesn't consume too much screen space. If you've expanded a track and want to collapse it, simply click the Collapse/Expand icon again.

- **Toggle Track Output:** Clicking the eye icon toggles track output on and off, which prevents the track from being viewed in the Program Monitor panel during playing or when exporting. To turn output on again, click the button again; the eye icon returns, indicating that the track will be viewed in the Program Monitor panel and output when exporting.

FIGURE 5.3

Timeline track options

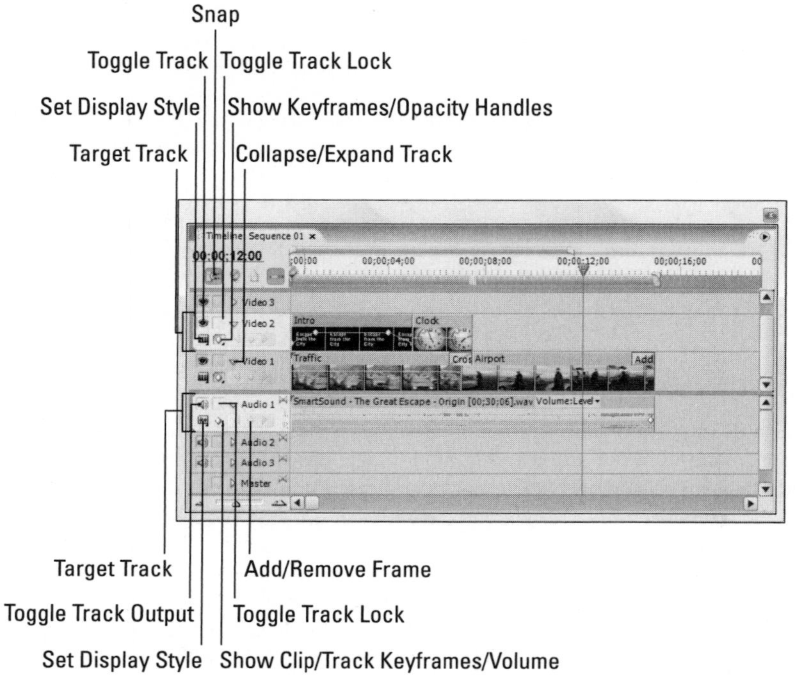

Snap

Toggle Track | Toggle Track Lock

Set Display Style | Show Keyframes/Opacity Handles

Target Track | Collapse/Expand Track

Target Track | Add/Remove Frame

Toggle Track Output | Toggle Track Lock

Set Display Style | Show Clip/Track Keyframes/Volume

- **Toggle Track Lock:** The track lock is a safety feature to prevent accidental editing. When a track is locked, no changes can be made to the track. Clicking the Toggle Track Lock icon locks the track. When you click the Lock Track icon, a lock appears, indicating that the track is locked. To unlock the track, click the icon again.

- **Set Display Style:** Clicking this drop-down menu allows you to choose how and whether thumbnail images appear in the Timeline tracks. The choices are Head and Tail, Show Head Only, Show Frames, and Show Name only. To view footage in the frames throughout a clip, choose Show Frames.

- **Show Keyframes/Opacity Handles:** Clicking this drop-down menu allows you to view or hide keyframes or opacity handles in the Timeline's effects graph line. Keyframes indicate control points for special effects that are chosen in the Effects panel. Opacity indicates transparency in frames. After you create effects with keyframes, the effect names appear in a drop-down menu in the effects graph line in the Timeline. After selecting an effect in this drop-down menu, you can adjust it by clicking and dragging its keyframes in the Timeline. If you are working with opacity handles, dragging down lowers opacity, and dragging up raises opacity.

- **Add/Remove Keyframe:** Clicking this button allows you to add or remove a keyframe from a track's effects graph line. To add a keyframe, move the CTI to where you want the keyframe to appear and click the Add/Remove Keyframe button. To remove a keyframe, move the CTI to the keyframe and click the Add/Remove Keyframe button. To move from keyframe to keyframe, click either the left- or right-arrow icon.

TIP Because the Timeline's effects graph line can show only one control for an effect at a time, you should create and edit most effects in the Effect Controls panel. The Effect Controls panel contains all of the controls for each effect. However, effects such as Opacity, which have one control that changes only one value, can easily be managed in the Timeline.

TIP You can also create and remove keyframes by Ctrl/⌘-clicking with the Selection or Pen tool.

Audio track icons and options

Audio track Timeline controls are similar to video track controls. Using the audio track Timeline options, you can adjust audio volume, choose which tracks are exported, and show and hide keyframes. Premiere Pro provides a variety of different audio tracks: standard audio, Submix tracks, Master tracks, and 5.1 tracks. Use the standard audio tracks for WAV and AIFF clips. Submix tracks allow you to create effects with a subset of your tracks, rather than all of them. Audio is placed in the Master and Submix tracks using Premiere Pro's Audio Mixer. The 5.1 tracks are special tracks used only for surround-sound audio. Figure 5.3 shows the audio section of the Timeline with a Master, Submix, and 5.1 track.

CROSS-REF Chapter 7 covers using audio in the Timeline and creating audio effects. Chapter 8 covers the Audio Mixer, as well as Master and Submix tracks.

NOTE If you drag a video clip that contains audio to a video track, the audio is automatically placed in the corresponding audio track. You can also simply drag music audio to an audio track. When your project plays, the video and corresponding audio also play.

The following list describes many of the audio icons and options that are shown in Figure 5.3:

- **Target Track:** As you edit, Premiere Pro alters the target track. The target track in Figure 5.3 is Audio 1. Note that the target audio has rounded corners. You can click a target track to select it. To turn a track into a target track, you click its left edge.

- **Toggle Track Output:** Clicking this icon turns audio output off and on for the track. When output is off, audio is not output when you play it in the Program Monitor panel or when you output the project.

- **Toggle Track Lock:** This option locks the track so it cannot be altered. Clicking the Toggle Track Lock icon toggles track locking on or off. When a track is locked, a lock icon appears.

- **Set Display Style:** Click this drop-down menu to choose whether audio clips display by name or as a waveform.

- **Show Clip/Track Keyframes/Volume:** This drop-down menu allows you to choose to view or hide keyframes or volume settings for either audio clips or the entire track. Keyframes in the audio track indicate changes in audio effects. If you choose to show volume settings for clips or the entire track, you can adjust the volume in the Timeline using the Pen or Selection tool. After you create audio effects with keyframes, the effect names appear in a drop-down menu in the audio effects graph line in the Timeline. After selecting an effect in this drop-down menu, you can adjust it by clicking and dragging its keyframes in the Timeline.

- **Add/Remove Keyframe:** Clicking this button allows you to add or remove a keyframe from a track's volume or from the graph line for an audio effect. To add a keyframe, move the CTI to where you want the keyframe to appear and click the Add/Remove Keyframe button. To remove the keyframe, move the CTI to the keyframe and click the Add/Remove Keyframe button.

- **Master Track:** The Master track is used in conjunction with the Audio Mixer (see Chapter 8). Like other audio tracks, the Master track can be expanded; you can show keyframes and volume, and you can set or remove keyframes.

Track Commands

As you work with the Timeline, you may want to add, remove, or rename audio and video tracks. This section reviews the commands for renaming, adding, and deleting tracks, as well as for changing the Snap options and the starting point of a sequence (the sequence zero point). You can activate some of these commands by right-clicking/⌘-clicking in the Timeline panel; you activate others through menu commands.

- **Rename Track:** To rename an audio or video track, right-click its name, and then choose Rename in the drop-down menu that appears.

- **Add Tracks:** To add a track, choose Sequence ⇨ Add Tracks (or right-click a track name and choose Add Track). This opens the Add Tracks dialog box, shown in Figure 5.4. Here you can choose what type of track to create and where to place it.

- **Delete Track:** Before deleting a track, decide whether you want to delete a target track or empty tracks. If you want to delete a target track, click at the left side of the track to select it and choose Sequence ⇨ Delete Tracks (or right-click the track name and choose Delete Track). This opens the Delete Tracks dialog box, where you can choose to delete empty tracks, the target tracks, or Submix tracks.

- **Snap:** The Snap icon (magnet) toggles Premiere Pro's Snap Edges command. When you activate it, clips snap together automatically when you click and drag one near the other. This prevents Timeline gaps between edits. To enable Snap, you can also choose Sequence ⇨ Snap.

- **Sequence Zero Point:** You can change the zero point of a sequence by choosing Sequence Zero Point from the Timeline panel drop-down menu. Then enter the frame that you want to set as your zero point. Why change the sequence zero point? You may start your production with a countdown, or other sequence, but not want the duration of this opening sequence to be added to the Timeline frame count.

FIGURE 5.4

Use the Add Tracks dialog box to specify options for new tracks.

■ **Display Audio Units:** By default, Premiere Pro shows Timeline intervals in frames. You can change the Timeline interval to display audio samples by choosing Audio Units in the Timeline panel drop-down menu. If you choose Audio Units, the display shows audio units in milliseconds or audio samples. You specify the audio unit to be either milliseconds or samples in the Project Settings dialog box, when you first create a project or new sequence.

Using Multiple Sequences

An assembled production in a Timeline is called a *sequence*. Why differentiate between the Timeline and the sequence within it? The answer is that you can place multiple sequences within a Timeline, with each sequence featuring different footage. Each sequence also has a name and can be renamed. You may want to use multiple sequences to divide your project into smaller elements. After you finish editing the smaller sequences, you can combine them into one sequence before exporting. You may also want to copy and paste footage from one sequence into another to experiment with different edits, effects, or transitions. Figure 5.5 shows a Timeline panel containing two sequences.

NOTE   If you import one Premiere Pro project into another Premiere Pro project, the imported project displays in a separate sequence that Premiere Pro places in a bin (folder) in the Project panel. The bin name is the name of the imported project. To make the sequence appear in the Timeline panel, open the bin and double-click the Sequence icon.

Creating a new sequence

When you create a new sequence, it is automatically added to the active Timeline panel as a new tab in the panel, as shown in Figure 5.5. Creating a sequence is easy; simply choose File ⇨ New ⇨ Sequence. This opens the New Sequence dialog box, shown in Figure 5.6. Here you can rename the sequence and choose how many tracks to add. Clicking OK creates a new sequence and adds it to the currently selected Timeline. After you place two sequences onscreen, you can cut and paste from one to the other or edit a sequence and nest it into another sequence.

FIGURE 5.5

The Timeline window with two sequences

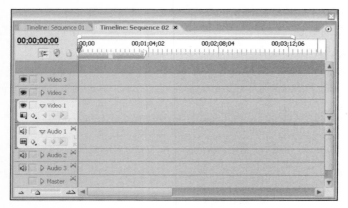

FIGURE 5.6

The New Sequence dialog box controls how tracks are created in new sequences.

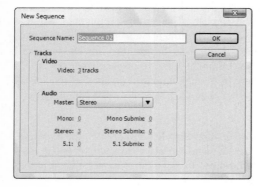

To move from one sequence to another in the Timeline panel, click the sequence's tab. If you want to separate a sequence into a separate window, click its tab, press Ctrl, and drag it away from the Timeline panel. Next, release the mouse and then the Ctrl key. If you open multiple windows onscreen, you can activate a window that contains a sequence by choosing Window ➪ Timelines and choosing the sequence name in the submenu.

Nesting sequences

After you add a new sequence to a project, you can place footage in it and add effects and transitions. Later, if desired, you can embed or nest it into another sequence. You can use this feature to gradually create a project in separate short sequences, and then assemble them all into one sequence (with the short sequences nested within the one sequence).

One advantage of nesting is that you can reuse an edited sequence again and again by simply nesting it several times in a Timeline. Each time you nest one sequence in another, you can trim it or change the transitions surrounding it in the Timeline. When you apply an effect to a nested sequence, Premiere Pro applies the effect to all of the clips in the sequence, saving you from having to apply the same effect to multiple clips.

If you are going to nest sequences, be aware that nested sequences always refer to their original source clips. If you change the original source clips, the change is reflected in the sequences in which it is nested.

Figure 5.7 shows how a nested sequence appears in the Timeline panel. In this figure, Sequence 02 was nested within Sequence 01, and audio and video transitions were added between the two sequences.

 The video in Sequence 01 is Artbeats clip RL104. mov; the video clip in Sequence 02 is Artbeats SP123.mov. You can find both in the Artbeats folder on the DVD.

FIGURE 5.7

Sequence 02 is nested within Sequence 01.

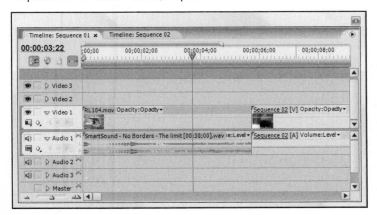

Follow these steps to nest one sequence within another:

1. **Create a new sequence by choosing File ⇨ New ⇨ Sequence.**

2. **In the new sequence, add footage, and create edits, transitions, and effects as needed.**

3. **To nest one sequence in another sequence, click and drag the sequence from the Project panel or from the Source section of the Monitor window into the track of the other sequence.**

 To open a sequence in the Source Monitor, Ctrl+double-click it in the Project panel or in the Timeline panel.

 To quickly return to the original sequence of a nested sequence, double-click the nested sequence in the Timeline panel.

Clip Project Management

Although the Timeline keeps program footage organized in a consistent linear structure, if you want to work efficiently, you also need to keep your source footage organized. Fortunately, Premiere Pro provides several features to keep your source clips organized while you work. The following sections review a variety of menu commands and options that can help you work efficiently with clips. Here's a summary of the primary topics in this section:

- **Project Manager:** Creates a new version of your project and can remove unused footage and extraneous frames from clips.

- **Subclips:** Allows you to divide up longer clips into multiple shorter clips.

- **Clip Notes:** Allow you to create PDF versions of a project for workgroup review. Members of the workgroup can view the video in Adobe Acrobat Reader.

- **Adobe Bridge:** An asset management application that is included with Adobe Premiere Pro, and that allows you to drag and drop files from Bridge directly into a project.

As discussed in Chapter 2, organizing footage in bins in the Project panel also provides a way to keep clips organized. To create a new bin, click the folder icon in the Project panel. Next, name your bin and drag footage into it. To view the contents of a bin, double-click it. If you would like to see bin footage by clicking a tab, change Bins preferences in the General preferences dialog box by clicking Edit ⇨ Preferences ⇨ General.

Using the Project Manager

Premiere Pro's Project Manager provides the fastest method to reduce the file size of a project and remove extraneous clips. The Project Manager conserves hard drive space by creating a new trimmed version of your work; it does this by removing files that aren't being used and removing extra frames before in points and after out points. The Project Manager provides two options: to create a new trimmed project or to copy all or some of the project files to a new location.

To use the Project Manager, choose Project ➪ Project Manger. This opens the Project Manager dialog box, shown in Figure 5.8, where you can choose from the following options:

- **Exclude Unused Clips:** This option removes unused clips from the new project.

- **Make Offline:** Select this option to take project clips offline so that you can recapture them using Premiere Pro's Batch Capture command (choose File ➪ Batch Capture). This option can be very useful if you are using low-resolution versions of footage. (See Chapter 4 for more information about batch capturing.)

- **Include Handles:** This option allows you to choose the number of extra frames before the in point and after the out point of project clips.

FIGURE 5.8

Use the Project Manager dialog box to reduce project file size and remove extraneous clips.

- **Include Preview Files:** This option allows preview files of rendered footage to be included in the new project. If you deselect this option, you create a smaller project, but you need to re-render effects to view the effects in the new project. You can only select this option if you choose Collect Files and Copy to New Location.

- **Include Audio Conform Files:** This option keeps conformed audio files in the new project. If you do not select this option, the new project consumes less hard drive space; however, Premiere Pro must conform the audio files in the new project — which may be time-consuming. (For more information about audio files, see Chapter 7.) You can only select this option if you choose Collect Files and Copy to New Location.

- **Rename Media Files to Match Clip Names:** If you renamed clips in the Project panel, this option ensures that those new names are maintained in the new project. Note that if you rename a clip and then set its status to offline, the original filename is maintained.

- **Project Destination:** This option allows you to specify a location for the project folder that contains the trimmed project material. Click Browse to choose the location.

- **Disk Space:** This option compares the file size of the original project and the new trimmed project. Click Calculate to update file sizes.

 **TIP**   If you want to remove only unused clips from your project, choose Project ⇨ Remove Unused.

Managing clips

If you are working on a long video project, organizing video and audio clips efficiently can help to ensure that you are working productively. Premiere Pro provides a variety of handy features for clip management. You can rename clips, create subclips out of longer clips, and take clips that you no longer need offline. However, before you begin to use these features, you should understand the relationship among master clips, clip instances, and subclips.

- **Master Clip:** When you first import a clip, it appears as a master clip in the Project panel. The master clip is a screen representation of the media hard drive file. You can rename and delete the master clip in the Project panel without affecting the original hard drive file.

- **Instance:** When you place a clip in the Timeline, you create an *instance* of the master clip. Premiere Pro allows you to create multiple instances of the master clip in the Timeline. If you delete the instance from the Timeline, the master clip remains in the Project panel. However, if you remove a master clip from the Project panel, all instances disappear from the Timeline.

- **Subclip:** A subclip is a shorter, edited version of a master clip that is independent of the master clip. For example, if you capture a long interview, you can divide different topics into multiple subclips and quickly access them in the Project panel. When editing, working with shorter clips is more efficient than taking one longer clip and using different instances of it in the Timeline. If you delete a master clip from the project, its subclips still remain in the project. You can recapture subclips from the Project panel using Premiere's Batch Capture options.

- **Duplicate Clip:** A duplicate clip is another instance of the master clip in the Project panel. It exists independently of the original and can be renamed. If the master clip is deleted from the Project panel, the duplicate remains. In the current version of Premiere Pro, most users will use subclips instead of duplicate clips. In previous versions of Premiere, many users would use duplicate clips in a similar fashion to Premiere Pro's subclips. However, subclips are more efficient because they do not contain all of the master clip footage.

Creating subclips

After you understand the relationship between master clips, clip instances, and subclips, you'll undoubtedly want to start using subclips in your projects. As mentioned, Premiere Pro allows you to reproduce parts of footage from one long clip in one or more shorter clips called subclips. This feature allows you to work with shorter child clips that exist independently of the master clip. Follow these steps to create a subclip:

1. **Double-click the master clip's icon in the Project panel.** This opens the clip in the Source Monitor. Alternatively, drag the clip from the Project panel to the Source Monitor.

2. **Set in and out points for the clip.** To set the in point, move the Source Monitor's CTI to the desired frame and then click the Set In Point button. Next, move the CTI to the desired out point and click the Set Out Point button.

3. **If you don't want the audio of a master clip to be included in a subclip, click the Toggle Take Audio and Video icon in the Source Monitor and click the Toggle Take Video icon (or click Take Video in the Source Monitor panel menu).**

4. **Choose Clip ⇨ Make Subclip, or drag the clip from the Source Monitor to an empty area of the Project panel.** This opens the Make Subclip dialog box, shown in Figure 5.9.

FIGURE 5.9

The Make Subclip dialog box

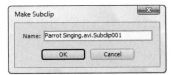

5. **In the Make Subclip dialog box, enter a name for the subclip.** This creates a new subclip in the Project panel.

Editing a subclip

After you create a subclip, you can edit its in and out points, or you can convert it to a master clip. To edit a subclip, select the subclip in the Project panel and choose Edit ⇨ Subclip. In the Edit Subclip dialog box, shown in Figure 5.10, edit the in and out points.

To convert the clip to a master clip, select Convert to Master Clip and click OK. After the master clip is created, its icon changes to a full clip in the Project panel, rather than a clip within a clip.

 If you use the Edit Subclip command to change the in and out points of a clip that is not a subclip, Premiere Pro creates a subclip with the in and out points.

FIGURE 5.10

The Edit Subclip dialog box

Offline and online clips

As you work with master and subclips, you may want to take a clip offline. This removes the link from a clip in the Project panel to its disk file. If you remove the link, Premiere Pro no longer attempts to access the footage when the project is open. After a clip is offline, you can re-link it to disk hard drive media and recapture it in a batch capture session.

To take a clip offline, right-click it in the Project panel and choose Make Offline in the drop-down menu. This opens the Make Offline dialog box, where you can specify whether to delete the original file footage from your storage media.

If you want to later link the files to another file, right-click the offline file in the Project panel and choose Link Media. In the Link Media dialog box, navigate to the file to which you want to link.

 You can replace one or more offline files with captured footage on a hard drive by first selecting the offline files in the Project panel and then choosing Project ➪ Link Media.

Master and subclip relations

Because subclips are children of parent master clips and both can inhabit a project simultaneously, you must understand their relationship to the original source footage and what happens if either clip is offline. Here are some tips for managing master clips and subclips:

■ If you take a master clip offline or delete it in the Project panel, but you don't delete the clip's file from disk, the subclip and subclip instances stay online.

■ If you take a clip offline and delete the clip's file from disk, the subclip and its master clip are taken offline.

■ If you delete a subclip from a project, the master clip is not affected.

- If you take a subclip offline, instances of the subclip are taken offline in Timeline sequences, but duplicates of the subclip remain online. Other subclips based on the master clip also remain online.

- If you recapture a subclip, the subclip becomes a master clip. Instances of the subclip in sequences are linked to the new subclip footage. They are no longer linked to the old subclip material. (See Chapter 4 to learn more about batch capturing.)

Duplicating, renaming, and deleting clips

Although using subclips is more efficient than duplicating and renaming clips, from time to time you may want to duplicate an entire clip so that you have another instance of the master clip in the Project panel.

To duplicate and rename a clip, follow these steps:

1. **Select the clip in the Project panel.**

2. **Choose Edit ⇨ Duplicate.** A duplicate of the clip appears in the Project panel with the word *copy* following the original clip name.

3. **Rename the clip by choosing Edit ⇨ Rename.**

TIP You can duplicate a master clip in the Project panel by pressing Ctrl/⌘ and dragging it below the last item in the panel. Release the mouse, and then release the Ctrl/⌘ key. If you want to delete a clip from the Project panel or from the Timeline, select it and press Backspace, or choose Edit ⇨ Cut or Edit ⇨ Clear. (Edit ⇨ Cut places the clip in the Clipboard, so that you can paste it into Premiere Pro again.) You can also delete a clip by right-clicking it and choosing Edit ⇨ Cut or Edit ⇨ Clear.

Enabling and disabling clips

While editing, you may decide that you don't want to see a clip's video when you play your project in the Program Monitor. Rather than deleting the clip, you can disable it — which also prevents it from being exported. To disable the clip, select the clip in the Timeline and choose Clip ⇨ Enable. This toggles the clip to a disabled state, and the check mark is removed from the Enable menu item. To re-enable the clip, choose Clip ⇨ Enable. This toggles the clip back to its original enabled state.

Using Clip Notes for workgroup review

If you are working as a member of a production team, Premiere Pro's Clip Notes option allows you to share your project with co-workers who aren't video editors. Clip Notes are exported from Premiere Pro as an Adobe PDF file, and thus can be read in Adobe Acrobat Reader. When you export your project using a Clip Note, Premiere Pro embeds either the entire project or the work area into the PDF file. When team members open the PDF file, they can review your project by clicking the Play button, shown in Figure 5.11. Reviewers can later export comments that can be imported into your Premiere Pro project.

To export a Clip Note file in PDF format, follow these steps:

1. **Select the Timeline panel that includes the sequence that you want to export.**

2. **Choose Export ⇨ Adobe Clip Notes.** This opens the Adobe Media Encoder's Export Settings dialog box.

3. **In the Export Settings dialog box, enter the format, range, and video preset in the Export Settings section.**

4. **Click the Clip Notes tab and enter a password, if desired.** You can also enter comments.

5. **Click OK.**

6. **In the Save File dialog box, enter a name for your PDF file, specify a location for the file, and then click Save.**

After you create the PDF file, you can open it in Adobe Acrobat Reader, as shown in Figure 5.11. In the PDF file, team members can enter comments and then click Export to export the file in XML Forms Data Format (.xfdf). You can import the XFDF file into the Premiere project by choosing File ⇨ Import. When imported, the comments appear as marker comments in the Timeline. To see a reviewer's comments, you can double-click the marker icon in the Timeline.

FIGURE 5.11

A Premiere Pro project viewed in Adobe Acrobat Reader

Timecode for Workgroup Review

If you want different members of your workgroup to review footage and edits, you can temporarily place timecode over video footage. To do this, you can add transparent video to a track above your footage and then apply the Time Code video effect to the transparent video. The result is timecode overlaying your footage, simulating what is often called a *window dub*. This allows everyone in your workgroup to refer to the same timecode as they view footage and compile editing comments.

To create transparent video, choose File ⇨ New ⇨ Transparent Video. After the transparent video appears in the Project panel, drag it to a track above your footage in the Timeline. Next, extend the transparent video by clicking and dragging the clip edge or by selecting it and choosing Clip ⇨ Speed/Duration. (In the Speed/Duration dialog box, enter the duration for the transparent video.) After you lay down the transparent video, drag the Timecode effect over it. (The Timecode effect can be found in the Video bin, in the Video Effects bin in the Effects panel.) Once you finish reviewing the project, you can remove the timecode by deleting the transparent video track or by turning off track output for the transparent video track. To learn more about applying video effects, see Chapter 13.

Using Adobe Bridge

Adobe Bridge is a file and asset management application that you can access directly from Premiere Pro. You can use Adobe Bridge to organize project files, add metadata, and preview video files. You can also import files directly from Adobe Bridge into Premiere Pro by double-clicking the file or dragging it into Premiere Pro's Project panel.

Although using Adobe Bridge is certainly not a necessity for creating Premiere Pro projects, it can prove helpful, particularly when organizing media before you create your projects. For example, you can add metadata to all files that you will be using in a project, and quickly search for them in Adobe Bridge. After files are found, you can place them in an Adobe Bridge Collection. By clicking an Adobe Bridge Collection icon, you can immediately access the files in the collection. This section provides an overview of features that Premiere Pro users may find useful when planning and editing projects.

Opening Adobe Bridge

Premiere Pro provides two options for opening Adobe Bridge directly from a project:

- **To open Adobe Bridge from Premiere Pro, choose File ⇨ Browse.** Figure 5.12 shows files being displayed in Adobe Bridge.

- **If you want to quickly find an online file's location on your hard drive and view it in Adobe Bridge, select the file in Premiere Pro's Project panel and choose File ⇨ Reveal in Bridge.**

FIGURE 5.12

Files in Adobe Bridge

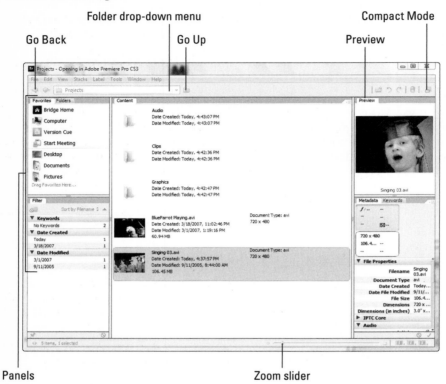

Panels

Zoom slider

Viewing files in Adobe Bridge

The best way to become familiar with Adobe Bridge is to use it to navigate through your hard drive. Here are few techniques for navigating and viewing files:

- **To view the contents of any folder, simply double-click the folder.** (If you double-click a file, it is imported into Premiere Pro.) When you double-click, the main viewing area of Adobe Bridge reveals the contents of the folders. To go back one level to the previous folder, click the Go Up folder at the top of the screen (shown in Figure 5.12).

- **To quickly jump to a folder, click in the drop-down menu at the top of the Adobe Bridge screen.** As you work, folders that you use are automatically added to the drop-down menu.

- **If you want to zoom in to view the images displayed in the Adobe Bridge file area, you can click and drag the zoom slider at the bottom of the screen.** You can also pick a view from the Window menu.

- **Premiere Pro users who want to access Adobe Bridge and use it while working in Premiere Pro will most likely prefer to work in Compact mode.** Compact mode shrinks the Adobe Bridge window so that you can view Premiere Pro panels and Adobe Bridge at the same time. To switch to Compact mode, click the Compact Mode icon in the top-right corner of the Adobe Bridge screen.

Bridge panels

After you start using Adobe Bridge, you'll see that it provides a visual alternative to Windows Explorer. Its panels also provide another graphic interface to help keep you organized. These panels, which appear along the left side of the Adobe Bridge screen (see Figure 5.12), allow you to create keywords, view metadata, and copy files into favorites. To open a panel, click the View menu and then choose the panel that you want to open. Adobe Bridge panels include the following:

- **Favorites:** This panel shows commonly used folders and files. To add to the favorites list, drag a file or folder from the main file area into the Favorites panel.

- **Preview:** Use this panel to preview audio and video files. Click and drag a file into the Preview panel, and then click the Play button to play video.

- **Keywords:** This panel allows you to view and add keywords to a file. Keywords can be used to describe a file, and can later be used for searching. Keywords are primarily used with Adobe's Photo Collection and images from Adobe's Creative Suite. Premiere Pro users who want to embed descriptive attributes in a file should use metadata.

- **Metadata:** This panel allows you to add metadata to a file. Metadata provides descriptive information about a file that remains with the file when it is used in different applications.

 If you want to view or hide the panels quickly, click Show/Hide Panels in the lower-left corner.

Using metadata in Adobe Bridge

Using Adobe Bridge's metadata capabilities, you can tag files with metadata information and search using metadata criteria. Some common fields for metadata include Title, Author, Description, and Copyright Information. Several video data metadata fields are shown in Figure 5.12. To add metadata, simply click the pencil icon that is adjacent to the field name and enter the appropriate information. After you finish entering metadata, click the check mark icon at the bottom of screen to save the changes, or click the circle bar icon to cancel.

The fields in the metadata section are controlled by the Metadata preferences. To change these preferences, click Preferences in the flyout menu and select which fields you want to include in the metadata panel.

 In the metadata panel, you can specify metadata according to the International Press Telecommunications Council (IPTC) standards.

Finding files using metadata criteria

If you begin embedding metadata to files, you can find and group your files based upon metadata criteria. To find data in Adobe Bridge based upon metadata criteria, start by choosing Edit ⇨ Find. In the Find dialog box, specify the search folder in the Look in drop-down menu.

Choose All Metadata in the Criteria drop-down menu, as shown in Figure 5.13. Enter the search criteria in the Enter Text search field.

FIGURE 5.13

Using metadata criteria to find files

After the data is found, a dialog box allows you to save the pictures in a collection. After you name the collection, a Collections icon appears in the Favorites panel. When you click the Collections icon, you can see the files that you have stored in the collection.

Other Adobe Bridge options

Adobe Bridge provides numerous other features for renaming and organizing files using ratings and labels. You can easily access these features from Adobe Bridge's View. However, despite all that Adobe Bridge has to offer, Premiere Pro users should generally not move and rename files after importing them into Premiere Pro. Otherwise, Premiere Pro cannot find them when you first load your project. Your best bet is to arrange and rename source files before you import them.

Summary

Premiere Pro provides numerous project management features. Its Timeline panel controls how clips are viewed and exported. In the Timeline panel you can work with multiple sequences and embed one sequence in another. In this chapter, you learned about the following:

■ Using Timeline ruler options to change zoom levels.

■ Selecting a track by clicking the head of the track to make it the target track.

■ Locking and hiding tracks.

■ Viewing keyframe and opacity settings in video tracks.

■ Creating a new sequence, by choosing File ➪ New ➪ Sequence.

■ Nesting one sequence in another, by clicking and dragging the sequence from the Project panel into a track in the Timeline window of another sequence.

■ Using the Project Management dialog box to trim projects.

■ Using subclips to create shorter source clips from master clips.

■ Exporting a project for review using Premiere Pro's Clip Notes option.

Chapter 6

Basic Editing with the Source Monitor and Timeline Panels

E diting drives a video program. The careful assembly of sound and video clips can control excitement, tension, and interest. Fortunately, Premiere Pro makes this crucial element of digital video production a logical, creative, and rewarding process rather than a tedious and frustrating one. Premiere Pro's interface — which features its Timeline and Monitor panels — combines with its track selection and editing tools to provide a fully integrated and powerful working environment.

This chapter introduces the basic techniques of editing in Premiere Pro. It begins with an overview of the editing process and provides details on creating insert and overlay edits using the Source Monitor and Timeline panels. The chapter concludes with a discussion of how to create lift and extract edits in the Timeline. Premiere Pro's advanced editing techniques are discussed in Chapter 12.

ON the DVD The images used in the figures in this chapter are from BG113.mov, BG117.mov, and SP123.mov. These clips are in the Artbeats folder on the DVD.

Basic Editing Concepts and Tools

Before you begin editing video in Premiere Pro, you should be familiar with the different techniques that you can use to edit a digital video production. Premiere Pro provides two main areas for editing clips and assembling them — the Monitor panels and the Timeline panel. As discussed earlier in this book, the Timeline provides a visual overview of your project. You can begin creating a rough edit by simply dragging clips from the Project panel into the Timeline. Using the selection tools in the Timeline, you can begin arranging the clips in a logical order. However, you can work even more efficiently by editing a clip's in and out points in the Source Monitor panel.

The Source Monitor displays clips that are not in a sequence in the Timeline, while the Program Monitor plays clips that are already edited in a Timeline sequence. Using controls in the Source Monitor panel, you can change the in and out points of clips, and then use an insert or overlay edit to place the clips in the Timeline. The steps and examples in this chapter show you how to create, insert, and overlay edits.

To further fine-tune your editing work, you can use Premiere Pro's editing tools to perform ripple, slide, and slip edits. These and more sophisticated editing techniques that can be performed in the Source Monitor panel — such as three- and four-point editing — are discussed in Chapter 12.

> **NOTE** When you are performing edits, you may find that using keyboard shortcuts saves time. To display the keyboard commands, choose Edit ➪ Keyboard Customization. Choose Panels in the pop-up menu, and then open the section for Monitor and Trim panels.

The workspace

An important consideration before actually editing a project is to plan how you want to set up your workspace. To select a predefined workspace, choose Window ➪ Workspace and then choose from the four available choices: Audio, Color Correction, Editing, Effects.

In the Editing workspace, shown in Figure 6.1, the Project, Monitor, Effects, Tools, and Timeline panels consume the entire screen. These are the most important panels that you will use as you assemble a project. You can drag clips from the Project panel into the Source Monitor panel, or you can drag them directly from the Timeline. As explained later in this chapter, you can edit the clips in either the Timeline panel or the Monitor panel.

At any point in time, you can change the arrangement of panels onscreen and save your workspace by choosing Window ➪ Workspace ➪ New Workspace. This command allows you to save a workspace to disk. It then adds the workspace name to the Window ➪ Workspace submenu. When you want to reload your workspace, simply choose Window ➪ Workspace and select your workspace name from the menu.

Getting started

After you import your video, audio, and still footage into the Project panel, you may be tempted to immediately start dragging clips to the Timeline to begin editing your production. If you're working on a long project with many production elements, you undoubtedly want to plan your production on paper beforehand. If you work from a script that describes the video elements and includes all narration, you can save yourself hours of time when you begin to edit your production. To help you visualize your production or various parts of it, you may also want to create a storyboard, which contains drawings or printouts of the video. After you load the various production elements into bins in the Project panel, you may also find it helpful to double-click each clip in the Project panel and click the Play button in the Source Monitor panel to view each clip before editing.

FIGURE 6.1

The Editing workspace

For beginners who are working on new projects, another good idea is to practice editing short video and audio sequences so that you become familiar with the basic techniques of creating a production. In Premiere Pro, you can edit clips in either the Source Monitor panel or the Timeline panel. Beginners may be tempted to drag all clips into the Timeline and click and drag to edit them there. However, for precision editing, the Source Monitor panel provides better controls for fine-tuning your work. After you have edited a clip's in and out points in the Source Monitor, you can then drag the clip to a sequence in the Timeline, or you can click the Source Monitor's Insert button or Overlay button to place the clip in the sequence.

Working with the Monitor Panels

The Source, Program, and Trim Monitor panels are not only used for previewing your production as you work, but they can also be used for precise editing and trimming. You can use the Source Monitor panel, shown in Figure 6.2, to trim clips before placing them in a video sequence.

FIGURE 6.2

The Source Monitor panel

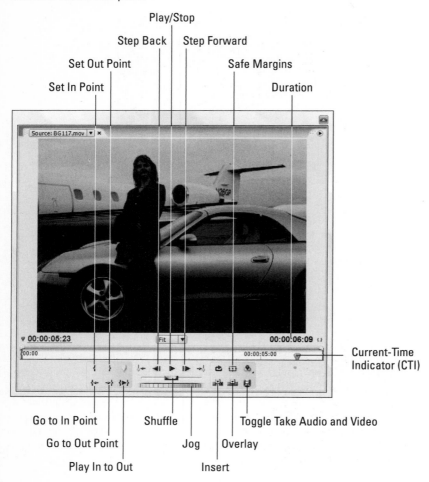

You can use the Program Monitor, shown in Figure 6.3, to edit footage that is already placed on the Timeline. You can also open the Trim Monitor panel, shown in Figure 6.4, to fine-tune your edits. In the Trim Monitor panel, the frame to the left and the frame to the right of an edit are represented in separate sections to provide greater precision for setting in and out points. To open the Trim Monitor panel (covered in Chapter 12), click the Trim button in the Program Monitor.

In most editing situations, you want to keep the Source Monitor and Program Monitor open onscreen. This enables you to view source clips (clips to be used in the program) and the program material (the clips that are already placed in a sequence in the Timeline panel) simultaneously. Before you use more sophisticated editing techniques, you should become familiar with both panels. Beneath the Source Monitor's video area is the source controller, which enables you to play source clips that haven't been added to the Timeline. The Set In Point and Set Out Point buttons enable you to set in and out points of source clips.

Beneath the Program Monitor's video area is the program controller, which enables you to play the program that exists on the Timeline. Clicking the In Point and Out Point buttons in the Program Monitor changes the in and out points of the sequence that is already on the Timeline. You use the sequence Set In Point and Set Out Point buttons before performing lift and extract edits, which remove footage from the current sequence, and when you create three-point edits. (Three-point edits are covered in Chapter 12.)

FIGURE 6.3

The Program Monitor panel

Current-Time Indicator   Lift Extract

FIGURE 6.4

The Monitor panel in Trim view

Left frame of edit   Right frame of edit

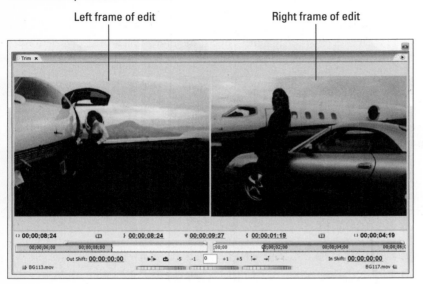

Both the Source Monitor and the Program Monitor allow you to view safe margin areas. Monitor-safe margins enable you to show the safe zones for movement and for titles. These margins indicate that the image area is safely within the monitor viewing area, as well as the image area that might be overscanned. A safe zone is needed because television screens (as opposed to a video production monitor, or your computer screen) may not show the full video fame that the camera actually shoots. To view the safe-margin markers in the Monitor panel, choose Safe Margins from the Monitor's panel menu or click the Monitor's Safe Margins button. When the safe-zone margins appear in the Monitor, the inner safe zone is the title-safe area, and the outer safe zone is the action-safe area.

Trimming clips in the Source Monitor panel

Before placing clips in a video sequence in the Timeline, you may want to first trim them (set the in and out points) in the Source Monitor panel, because captured clips invariably contain more footage than needed. If you trim a clip before placing it in a video sequence in the Timeline, you may find that you save time that would otherwise be spent clicking and dragging clip edges in the Timeline. Follow these steps for setting the in and out points of a clip in the Source Monitor panel:

TIP   To practice, import a clip into your project or load a clip from the Chapter 1 folder on the DVD that accompanies this book. To import the clip, choose File ➪ Import and then select the clip from your hard drive or the DVD. (You can work faster if you copy clips from the DVD to your hard drive.)

1. **To display a clip in the Source Monitor panel, double-click it in the Project panel.** Alternatively, you can click and drag a clip from the Project panel to the Source Monitor panel. When the clip appears in the Source Monitor panel, you can use the controls shown in Figure 6.1 to play the clip.

NOTE If you double-click footage that is already placed in a sequence in the Timeline window, the video portion appears in the Source Monitor. If you double-click an unlinked audio track, Premiere Pro displays the audio portion in the Source Monitor. (See Chapter 7 for more information about editing audio.)

2. **Click the Play button to play the entire clip.** (You can replay the clip continuously by clicking the Loop button.) When you find a section you want to edit, you can stop it by clicking the Stop button. When you stop the clip, look at the time display in the left side of the Source Monitor to see at which frame you have stopped. This can help you when setting in and out points and when setting markers.

3. **To precisely access the frame that you want to set as your in point, start by clicking and dragging the current-time indicator (CTI), a blue triangle, over the ruler area in the Monitor panel.** As you click and drag, the Source Monitor's time display indicates your frame location. If you don't stop at the correct frame, you can click the Step Forward and Step Backward buttons to slowly move one frame at a time forward or backward. You can also click and drag the shuttle (refer to Figure 6.2) or the jog tread area to move back and forth through your clip. If you prefer to use the keyboard, press the left- or right-arrow keys to move back and forth frame by frame.

TIP You can jump to a specific frame in a clip by double-clicking the Time display in the bottom-left corner of the Source Monitor. Make sure that the entire timecode readout is selected (you might need to double-click twice), and then type a specific timecode position. You do not need to type colons or semicolons. For example, when you type 50, it is read as 50;00. If you type +50, the CTI jumps forward 50 frames; type –50 and the CTI jumps back 50 frames. These shortcuts also work in the Timeline panel.

TIP If you want to enlarge the time ruler intervals in the Source Monitor, click and drag its Viewing Area bar. The Viewing Area bar is the gray bar with curved edges above the panel's time ruler.

4. **When you reach the in point, click the Set In Point button or press I, or choose Marker ⇨ Set Clip Marker ⇨ In.** A left brace appears in the ruler area.

5. **Locate the frame that you want to set as the out point, and click the Set Out Point button or press O, or choose Marker ⇨ Set Clip Marker ⇨ Out.** A right brace appears in the ruler area. After you set the in and out points, you can easily edit their positions by clicking and dragging one of the brace icons. After you set the in and out points, note the time display on the right side of the monitor. This number indicates the duration from the in point to the out point.

6. **Play the edited sequence in the Source Monitor by clicking the Play In to Out button.**

Shuttle Keyboard Commands

You can use these keyboard combinations to shuttle through footage:

Forward frame by frame	Press and hold K, while tapping L
Reverse frame by frame	Press and hold K, while tapping J
Play forward at 8 fps	Press and hold K and L simultaneously
Reverse at 8 fps	Press and hold K and J simultaneously
Forward five frames	Shift+right arrow
Back five frames	Shift+left arrow

TIP   **If you want to play a short video segment near the CTI, press Alt/Option while clicking the Play In to Out button. (This converts the Play In to Out button to a Play Around button.) The footage backs up to the preroll time set in the General Preferences dialog box and plays to the postroll time. You can set the preroll and postroll times by choosing Edit ➪ Preferences ➪ General.**

After you edit a clip in the Source Monitor panel, you can insert it or overlay it in the Timeline. Insert and overlay edits are discussed in the "Creating Insert and Overlay Edits" section later in this chapter.

Choosing clips in the Source Monitor panel

After you start working with clips in the Source Monitor panel, you can easily return to previously used clips. When you first work with a clip in the Source Monitor panel, the clip's name appears in the tab at the top of the Source Monitor panel. If you want to return to a clip that you previously used in the Source Monitor, simply click the tab's down arrow. This opens a drop-down menu in which you can pick previously used clips. After you choose the clip in the drop-down menu, it appears in the Source window.

"Taking" audio and/or video

When working with clips in the Source Monitor, you can specify whether to use both audio and video, video only, or audio only. If the clip that you are editing in the Source Monitor includes both video and audio, you can use the Take Audio and Video button to "take" only audio or video. If you want to edit using only a clip's video, click the Toggle Take Audio and Video button in the Source Monitor panel (refer to Figure 6.2) until it changes to the Take Video button. If you want to edit using only audio from the clip, click the Toggle Take Audio and Video button until the Take Audio button appears. (If your clip doesn't include an audio track, the audio button does not appear.) When you perform an insert or overlay edit, Premiere Pro creates the edit using the audio and video, the video only, or the audio only, depending on the setting of the Toggle Take Audio and Video button.

 You can also choose Take Audio and Video, Take Video, and Take Audio from the Source Monitor's panel menu.

Creating Insert and Overlay Edits

Once you edit the in and out points of a clip, your next step to place it into a sequence on the Timelime. Once the clip is in the Timeline, it plays in the Program Monitor. As you place clips in the Timeline, you can insert clips between other footage or you can overlay them. When you create an overlay edit, you replace old footage with new footage; when you insert footage, the new footage is added to the Timeline, but no footage is replaced.

For example, the footage in the Timeline may include a galloping horse, where you want to edit in a three-second close-up of the jockey on the horse. If you perform an insert edit, the clip is split at the current edit point, and the jockey is inserted into the clip. The entire Timeline sequence becomes three seconds longer. If you perform an overlay edit instead, the three-second jockey footage replaces three seconds of horse footage. An overlay edit enables you to continue using the audio track that is linked to the galloping horse clip.

Inserting and overlaying from the Source Monitor

Creating an insert edit or overlay edit from the Source Monitor is easy. First, choose the clip you want to edit in the Source Monitor. If the clip isn't already in the Source Monitor, double-click it or drag it from the Project panel to the Source Monitor. Once the clip is in the Source Monitor, set the in and out points (as described in the section, "Trimming clips in the Source Monitor panel"). If you only want to insert or overlay video without audio, set the Toggle Take Audio and Video button to Take Video (or choose Take Video from the Source Monitor panel menu). Then follow these steps to insert or overlay a clip in the Timeline:

1. **Select the target track in the Timeline.** The target track is where you want the video to appear. To select a target track, click the left edge of the track. After you select it, it displays rounded edges.

2. **Move the CTI to the point where you want the clip to appear in the sequence in the Timeline.**

3. **Create the insert or overlay edit.**

    ■ To create an insert edit, click the Insert button in the Source Monitor panel or choose Clip ⇨ Insert.

   ■ To create an overlay edit, click the Overlay button in the Source Monitor panel or choose Clip ⇨ Overlay.

Inserting and overlaying by clicking and dragging

If you prefer using the mouse, you can create insert and overlay edits by dragging clips directly to the Timeline.

 ■ **To create an insert edit on the Timeline, press and hold Ctrl/⌘.** Click and drag a clip from the Source Monitor or Project panel over a clip in the Timeline. As you move one clip over the other, the mouse pointer changes to an Insert icon (an arrow pointing to the right). When you release the mouse (make sure Ctrl/⌘ is still pressed), Premiere Pro inserts the new clip in the Timeline and pushes the footage at the insert point to the right. Figure 6.5 shows the Timeline before and after an insert edit.

In Figure 6.5, the frames from the Players clip now appear after the inserted Ball clip. The arrows in the middle of the figure indicate that the edit affects all tracks (a gap is inserted into other tracks). To insert only into the target track, press Ctrl+Alt/⌘+Option while clicking and dragging. Release the mouse before releasing the keys.

FIGURE 6.5

The sequence in the Timeline panel before and after an insert edit

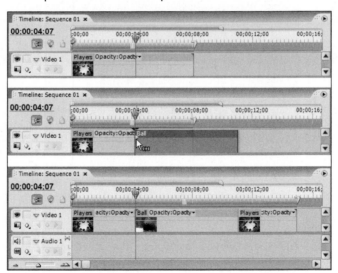

■ **To create an overlay edit on the Timeline, click and drag a clip from the Source Monitor or Project panel over a clip in the Timeline.** As you drag one clip over the other, the mouse pointer changes to an Overlay icon (an arrow pointing downward). When you release the mouse, Premiere Pro places one clip over the other and removes the underlying video. Figure 6.6 shows the Timeline before and after an overlay edit.

FIGURE 6.6

The sequence in the Timeline panel before and after an overlay edit

 You can add a video or audio track to the Timeline by clicking a clip in the Timeline or the Source Monitor panel and dragging it above the top video track or below the last audio track.

Replacing one clip with another

If you have edited a clip and placed it into the Timeline, and you later need to replace the clip with another, you can replace the original and have Premiere Pro automatically edit the replacement clip so that its duration matches the original. To do this, press Alt/Option and then click and drag a clip from the Project panel over a clip in the Timeline.

You can also replace a clip in the Timeline with a clip in the Source Monitor panel, and have the clip begin at the frame you select in the Source Monitor panel. To do this, follow these steps:

1. **In the Timeline, select the clip that you want to replace.**

2. **In the Source Monitor panel, move the CTI to the frame that you want to use as the starting replacement frame.**

3. **Choose Clip ➪ Replace with Clip from Source Monitor, Match Frame.**

NOTE You can also use the Clip ➪ Replace with Clip command to replace the currently selected clip in the Timeline with the clip displayed in the Source Monitor, or the currently selected clip in a bin in the Project panel.

155

Using Clip Markers

If you want to return to a particular frame in a clip, you can set a marker as a reference point.

Markers appear as triangles in the Source Monitor panel or in sequences in the Timeline panel. To set a marker for a source clip, move the Source Monitor's CTI to the frame where you want to create the marker, and then click the Marker button in the Source Monitor. To return to a clip marker, you can jump to it by clicking the Go to Next Marker button or the Go to Previous Marker button in the Source Monitor panel.

If you would like to place a numbered or unnumbered marker on a clip in the Timeline, select the Timeline and then move the CTI to the frame where you want the marker to be. Next, choose Marker ⇨ Set Marker ⇨ Unnumbered, or Marker ⇨ Set Marker ⇨ Next Available Marker. Markers appear in the portion of the Timeline that contains the Time Ruler/Work Area bar.

To jump to a marker in a sequence, select the sequence, and then choose Marker ⇨ Go to Clip Marker ⇨ Next, or Marker ⇨ Go to Clip Marker ⇨ Previous. If you choose Marker ⇨ Go to Clip Marker ⇨ Numbered, a dialog box appears listing all clip markers. You can then click an item in the list to go to a specific marker. To clear a clip marker, choose Marker ⇨ Clear Clip Marker and then choose the type of marker that you want to clear from the Clip Marker submenu.

Editing in the Timeline

As discussed in Chapter 5, Premiere Pro's Timeline provides a graphical representation of your project. By simply analyzing the effects and transitions in a video sequence in the Timeline, you can get a visual sense of your production without actually viewing the footage. Premiere Pro provides a variety of ways to place clips into the Timeline:

- Click and drag the footage or image from the Project panel into the Timeline.

- Select a clip in the Project panel, and then choose Clip ⇨ Insert or Clip ⇨ Overlay. The clip is inserted or overlaid into the target track at the CTI. When you insert a clip, it is dropped into the sequence and pushes footage to the right. When you overlay a clip, it replaces footage.

- Double-click the clip in the Project panel to open it in the Source Monitor panel. After setting in and out points, click the Insert or Overlay button in the Source Monitor panel (or select Clip ⇨ Insert or Clip ⇨ Overlay). Alternatively, drag the clip from the Source Monitor panel to the Timeline. As discussed earlier, pressing Ctrl/⌘ inserts footage into the Timeline, and dragging without pressing Ctrl/⌘ overlays footage.

- If you want to place multiple clips in the Timeline to create a rough cut of your work, you can use the Automate to Sequence command described in the next section.

 To make a track the target track, click in the track's header area.

Automate to Sequence

Premiere Pro's Automate to Sequence command provides a fast way to assemble a project in the Timeline. Automate to Sequence not only places clips from the Project panel into the Timeline, but it can also add default transitions between clips. Thus, you may view this command as an efficient way to create a quick rough cut. However, if the clips in the Project panel contain too much extraneous footage, your best option is to trim the clips in the Source Monitor panel before executing Automate to Sequence. Follow these steps for using Automate to Sequence:

TIP   Automate to Sequence places clips in the first non-locked track in the Timeline. If you want to place clips in tracks other than the Video 1 track, lock the preceding tracks. Be sure to re-select the Project panel before executing Automate to Sequence.

1. **Move the CTI to the location in the Timeline where you want the footage to begin.**

2. **Select the clips in the Project panel that you want to place in the Timeline.** To select a group of adjacent clips, click the first clip you want to include in the sequence and press Shift. While holding Shift, click the last clip you want in the sequence.

TIP   To select non-adjacent clips, Ctrl/⌘-click different clips in the Project panel.

3. **To add the selected clips to the Timeline, choose Project ⇨ Automate to Sequence or click the Automate to Sequence button in the Project panel.** This opens the Automate to Sequence dialog box, shown in Figure 6.7.

FIGURE 6.7

The Automate to Sequence dialog box

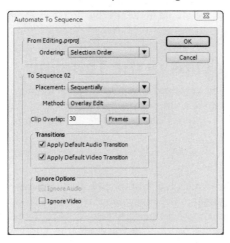

4. **In the Automate to Sequence dialog box, choose the options to control how the clips are placed on the Timeline.** These are your choices:

    ▪ **Ordering:** This option allows you to choose to have the clips placed in their sorted order in the Project panel or according to the order in which you selected them in the Project panel.

    ▪ **Placement:** You can choose to have the clips ordered sequentially or at each unnumbered marker in the Timeline. If you choose the Unnumbered Marker option, Premiere Pro disables the Transitions option in the dialog box.

    ▪ **Method:** This option allows you to choose Insert or Overlay edit. If you choose Insert, clips already in the Timeline are pushed to the right. If you choose Overlay, clips from the Project panel replace clips in the Timeline.

    ▪ **Clip Overlap:** This option allows you to specify how many seconds or frames are used for the default transition. In a 30-frame-long transition, 15 frames overlap from two adjacent clips.

    ▪ **Apply Default Audio/Video Transition:** This option applies the currently set default transition between clips.

    ▪ **Ignore Audio:** If you select this option, Premiere Pro doesn't place the audio that is linked to clips.

    ▪ **Ignore Video:** If you select this option, Premiere Pro doesn't place the video in the Timeline.

5. **To execute the Automate to Sequence command, click OK.**

> **TIP** You can sequentially place selected clips from the Project panel into the Timeline. First, sort the clips in the Project panel so that they appear in the order that you want to view them in the Timeline. Next, Shift-click to select more than one clip in the Project panel, and then drag one of the clips to the Timeline. The clips are placed in the Timeline in the same order as they appear in the Project panel.

Selecting and moving clips in the Timeline

After you place clips in the Timeline, you may need to reposition them as part of the editing process. You can choose to move one clip at a time, or you can move several clips at the same time. (You can also move either the video or audio of a clip independently. To do this, you need to temporarily unlink the clip.)

Using the Selection tool

 The simplest way to move a single clip is to click it with the Selection tool and move it in the Timeline panel. If you want the clip to snap to the edge of another clip, make sure that the Snap to Edges option is selected. You can either choose Sequence ⇨ Snap or click the Snap button (a magnet) in the upper-left corner of the Timeline panel. After you select the clips, you can move them by clicking and dragging them, or delete them from a sequence by pressing Delete. These tips can help you select clips and tracks using Premiere Pro's Selection tool:

- **To select a clip, activate the Selection tool and click the clip.**

- **To select more than one clip, press and hold Shift.** Click the clips that you want to select. Alternatively, you can click and drag to create a marquee selection around the clips that you want to select. After you release the mouse, the clips within the marquee are selected. You can also use this technique to select clips that are on different tracks.

- **If you want to select the video without the audio portion of a clip, or the audio without the video, Alt/Option-click the video or audio track.**

- **To add or subtract a clip or a selection of clips to or from a selection, press Shift.** Click and drag a marquee selection around the clip or clips.

> **TIP**   You can move a clip a specific number of frames right or left in the Timeline by selecting the clip and then pressing + or − on the numeric keyboard. Next, enter the number of frames to move and press Enter.

Using the Track Select tool

 If you want to quickly select several clips on a track or to delete clips from a track, you can use the Track Select tool. The Track Select tool does not select all clips on the track. It selects all clips from the point at which you click. Thus, if you place four clips on the Timeline and you want to select the last two, click the third clip. Figure 6.8 shows clips selected with the Track Select tool.

FIGURE 6.8

Clips selected with the Track Select tool

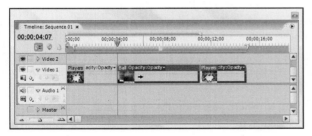

If you want to quickly select multiple clips on different Timeline tracks, press and hold Shift while you click in a track with the Track Select tool. This selects all clips on all tracks, starting at the point where you first click.

Grouping clips

If you need to select the same clips multiple times, you should place them in a group. After you create a group of clips, you can select every member of the group by clicking any group member. You can also delete all clips in a group by selecting any member of the group and pressing Delete.

To create a group of clips, start by selecting the clips and then choose Clip ➪ Group. To ungroup the clips, choose Clip ➪ Ungroup.

If you move a clip on the Timeline that is grouped to another clip — such as a video clip that is linked to its audio clip — the linked clips move together.

Setting In and Out Points in the Timeline Panel

When you are familiar with how to select clips in the Timeline, you can easily perform edits. You can edit by using the Selection tool or by setting in and out points using markers.

Using the Selection tool to set in and out points

One of the simplest ways to edit in the Timeline panel is to set in and out points using the Selection tool. To edit an in or out point with the Selection tool, follow these steps:

1. **Click the Selection tool in the Tools panel.**

2. **To set a clip's in point, move the Selection tool over the left edge of the clip in the Timeline.** The Selection tool changes to an Edge icon.

3. **Click and drag the edge of the clip to where you want the clip to start.** As you click and drag, a timecode readout appears next to the clip, showing the editing change. The display in the Program Monitor panel changes to show the in point of the clip.

4. **To set a clip's out point, move the Selection tool over the right edge of the clip in the Timeline.** The Selection tool changes to an Edge icon.

5. **Click and drag the edge of the clip to where you want the clip to end.** As you click and drag, a timecode readout appears next to the clip, showing the editing change. The display in the Program Monitor panel shows the out point of the clip.

NOTE   If you don't want the Program Monitor to display timecode as you edit clips, deselect Timecode Overlay During Edit in the Program Monitor panel menu.

Cutting clips with the Razor tool

If you want to create an in or out point quickly, you can literally slice a clip in two with the Razor tool. Move the CTI to the frame that you want to slice (this allows you to see the frame in the Program Monitor panel), and then click the frame with the Razor tool. Alternatively, choose Sequence ➪ Razor at Current Time Indicator. To slice footage in multiple tracks simultaneously, press Shift while clicking a frame with the Razor tool.

Rearranging clips

As you edit, you may want to grab a clip in the Timeline and place it into another area. If you do this, you are left with a gap where you have removed the footage. This is called a *lift edit*. The opposite of a lift edit is an *extract edit*, which closes the gap after you remove footage. Premiere Pro provides a timesaving keyboard command that combines an extract edit with either an insert or overlay edit:

■ To rearrange footage using an extract edit (which closes the gap) and an *insert* edit, press Ctrl/⌘ as you drag a clip or a group of selected clips to a new location. Release the mouse and then release the Ctrl/⌘ key.

■ To rearrange footage using an extract edit (which closes the gap) and an *overlay* edit, press Ctrl/⌘ as you drag a clip or a group of selected clips to a new location. Release Ctrl/⌘ and then release the mouse.

Editing with Sequence Markers

You can also perform basic editing in the currently selected sequence by setting in and out points using the Marker ➪ Set Sequence Marker ➪ In, and Marker ➪ Set Sequence Marker ➪ Out commands. These commands set in and out points for the beginning and end of the Timeline sequence. After you create Sequence Markers, you can use them as in and out points for lift and extract edits, which remove frames from the Timeline panel (described in the next section).

Setting in and out points

Follow these steps to set in and out points on the Timeline using menu commands:

1. **Click and drag the CTI to where you want to set the sequence in point.**
2. **Choose Marker ➪ Set Sequence Marker ➪ In.** An In Point icon appears at the ruler line on the Timeline at the position of the CTI.
3. **Click and drag the CTI to where you want to set the out point.**
4. **Choose Marker ➪ Set Sequence Marker ➪ Out.** An Out Point icon appears on the Timeline at the position of the CTI.

 After you create the in and out points, you can easily move them by clicking and dragging them in the Timeline.

 You can also set in and out points for the current sequence by clicking the Set In Point and Set Out Point buttons in the Program Monitor.

161

Clearing in and out points

After creating Sequence Markers, you can easily clear them with the following menu commands:

- To clear both the in and out points and start all over again, choose Marker ⇨ Clear Sequence Marker ⇨ In and Out.

- To clear just the in point, choose Marker ⇨ Clear Sequence Marker ⇨ In.

- To clear just the out point, choose Marker ⇨ Clear Sequence Marker ⇨ Out.

Performing lift and extract edits at Sequence Markers

 You can use Sequence Markers to easily remove clip segments from the Timeline by executing the Sequence Lift command or the Sequence Extract command. When you perform a lift edit, Premiere Pro lifts a segment off the Timeline and leaves a blank space where the deleted clip existed. When you perform an extract edit, Premiere Pro removes a section of the clip and then joins the frames of remaining clip sections together so that no blank area exists.

To perform a lift edit using Sequence Markers, follow these steps:

1. **Set in and out Sequence Markers at the section that you want to delete.** The top of Figure 6.9 shows in and out points created with Sequence Markers in the Timeline panel. See the earlier section "Setting in and out points" for information on creating in and out points.

2. **To perform a lift edit, choose Sequence ⇨ Lift, or click the Lift button in the Program Monitor.** Premiere Pro removes the section bordered by the in and out markers and leaves a blank area in the Timeline, as shown at the bottom of Figure 6.9.

FIGURE 6.9

The sequence in the Timeline panel before and after a lift edit

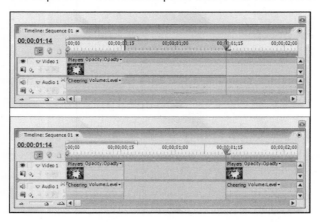

Adding Sequence Markers

You can add numerical markers to a sequence and use them as visual landmarks that you want to quickly return to later. These are especially useful with longer projects. To add a marker, move the CTI in the Timeline panel to where you want to add the marker and then choose Marker ⇨ Set Sequence Marker ⇨ Next Available Numbered.

You can jump to a marker by choosing Marker ⇨ Go To Sequence Marker ⇨ Next, or Marker ⇨ Go To Sequence Marker ⇨ Numbered. As mentioned earlier, you can also select a clip on a sequence and set a clip marker by moving the CTI to a frame and then choosing Marker ⇨ Set Clip Marker.

To perform an extract edit using Sequence Markers, follow these steps:

1. **Set in and out Sequence Markers at the section that you want to delete.** See the earlier section "Setting in and out points" for information on creating in and out points.

2. **To perform an extract edit, choose Sequence ⇨ Extract, or click the Extract button in the Program Monitor.** Premiere Pro removes the section bordered by the in and out markers and joins the edited sections together.

Summary

Premiere Pro provides graphical tools to aid in editing a digital video production. The Timeline, the Selection tools, and the monitor panels all come into play when you begin to assemble and fine-tune your production. When you edit in Premiere Pro, you can do the following:

- Drag clips to a sequence in the Timeline from the Project panel.

- Use the Selection tools to select and move clips in a sequence in the Timeline.

- Set in and out points in a sequence in the Timeline.

- Set in and out points in the Source Monitor panel.

- Perform lift and extract edits using the menu commands or the controls in the Program Monitor panel.

Chapter 7

Editing Audio

Just as a picture is worth a thousand words, sound can create a mood that could take a thousand words to describe. You can use sound to capture your audience's attention. The right background music can create a feeling of intrigue, comedy, or mystery. Sound effects can add realism and suspense to the visual elements that you present. Undoubtedly, the success of many of the best video productions and movies is related to the sound accompanying the video.

Fortunately, Premiere Pro provides a wealth of features that enable you to integrate sound into your video projects. When you place a video clip in the Timeline, Premiere Pro automatically takes the sound along with it. If you want to fade in or fade out background music or narration, Premiere Pro's Effect Controls panel provides the tools. If you want to add an audio effect that enhances an audio clip or add a special effect, you can simply drag it from the Effects panel to the clip. If you want to mix audio into a master track, Premiere Pro's Audio Mixer does the job.

This chapter focuses on audio track basics, audio enhancement, and special effects. It provides a look at how to use Premiere Pro's audio tracks and how to create effects in the Timeline. This chapter also includes an overview of Premiere Pro's many audio effects and concludes with a look at how to export audio.

CROSS-REF Chapter 8 covers creating audio effects and mixing tracks with the Audio Mixer. Soundbooth, Adobe's audio editing and composition program, is covered in Chapter 25.

What Is Sound?

Before you begin to use Premiere Pro's audio features, you need to have a fundamental idea of what sound is and the terms used to describe it. It is helpful to understand exactly what type of sound you're working with, as well as its quality. Terms such as *sample rate* of 32,000 kHz and *16-bit* appear in the Custom Settings dialog boxes, Export dialog boxes, and in the Project panel, as shown in Figure 7.1.

FIGURE 7.1

Audio information appears in the Project panel.

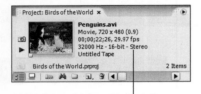

Audio sample rate and bit rate

To understand digital sound, we must start in the analog world, where a sound such as someone beating on a drum or playing a musical instrument in a concert hall travels to us through waves. We hear sounds because of the vibrations the waves create. The rate of this vibration is the sound's pitch. Thus, a high-pitch sound vibrates more than a low-pitch sound. The frequency of these vibrating sound waves is determined by how many cycles occur each second. Sound frequency (cycles per second) is measured in hertz (Hz). Humans can generally hear within a range from 20 Hz to about 20,000 Hz (20 kHz).

The magnitude of a soundwave — or its amplitude — is measured in *decibels*. The greater the curve, the greater its amplitude is and the louder the sound.

Sound bits and sampling

When sound is digitized, thousands of numbers represent *amplitude*, or the height and depth of waves. During this process, the sound is sampled and recreated digitally into a series of ones and zeroes, or *bits*. If you use Premiere Pro's Audio Mixer to record narration, the waves of sound from your voice are processed by a microphone and then digitized by your sound card. When you play back the narration, the sound card converts the ones and zeroes back to analog sound waves.

Higher-quality digital recording uses more bits. CD-quality stereo uses a minimum of 16 bits. (Older multimedia software sometimes used 8-bit sound rates, which provided poorer-quality sound, but produced smaller digital sound files.) Thus, one sample of CD-quality sound could be digitized into a series of 16 ones and zeroes to look like this:

```
1011011011101010
```

If the concept of bit rate is confusing, visual artists may find it easiest to think of a sound's bit rate as somewhat similar to image resolution: A higher bit rate produces a smoother-looking sound-wave, just as higher image resolution produces smoother images.

In digital sound, the frequency of the digital waves is determined by the *sample rate*. Many camcorders record sound at a sample rate of 32 kHz, thus recording 32,000 samples every second. The higher the sample rate, the greater the frequency range that the sound can reproduce.

To reproduce a specific frequency, sound generally should be sampled at double that frequency. Consequently, to reproduce the highest frequency of human hearing of 20,000 kHz, a sample rate of at least 40,000 samples is required (CDs are recorded at a sample rate of 44,100).

Figure 7.2 shows a spectral depiction of a low-frequency bass recording compared to the audio frequencies of a portion of Beethoven's *Ninth Symphony*. As you see later in this chapter, you can use several of Premiere Pro's audio effects to hone into specific frequency ranges to fine-tune and alter sound. The screen shots were taken in Adobe Audition, Adobe's audio-editing and composition application.

FIGURE 7.2

Audio frequency of bass recording, above; audio frequencies of Beethoven's Ninth Symphony, below

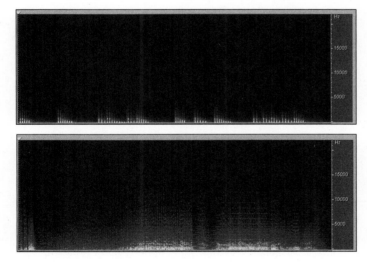

Digitized sound file sizes

As you might imagine, the larger a sound's bit depth and the larger its sample rate, the larger the sound's file size becomes. Because sound files, like video, can be very large, it can be important to estimate how large a sound file will be. You can estimate a sound file's size by multiplying the bit depth by the sample rate. Thus, one second of one-track mono at 16 bits with a sample rate of 44,100 (16-bit x 44,100) produces 705,600 bits per second (88, 200 bytes per second) — over 5MB per minute. A stereo clip would be twice as large.

Timeline Audio Tracks

When you edit in Premiere Pro, its Timeline panel provides a broad overview of the audio that accompanies your video. As you can see from Figure 7.3, audio tracks are grouped together beneath video tracks. If you click in the Set Display Style pop-up menu, you can choose to show an audio clip's name or its waveform. As with video clips, if you place audio clips into a sequence in the Timeline, you can click and drag to move them, use the Razor tool to slice audio, and use the Selection tool to adjust in and out points.

As you'll soon see, you can also edit the in and out points of audio clips in the Source Monitor, and store subclips of audio clips in the Project panel.

FIGURE 7.3

Audio tracks with submix and master tracks in the Timeline

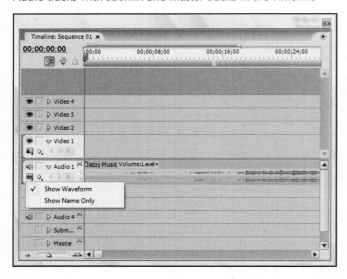

When you place a video clip into the Timeline, Premiere Pro automatically places its audio into the corresponding audio track. Thus, if you place a video clip with audio in the Video 1 track, the audio is automatically placed into Audio track 1. If you slice a video clip with the Razor tool, the linked audio is sliced along with it.

As discussed in Chapter 5, you can expand and compress audio track views by clicking the Collapse/Expand icon. After the track expands, you can choose from the following display options:

- You can view the audio by name or by waveform by choosing from the Set Display Style pop-up menu in the Timeline panel (shown in Figure 7.3).

■ You can view changes in audio levels for the clip or the entire track by choosing Show Clip Volume or Show Track Volume in the Show Keyframes pop-up menu, as shown in Figure 7.4.

■ You can view audio effect keyframes by choosing Show Clip Keyframes or Show Track Keyframes in the Show Keyframes pop-up menu (see Figure 7.4). The Show Keyframe mode also shows volume as an effect as well as other effects. Effects appear in a pop-up menu along the keyframe graph line.

FIGURE 7.4

The Show Keyframes pop-up menu offers different viewing options.

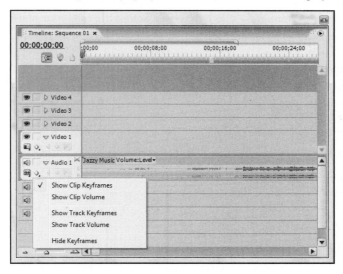

As you work with audio in Premiere Pro, you'll encounter different types of audio tracks. The Standard audio track allows for either Mono or Stereo (two-channel sound). The other tracks available include the following:

■ **Master track:** This displays keyframes and volume for the master track. You can mix sound from other tracks onto the master track using Premiere Pro's Audio Mixer.

■ **Submix tracks:** These are mixed tracks used by the Audio Mixer to mix a subset of other audio tracks.

■ **5.1 track:** These tracks are used in Dolby's Surround Sound; often used for surround sound DVD movies. In 5.1 sound, the left, right, and center channels are in front of the audience, with ambient sounds produced from two speakers behind. This requires a total of five channels; the extra .1 channel is a subwoofer that produces deep bass and some-times sudden explosive-type sounds. These low-frequency sounds are difficult to produce by the other speakers, which are usually smaller than the subwoofer.

169

Playing a Sound Clip

After you import a sound clip using Premiere Pro's File ➪ Import command, you can play it in the Project panel or Monitor panel.

ON the DVD The DVD includes practice sound clips from SmartSound. You can also download a free copy of Quicktracks for Adobe Premiere from SmartSound's Web site (`www.smart sound.com`). Quicktracks is a plug-in that resides in Adobe Premiere and allows you to search for music and customize music to fit the duration of a project. Quicktracks also comes with ten royalty-free music scores.

Here are the steps:

1. **Choose File ➪ Import ➪ File to import a sound file into your new project.**

2. **At this point, you can play the clip in the Project panel by clicking the Play button, as shown in Figure 7.5.** Alternatively, you can double-click the sound file in the Project window. The clip opens in the Source Monitor panel.

FIGURE 7.5

Click the Play button to play a clip in the Project window.

Play button

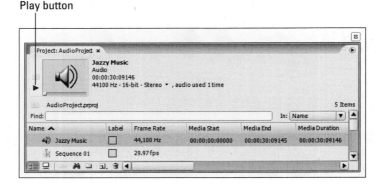

3. **If you opened the clip in the Source Monitor panel, you see the audio waveform in the Source Monitor.** Click the Source Monitor's Play button to play the clip.

NOTE You can view the audio waveform of a video clip by choosing Audio Waveform in the Source Monitor panel menu.

Editing Audio

Depending upon your needs, you can take several approaches to editing audio in Premiere Pro. You can slice the audio with the Razor tool in the Timeline as you edit video, clicking and dragging clips or clip edges as you work. If you need to work with audio independently of video, you can unlink the audio from the video. If you need to edit narration or sound effects, you can set in and out points for an audio clip in the Source Monitor. Premiere Pro also allows you to extract the audio from the video, so that it appears in the Project panel as another content source. If you need to edit your audio more precisely, you can select an audio-only master clip, subclip, or clip instance and choose Edit ⇨ Edit in Soundbooth (if Adobe Soundbooth is installed on your computer. Chapter 25 covers editing audio in Soundbooth). When you edit the audio in Soundbooth, the changes are saved to your hard drive and are reflected when you return to Premiere Pro. Finally, if you need to enhance or create transitions or audio effects, you can use the audio effects provided by Premiere Pro's Effects panel.

Using audio units

As you edit in the Monitor panels, the standard unit of measurement is the video frame. This is perfect for editing video where you can precisely set in or out points on a frame-by-frame basis. However, with audio, you may need more precision. For example, you may want to edit out an extraneous sound that is less than a frame long. Fortunately, Premiere Pro can display audio time in audio "units" as opposed to frames. You can view audio units in milliseconds or the smallest possible increment — the audio sample. These are your choices for working with audio units:

- To choose between milliseconds and audio samples, choose Project ⇨ Project Settings ⇨ General in the Audio Display Format drop-down menu, and then choose Milliseconds or Audio Samples.

- To view the audio units in the time display sections of the Source or Program Monitor panels, choose Audio Units in the panel menu.

- To view audio units in the Timeline's time ruler and time display, choose Audio Units in the Timeline's panel menu.

Editing audio on the Timeline

Although Premiere Pro is not a sophisticated audio-editing program, you can make simple edits in the Timeline panel. You can unlink audio from video and shift the audio so that it accompanies a different section of audio. You can also execute audio edits by zooming into the audio clips waveform in the Timeline panel and slicing audio with the Razor tool. Here are the basic steps for setting up the Timeline for audio editing:

1. **Click the Collapse/Expand button (the triangle in front of the audio track's name) to expand the audio track.**

2. **Click the Set Display Style icon in the Timeline, and choose Show Waveform.**

3. **Change units to audio samples by choosing Audio Units in the Timeline panel menu.** This changes the Timeline ruler display to audio units as either audio samples or milliseconds. (The default setting is audio samples; however, you can change this by choosing Project ⇨ Project Settings and choosing Milliseconds in the Audio Section Display Format drop-down menu.)

4. **Zoom in by clicking and dragging toward the right on the Timeline zoom slider.** Figure 7.6 shows the ruler with audio units in view. The time readout is shown in audio samples. Notice how much audio exists between two adjacent video frames in the audio track.

5. **Use editing tools to edit the audio.** You can click and drag either clip edge to change in and out points. You can also edit by activating the Razor tool in the Tools panel and clicking to slice the audio at a specific point.

FIGURE 7.6

Audio units and audio waveform in the Timeline

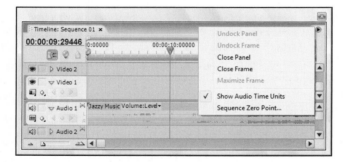

Unlinking and linking

If you place a clip with audio in the Timeline, you can edit its audio separately from the video. To do this, you first need to unlink the audio from the video; then you can edit audio in and out points separately from the video. For example, you may want to create a *j-cut,* where audio begins playing before the next video scene, or an *l-cut,* where the audio extends over the next video scene. Follow these steps to unlink video from audio:

1. **Select the clip in the Timeline.**

2. **Unlink the clip by choosing Clip ⇨ Unlink (you can also right-click either the audio or video clip and choose Unlink).**

3. **Deselect the audio and video tracks by clicking in an empty Timeline track.**

If you later want to relink the audio and video, you can select the audio and the video and choose Clip ⇨ Link.

TIP   If you've edited two clips together and unlinked the audio, you can use the Rolling Edit tool to simultaneously adjust the out point of one audio clip and the in point of the next. The Rolling Edit tool can be helpful in creating j-cuts and l-cuts. The Rolling Edit tool is discussed in detail in Chapter 12.

Unlinking and resyncing audio

Premiere Pro provides a temporary method of unlinking audio and video. You can temporarily unlink audio and video by pressing Alt/Option and then clicking and dragging either the audio or video portion of the clip. When you release the mouse, the clips are considered linked but are out of sync. If you use this temporary unlinking technique, Premiere Pro displays the out-of-sync frame difference at the in point of the clip on the Timeline. If you want to place the temporary unlinked clips back in sync, follow these steps:

1. Right-click/Ctrl-click the out-of-sync number at the in point of the clip in the Timeline.

2. In the drop-down menu that appears, choose one of the following:

   ▦ Choose Move into Sync to move the audio and video back into sync. Be aware that this can overwrite existing clips.

   ▦ Choose Slip into Sync to sync the clips without moving them. This choice uses a slip edit to create a new sync point for the clip.

NOTE   You can synchronize clips in multiple tracks to a clip in a target track by choosing Clip ↻ Synchronize. The Synchronize Clips dialog box allows you to synchronize clips at the start or end of a clip in the target track, at a numbered sequence marker, or by Timecode. See Chapter 12 for more information about using the Synchronize Clips command.

Linking multiple audio files

If you're working with multiple audio tracks that play simultaneously with video, you can link them all together. Later, if you need to apply effects, all tracks appear in the Effect Controls panel where you can selectively choose the tracks to which you want to apply the effects. Here's how to link multiple audio tracks:

1. **Place the audio into separate audio tracks.**

2. **Select the tracks by Shift-clicking the audio to be linked.** Note that you cannot mix track types. For example, you cannot link a stereo track to a mono track.

3. **Choose Clip ⇨ Link.**

Later, if you need to unlink the tracks, you can select one of the linked tracks and choose Clip ⇨ Unlink.

Editing source clips

Although you may find that editing audio in the Timeline meets most of your needs, you can also edit an audio clip's in and out points in the Source Monitor. In addition, you can use the Source Monitor to create subclips from one long audio clip, and then edit the subclips individually in the

Source Monitor or in the Timeline. (As discussed in Chapter 5, you create a subclip by setting in and out points in the Source Monitor, selecting it in the Source Monitor, and then choosing Clip ⇨ Make Subclip. Alternatively, you can drag the edited clip from the Source Monitor into an empty area of the Project panel.)

Taking audio only

When editing a clip with audio and video, you may find that you want to use the audio without the video. If you choose Take Audio in the Source Monitor, the video image is replaced by the audio's waveform. Follow these steps to take audio only and set in and out points in the Source Monitor:

1. **Drag the video clip to the Source Monitor window, or double-click it in the Project panel.**

2. **Click the Toggle Take Audio and Video button , and choose the Take Audio icon.** Alternatively, you can choose Take Audio in the Source Monitor panel menu. The audio waveform for the clip appears in the Source Monitor, as shown in Figure 7.7.

3. **Use the Set In Point and Set Out Point icons to edit the clip.** To set in and out points in the Source Monitor, you can use the same techniques used for video. You can click and drag the current-time indicator (CTI), use the scrubbing bar, or press the left- or right-arrow keys on your keyboard. As you reposition the CTI, Premiere Pro plays the audio. Click the Set In Point button. Move the CTI to the out point and click the Set Out Point button.

4. **If you want to change or choose a target track for the audio, click the left track edge to select it.**

5. **To place the edited audio into the target track, set the CTI in the Timeline to where you want to place the audio.** Click the Insert or Overlay button in the Source Monitor panel.

> **TIP** You can also replace one audio clip with another by right-clicking/Ctrl-clicking the clip in the Timeline and choosing Replace with Clip from the drop-down menu. You can replace a clip in the Timeline with a clip from the Source Monitor or the Project panel.

FIGURE 7.7

An audio waveform in the Source Monitor

> **TIP** If the display in the Source Monitor is set to Audio Units, use the Step Back or Step
> Forward button (or press the left- or right-arrow key) to step through the audio one
> audio unit at a time.

> **TIP** You can add an Audio In point and Audio Out point column to the Project panel.
> Choose Edit Columns in the Project panel menu, and then select Audio In point and
> Audio Out point in the Edit Columns dialog box.

Extracting audio from video

If you want to separate audio from its video so you can work with it as a separate media source in
the Project panel, you can have Premiere strip the audio from the video. To create a new audio file
from a video clip that includes audio, select a clip or multiple clips in the Project window and then
choose Clip ⇨ Audio Options ⇨ Extract Audio. The audio file then appears in the Project panel.

Editing in Adobe Soundbooth

If you have Adobe Soundbooth installed on your computer, your best option for editing audio is to
send your Premiere Pro audio clips to Soundbooth for a quick visit. After you edit the clip in
Soundbooth, the changes are reflected in Premiere Pro. To edit a clip in Soundbooth, select an
audio-only master clip, subclip, or clip instance and then choose Edit ⇨ Edit in Adobe
Soundbooth. Alternatively, right-click the clip in the Timeline and then choose Edit in Adobe
Soundbooth. After you save the changes in Soundbooth, the changes appear when you return to
Premiere Pro.

Mapping audio channels

As you work with audio, you may want to disable one channel from a stereo track or select a mono
audio clip and convert it into a stereo clip. You can do this using Premiere's Source Channel
Mapping command. Here are the steps to remap audio:

1. **Select an audio clip in the Project panel that hasn't previously been placed in a
   sequence on the Timeline.** If you want to select more than one clip, click the other clip
   while holding down the Shift key.
2. **Choose Clip ⇨ Audio Options ⇨ Source Channel Mappings.**
3. **In the Source Channel Mappings dialog box, shown in Figure 7.8, select the track
   format: Mono, Stereo, Mono as Stereo, or 5.1 audio.**

   If you want to disable a Source channel, deselect it in the Enable column (column of
   check boxes).
4. **Preview the sound by clicking the triangle at the bottom of the dialog box.**
5. **Click OK to remap the sound.**

> **TIP** If you want to simply make separate mono tracks from a stereo track, select the audio in
> the Project panel and choose Clip ⇨ Audio Options ⇨ Breakout to Mono. Two audio sub-
> clips are added to the Project panel.

FIGURE 7.8

Remap audio tracks in the Source Channel Mappings dialog box.

Gaining, Fading, and Balancing

One of the most common sound effects is to slowly fade in audio at the beginning of a clip and fade it out at the end. You can easily do this in Premiere Pro by setting keyframes on the keyframe graph line that appears when you choose Show Clip Volume in the Audio Tracks Display pop-up menu. You can also change the balance of a sound in a stereo channel. When you balance, you redistribute sound, removing a percentage of the sound information from one channel and adding it to the other. Premiere Pro also allows you to pan to create sounds that appear to come from different areas of a room. To pan, you alter a mono track when outputting to a multi-channel master or submix track.

You can also change the entire volume of a sound clip by using Premiere Pro's Gain command. The following sections show you how to adjust audio gain, fade audio in and out, and balance stereo channels.

Normalizing and adjusting gain

The Gain command enables you to change the sound level of an entire clip by raising or lowering audio gain in decibels. In audio recording, engineers generally raise or lower gain during recording. If sound levels dip, the engineer "riding the gain" raises the gain; if the levels go too high, they can lower the gain. Premiere's Gain command also allows you to click one button to normalize audio. This raises the level of the clip as high as possible without distortion. Normalizing is often an efficient way of ensuring that audio levels remain constant throughout a production. Here's how to use the Premiere Pro Gain command, which adjusts the uniform volume of the clip:

1. **Choose File ⇨ Import to import a sound clip or a video clip with sound.**

2. **Click the clip in the Project panel, or drag the sound clip from the Project panel to an audio track in the Timeline panel.**

3. **If the clip is in the Timeline, click the sound clip in the audio track in the Timeline panel.**

4. **Choose Clip ⇨ Audio Options ⇨ Audio Gain.** The Audio Gain dialog box appears, as shown in Figure 7.9.

5. **Type a value in the field in the Audio Gain dialog box.** The 0.0 dB setting is the original clip volume in decibels. A number greater than 0 increases the sound volume of the clip. A number less than 0 decreases the volume. If you click Normalize, Premiere Pro sets the maximum gain possible without audio distortion. Distortion can occur when an audio signal is too high.

FIGURE 7.9

Use the Audio Gain dialog box to adjust audio gain for an entire clip.

TIP Click and drag the mouse over the dB value in the Audio Gain dialog box to increase or decrease audio gain. Clicking and dragging right increases the dB level; clicking and dragging left decreases it.

Fading sound

Premiere Pro provides a variety of options for fading in or out a clip's volume. You can fade a clip in or out and change its volume using the Volume audio effect in the Effect Controls panel, or you can fade a clip in or out by applying a crossfade audio transition to the beginning or end of the clip. As shown in the following steps, you can also change volume using the Pen or Selection tool to create keyframes in the Timeline. After the keyframes are set, you can adjust volume by clicking and dragging the keyframe graph line.

When you fade sound, you can choose to fade the track's volume or a clip's volume. Note, however, that if you apply volume keyframes to a track (rather than a clip) and delete the audio in the track, the keyframes still remain in the track. If you apply keyframes to a clip and delete the clip, the keyframes are deleted as well.

Follow these steps to fade volume:

1. Choose File ⇨ Import ⇨ File to import a sound clip or a video clip with sound.

2. Drag the sound clip from the Project panel to an audio track in the Timeline panel.

3. Expand the audio track, and choose Show Track Volume or Show Clip Volume from the Show Keyframes drop-down menu (refer to Figure 7.4). A yellow graph line now appears in the middle of the audio track.

> **NOTE** You can also choose Show Clip Keyframes or Show Track Keyframes from the Show Keyframes drop-down menu. This causes a Volume drop-down menu to appear in the track. When you select Volume in the drop-down menu, you can adjust volume in the keyframes graph line.

4. If the Tools panel is not open, open it by choosing Window ⇨ Show Tools.

5. Activate the Selection tool, or select the Pen tool in the Tool panel.

6. Set the CTI to the Timeline location where you want the fade to end.

7. Move the Pen or Selection tool to the point where you want the fade to end. Then press Ctrl/⌘ (a plus sign appears) while you click in the graph line to create a keyframe. This keyframe icon serves as a placeholder for the sound to stay at 100 percent of its volume at the middle of the sound clip.

> **NOTE** You can also create a keyframe by clicking the Add/Remove Keyframe button on the left side of the track. When applying keyframes to clips, select the clip and move the CTI to where you want the keyframe to appear; then click the Add/Remove Keyframe button.

8. Move the Pen or Selection tool to the beginning of the clip, and create another keyframe there by Ctrl-clicking.

9. Drag the handle at the beginning of the graph line downward. This makes the audio clip fade in. Dragging it upward increases the sound. As you click and drag, a tiny read-out shows the current Timeline position and the change in decibels. Figure 7.10 shows the Timeline with the adjusted volume keyframes.

FIGURE 7.10

Audio fade created with keyframes

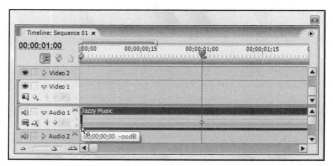

10. **To create a fade-out, repeat the preceding steps to create a keyframe at the end of the clip and a few seconds before the end of the clip.** Drag the keyframe at the end of the graph line downward to make the audio clip fade out.

If desired, you can use the Pen or Selection tool to add more keyframes to the graph line. Adding more keyframes to the graph line enables you to fade a sound clip into different sections within the clip.

 You can adjust overall volume for a clip or a track by showing track volume, and then clicking and dragging a track's volume graph line up or down with the Pen or Selection tool.

Creating a curve fade line

The previous example illustrates a linear fade, where the fade is created in a diagonal line. A curve fade line can produce a faster fade-in or fade with less time spent at lower sound levels. The resulting fade is less likely to display noise inhabiting lower sound levels.

To create a curve on the Timeline keyframe line, follow these steps:

1. **Create at least two keyframes on the Keyframe line by Ctrl-clicking with either the Selection tool or the Pen tool.**

2. **Move the cursor over one of the keyframes and press Ctrl.** When the cursor changes to a V-shaped symbol, click the mouse. A short, blue line appears.

3. **To create the curve, click and drag the blue line.** As you drag, a curve forms between the two keyframes.

If you later want to remove the curve, simply Ctrl/⌘ click the keyframe handle; the smooth "corner" changes to a sharp corner.

Removing keyframes

As you edit audio in the Timeline, you may want to remove keyframes. The easiest way to do this is to have Premiere Pro jump to the specific keyframe and then click the Add/Remove Keyframe button in the Timeline. Here's how to remove a keyframe from an audio track in a sequence:

1. **Move the CTI in front of the keyframe that you want to remove.**

2. **Click the Go to Next Keyframe button in the Timeline.**

3. **Click the Add/Remove Keyframe button.** The keyframe is removed.

TIP **You can also delete a keyframe by clicking it, and then pressing Delete; another way is to right-click it and choose Delete from the drop-down menu.**

Balancing stereo in the Timeline

Premiere Pro enables you to adjust stereo channel balance in a stereo track. When you balance a stereo track, you redistribute the sound from one track to another. When balancing, as you add volume to one track, you subtract it from the other. Although balancing is also covered in Chapter 8, it is included here because you can do it simply in the Timeline panel.

Here's how to balance a stereo track:

1. **Expand the audio track if it isn't already expanded.**
2. **Choose Show Track Keyframes from the Show Keyframes drop-down menu at the head of the track.** A Volume drop-down menu appears in the track.
3. **In the Volume drop-down menu, choose Panner.** In the Panner drop-down menu, choose Balance, as shown in Figure 7.11.
4. **If the Selection tool is not selected, click it in the Tools panel.**
5. **To adjust stereo levels, click and drag with the Selection tool on the track keyframe graph line.** (You can also use the Pen tool.) If you want to set keyframes, Ctrl-click/⌘-click and drag to adjust the balance.

FIGURE 7.11

Choosing the Balance audio effect in the Timeline panel

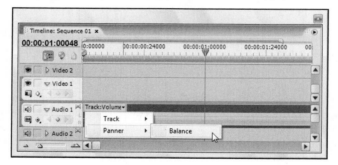

Creating Transitions Using Audio Effects

Premiere Pro's Audio Effects bin in the Effects panel provides audio effects and audio transitions that enable you to enhance and correct audio. The effects provided in the Audio Effects folder are similar to those used in professional audio studios.

To display the Effects window, shown in Figure 7.12, choose Window ➪ Effects. When the Effects panel opens, note that it includes folders for Mono, Stereo, and 5.1 tracks. In addition, note that the Audio Effects bin also includes audio transitions. To view the effects in the transitions or any other bin, click the triangle in front of the bin.

FIGURE 7.12

The Effects panel includes audio transitions and audio effects.

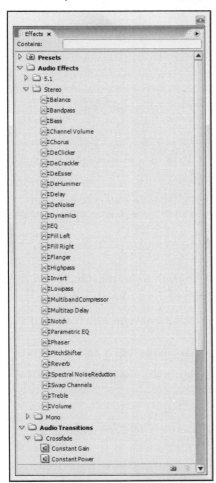

Creating bins in the Effects panel

In a project, you may need to apply effects that are in different bins again and again. If so, you may want to eliminate some unnecessary mouse clicks by creating a bin and placing these effects into it. To create a new bin, click the New Custom Bin icon at the bottom of the Effects panel, or choose New Custom Bin from the Effects panel menu. Premiere Pro adds the bin, naming it "Custom Bin" and assigning it a number. If you want to rename it, simply double-click the words Custom Bin and enter a new name. To populate the bin with effects, simply click and drag your favorite effects into it. Premiere Pro puts a copy of the effect into the new bin.

If you want to delete the bin or an effect within the bin, simply click it and click the Trash icon at the bottom of the panel. You can also right-click the item you wish to delete, and choose Delete from the drop-down menu.

Applying audio transitions

The Effects panel's Audio Transitions folder provides two crossfade effects that allow you to fade in and fade out audio. Premiere Pro provides two varieties of transitions: Constant Power and Constant Gain. Constant Power, the default audio transition, produces an effect that should sound like a gradual fading in and out to the human ear. Constant Gain produces a mathematical fade-in and fade-out.

Typically, crossfades are applied to create a smooth transition between two audio clips. However, when using Premiere Pro, you can place a crossfade transition at the front of an audio clip to create a fade-in, or at the tail end of the audio clip to create a fade-out.

> **NOTE** Before creating a transition, you must make sure that the Show Track/Clip Keyframes pop-up menu is not set to Show Track Keyframes or Show Track Volume. Otherwise, you will not be able to apply a transition.

Here are the steps for creating an audio transition:

1. **Place two audio clips so that they are next to each other on the Timeline.**

2. **Open the Effects panel by choosing Window ➪ Effects.**

3. **Open the Audio Transitions bin by clicking the small triangle to the left of the folder.**

4. **Open the Crossfade bin by clicking the small triangle to the left of the bin.**

5. **Drag the crossfade and drop it between the two clips in the audio track.** Don't worry if the transition does not drop directly over the middle of the two clips. You see the transition icon in the Timeline.

> **NOTE** If you can't see the transition in the Timeline, zoom in by clicking and dragging the zoom slider in the Timeline, or press = on your keyboard.

6. **If the Effect Controls panel is not open, choose Window ➪ Effect Controls, or double-click the transition in the Timeline.**

7. **To view the Timeline in the Effect Controls panel, click the Show/Hide Timeline view icon.** (If you don't see the icon, click and drag to make the panel larger.)

8. **To center the transition between the two clips, as shown in Figure 7.13, choose Center at Cut from the Alignment drop-down menu in the Effect Controls panel.**

9. **To change the duration of the transition, click and drag either end of the transition icon in the Effect Controls panel or in the Timeline.** You can also edit the Duration display in the Effect Controls window.

You can set the default audio transition duration by altering the Default Audio Transition Duration setting, found in the General Preferences dialog box. Choose Edit ⇨ Preferences ⇨ General. You can also change the default duration by choosing Default Transition Duration in the Effects panel menu.

10. To play the transition, in the Effect Controls panel, set the CTI before the transition and press the Spacebar.

FIGURE 7.13
_____

The Crossfade transition with alignment set to Center at Cut

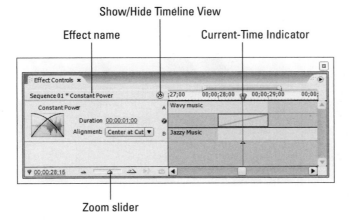

Zoom slider

Using the default audio transition

If you know that you will be using the same audio transition again and again, you can easily apply it using Premiere Pro's Apply Audio Transition command. If you want to set the default audio transition, select the transition in the Effects panel, and then choose Set Selected as Default Transition.

Follow these steps to apply the default audio transition:

1. Place two audio clips so that they are next to each other in a track in the Timeline.

2. Select the left edge of the track to set it as the target track.

3. Move the CTI between the two audio clips.

4. Choose Sequence ⇨ Apply Audio Transition.

Fading in and out using a Crossfade transition

Earlier in this chapter, you saw how to manually create fade-in and fade-out effects using keyframes in the Timeline. You can also create a fade-in or fade-out by using a Crossfade transition, as follows:

1. **Drag a Crossfade transition from the Crossfade bin (in the Audio Transitions bin) to the front of the in point of the audio clip.**

2. **In the Effect Controls panel, choose Start at Cut from the Alignment pop-up menu.**

Here's how to create a fade-out using a Crossfade transition:

1. **Drag a Crossfade transition from the Crossfade bin (in the Audio Transitions bin) to the back of the out point of the audio clip.**

2. **In the Effect Controls window, choose End at Cut from the Alignment drop-down menu.**

Applying an audio effect

Like transitions, you can access audio effects from the Effects panel, and you can adjust them using controls in the Effect Controls panel. To display the Effect Controls panel, shown in Figure 7.14, choose Window ➪ Show Effect Controls.

To apply an audio effect to an audio clip, follow these steps:

1. **Select the audio clip in the Timeline panel.** If the clip is linked to video, unlink it by choosing Clip ➪ Unlink.

2. **Select the effect in the Effects panel; either drag it into the Effect Controls panel or drag it over the audio in the audio track in the Timeline; and release the mouse.**

Most audio effects provide settings that allow you to fine-tune them. If an audio effect provides settings that you can adjust, the settings appear in the Effect Controls panel when the effect is expanded. To expand or collapse the effect, click the triangle in front of the effect's name.

FIGURE 7.14

You can adjust audio effects in the Effect Controls panel.

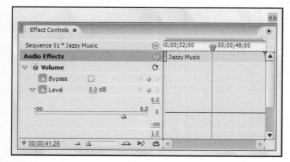

You can adjust the effect in the Effect Controls panel either by dragging the sliders in the panel or by entering a value into a control's field. In Figure 7.14, the slider allows you to change the decibel level for the Volume effect. The panel also features a Play button, enabling you to play the sound.

NOTE Volume is called a fixed effect because you do not need to drag it from the Effects panel. Other effects, called Standard effects, must be dragged over a clip or into the Effect Controls panel.

You delete an audio effect (other than the fixed Volume effect) from the Effects panel by right-clicking its name and choosing Clear from the pop-up menu. If you want to prevent an effect from playing, then click the ƒ button next to the effect's name; this essentially turns it off. To turn the effect back on, click the ƒ button again.

CROSS-REF You can also apply audio effects to audio tracks from Premiere Pro's Audio Mixer window. See Chapter 8 for details.

Applying an audio effect over time

If you want to change the settings of an effect as an audio clip plays, you need to apply an effect over time and set keyframes where you want to make a change. A *keyframe* stores the effect at a specific point on the effects graph line in the Timeline in the Effect Controls panel.

To apply an audio effect over time, you should have a project open that contains an audio clip in an audio track. If don't have an audio clip, use an audio clip from the SmartSound folder on the Premiere Pro Bible CS3 DVD, and try out a simple effect, such as Treble or Bass.

Then follow these steps:

1. **If the Effect Controls panel is not open, choose Window ➪ Effect Controls to display the Effect Controls panel.** If the Effects panel is not open, choose Window ➪ Effects.
2. **Select the clip in the Timeline to which you want to apply the effect.**
3. **Open the Audio Effects bin in the Effects folder by double-clicking it or by clicking the right-pointing triangle to the left of the bin.**
4. **Open a bin corresponding to the selected audio track (for example, Stereo) by double-clicking it or by clicking the triangle next to the bin name.**
5. **Drag an audio effect from the bin to the Effect Controls panel, or drop the effect over the clip.** (If you drop the effect over a clip, you don't need to select it first.)
6. **If the Timeline is not visible in the Effect Controls panel, click the Show/Hide Timeline View button.**

NOTE If the Timeline doesn't appear in the Effect Controls panel, the panel is not wide enough to display it. Click and drag the right edge of the panel to widen it, and then click the Show/Hide Timeline View button.

7. **Turn on Keyframe mode by clicking the Toggle animation button (Stopwatch icon to the left of the effect name).** The Add/Delete Keyframe button appears in the Effect Controls panel.

8. **Click and drag the CTI in the Effect Controls panel to a new position.**

9. **Adjust a setting for the effect in the Effect Controls panel.** This creates a keyframe.

10. **If needed, repeat the previous step to create new keyframes.** Figure 7.15 shows the Timeline in the Effect Controls window with various keyframes.

> **TIP** As you create keyframes, you can manipulate them and create curves using the same techniques used when working with keyframes in the Timeline. For example, you can also click and drag up or down on the keyframe graph line. You can Ctrl-click with the Selection or Pen tool on a keyframe in the graph line and drag it to create a curved line. You can also right-click a keyframe above the graph line in the Effect Controls panel and choose Ease In or Ease Out in the drop-down menu (this changes the keyframe into a Bezier keyframe). For more information about editing effects in the Effects panel, see Chapter 14.

FIGURE 7.15

Effect Controls panel keyframes created in Audio Effects

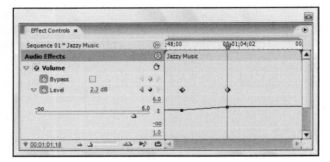

11. **To delete a keyframe, move the CTI over the keyframe that you want to delete.** Alternatively, you can click the Next or Previous Keyframe button and then click the Add/Delete Keyframes button. (You can also press Backspace on your keyboard.)

12. **To play the effect, click the Play button in the Effect Controls panel.**

> **NOTE** If you want to delete all keyframes for one of an effect's controls, click the Stopwatch icon for that control. To delete all effects for a clip, choose Delete All Effects from Clip in the Effect Controls panel menu.

> **TIP** You can copy and paste keyframes in the Effect Controls panel. First, select the keyframe or keyframes that you want to copy, and then move the CTI in the Effect Controls panel to where you want the keyframe or keyframes to appear. Then choose Edit ➪ Paste. Note also that you can select another clip before pasting the keyframes. If you need to view more of the Timeline in the Effect Controls panel, deselect Pin to Clip in the Effect Controls panel menu, and then widen the panel or scroll using the horizontal scroll bar.

Premiere Pro's audio effects

Premiere Pro's audio effects provide an assortment of effects that can help you improve sound quality or create unusual sound effects. The following sections provide a review of Premiere Pro's audio effects. Because many effects from the Stereo bin also reside in the Mono and 5.1 folders, this audio effects overview is based on the contents of the Stereo folder. As you read through the overview of each effect, try them out. Remember that after you apply an audio effect, you can listen to it by clicking the Play button in the Effect Controls panel.

In order to help you apply audio effects while you're working on a project, they are grouped according to functionality.

NOTE   Premiere Pro's audio effects conform to the Steinberg VST (Virtual Studio Technology) plug-in standard. This means that you can apply third-party VST audio effects from within Premiere Pro. They also appear in the Effects window with other plug-ins.

Amplitude

Amplitude measures the magnitude of the sound wave. Effects that control Amplitude generally produce a change in volume or the balance among audio channels.

Balance

This effect changes the volume of the left and right stereo channels in a stereo clip. A positive number adds volume to the right channel and subtracts volume from the left. Negative values subtract volume from the right channel and add volume to the left. The controls for the Balance audio effect are shown in Figure 7.16.

FIGURE 7.16

Balance audio effect options

Channel Volume

Use this effect to adjust channel volume in stereo or 5.1 clips or tracks. Unlike Balance, Channel Volume adjusts channels independently of other channels.

Fill Left

This effect copies the audio in the left stereo channel and fills the right channel with it — replacing the previous audio in the channel.

Fill Right

This effect copies the audio in the right channel and fills the left channel with it — replacing the previous audio in the channel.

Swap Channels

This effect swaps or exchanges left and right channels in stereo tracks.

Volume

Use this effect instead of Premiere's *fixed* Volume effect when you want to have volume rendered first. If you use Premiere's fixed Volume effect, volume is rendered after other standard effects are applied in the Effect Controls panel.

The Volume effect prevents distortion by preventing clipping when you increase volume. You can increase volume with positive values and decrease volume with negative values.

Delay effects

These effects repeat and play back sound sounds after a delay. Although some delay effects repeat a sound or a word, others can transform the sound to seemingly bounce around a large room or echo through the Grand Canyon. A commonly used delay effect is Reverb, which creates room tone effects by simulating multiple sound waves bouncing in a room.

Delay

Use this effect to create an echo that occurs after the time entered in the Delay field. Feedback is a percentage of the audio that is popped back into the delay. Use the Feedback option to create a series of delaying echoes. Use the Mix option to specify how much echo occurs in the effect.

Multitap Delay

The Multitap Delay Settings dialog box enables you to use four delays or taps (a *tap* is a delay effect) to control the overall delay effect. Use Delay 1 through Delay 4 controls to set the time of the delay. To create multiple delaying effects, use the Feedback 1 through Feedback 4 controls. The feedback controls add a percentage of the delayed signal back into the delay. Use the mix field to control the percentage of delayed to non-delayed echo.

Reverb

Reverberation refers to sound waves bouncing off an interior space. Reverb effects are commonly applied to simulate the sound or acoustics of a room. Thus, you can use Reverb to add ambience and a sense of humanity to dry electronic sound. Figure 7.17 shows the Reverb controls. Notice that a pop-up menu allows you to automatically generate settings for specific environments. You can also control the effect by clicking and dragging the figures in the room area of the effect display. These controls are available in the Reverb panel:

- **PreDelay:** Use to simulate the time it takes for sound to hit a wall and bounce back to the audience.

- **Absorption:** Use to set sound absorption. This effect simulates a room that absorbs sound.

- **Size:** Use to set room size in percentage. The larger the percentage, the larger the room is.

- **Density:** Use to set the size or density of the "tail" of the reverberation.

- **Lo Damp:** Use to set low-frequency dampening.

- **Hi Damp:** Use to set high-frequency dampening.

- **Mix:** Use to set how much reverb effect is added to the sound.

FIGURE 7.17

Use the Reverb audio effect controls to adjust room tone.

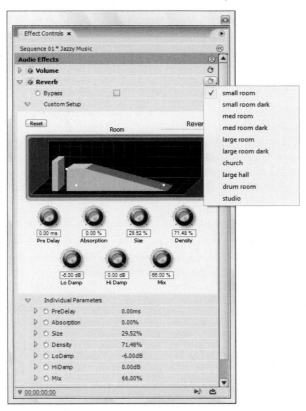

Filters

Filter effects are used to improve and restore sound by providing adjustments to specific frequencies. Thus, if you want to adjust only the bass or treble frequency of a sound, you could use the Bass or Treble filter to hone into the sound and raise or lower just the high or low frequency. Some filters, such as Notch, are used to filter out hiss and other noise from sounds.

Bandpass

Use this filter to remove frequencies beyond a frequency band. The Center field indicates the center of the frequency band to keep. The Q settings indicate the frequency band range that you want to preserve. To create a wide range of frequencies to preserve, use a low setting; to preserve a narrow band of frequencies, use a high setting.

Bass

Use this filter to adjust lower frequencies (200 Hz and below). Use the Boost option to raise or lower decibels.

Treble

Use this filter to adjust higher frequencies (4000 Hz and above). Use the Boost slider to adjust the effect. Dragging right increases the amount in decibels; dragging left decreases it.

Dynamics

This filter provides a diverse set of options that you can use to adjust audio, as shown in Figure 7.18.

- **AutoGate:** This option shuts the gate on unwanted audio signals. It removes the unwanted signal when its level drops below the dB setting for the Threshold control. When the signal goes beyond the Threshold, the Attack option determines the time interval for the gate to open, and the Release option determines the time interval for the gate to close. When the signal drops below the Threshold, the Hold time determines how long the gate stays open.

- **Compressor:** This option attempts to balance the clip's dynamic range by boosting soft sound levels and decreasing loud sound levels (*dynamic range* is the range from the highest level to the lowest level).

- **Expander:** This option produces a subtle AutoGate effect by dropping signals that are below the Threshold setting to the Ratio setting. A ratio setting of 2:1 would expand the decrease from 1 dB to 2 dB.

- **Limiter:** This option allows you to level out audio peaks to reduce clipping. Use the Threshold option to adjust the maximum signal level. Use the Release option to set the time necessary for gain to drop to its normal level after clipping.

- **SoftClip:** Like Limiter, SoftClip also reduces clipping when signals peak.

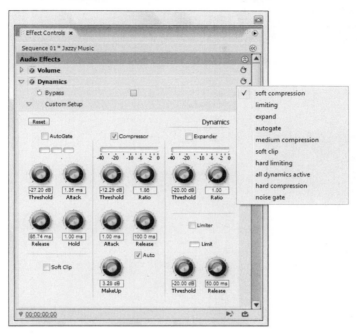

FIGURE 7.18

The Dynamics audio effect controls

EQ

EQ effects cut or boost specific frequency ranges. The EQ effect serves as a *parametric equalizer*. These equalizers allow you to precisely focus your audio corrections on specific frequencies. EQ controls frequency, bandwidth (called Q), and level using several bands — low, middle, and high. Figure 7.19 shows the EQ audio effect controls. Here is a summary of the controls:

- **Frequency:** Increases or decreases frequency between 20 and 2000 Hz.
- **Gain:** Adjusts the gain between −20 and 20 dB.
- **Cut:** Switches the low and high bands from a shelving filter that can boost or lower part of a signal to a cutoff filter, which excludes or cuts off the signal at specified frequencies.
- **Q:** Specifies filter width between 0.05 and 5.0 octaves. This specifies the spectrum over which EQ adjustments are made.

FIGURE 7.19

EQ effect controls

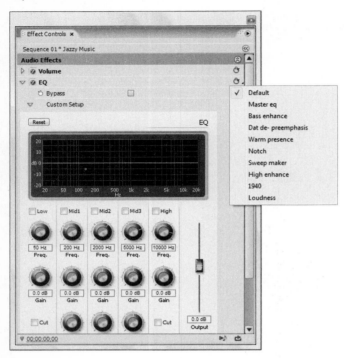

Notch

Use this filter to remove hum and other extraneous "noises." Use the Center control to set the frequency that you want to exclude. Use the Q setting to control the bandwidth of the frequency.

Highpass

Use this filter to remove frequencies above the Cutoff frequency.

Invert

Use this filter to invert the audio phase of each channel.

Lowpass

Use this filter to remove frequencies below the Cutoff frequency.

MultibandCompressor

Compressors are used to smooth out sound variations and maintain consistent volume.

Use the MultibandCompressor, shown in Figure 7.20, for compressing sounds according to three bands that correspond to low, middle, and high frequencies.

FIGURE 7.20

MultibandCompressor effect controls

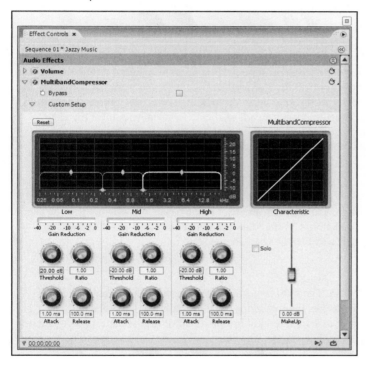

Adjust the handles for controlling gain and frequency range. Use Band Select to select a band and Crossover Frequency to change the frequency range for the selected band. The MultibandCompressor produces a softer effect than the Dynamics audio effect. This can apply to an individual stereo track.

Parametric EQ

Parametric EQ allows you to boost or lower frequency near a specified Center frequency. Use the Center control to set the frequency. Use the Q control to set the range of frequency (bandwidth) that you want to affect. A high setting affects a wide range; a low setting affects a low range. The Boost control allows you to specify how many decibels you want to boost or lower the frequency range — between –20 and 20 dB.

Restoration

Restoration effects are filter effects that restore audio. Some, such as DeNoiser, can be used to remove audio noise.

DeCrackler

As you might expect, the DeCrackler effect removes crackling noise from audio. Using the effect is quite simple. The Threshold slider controls the starting level at which you want the correction to occur. Use the Adjustment slider to set the amount of decrackling correction. Set the Audition to On if you want to hear the crackling noises as you adjust them. To visually monitor the effect of the DeCrackler effect, click the Custom button in the Effect Controls panel. This displays the Detected Crackles and Output graphs, which are updated as you adjust the effect while audio plays.

DeEsser

This effect removes "sss," or sibilant sounds that can occur in narration and singing. Use the Gain control to set the level of "sss" reduction. Use the Male and Female controls to set DeEsser to remove the "sss," based upon Male and Female voice frequencies.

DeHummer

This effect removes hum from audio. The hum removal range is from 50 Hz (often found in European and Japanese audio) to 60 Hz, the frequency often found in the United States and Canada. Use the Reduction control to set the level of hum reduction. Adjust the Frequency setting to specify the center of the hum frequency range. The filter applies the DeHummer to harmonic frequencies that are multiples of the DeHummer Frequency setting.

DeNoiser

Use this effect to automatically remove noise from audio. Figure 7.21 shows the DeNoiser audio effect controls. In the Custom Setup area, you can click and drag the knob icons to adjust the effect. To set keyframes, use the Individual Parameters section.

- **Noisefloor:** This setting indicates the noise floor in decibels when the clip plays.
- **Freeze:** Click Freeze to halt the Noisefloor readout at its current decibel level.

- **Reduction:** Click and drag to indicate how much noise to remove. The range is −20 to 0 dB.
- **Offset:** This control sets an offset value or range for denoising between the Noisefloor and the values from −10 and +10 dB.

FIGURE 7.21

The DeNoiser audio effect controls

Spectral Noise Reduction effect

This effect provides a spectral audio display as it reduces buzzing and whistling noises. The effect uses three filter banks to clean up audio problems. You can turn any of the three filters on or off by clicking the Filter check box. After you activate a filter, you can use the filter's Frequency and Reduction controls. The Frequency option controls the center frequency for the specific filter. The Reduction option controls the amount of reduction.

The MaxLevel slider (vertical slider in the custom setup) controls how much noise will be removed from the signal. If you click the Cursor check box, and click the Cursor radio button for a Filter bank, you can click and drag in the Custom Set Up display area to change Frequency. This means that you can click and drag the mouse to change Frequency settings for a filter as your audio plays.

195

Pitch

Pitch effects change pitch. They are often used to change the pitch of a narrator or vocalist.

PitchShifter

As its name suggests, you can use the PitchShifter effect to alter pitch, particularly when you want to produce a change in voice. As you might expect, playing with pitches can also produce special effects, particularly if you want your narrator to sound as if they are from outer space.

Use the Pitch control to alter pitch in semitones. Fine-tune the effect with the Finetune control. FormantPreserve prevents high-pitched voices from sounding like cartoon characters by preventing PitchShifter from altering formants (a *formant* is a resonant frequency). Try recording yourself singing with the Audio Mixer, and see whether the pitch shifter can put you back on key.

Exporting Sound Files

After you've edited and refined your audio tracks, you may want to export them as separate sound files so that you can use them in other programs or other Premiere Pro projects. When you export a sound clip, you can export it in a variety of formats, such as Windows Waveform (.wav), QuickTime (.mov), and Microsoft AVI (.avi). Follow these steps for exporting an audio file from Premiere Pro:

1. **Select the audio track with the audio clip you want to export by clicking the left edge of the track.**

2. **Choose File ⇨ Export ⇨ Audio.** The Export Audio dialog box appears.

3. **Type a name for your audio file.**

4. **Click the Settings button.**

5. **In the General section of the Export Audio Settings dialog box, set the File Type drop-down menu to Audio Interchange File Format (used by Mac OS computers), Windows Waveform, QuickTime, or the AVI choice.** You can set the Range drop-down menu to be either the entire sequence or only the work area.

6. **If you want to be able to open the project file by choosing File ⇨ Edit Original in another Adobe application, leave the Embedding Options setting at Project; otherwise choose None.**

7. **Click the Audio listing to choose Sample Rate, Sample Type, and Channels (for example, Stereo or Mono).**

8. **If you want to compress the exported audio, choose from the Compressor drop-down menu.** Compressor choices are discussed in Chapter 23. Note that some applications do not support compressed audio.

9. **For most standard hard drives, leave the Interleave setting to one-half or one frame.** Higher settings consume more RAM. The Interleave setting controls how often audio is slipped in between video frames.

10. **Click OK to close the dialog box.**

11. **Click Save to save the audio file.**

Summary

Premiere Pro provides numerous features for adjusting and editing audio. You can control fade-ins and fade-outs in the Timeline panel. You can adjust and create professional audio effects using Premiere Pro's audio effects and transitions. This chapter covered these topics:

- You can edit audio in the Timeline with the Razor and Selection tools.
- In and out points for audio can be set in the Source Monitor panel.
- Using keyframes, you can fade in, fade out, and adjust the volume of audio clips.
- You can adjust audio gain by choosing Clip ➪ Audio Options ➪ Gain.
- You can use Premiere Pro's audio transitions to create crossfades.
- You can use the effects in the Premiere Pro Effects panel to enhance and correct audio.

Chapter 8

Mixing and Creating Effects with the Audio Mixer

Creating the perfect blend of music, narration, and effects is certainly an audio art. The audio engineer who blends or mixes various tracks together into a master track must have a deft touch and a sensitive ear. Music and narration can't be overpowering, and sound effects must sound real. Mixing these together at the perfect sound levels produces audio that truly enhances the accompanying video.

In a recording studio, engineers use a mixing console to control the mixing of music tracks. In Premiere Pro, you can create a mix using its Audio Mixer. Using the Premiere Pro Audio Mixer, you can mix sound from a maximum of five tracks onto a master track, or you can apply effects to several tracks at once using a submix track, which can also be routed into the master track. Like a professional mixer, Premiere Pro allows you to adjust audio levels, fade in and fade out, balance stereo, control effects, and create effects sends. Premiere Pro's Audio Mixer also allows you to record audio and isolate and listen to one "solo" track, even while others play. You can even use it to add and adjust many of the audio effects found in the Effects panel.

This chapter provides a thorough look at the Audio Mixer and how to use it. After touring the Audio Mixer panel, this chapter covers the Audio Mixer's Automation settings, which allow you to adjust audio while it plays. After you learn how to create a mix, you then learn to balance and pan audio, add effects, and create submixes.

Audio Mixer Tour

Premiere Pro's Audio Mixer is undoubtedly one of its most complex and versatile utilities. To use it efficiently, you should become familiar with all of its controls and functionality. If the Audio Mixer isn't open on-screen, open it by choosing Window ⇨ Audio Mixer. If you would like to open the Audio Mixer in Premiere Pro's Audio Workspace, choose Window ⇨ Workspace ⇨ Audio. When the Audio Mixer (shown in Figure 8.1) opens on-screen, it automatically shows at least two tracks and the master track for the current active sequence. If you have more than two audio tracks in the sequence, click and drag the lower-right corner of the Audio Mixer panel to extend the panel. Although the sight of so many knobs and levels probably wouldn't intimidate an audio engineer, you must understand and thoroughly examine the buttons and features. Note that the Audio Mixer offers two major views: the collapsed view (refer to Figure 8.1), which does not show the Effects area, and the expanded view, which shows effects for the different tracks. To switch from one view to another, click the small triangle to the left of Audio track 1.

> **NOTE** The Audio Mixer shows only the current active sequence's audio tracks. If you want to show tracks from different sequences in the Audio Mixer panel simultaneously, you must nest the sequences in the current active sequence. Chapter 5 covers how to nest one sequence into another.

FIGURE 8.1

The Audio Mixer collapsed view

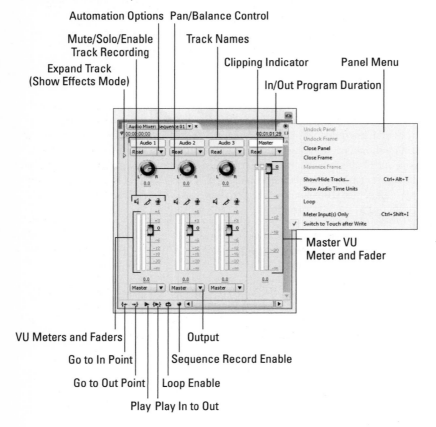

200

Tracks versus Clips

Before you begin working with Premiere Pro's Audio Mixer, you must understand that the Audio Mixer affects the audio in an entire track. When you work in the Audio Mixer, you make audio track adjustments, not audio clip adjustments. When you create and alter effects in the Audio Mixer, you apply audio effects to tracks, not to specific clips. As discussed in Chapter 7, when you apply effects in the Effect Controls panel, you apply them to clips. The current sequence's Timeline panel can provide an overview of your work and shouldn't lose track (no pun intended) of whether clip or track keyframes are displaying in the Timeline panel. Here's a review of audio track display options:

- To view audio adjustments for clips, choose Show Clip Volume or Show Clip Keyframes in the audio track's Show Keyframes pop-up menu. Note that the keyframe graph line for a clip extends from the in point to the out point of the clip, not to the entire track.

- To view audio adjustments for the entire track, choose Show Track Volume or Show Track Keyframes in the audio track's Show Keyframes pop-up menu. The graph line for keyframes in a track extends throughout the entire track. When you apply audio effects using the Audio Mixer, these effects appear by name in a Track pop-up menu in the Audio track's graph line. If you choose the effect from the pop-up menu in the audio track graph line, the keyframes for the effect appear on the graph line.

For both clip and track graph lines, you can create keyframes by Ctrl/⌘-clicking with the Pen tool. You can make adjustments to keyframe placement by clicking and dragging with the Pen tool.

To become familiar with the Audio Mixer, start by examining the track area of the Audio Mixer. The vertical areas headed by Audio 1, Audio 2, and so on correspond to the tracks on the active sequence. When you are mixing, you can see audio levels in the displays in each track column and make adjustments using the controls in each column. As you make adjustments, the audio is mixed or blended together into a master track or submix track. Note that the drop-down menu at the bottom of each track indicates whether the current track signal is being sent to a submix track or the master track. By default, all tracks are output to the master track (refer to Figure 8.1).

NOTE   You can set the master track to be mono, stereo, or 5.1 by choosing master track settings in the Default Sequence section of the New Project dialog box (you must first click the Custom Settings tab after creating a new project) or in the New Sequence dialog box (File ➪ New Sequence).

Below the track names are the track Automation options. In Figure 8.1, Automation is set to Read. When the Automation is set to Read, track adjustments written to the tracks with keyframes are read by the track. If you change Read to Write, Touch, or Latch, keyframes are created in the current sequence's audio tracks, reflecting adjustments made in the Audio Mixer.

The following sections discuss the major controls and areas of the Audio Mixer, including the controls for Automation, Mute/Solo/Record, Pan/Balance, Volume, and Playback, as well as the Audio Effects menu and the Audio Sends area that appear in the expanded view (see "Effects and Sends options," later in this chapter).

Automation

The Automation options (Off, Read, Latch, Touch, and Write) determine whether Premiere Pro reads or saves the adjustments you make in the Audio Mixer as keyframes in the Timeline panel. A detailed description of each option is provided later in this chapter in the section "Mixing Audio."

The Mute, Solo, and Record buttons

The Mute and Solo buttons below the Automation options enable you to choose which audio tracks you want to work with and which ones you don't. The Record button allows you to record analog sound (which could be from a microphone attached to a computer audio input).

- Click the Mute button to mute or silence tracks that you don't want to hear during Audio Mixer playback. When you click the Mute button, no audio levels are shown in the Audio Mixer VU (audio level) meter for the track. Using the Mute feature, you can set levels for one or more tracks without hearing others. For example, assume that your audio includes music and sound effects of footsteps nearing a pond of croaking frogs. You could mute the music and adjust levels for only the footsteps and croaking frogs as the video shows the pond coming into view.

NOTE If a track is in Mute mode, its Automation setting is not disabled. If you want to completely stop audio output from a track, click the track's Speaker icon in the Timeline panel. Automation settings are covered in the "Automation settings" section later in this chapter.

- Click the Solo button to isolate or work with one specific track in the Audio Mixer panel. When you click Solo, Premiere Pro mutes all other tracks, except the Solo track.

- Click the Enable Track Recording button to record to the enabled track. To record audio, you must then click the Sequence Record button at the bottom of the panel and then click the Play button. Using the Audio Mixer to capture sound is covered in Chapter 4.

NOTE To completely turn off output for an audio track in the Timeline, click the Toggle Track Output button (Speaker icon). After you click, the Speaker icon disappears. To turn audio output back on, click the Toggle Track Output button again.

The Pan and Balance controls

Panning allows you to control levels of mono tracks when outputting to stereo or 5.1 tracks. Thus, by panning, you can increase a sound effect such as birds chirping in the right channel as trees come into view in the right side of your video monitor.

Balancing allows you to redistribute output in stereo and 5.1 tracks. As a result, as you add to the sound level in one channel, you subtract from another, and vice versa. Depending upon the type of track that you are working with, you control either balance or panning by using the Pan/Balance knob.

As you pan or balance, you can click and drag over the Pan/Balance knob or click and drag over the numeric readout below the knob. You can also click the numeric readout and type a value using your keyboard. (For more information, see the section "Panning and Balancing," later in this chapter.)

Volume

Dragging the Volume Fader control up or down adjusts track volume. Volume is recorded in decibels. The decibel volume displays in the field below the Volume Fader control. When you change the volume of an audio track over time by clicking and dragging the Volume Fader control, Audio Mixer Automation settings can place keyframes in the track's audio graph line in the Timeline panel. You can further adjust the volume by dragging the keyframes on the graph line in the track with the Selection tool. Note that when the VU meter (to the left of the Volume Fader control) turns red, it is a warning that clipping or sound distortion may be occurring. Also note that mono tracks display one VU meter, stereo tracks display two VU meters, and 5.1 tracks display five VU meters.

 To view the VU meters without opening the Audio Mixer, choose Window ➪ Audio Master Meters.

Playback

Six buttons appear at the lower-left side of the Audio Mixer panel. They are Stop, Go to In Point, Go to Out Point, Play/Stop, Play In to Out, Loop, Record. Click the Play button to play an audio clip. To work with only a portion of the sequence in the Timeline panel, set in and out points and then jump to the in points by clicking the Go to In Point button. Next, click the Play In to Out button to mix only the audio between your in and out points. If you click the Loop button, playback is repeated so that you can continue to fine-tune the audio between the in and out points without starting and stopping playback.

 You can set in and out points in a sequence by clicking the Set In Point and Set Out Point buttons in the Program Monitor or by moving the current-time indicator and choosing Marker ➪ Set Sequence Marker ➪ In, or Marker ➪ Set Sequence Marker ➪ Out. You can also select a clip in the sequence and choose Marker ➪ Set Sequence Marker ➪ In and Out around Selection.

Audio Mixer menu

Because the Audio Mixer contains so many icons and controls, you may want to customize it to display just the controls and features that you want to use. This list explains custom settings that are available in the Audio Mixer menu that is shown in Figure 8.1.

- **Show/Hide Tracks:** Shows or hides individual tracks.
- **Meter Input(s) Only:** Displays hardware (not track) input levels when recording. To display hardware input levels on the VU meters (not track levels in Premiere Pro), choose Meter Input(s) Only. When this option is on, you can still monitor audio in Premiere Pro for all tracks that aren't being recorded.
- **Audio Units:** Sets the display to audio units. If you want to display units in milliseconds rather than audio samples, change this setting in the General tab of the Project Settings window (Project ⇨ Project Settings). The Audio setting changes the time display in the Timeline and Monitor panels, as well.
- **Switch to Touch after Write:** Automatically switches the Automation mode from Write mode to Touch mode after using Write Automation mode.

Effects and Sends options

The Effects and Sends options that appear in the expanded view of the Audio Mixer are shown in Figure 8.2. To display the effects and sends, click the triangle to the left of the Automation options drop-down menus. To add an effect or send, click any of the triangles on the right side of the effects and sends lists. Figure 8.2 shows several of these triangles, which appear vertically down the effects and sends portion of each track.

Choosing Audio Effects

Clicking a triangle in the Audio Effects area allows you to choose an audio effect. You can place up to five effects in each track's Effects area. When an effect is loaded, you can adjust settings for the effect at the bottom of the Effects area. Figure 8.2 shows the Notch and Reverb effects loaded in the Audio Effects panel. The PreDelay adjustment for the Reverb effect is shown at the bottom of the Effects area.

Effects Sends area

Below the Effects area is the Effects Sends area. Figure 8.2 shows the pop-up menu that creates sends. Sends allow you to *send* a proportion of a track's signal to a submix track using a volume control knob. To learn more about sends, see the section "Creating Sends," later in this chapter.

FIGURE 8.2

The Audio Mixer expanded view

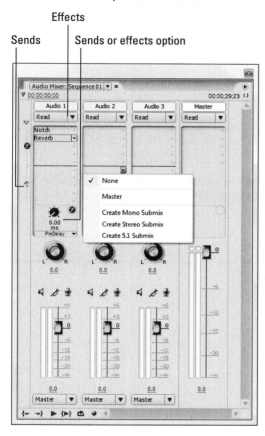

Mixing Audio

When you use the Audio Mixer to mix audio, Premiere Pro can add keyframes in the Timeline panel for the currently selected sequence. As you add effects, the effect names also display in a track's pop-up menu in the Timeline panel. After you've placed all of your audio clips in Premiere Pro tracks, you're almost ready to start a trial mix. Before you begin, you should understand the Audio Mixer's Automation settings, because these control whether or not keyframes are created in an audio track.

ON the DVD   If you would like to practice using the Audio Mixer, you can use the audio clips in the Chapter 7 and Chapter 10 folders of the DVD.

Automation settings

Premiere Pro's Audio Mixer uses the term *automation* because it allows you to automate audio track adjustments that are saved as keyframes. After you've made adjustments to one track, you can replay the audio sequence and adjust another track. As the Audio Mixer plays, you can hear the changes you made to the first track and see the fader handles move up and down in that track's section of the Audio Mixer.

You cannot successfully mix audio with Automation unless you make the proper settings at the top of each track in the Audio Mixer. For example, in order to record your track adjustments with keyframes, you need the Automation drop-down menu set to Write, Touch, or Latch. After you make adjustments and stop audio playback, your adjustments are represented by keyframes in the Timeline panel (in the track graph line). Figure 8.3 shows the master track with the Automation pop-up menu displayed.

> **NOTE**   To see Audio Mixer keyframes in the Timeline panel, choose Show Track Keyframes in the audio track's Show Keyframe pop-up menu. You don't see the keyframes if you have the pop-up menu set to Show Clip Keyframes.

FIGURE 8.3

Automation pop-up menu choices

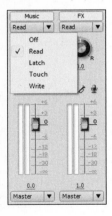

Here is a brief description of each Automation setting:

- **Off:** This setting disregards the stored Automation settings during playback. Thus, if you adjust levels using an Automation setting such as Write, and play back the track with the Automation mode set to Off, you don't hear the original adjustments.

- **Read:** This setting plays each track's Automation setting during playback. If you adjust a setting (such as volume) during playback, you hear the change and see the change in the track's VU meters, and the entire track remains at that level.

If you previously made adjustments using an animation mode such as Write to record changes to a track and then play back in Read mode, settings return to the recorded values after you stop making adjustments in Read mode.

Like Touch, the rate of return is based on the Automatch Time preference.

- **Latch:** Like Write, this setting saves adjustments and creates keyframes in the Timeline. But automation does not start until you begin to make adjustments. However, if you change settings (such as volume) when playing back a track that already has recorded automation, the settings do not return to their previous levels after current adjustments are made.

- **Touch:** Like Latch, the Touch setting creates keyframes in the Timeline and does not make adjustments until you change control values. However, if you change settings (such as volume) when playing back a track that already has recorded automation, the settings return to their previous levels.

- **Write:** This setting immediately saves adjustments made for the track and creates keyframes in the Timeline panel that represent the audio adjustments. Unlike Latch and Touch, the Write setting starts writing as soon as playback starts, even if changes are not made in the Audio Mixer. Thus, if you set a track to Write, change volume settings, and then start playing back the track, a keyframe is created at the start of the track — even if you do not make further adjustments. Note that you can choose Switch to Touch after Write in the Audio mixer menu. This changes all tracks from Write to Touch mode.

> **NOTE** You can right-click a fader pan/volume or effect and choose Safe During Write to prevent changes to the setting while Write Automation is in effect. You can also have Write mode switch to Touch mode automatically when playback is finished by choosing Switch to Touch after Write in the Audio Mixer panel menu.

> **NOTE** The rate of return for values when Touch is the Automation setting is controlled by the Automatch Time preference. You can change this preference by choosing Edit ⇨ Preferences ⇨ Audio. The default time is one second.

> **NOTE** The default minimum time for the interval between keyframes created by automation in Premiere Pro is 2000 ms. If you want to decrease the keyframes time interval, choose Edit ⇨ Preferences. In the Preferences dialog box, click the Audio tab. In the Minimum Time Interval Thinning field, enter the desired value in milliseconds.

Creating a mix

After you review the Automation settings and are familiar with Audio Mixer controls, you're ready to try out a mix. The following steps outline how to do so. Before you begin, place audio in a minimum of two tracks in the current sequence in the Timeline panel. Choose Show Track Keyframes in each audio track's Keyframe pop-up menu.

> **TIP** As you experiment with the Audio Mixer, you can quickly undo your changes by clicking previous history states in the History panel.

1. **In the Audio Mixer panel or Timeline panel, set the current-time indicator to the position where you want to start the mix.**

2. **Preview the audio by clicking the Play button with automation set to Read.** As the audio plays, you may want to see how changing levels with the fader controls affects the audio. After previewing the audio, proceed to step 3.

3. **At the top of the tracks for which you want to set automation, choose an Automation setting such as Latch, Touch, or Write.** If you want a keyframe to be created based upon the settings before changing them, set automation to Write. If you want keyframes to be created when you start making adjustments, set automation to Latch or Touch. Note that the drop-down menu at the bottom of the track indicates where the signal is being sent. By default, track output is routed to the master track, although you can change it to a submix track (which can output to the master track).

> **NOTE**   If you don't want a control such as the Volume Fader to affect the track, right-click it and choose Safe During Write.

4. **Click the Play button in the Audio Mixer panel.** If you want to play from the sequence in point to the out point, click the Play In to Out button.

5. **While the tracks play, make adjustments to the controls in the Audio Mixer.** If you work with the fader controls, you can see the changes in the meters for the different tracks.

6. **When you have finished making adjustments, click the Stop button in the Audio Mixer.** If the Timeline panel is open and the Show Keyframe pop-up menu is set to Track Keyframes, you can click the Track pop-up menu to show Volume, Balance, or Panning keyframes.

7. **To play back the adjustments, return the current-time indicator to the beginning of the audio and click the Play button.**

8. **Repeat steps 1 to 6 for each track that you want to adjust.**

Panning and Balancing

As you work a mix in the Audio Mixer, you can pan or balance. *Panning* allows you to adjust a mono track to emphasize it in a multitrack output. For example, as mentioned before, you could create a panning effect to increase the level of a sound effect in the right channel of a stereo track as an object appears in the right side of the video monitor. You can do this by panning as you output mono tracks to a stereo or 5.1 master track.

Balancing redistributes sound in multichannel tracks. For example, in a stereo track, you could subtract audio from one channel and add it to the other. As you work, you must realize that the ability to pan or to balance depends upon the tracks you are playing back and to which you are outputting. For example, you can pan a mono track if you are outputting to a stereo or 5.1 surround track. You can balance a stereo track if you are outputting to a stereo or 5.1 track. If you output a stereo track or 5.1 surround track to mono, Premiere Pro *downmixes*, or puts the sound tracks into fewer channels.

You can set the Master track to be mono, stereo, or 5.1 by choosing Master track settings in the Default Sequence section of the New Project dialog box (you must first click the Custom Settings tab after creating a new project) or in the New Sequence dialog box (File ➪ New Sequence).

If you are panning or balancing a mono or stereo track, simply set up the Audio Mixer to output to a stereo submix or master track and use the round knob shown in Figure 8.4 to adjust the effect. If you are panning to a 5.1 submix or master track, the Audio Mixer replaces the knob with a "tray" icon. To pan using the tray, slide the puck icon within the tray area. The "pockets" along the edges of the tray represent the five surround-sound speakers. You can adjust the center channel by clicking and dragging the Center percentage knob (upper-right area of the tray). You can adjust the subwoofer channel by clicking and dragging the knob above the Bass Clef icon.

After you complete a panning or balancing session using the Audio Mixer, you can see recorded automation adjustments in the keyframe graph line for the adjusted audio tracks in the Timeline panel. To see the keyframes in the graph line, the Show Keyframe pop-up menu in the adjusted tracks should be set to Show Track Keyframes. In the Track pop-up menu that appears in the keyframe graph line, choose either Panner or Balance.

FIGURE 8.4

Panning/Balance controls for stereo and 5.1 surround track

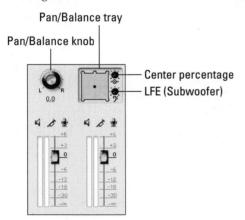

Pan/Balance tray

Pan/Balance knob

Center percentage

LFE (Subwoofer)

You can copy a stereo track into two mono tracks by selecting it in the Project panel and choosing Clip ➪ Audio Options ➪ Breakout to Mono Clips. You can convert a mono audio clip to stereo by selecting it in the Project panel and choosing Treat as Stereo.

You can pan or balance in the Timeline without using the Audio Mixer. To do this, set the Show Keyframes pop-up menu to Show Track Keyframes. In the Track pop-up menu, choose Panner ➪ Pan or choose Panner ➪ Balance. Use the Pen tool to adjust the graph line. If you want to create keyframes, Ctrl/⌘-click with the Pen tool.

Applying Effects Using the Audio Mixer

After you become familiar with the Audio Mixer's ability to adjust audio on the fly, you'll probably want to start using it to apply and adjust audio effects for audio tracks. Adding effects to the Audio Mixer is quite easy: You load the effects into the Effects area and then adjust individual controls for the effects (a control appears as a knob). If you intend to apply many effects to a track, be aware that the Audio Mixer allows you to add only five audio effects. The following steps show you how to load an effect and adjust it:

1. **Place an audio clip in an audio track, or place a video clip that contains audio in a video track.**

2. **If the Effects area of the Audio Mixer is not open, open it by clicking the small Expand/Collapse triangle icon (refer to Figure 8.1).**

FIGURE 8.5

Choosing effects in the Audio Mixer panel

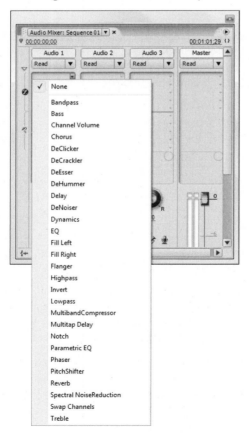

210

3. **In the track to which you want to apply the effect, click the down triangle in the Effects area.** This opens a list of audio effects, as shown in Figure 8.5.

4. **Choose the effect that you want to apply from the list of effects.** After you select the effect, its name displays in the Effects area of the Audio Mixer panel.

5. **If you want to switch to another control for the effect, click the down arrow to the right of the control name and choose another control.** (The controls are near the Pan/Balance knob.)

6. **Proceed to set automation for the track.**

7. **Click the Play button in the Audio Mixer panel.** Adjust effect controls as desired.

Removing effects

If you want to remove an effect from an Audio Mixer track, select the triangle for the effect and choose None in the drop-down list.

Bypassing an effect

You can turn off or bypass an effect by clicking the *f* (Bypass) icon that appears to the right of the effect's control knob. After you click, a slash appears through the icon. To turn the effect back on, simply click the Bypass icon again.

Applying Fill Left, Fill Right, and Swap Channels

The latest version of Premiere Pro adds Fill Left, Fill Right, and Swap Channels to the effects that are available in the Audio Mixer. The Swap Channels effect transfers the audio from the left channel into the right channel and vice versa; the Fill Left effect fills the right stereo channel with audio from the left channel, and Fill Right does the opposite.

If you want to quickly apply one of these effects in the Audio Mixer, you can experiment using an audio file in the SmartSounds folder on the DVD that accompanies this book.

1. **Create a new project in Premiere Pro by choosing File ⇨ New Project.** Alternatively, you can create a new sequence by choosing File ⇨ New Sequence.

2. **If you don't have a stereo audio file to use, load one of the audio files from the Chapter 8 folder on the DVD by choosing File ⇨ Import.**

3. **Remove the Right stereo track by selecting the audio file in the Project panel and choosing Clip ⇨ Audio Options ⇨ Source Channel Mappings.** In the Source Channel Mappings dialog box, deselect the Right channel check box and then click OK.

4. **Drag the audio file to Audio Track 1 in the new sequence.**

5. **Choose Window ⇨ Audio Mixer.** Choose the sequence containing your audio in the submenu.

6. **In the Audio Mixer, click the Show Effects button to switch to Effects view, as shown in Figure 8.5.**

7. **Click the Play or Play In to Out button in the Audio Mixer.** This plays the audio and confirms that the narration is only in the left stereo channel.

8. **From the Effects area of Track 1, click the Effects triangle to open the drop-down list of effects.** Choose either Fill Left or Swap Channels.

9. **Switch out of Effects view in the Audio Mixer by clicking the Show Effects button.** This displays the VU meters and faders.

10. **Click the Audio Mixer's Play button.** As the audio plays, view the track meters to see how the audio that was in the left track has been switched to the right track. Note also that the clip itself hasn't been changed. The effect is applied to the track, not the clip.

Creating a Submix

Premiere Pro's Audio Mixer not only allows you to mix audio into a master track, but it also allows you to combine audio from different tracks into a submix track. Why use a submix track? Assume that you have four audio tracks and you want to apply the same effects to two of the tracks simultaneously. Using the Audio Mixer, you can route the two tracks to the submix track and apply the effect to this track, which could in turn output it to the master track. Applying the effect to one submix track instead of two standard audio tracks can be easier to manage and drains fewer computer resources. When using submix tracks, you can't manually drag clips into them in the Timeline. Their input is solely created from settings in the Audio Mixer. Follow these general steps for setting up a submix track:

1. **Create a submix by choosing Sequence ➪ Add Track.** In the Add Tracks dialog box, shown in Figure 8.6, type **1** in the Add Audio Submix Track(s) field. In the Track Type drop-down menu, choose whether you want the submix track to be mono, stereo, or 5.1. You may want to type **0** in other fields so that you do not add other audio or video tracks.

FIGURE 8.6

Creating a submix track

2. **In the Audio Mixer panel, set the output for the submix track if necessary.** (You could output a submix track to another submix track, depending upon your track setup.)

3. **In the Output drop-down menu at the bottom of the track, set the output for individual tracks that you want routed to the submix track.**

4. **Choose effects for the submix track by clicking one of the effects triangle icons and selecting an effect.** Figure 8.7 shows one possible submix setup. After you choose an effect or effects, you can then set Automation settings as needed.

FIGURE 8.7

The submix setup in the Audio Mixer

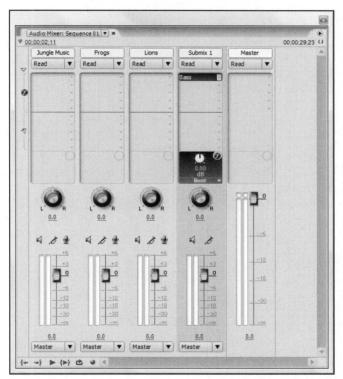

Creating Sends

Premiere Pro's Audio Mixer allows you to create *sends*, which you can use to send a portion of a track's signal to a submix track. When you create a send, a control knob appears at the bottom of the track's area, as shown in Figure 8.8. (In Figure 8.8, the control knob is set to Volume. However, by clicking the word *Volume*, you may be able to set the knob to Balance or Pan, depending upon whether you are working with mono or multichannel tracks.)

FIGURE 8.8

Effects send created for a submix

Send Properties pop-up menu

Send Control knob

Send Assignment pop-up menu

Mute button

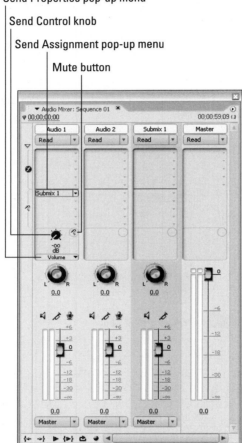

This control knob allows you to adjust how much of a track's signal is duplicated to the submix track. In audio terminology, this is akin to the track portion of the signal being referred to as "dry," and the submix portion being referred to as "wet." When you create a send, you can choose to set the send to be Pre-Fader or Post-Fader (the default choice). This allows you to control whether the signal is sent from the track before or after its fader control is adjusted. If you choose Pre-Fader, raising or lowering the send track's fader does not affect the send output. Choosing Post-Fader uses the control knob setting as you change volume in the send track.

You can choose between Pre-Fader and Post-Fader settings by right-clicking the listed send in the Audio Mixer panel. In Figure 8.8, right-clicking Submix 1 opens the Pre-Fader/Post-Fader pop-up menu.

Follow these steps for creating a submix track in the Audio Mixer and then creating the effects send:

1. **If the Effects/Send area of the Audio Mixer is not open, expand it by clicking the Expand/Collapse triangle icon (refer to Figure 8.1).**

2. **Click one of the triangles in a track's Send area to open the Send area pop-up menu.**

3. **If you haven't created a submix track, you can create it by choosing one of the create submix choices in the pop-up menu.** After you make the choice, a send is automatically created for the submix track. You can see the send in Audio Track 1 in Figure 8.8. If the submix track already exists in the Audio Mixer, choose it from the Send pop-up menu.

4. **When the send is created, a Volume knob appears.** This allows you to control the proportion of the track signal that is sent to the submix track when you mix the tracks.

5. **If desired, you can change send properties:**
   - Right-click the Send Properties pop-up menu, and choose Pre-Fader or Post-Fader.
   - Click the Mute button to mute the send.
   - Delete a send by choosing None in the Send Assignment pop-up menu.

Audio Processing Order

With all of the controls available for audio, you may wonder what order Premiere Pro uses to process audio. For example, are clip effects processed before track effects, or vice versa? Here's an overview: First, Premiere Pro processes audio according to the audio settings that you set in the New Project dialog box. When audio is output, Premiere Pro follows this general order:

1. **Clips adjusted with Premiere Pro's Audio Gain command**

2. **Clip effects**

3. **Track effect settings such as Pre-Fader effects, Fader effects, Post-Fader effects, and then Pan/Balance**

4. **Track volume from left to right in the Audio Mixer, with output routed through any submix tracks to the master track**

You certainly don't need to memorize this, but having a general idea of the order in which audio is processed may prove helpful as you work on complex projects.

Summary

The Premiere Pro Audio Mixer provides a variety of utilities for mixing audio. After you set the Automation mode in the Automation pop-up menu, you can mix to a master or submix track during playback. These topics were covered in this chapter:

- You can use the Audio Mixer Automation controls to save changes to tracks when mixing.
- You can use the Audio Mixer to pan and balance.
- You can use a submix track to apply one effect to multiple tracks.
- You can add effects and adjust them in the Audio Mixer during playback.
- You can create effects sends in the Audio Mixer.

Chapter 9

Creating Transitions

A cut from one scene in your video production to another provides an excellent transition for action clips or for clips that move the viewer from one locale to another. However, when you want to convey the passage of time or create an effect in which a scene gradually transforms into the next one, a simple cut just won't do. To artistically show passage of time, you may want to use a *cross dissolve,* which gradually fades one clip in over another. For a more dramatic and abrupt effect, you can use a *clock wipe,* in which one scene is rotated onscreen, as if it were swept into the frames by the hands of a clock.

Whether you're trying to turn night into day, day into night, youth into age — or simply wake up your audience with a startling special effect that bridges one scene to another — you should find what you're looking for with Adobe Premiere Pro's Video Transitions. This chapter takes you on a tour of this feature.

IN THIS CHAPTER

Touring the Video Transitions bin

Exploring Premiere Pro's transitions

Touring the Video Transitions Bin

The Video Transitions bin (folder) in the Effects panel stores more than 70 different transitional effects. To view the Video Transitions bin, choose Window ⇨ Effects. To see a list of the transition categories, click the triangle icon in front of the Video Transitions bin in the Effects panel. As shown in Figure 9.1, the Effects panel keeps all of the video transitions organized into subfolders. To view the contents of a transition bin, click the triangle icon to the left of the bin. When the bin opens, the triangle icon points down. Click the downward-pointing triangle icon to close the bin.

FIGURE 9.1

The Effects panel contains more than 70 different video transitions.

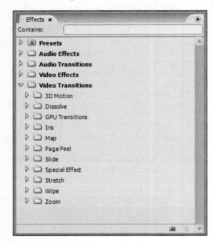

Navigating within the Video Transitions bin

The Effects panel can help you locate transitions and keep them organized. To find a video transition, click in the Contains field in the Effects panel and start typing the name of the transition. You don't need to type the full name. For example, if you type the word **cross**, Premiere Pro opens all of the bins that have the word *cross* in the effects. If you type the word **invert**, Premiere Pro opens all the bins that have the word *invert* in the effects.

To organize your bin, you can create new custom bins to group together the transitions that you use most often. To create a new custom bin, click either the New Custom Bin icon at the bottom of the Effects panel or the triangle icon in the upper-right corner of the panel and choose New Custom Bin. To rename a custom bin, first select the custom bin and then click the name of the bin. When the name is highlighted, begin typing the new name. To delete a custom bin, either click it to select it and click the Delete Custom Items icon, or choose Delete Custom Item from the panel drop-down menu. When the Delete Item dialog box appears, click OK to delete the bin.

The Effects panel also allows you to set a default transition. By default, the video transition is set to Cross Dissolve. The default transition has a red frame around its icon. The video transition default duration is set to 30 frames. To change the duration of the default transition, click the Default Transition Duration command, located in the Effects panel drop-down menu. In the Preferences ⇨ General dialog box, you can change the duration of the default video transition by entering a new number in the appropriate field. To select a new transition as the default, first select a video transition and then click Set Selected as Default Transition in the Effects panel drop-down menu.

Applying a transition

Premiere Pro allows you to apply transitions similar to traditional video editing: You place the transition between two clips in the track. The transition uses the extra frames at the out point of the first clip and the extra clips at the in point of the second clip as the transitional area. When you use Single-Track editing, extra frames beyond the out point of one clip and the extra frames before the in point of the next clip are used as the transitional area. (If no extra frames are available, Premiere Pro enables you to repeat ending or beginning frames.)

Figure 9.2 shows a sample transition project with its panels. In the Timeline panel, you can see all of the clips used to create the transition project: a Title clip and Black Video clips and three video clips. The Black Video clips, created using Video Effects, were used as backgrounds. (You can find more information on creating the background clips later on in this chapter.)

FIGURE 9.2

You can use Premiere Pro's Effects workspace when creating a Transition project.

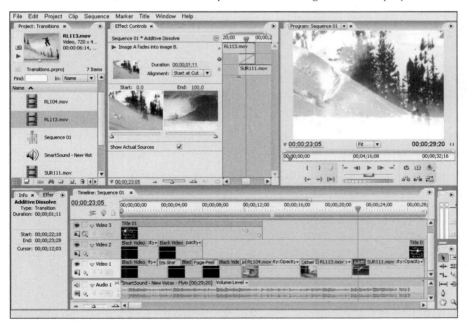

The Title clip in the Video 3 track extends over the background clips (Black Video clips) in the Video 1 and 2 tracks. Figure 9.3 shows two frames of the Title clip over the two different backgrounds. The Title clip slowly fades out into the first video clip.

Figure 9.4 shows the Title clip over the first video clip. There are three video clips with transitions. The first video clip is of a skydiver, the second clip is of a snowboarder, and the third is of a surfer. The three video clips start at the 12-second mark (shown in the Timeline panel in Figure 9.2). At the beginning of the project, there is a 12-second opening (shown in the Timeline panel in Figure 9.2). The opening consists of a few background clips with a Title clip superimposed over them. At the end of the project, the Title clip is once again superimposed over the end of the third video clip (shown in Figure 9.5). The Info panel shows information on the selected transition. The Effect Controls panel displays the options for the selected transition. In the Program Monitor panel, you can see a preview of the selected transition.

FIGURE 9.3

Two frames of the Title clip superimposed over two different backgrounds in the Transition project

TIP The Effects workspace helps you organize all the windows and panels you need onscreen when working with transitions. To set your workspace to Effects, choose Window ➪ Workspace ➪ Effects.

FIGURE 9.4

A frame of a Title clip superimposed over the beginning of the first video clip in the Transition project. The clip is Artbeats RL104.

FIGURE 9.5

A frame from the Title clip superimposed over the end of the third video clip in the Transition project. The clip is Artbeats SUR111.

The Iris Box transition is applied to the opening title and the background part that overlaps the first video clip (Artbeats RL104), as shown in Figure 9.6. The Dither Dissolve transition is applied between the first video clip (Artbeats RL104) and the second video clip (Artbeats RL113), and the Additive Dissolve transition is applied between the second video clip and the third video clip (Artbeats SUR111). Figure 9.7 shows the frames from the Dither Dissolve transition. Figure 9.8 shows the frames from the Additive Dissolve transition.

FIGURE 9.6

A frame showing an Iris Box transition applied to a video clip and a background clip. The video clip is Artbeats RL104. The Iris Box transition controls are shown in the Effect Controls panel.

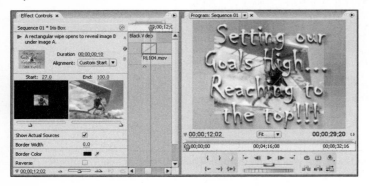

ON the DVD The three video clips used to create the Transition project shown in Figure 9.2 are from Artbeats. They include the following: Artbeats RL104; Artbeats RL113; and Artbeats SUR111. The sound clip is SmartSound's New Vistas sound clip. You can find the clips in the Artbeats and SmartSound subfolders in the Tutorial Projects folder on the DVD that accompanies this book.

FIGURE 9.7

Frames from a transition project showing a Dither Dissolve effect. The clips used are Artbeats RL104 and Artbeats RL113.

FIGURE 9.8

Frames from a transition project showing an Additive Dissolve effect. The clips used are Artbeats Lifestyles RL113 and Artbeats SUR111.

Here are the steps for creating a transition to video clips in Single-Track editing:

1. **Create a new project by choosing File ➪ New ➪ Project.** In the New Project dialog box, pick a preset or create a custom setting. Name your new project and click OK to create the new project.

2. **Choose Window ➪ Workspace ➪ Effects to set Premiere Pro's workspace to Effects mode.** In the Effects workspace, all of the necessary panels needed to apply and edit transitions are onscreen.

3. **Choose File ➪ Import to import video clips.** In the Import dialog box, select the clips that you want to import. Then click Open to import a video clip into the Project panel. If you want to import a folder, click the folder and then click the Import Folder button in the Import dialog box.

4. **Drag one video clip from the Project panel into the Video 1 track of the Timeline.** If you want to have a title and background clip at the beginning of the Transition project, you need to make room for it. In Figure 9.2, 12 seconds are used for the opening, and so the first video clip is placed at the 12-second mark.

5. **Drag the second video clip next to the first video clip.** Set the out point of the first clip and the in point of the second clip. The first clip should have extra frames that extend beyond the out point. The second clip should have extra frames that extend beyond the in point. Premiere Pro uses these extra frames to determine the length of the transition.

   When you set the in and out points, each clip should have an equal number of extra frames. The extra frames determine the length of the transition. For example, to create a 30-frame dissolve, each clip should contain 15 extra frames. You can set in and out points by using the Selection tool, Timeline markers, the Source Monitor, or the Program Monitor panel. For more information on setting in and out points, refer to Chapter 6.

6. **Another way to overlap two clips in the Timeline is to use the Snap option and the current-time indicator (CTI).** To do so, drag a clip to the Timeline panel and then move the CTI toward the end of the first clip. Now drag the second clip to the CTI. As you drag, notice that the second clip snaps to align at the left, right, or center of the CTI.

7. **Pick a transition from the Effects panel, and place it over the area where the two clips meet.** Premiere Pro highlights the area where the transition occurs and then places the transition within the track. If the number of extra frames for each clip is not sufficient to create the transition, a prompt appears, displaying the message, "Insufficient media." This transition will contain repeated frames. You can either change the duration of the transition or click OK to have Premiere Pro repeat the last and first frames of the clips to accommodate the transition.

8. **You can edit a transition in the Timeline panel either by moving the clip to the right or left or by changing its duration by moving one of the transition's edges.**

 If you move a transition edge, you may also move the edge of a clip. To move a transition edge without affecting any clips, press Ctrl/⌘ while you click and drag the Transition edge.

9. **To see the overlapping areas and the transition displayed below the first clip and above the next clip (as shown in Figure 9.9), double-click the transition in the Timeline panel.** Display the Effect Controls panel. To see the clips and transition in the Timeline of the Effect Controls panel, select the Show/Hide Keyframes option. You can edit the transition using either the Timeline features or the Duration and Alignment options in the Effect Controls panel. These features are discussed in the next section.

FIGURE 9.9

The Effect Controls panel and the Program Monitor panel with a preview of a transition

10. **To preview a transition in the Effect Controls panel (shown in Figure 9.9), click the Play the Transition button, or select the Show Actual Sources check box and move the sliders below the Start and End previews.**

11. **To preview a transition in the Program Monitor panel (shown in Figure 9.9), either use the shuttle or jog slider or click the Play button.** You can also view the transition in the Program Monitor panel when you move the CTI in the Timeline panel. By default, the Program Monitor panel displays the preview in Automatic Quality. To change the preview quality, click the Program Monitor panel drop-down menu and choose either Highest Quality or Draft Quality.

    You can also import a sound clip and place it in Audio Track 1.

12. **To render the work area, choose Sequence ⇨ Render Work Area.**

13. **Save your work by choosing File ⇨ Save.**

14. **To make a movie from your Premiere Pro project, choose File ⇨ Export ⇨ Movie.**

Proceed to the next section to learn how to edit transitions.

Editing transitions

After you apply a transition, you can either edit it in the Timeline panel or use the Effect Controls panel. To edit a transition, you first need to select it in the Timeline panel. Then you can either move the transition's alignment or change its duration.

Changing a transition's alignment

To change a transition's alignment using the Timeline panel, click the transition and then drag it left or right, or center it. When you drag left, you align the transition to the end of the edit point. When you drag right, you align the transition to the beginning of the edit point. When you center the transition, you align the transition so that it is centered within the edit point.

The Effect Controls panel allows you to make more editing changes. To change a transition's alignment using the Effect Controls panel, first double-click the transition in the Timeline panel. To view the clips and transition in the Timeline of the Effect Controls panel, you must select the Show/Hide Keyframes option. Then choose an option from the Alignment drop-down menu to change the transition's alignment. To create a custom alignment, manually move the transition in the Timeline of the Effect Controls panel.

Changing a transition's duration

In the Timeline panel, you can increase or decrease the number of frames to which the transition is applied by dragging one of its edges. For accuracy, be sure to use the Info panel when making adjustments on the Timeline.

To change a transition's duration using the Effect Controls panel, first double-click the transition in the Timeline panel. To view the clips and transition in the Timeline of the Effect Controls panel, you must select the Show/Hide Keyframes option. Then click and drag the Duration value to change the duration.

The alignment and duration of a transition work together. The results of changing the transition's duration are affected by its alignment. When you set the alignment to Center at Cut or Custom Start, changing the Duration value affects both the in and out points. When you set alignment to Start at Cut, changing the Duration value affects the out point. When you set alignment to End at Cut, changing the Duration value affects the in point. Besides using the Duration value to change the duration of a transition, you can also manually adjust the duration of the transition by clicking the right or left edge of the transition and dragging outward or inward.

Changing a transition's settings

Many of the transitions include setting options that enable you to change how a transition appears onscreen. After you apply a transition to a clip, you can find the settings for that transition at the bottom of the Effect Controls panel. To preview the settings for a transition (as shown in Figure 9.10), you may need to lengthen the Effect Controls panel.

After you apply a transition, you can edit the transition direction by clicking the Reverse check box in the Effect Controls panel (refer to Figure 9.9). By default, a clip transitions from the first clip to the second (A to B). Occasionally, you may want to create a transition in which scene B transitions to scene A — even though scene B appears after scene A. To see a preview of the transition effect, click and drag the A or B slider. To see the actual clips previewed in the window, select the Show Actual Sources check box and then click and drag the sliders (as shown in Figure 9.9). To preview the transition, you can also click the Play the Transition button.

FIGURE 9.10

The Effect Controls panel with the Dither Dissolve settings

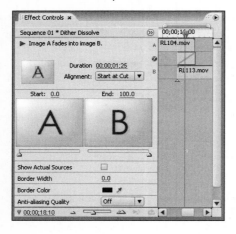

Many transitions enable you to reverse the effect. For example, the Curtain Transition in the 3D Motion bin normally applies the transition with Clip A onscreen — the curtain opens to display Clip B. However, by clicking the Reverse check box at the bottom of the Effect Controls panel, you can make the curtain close to reveal Clip B. The Doors Transition is quite similar. Normally the doors open to reveal Clip B. However, if you click the Reverse check box, the doors close to reveal Clip A.

Several transitions also enable you to smooth the effect or create a soft-edge effect by applying anti-aliasing to the transitions. To smooth the effect, click the Anti-aliasing Quality drop-down menu (shown in Figure 9.10) and choose Anti-aliasing Quality. Some transitions also allow you to add a border. To do so, click and drag the Border Width value to set the width of the border, and then pick a border color. To pick a border color, use the Eyedropper tool or the Border Color swatch.

Creating a default transition

If you are applying the same transition many times throughout a project, you can set a default transition. After you specify a default transition, you can easily apply it without having to drag it to the Timeline from the Effects panel.

Here are the steps for creating a default transition:

1. **If the Effects panel is not open, open it by choosing Window ⇨ Effects.**

2. **In the Effects panel, click the transition that you want to set as the default.** By default, Premiere Pro sets the Cross Dissolve transition as the default transition.

3. **In the Effects panel menu, choose Set Selected as Default Transition.**

 The default transition remains the default for all Premiere Pro projects until you choose another default transition.

Applying a default transition

To use a default transition, organize the clips in the Video 1 track as you would for a normal transition. You must position the clips so that the in and out points meet in the track. Follow these steps to apply the transition:

1. **Select the target track that includes the video clips by clicking the left edge of the track.**

2. **Move the CTI between the two clips.**

3. **Choose Sequence ⇨ Apply Video Transition.** Alternatively, you can apply the default transition by pressing Ctrl+D/⌘+D.

 You can create a keyboard shortcut for applying a default transition. See Chapter 2 for more information on creating keyboard shortcuts.

Replacing and deleting transitions

After you create a transition, you may decide that it doesn't provide the effect that you originally intended. Fortunately, replacing or deleting transitions is easy. You can do it in either of these ways:

- To replace one transition with another, simply click and drag a transition from the Effects panel over the transition that you want to replace in the Timeline. The new transition replaces the old transition.

- To delete a transition, simply click to select it and then press the Delete or Backspace key.

Creating animated backgrounds using video transitions and Title clips

You can create a simple graphic file in Photoshop using filters, import it into Premiere Pro, and apply video effects and video transitions to it to make a really interesting animated background. You can also take that simple graphic file and animate it using Photoshop filters and Photoshop's Animation panel. (For more information on using Photoshop's Animation panel to create animations, see Chapter 28.) An animated background can be used in any project as the backdrop of a title, or it can be superimposed onto another clip.

Here's how to create the background clips and Title clip in the Transition project, shown in Figure 9.2:

1. **Start by creating a Black Video clip.** Select File ⇨ New ⇨ Black Video.

2. **Drag the Black Video clip from the Project panel to the beginning of the Video 1 track in the Timeline panel.**

3. **Apply different video effects to create the desired background effect.** The Transition project in Figure 9.2 used these video effects: 4-Color Gradient, Color Balance (HLS), and Mosaic (as shown in Figure 9.11).

FIGURE 9.11

A background clip created by applying various video effects to a Black Video clip

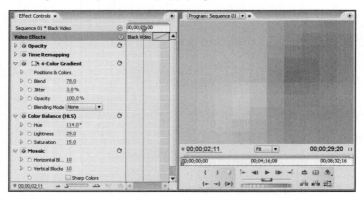

4. **Drag the Black Video clip from the Project panel two more times to the Video 1 track in the Timeline panel.** Each time you drag the Black Video clip to the Timeline panel, make it overlap the previous clip. The overlapping area is where you apply a transition.

   In this example, the Iris Star transition (shown in Figure 9.12) is applied between the first and second background clips in the Video 1 track.

   The Page Peel transition (shown in Figure 9.13) is applied to the second and third background clips in the Video 1 track. The Iris Box transition (shown in Figure 9.14) is applied between the third background clip and the first video clip in the Video 1 track.

5. **For all of the background clips in the Video 1 track to have the same video effects, select the first background clip.** Choose Edit ⇨ Copy. Select the second background clip and choose Edit ⇨ Paste Attributes. Repeat this for the third background clip in the Video 1 track. For the three background clips to look a little different, you can adjust the Color Balance (HLS) video effect to slightly change the clips' colors.

FIGURE 9.12

Various frames from the Iris Star transition to a background video clip. You can find this transition in the Iris bin.

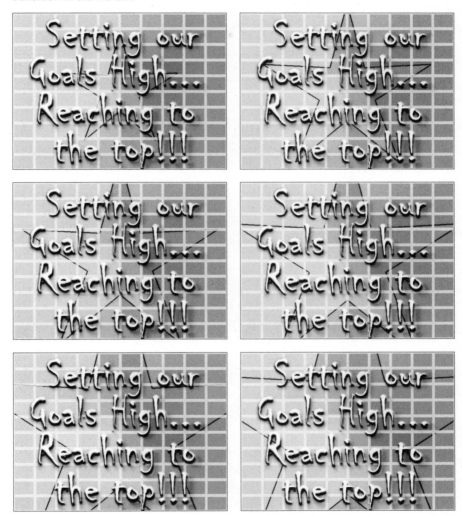

6. **To make the first and second background clips in the Video 1 track more interesting, drag the Black Video clip two separate times from the Project panel to the Timeline.** Place the clips side by side so that they overlap each other. In the overlapping area, place the Cross Dissolve transition. To the first Black Video clip in the Video 2 track,

apply the CheckerBoard video effect (shown in Figure 9.15). Set the white checkerboard Opacity to 38 percent so that you can see the background clip in the Video 1 track. To the second Black Video clip, apply the Grid video effect (shown in Figure 9.16). Set the white grid Opacity to 34 percent to see the background in the Video 1 track.

Various frames from the Page Peel transition to a background video clip. You can find this transition in the Page Peel bin.

FIGURE 9.14

Various frames from the Iris Box transition to a background video clip. You can find this transition in the Iris bin.

FIGURE 9.15

The Checkerboard video effect is applied to a Black Video clip.

7. **To create the Title clip, choose File ➪ New ➪ Title.** In the Titler, set the font to Chiller and the font size to 157 points. Activate the Type tool and type **Setting our Goals High...Reaching to the top!!!** (as shown in Figure 9.17).

233

FIGURE 9.16

The Grid video effect is applied to a Black Video clip.

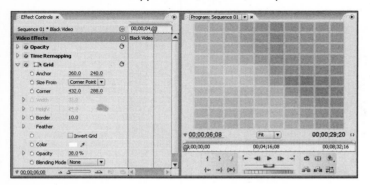

When you finish typing the text, close the Titler window. Then drag the Title clip to the beginning of the Video 3 track. To give the text depth, apply a few Perspective video effects: Bevel Alpha, Bevel Edges, Drop Shadow, and Radial Shadow. The Effect Controls panel is shown in Figure 9.18, with the video effects that you applied to the Title clip. The clip slowing fades out. (See Chapter 14 for more information on fading a clip.) The Title clip also appears at the end of the project over the last video clip (in the Video 2 track), as shown in Figure 9.2.

FIGURE 9.17

You can use the Titler window to create Title clips.

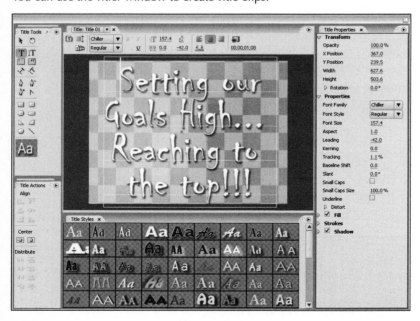

FIGURE 9.18

You can use Perspective video effects to add dimension to a Title clip.

Here's how to use video transitions to animate a graphic background:

1. **Create a new project.**

2. **Import a background clip into the Premiere Pro Project panel.** Import a file that you created in Adobe Illustrator or Photoshop using graphics, paint tools, and filters, or import a generic-looking video clip, to which you can apply various Premiere Pro video effects to turn it into an interesting background clip. You can also create a background clip using Premiere Pro's video effects and a Black Video clip (File ➪ New ➪ Black Video) or a color matte (File ➪ New ➪ Color Matte).

3. **Drag the background clip from the Project panel to the Video 1 track of the Timeline panel.** If you want to apply a video effect to it, click and drag a video effect over the clip in the Timeline panel. For more information on using video effects, see Chapter 13.

4. **Drag the same background clip from the Project panel so that it overlaps the clip already in the Video 1 track.** Alternatively, you can drag another background clip.

5. **If you use the same background clip, apply a video effect to the second clip in the Timeline, so that it is not exactly the same as the first clip.** You can use the Color Balance video effect to change the color of the clip. The Color Balance (HLS) video effect is in the Image Control bin.

6. **Click and drag a video transition onto the overlapping area of two clips in the Timeline panel.** For a more animated feel, you can try a transition from the Wipe, Slide, Page Peel, or Iris bin.

7. **Repeat steps 5 and 6 as many times as you want.**

8. **Click the Play button in the Program Monitor panel to preview the project.**

9. **If you want, import a sound and place it in the Audio 1 track.**

10. **Remember to save your work.**

Exploring Premiere Pro's Transitions

Premiere Pro's Video Transitions bin contains ten different transition bins: 3D Motion, Dissolve, Iris, Map, Page Peel, Slide, Special Effect, Stretch, Wipe, and Zoom. Each bin features its own set of eye-catching transitions. To view the video transitions in the Effects panel, choose Window ⇨ Effects. In the Effects panel, click the triangle in front of the Video Transitions bin to display the video transition bins.

This section features a tour of virtually every transition in each bin, along with examples of some of the transitions. The examples shown in the figures use these video clip files from Artbeats SP123 and SP127. These clips are in the Artbeats folder in the Tutorial Projects folder on the DVD that accompanies this book. If you want, you can also try creating still images in Adobe Photoshop and Illustrator and applying transitions to them. When using Adobe Illustrator files, you may want to use the Scale to Frame Size command to scale the Illustrator file to the project frame size. To use the Scale to Frame Size command, first import an Illustrator file, and then click it in the Project panel. Choose Clip ⇨ Video Options ⇨ Scale to Frame Size. The command immediately takes effect. When you are ready to use the Illustrator clip, drag it to a video track in the Timeline panel.

ON the DVD The two video clips used in the transition examples are from Artbeats SP123 and SP127. These clips are found in the Artbeats folder in the Tutorial Projects folder on the DVD that accompanies this book.

NOTE To help describe the transitions, we call the first clip in the Video track *Clip A*, and the second clip in the Video track *Clip B*. In the following sections, we describe how Clip A transitions to Clip B. However, note that you can reverse many transitions so that Clip B transitions to Clip A.

3D Motion

The 3D Motion bin features ten transitions: Cube Spin, Curtain, Doors, Flip Over, Fold Up, Spin, Spin Away, Swing In, Swing Out, and Tumble Away. Each one of the transitions includes motion as the transition occurs.

Cube Spin

This transition uses a spinning 3-D cube to create the transition from Clip A to Clip B. In the Cube Spin settings, you can set the transition to be from left to right, right to left, top to bottom, or bottom to top. Drag the Border slider to the right to increase the border color between the two video tracks. Click the color swatch if you want to change the border color. You can see the Cube Spin controls in the Effect Controls panel and a preview of the effect in the Program Monitor panel, as shown in Figure 9.19.

Curtain

This transition simulates a curtain that opens to reveal Clip B replacing Clip A. You can see the Curtain settings in the Effect Controls panel and a preview of the effect in the Program Monitor panel, as shown in Figure 9.20.

FIGURE 9.19

Cube Spin controls and a preview of the effect

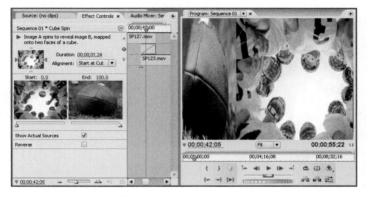

FIGURE 9.20

The Curtain controls and a preview of the effect

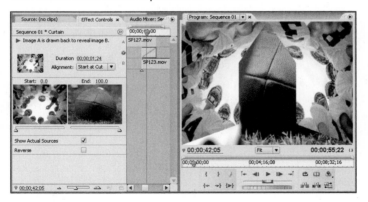

Doors

This transition simulates opening a door. What's behind the door? Clip B (replacing Clip A). You can have the transition move from left to right, right to left, top to bottom, or bottom to top. The Doors controls, shown in Figure 9.21, include a Border slider. Drag the Border slider to the right to increase the border color between the two video tracks. Click the color swatch if you want to change the border color.

FIGURE 9.21

The Doors controls and a preview of the effect

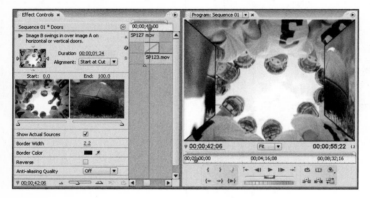

Flip Over

This transition flips Clip A along its vertical axis to reveal Clip B. Click the Custom button at the bottom of the Effect Controls panel to display the Flip Over Settings dialog box. Use this dialog box to set the number of bands and cell color. Click OK to close the dialog box.

Fold Up

This transition folds up Clip A (as if it were a piece of paper) to reveal Clip B.

Spin

Spin is very similar to the Flip Over transition, except that Clip B spins onto the screen, rather than flipping, to replace Clip A. Figure 9.22 shows the Spin controls in the Effect Controls panel and a preview of the effect in the Program Monitor panel.

FIGURE 9.22

The Spin controls and a preview of the effect

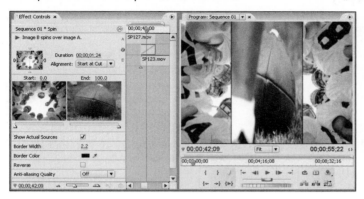

Spin Away

In this transition, Clip B spins onscreen similarly to the Spin transition. However, in Spin Away, Clip B consumes more of the frame than the Spin transition. The Spin Away controls in the Effect Controls panel and a preview of the effect in the Program Monitor panel are shown in Figure 9.23.

FIGURE 9.23

The Spin Away controls and a preview of the effect

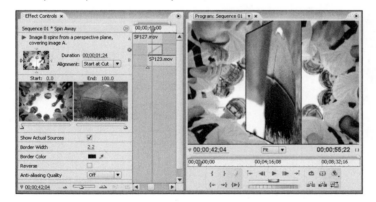

Swing In

In this transition, Clip B swings onto the screen from the left, like a gate that is open and is being shut.

Swing Out

In this transition, Clip B swings onto the screen from the left, like a gate that is closed and is being opened.

Tumble Away

In this transition, Clip A spins and gradually becomes smaller as it is replaced by Clip B. The Tumble Away controls in the Effect Controls panel and a preview of the effect in the Program Monitor panel are shown in Figure 9.24.

Dissolve

The Dissolve transition gradually fades in one video clip over another. You can choose from seven Dissolve transitions: Additive Dissolve, Cross Dissolve, Dip to Black, Dip to White, Dither Dissolve, Non-Additive Dissolve, and Random Invert.

Additive Dissolve

This transition creates a fade from one clip to the next.

FIGURE 9.24

The Tumble Away controls and a preview of the effect

Cross Dissolve

In this transition, Clip B fades in before Clip A fades out.

Dip to Black

In this transition, Clip A gradually fades to black, and then to Clip B.

Dip to White

In this transition, Clip A gradually fades to white, and then to Clip B.

Dither Dissolve

In this transition, Clip A dissolves to Clip B, as tiny dots appear onscreen.

Non-Additive Dissolve

In this transition, Clip B gradually appears in colored areas of Clip A.

Random Invert

In this transition, random dot patterns appear as Clip B gradually replaces Clip A.

Iris

The Iris transitions all begin or end at the center point of the screen. The Iris transitions are Iris Box, Iris Cross, Iris Diamond, Iris Points, Iris Round, Iris Shapes, and Iris Star.

Iris Box

In this transition, Clip B gradually appears in an ever-growing square that gradually consumes the full frame.

Iris Cross

In this transition, Clip B gradually appears in a cross that grows bigger and bigger until it takes over the full frame. The Iris Cross controls in the Effect Controls panel and a preview of the effect in the Program Monitor panel are shown in Figure 9.25.

FIGURE 9.25

The Iris Cross controls and a preview of the effect

Iris Diamond

In this transition, Clip B gradually appears in a diamond that gradually takes over the full frame.

Iris Points

In this transition, Clip B appears in the outer edges of a large cross, with Clip A in the cross. As the cross becomes smaller, Clip B gradually comes full screen. The Iris Points controls in the Effect Controls panel and a preview of the effect in the Program Monitor panel are shown in Figure 9.26.

Iris Round

In this transition, Clip B gradually appears in an ever-growing circle that consumes the full frame. The Iris Round controls in the Effect Controls panel and a preview of the effect in the Program Monitor panel are shown in Figure 9.27.

Iris Shapes

In this transition, Clip B gradually appears inside diamonds, ovals, or rectangles that grow and consume the frame. When you choose this transition, you can click the Custom button in the Effect Controls panel to display the Iris Shapes Settings dialog box. This dialog box allows you to pick the number of shapes and the shape type.

Iris Star

In this transition, Clip B appears in an ever-growing star that gradually consumes the full frame.

FIGURE 9.26

The Iris Points controls and a preview of the effect

FIGURE 9.27

The Iris Round controls and a preview of the effect

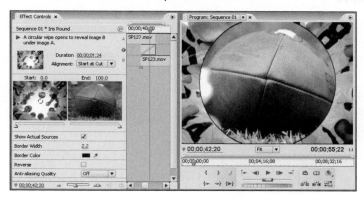

Map transitions

The Map transitions remap colors during the transition. These transitions are Channel Map and Luminance Map.

Channel Map

This transition enables you to create unusual color effects by mapping image channels to other image channels. When you use this transition, you can click the Custom button in the Effect Controls panel to display the Channel Map Settings dialog box, as shown in Figure 9.28. In this dialog box, select the channel from the drop-down menu and choose whether to invert the colors. Click OK, and then preview the effect in the Effect Controls panel or the Program Monitor panel.

FIGURE 9.28

The Channel Map Settings dialog box

Luminance Map

This transition replaces the brightness levels of one clip with another. Figure 9.29 shows the Luminance Map controls in the Effect Controls panel and a preview in the Program Monitor panel.

FIGURE 9.29

The Luminance Map controls and a preview of the effect

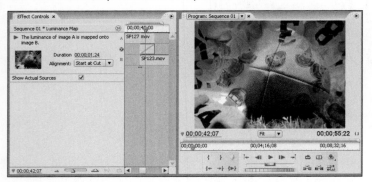

Page Peel

The transitions in the Page Peel bin simulate one page of a book turning to reveal the next page. On the first page is Clip A, and on the second page is Clip B. This transition can be quite striking, as Premiere Pro renders the image in Clip A curled onto the back of the turning page.

Center Peel

This transition creates four separate page curls that rip out of the center of Clip A to reveal Clip B. Figure 9.30 shows the Center Peel settings and a preview of the effect.

Page Peel

This transition is a standard peel where the page curls from the upper left of the screen to the lower right to reveal the next page.

Page Turn

With this transition, the page turns, but it doesn't curl. As it turns to reveal Clip B, you see Clip A reversed on the back of the page.

FIGURE 9.30

The Center Peel controls and a preview of the effect

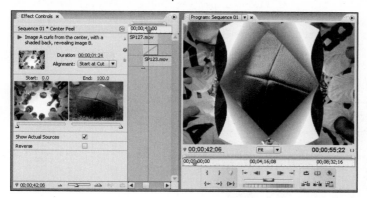

Peel Back

In this transition, the page is peeled back from the middle to the upper left, then to the upper right, then the lower right, and then the lower left.

Roll Away

In this transition, Clip A rolls from left to right off the page (with no curl) to reveal Clip B.

Slide

The Slide transitions enable you to slide clips in and out of the frame to provide transitional effects.

Band Slide

In this transition, rectangular bands appear from screen right and screen left, gradually replacing Clip A with Clip B. When you use this transition, you can click the Custom button in the Effect Controls panel to display the Band Slide Settings dialog box. In this dialog box, type the number of band slides you want.

Center Merge

In this transition, Clip A gradually shrinks and squeezes into the center of the frame as it is replaced by Clip B.

Center Split

In this transition, Clip A is split into four quadrants and gradually moves from the center out as it is replaced by Clip B.

Multi-Spin

In this transition, Clip B gradually appears in tiny spinning boxes that grow to reveal the entire clip. Click the Custom button in the Effect Controls panel to display the Multi-Spin Settings dialog box, where you can set the horizontal and vertical values. Click OK to close the dialog box. Figure 9.31 shows the Multi-Spin controls in the Effect Controls panel and a preview of the effect in the Program Monitor panel.

FIGURE 9.31

The Multi-Spin controls and a preview of the effect

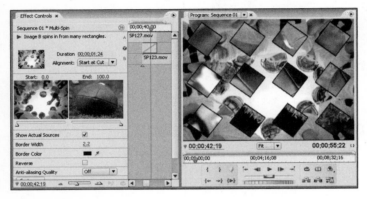

Push

In this transition, Clip B pushes Clip A to one side. You can set the transition to push from West to East, East to West, North to South, or South to North.

Slash Slide

In this transition, diagonal slashes filled with pieces of Clip B gradually replace Clip A, as shown in Figure 9.32. You can set the slashes to move from Northwest to Southeast, Southeast to Northwest, Northeast to Southwest, Southwest to Northeast, West to East, East to West, North to South, or South to North. When you use this transition, the Slash Slide Settings dialog box appears. In the dialog box, set the number of slashes that you want. Click the Custom button at the bottom of the Effect Controls panel to change the number of slashes.

Slide

In this transition, Clip B gradually slides over Clip A. You can set how the transition slides. The transition can slide from Northwest to Southeast, Southeast to Northwest, Northeast to Southeast, Southwest to Northeast, West to East, East to West, North to South, or South to North.

FIGURE 9.32

The Slash Slide controls and a preview of the effect

Sliding Bands

In this transition, Clip B begins in a compressed state and then gradually stretches across the frame to replace Clip A. The sliding bands can be set to move from North to South, South to North, West to East, or East to West.

Sliding Boxes

In this transition, vertical bands composed of Clip B gradually move across the screen to replace Clip A. When you use this transition, you can click the Custom button in the Effect Controls panel to display the Sliding Boxes Settings dialog box. In the dialog box, set the number bands that you want. Figure 9.33 shows the Sliding Boxes controls in the Effect Controls panel and a preview of the effect in the Program Monitor panel.

Split

In this transition, Clip A splits apart from the middle to reveal Clip B behind it. The effect is like opening two sliding doors to reveal the contents of a room.

Swap

In this transition, Clip B swaps places with Clip A. The effect almost looks as if one clip moves left or right, and then behind the previous clip.

Swirl

In this transition, shown in Figure 9.34, Clip B swirls onto the screen to replace Clip A. When you use this transition, you can click the Custom button in the Effect Controls panel to display the Swirl Settings dialog box. In this dialog box, you can set the horizontal, vertical, and rate amount.

FIGURE 9.33

The Sliding Boxes controls and a preview of the effect

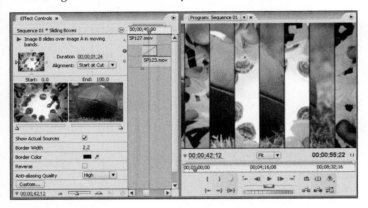

FIGURE 9.34

The Swirl controls and a preview of the effect

Special Effects

The transitions in the Special Effects bin include a variety of transitions that create special effects, many of which change colors or distort images. The Special Effects transitions are Direct, Displace, Image Mask, Take, Texturizer, and Three-D.

Direct

This transition is actually a cut. When you place the transition between two overlapping clips, the scene cuts from A to B with audio from track A. By clicking and dragging the transition edge, you can control the in and out points of Clip B without actually editing Clip B. This transition is most useful when you need to drop in a short piece of video. In other words, you can have Clip A play and use the Direct transition to create a short insert edit to Clip B before the program returns to Clip A.

Displace

In this transition, the colors in Clip B create an image distortion in Clip A. When you use this transition, you can click the Custom button in the Effect Controls panel to display the Displace Settings dialog box. This dialog box allows you to change the Scale settings. The lower the scale, the larger the displacement is. If the displacement would cause the image to stretch beyond the frame, then the Wrap Around option tells Premiere Pro to wrap the pixels to the other side of the frame. The Repeat Pixels option repeats the pixels along the image edges instead of wrapping them on the other side of the frame.

Image Mask

This transition uses a black-and-white mask image to determine how the transition appears. When you apply this transition, you can click the Custom button in the Effect Controls panel to display the Image Mask Settings dialog box. Click the Select Image button to select a black-and-white image to use as a mask. Click OK. You can see Clip B through white areas of the mask. You can see Clip A through black areas of the mask.

NOTE If you select a grayscale image to use as a mask, the transition converts all pixels below 50 percent black to white and all pixels above 50 percent black to black. This can result in a very aliased (jaggy) transition if you are not careful in choosing the mask image.

Take

This transition is similar to Direct, providing a cut from Clip A to Clip B. If you click and drag the end of the transition beyond Clip B, Premiere Pro inserts black rather than returning to Clip A.

Texturizer

This transition maps color values from Clip B into Clip A. The blending of the two clips can create a textured effect.

Three-D

This transition distorts the colors in Clips A and B, creating a composite between the two images. The brightness values of Clip A applied to Clip B can create a three-dimensional effect.

Stretch transitions

The Stretch transitions provide a variety of effects that usually stretch at least one of the clips during the effect. These transitions include the following: Cross Stretch, Funnel, Stretch, Stretch In, and Stretch Over.

Cross Stretch

This transition is more like a 3-D cube transition than a stretch. When the transition occurs, the clips appear as if on a cube that turns. As the cube turns, Clip B replaces Clip A.

Funnel

In this transition, Clip A is gradually transformed into a triangular shape and then sucked out the point of the triangle, to be replaced by Clip B.

Stretch

In this transition, Clip B is first compressed and then gradually stretches across the frame to replace Clip A.

Stretch In

In this transition, Clip B appears stretched over Clip A, but then gradually unstretches. When you use this transition, you can click the Custom button in the Effect Controls panel to display the Stretch In Settings dialog box. In this dialog box, you can choose the number of bands that you want. The Stretch In controls in the Effect Controls panel and a preview of the effect in the Program Monitor panel are shown in Figure 9.35.

FIGURE 9.35

The Stretch In controls and a preview of the effect

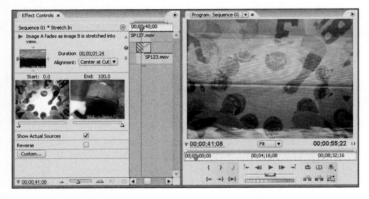

Stretch Over

In this transition, Clip B appears over Clip A in a thin, elongated stretch but then gradually unstretches. Figure 9.36 shows the Stretch Over controls in the Effect Controls panel and a preview of the effect in the Program Monitor panel.

Wipe transitions

The Wipe transitions wipe away different parts of Clip A to reveal Clip B. Many of the transitions provide a very modern-looking digital effect. The choices include Band Wipe, Barn Doors, Checker Wipe, CheckerBoard, Clock Wipe, Gradient Wipe, Inset, Paint Splatter, Pinwheel, Radial Wipe, Random Blocks, Random Wipe, Spiral Boxes, Venetian Blinds, Wedge Wipe, Wipe, and Zig-Zag Blocks.

FIGURE 9.36

The Stretch Over controls and a preview of the effect

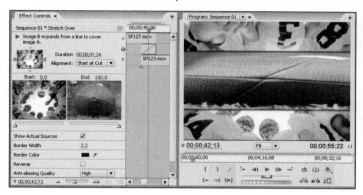

Band Wipe

In this transition, rectangular bands from screen left and screen right gradually replace Clip A with Clip B. When you use this transition, you can click the Custom button in the Effect Controls panel to display the Band Wipe Settings dialog box. In the dialog box, you can type the number of bands that you want, and then click OK to apply the setting.

Barn Doors

In this transition, Clip A opens to reveal Clip B. The effect is more like sliding doors than barn doors that swing open.

Checker Wipe

In this transition, a checkerboard pattern of squares that contains Clip B slices across the screen. When you use this transition, the Checker Wipe Settings dialog box appears, allowing you to choose the number of horizontal and vertical slices. To change the number of slices, click the Custom button at the bottom of the Effect Controls panel. Figure 9.37 shows the Checker Wipe controls in the Effect Controls panel and a preview of the effect in the Program Monitor panel.

CheckerBoard

In this transition, a checkerboard pattern that contains Clip B gradually replaces Clip A. This effect provides more squares than the Checker Wipe transition. When you use this transition, you can click the Custom button in the Effect Controls panel to display the CheckerBoard Settings dialog box, where you can choose the number of horizontal and vertical slices.

Clock Wipe

In this transition, Clip B appears gradually onscreen and is revealed in a circular motion. The effect is as if the rotating hand of a clock is sweeping the clip onscreen.

FIGURE 9.37

The Checker Wipe controls and a preview of the effect

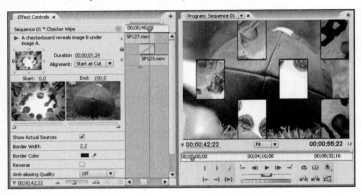

Gradient Wipe

In this transition, Clip B gradually wipes across the screen using the brightness values of a user-selected grayscale image to determine which image areas in Clip A to replace. When you use this wipe, you can click the Custom button to display the Gradient Wipe Settings dialog box (shown in Figure 9.38). In this dialog box, you can load a grayscale image by clicking the Select Image button. When the wipe appears, image areas of Clip B corresponding to the black areas and dark areas of Clip A show through first. In the Gradient Wipe Settings dialog box, you can also click and drag the softness slider to soften the effect. Click OK to apply the settings. To return to these settings, click the Custom button at the bottom of the Effect Controls panel. Figure 9.39 shows the Gradient Wipe controls in the Effect Controls panel and a preview of the effect in the Program Monitor panel.

FIGURE 9.38

The Gradient Wipe Settings dialog box allows you to pick a grayscale image to use in the Gradient Wipe transition.

Inset

In this transition, Clip B appears in a small rectangular box in the upper-left corner of the frame. As the wipe progresses, the box grows diagonally until Clip B replaces Clip A.

FIGURE 9.39

The Gradient Wipe controls and a preview of the effect

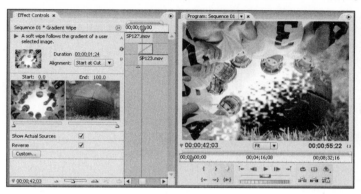

Paint Splatter

In this transition, Clip B gradually appears in splashes that look like splattered paint. Figure 9.40 shows the Paint Splatter controls in the Effect Controls panel and a preview of the effect in the Program Monitor panel.

FIGURE 9.40

The Paint Splatter controls and a preview of the effect

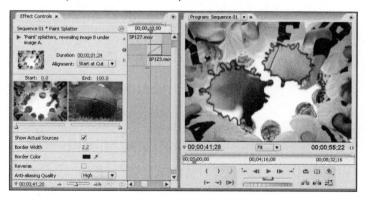

Pinwheel

In this transition, Clip B gradually appears in a growing star that eventually consumes the full frame. When you use this transition, you can click the Custom button in the Effect Controls panel to display the Pinwheel Settings dialog box. In the dialog box, you can choose the number of wedges that you want. Figure 9.41 shows the Pinwheel controls in the Effect Controls panel and a preview of the effect in the Program Monitor panel.

FIGURE 9.41

The Pinwheel controls and a preview of the effect

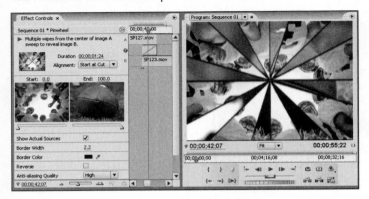

Radial Wipe

In this transition, Clip B is revealed by a wipe that begins horizontally across the top of the frame and sweeps through a clockwise arc, gradually covering Clip A.

Random Blocks

In this transition, Clip B gradually appears in tiny boxes that appear randomly onscreen. When you use this transition, you can click the Custom button in the Effect Controls panel to display the Random Blocks Settings dialog box. In the dialog box, you can set the value for how wide and how high you want the boxes to be. Click OK to apply the changes.

Random Wipe

In this transition, Clip B gradually appears in small blocks that drop down the screen.

Spiral Boxes

In this transition, a rectangular border moves around the frame, gradually replacing Clip A with Clip B. When you use this transition, you can click the Custom button in the Effect Controls panel to display the Spiral Boxes Settings dialog box. In the dialog box, you can set the horizontal and vertical value. Click OK to apply the changes.

Venetian Blinds

In this transition, Clip B appears as if seen through Venetian blinds that open gradually to reveal Clip B's full frame. When you use this transition, you can click the Custom button in the Effect Controls panel to display the Venetian Blinds Settings dialog box. In the dialog box, you can choose the number of bands that you want to appear. Click OK to apply the changes.

Wedge Wipe

In this transition, Clip B appears in a pie wedge that becomes larger, gradually replacing Clip A. Figure 9.42 shows the Wedge Wipe controls in the Effect Controls panel and a preview of the effect in the Program Monitor panel.

FIGURE 9.42

The Wedge Wipe controls and a preview of the effect

Wipe

In this simple transition, Clip B slides in from left to right, replacing Clip A.

Zig-Zag Blocks

In this transition, Clip B gradually appears in horizontal bands that move from left to right and right to left down the screen. When you use this transition, you can click the Custom button in the Effect Controls panel to display the Zig-Zag Blocks Settings dialog box. In the dialog box, you can choose the number of horizontal and vertical bands that you want. Click OK to apply the changes.

Zoom transitions

The Zoom transitions provide effects in which the entire clip zooms in or out, or boxes zoom in and out to replace one clip with another. The choices are Cross Zoom, Zoom, Zoom Boxes, and Zoom Trails.

Cross Zoom

This transition zooms into Clip B, which gradually grows to consume the full frame.

Zoom

In this transition, Clip B appears as a tiny dot and then gradually enlarges to replace Clip A. Figure 9.43 shows the Zoom controls in the Effect Controls panel and a preview of the effect in the Program Monitor panel.

FIGURE 9.43

The Zoom controls and a preview of the effect

Zoom Boxes

In this transition, tiny boxes filled with Clip B gradually enlarge to replace Clip A. When you use this transition, you can click the Custom button in the Effect Controls panel to display the Zoom Boxes Settings dialog box. In the dialog box, you can choose the number of shapes that you want. Click OK to apply the changes.

Zoom Trails

In this transition, Clip A gradually shrinks (a zoom-out effect), leaving trails as it is replaced by Clip B. When you use this transition, you can click the Custom button in the Effect Controls panel to display the Zoom Trails Settings dialog box. In the dialog box, you can choose the number of trails that you want. Click OK to close the dialog box. Figure 9.44 shows the Zoom Trails controls in the Effect Controls panel and a preview in the Program Monitor panel.

FIGURE 9.44

The Zoom Trails controls and a preview of the effect

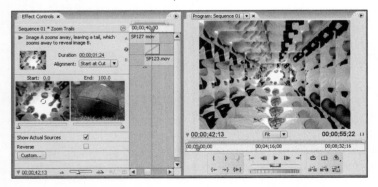

Summary

Premiere Pro's video transitions provide a variety of transitions that you can use to smooth the flow from one clip to another. This chapter covered the following topics:

- Adding a transition between two clips in Single-Track editing mode, by dragging the transition from the Effects panel and placing it between two overlapping video clips.

- Editing a transition, by using the Effect Controls panel or clicking the transition in the Timeline panel.

- Replacing one transition with another, by clicking and dragging the new transition over the old transition.

- Specifying a default transition, by selecting the transition in the Effects panel and then choosing Set Selected as Default Transition from the Effects panel menu.

Part III

Working with Type and Graphics

Chapter 10

Creating Titles and Graphics with Title Designer

U sed effectively, titles at the beginning of a production can help build expectations, introduce a subject, establish a mood, and, of course, provide the title of the production. Throughout a video production, titles can provide transitions between one segment and another; they can also help introduce speakers and locales. Titles used with graphics can help convey statistical, geographical, and other technical information. At the end of the production, you can use titles to give yourself and your production crew the credit you so richly deserve for your creative efforts.

Although you can create titles in graphics programs, such as Adobe Photoshop and Adobe Illustrator, you may find that Premiere Pro's Title Designer offers all the titling capabilities you need for many productions without ever leaving the Premiere Pro environment. As you will soon see, the Title Designer not only enables you to create text and graphics, but it also enables you to create drop shadows and animation effects with crawling and rolling text.

This chapter provides a step-by-step look at how to create production titles using Premiere Pro's Title Designer. It then shows you how to integrate your titles into your digital video productions.

Exploring the Title Designer

The Title Designer provides a simple and efficient means of creating text and graphics that you can use for video titles in Premiere Pro projects.

To display the Title Designer, you first need to launch Premiere Pro and either create a new project or open a project. When creating a new project, be sure to use the frame size you want your Title drawing area to have. The

Title drawing area takes on the frame size of the existing project. When the title and the output dimensions are the same, your titles appear exactly where you want them to be in your final production.

To create a project using custom settings, choose File ➪ New ➪ Project. In the New Project dialog box, click the Custom Settings tab. Click the Editing Mode drop-down menu and choose Desktop. To create a custom preset, type the appropriate frame size in the horizontal and vertical fields. To save the custom preset, click the Save Preset button. In the Save Project Settings dialog box, name the preset, give it a description, and then click OK. In the New Project dialog box, name the file project and click OK.

Creating a simple title

To become familiar with the core tools and features of the Title Designer, use the following steps to create and save a simple title clip for use in a Premiere Pro project:

1. **Choose File ➪ New ➪ Project to create a new project.** The New Project dialog box appears. Name your project, pick a preset, or create a custom preset. Click OK to create the new project. For more information on Premiere Pro digital video project settings, see Chapter 3. If you want, you can also load a Premiere Pro project.

2. **Choose File ➪ New ➪ Title, or Title ➪ New Title ➪ Default Still, to create a new title.** When the New Title dialog box appears, as shown in Figure 10.1, you can name your title in the Name field. Click OK to create the new title. The title is automatically placed in the current project's panel and is saved with the project. The Title panel appears onscreen, as shown in Figure 10.2. The drawing area of the Title panel is the same size as the project frame size.

FIGURE 10.1

The New Title dialog box allows you to name your title.

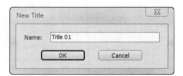

If you plan to output your titles to film or videotape, you should display the safe title margin and safe action margin areas. By default, these margins are already displayed. To view and hide these margins, choose Title ➪ View ➪ Safe Title Margin, and Title ➪ View ➪ Safe Action Margin. You can also select these options from the Title panel menu. To have Premiere Pro display a video clip in the Timeline panel, either click the Show Video check box in the Title panel or choose Show Video from the Title menu. The Title menu also allows you to display the Tools, Styles, Actions, and Properties panels.

FIGURE 10.2

Use the Title Designer to create text and graphics for production titles.

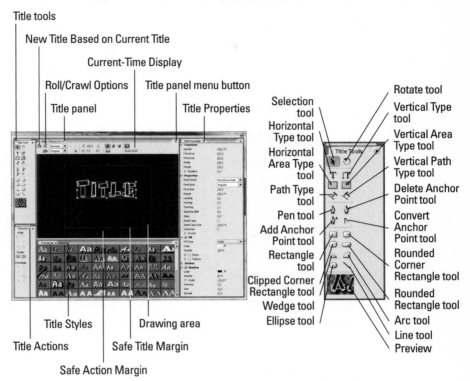

The tools in the Tools panel and drawing area in the Title panel resemble those found in simple drawing and painting programs. Five panels make up the Title Designer: Title, Title Tools, Title Actions, Title Styles, and Title Properties. You can display the Title Designer panels by selecting them from the Window menu. You can group some of the Title Designer panels to create a custom workspace. (To save a custom workspace, choose Window ⇨ Workspace ⇨ Save Workspace.) The Title Designer is divided into the following sections:

■ **Title:** The Title panel consists of the drawing area and the main toolbar. The main toolbar options allow you to specify whether you are creating still, crawling, or rolling text, or whether you are basing the title on a current title, and they allow you to pick a font and alignment. These options also allow you to show a video clip in the background.

▪ **Title Tools:** This panel contains the text and graphic tools, as well as a preview area displaying the current style.

▪ **Title Actions:** The icons in this panel enable you to align and distribute text and graphic objects.

▪ **Title Styles:** The icons in this panel enable you to apply preset custom styles to text and graphic objects.

▪ **Title Properties:** The settings in this panel enable you to transform and stylize text and graphic objects.

3. **Click the Horizontal Title tool (the "T" next to the arrow).** Move the mouse to the center of the drawing area.

4. **Click the mouse.** Then type **Title**.

5. **Format your text using the options in the Title Properties panel.** If you want to format just one letter, click and drag over the letter you want to format. The Title Properties panel contains the Font and Font Size, Fill, Strokes, and Shadow text options. You can change the following parameters:

▪ **Font or font size:** Click the triangle beside the word Properties to expand the Properties section. Click the Font drop-down menu to change the font, and click and drag through the Font Size value to change the font size. For more information on stylizing type, see the section "Creating and Stylizing Type" later in this chapter.

▪ **Font color:** Click the triangle beside the word Fill to expand the Fill section. Leave the Fill Type menu set to Solid, and click the Color Swatch icon next to the Color option. In the Color Picker dialog box that appears, click a color and then click OK. The new color is applied to the title text. For more information on working with color in the Title Designer, see the section "Using Color" later in this chapter.

6. **To add the title file to your project, close the Title Designer.** Drag the title file from the Project panel to a video track in the Timeline panel.

7. **To save the Title file to your hard drive, so that you can import it into other Premiere Pro projects, click the title in the Project panel.** Choose File ➪ Export ➪ Title. In the Save Title dialog box, you can rename your title using the File Name drop-down menu. Locate a place on your hard drive to save your title, and then save it in PRTL format.

Touring the Title tools

The tools in the Title Tools panel enable you to create graphics and text. Table 10.1 reviews the tools and other graphic controls.

TABLE 10.1

Tool Items in the Title Tools Panel

Shortcut Key	Name	Description
V	Selection tool	Selects objects so that they can be moved or resized (stretched or shrunk); you can also use it to select text before changing text attributes
O	Rotation tool	Allows you to rotate text
T	Horizontal Type tool	Creates type horizontally
C	Vertical Type tool	Creates type vertically
	Horizontal Area Type tool	Creates wrapped text horizontally
	Vertical Area Type tool	Creates wrapped text vertically
	Path Type tools	Creates text along a path
P	Pen tool	Creates curved shapes using Bezier curves
	Add Anchor Point tool	Adds anchor points to a path
	Delete Anchor Point tool	Deletes anchor points from a path
	Convert Anchor Point tool	Converts a curved point to a corner point, and vice versa
R	Rectangle tool	Creates rectangles
	Clipped Corner Rectangle tool	Creates rectangles with dog-eared corners
	Rounded Corner Rectangle tool	Creates rectangles with round corners
W	Wedge tool	Creates triangular shapes
A	Arc tool	Creates curved shapes
E	Ellipse tool	Creates ellipses
L	Line tool	Creates lines

Using the Title menu

Premiere Pro's Title menu enables you to change visual attributes of text and graphic objects. For example, you can use the Title menu to set the font, size, and style of the text that you create in the Title Designer. You can also use it to set the speed and direction of rolling title text. Table 10.2 summarizes the Title menu commands. The Title menu appears when the Title Designer is open onscreen.

TABLE 10.2

The Title Menu Commands

Menu Command	Description
New Title	Allows you to create a new still, roll, or crawl title. You can also choose whether you want the title to be based on the current title or on a template.
Font	Changes the typeface.
Size	Changes the size of text/
Type Alignment	Sets text to flush left, flush right, or centered.
Orientation	Sets text to be horizontal or vertical.
Word Wrap	Sets text to wrap when it reaches the safe title margin.
Tab Stops	Enables you to create tabs within a text box.
Templates	Enables you to apply, create, and edit templates.
Roll/Crawl Options	Provides options for setting direction and speed of rolling and crawling text.
Logo	Enables you to insert logos in the entire Title Designer drawing area as a background, in a portion of the drawing area, or within a text box.
Transform	Enables you to change the position, scale, rotation, and opacity of an object or text.
Select	Enables you to select from a stack of objects, the first object above, next object above, next object below, or last object below.
Arrange	Enables you to bring selected objects to the front or forward, or to send selected objects to the back or backward in a stack of objects.
Position	Moves an object so that it is either horizontally or vertically centered, or moves it to the lower-third part of the Title Designer drawing area. The lower-third part of the screen is frequently used for text that must be read without covering up the onscreen image.
Align Objects	Enables you to align selected objects horizontally left, right, or centered and vertically top, bottom, or centered
Distribute Objects	Enables you to distribute selected objects horizontally left, right, centered, or evenly spaced and vertically top, bottom, centered, or evenly spaced
View	Enables you to the view safe title margin, the safe action margin, text baselines, and tab markers. It also allows you to view a video from the Timeline in the drawing area.

Saving, Opening, and Copying a Title File

After you have created some stunning text and graphics with the Title Designer, you may want to reuse it in various other Premiere Pro projects. To do so, you need to export your title files, save them to your hard drive, and then import them into the projects you want to use them in.

NOTE If you save your title to your hard drive, you can always load the title into any project.

To save your title to your hard drive, click the title in the Project panel and then choose File ⇨ Export ⇨ Title. In the Save Title dialog box, you can rename your title using the File Name drop-down menu. Locate a place on your hard drive to save your title, and then save it in PRTL format.

To import a saved title to a Premiere Pro project, choose File ⇨ Import. In the Import dialog box, locate and select the title file you want to import and then click Open. The New Title dialog box that appears allows you to rename the title file. Rename the title, and then click OK. The imported title file appears in the Project panel ready to be placed in a video track in the Timeline panel.

TIP Double-clicking a title clip in the Project panel opens that title in the Title Designer.

To edit the title file, double-click the title file in the Project panel. When the title appears in the Title Designer, make the changes you want. Making changes to the title replaces the old one. If you do not want to replace the current title, click the New Title Based on Current Title icon in the Title panel. To make a copy of the current title, you can also choose Title ⇨ New Title ⇨ Based on Current Title. When the New Title dialog box appears, change the name of the title and click OK.

NOTE You can create one title as a template and then load it, edit the text and graphics, and save it under a new name.

Creating and Stylizing Type

Premiere Pro's horizontal and vertical Type tool works very much like the Type tools in graphics programs. Creating text, selecting and moving it, and stylizing fonts works very much the same as with most other Type tools. Changing type color and adding shadows is somewhat different but very simple when you are familiar with it. The Path Type tool even enables you to create text along a Bezier path.

CROSS-REF Creating text along a path with the Path type tool, along with creating Bezier paths and shapes with the Pen tool, is covered later in this chapter in the section "Working with the Bezier Tools."

Using the Horizontal Type and Vertical Type tools

Text in video productions should be clear and easy to read. If viewers need to strain their eyes to read your titles, they either stop trying to read them or they ignore the video and audio as they try to decipher the text onscreen.

Premiere Pro's Type tools provide the versatility that you need to create clear and interesting text. Not only can you change size, font, and color by using the options in the Title Properties panel, but you also can create drop shadows and emboss effects.

Premiere Pro's Type tools enable you to place type anywhere in the Title panel drawing area. As you work, Premiere Pro places each block of text within a text *bounding box* that you can easily move, resize, or delete.

Follow these steps to create horizontal and vertical text:

1. **Choose File ⇨ New ⇨ Project to create a new project.** Set the preset to the size of your title and production.

2. **Choose File ⇨ New ⇨ Title to create a new title.** In the New Title dialog box that appears, name your title and then click OK. The Title Designer window appears. Make sure the Title Type option is set to Still because you are creating still text rather than rolling or crawling text. To view the Title Type option, click the Roll/Crawl Options icon in the Title panel.

 To learn how to create rolling and crawling text, turn to the section "Rolling and Crawling Titles" later in this chapter.

3. **Click either the Horizontal Type or Vertical Type tool in the Title Tools panel.** The Horizontal Type tool creates text horizontally from left to right, and the Vertical Type tool creates text vertically.

4. **Drag the I-beam cursor to where you want your text to appear, and then click the mouse.** A blinking cursor appears.

NOTE Select the Horizontal Paragraph and Vertical Paragraph Type tools to create horizontal and vertical text that wraps.

5. **Type your title text.** If you make a mistake and want to delete the last character you typed, press Backspace. Figure 10.3 shows text being entered in a bounding box, with a video clip in the background. To display a video clip in the Title panel, you first need to import a clip into the Project panel. Then drag the clip from the Project panel into the Timeline panel. When you open the Title panel, the clip appears in the drawing area. The clock video clip is on the DVD that accompanies this book. It is FilmDisc bc0104.

TIP You can choose Edit ⇨ Undo to undo your last entry, or File ⇨ Revert to revert back to the last time you saved your file.

Editing with the Type tools

If you want to edit text after you finish using the Type tool, you must reselect the text with the Type tool. Move the I-beam cursor over the characters that you want to edit and then click. The blinking cursor appears where you clicked; you can then edit your text. To select all the text within a text box, click the text with the Selection tool.

If you are using the Horizontal Type or Vertical Type tool and you want to create a new line, press Enter and then begin typing. Before you press Enter, make sure that the I-beam cursor is set to where you want the new line to begin.

FIGURE 10.3

Text created with Premiere Pro's Horizontal Type tools. The background video clip is FilmDisc bc0104.

Wrapping text

The Horizontal Type and Vertical Type tools do not automatically wrap text to the next line. If you want to have Premiere Pro automatically wrap text created with the Horizontal Type or Vertical Type tool, choose Title ➪ Word Wrap. The Horizontal Paragraph and Vertical Paragraph Type tools automatically wrap text to the next line. To use the Horizontal Paragraph and Vertical Paragraph Type tools, select the tool from the toolbox. Move the tool to the drawing area, click and drag to create a text box, and begin typing. Notice that as you type, the text automatically wraps to the next line.

Using tabs

You can add spacing between words and align them left, center, or right using tabs. Tabs can help make your titles (or rolling and crawling text) more readable. To apply tabs to your text, you need to use the tab ruler in the Tab Stops dialog box. Before you display the tab ruler, you may want to display the tab markers. When you display tab markers, Premiere Pro displays lines where you set your tabs. By displaying the tab markers as lines, you can better visualize how your tabs will appear within your text. To display tab markers, choose Title ➪ View ➪ Tab Markers or choose Tab Markers from the Title menu. To display the tab ruler, choose Title ➪ Tab Stops. To create a tab, just click the ruler with the left, center, or right tab selected. To move a tab, click and drag it. To apply the tab marks, click OK to close the Tab Stops dialog box. Then move the text I-beam cursor in front of where you want to apply a tab, and press the Tab key. If you want to change the tabs after you have closed the Tab Stops dialog box, just reopen the Tab Stops dialog box and then click and drag the tab on the ruler to the desired location. The text is automatically updated. To delete tab markers, just click the tab and drag it off to either side of the ruler.

Moving text onscreen

You can move a text box by using the Selection tool, by choosing Title ➪ Transform ➪ Position, or by changing the X and Y Position in the Transform section of the Title Properties panel. The Selection tool, the Title ➪ Transform ➪ Rotation menu, and the Transform options (in the Title Properties panel) can also be used to rotate the text box onscreen. You can also rotate text by moving the mouse over one of the corners of the text bounding box. When the mouse icon changes to a curved, double-sided arrow, press and hold the mouse while you drag left or right.

 A quick way to display the Transform commands is to right-click the mouse while a text bounding box is selected.

Manipulating text with the Selection tool

You can quickly move the type's bounding box by following these steps:

1. **In the Title panel, click inside the text bounding box with the Selection tool.**

2. **Drag the text to a new location.** The X and Y Position values change in the Transform area in the Title Properties panel.

The Selection tool enables you to resize a text bounding box. To do so, follow these steps:

1. **Move the Selection tool over one of the bounding box handles.** The cursor changes to a small, straight line with two arrows at either end of it.

2. **Click and drag to increase or decrease the bounding box and font size.** Notice that the Width, Height, X Position, and Y Position values change in the Transform section of the Title Properties panel.

You can also use the Selection tool to rotate a bounding box. To do so, follow these steps:

1. **Move the Selection tool over one of the bounding box handles.**

2. **When the cursor icon changes to a small, curved line with two arrows at either end of it, click and drag to rotate the bounding box and text size.** Notice that the Rotation value changes in the Transform section of the Title Properties panel.

TIP To rotate a bounding box, you can use the Rotation tool in the Title Tools panel. To use the Rotation tool, click it in the Title Tools panel. Then move it to the bounding box, and click and drag in the direction you want to rotate the text box.

Manipulating text with the Transform values

You can use the Transform values (located in the Title Properties panel) to move, resize, and rotate a bounding box. Before you can move, resize, or rotate a bounding box, you must select the bounding box by clicking inside it with the Type tool or the Selection tool. You can manipulate text in these ways:

- **Changing the opacity of a bounding box:** Click and drag to the right or left on the Opacity value to change it. Values less than 100 percent make the items in the bounding box translucent.

- **Moving a bounding box:** In the Transform section of the Title Properties panel, click and drag to the right or left on the X and Y Position values to change them. To move the text bounding box in increments of ten, press and hold the Shift key as you drag to the right or left on the X and Y Position values.

- **Resizing a bounding box:** In the Transform section of the Title Properties panel, click and drag to the right or left on the Width and Height values to change them. Pressing the Shift key as you drag right or left increases the values in increments of ten.

- **Rotating a bounding box:** In the Transform section of the Title Properties panel, click the Rotation value and drag to the left or right to change it. Dragging left rotates the box counterclockwise, and dragging right rotates the box clockwise.

Manipulating text with the Title menu

Before you can move, resize, or rotate a bounding box, you must select it. If it is not already selected, click inside the text bounding box with either the Type tool or the Selection tool. Here are some things you can do:

- **Moving the bounding box:** Choose Title ➪ Transform ➪ Position. In the Position dialog box, type a value for the X and Y Position and then click OK. The Title ➪ Position command enables you to move the box horizontally center, vertically center, and to the lower-third area.

- **Resizing the bounding box:** Choose Title ➪ Transform ➪ Scale. In the Scale dialog box, type a scale percentage. You can choose to scale uniformly or nonuniformly. Click OK to apply the scale.

- **Rotating the bounding box:** Choose Title ➪ Transform ➪ Rotation. In the Rotation dialog box, type the degrees you want to rotate the text box, and then click OK.

As you move, resize, and rotate the text bounding box, notice that the options in the Transform section in the Title Properties panel are updated to reflect the changes.

Changing text attributes

When you first type with the Type tool, Premiere Pro places the type onscreen in its default font and size. You can change type attributes by changing the properties in the Title Properties panel or by using the menu commands found in the Title menu. The Properties section in the Properties panel allows you to change font and font size; set the aspect ratio, kerning, tracking, leading, baseline shift, and slant; apply small caps; and add an underline. You can use the Type menu to change the font and size, and you can change the type orientation from horizontal to vertical, and vice versa.

Changing font and size attributes

You can use both the Title menu and the Properties options in the Title Properties panel to change the font and size of your type. The Title Designer offers three basic techniques for editing font and size attributes.

To change the font and size text attributes before typing, follow these steps:

1. **Click a Type tool.**

2. **Click where you want the text to appear.**

3. **Change the settings for the font and size by using the Title ⇨ Font command and the Title ⇨ Size command.** You can also change the font and size from the Font drop-down menu in the Properties section of the Title Properties panel, or by clicking the Browse icon (which is next to the Roll/Crawl Options icon) at the top of the Title panel. As you type, the new text you type features the attributes of the current font and size settings.

To change individual characters or words, follow these steps:

1. **Select the text with the Type tool by clicking and dragging over the character or word.**

2. **Change type attributes using either the Title menu commands or the Properties options in the Title Properties panel.**

> **TIP**   To browse through the available fonts, choose Title ⇨ Font ⇨ Browse. In the Font Browser dialog box, click the down arrow to see a preview of the fonts. You can change the character display in the Font Browser dialog box. To do so, choose Edit ⇨ Preferences ⇨ Titler. In the dialog box that appears, change the letters in the Font Browser field.

If you want to change all text in a text block, click the text with the Selection tool. Then change the font and size attributes of the text.

Changing spacing attributes

Typically, a typeface's default *leading* (space between lines), *kerning* (space between two specific letters or characters), and *tracking* (space between all letters throughout a selected area of text) provide readable type onscreen. However, if you begin using large type sizes, white space between lines and letters may look awkward. If this happens, you can use Premiere Pro's leading, kerning, and tracking controls to change spacing attributes.

Follow these steps to change leading (the spacing between lines):

1. **Use either the Horizontal Paragraph Type or Vertical Paragraph Type tool to create more than one line of text in the drawing area of the Title panel.**

2. **Click and drag left or right on the Leading value.** The Leading field is in the Properties section of the Title Properties panel. Increase the Leading value to add space between lines. Decrease the Leading value to remove space between lines. If you want to reset spacing to its original leading, type **0** in the Leading field.

You can use the Baseline Shift property to move the baseline of a selected letter, word, or sentence up or down. Increasing the Baseline Shift value moves text up. Decreasing the Baseline Shift value moves text down. Follow these steps to change the baseline shift:

1. **Use the Horizontal Type or Vertical Type tool to create more than one line of text.**

2. **Click the triangle next to the Properties section (in the Title Properties panel) to display the properties.** The Baseline Shift property is located below the Tracking property.

3. **Click and drag the Baseline Shift value to change it.** Increasing the Baseline Shift moves the baseline of the text up. Decreasing the Baseline Shift moves the baseline of the text down.

Follow these steps to change kerning (the spacing between two specific letters or characters to allow for their specific shapes):

1. **Use a Type tool to create a word in the drawing area of the Title panel.**

2. **Click between the two letters whose spacing you want to change.**

3. **Increase or decrease the kerning values in the Properties section of the Title Properties panel.** As you increase the kerning value, the space between the two letters increases. If you decrease the kerning value, the space between the two letters decreases.

Follow these steps to change tracking (the spacing between all letters in a selected area of text):

1. **Use a Type tool to type some text in the drawing area of the Title Properties panel.**

2. **Click and drag over the text with the Type tool.**

3. **Increase or decrease the Tracking value in the Properties section of the Title Properties panel.** Increasing the Tracking value increases the spacing between the letters. Decreasing the Tracking value decreases the spacing between the letters.

Changing other text attributes

Some of the other text attributes allow you to change the appearance of the text. These are the Aspect, Slant, Distort, Small Caps, and Underline attributes. Figure 10.4 shows text before and after changing the Aspect, Slant, and Distort attributes. Each letter was selected separately and then the text attributes were changed. This gives each letter its own unique appearance. In Figure 10.4, the colors of the text and shadow are also changed. Proceed to the next section to learn more about using color.

FIGURE 10.4

Text before and after changing the Aspect, Slant, and Distortion attributes. The background video clip is FilmDisc bc0104.

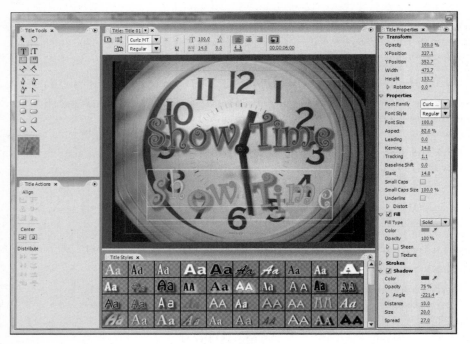

Follow these steps to change the appearance of your text using some of the text attributes in the Properties section of the Title Properties panel:

1. Select a font and font size.

2. Type a word using the Horizontal Type tool.

3. Click and drag to the right or left on the Aspect value to increase or decrease the horizontal scale of the text.

4. **To slant the text to the right, click and drag the Slant value to the right.** To slant the text to the left, click and drag the Slant value to the left.

5. To distort the text, click the X and Y values in the Distort section.

6. If you want to underline or convert the text to small caps, click to select the Small Caps check box.

Using Color

The colors you choose for text and graphics can add to the mood and sophistication of your video project. Using the Premiere Pro color tools, you can pick colors, as well as create gradients from one color to another. You can even add transparency effects that show background video frames through text and graphics.

How do you know what colors to pick when creating titles? The best guide is to use colors that stand out from background images. When watching broadcast television, pay special attention to titles. Many television producers simply use white text against a dark background, or they use bright text with drop shadows to prevent the titles from looking flat. If you are creating a production that includes many titles, keep the text the same color throughout the production to avoid distracting the viewer. An example of this type of title is *lower thirds,* which are graphics that appear at the bottom of the screen and often provide information such as the names of speakers.

Choosing color with the Color Picker

Whenever you select a color in Premiere Pro, you are using Premiere Pro's Color Picker. Picking colors in Premiere Pro can be as simple as clicking the mouse. To see how easy it is to pick a color in Premiere Pro, open the Color Picker, shown in Figure 10.5, by clicking the Solid Fill Color Swatch. Click the Fill triangle to expand the Fill section and display the color swatch. (The Fill section is found below the Properties section in the Title Properties panel.) For the Solid Fill Color Swatch to appear, you must set the Fill Type drop-down menu to Solid.

FIGURE 10.5

Use Premiere Pro's Color Picker to select colors.

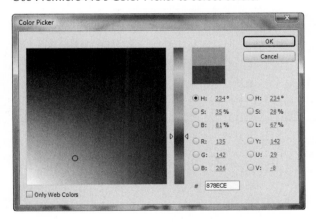

You can pick colors for text and graphic objects in the Color Picker window by clicking in the main color area of the dialog box, or you can enter specific RGB values. As you work in the Color Picker, the color that you are creating is previewed in the bottom color swatch in the upper-right corner of the Color Picker dialog box. The top color swatch displays the original color. If you want to return to the original color, simply click the top color swatch.

If you pick a color that falls beyond the NTSC video color gamut, Premiere Pro displays a gamut warning signal that looks like an exclamation mark inside a gray triangle (shown in Figure 10.5). To drop the color back to the nearest NTSC color, simply click the gamut warning signal. If you want to work with colors that are specifically for the Web, click the Only Web Colors option in the bottom-left corner of the Color Picker dialog box.

 PAL and SECAM video use larger color gamuts than NTSC video. You can ignore the gamut warning if you are not using NTSC video.

Understanding RGB colors

Computer displays and television video monitors create colors by using the red, green, and blue color model. In this model, adding different values of red, green, and blue light creates millions of colors.

Premiere Pro's Color Picker simulates adding light by enabling you to enter values into its Red, Green, and Blue fields. Some of the color values are shown in Table 10.3.

The largest number that you can enter into one of the color fields is 255, and the smallest is 0. Thus, Premiere Pro enables you to create over 16 million colors ($256 \times 256 \times 256$). When each RGB value equals 0, no light is added to create colors; the resulting color is black. If you enter 255 in each of the RGB fields, you create white.

To create different shades of gray, you must make all field values equal. Values of R 50, G 50, B 50 create a dark gray; values of R 250, G 250, B 250 create a light gray.

TABLE 10.3

The Color Values for RGB Colors

Color	Red Value	Green Value	Blue Value
Black	0	0	0
Red	255	0	0
Green	0	255	0
Blue	0	0	255
Cyan	0	255	255
Magenta	255	0	255
Yellow	255	255	0
White	255	255	255

Choosing colors using the Eyedropper tool

Apart from the Color Picker, the most efficient way to pick colors is to click a color with the Eyedropper tool. The Eyedropper tool automatically copies the color you click into the color swatch. Therefore, you can recreate a color with one click of the mouse, rather than wasting time experimenting with RGB values in the Color Picker.

You can use the Eyedropper tool to do the following:

- Select a color from a type or graphic object in the drawing area.
- Select a specific color from a logo, style, or template.
- Copy a specific color from a video clip in the background of the Title panel.

The Eyedropper tool can be very handy for selecting colors from a video clip, logo, style, or template. Follow these steps to use the Eyedropper tool:

1. **Create a new project using the presets you want your title to have.** If you want to use the Eyedropper tool to select a color from a video frame, you need to import a video clip into your project by choosing File ➪ Import.

 If you don't have a video clip to use, you can use one of the video clips in the Tutorial Projects folder on the DVD that accompanies this book.

2. **Drag the video clip from the Project panel to a video track in the Timeline panel.**

3. **Choose File ➪ New ➪ Title to create a new title.** When the New Title dialog box appears, name your title and click OK.

4. **To display the video clip in the Title panel, click the Show Video check box to display the video clip.**

5. **Click and drag in the Timeline location area to display the frame you want to appear in the background of the Title drawing area.** Notice that the Fill, Strokes, and Shadow sections all have Eyedropper tools. Using the Fill Eyedropper tool changes the Fill Color Swatch. Using the Strokes Eyedropper tool changes the Strokes Color Swatch. Using the Shadow Eyedropper tool changes the Shadow Color Swatch. Click the Eyedropper tool you want to use.

TIP To import a graphic file as the background or as a logo into the Title panel drawing area, choose Title ➪ Logo ➪ Insert Logo. To insert a logo into text, choose Title ➪ Logo ➪ Insert Logo into Text. To import a template into the drawing area of the Title panel, choose Title ➪ Templates.

6. **Move the Eyedropper tool over the color you want to select, and click the mouse.** The color swatch changes to the new color.

Applying solid colors to text and graphics

After you have created a graphic object or some text, applying a solid fill color using Premiere Pro's Color Picker is quite simple. Follow these steps:

1. **Use a Type tool to create a text object, or use a Graphic tool to create a graphic object onscreen.** You can use the Selection tool to select a text or graphic object that is already onscreen.

2. **Ensure that the Fill option is selected in the Title Properties panel.** Deselecting the Fill check box removes the fill.

3. **Click the triangle next to the Fill option to display the options.**

4. **Set the Fill Type drop-down menu to Solid.**

5. **Click the color swatch to open the Color Picker.**

6. **Pick your new color, and close the Color Picker.** You can also use the Eyedropper tool to pick a color from an object in the drawing area or from a video clip in the background (see the preceding section).

7. **To make the color transparent so that you can see through it, reduce the opacity percentage.** The lower the opacity, the more transparent the object is. You can change the opacity percentage by using the Opacity field in either the Object Style section or in the Transform section. You can also use the Title ➪ Transform ➪ Opacity command. By lowering the opacity in an object, you can create interesting graphic effects where portions of objects below show through the object above.

Applying highlights and textures with text and graphic objects

You can also add a highlight and a texture to the fill and stroke of text or a graphic object. To add a highlight, use the Sheen option. First click the triangle next to Fill to display the Fill options. The Sheen option is located within the Fill section. To view the Sheen option, select the Sheen option check box and then click the triangle next to the Sheen option to display all of the properties.

Adding a highlight

Follow these steps to create a sense of light and shadow in your text or graphic:

1. **In the Title Properties panel, with an object selected, click the triangle next to the Fill property to display the Sheen option.** Then click to select the Sheen check box.

2. **Click the triangle next to the Sheen check box to display the Sheen options.**

3. **Click the color swatch to pick a color.** You can also use the Eyedropper tool to pick a color from an object onscreen or from a background video clip.

4. **Click and drag over the Size value to change the size of the highlight.** Drag to the right to increase the size. Drag to the left to decrease the size.

5. **Click and drag over the Angle value to change the value of the highlight.**

6. **Click and drag over the Offset value to move the highlight up or down.** Increasing the Offset value moves the highlight up, and decreasing the Offset value moves the highlight down.

7. **Change the Opacity value to make the highlight transparent.** Reducing the Opacity value makes the highlight more transparent.

Adding a texture to text or graphics

You can easily make text and graphics more realistic by applying a texture. Figure 10.6 shows the objects and text with textures applied to them. The two rectangle objects have the 1080_blueprint_bkg1.png and the 1080_summer_bkg.png textures applied to them. The 1080_abstract_bkg2.png texture is applied to the text.

FIGURE 10.6

In the Title Designer, you can see textures applied to text and graphics.

Follow these steps to apply textures:

1. **Use one of the graphic tools or the Type tool to create an object in the drawing area of the Title panel.** Select the object or text in the Title Designer, and click the triangle next to the Fill property to display the Texture option. Then click the Texture check box.

2. **Click the triangle next to the Texture check box to display the Texture options.**

3. **Click the Texture Swatch to display the Choose a Texture Image dialog box.**

4. **In the Choose a Texture Image dialog box, pick a texture from the Premiere Pro Textures folder.**

5. **Click Open to apply the texture to the selected object.**

NOTE You can create your own textures. For example, you can use Photoshop to save any bitmap file as a PSD, JPEG, TARGA, or TIFF file. You can also use Premiere Pro to output a frame from a video clip.

6. **Specify optional settings.** These are your choices:

■ **Flip with Object or Rotate with Object:** Premiere Pro flips or rotates a texture with the object.

■ **Scaling:** Premiere Pro scales the texture. First, click the triangle next to the option, and then click and drag over the Horizontal and Vertical values.

The Scaling section also contains the Tile X and Tile Y options, which you use to specify whether you want the texture to be tiled to an object.

You use the Object X and Object Y drop-down menus in the Scaling section to determine how the texture is stretched along the X and Y axes. The four choices from the drop-down menus are Clipped Face, Arbitrary, Face, and Extended Character. The choice you pick determines how the texture is stretched. By default, the Clipped Face option is selected.

■ **Alignment:** Use the Object X and Object Y drop-down menus to determine how the texture aligns with the object. The four choices from the drop-down menus are Clipped Face, Arbitrary, Face, and Extended Character. The choice you pick determines how the texture is aligned. By default, the Clipped Face option is selected.

You use the Rule X and Rule Y check boxes in the Alignment section to determine how the texture is aligned. You can choose Top Left, Center, or Bottom Right.

You use the X Offset and Y Offset values to move the texture within the selected object.

■ **Blending:** Use the Mix value in the Blending section to blend the texture with the fill color. Decreasing the Mix value increases the fill color and decreases the texture.

The Fill Key and Texture Key check boxes in the Blending section take into consideration the transparency of an object.

Lowering the Alpha Scale value in the Blending section makes the object more transparent. The Composite Rule drop-down menu allows you to pick which channel is going to be used in determining the transparency. Clicking the Invert Composite check box inverts the alpha values.

Creating and applying gradients to text and graphics

Premiere Pro's color controls enable you to apply gradients to text and graphic objects that are created in the Title Designer. A *gradient*, which is a gradual blend from one color to another, can help add interest and depth to otherwise flat color. Used effectively, gradients can also help simulate lighting effects in graphics. The three types of gradients you can create in the Type Designer are Linear Gradient, Radial Gradient, and 4 Color Gradient. Linear and radial gradients are created from two colors. The 4 Color Gradient is created from four colors. Figure 10.7 shows the 4 Color Gradient being used on the background rectangle object and the text. The font used to create the text is Rosewood Std.

 If you want to apply a gradient to specific letters in a text block, select the text by clicking and dragging over it with the Type tool.

 If you are outputting to video, gradients created in small text may make the text unreadable on a television monitor.

FIGURE 10.7

A graphic object and text created using the 4 Color Gradient effect

Follow these steps to create a linear and radial gradient:

1. **In the Title Designer, create text or a graphic with the tools in the Title Tools panel.** Alternatively, select text or a graphic with the Selection tool.

2. **Ensure that the Fill check box is selected, and that the triangle next to the check box is facing downward.** The Fill option is found in the Title Properties panel.

3. **From the Fill Type drop-down menu, choose Linear Gradient, Radial Gradient, or 4 Color Gradient.**

Moving the Gradient Start and End Color Swatches

You can move the gradient start color swatch and the gradient end color swatch. Moving the swatches changes how much color of each swatch is applied to the gradient.

The Color Stop Color Swatch allows you to change the color of the selected color swatch. The Color Stop Opacity setting allows you to change the opacity of the selected color swatch. The selected color swatch is the color swatch with a black triangle above it.

To change the angle in a linear gradient, click and drag over the Angle value.

To increase the number of repeats in the linear or radial blend, click and drag over the Repeat value.

4. **To set the start and ending colors of the gradients, use the gradient start and end color swatches.** The 4 Color Gradient has two start swatches and two end color swatches. For linear and radial gradients, the start and end color swatches are the two tiny rectangles below the gradient bar. For the 4 Color Gradient, the color swatches are two tiny rectangles below and above the gradient. Pick the starting gradient color by double-clicking the gradient start color swatch. When the Color Picker opens, pick a color. Double-click the gradient end color swatch. When the Color Picker opens, pick an ending gradient color.

Creating and applying bevels to text and graphic objects

Premiere Pro enables you to create some really interesting bevels in the Title Designer. You can add a three-dimensional effect to your text and graphic objects by beveling them, as shown in Figure 10.8.

Follow these steps to bevel an object:

1. **In the Title Designer, create either text or a graphic with the tools in the Title Tools panel.** Alternatively, select text or a graphic with the Selection tool.

2. **Ensure that the Fill check box is selected.** Also check that the triangle next to the check box is facing downward.

3. **From the Fill Type drop-down menu, choose Bevel.**

4. **Click the Highlight Color Swatch or use the Eyedropper tool to pick a highlight color.** Then click the Shadow Color Swatch or the Eyedropper tool to pick a shadow color.

5. **Click and drag the Size slider to the right to increase the bevel size.**

6. **To increase or decrease the highlight color, click and drag over the Balance value.** Increasing the highlight color decreases shadow color, and vice versa.

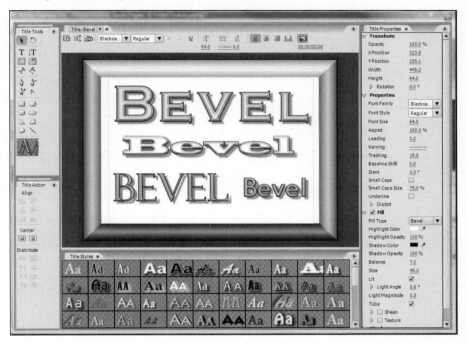

FIGURE 10.8

Rectangle and text objects with a bevel

7. **To make your bevel look more decorative, click the Tube check box.** A tubular border appears between the highlight and shadow area, as shown in Figure 10.8.

8. **Click the Lit check box to increase the bevel effect and make the object more three-dimensional.** Click and drag over the Light Angle value to change the angle of the light. Click and drag over the Light Magnitude value to increase or decrease the amount of light.

9. **If you want to make the bevel translucent, click and drag to the left over either the Highlight Opacity or Shadow Opacity value.**

Applying shadows to text and graphics

To add a finishing touch to your text or graphic object, you may want to add a shadow to it. You can add either an inner or outer stroke to an object. Follow these steps:

1. **In the Title Designer, create text or a graphic with the tools in the Title Tools panel.** Alternatively, select text or a graphic with the Selection tool.

> **TIP** If you want to fill the selected object with a shadow, set the object's Fill Type to Ghost Fill.

283

2. Click the Shadow check box to select it.

3. To see all of the Shadow options, click the triangle next to the Shadow option so that it is facing downward.

4. Click and drag over the Size value to set the size of the shadow.

5. Click and drag over the Distance and Angle values to move the shadow to the desired location.

6. Click and drag over the Spread value to soften the edges of the shadow.

7. **Double-click the color swatch to change the color for the drop shadow.** You can also use the Eyedropper tool to pick a color from a background video clip or template.

8. **Reduce the Opacity value if you want to make the shadow transparent.**

 Don't let a shadow fool you. If you are changing the opacity of an object that has a solid shadow, the opacity effect you desire may not be possible until you remove the shadow or make the shadow transparent.

Applying strokes to text and graphics

To separate the fill color from the shadow color, you may want to add a stroke to it. You can add either an inner or outer stroke to an object. Follow these steps:

1. **In the Title Designer, create text or a graphic with the tools in the Title Tools panel.** Alternatively, select text or a graphic with the Selection tool.

 If you want the selected object to have a stroke, but no fill or shadow, set the object's fill type to Eliminate Fill. This way, you can use the selected object as a frame.

2. Click the triangle next to the Strokes option so that it is facing downward.

3. Click Add next to the Inner Strokes and/or Outer Strokes option to add inner and/or outer strokes to the selected object.

TIP You can click the Object Style menu — the tiny circle with an arrow surrounding it — to add, delete, or move a stroke.

4. Click the Stroke Type drop-down menu to pick a stroke type.

5. Click and drag over the Size value to change the stroke size.

6. Click and drag over the Angle value to change the angle of the Depth and Drop Face stroke type.

7. Click the Fill Type drop-down menu to pick a fill type.

8. **Double-click the color swatch to pick a color for the drop shadow.** You can also use the Eyedropper tool to pick a color from a background video clip or template.

9. Reduce the Opacity value if you want to make the stroke translucent.

Using Styles

Although setting text attributes is quite simple, sometimes finding the right combination of font, size, style, kerning, and leading can be time-consuming. After you have spent time fine-tuning text attributes in one text block, you may want to apply the same attributes to other text in the Title Designer or to other text that you have previously saved. You can save attributes and color by using styles. Figure 10.9 shows rectangles and text with styles applied to them.

The Premiere Pro Title Styles panel enables you to save and load preset styles for text and graphics. Thus, instead of picking the font, size, and color each time you create a title, you can apply a style name to the text and have all of the attributes applied at once. Using one or two styles throughout your project helps to ensure consistency. If you don't want to create your own styles, you can use the preset styles that appear in the Title Styles panel. To display the Title Styles panel, choose Window ⇨ Title Styles or click the Title panel menu and choose Styles. All you need to do to apply a style is to select some text and click the style swatch that suits your needs.

FIGURE 10.9

Some styles applied to rectangles and text

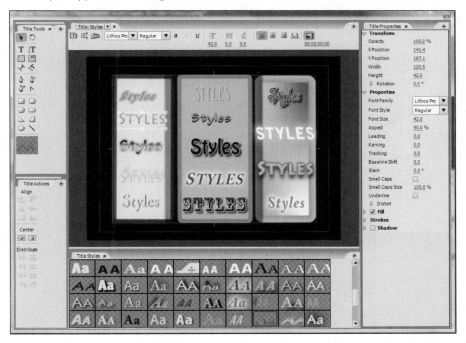

The choices for styles are hidden within the Title Styles panel. You can access the style choices by clicking the Styles menu — the tiny arrow with a circle surrounding it. Clicking the Styles menu arrow displays commands that allow you to create styles, save them to disk, and change the way styles appear onscreen.

Follow these steps to create a style:

1. **Create text using attributes from the Title menu or the Title Properties panel.**
2. **Choose New Style from the Styles menu.**
3. **Enter a name for the style.** Click OK. Either you see a swatch of the new style, or the style name appears in the Styles area.

Styles remain only during the current Premiere Pro project session. If you want to use a style again, you must save the style into a styles file. Follow these steps to save a styles file:

1. **Select the name of the style you want to save, or select its thumbnail.**

 You can also start by selecting each object containing the style that you want to save.

2. **Choose Save Style Library from the Styles menu.**
3. **Enter a name for the style.** Designate its location on your hard drive.
4. **Click Save.** Premiere Pro saves the file using a .prtl file extension.

NOTE You can replace a preexisting style name with a new style name by choosing Rename Style. To create a new style, choose New Style. To create a copy of the style, choose Duplicate Style.

Loading and applying styles

If you want to load a style from the hard drive to use in a new Premiere Pro session, you must load the style library before you can apply it.

Follow these steps to load styles from the hard drive:

1. **Click the triangle in the Styles section to display the Styles menu.** Choose Load Style Library from the Styles menu.
2. **Use the mouse to navigate to the hard drive location containing your style.**
3. **Select the style.** Click Open. After styles are loaded, you can easily apply a style by clicking the text or object and then simply clicking the swatch for the style that you want to apply.

Renaming, deleting, and changing style swatches

You can duplicate and rename styles, and you can delete saved styles that you don't need to use anymore. You can also change the way the style swatches appear in the Title Designer.

Follow these steps to duplicate, rename, and delete styles:

1. **With a style selected, choose Duplicate Style from the Styles menu.**

2. **To rename a style, first select it.** Choose Rename Style from the Styles menu.

3. **In the dialog box that appears, type a new name.**

4. **To delete a style, select it from the Styles section.**

5. **With the style selected, choose Delete Style from the Styles menu.** In the dialog box that appears, click OK to delete the selected style.

If you feel the style swatches consume too much screen space, you can change the display of styles so that they appear as text or as small icons. To change the display, simply click the Styles menu and then choose Text Only, Large Thumbnails, or Small Thumbnails.

> **TIP**   To change the two characters that appear in the style swatch, choose Edit ⇨ Preferences ⇨ Titler. In the dialog box that appears, type the two characters that you want in the Style Swatches field.

Placing a Title in a Project

To use the titles you create in the Title Designer, you need to add them to a Premiere Pro project. When you save a title, Premiere Pro automatically adds the title to the Project panel of the current project. After the title is in the Project panel, you add titles to the Timeline panel in much the same way as you add video clips and other graphics — by dragging and dropping them from the Project panel to the Timeline panel. Titles can be placed either in a video track above a video clip or in the same track as a video clip. Typically, you could add a title to the Video 2 track so that the title or title sequence appears over the video clips in the Video 1 track. If you want to have a title file gradually transition into a video clip, you can place the title file in the same video track, so that the title overlaps the video clip at the beginning or at the end. The transition is applied to the overlapping section. For more information on working with video transitions, refer to Chapter 9.

You can add a preexisting title to a project onscreen by importing it into the project. Follow these steps to add a title to the Project pane, by using the Import command:

1. **Choose File ⇨ Open to open the project file that you want to work with.**

2. **Choose File ⇨ Import to import the title file that you want to use.** Choose File ⇨ New ⇨ Title to create a new title. You should have the title file in the Project panel of the project file.

3. **Drag the title file from the Project panel to the Video 2 track of the Timeline panel.** If the Timeline panel is not open, you can open it by choosing Window ⇨ Timelines or by double-clicking Sequence 01 in the Project panel.

4. **After you add your title to a Video 2 track in the Timeline panel, you will probably want to preview your project.** In the Timeline panel, move the current-time indicator (CTI) over the area you want to preview. Then open the Monitor panel (choose Window ⇨ Program Monitor ⇨ Sequence 01). Press the Play button to have Premiere Pro play the clip

in the Program Monitor panel. (For more information about previewing Premiere Pro projects, see the QuickStart chapter.)

 **TIP** After you place a title file into a Premiere Pro project, you can edit the title file by double-clicking it. When you double-click, the Title Designer appears.

5. **Choose File ⇨ Save to save your work.**

Adding a Background to a Title Clip

In this section, you create a new project. In the project, you import a video clip to use behind the title that you create using the Premiere Pro Title Designer. You then save the title and place it in your production. Figure 10.10 shows the Premiere Pro layout of a production created using a title superimposed over a video clip. In the Program Monitor panel, you can see the title file superimposed over the video clip. In the Timeline panel, the title file is selected. Premiere Pro creates title files with transparent backgrounds, allowing you to see a video clip below the title file. Notice that in the Timeline panel, the title file appears in the Video 2 track, the video clip appears in the Video 1 track (ArtBeats SNY127), and a sound clip appears in the Audio 1 track (SmartSound Synergy).

FIGURE 10.10

The production layout of a Premiere Pro project with a title superimposed over a video clip

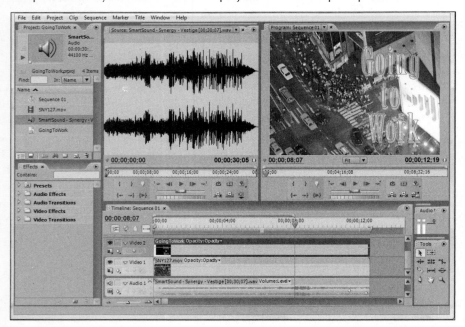

Follow these steps to create a title and to overlay it onto a video clip:

1. **Choose File ⇨ New ⇨ Project to create a project.** Make sure that you use the proper preset.

2. **Choose File ⇨ Import to import the video clip you want to appear behind the title.** This example uses the ArtBeats SNY127 video clip. This video clip is located in the ArtBeats folder in the Tutorial Projects folder on the DVD that accompanies this book.

ON the DVD If you want, you can use the video clip that appears in Figure 10.10. It is found in the ArtBeats folder, inside the Tutorial Projects folder on the DVD that accompanies this book. The video clip is ArtBeats SNY127. The sound clip is found in the SmartSound folder on the DVD that accompanies this book, and is the Synergy sound clip.

3. **Drag the video clip from the Project panel to the Video 1 track in the Timeline panel.**

4. **Choose File ⇨ New ⇨ Title to create a new title.** When the New Title dialog box appears, name your title and click OK.

5. **Make sure to select the Show Video check box to display the video clip in the drawing area of the Title panel.** Premiere Pro places the frame in the background where the CTI is located. To use a different frame in the video clip, move the CTI in the Timeline panel, or click and drag the Timeline values to the right of the Show Video check box.

NOTE If you are outputting to video or film, you want to have the Safe Title Margin and Safe Action Margin displayed. If they are not displayed, choose Type ⇨ View ⇨ Safe Title Margins, and Type ⇨ View ⇨ Safe Action Margins. If you are outputting to the Web, you don't need to select these options.

6. **Click the Type tool.** Move the I-beam cursor to the drawing area of the Title panel. Type the text you want. This example uses the text "Going to Work," as shown in Figure 10.11.

7. **Choose a style.** You can change the text attributes, color, and shadow as desired using the Title Properties panel.

8. **Close the Title Designer.** The title automatically appears in the Project panel of the project. If you want to save the title to your hard drive, click the title in the Project panel and choose File ⇨ Export ⇨ Title. In the Save Title dialog box, click Save.

9. **Drag the title from the Project panel to the Video 2 track of the Timeline panel.** Move the title into position. The title shown in Figure 10.10 is adjusted so that it lines up with the video clip in the Video 1 track.

10. **If you need to extend the title so that it matches the length of the video clip, click the right side of the title in the Timeline panel and drag to the right.**

NOTE You can change the duration of a title by clicking the title in the Timeline panel and choosing Clip ⇨ Speed/Duration. In the Clip Speed/Duration dialog box, click the chain to unlink the speed and duration. Then type the new duration. Click OK to activate the changes.

FIGURE 10.11

The Title Designer for the production shown in Figure 10.10

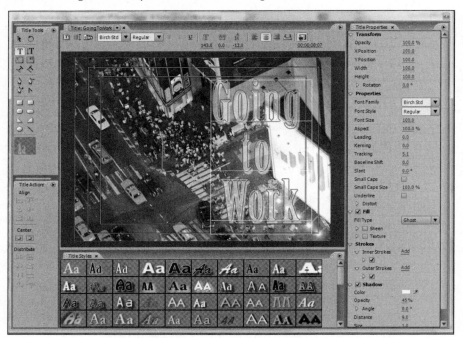

11. **Display the Monitor panel, if it is not already open, by choosing Window ⇨ Program Monitor ⇨ Sequence.** Click the Play button to play the project.

NOTE   You can animate your title by using the Perspective Video Effect, the Basic 3D Video Effect, or the Motion options in the Effect Controls panel. Click the triangle next to Motion in the Effect Controls panel to display the Motion options. The Motion options are Position, Scale, Rotation, and Anchor Point. For more information on using the Motion options, see Chapter 16.

12. **To add sound to your clip, choose File ⇨ Import.** Locate the sound you want to import. When the sound clip is in the Project panel, click and drag it to the Audio 1 track of the Timeline panel. If the sound clip is too long, you can cut it using the Razor tool. You may also want to gradually fade out the sound.

    For more information on editing sound, refer to Chapter 7. This example uses SmartSound's Synergy sound clip. This sound clip is located in the SmartSound folder in the Tutorial Projects folder on the DVD that accompanies this book. You can also choose File ⇨ New ⇨ SmartSound to import a SmartSound sound clip. To download SmartSound's QuickTrack software, go to www.smartsound.com/premiere/index.html.

13. **Choose File ⇨ Save to save the project.** To preview the project with sound, click the Play button in the Program Monitor panel.

Working with Logos

Logos can be imported into the Title Designer and used in a portion of the drawing area or in the entire area. A logo can be a graphic or a photograph. The title in Figure 10.12 is created by inserting two logos: a photograph of waves in the background and a graphic SunSurf logo in the center of the drawing area. The waves image is a frame from the Waves video clip found on the DVD, and the SunSurf logo is created using shapes and paths in Adobe Photoshop (you could also create the logo in Adobe Illustrator). To create the text, this example uses the font Baveuse with different fills and font sizes.

FIGURE 10.12

A title created by inserting two logos into the Title Designer

Follow these steps to import a logo into a title:

1. **Choose File ⇨ New ⇨ Project to create a new project.** In the New Project dialog box, choose a preset. Name your project and click OK.

2. **Choose File ⇨ New ⇨ Title to create a new title.** In the New Title dialog box that appears, name your title and click OK. Stylize the text as desired.

3. **In the Title Designer, choose Title ⇨ Logo ⇨ Insert Logo.** In the Import Image as Logo dialog box, pick a file to import into the Title drawing area. You can either use one of the logos in the Logo or Texture folder that comes with Premiere Pro, or make your own by using Adobe Illustrator or Adobe Photoshop.

 If you want, you can use the images that appear in Figure 10.12 (SunSurfLogo.png and Waves.bmp). These images are found in the MoreClips folder, inside the Tutorial Projects folder on the DVD that accompanies this book.

TIP   To insert a logo in a text box, double-click the text box with the Selection tool. Then choose Title ⇨ Logo ⇨ Insert Logo into Text.

4. **To change the logo in the drawing area to a different graphic, click the box to the right of Logo Bitmap in the Properties section.** When the dialog box appears, pick a file.

5. **After the logo is in the drawing area, you can move, resize, and rotate it with the Selection tool.** You can also use the Transform commands in the dialog box or the Title menu.

6. **To restore the logo to its original settings, choose Title ⇨ Logo ⇨ Restore Logo Size, or Title ⇨ Logo ⇨ Restore Logo Aspect Ratio.**

Using Templates

Creating titles using preexisting styles and templates can help reduce the time it takes to create a Premiere Pro project. Creating a title using a template is easy. Follow these steps to use a template:

1. **Choose File ⇨ New ⇨ Project to create a new project.**

2. **Choose File ⇨ New ⇨ Title to create a new title.** When the New Title dialog box appears, name your title and click OK.

3. **Choose Title ⇨ Templates.** In the Templates dialog box that appears, pick a template from one of the folders. Then click Apply to apply the template to the drawing area.

You can use the Templates menu in the Templates dialog box to save a title as a template, rename a template, delete a template, and perform other actions. Follow these steps:

1. **Create a new title or open an existing title.**

2. **Choose Title ⇨ Templates.**

3. **Click the triangle in the Templates dialog box to display the Templates menu.**

4. **To save the title that appears onscreen as a template, choose Save as Template.**

5. **To rename or delete a template, click the template you want to change and then choose Rename Template or Delete Template from the Templates menu.**

6. **To import a file as a template, select a file and then choose Import File as Template.**

7. **Click Apply to close the Templates dialog box.**

After the template is in the Title Designer, you can change it to meet your needs. Click and drag over the text in the template with the Type tool to edit the text. If you want, you can also change the style of the text. You can select items in the template with the Selection tool and move them to a new position. You can also change the fill style and color.

Using a Title Created from a Template

In this section, you create a Business Meeting project with two different titles using templates. One title goes at the beginning of the Business Meeting project in the Video 2 track; the other title is at the end of the project, also in the Video 2 track. The first title template is used as an opening screen, which gradually fades out to the first video clip that is in the Video 1 track, and the second title template is used as a closing screen. The second template fades in over the video clip that is in the Video 1 track. Figure 10.13 shows the Premiere Pro Timeline, Project, Effect Controls, and Program Monitor panels for the Business Meeting project. Figure 10.14 shows frames from the Business Meeting project created by using two template titles, two video clips (ArtBeats BG113 and BG117), and a sound clip (SmartSound No Borders).

FIGURE 10.13

The Business Meeting project was created using two template titles, two video clips (ArtBeats BG113 and BG117), and a sound clip (SmartSound No Borders).

Follow these steps to create a project using two titles created from templates:

1. **Choose File ⇨ New ⇨ Project to create a project.** Make sure that you use the proper preset.

2. **Choose File ⇨ New ⇨ Title to create a new title.** When the New Title dialog box appears, name your title and click OK. The Title Designer appears.

3. **Choose Title ⇨ Templates.** In the Templates dialog box that appears, pick a template from one of the folders. For the Business Meeting project, you need to create two titles. The first template is used at the beginning of the project, and the second template is used at the end of the project. Start by creating the first title. The first title in the project has a title at the top and a subtitle at the bottom. Select a template. Click Apply for the template to appear in the drawing area of the Title Designer. Figure 10.15 shows the template that is used for the introduction. The template is the Number_HD_side title template in the Numbers folder, which is in the Corporate folder in the Title Designer Preset folder. The Title Designer Preset folder is located in the User Preset folder.

FIGURE 10.14

Frames from the Business Meeting project. This project is created from two template titles, two video clips (ArtBeats BG113 and BG117), and a sound clip (SmartSound No Borders).

4. **Ensure that the title elements are aligned the way you want.** In this example, everything in the template in Figure 10.16 is flush left, but you want everything to be flush right. Choose Edit ⇨ Select All. Then use the Selection tool to move everything to the right. You may need to individually select separate items to achieve the desired effect.

   Now use the Horizontal Type tool to type the heading **CORPORATE BUSINESS MEETING**. Use the Horizontal Type tool to type the subheads **Budget**, **Income**, **Expenses**, **Marketing**, and **Research**, as shown in Figure 10.16. In order to have the text fit within the drawing area, you might need to reduce the font size of the subtitle text. When you are finished, close the Title Designer. The title appears in the Project panel.

5. **Now that you have created the first title of your project (shown in the Video 2 track in Figure 10.13), create the second title (shown in the Video 2 track in Figure 10.13) by choosing Title ⇨ New Title ⇨ Based on Template.** In the Templates dialog box, select a template. Click OK for the template to appear in the drawing area of the Title Designer. Figure 10.17 shows the template that is chosen for the conclusion. The template is Number_low3 in the Numbers folder, which is in the Corporate folder in the Title Designer Preset folder. The Title Designer Preset folder is located in the User Preset folder.

FIGURE 10.15

The template for the introduction in the Templates dialog box

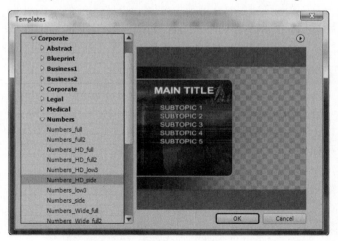

FIGURE 10.16

The template from Figure 10.15 after it is edited

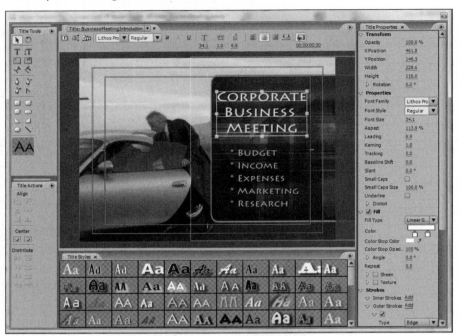

FIGURE 10.17

The template for the conclusion in the Templates dialog box

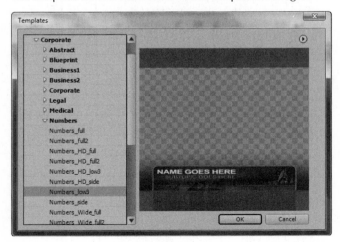

6. **Use the Horizontal Type tool to type a heading.** This example creates the heading CORPORATE BUSINESS MEETING, as shown in Figure 10.18. You may need to reduce the size of the font of the title text. Use the Horizontal Type tool for the subhead. Type a company name and Web site, as shown in Figure 10.18. When you are finished, close the Title Designer. The title appears in the Project panel.

7. **Click and drag the first title you created at the beginning of the Video 2 track, as shown in Figure 10.13.** Then click and drag the second title to the Video 2 track, as shown in Figure 10.13. The end of the second title lines up with the end of the last video clip in the Video 1 track. To extend the title duration, click and drag the end of the title left or right.

TIP Whenever you want to edit a title while you are working in a project, just double-click the title in either the Timeline panel or the Project panel to display the Title Designer.

FIGURE 10.18

The template from Figure 10.17 after it is edited

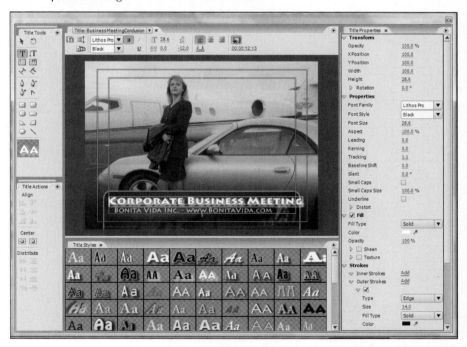

8. **Choose File ⇨ Import to import the video clip that you want to appear at the beginning of the project.** Then import the video clip that you want to appear at the end of the project.

9. **Drag one video clip to the beginning of the Video 1 track and another video clip so that it overlaps the first video clip in the Video 1 track, as shown in Figure 10.13.** This example places ArtBeats BG113 at the beginning of the Video 1 track and ArtBeats BG117 in the Video 1 track so that it overlaps video clip ArtBeats BG113.

10. **In the Effects panel, click the triangle next to the Video Transitions folder.** Click the triangle next to the Dissolve bin (folder), and click the Dither Dissolve transition. Drag the Dither Dissolve transition to the Video 1 track, to where the two video clips overlap.

11. **For a quick preview of the transition, use the Effect Controls panel.** To open the Effect Controls panel (shown in Figure 10.19), choose Window ⇨ Effect Controls. Next, click the transition in the Video 1 track. To preview the transition with the video clips, click the Show Actual Sources check box, and then click the Play the Transition button. You can also use the settings and the Timeline in the Effect Controls panel to edit the transition. For more information on using transitions, turn to Chapter 9.

FIGURE 10.19

The Dither Dissolve transition is used between the two video clips in the Video 1 track.

12. **To fade out the first title into the first video clip, click the first title to select it.** Then click the triangle next to the words *Video* 2 to expand the Video track. Next, click the Show Keyframes icon, and choose Show Opacity Handles. To fade out the title into the first video clip, you have to create two handles (keyframes) at the end of the Opacity line and then drag the last handle (keyframe) downward.

    To create the first handle (keyframe) (shown in Figure 10.13), move the current-time indicator (CTI) to the middle of the title. Then click the Add/Remove Keyframe button to add a handle. To create the last handle (keyframe) (shown in Figure 10.13), move the CTI to the end of the title. Then click the Add/Remove Keyframe button to add a handle. Use the Selection tool to click and drag down the last handle on the Opacity line.

13. **To preview the fade-out from the first title to the first video clip, click and drag the CTI in the Timeline over the areas.**

14. **To gradually fade the last title into the last video clip, you must add two handles at the beginning to the second title's Opacity line.** First, select the last title in the Timeline panel. Move the CTI to the beginning of the second title, and then click the Add/Remove Keyframe button to add the first handle (keyframe). Move the CTI toward the middle of the second title, and then click the Add/Remove Keyframe button to create a second handle (keyframe). Use the Selection tool to click and drag down the first handle (keyframe) on the Opacity line. For more information on fading video clips, turn to Chapter 14.

15. **To preview your project, click the Play button in the Program Monitor panel.**

16. **To add sound to your project, click and drag the sound clip from the Project panel to the Audio 1 track of the Timeline panel.** Then edit the sound so that it ends at the same place that the video and title end. For more information on working with sound clips, refer to Chapter 7.

17. **To build a preview, press Enter.** Press the Play button in the Program Monitor panel to play the project. Choose File ➪ Save to save your project.

Rolling and Crawling Titles

If you are creating production credits or a long sequence of text, you probably want to animate the text so that it scrolls up or down or crawls left or right across the screen. Premiere Pro's Title Designer provides just what you need — it enables you to create smooth, attractive titles that stream across the screen. Follow these steps to create rolling or crawling text:

1. **Create a new project, or load a project.**
2. **Create a new title by choosing File ➪ Title ➪ Default Crawl, or File ➪ Title ➪ Default Roll.** To roll text vertically up or down, choose Default Roll. To make the text crawl across the screen, choose Default Crawl.
3. **In the New Title dialog box, name your title and click OK.** The Title Designer appears.

NOTE   If you want to place a graphic in the background of the scrolling titles, you can choose Title ⇨ Logo ⇨ Insert Logo, or Title ⇨ Logo ⇨ Insert Logo into Text. In Figure 10.20, a template is applied to the background. To add a template to the Title Designer, choose Title ⇨ Templates. In the Templates dialog box, choose a template. This example uses the Tropical List template located in the Tropical folder in the Travel folder. To make room for the title credits, you must delete the list of text.

4. **Select a Type tool.** Position the cursor in the area where you want the titles to appear, and then click. Start typing the text that you want to scroll across the screen. For rolling text, press Enter to add new lines. Figure 10.20 shows rolling text.

5. **Use the techniques described earlier in this chapter to stylize the text that you want to roll or crawl.** If you want to reposition the bounding box, click in the middle and drag it to reposition it onscreen. To resize the box, click one of the four handles and drag with the mouse.

FIGURE 10.20

The Title Designer with rolling text

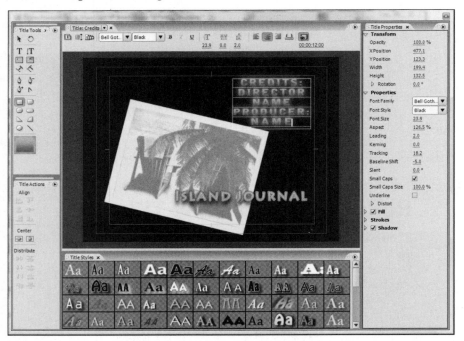

6. **Set the rolling and crawling options by clicking the Roll/Crawl Options icon at the top of the Title panel.** The Roll/Crawl Options dialog box provides the following options to customize the roll or crawl:

   ▪ **Start Off Screen:** Choose this option to have the roll or crawl effect begin with the text off screen.

   ▪ **End Off Screen:** Choose this option to have the roll or crawl effect end with the text off screen.

   ▪ **Preroll:** If you want the text to appear motionless before the animation begins, enter the number of static frames in this field.

   ▪ **Ease-In:** Enter the number of frames that you want to ramp up, or gradually accelerate, until normal playing speed.

   ▪ **Ease-Out:** Enter the number of frames that you want the titles to ramp down, or gradually slow down, to a complete stop.

   ▪ **Postroll:** If you want the text to appear motionless after the animation ends, enter the number of static frames in this field.

7. **Choose a rolling and crawling option from the Roll/Crawl Options dialog box, and click OK to close the dialog box.**

> **NOTE** You can create templates from your rolling and crawling text. To save the rolling or crawling title onscreen as a template, choose Titles ⇨ Templates. In the Templates dialog box, click the triangle to display the Templates menu. Choose Save as Template, and then click Apply to save the title onscreen as a template.

8. **After you create the rolling and crawling title, close the Title Designer.** Notice that the icon for the title in the Project panel is a video clip rather than a still clip. You can preview the rolling and crawling title by clicking the Play button next to the Title preview in the Project panel. To put the rolling or crawling type into action, drag the title from the Project panel to a video track in the Timeline panel.

> **TIP** To save the rolling and crawling text to your hard drive, click the title in the Project panel and choose File ⇨ Export ⇨ Title. In the Save Title dialog box, click Save to save the title file as a PRTL file.

Creating Basic Graphics

Premiere Pro's graphic tools enable you to create simple objects and shapes such as lines, squares, ovals, rectangles, and polygons. You can find these basic graphic tools in the Title Tools panel. They are the Rectangle, Clipped Corner Rectangle, Rounded Corner Rectangle, Wedge, Arc, Ellipse, and Line tools. Follow these steps to create a rectangle, a rounded rectangle, an ellipse, or a line:

> **NOTE** Before you go to step 1, you need to have a project open with a title, and with the Title Designer onscreen.

1. **Select one of Premiere Pro's basic graphic tools, such as the Rectangle, Rounded Rectangle, Ellipse, or Line tool.**

2. **Move the pointer into the Title Designer drawing area where you want to have the shape appear, and click and drag onscreen to create the shape.** To create a perfect square, rounded square, or circle, press the Shift key as you click and drag. To create a line at 45-degree increments, press the Shift key while dragging with the Line tool. Press and hold the Alt key to create a shape from its center out.

3. **As you drag, the shape appears onscreen.** Release the mouse after you finish drawing the shape.

4. **To change a graphic from one shape to another, click the Graphic Type drop-down menu and make a selection.** The Graphic Type drop-down menu is located in the Properties section of the Title Properties panel.

5. **To distort a graphic shape, change the X and Y values in the Distort section.** The Distort section is located below the Graphic Type section.

6. **Click the triangle next to the Distort option to display the X and Y values.** Adjust the X and Y values as needed.

Transforming Graphics

After you create a graphic object or shape in Premiere Pro, you may want to move or resize it. The following sections provide step-by-step instructions on how to move and resize graphic objects or shapes.

Moving graphic objects

To move a graphic object or shape, follow these steps:

1. **Click the Selection tool, and click a graphic object or shape to select it.**

NOTE If you have various shapes that overlap each other onscreen, and you are having difficulty selecting a specific shape, you may want to use one of the Title ⇨ Select commands or the Title ⇨ Arrange commands.

2. **With the Selection tool activated, click and drag the shape to move it.** As you move the shape, notice how the X and Y position changes in the Transform section of the Title Properties panel.

   ■ If you want, you can change the position of a shape by changing either the X position or the Y position in the Transform section of the Designer Type window; you can also use the Title ⇨ Transform ⇨ Position command.

   ■ To center a graphic horizontally, vertically, or in the lower-third section of the Title drawing area, choose one of the Title ⇨ Position commands.

NOTE If you have various shapes selected onscreen and you are having difficulty distributing or aligning them horizontally or vertically, you may want to use one of the Title ⇨ Align Objects commands or the Title ⇨ Distribute Objects commands.

Resizing graphic objects

Follow these steps to resize and rotate a graphic object or shape:

1. **Click the Selection tool.**

2. **Resize the shape by moving the mouse pointer to one of the shape's handles.** When the icon changes to a line with arrows at either end of it, click and drag the shape's handle to enlarge or reduce the shape. As you resize the shape, notice that the X and Y position changes as well as the Width and Height values in the Transform section of the Title Properties panel.

NOTE Pressing and holding the Shift key while resizing a shape with the Selection tool keeps the shape's proportions. Press and hold Alt as you resize with the Selection tool to create a shape from its center out.

3. **If you want, you can change the size of a shape by changing the Width or Height values in the Transform section of the Title Properties panel.** Alternatively, you can use the Title ⇨ Transform ⇨ Scale command.

4. **Rotate the shape by moving the mouse pointer to one of the shape's handles.** When the icon changes to a curved line with arrows at either end of it, click and drag the shape's handle to rotate the shape. As you rotate the shape, notice that the Rotation value changes in the Transform section of the Title Properties panel.

   ▪ There are other ways that you can change the rotation of a shape: You can change the Rotation value in the Transform section of the Title Properties panel; you can select the Title ⇨ Transform ⇨ Rotation command; or you can use the Rotate tool in the toolbox.

Stylizing Graphic Objects

After you have created a graphic object or shape, you may want to change the attributes and stylize it. For example, you can change the fill color, fill style, opacity, stroke, and size, and you can apply a shadow to it. You can also change the shape of a graphic. All of these effects can be changed using the options in the Title Properties panel.

Changing the fill color

Follow these steps to change the fill color of a graphic object or shape:

1. **Use the Selection tool to select the shape you want to change.**

2. **Click the Fill Type drop-down menu, and select a fill style.**

NOTE For more information on selecting a color and fill style, see the section "Using Color."

3. Click the color swatch, and pick a color from Premiere Pro's Color Picker.

4. **If desired, you can change the opacity to make your object translucent.** Decreasing the Opacity value makes your object more translucent.

5. **You can also add a sheen (a highlight) or texture to your object.** Add a sheen by clicking the Sheen check box; add texture by clicking the Texture check box. Then click the triangle next to the Sheen or Texture section to display their options.

Adding a shadow

Follow these steps to add a shadow to your graphic object or shape:

1. Use the Selection tool to select the shape you want to change.

2. **Click to select the Shadow check box.** Then click the triangle next to the check box to expand the Shadow section.

3. **By default, the shadow color is black.** If you want to change the shadow color, click the Shadow Color Swatch to change the color. If you have either a video clip or a graphic in the background of the Title Designer, you can use the Eyedropper tool to change the shadow color to one of the colors in the background. Just click the Eyedropper tool, and then click the color to which you want to change the Shadow Color Swatch.

4. **Use the Size, Distance, and Angle options to customize the magnitude and direction of the shadow.** To soften the edges of the shadow, use the Spread and Opacity options.

5. **To remove the shadow, click to deselect the Shadow check box.**

Applying a stroke

Follow these steps to add a stroke to your graphic object or shape:

1. Select the filled object with the Selection tool.

2. Click the triangle next to Strokes to expand the Strokes section.

3. To add a stroke using the default settings, click Add after the words Inner Strokes or Outer Strokes, or both.

4. To customize the inner stroke or outer stroke, click the triangle next to Inner Stroke and Outer Stroke.

5. Pick a stroke type and size, as well as a fill type and fill color. If you want, you can add a sheen and pattern.

6. To remove a stroke, click to deselect the Inner Stroke or Outer Stroke check box, or both.

Working with the Bezier Tools

Premiere Pro features a Pen tool (as found in Adobe Illustrator), which is a curve-drawing tool that enables you to create freeform shapes with round and corner edges. These freeform polygon shapes are created from anchor points, lines, and curves. You can edit these Bezier shapes by using the Selection tool to move anchor points, or by using the Add Anchor Point or Delete Anchor Point tools to add or delete anchor points. You can also use the Convert Anchor Point tool for rounding the corners of polygons or for making rounded corners into pointed corners. For example, you can transform large triangles into mountains, or many small triangles into waves.

Follow these steps to use the Pen tool to create a line (before continuing, you should have the Title Designer open):

1. **Select the Pen tool.**

2. **Move the Pen tool to the left side of the Title Designer work area, and click the mouse to establish an anchor point.**

3. **To create a straight line, move the Pen tool to the right side of the Title Designer work area.** Press and hold the Shift key as you click the mouse. Now you have two anchor points connected by a straight line.

4. **If you click again, the Pen tool keeps creating anchor points and lines.** To have the Pen tool stop creating anchors, click the Selection tool. If you accidentally create an extra anchor point, you can delete it by selecting it with the Delete Anchor Point tool.

Follow these steps to convert a rectangle into a diamond:

1. **Select the Rectangle tool.**

2. **In the Title Designer drawing area.** Click and drag to create a rectangle.

3. **Notice that the Graphic Type drop-down menu is set to Rectangle**. Change it to Closed Bezier. The rectangle now has four anchor points, one at each corner.

4. **Use the Pen tool to click the anchor points and drag them to convert the rectangle into a diamond.**

5. **To fill the diamond, click the Graphic Type drop-down menu.** Choose Filled Bezier. Then use the Fill options to customize the fill. You can also add a shadow and strokes to the diamond using the Shadow and Stroke options. In Figure 10.21, the diamond is filled with a texture. A stroke and a drop shadow are also added.

6. **After you have finished creating and filling the diamond, you can use the Rotate tool to rotate it, or use the Title ⇨ Transform commands to transform it.** In Figure 10.21, after the diamond is created and rotated, a rectangle is created, filled with a texture, and sent to the background by choosing Title ⇨ Arrange ⇨ Send to Back. Some text is also added.

FIGURE 10.21

A rectangle converted to a diamond shape using the Pen tool

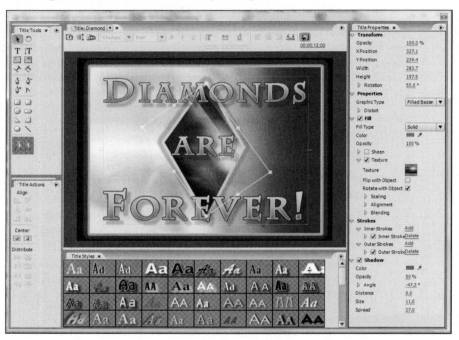

To convert a pointed corner to a rounded corner, follow these steps:

1. **Use the Pen tool to create four small, adjoining, upward-pointing corners, as shown in Figure 10.22.** If you need to, you can use the Pen tool to edit the points so that the points at the top and bottom align.

2. **Select the Convert Anchor Point tool from the toolbox.**

3. **Click and drag the anchor points with the Convert Anchor Point tool to convert a pointed corner to a rounded corner, as shown in Figure 10.22.** Whenever you want to move a point, use the Pen tool. For the background in Figure 10.22, a rectangle is created and filled with a texture.

   You can use the Add Anchor Point, Delete Anchor Point, and Pen tools to transform objects. As shown in Figure 10.23, a rectangle is created in the background and then filled with a texture.

Follow these steps to transform an object:

1. **Start by creating a square using the Rectangle tool.** As you use the Rectangle tool, press and hold Shift to constrain the aspect ratios.

2. **To edit the object, choose Closed Bezier from the Graphic Type drop-down menu.**

3. **To turn the square into a house shape, you need to use the Add Anchor Point tool to add an anchor point in the middle of the top two anchor points.**

4. **Use the Pen tool to drag the anchor point up, as shown in Figure 10.23.**

5. **Now use the Convert Anchor Point tool to click the new anchor point to convert it from a curve anchor point to a corner anchor point.**

6. **To convert the house shape into a triangle (shown in Figure 10.23), use the Delete Anchor Point tool to delete the two anchor points below the newly added anchor point.**

FIGURE 10.22

This path is created from pointed anchor points using the Pen tool, and then converted to rounded anchor points using the Convert Anchor Point tool.

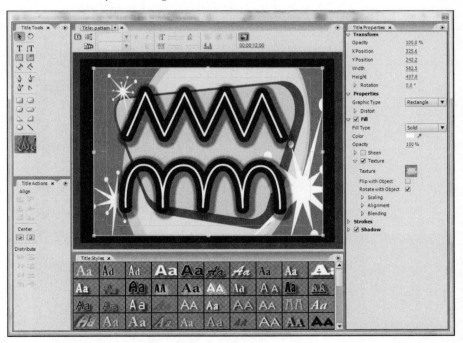

7. **To convert the triangle into a dome shape (shown in Figure 10.23), use the Convert Anchor Point tool to click and drag the point of the triangle to convert it into a rounded anchor point.**

8. **To fill the shape, set the Graphic Type drop-down menu to Filled Bezier.** Then use the Fill, Shadow, and Stroke options to customize the fill.

To create curves with the Pen tool, follow these steps:

1. **Select the Pen tool from the toolbox.**

2. **Move the mouse to the left side of the Title Designer.** Click to establish an anchor point. Don't release the mouse. Instead, drag straight up about one-half inch (shown in Figure 10.24). Then release the mouse. The line that appears above and below the anchor point is called a directional line. The angle and direction at which the directional line is created determines the angle and direction of the curve being created. By extending the anchor point up rather than down, the first part of the curve bump points up rather than down.

FIGURE 10.23

A square is converted into a house shape, and a triangle into a triangle with a rounded point using the Add Anchor Point and Delete Anchor Point tools.

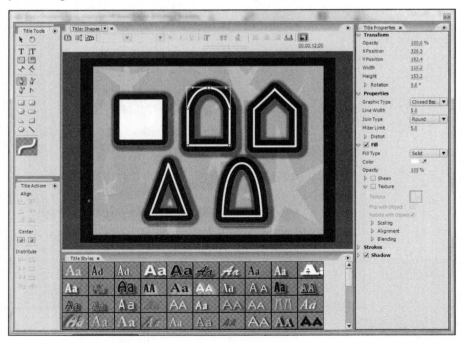

3. **Move the mouse about one-half inch to the right of the anchor point you created in step 2.** Then click and drag straight down about one-half inch. As you drag down, notice that a new directional line appears. Release the mouse to create a curve that has the first part of the curve bump pointing up and the last part of the curve bump pointing down. Congratulations, you have just created your first curve.

4. **If you want, you can edit the curve.** Use the Pen tool to move the curve's directional lines. As you move the directional lines, the curve's shape alters.

5. **To continue drawing curves, move the mouse about one-half inch to the right from the anchor point you created in step 3.** Click and drag straight up about one-half inch to create a curve pointing down.

6. **To draw another curve pointing up, move the mouse about one-half inch to the right of the anchor point you created in step 5.** Then click and drag straight down about one-half inch.

7. **To continue creating curves going down and up, repeat steps 3 and 5.**

FIGURE 10.24

Bezier curves created with the Pen tool

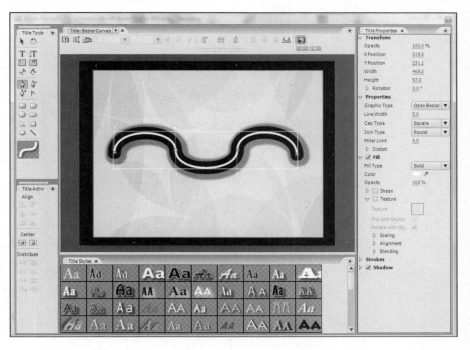

To create curves that connect to line segments, follow these steps:

1. **Select the Pen tool from the toolbox.**

2. **Create a curve using the Pen tool.** Move the mouse to the left side of the Title Designer, and click and drag straight up about one-half inch. Move the mouse about an inch to the right of the anchor point you just created. Then click and drag straight down about one-half inch to create a curve. If you want your curve to point down instead of up, you need to reverse the dragging part of this step. Instead of starting by clicking and dragging up, you start by clicking and dragging down, and you finish by clicking and dragging up.

3. **Connect a line to the curve, as shown in Figure 10.25.** Move the mouse cursor over to the last anchor point you created in step 2. Press and hold Alt/Option (a tiny diagonal line appears at the bottom of the Pen tool icon). Click the anchor point to create a corner point. After you convert the point to a corner point, the shape of the curve may change. To adjust the shape of the curve, click the directional line above the corner point and move it to adjust the curve. To create the line segment, move the mouse pointer about an inch to the right and click the mouse. If you need to adjust the position of the line, use the Pen tool.

FIGURE 10.25

A curve connected to a line segment

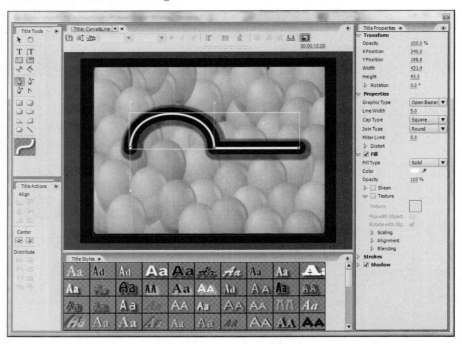

To create lines that connect to curve segments, follow these steps:

1. **If you have the curve and line segment onscreen from the preceding section, click the Selection tool to deselect the curve and line segment.**

2. **Select the Pen tool so that you can create a Bezier outline.**

3. **Use the Pen tool to create a line.** To create a line, click in the middle of the screen, move the mouse over about an inch to the right, and click again. Then press and hold Alt/Option as you click the anchor point, and drag up and to the right to establish a directional line.

4. **To connect a curve to the line you just created (shown in Figure 10.26), move the mouse straight to the right about an inch, and then click and drag down about one-half inch.** The curve you created is pointing up. If you want the curve to point down, make the directional line point down, rather than up; then click and drag up with the mouse, rather than down.

FIGURE 10.26

A line connected to a curve

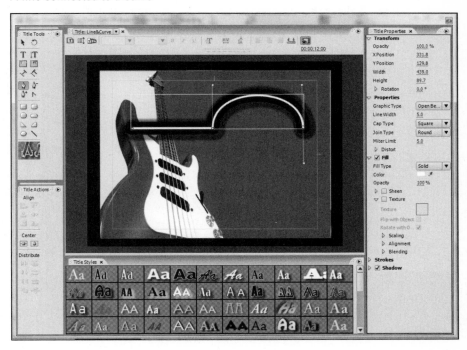

Creating Text on a Bezier Path

You can use the Path Type tool to create text on a path. To use the Path Type tool, you first need to create a path and then begin typing alongside it. Figure 10.27 shows text along a curved path. A rectangle is created in the background, and filled with a Premiere Pro texture.

Follow these steps to use the Path Type tool:

1. **In the Title Designer, select the Path Type tool from the toolbox.**

2. **Use the Path Type tool to create a path.** The Path Type tool creates paths the same way as the Pen tool. To review how to use the Pen tool, go to the preceding section.

3. **If you want to create a curved path and still don't feel confident in creating curves, create a path by using the Path Type tool to create corner anchor points.** Then use the Convert Anchor Point tool to convert the corner anchor points to curve anchor points.

4. **Use the Pen tools to edit the path to the way you want it.**

5. **Switch back to the Path Type tool, and start typing.**

6. **Use a style to stylize your text.** Use the Object Style options to edit the style.

7. **If you want, you can create a shape and then fill it with a texture.** This example creates a rectangle with the Rectangle tool, as shown in Figure 10.27. After you have finished creating the shape, click the triangle next to the Fill option, click the triangle next to the Texture option, and then click the Texture swatch. Locate the Premiere Pro Texture folder, click a texture, and then click Open to apply the texture to the selected shape.

If you want, you can edit the text, stylize it, or apply one of the styles to it. As you edit the text and stylize it, you may find that you need to edit the path.

Creating a Logo

Logos may appear at the beginning, at the end, or throughout a video clip. You can import a logo created in another program or create logos using the Premiere Pro Title Designer. Figure 10.28 shows a Robot Logo project that was created by using Premiere Pro's graphic tools and the Type tools in three different titles: a robot that was created with various graphic tools and filled with a bevel; the background, which was created using the Rectangle tool and then filled with a Premiere Pro texture; and the text.

FIGURE 10.27

Text created along a curved path by using the Path Type tool

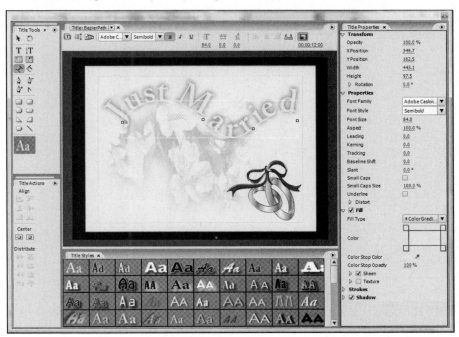

For the Robot Logo project, the background title is placed in the Video 1 track, the robot title is placed in the Video 2 track, and the Text Title is placed in the Video 3 track. The robot and the text are then animated in a 3-D plane using the Basic 3D video effect (found in the Perspective bin). In order to animate the robot and text over time, you can set keyframes for the Swivel, Tilt, and Distance controls of the Basic 3D video effect. Figure 10.29 shows a few frames from the Robot Logo project.

FIGURE 10.28

The panels used to create the Robot Logo project

Follow these steps to create the Robot Logo project:

1. **Choose File ⇨ New ⇨ Project to create a new project.**

2. **Before you create the robot, first create a new title that you will use for the background.** Choose File ⇨ New ⇨ Title to create a new title. In the New Title dialog box, name your title LogoBackground and click OK. The Title Designer appears.

3. **Use the Rectangle tool to create a rectangle in the Title drawing area.** Then fill it with a texture. This example uses Medical Title Bkgd_7.tga, found in the Texture folder of Premiere Pro.

4. **Close the Title Designer, and drag the LogoBackground title to the Video 1 track.** Next, create a robot. Feel free to use the graphic tools to create your own robot or follow the steps below to create the robot shown in Figure 10.28.

5. **Choose File ⇨ New ⇨ Title to create a new title in which you will create your robot.** In the New Title dialog box, name your title RobotLogo and click OK. The Title Designer appears.

FIGURE 10.29

Frames from the Robot Logo project

6. **Use the Clipped Corner Rectangle tool to create the head of the robot.** Press Shift while clicking and dragging to create a perfect circle. Press Alt/Option while clicking and dragging to create a clipped-corner rectangle from the center out.

7. **To fill the clipped-corner rectangle with a bevel, as shown in Figure 10.28, click the triangle next to the Fill option.** Then click the Bevel option from the drop-down menu. Set the shadow color to black and the highlight color to off-white. Next, increase the Balance and Size values and select the Lit option.

8. **Use the Rectangle tool to create the robot's body.**

9. **Use the Rounded Rectangle tool to create the legs.** Create one leg, and then press and hold Shift+Alt/Shift+Option while you drag to create the second leg.

10. **Use the Rounded Rectangle tool to create the arms.** Create one arm, and then press and hold Shift+Alt/Shift+Option while you drag to create the second arm. Use the Rotate tool to rotate the arms.

11. **To give the robot a face, use the Ellipse and Line tools to create the eyes.** Use the Triangle tool to create the nose, and the Rounded Rectangle tool to create the mouth. To create the antennas, you can use the Arch and Line tools. Use the Line tool to create a line between the head and the body, and a line between the body and the legs.

 Use the Title ➪ Arrange commands to shift different shapes forward or backward as needed. Use the Title ➪ Position commands to horizontally and vertically center the geometric pieces.

12. **Close the Title Designer.**

13. **Drag and drop the Robot Title from the Project panel to the Video 2 track in the Timeline panel of the Robot Logo project.** Move the Robot Title to the beginning if you want it to appear there. If not, drag it to the location where you want it. To stretch the logo over time, click and drag the edge of the clip outward.

14. **Choose File ➪ New ➪ Title to create a new title for the text.** In the New Title dialog box, name your title LogoText and click OK. The Title Designer appears.

15. **Use the Vertical Type tool to create the text.** Set the attributes and color. This example uses the Rosewood Black 100 style to stylize the text.

16. **Close the Title Designer.**

17. **Drag the LogoText Title to the Video 3 track.**

18. **Drag the Basic 3D video effect to the Video 2 and Video 3 tracks.** Use the Effect Controls panel to animate the robot and the text using the Basic 3D video effect. For more information on using video effects, turn to Chapter 13.

19. **To preview the robot logo in the Robot Logo project, display the Program Monitor panel (Window ➪ Program Monitor ➪ Sequence).** Click the Play button to view the preview.

 If you want, you can import a sound to use in the Audio 1 track.

20. **Choose File ➪ Save to save the changes to the Robot Logo project to your hard drive.**

Summary

Premiere Pro's Title Designer provides an easy-to-use interface for creating digital video titles. By using the Title Designer, you can quickly create text and graphics to introduce video segments or to roll your final credits. This chapter covered the following topics:

- Using the tools in the Title Tools panel to create text and graphics.
- Editing object attributes by using the Title menu or the options in the Title Properties panel.
- Dragging titles from the Project panel to the Timeline panel.
- Creating titles using styles, templates, and logos.
- Creating rolling and crawling text by using the Rolling and Crawling options.
- Creating graphics using the Title Designer.

Chapter 11

Creating Type and Graphic Effects with Photoshop and Illustrator

A dobe Premiere Pro packs enormous power as a digital video production tool. However, if you're creating a sophisticated project, designed to appeal to and impress viewers, you may need to turn to other applications to create your text and graphics. During the course of production, many Premiere Pro producers turn to such graphics applications as Adobe Photoshop and Adobe Illustrator to create eye-catching text and graphics.

This chapter provides several tutorials to teach you how to create text and graphic effects in Adobe Photoshop and Adobe Illustrator. After you see how to create the graphic effects, you integrate them into Premiere Pro projects. Once your graphics are loaded into Premiere Pro, you can use Premiere Pro's effects to create some digital magic.

IN THIS CHAPTER

Creating and importing graphics from Adobe Photoshop

Using Premiere Pro to animate Adobe Illustrator type and graphics

Creating and Importing Graphics from Adobe Photoshop

Adobe Photoshop is one of the most powerful digital imaging programs available for both PCs and Macs. Photoshop easily surpasses Premiere Pro in its capability to create and manipulate graphics. For example, by using Photoshop, you can create three-dimensional text or grab a piece of text or graphics and bend, twist, or skew it. Because both Premiere Pro and Photoshop belong to the Adobe family of graphics products, it's not surprising that you can create graphics, text, or photomontages in Photoshop and then import them to use as titles and backgrounds in Premiere Pro.

You can also create your Photoshop titles, graphics, or backgrounds from within a Premiere Pro project by choosing File ➪ New ➪ Photoshop File.

This launches Photoshop and creates a new Photoshop file that will appear in your Premiere Pro project. You can also create a Photoshop file from within Adobe After Effects by choosing File ➪ New ➪ Photoshop File. Premiere Pro and After Effects files (in the Project panel) or tracks (in the Timeline panel) can be copied back and forth.

You can use Photoshop's layers to output a Sequence file, and then import the file into Premiere Pro to create either an animation or presentation project. You can also use Photoshop's layers and Animation palette to create an animation from the individual layers, and then export the animation as a QuickTime or AVI movie. After you create a QuickTime or AVI movie, you can import the file into Premiere Pro to add sound and make a slide show presentation. In Photoshop CS3 Extended, you can open a movie that you have made in either Premiere Pro or After Effects and edit it using filters, add type and graphics, and take advantage of other useful Photoshop features. For more information on using Photoshop, turn to Chapter 28. For more information on using Photoshop for retouching movies, turn to Chapter 17. For more information on using Photoshop for creating background mattes, turn to Chapter 15. For more information on using After Effects, turn to Chapters 30, 31, and 32.

Creating a Photoshop layer file to animate with Premiere Pro

You can use Adobe Photoshop to create a layered file and then import the layered file into Premiere Pro to create an animation or presentation. Figure 11.1 shows a Photoshop file with a background layer and five other layers. In this example, the Photoshop layer file is imported into Premiere Pro for animating. (You can also animate using the Photoshop CS3 Extended Animation palette.) The following steps show you how to create a Photoshop layer file for use in Premiere Pro.

 For more information on using Photoshop CS3 Extended for animating, turn to Chapter 28.

1. **Launch Adobe Photoshop, and choose File ➪ New.**

2. **In the New dialog box, name your file.** Because you will probably import this file into a Premiere Pro project, click the Preset drop-down menu and choose Film & Video. Next, click the Size drop-down menu and select an option, such as NTSC DV. Click OK to create the file.

3. **In Figure 11.1, the background layer is left white.** All of the graphics and text are created in separate layers. You can create a new layer in one of these ways: you can click the Create New Layer icon at the bottom of the Layers palette; you can choose New Layer from the Layer menu; or you can choose Layer ➪ New ➪ Layer.

 At any time, you can double-click the layer name in the Layers palette to rename it.

FIGURE 11.1

You can import a Photoshop layer file in Premiere Pro as a Sequence file so that you can animate the individual layers.

4. **To create a graphic in the new layer, you can use the Selection tools, Pen tool, or Shape tool.** The example in Figure 11.1 uses the Custom Shape tool to create the umbrella. Before you create the umbrella, first pick a Foreground color. Then click the Custom Shape tool and make sure that the Shape Layers option is selected in the toolbar at the top of the screen, as shown in Figure 11.2. Click to display the Shape drop-down menu and choose Umbrella. To create the umbrella, click and drag toward the bottom of the drawing area. The umbrella is created.

FIGURE 11.2

The Custom Shape tool allows you to create shape layers.

5. **Now you are ready to create some text.** Select the Horizontal Type tool from the tool-box. Then choose a font and size (this example uses the font Mufferaw with a font size of 24) by using either the Character palette or the options on the Type tab. Pick a color. You can change the color by using the Type bar, the Colors palette, or the Swatches palette. Use the Horizontal Type tool to create the text BRING YOUR UMBRELLA.

6. **To move the text onscreen, use the Move tool.**

7. **Now you are ready to create some warped, beveled type, as shown in Figure 11.1.** Select the Horizontal Type tool from the toolbox. Select a font, size, and color, and then type **It's Raining**. This example uses the font Kristen ITC with a font size of 44 points. To warp the text, click the Warp button in the Type bar. In the Warp Text dialog box, shown in Figure 11.3, select a warp option to warp the text. Then click OK to close the dialog box and apply the effect.

   To bevel the text and add a drop shadow, choose Layer ⇨ Layer Style ⇨ Blending Options to stylize your text. In the Layer Style dialog box, click the style you want and then customize it. Figure 11.4 shows the Layer Style dialog box with the settings that were used to create the text shown in Figure 11.1.

   The effects applied in Figure 11.1 include a drop shadow, an inner shadow, a bevel and emboss with contour and texture, and a 1-pixel black stroke.

FIGURE 11.3

Photoshop's Warp Text dialog box allows you to warp type.

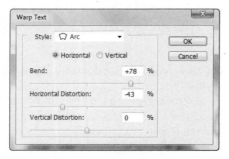

8. **Create two new layers in which to create graphic shapes using paths.** Call one layer Clouds and the other layer WaterDrops. The example in Figure 11.1 uses the Custom Shape tool to create paths for the clouds, and a path for the raindrops. The clouds and the raindrops are created in separate layers. The Clouds layer should be above the WaterDrops layer.

9. **Now you are ready to create shapes from paths.** To create a Raindrop path, click the Custom Shape tool and make sure the Paths option is selected in the toolbar at the top of the screen, as shown in Figure 11.5. Click to display the Shape drop-down menu and choose Raindrop. Click and drag in the drawing area.

A path of a raindrop appears onscreen and in the Paths palette, as shown in Figure 11.6. To save and name your path, double-click Work Path in the Paths palette. In the Save Path dialog box that appears, name your path Raindrops (see Figure 11.7). Then click OK.

FIGURE 11.4

The Layer Style dialog box in Photoshop allows you to bevel and emboss text, as well as add a drop shadow and a stroke.

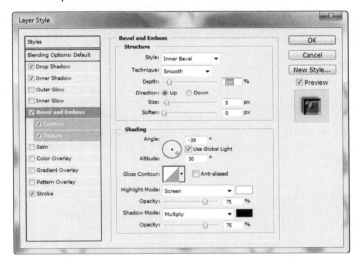

FIGURE 11.5

The Custom Shape tool allows you to create paths.

FIGURE 11.6

You can use the Custom Shape tool to create water drop paths in the drawing area, which appear in the Paths palette.

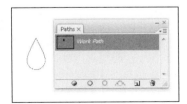

The Save Path dialog box allows you to save and name your path.

10. **To fill a path, you must first select it in the Paths palette.** Then choose Make Selection from the Paths menu. In the Make Selection dialog box that appears (shown in Figure 11.8), you can enter a Feather value. This gives the fill soft rather than hard edges. Because the raindrop selection is small, you should enter a small Feather value, such as 2.

Click OK to make the selection. Now set the Foreground color to the color you want to fill the raindrop. Then choose Edit ➪ Fill. In the Fill dialog box, shown in Figure 11.9, select Foreground Color in the Use drop-down menu. Leave the Mode drop-down menu to Normal unless you want to create a special effect and use another mode. Leave the Opacity at 100 percent unless you want to make the fill transparent. Click OK to fill the selection.

NOTE   You can export a path from Photoshop to Illustrator by choosing File ➪ Export ➪ Paths to Illustrator. In the Export Paths dialog box, click the Paths drop-down menu to select the path that you want to export, or choose All Paths to export all of the paths. Then click Save to export the path as an Illustrator file. To open the exported path in Illustrator, choose File ➪ Open. In the Open dialog box, locate the file and then click Open. In Illustrator, use the Selection tool to select the path. To fill or stroke the path, use the Color palette (Window ➪ Color). If you want to make the object 3-D, choose Effect ➪ 3D ➪ Extrude & Bevel. Use the options in the Extrude & Bevel dialog box to make your object 3-D, and then click OK.

The Make Selection dialog box allows you to specify a Feather Radius value for your selection.

11. **You can use the Raindrop path that you have created to add raindrops to the Raindrop layer that you have made.** With the Rectangular Marquee tool, select the rain-drop and move it to a place where you want to create a new raindrop. To fill the selection, choose Edit ➪ Fill. Click OK in the Fill dialog box to fill the raindrop selection. To add a stroke to a raindrop selection, choose Edit ➪ Stroke. In the Stroke dialog box, shown in Figure 11.10, enter a value for the Width field. Use a small number such as one. Choose a stroke location. Set the Mode to Normal and the Opacity to 100 percent. Click OK to stroke the selection.

FIGURE 11.9

The Fill dialog box allows you to fill a selection with the Foreground color.

FIGURE 11.10

The Stroke dialog box allows you to add a stroke to a selection with the Foreground color.

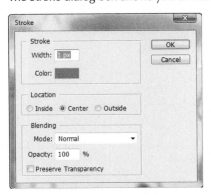

12. **Repeat step 11 to add more raindrops.**

13. **To create the clouds, first click the Clouds layer in the Layers palette.** Then deselect any paths in the Paths palette. Next, click the Custom Shape tool and make sure that the Paths option is selected in the toolbar at the top of the screen, as shown in Figure 11.5. Then click the Shape drop-down menu and choose Cloud 1. To create a cloud path, click and drag in the top-left side of the drawing area.

    A path of a cloud appears onscreen and in the Paths palette, as shown in Figure 11.11. Click and drag to the right of the path cloud to create a second path cloud. To save and name your cloud path, double-click Work Path in the Paths palette. In the Save Path dialog box that appears, name your path Clouds. Then click OK.

14. **To fill the cloud paths, choose Make Selection from the Paths palette.** In the Make Selection dialog box, enter a feather radius of four or five. Then click OK to make the cloud selections. Use the Gradient tool to fill the clouds.

15. **Choose File ⇨ Save to save the file in Photoshop format.** Photoshop format saves a file with all of its layers.

FIGURE 11.11

The Custom Shape tool can be used to create paths in the drawing area, which appear in the Paths palette.

Importing a Photoshop layer file into Premiere Pro as a Sequence file for animation

After you have created graphics and text in various Photoshop layers and saved the file in Photoshop format, you are ready to transform the Photoshop layers into a digital movie. Follow these steps:

1. **Launch Premiere Pro.** Then choose File ➪ Import. In the Import dialog box that appears, locate the Photoshop layer file and click Open. In the Import Layered File dialog box (shown in Figure 11.12), set the Import As drop-down menu to Sequence. Click OK to import the Photoshop file as a Sequence file.

FIGURE 11.12

The Import Layered File dialog box allows you to import the It'sRaining Photoshop file with layers as a Sequence file, merge all of the layers, or choose a layer.

2. **The ItsRaining layers appear in a folder in Premiere Pro's Project panel.** Click the triangle in front of the ItsRaining folder to open it. Notice that the Photoshop layers appear along with an ItsRaining sequence. By placing each item on a separate layer, the background transparent areas in Photoshop are automatically read as transparent areas in Premiere Pro.

3. **To place each Photoshop layer in a video track in the Timeline panel, double-click the Sequence file in the ItsRaining folder.** Figure 11.13 shows the Photoshop layers in video tracks in the Timeline panel.

4. **To animate the raindrops, click the WaterDrops video track to activate it.** Next, click the triangle beside the word *Motion* in the Effect Controls panel. In the Effect Controls panel, move the current-time indicator (CTI) to the beginning of the WaterDrops clip. Now, click the stopwatch icon beside the word *Position* to set a keyframe. To create a second keyframe, move the CTI to the right, and then click the word *Motion* and move the raindrops in the Program Monitor panel down a little. Notice that a second keyframe is created. To create a third keyframe, move the CTI to the right one more time. Then move the raindrops farther down in the Program Monitor. A third keyframe is created, as shown in Figure 11.13.

NOTE For more information on using the Motion effect in the Effect Controls panel to animate, turn to Chapter 16.

5. **Click the Play button in the Program Monitor panel to preview the raindrop animation.**

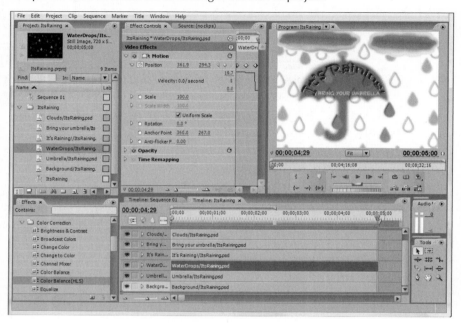

FIGURE 11.13

The panels used to create the ItsRaining Premiere Pro project.

6. **In the ItsRaindrop Premiere Pro project, the Bring your Umbrella text is also ani-mated**. You can animate the color of the text by using the Color Balance (HLS) video effect (found in the Color Correcting bin). To use the effect, drag it over the Bring your Umbrella video track in the Timeline panel. Next, click the triangle in front of the Color Balance (HLS) effect in the Effect Controls panel. In the Effect Controls panel, move the CTI to the beginning of the Bring your Umbrella clip. Now, click the stopwatch icon beside the word *Hue* to set a keyframe.

To create a second keyframe, move the CTI to the right, and then click the Hue value and drag to the right. Notice that a second keyframe is created. To create a third keyframe, move the CTI to the right one more time. Then click and drag the Hue value to the right some more. A third keyframe is created. If you like, you can create more keyframes.

7. **Click the Play button in the Program Monitor panel to preview the Bring your Umbrella animation.**

8. **To add sound, choose File ➪ Import.** In the Import dialog box, locate a sound clip and click Open to import the clip into the Project panel. Drag the sound clip from the Project panel to the Audio 1 track of the Timeline panel. If the sound clip is too long, click the end of the sound clip and drag left.

CROSS-REF For more information on working with sound clips, see Chapters 7 and 8.

9. **Choose File ⇨ Save to save your Premiere Pro project.** To output your project as a movie, choose File ⇨ Export ⇨ Movie.

CROSS-REF For more information on exporting a Premiere Pro project as a movie, see Chapter 18.

Using Premiere Pro to Animate Adobe Illustrator Type and Graphics

Adobe Illustrator is known as a powerful digital drawing tool. By using Adobe Illustrator, you can create precision drawings and type effects. After creating graphics in Illustrator, you can apply effects and filters to distort them or to make them 3-D. You can also import them into Premiere Pro. (If you prefer, you can import or copy and paste the graphics into Photoshop first, apply more filters, and then import into Premiere Pro.) This project (LasVegasTrip) shows you how to create 3-D text and graphics in Illustrator and then import them into a Premiere Pro project for a slide show presentation. The Illustrator palettes for the LasVegasTrip project are shown in Figure 11.14. Figure 11.15 shows the Premiere Pro panels for the LasVegasTrip project.

FIGURE 11.14

The palettes used to create the LasVegasTrip Illustrator project

FIGURE 11.15

The panels used to create the LasVegasTrip Premiere Pro project

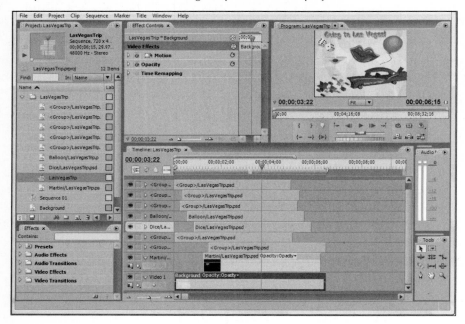

Creating graphics and text using layers in Illustrator

To get the Illustrator file ready for Premiere Pro, you can create text and graphics in separate layers. That way, when you import the Illustrator file into Premiere Pro, the layers can easily be converted into separate video tracks.

 **For more information on using Adobe Illustrator, turn to Chapter 29.**

Follow these steps to create the graphics and text for the LasVegasTrip Illustrator project (shown in Figure 11.14):

1. **Create a new file in Illustrator by choosing File ➪ New.** In the New Document dialog box, name your document in the Name field. Then click the New Document Profile drop-down menu and choose Basic RGB. Click OK to create a new document.

2. **The Layers palette should be onscreen.** To display it, choose Window ➪ Layers. Note that the Layers palette appears with one layer called Layer 1, as shown in Figure 11.16. Anything you do in the drawing area is added to Layer 1. Make sure that every item in your document is created on a separate layer. That way, each layer can be placed in a separate video track in Premiere Pro. To have separate items in separate layers, you need to

create new layers. If you accidentally make two objects in one layer, you should cut and paste one of the objects into a new layer.

3. **To add a new layer, choose New Layer from the Layers palette menu.** When the Layer Options dialog box appears, you can name the layer. If you don't want to name the layer, click OK to create a new layer. You can always rename a layer.

The Layers palette with Layer 1

4. **To name your layer, double-click the layer name in the Layers palette.** In the Layer Options dialog box that appears, enter a name in the Name field and click OK.

5. **Use the Symbols palette to create 3-D graphics.** Choose Window ➪ Symbols Libraries ➪ 3D Symbols to display the 3D Symbols library palette, shown in Figure 11.17. Click a 3-D symbol and drag it to the drawing area of your document. The example shown in Figure 11.14 uses the Dice 3D symbol. Now you have a 3-D symbol in the drawing area of your project and in Layer 1 of the Layers palette.

The 3D Symbols library

6. **You can add a 2-D graphic to the drawing area using some of the other symbols libraries.** Choose Window ➪ Symbols Libraries, and then select a library. The example in Figure 11.14 uses the Balloon 3 and Confetti symbols from the Celebration Symbols library (shown in Figure 11.18); the Lips symbol from the Retro Symbols library (shown in Figure 11.19); and the Automobile and the Martini symbols from the Tiki Symbols Library (shown in Figure 11.20). Note that each graphic is created in a separate layer (shown in Figure 11.14).

FIGURE 11.18

The Celebration Symbols library

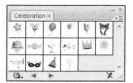

FIGURE 11.19

The Retro Symbols library

FIGURE 11.20

The Tiki Symbols library

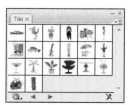

7. **You can rearrange the items in the layers.** This moves different items to the front or the back by moving them up and down in the Layers palette.

8. **To add text to your document, click the Type tool.** Then select a font, font size, and color. Next, move the Type tool to the drawing area of your document and start typing. To stylize the text, click and drag to select it, then stylize it.

   The example shown in Figure 11.14 adds text twice: once at the top of the document and again at the bottom of the document (on top of the car). The second time the text is created, the font size is reduced and the text is rotated. Each text block is created in a separate layer. That way, they can be moved separately.

9. **To make your text 3-D (as shown at the top of the drawing area in Figure 11.14), select the text and then choose Effect ⇨ 3D ⇨ Extrude & Bevel.** In the 3D Extrude & Bevel Options dialog box, click the Preview check box. Then click the 3-D cube in the dialog box and move it to the position where you want your 3-D object. To change the depth of your 3-D object, click the Extrude Depth value and make a selection. Click OK to convert your 2-D text to 3-D. Figure 11.21 shows the 3D Extrude & Bevel Options dialog box, along with a preview of the text being extruded.

CROSS-REF Turn to Chapter 13 to learn how to use the Effect ⇨ 3D ⇨ Revolve command to create a 3-D trophy.

FIGURE 11.21

The 3D Extrude & Bevel Options dialog box allows you to turn 2-D text and graphics into 3-D by extruding and beveling them.

10. **To make your 2-D graphics 3-D, select a graphic object and then choose Effect ⇨ 3D ⇨ Extrude & Bevel.** In the 3D Extrude & Bevel Options dialog box, click the Preview check box. Then click the 3-D cube in the dialog box and move it to the position where you want your 3-D object. To change the depth of your 3-D object, click the Extrude Depth value and make a selection. Click OK to convert your 2-D graphic to 3-D.

11. **Choose File ⇨ Save.** Save your work in Adobe Illustrator format.

12. **Choose File ⇨ Export.** Export your work in Photoshop format to save the file with layers. In the Photoshop Export Options dialog box, set the resolution to Screen and make sure that the Write Layers option is selected. This way, the layer information is saved with the document. Click OK to export your Illustrator file as a Photoshop file with layers. You should now have two versions of the LasVegasTrip file: one in Illustrator file format and the other in Photoshop file format.

Animating the LasVegasTrip project using Premiere Pro

After you have used Illustrator to create graphics and text in separate layers, you are ready to transform your Illustrator layers into a digital slide show using Premiere Pro. Follow these steps:

1. **Launch Premiere Pro.** Then choose File ⇨ Import. In the Import dialog box that appears, locate the Illustrator layer file that you exported as a Photoshop file. Click Open. In the Import Layered File dialog box, shown in Figure 11.22, set the Import As drop-down menu to Sequence. Click OK to import the Photoshop file as a Sequence file.

 The Illustrator LasVegasTrip file, shown in Figure 11.14, is found in the MoreClips folder of the DVD that accompanies this book.

FIGURE 11.22

The Import Layered File dialog box allows you to choose to import the LasVegasTrip file with layers as a Sequence file, merge all of the layers, or select a layer.

2. **The LasVegasTrip layers appear in a folder in Premiere Pro's Project panel.** Click the triangle beside the LasVegasTrip folder to open it. Notice that all of the layers appear along with a LasVegasTrip sequence. By placing each item on a separate layer, the background transparent areas in Photoshop and Illustrator are automatically read as transparent areas in Premiere Pro.

3. **To place each layer in a video track in the Timeline panel, double-click the Sequence file in the LasVegasTrip folder.** Figure 11.15 shows the layers in video tracks in the Timeline panel.

4. **Move the layers in the video tracks so that the objects start at different times, as shown in Figure 11.15.**

5. **Click the Play button in the Program Monitor panel to preview the LasVegasTrip animation.**

6. **If you want, you can set keyframes with the Motion effect to move an object over time.** You set keyframes and use the Basic 3D video effect (found in the Perspective bin) to move an object in a 3-D plane. The LasVegasTrip example animates the 3-D dice and text.

7. **Create a new track before the first video track to use it as a background for the LasVegasTrip project.** Choose Sequence ⇨ Add Tracks. In the Add Tracks dialog box (shown in Figure 11.23), click the Placement drop-down menu and choose Before First Track. Click OK to add the video track.

FIGURE 11.23

The Add Tracks dialog box allows you to add a video or sound track either before or after the tracks in the Timeline panel.

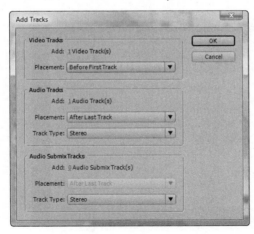

8. **You can import a video clip to use in the Video 1 track for the background, import a graphic file from Photoshop or Illustrator.** Alternatively, you can use the Title Designer to create a background, as in this example.

   To use the Title Designer, choose File ➪ New ➪ Title. In the New Title dialog box that appears, name the title *Background*. Click OK to display the Title Designer. Use the Rectangle tool to create a rectangle in the drawing area of the Title panel. Fill the rectangle with a texture. This example uses Premiere Pro's 1080_presents_bkg.png texture. Close the Title Designer and drag the title to the Video 1 track. The title should extend the entire length of the clip. Figure 11.24 shows the Title Designer with the rectangle and texture that are used to create the background for the LasVegasTrip Premiere Pro project.

9. **To add sound, choose File ➪ Import.** In the Import dialog box, locate a sound clip and click Open to import the clip into the Project panel. Drag the sound clip from the Project panel to the Audio 1 track of the Timeline panel. If the sound clip is too long, click the end of the sound clip and drag left. For more information on working with sound clips, see Chapters 7 and 8.

10. **Choose File ➪ Save to save your Premiere Pro project.** To output your project as a movie, choose File ➪ Export ➪ Movie. For more information on exporting a Premiere Pro project as a movie, see Chapter 18.

FIGURE 11.24

You can use Premiere Pro's Title Designer to create a background for a Premiere Pro project.

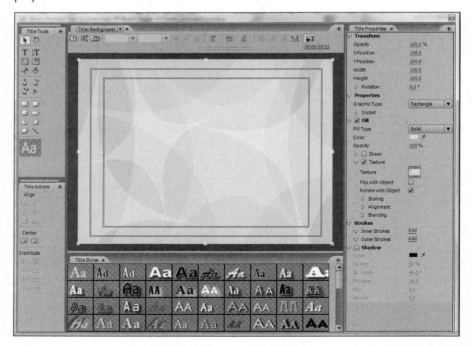

Summary

To create the most attractive and elaborate text and graphics effects, you may need to use the digital power of such programs as Adobe Photoshop and Adobe Illustrator in conjunction with Premiere Pro. This chapter covered these topics:

- Both Photoshop and Illustrator provide excellent text and graphic features that you can use in conjunction with Premiere Pro.
- Premiere Pro successfully interprets Photoshop layers into video tracks.
- Background transparent areas in Photoshop and Illustrator are automatically read as transparent areas (alpha channel masks) in Premiere Pro.
- You can create a variety of different transparency effects using Premiere Pro and Photoshop or Illustrator.

Part IV

Advanced Techniques and Special Effects

Chapter 12

Working with Advanced Editing Techniques

Premiere Pro is so versatile that you can create and edit an entire project using little more than Premiere Pro's Selection tool. However, if you need to make precise edits, you should explore Premiere Pro's advanced editing functions. For example, Premiere Pro's Trim panel enables you to shave one frame at a time from the in or out point of a clip by simply clicking the mouse. As you click, you can see the last frame of one out point in one side of the monitor, and the first frame of the adjacent in point in another side of the monitor.

Premiere Pro also enables you to create sophisticated three-point edits where you can specify an in or out point to maintain in a source clip, and an in and out point for placement in your program. When you perform the edit, Premiere Pro calculates the precise section of the source clip to overlay into your program material.

This chapter provides a guide to Premiere Pro's intermediate and advanced editing features. It starts with a look at some basic editing utilities, such as copying and pasting clip attributes, and then proceeds to discuss Premiere Pro's tool panel editing tools — the Ripple Edit, Rolling Edit, Slip, and Slide tools. The chapter continues with a look at three-point and four-point editing, how to trim using the Trim Monitor, and how to edit using the Multi-Camera Monitor. This chapter is designed to enable you to quickly move from subject to subject so that you can learn or review editing features and immediately put them to use.

Editing Utilities

From time to time, you may want to edit by simply copying clips from one section and pasting them into another. To aid in editing, you may want to unlink audio from video. This section provides a review of several different commands that can aid you as you edit your production. It starts with a discussion of the History panel, which enables you to quickly undo different stages of your work.

Undoing edits with the History panel

Even the best editors change their minds and make mistakes. Traditional non-linear editing systems enable you to preview edits before actually recording the source material onto the program videotape. However, traditional editing systems can't provide as many levels of undo as Premiere Pro's History panel, shown in Figure 12.1.

FIGURE 12.1

The History panel

As discussed in Chapter 1, the History panel records your editing activity while using Premiere Pro. Each step appears as a separate entry in the History panel. If you want to return to a previous step, you can simply click it in the History panel to return to it. When you go forward with your work, the previously recorded steps (after the step you returned to) disappear.

If the History panel is not open onscreen, you can open it by choosing Window ➪ History. To see how the History panel works, open a new or existing project, and drag several clips to the Timeline. As you drag, watch how the states are recorded in the History panel. Now select one of the clips in the Timeline, and delete it by pressing Delete. Then delete another clip. Again, note how each state is recorded in the panel.

Now assume that you want to return the project to the state it was in before you deleted any clips. Just click in the History panel to the left of the first Delete state in the panel. The project returns to its state before any of the deletions. Now move one of the clips in the Timeline using the Selection tool. As soon as you move the clip, a new state is recorded in the History panel, removing the second Delete state from the History panel. After you return to one state in the History panel and begin to work, you can't go forward again.

Cutting and pasting clips

If you have ever used a word processor to edit text, you know that one of the easiest ways to rearrange your work is to copy and paste from one part of the text to another. In Premiere Pro, you can easily copy and paste, or cut and paste, a clip from one part of the Timeline panel to another. In fact, Premiere Pro provides three paste commands — Paste, Paste to Fit, and Paste Attributes.

Splitting a clip with the Razor and Multiple Razor tools

 Before copying and pasting or moving a clip, you may want to splice it into two pieces and paste or move only a portion of the clip. An easy way to splice a clip is to use Premiere Pro's Razor tool. One click of the Razor tool splits a clip into two pieces. If you need to slice more than one track, press Shift while clicking the Razor tool. Follow these steps to use the Razor tool:

1. **If you want to splice one clip in one unlocked track into two pieces, select the Razor tool.** If you want to split all unlocked tracks into two separate pieces, press and hold the Shift key (the Razor tool icon changes to show two razors). To slice video without audio, or vice versa, press Alt/Option.

 **Press C to activate the Razor tool.**

2. **Move the current-time indicator (CTI) to the frame where you want to create a cut.**

3. **In the sequence that you want to edit, click the clip to cut it with the Razor tool, as shown in Figure 12.2.** (You can also choose Sequence ➪ Razor at Current Time Indicator.) After you click with the Razor tool, you can move the cut portion of the clip independently of the rest of the clip.

FIGURE 12.2

Cutting with either the Razor or Multiple Razor tool splits the clip into two sections.

Pasting clips

After you have split a clip, you may want to copy and paste it or cut and paste it to another location in the Timeline.

If the area into which you want to paste the clip already has clips within it, you can use Premiere Pro's Paste, Paste Insert, or Paste Attributes command. Premiere Pro's Paste command pastes a clip over any clip at the CTI position; the Paste Insert command inserts the pasted clip in a Timeline gap; and the Paste Attributes command copies the motion, opacity, volume, and color settings of one clip into another clip.

Using Paste to overlay clips

Premiere Pro's Paste command enables you to paste clips into gaps in the Timeline. It also provides options for how you want the inserted clips to fit within your production. Follow these steps to paste a clip so that it overlays or replaces clips in the current sequence in the Timeline:

1. **Select the clip or clips that you want to copy or paste.**
2. **Choose Edit ➪ Cut or Edit ➪ Copy.**
3. **Move the CTI to where you want to overlay the clip or clips.**
4. **Select the target track by clicking the track header (left end of the track).**
5. **Choose Edit ➪ Paste.** Premiere Pro drops the new material over any clip at the CTI.

Using Paste Insert to insert clips

Premiere Pro's Paste Insert command enables you to paste clips into gaps in the Timeline. It also provides options for inserting clips to fit within your production. Follow these steps to use Paste Insert to insert a clip:

1. **Select the clip or clips that you want to copy or paste.**
2. **Choose Edit ➪ Cut or Edit ➪ Copy.**
3. **Move the CTI to where you want to insert the clip or clips.**
4. **Select the target track by clicking the track header (left end of the track).**
5. **Choose Edit ➪ Paste Insert.** Premiere Pro drops the clip at the CTI and pushes all subsequent clips to the right.

Using Paste Attributes

Premiere Pro's Paste Attributes command allows you to copy one clip's attributes and apply them to another clip. For example, using Paste Attributes, you can copy the color settings, opacity, volume, and effects of one clip and apply them to another. To use the Paste Attributes command, follow these steps:

1. **Select the clip or clips that that have the attributes that you want to copy.**
2. **Choose Edit ➪ Cut or Edit ➪ Copy.**

3. Select one or more clips.

4. Choose Edit ⇨ Paste Attributes.

Removing sequence gaps

During the course of editing, you may purposely or inadvertently leave gaps in the Timeline. Sometimes the gaps aren't even visible because of the zoom level in the Timeline panel. Here is how to automatically remove a gap in the Timeline:

1. **Right-click the mouse in the gap in the Timeline.** You may need to zoom in to see small gaps.

2. **Choose Ripple Delete from the drop-down menu that appears in the sequence, as shown in Figure 12.3.** Premiere Pro removes the gap.

FIGURE 12.3

Right-click and choose Ripple Delete to remove gaps.

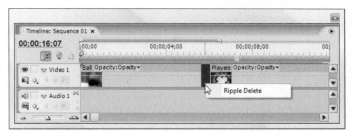

Unlinking and linking audio and video

While performing video edits, you may want to create audio effects where the audio from one clip plays over the next video clip (called a *split edit*). Although editing the video is a simple process, you may find that you need to *unlink* the audio from the video to create the effect you want.

When you capture video using the Premiere Pro Capture command, Premiere Pro links the video information to the audio. This relationship is evident as you work. When you drag a clip to the Timeline, its audio automatically appears in an audio track. When you move the video, the audio moves with it. If you delete the video from the track, the audio is deleted. However, during editing, you may want to separate the video from its audio to create effects or to replace the audio altogether.

TIP If you are trying to sync audio to video, viewing the audio's waveform in the audio track is helpful. To view the waveform, expand the audio track by clicking the triangle in front of the track. Then choose Show Waveform from the Set Display Style drop-down menu.

To unlink video from audio, follow these steps:

1. **Select the audio track that you want to unlink.** Note that the names of linked clips are underlined.

2. **Choose Clip ⇨ Unlink.** You can also right-click the clip and choose Unlink from the pop-up menu, as shown in Figure 12.4. After unlinking, you can also delete the audio independently of the video, or vice versa.

FIGURE 12.4

Right-click a linked clip, and choose Unlink to unlink it.

CROSS-REF   For more information about linking and unlinking audio and video, see Chapter 7.

Using Keyboard Commands

As you work with Premiere Pro, you may find it difficult to fine-tune the movement of clips using the mouse. Fortunately, you can move clips a specific number of frames using the keyboard: Start by selecting the clip, pressing + or – on the numeric keypad, and then typing a number using the numeric keypad. Thus, +5 moves a clip forward five frames, and –5 moves a clip backward five frames. If the Timeline panel view is in Audio Units, the clip moves forward or backward in audio units. You can also move a selected clip one frame to the left by pressing Alt/Option+,. You can move it five frames to the right by pressing Alt/Option+Shift+,. You can move a selected clip one frame to the right by pressing Alt/Option+. You can move it five frames to the right by pressing Alt/Option+Shift+..

When working with the editing tools, keyboard commands can also speed up your work. Pressing + zooms in, and pressing – zooms out. You can use the left-arrow key and right-arrow key to move forward and backward one frame at a time. You can also use the following JKL keyboard combinations:

Play forward frame by frame	Hold K, while pressing L repeatedly
Play in reverse frame by frame	Hold K, while pressing J repeatedly
Play forward at 8 fps	Press K and L simultaneously (and keep the keys pressed)
Play in reverse at 8 fps	Press K and J simultaneously (and keep the keys pressed)

Using a Reference Monitor

A Reference Monitor is a second Program Monitor that can display program footage independently of the Program Monitor. You may want to use the Reference Monitor to show footage just before or after the sequence you are editing in the Program Monitor to help you preview the effect of the edit. You can also use the Reference Monitor to display Premiere's scopes, such as vectorscope and YC Waveform, while the actual program footage runs. When doing this, you may want to *gang* the Reference Monitor and the Program Monitor so that each is displaying the same frames, with the Program Monitor showing the video and the Reference Monitor displaying the scopes.

To view the Reference Monitor, choose Window ➪ Reference Monitor. By default, the Gang to Reference Monitor option is turned on in the Program Monitor menu, as shown in Figure 12.5. If you want to turn it off, simply click Gang to Reference Monitor in the Program Monitor menu.

FIGURE 12.5

Choose the Gang to Reference Monitor option in the Program Monitor menu in order to sync the Program monitor to the reference monitor.

Editing with the Tool Panel Tools

After you have edited two clips together in a sequence Timeline, you may want to fine-tune the edit by changing the out point of the first clip. Although you can use the Selection tool to change the edit point, you may prefer to use Premiere Pro's editing tools, such as the Rolling Edit and Ripple Edit tools. Both tools enable you to quickly edit the out point of adjacent clips.

If you have three clips edited together, the Slip and Slide tools provide a quick way to edit the in or out point of the middle clip. The following sections describe how to use the Rolling Edit and Ripple Edit tools to edit adjacent clips, and how to use the Slip and Slide tools to edit a clip between two other clips. As you experiment with these tools, keep the Program Monitor open. It provides an enlarged view of the clips. When using the Slip and Slide tools, the Program Monitor panel also shows how many frames have been edited. Figure 12.6 shows the Ripple Edit, Rolling Edit, Slip, and Slide tools.

ON the DVD   The sports clips shown in this chapter use video footage from the Artbeats folder on the Premiere Pro CS3 Bible DVD. The animal clips are in the MoreClips folder.

FIGURE 12.6

The Ripple Edit, Rolling Edit, Slip, and Slide tools

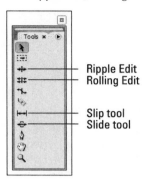

Ripple Edit
Rolling Edit

Slip tool
Slide tool

Creating a rolling edit

 The Rolling Edit tool enables you to click and drag the edit line of one clip and simultaneously change the in or out point of the next clip on the edit line. When you click and drag the edit line, the duration of the next clip is automatically edited to compensate for the change in the previous clip. For example, if you add five frames to the first clip, five frames are subtracted from the next clip. Thus, a rolling edit enables you to edit one clip without changing the duration of your edited program. Follow these steps to create a rolling edit, as shown in Figure 12.7:

1. **Open a project with at least two adjacent clips in a video track in the Timeline panel.** Display the Program Monitor as you work, so that you can preview the edit.

2. **Click the Rolling Edit tool to select it, or press N.**

3. **Move the Rolling Edit tool to the edit line between two adjacent clips.**

4. **Click and drag either left or right to trim the clips.** If you drag right, you extend the out point of the first clip and reduce the in point of the next clip. If you click to the left, you reduce the out point of the first clip and extend the in point of the next clip. In Figure 12.7, dragging the Rolling Edit tool right simultaneously changes the in point of the clip on the right and the out point of the clip on the left. The figure also shows how the Program Monitor previews the in and out points of the edit.

FIGURE 12.7

You can simultaneously change in and out points of two different clips with a rolling edit.

Creating a ripple edit

 The Ripple Edit tool enables you to edit a clip without affecting the adjacent clip. Performing a ripple edit is the opposite of performing a rolling edit. As you click and drag to extend the out point of a clip, Premiere Pro pushes the next clip to the right to avoid changing its in point — this creates a ripple effect throughout the production, changing its duration. If you click and drag to the left to reduce the out point, Premiere Pro doesn't change the in points of the next clips. To compensate for the change, Premiere Pro shortens the duration of the sequence. Follow these steps to perform a ripple edit with the Ripple Edit tool, as shown in Figure 12.8:

1. **Open a project with at least two clips touching side by side in a video track in the Timeline panel.** Display the Program Monitor, so that you can preview the edit.

2. **Click the Ripple Edit tool to select it, or press B.**

3. **Move the Ripple Edit tool to the out point of the clip you want to trim.**

FIGURE 12.8

The in point of the Penguins clip remains unchanged as you perform a ripple edit.

4. **Click and drag right to increase the clip's length, or left to decrease the clip's length.**
   The duration of the next clip remains unchanged, but the duration of the sequence is changed. In the figure, the in point of the Penguins clip remains unchanged, as the out point of the Parrot clip (on the left) is extended.

 If you want to perform a ripple edit without affecting audio, press Alt/Option while clicking and dragging the Ripple Edit tool.

 To edit only the audio or video of a linked clip, Alt/Option-drag with the Ripple Edit or Rolling Edit tool.

Creating a slip edit

 A slip edit enables you to change the in and out points of a clip that is sandwiched between two other clips while maintaining the middle clip's original duration. As you click and drag the clip, the clip's neighbors to the left and right do not change, and so neither does the sequence duration. Follow these steps to perform a slip edit with the Slip tool, as shown in Figure 12.9:

FIGURE 12.9

A slip edit changes the in and out points of the selected clip, but not the duration of the sequence.

1. **Open a project that contains at least three clips side by side in a video track in the Timeline panel.** If you want to preview the edit as you work, display the Program Monitor.

2. **Click the Slip tool to select it, or press Y.**

3. **With the Slip tool selected, click a clip that is in the middle of two other clips.**

4. **To change the in and out points without changing the duration of the sequence, click and drag left or right.** In the figure, the middle clip is dragged to the left, which changes its in and out points.

 Although the Slip tool is generally used to edit one clip between two others, you can edit the in and out points of a clip with the Slip tool even if it is not between other clips.

Creating a slide edit

 Like the slip edit, you perform the slide edit on one clip placed between two others in a sequence. A slide edit, as shown in Figure 12.10, maintains the in and out points of the clip that you are dragging while changing the duration of the adjacent clips.

FIGURE 12.10

Dragging right to create a slide edit extends the out point of the clip on the left and causes the in point of the clip on the right to occur later.

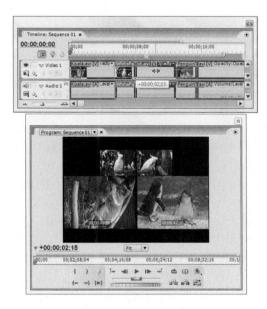

When you perform a slide edit, dragging right extends the out point of the previous clip as well as the in point of the next clip (making it occur later). Dragging left on a clip reduces the out point of the previous clip, as well as the in point of the following clip (causing it to occur earlier). As a result, the duration of the edited clip and the entire edited program do not change. Follow these steps to perform a slide edit with the Slide tool:

1. **Open a project that contains at least three clips side by side in a video track in the Timeline.** If you open the Program Monitor, you can preview the edit as you work.

2. **Click the Slide tool to select it, or press U.**

3. **Click and drag a clip that is between two other clips to move it.** Dragging left shortens the previous clip and lengthens the following clip. Dragging right lengthens the previous clip and shortens the following clip. In the figure, the Program Monitor shows the
   effect on all clips. As the Parrot clip is dragged right, the out point of the Koala clip (on
   the left) is extended, which causes the in point of the Penguin clip to occur later.

Creating a Three-Point or Four-Point Edit

Three-point and four-point edits are commonly performed in traditional non-linear video editing
studios, using a monitor setup that is similar to Premiere Pro's Source and Program Monitor panels.
As discussed in Chapter 6, the Source Monitor typically displays source clips that haven't been
added to the Timeline, while the Program Monitor displays program material that has been added
to the Timeline.

Performing a three-point edit

Typically, a three-point edit is used to overlay or replace a section of the program footage with a
portion of the source clip. Before you perform the edit, three crucial points are specified. The three
points are usually as follows:

- **The in point of the source clip:** This is the first frame of the source clip that you eventually want to view in the program.

- **An in point of the program footage:** This is first frame of the program footage that you
  want to be replaced by the source footage.

- **An out point of the program footage:** This is the frame where you want the source
  replacement to end.

> **NOTE**   You can perform a three-point edit with virtually any combination of three edit points.
> You could also set the in and out points of the source clip and the in point or out point
> of the program footage.

When you perform the edit, Premiere Pro automatically calculates the exact section of the source clip
that is needed to replace the program footage. You could use a three-point edit in the following situa-
tion: Assume that you have placed action footage in the Timeline and you want to replace a 2-second
cutaway. To set this up, you open the clip that you wish to appear as a cutaway in the Source Monitor
and set its in point. Next, in the Program Monitor, you set in and out points within the action clip.
When you perform the three-point edit, the cutaway appears within the in and out points that you
just set in the action footage. Figure 12.11 shows a graphic depicting a three-point edit.

FIGURE 12.11

A three-point edit

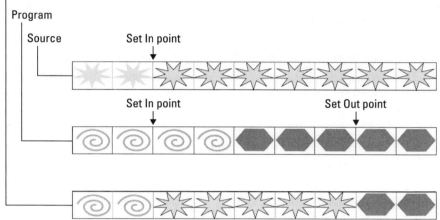

Program after edit

Program

Source

Set In point

Set In point   Set Out point

If you want to practice using one of the tutorial files, start by importing the SP127.mov file from the Artbeats folder on the DVD. This clip shows football players in a huddle. After you import the file, drag it into the Video 1 track in the Timeline. This clip appears in the Program Monitor panel. Next, import the SP123.mov clip from the DVD. This clip shows hands on a football. Don't place this clip on the Timeline; Premiere Pro does this for you when you create the three-point edit. The three-point edit creates a cutaway from the players to the ball for a few seconds, before returning to the players clip. Follow these steps to perform the three-point edit:

1. **Make sure that the target track is selected.** If it isn't, select the target track in the Timeline by clicking the far left of the track.

2. **Open a clip in the Source Monitor.** If you are using this book's DVD tutorial files, double-click the SP123.mov clip in the Project panel. The clip should appear in the Source Monitor, and its name should appear in the Source Monitor's tab. Note that you may be able to choose another clip from the source clip's drop-down menu if you have already been working with clips in the Source Monitor.

3. **In the Source Monitor, move the CTI to the in point for the source clip.** This is the first frame that you want overlaid into the program. If you are using the tutorial files, set the in point about two seconds from the beginning of clip SP123.mov. To move to the frame, click and drag in the jog tread control or the CTI in the Source section and then use the Step Forward or Step Backward button to navigate to the precise frame.

4. **Click the Set In Point button in the Source Monitor.**

5. **In the Program Monitor, move to the first frame that you want to replace with the source clip.** If you are using the tutorial files, move to about four seconds from the beginning of clip SP127. To move to the frame, click and drag in the job tread or CTI in the Program Monitor, and then use the Step Forward or Step Backward button to navigate to the precise frame. Alternatively, you can click and drag the edit line in the Timeline.

6. **Set the in point by clicking the Set In Point button in the Program Monitor.**

7. **In the Program Monitor, move to the last frame that you want to be replaced by the source clip.** If you are using the tutorial files, move about six seconds into clip SP127.

8. **Click the Set Out Point button.**

9. **To perform the edit, click the Overlay button in the Source Monitor, to the left of the Toggle Take Audio and Video button.** When Premiere Pro performs the edit, it automatically calculates the out point for clip SP123.

NOTE   When performing a three-point edit, the Fit Clip dialog box may appear when the source clip's duration doesn't match the duration specified in the program sequence's in to out point duration. When the Fit Clip dialog box appears, you can choose to have Premiere Pro change the speed of the source clip to fit, trim the front or the tail portion of the source clip, or ignore the sequence in point or out point.

Performing a four-point edit

Three-point edits are performed more frequently than four-point edits because you only need to specify three points. In a four-point edit, you specify the in and out points of the source clip as well as the in and out points of the program clip.

Before performing the edit, make sure that the target track is set. If it is not, choose the track that you want to have the clip dropped into on the Timeline by clicking the far-left side of the track.

Otherwise, performing a four-point edit (see Figure 12.12) is identical to performing a three-point edit, except that you must set an out point as well as an in point in the Source Monitor. What happens if the source duration (the duration between in and out source points) does not match the duration between the program's in and out points? Premiere Pro displays an alert, enabling you to choose whether you want to trim the source clip or change the speed of the source clip.

FIGURE 12.12

A four-point edit

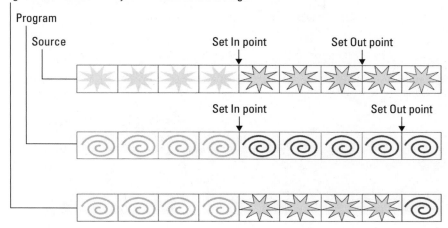

Fine-Tuning Edits Using the Trim Monitor Panel

The Trim Monitor panel enables you to precisely change the edit points of clips on the Timeline. When you work in the Trim Monitor panel, shown in Figure 12.13, you can click to move from edit point to edit point, and then remove or add frames on either side of the edit line. The Trim Monitor panel enables you to create ripple edits and rolling edits by simply clicking and dragging in the panel. When you create a ripple edit, the project duration increases or decreases, depending on whether frames are added to or subtracted from the edit. If you create a rolling edit, the project duration remains the same. Premiere Pro does this by adding frames from one side of the edit as it subtracts from the other, and by subtracting from one side of the edit while it adds to the other.

Before you use the Trim Monitor panel, you should have at least two separate clips on the Timeline that are adjacent to each other. If you keep the Timeline panel open, you can see the effects of the edit in the Timeline as you work. To use the Trim Monitor panel to trim an edit, follow these steps:

1. **Select the target track by clicking the far-left side of the track.**
2. **Move the CTI close to the area that you want to fine-tune.** Alternatively, use the controls in the Program Monitor to move close to the area that you want to edit.

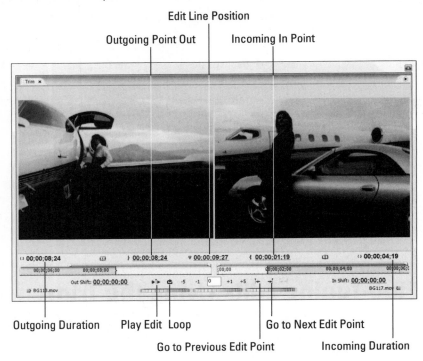

FIGURE 12.13

The Trim Monitor panel

3. **Open the Trim Monitor panel.** Click the Trim button in the Program Monitor (lower-right corner), or choose Trim in the Program Monitor panel menu.

4. **Click the Go to Next Edit Point button or the Go to Previous Edit Point button to move to the edit that you want to adjust.** The Out Shift section of the panel shows the left side of the edit; the In Shift section of the panel shows the right side of the edit (as if you were standing in the Timeline in the middle of a cut). Note that onscreen, the Trim Monitor panel shows you the outgoing out point, the current edit point position, and the incoming in point.

5. **Edit the clip in one of the following ways:**

   ▪ To create a ripple edit, follow these steps:

   a. **Click and drag either clip in the Trim Monitor panel.** If you click and drag left on the clip in the left window, you make this clip's duration shorter (changing its out point), without affecting the duration of the clip on the right. If you click and drag right on the clip in the right window, you delay its in point (causing it to be farther into the clip), thereby shortening this clip, but not changing the duration of the clip on the left.

b. **After you start the process of creating a ripple edit, you can add or remove frames by clicking in the bordered frame (below and between the two clips) and entering a positive or negative number.** Enter a positive number of frames if you want to add frames to the last selected clip; enter a negative number to subtract frames from the selected clip.

Clicking the −5 or −1 button removes five frames or one frame from the last selected clip. Clicking the +5 or +1 button adds five frames or one frame to the last selected clip.

You can also create a ripple edit by clicking the Jog In Point or Jog Out Point treads, clicking and dragging the In Point or Out Point buttons, or clicking and dragging the timecode display of the incoming, outgoing, and current edit position.

▨ To create a rolling edit, follow these steps:

a. **Click and drag in the middle of the two clips.** If you click and drag right, you simultaneously change the in point of the clip on the right (making it later in the clip) and the out point of the clip on the left (also making it later). Clicking and dragging left produces the opposite effect.

You can also create a rolling edit by clicking the Jog In Point and Jog Out Point treads.

b. **After you start the process of creating a rolling edit, you can add or remove frames by clicking in the bordered frame (below and between the two clips) and entering a positive or negative number.** Enter a positive number to specify the number of frames that you want to add to both clips, or enter a negative number to specify the number of frames to delete from both clips.

Clicking the −5 or −1 button removes five frames or one frame from both clips. Clicking the +5 or +1 button adds five frames or one frame to both clips.

6. **To play back the edit, click the Play Edit button.**

 You can also edit in the Trim Monitor by clicking and editing jog controls, by clicking the Set In Point and Set Out Point buttons, or by editing the timecode numbers in the Incoming In Point and Outgoing Out Point timecode fields and then pressing Enter.

TIP To change the default trim amount (set to 5), choose Edit ➪ Preferences ➪ Trim.

Multi-Camera Editing

If you shoot footage from a live event such as a concert or a dance performance with several cameras, editing the footage together sequentially can be quite time-consuming. Fortunately, Premiere Pro's multi-camera editing feature can simulate some of the features of a video switcher (which allows you to choose shots from the cameras on the fly). Using Premiere Pro's Multi-Camera Monitor, you can view up to four video sources simultaneously and quickly select the best shot to record into a video sequence. As the video rolls, you can keep selecting from any of the four synchronized sources, making cuts from one source to the other. You can also choose to monitor and use the audio feed from different sources.

Although it is easy to edit using the Multi-Camera Monitor, the setup is somewhat involved: You synchronize your source footage in one Timeline sequence; embed this source sequence in a target Timeline sequence (where the edits are recorded); enable multi-camera editing; and start recording in the Multi-Camera Monitor.

After you complete a multi-camera edit session, you can return to the sequence and easily substitute footage from one camera to another camera. The following sections detail these procedures.

 **Although Premiere Pro's multi-camera editing feature is primarily designed to allow edits from multi-camera shoots, you can use it to edit any footage, including graphics.**

Setting up multi-camera clips

After you import your footage into Premiere Pro, you are ready to try out a multi-camera edit session. As mentioned earlier, you can create a multi-camera session from up to four video sources. Follow these steps to set up a multi-camera edit:

1. **Create a new sequence by choosing File ➪ New Sequence.** In the New Sequence dialog box, choose the number of tracks you need. You can have up to four tracks feeding the Multi-Camera Monitor.

2. **Place all footage on individual tracks so that they are parallel to one another.**

3. **Line up the footage in the tracks using the Clip ➪ Synchronize command.** When you execute the Clip Synchronize command, Premiere Pro syncs all clips to the clip on the target track. Select a target track by clicking the left edge of a track. Next, Ctrl/⌘-click each clip that you want to synchronize. Then choose Clip ➪ Synchronize. The Synchronize Clips dialog box, shown in Figure 12.14, provides the following options:

FIGURE 12.14

Clips must be synchronized before you can use them as multi-camera sources.

- **Clip Start:** This option syncs on the clip's in point.
- **Clip End:** This option syncs on the clip's out point.

▪ **Timecode:** Use this option by clicking and dragging in the timecode readout area, or entering a timecode from the keyboard. If you want to sync using only minutes, seconds, and frames, leave the Ignore Hours option selected.

▪ **Numbered Clip Marker:** This option syncs to a clip marker that you choose.

When you click OK, Premiere Pro synchronizes the clips on the tracks.

4. **Create a new sequence to be the target sequence (for recording the final cuts) by choosing File ⇨ New Sequence.**

5. **Select the target sequence tab (from step 4) so that it is visible in the Timeline.**

6. **Nest the source sequence into the target sequence.** Drag the source sequence (with the synchronized video) from the Project panel into a track in the target sequence (created in step 4).

7. **Click to select the left area of the track header to designate it as the target track.**

8. **Click the embedded sequence to select it in the target track.**

9. **Turn on multi-camera editing by choosing Clip ⇨ Multi-Camera ⇨ Enable.** (You cannot access this command unless the embedded sequence is selected in the Timeline.)

Viewing multi-camera footage

After you properly set up your source and target tracks and enable multi-camera editing, you are ready to view your footage in the Multi-Camera Monitor. Follow these steps:

1. **Open the Multi-Camera Monitor by choosing Multi-Camera Monitor in the Program Monitor panel menu.** The Multi-Camera Monitor is shown in Figure 12.15.

2. **Play the footage in the Multi-Camera Monitor to view the clips simultaneously.** Here are some options for playing video:

   ▪ To view the footage, click any of the standard monitor transport controls: Step Forward, Step Backward, Play, Shuttle, and Job.

   ▪ Click the Play Around button, which backs up the CTI to the preroll position and plays to the postroll position.

 You can set the preroll and postroll settings in the General Preferences dialog box (Edit ⇨ Preferences ⇨ General).

   ▪ Press the Spacebar to start and stop video; use the left-arrow key or right-arrow key to step forward or back; or use the JKL keyboard combinations.

NOTE If you click camera 1, 2, 3, or 4 while playing footage in the Multi-Camera Monitor, the camera border turns red and the footage is automatically recorded to the Timeline.

FIGURE 12.15

The Multi-Camera Monitor with four video sources

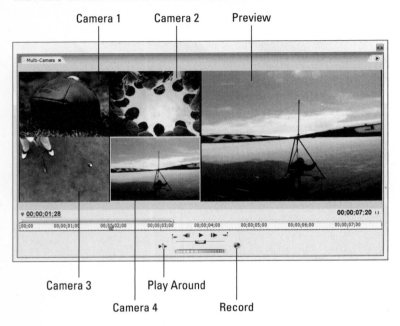

Recording multi-camera edits

After you open the Multi-Camera Monitor to display your footage, you are ready to start choosing shots to be recorded to the target sequence in the Timeline. When you record, you can choose to record video and audio from the different source footage. Follow these steps to record multi-camera edits:

1. **Turn on recording by clicking the Record button.**

2. **Choose the first shot by clicking a camera in the Multi-Camera Monitor.**

3. **Set Audio as the audio source.** By default, multi-camera editing uses the Audio 1 track in the source footage. If you want audio to correspond to your camera-editing choices, choose Audio Follows Video from the Multi-Camera Monitor panel menu. Otherwise, make sure that the Audio Follows Video option is deselected.

4. **Play the sequence by pressing the Spacebar or clicking the Play button in the Multi-Camera Monitor.**

5. **As the sequence plays, choose shots by clicking in the video from one of the cameras in the Multi-Camera Monitor or by pressing 1, 2, 3, or 4.**

6. **Stop recording by pressing the Spacebar or clicking the Stop transport control.**

Replacing multi-camera scenes

After you finish recording a multi-camera session, you may decide that you would like to replace a scene from one camera with footage from a different camera. You can do this by simply selecting the footage in the target sequence, choosing Clip ⇨ Multi-Camera, and then choosing one of the cameras from the Multi-Camera submenu. For example, you may select footage recorded from Camera 1 in the Timeline and then choose Clip ⇨ Multi-Camera ⇨ 2. Footage from Camera 2 replaces the selected footage in the target sequence.

You can also return to a specific area of the target sequence and record over it. To record over a sequence, set the CTI at the point you want to start editing and then re-record using the recording steps described in the preceding section. You can also use the editing features described in this chapter to further enhance the multi-camera sequence.

Editing a Clip Using Clip Commands

When editing a production, you may find that you need to adjust a clip to maintain continuity in a project. For example, you may want to slow the speed of a clip to fill a gap in your production or to freeze a frame for a moment or two.

Various commands in the Clip menu enable you to edit a clip. Premiere Pro enables you to change the duration and the speed of a clip using the Clip ⇨ Speed/Duration command. You can change the frame rate of a clip using the Clip ⇨ Video Options ⇨ Frame Hold command. You can also use the Clip ⇨ Video Options ⇨ Frame Hold command to freeze a video frame.

Using the Duration and Speed commands

You can use the Clip ⇨ Speed/Duration commands to change the length of a clip, to speed up or slow down a clip, or to play a clip in reverse.

Follow these steps to change the duration of a clip:

1. **Click the clip in a video track or in the Project panel to select it.**
2. **Choose Clip ⇨ Speed/Duration.** The Clip Speed/Duration dialog box appears, as shown in Figure 12.16.
3. **Click the Link button to unlink speed and duration.**
4. **Enter a duration.** You can't expand the clip to extend it past its original out point.
5. **Click OK to close the dialog box and set the new duration.**

 You can also change the duration of a clip by extending its edge with the Selection tool in the Timeline.

FIGURE 12.16

Use the Clip Speed/Duration dialog box to change a clip's speed or duration.

Follow these steps to change the speed of a clip.

1. **Click the clip in a video track, or select it in the Timeline.**

2. **Choose Clip ➪ Speed.** The Clip Speed/Duration dialog box appears.

3. **Type a value in the Speed field.** Type a value greater than 100 percent to speed up the clip, or type a value between 0 percent and 99 percent to slow down the clip. If you want to reverse the clip, click the Reverse Speed check box.

4. **Click OK to close the Clip Speed/Duration dialog box and apply the new speed.**

 You also can change a clip's speed in the Timeline panel by clicking and dragging either edge of the clip with the Rate Stretch tool.

Using the Frame Hold command

Premiere Pro's Frame Hold command allows you to freeze one frame of a clip so that the frame appears from the in point to the out point of the clip. You can create a freeze frame from the in point, the out point, or at Marker point 0:

1. **Click a clip in a video track to select it.**

2. **If you want to freeze at a specific frame other than the in point or out point, set an unnumbered marker for the clip in the Source Monitor.**

3. **Choose Clip ➪ Video Options ➪ Frame Hold.** This opens the Frame Hold Options dialog box, shown in Figure 12.17.

4. **In the pop-up menu, choose whether to create the freeze frame on the In Point, on the Out Point, or at Marker 0.** If you want to freeze on a specific frame, set Marker 0 at the frame you want to freeze in the Source Monitor panel, and choose the Marker 0 option.

5. **Click the Hold On check box.**

6. **If you want to prevent keyframe effects from being viewed, click the Hold Filters check box.**

7. **To remove the effects of video interlacing, click the Deinterlace check box.** The Deinterlace option removes field artifacts from interlaced video by removing one of the two fields from the frame and then repeating the other field from the frame.

FIGURE 12.17

Use the Frame Hold Options dialog box to create a freeze frame.

More clip commands and utilities

As you edit in Premiere Pro, you are likely to use a variety of clip utilities, some of which have been described in preceding chapters. Here is a summary of commands that may prove useful when editing:

- **Clip ⇨ Group:** This command groups clips together, allowing you to move or delete several clips as one entity. Grouping clips can help you avoid inadvertently separating titles and unlinked audio in one track from footage in another. When clips are grouped, you can click and drag clip edges in the Timeline to edit all clips simultaneously. To group clips, select all of the clips and then choose Clip ⇨ Group. To ungroup them, select one of the clips and choose Clip ⇨ Ungroup. To select one member of a group independently of others, press Alt/Option and then click and drag the clip. Note that you can simultaneously apply commands from the Clip menu to clips that are in a group.

- **Clip ⇨ Scale to Frame Size:** This command scales the selected clip to match the project frame size.

- **Clip ⇨ Video Options ⇨ Frame Blend:** The Frame Blend option prevents choppy video when you have changed the speed or frame rate of clips. By default, Frame Blend is on.

- **Clip ⇨ Video Options ⇨ Field Options:** This command provides options for reducing flicker and removing interlacing in clips.

- **File ⇨ Get Properties For ⇨ Selection:** This command provides data rate, file size, image size, and other file information about the selected file in the Project panel.

Summary

Premiere Pro provides numerous tools and commands that enable you to quickly and precisely edit a digital video production. Premiere Pro's editing tools can be found in the Timeline tool panel. Most other editing utilities reside in the Source, Program, Trim, and Multi-Camera Monitors. This chapter covered the following topics:

- You can use the Ripple Edit and Rolling Edit tools to change the in and out points of clips in the Timeline. A ripple edit changes the project duration; a rolling edit does not.

- You can click and drag with the Slip or Slide tools to edit the in and out points of a clip in between two other clips. The Slip tool does not change project duration; the Slide tool does.

- You can use the Source and Program Monitors to create three-point and four-point edits.

- You can use the Trim Monitor to precisely shave frames from clips.

- You can use the Multi-Camera Monitor to edit footage from up to four video sources.

Chapter 13

Using Video Effects

Adobe Premiere Pro's special effects can wake up even the dullest video production. For example, using the video effects in Premiere Pro's Effects panel, you can blur or skew images and add bevels, drop shadows, and painterly effects. Some effects can correct and enhance video; others can make it seem as though the video is out of control. By changing controls for the effects, you can also create startling motion effects, such as making it appear as if an earthquake or tornado has struck your clip.

As this chapter illustrates, Premiere Pro's video effects work in sync with the keyframe track, enabling you to change effect settings at specific points on the Timeline. All you need to do is specify the settings for the start of an effect, move to another keyframe, and set the ending effect. When you create a preview, Premiere Pro does the rest: It interpolates the video effect, editing all of the in-between frames to create a fluid effect over time.

If you haven't been adding effects to your video, this chapter provides everything you need to get up and running. You'll explore every video effect in the Effects panel and you'll see how the Effect Controls panel enables you to change effect settings. You also have a chance to practice creating effects with keyframes and image mattes using sample clips from the DVD that accompanies this book.

If you've already started working with Premiere Pro effects, this chapter shows you how to use Premiere Pro's keyframe track and provides a reference for every effect in the Effects panel.

Exploring the Video Effects

Premiere Pro's Effects panel is a storehouse of video effects. However, before you begin to use the effects, you should become familiar with the window interface. To display the Effects panel, choose Window ➪ Effects. The Effects panel, shown in Figure 13.1, not only contains the Video Effects bin, but also the Audio Effects, Audio Transitions, and Video Transitions bins. To view the video effects, click the triangle to the left of the Video Effects bin (folder) in the Effects panel. Within the Video Effects bin are 18 bins (folders) that contain different video effects.

FIGURE 13.1

Premiere Pro's Effects panel provides access to the video effects.

Open a bin within the Video Effects bin to view a video effect. After you open the bin, it displays a list of effects. An icon to the left of the video effect's name represents each effect. After you open a bin, you can apply a video effect to a video track by clicking and dragging it over a clip in the Timeline panel. To close a bin, click the triangle to the left of the bin.

Navigating within the video effects

The Effects panel features options that can help you keep organized while using Premiere Pro's many video effects. The following is a brief description of these options:

■ **Find:** The Contains field at the top of the Effects panel helps you to locate effects. In the Contains field, type the name of the effect that you want to find. Premiere Pro automatically starts the search.

- **New Custom Bin:** When you create custom bins (folders), you can use them to organize effects. To create a custom bin, either click the bin icon at the bottom of the Effects panel or click the Effects drop-down menu and choose New Custom Bin. After you create a bin, drag the effects into it. With all of your chosen effects in one bin, you'll find that they are easier to locate and use.

- **Rename:** You can change the name of a custom bin at any time by selecting the bin and then clicking the name. When the name of the bin is highlighted, type the name that you want in the Name field.

- **Delete:** If you have finished using a custom bin, you can delete it by selecting it and choosing Delete Custom Item from the Effects drop-down menu or by clicking the Delete icon at the bottom of the panel. A prompt appears, asking whether you want to delete the item. If you do, click Yes.

The Effect Controls panel

When you apply a video effect to an image, the effect appears in the Effect Controls panel, as shown in Figure 13.2.

FIGURE 13.2

The settings for a video effect appear in the Effect Controls panel after a video effect is applied to a clip.

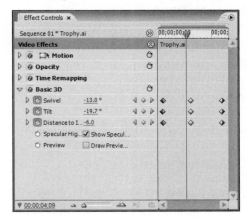

The name of the selected clip appears at the top of the panel. To the right of the clip name is a button that enables you to create as well as show or hide keyframes over a Timeline. At the bottom left of the Effect Controls panel is a time display showing you where the clip appears in the Timeline. To the right of the time display are options allowing you to zoom out or in.

Below the name of the selected sequence and clip name appear the Fixed Effects — Motion and Opacity. Below the Fixed Effects appear the Standard Effects. If you have applied a video effect to the selected clip, a Standard Effect displays below the Opacity option. All of the video effects that you have applied to the selected clip display below the Video Effects heading. The video effects appear in the order in which you have applied them. If you like, you can click and drag the standard video effects up or down to change the order. To the left of the Fixed Effects (Motion Opacity and Time Remapping) and the Video Effects name appears a box containing an ƒ symbol. The ƒ symbol means that this effect is enabled. You can disable the effect by clicking the ƒ symbol or by deselecting Effect Enabled in the Effect Controls drop-down menu. Also next to the effect name is a small triangle. If you click the triangle, the settings appear for that effect.

Many effects also feature a dialog box that includes a preview area. If the effect provides a dialog box, a little dialog box icon appears to the right of the name of the video effect in the Effect Controls panel. Click the icon to access the Setup dialog box. You can apply many effects with Premiere Pro's keyframe and graph option. If you do so, a small stopwatch icon appears in front of the name of the effect. To enable keyframing, click the stopwatch icon. After you click it, a small blue frame appears around the stopwatch icon. (Keyframing is explained later in this chapter.)

NOTE You can copy and paste effects from one clip to another. In the Effect Controls panel, click the effect that you want to copy. Shift-click to select more than one effect. Then choose Edit ⇨ Copy. In the Timeline panel, select the clip that you want to apply the effects to, and then choose Edit ⇨ Paste.

The Effect Controls drop-down menu

The Effect Controls drop-down menu provides control over all of the clips in the panel. The menu enables you to turn previewing on and off and to select preview quality, as well as to enable and disable effects. The following is a brief description of the Effect Controls drop-down menu commands:

- **Effect Enabled:** Click this command to disable or enable effects. By default, Effect Enabled is selected.
- **Delete Selected Effect:** This command removes the selected effect from the clip.

NOTE You can also remove an effect from the panel by selecting it in the Effect Controls panel and pressing Delete.

- **Delete All Effects from Clip:** This command removes all effects from the clip.

NOTE The Audio commands in the Effect Controls drop-down menu are covered in Chapters 7 and 8.

Applying a Video Effect

You can apply one video effect or multiple video effects to an entire video clip by dragging the effect from the Effects panel to the Timeline. The video effects allow you to change the color of a clip, blur it, or even distort it.

Follow these steps to apply a video effect to a clip in the Timeline:

1. **Create a new project.** Name it as VideoEffects.

CROSS-REF Refer to Chapter 3 for information on choosing a project preset.

2. **Choose Window ⇨ Workspace ⇨ Effects to display all the panels you need.**

3. **Choose File ⇨ Import to import a video clip to use as the background.** Figure 13.3 shows a video clip of a Polo match as the background. If you want, you can use the Artbeats LM229 video clip as the background.

ON the DVD Artbeats LM229 is in the Artbeats folder in the Tutorial Projects folder on the DVD that accompanies this book.

4. **Drag the background (Polo match) video clip from the Project panel to the Video 1 track of the Timeline panel.**

5. **To apply an effect to the background (Polo match), you first need to select it in the Timeline panel.** Click the background (Polo match) clip in the Video 1 track.

6. **Choose an effect by clicking it.** For a simple effect, try the Sharpen effect, located in the Blur & Sharpen folder. In Figure 13.3, the grass is made to look greener in the Polo field by using the Change to Color effect, which is located in the Color Correction folder.

FIGURE 13.3

The preview of the Change to Color video effect in the Program Monitor panel

7. **To apply the effect, drag the effect from the Effects panel directly onto the clip in the Video 1 track or into the Effect Controls panel.** To adjust the settings of the effect, use the options located beneath the effect's name in the Effect Controls panel. To set an effect to its default settings, click the Reset button to the right of the effect's name. For a full discussion of the video effects and their options, see the section "Touring Premiere Pro's Video Effects" in this chapter.

8. **Try different effects, such as those found in the Adjust, Distort, Image Control, Generate, Stylize, Time, and Transform folders.** To turn the effect on or off, click the small *f* symbol in front of the effect's name in the Effect Controls panel. To delete an effect, click the effect in the Effect Controls panel and press Delete, or click the Effect Controls drop-down menu and choose Delete Selected Effect. To remove all of the effects from a clip, click the Effect Controls drop-down menu and choose Delete All Effects from Clip.

 You can add multiple effects to an image. You can also add the same effect with different effect settings to the same image.

9. **Click the Play button in the Program Monitor panel to see a preview of the effects.** As you work, you can watch the preview in the Program Monitor panel.

10. **Choose File ⇨ Import to import a sound clip, and drag the sound clip to the Audio 1 track.** This example uses SmartSound's No Borders sound clip. You can also choose File ⇨ New ⇨ SmartSound to import a SmartSound sound clip. To download SmartSound, go to www.smartsound.com/premiere/index.html.

    If the sound clip is too long, click the left side of the clip and drag it inward. For more information on working with sound clips, see Chapter 7.

ON the DVD SmartSound's No Borders sound clip is in the SmartSound folder in the Tutorial Projects folder on the DVD that accompanies this book.

11. **Choose Sequence ⇨ Render Work Area.** Choose File ⇨ Save to save your project so that you can use it in the next section.

Applying a video effect to a clip with an alpha channel

Not only can you apply an effect to a video clip, but you can also apply an effect to a still image that has an alpha channel. In a still image, an alpha channel is used to isolate an object from its background. To apply an effect to just an image and not its background, the image must have an alpha channel. You can use Adobe Photoshop to mask an image and save the mask as either an alpha channel or a layer. For more information on creating alpha channels using Photoshop, see Chapter 28.

You can also use Adobe Illustrator to create a graphic. When you import an Illustrator file into Premiere Pro, Premiere Pro reads the transparent areas and creates an alpha channel. To create the 3-D Trophy image shown in Figures 13.3, 13.5, and 13.6, you can use Illustrator's Pen tool to create a wireframe of one side of the trophy shape. Use the Effect ⇨ 3D ⇨ Revolve command to make the 3-D shape of the trophy. Next, create one of the handles of the trophy by using Illustrator's Pen tool to create a wireframe.

To create the second handle, use the Reflect tool to reflect the wireframe vertically and make a copy. Then use the Effect ⇨ 3D ⇨ Extrude & Bevel command to extrude the wireframe handles. After the 3-D Trophy shape is complete, use the Pen tool to create the red rectangle area at the bottom of the trophy. Towards the bottom of the red rectangle, make a curve and use the Type on a Curve tool to type the text **1ˢᵗ Place**. Figure 13.4 shows the wireframes and the 3-D command dialog boxes.

CROSS-REF For more information on using Adobe Illustrator, see Chapter 29.

FIGURE 13.4

Illustrator's 3-D command allows you to create 3-D images out of wireframes.

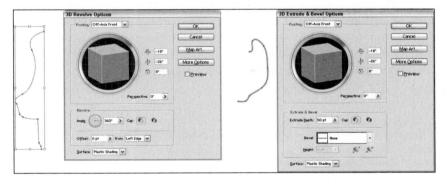

Follow these steps to apply a video effect to a file with an alpha channel:

ON the DVD If you want to apply an effect to an image with an alpha channel, you can apply video effects to the Trophy image (shown in Figure 13.5) and use the Artbeats LM229 video clip as the background. These files are located in the More Clips folder and the Artbeats folder in the Tutorial Projects folder on the DVD that accompanies this book.

Before you start, load the video effects project from the previous section, or create a new project, import a video clip, and drag it into the Video 1 track.

1. Choose Window ⇨ Workspace ⇨ Effects to display all of the panels that you need.

2. **Choose File ⇨ Import to load a file with an alpha channel.** This example imports the Trophy Illustrator file that is shown in Figure 13.3.

3. **In the Import dialog box, locate the file that has an alpha channel (Trophy) so that only the image, and not the background, is imported.** This example uses the Trophy image (found in the More Clips folder in the Tutorial Projects folder on the DVD that accompanies this book). After you locate the file, click Open. Click OK. The file and its alpha channel appear in the Project panel.

4. **Drag the file with an alpha channel (Trophy file) from the Project panel to the Video 2 track.** Place it directly above the background clip in the Video 1 track. The Timeline Marker should be over both clips.

5. **Double-click the file with the alpha channel (Trophy file) in the Timeline panel to display it in the Program Monitor panel.** On one side of the Program Monitor panel, the alpha channel file (Trophy file) appears on a black background (Polo match). On the other side of the image, the alpha channel file (Trophy file) appears over the selected background (Polo match) from the Video 1 track, as shown in Figure 13.5. The alpha channel file (Trophy file) from the Video 2 track takes on the background (Polo match) of the clip from the Video 1 track because it has an alpha channel.

6. **To see the alpha channel (Trophy) file, click the Program Monitor panel drop-down menu and choose Alpha.** Figure 13.6 shows the Trophy Illustrator file with and without the alpha channel. To return to standard view, click Composite Video from the drop-down menu.

7. **Select the alpha channel (Trophy) file in the Video 2 track.**

8. **Drag the desired video effect from the Effects panel onto the alpha channel (Trophy) file in the Video 2 track or into the Effect Controls panel.** This example applies the Drop Shadow effect, which is found in the Perspective folder. In the next section, you apply the Basic 3D video effect, using keyframes. The Basic 3D video effect is found in the Perspective folder. It allows you to move an object in a three-dimensional plane. By setting keyframes, you can change the effect over time. Proceed to the next section if you want to learn how to use video effects with keyframes.

9. **To preview your work, click and drag the shuttle or jog slider in the Program Monitor panel.** You can also move the Timeline Marker in the Timeline. To preview your entire clip, click the Play button in the Program Monitor panel.

FIGURE 13.5

The Program Monitor panel displays the Trophy Illustrator file with an alpha channel over a Polo match scene that is used as the background. The Polo match scene video clip is in the Video 1 track of the Timeline panel, and the Trophy Illustrator file is in the Video 2 track.

FIGURE 13.6

The Trophy Illustrator file with and without the alpha channel

 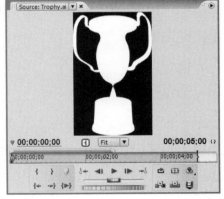

10. **Choose File ⇨ Import to import a sound clip, and then drag the sound clip to the Audio 1 track.** This example uses SmartSound's No Borders sound clip. You can also choose File ⇨ New ⇨ SmartSound to import a SmartSound sound clip. To download SmartSound, go to www.smartsound.com/premiere/index.html.

If the sound clip is too long, click the left side of the clip and drag it inward. For more information on working with sound clips, see Chapter 7.

 The SmartSound clip is found in the SmartSound folder in the Tutorial Projects folder on the DVD that accompanies this book.

11. **Choose Sequence ⇨ Render Work Area.** Then choose File ⇨ Save to save your work so that you can use it in the next section.

Applying video effects with markers

Premiere Pro allows you to go through your project and set markers in designated areas where you would like to add video effects to individual video clips. You can set In and Out markers, Unnumbered markers, Numbered markers, or Other Numbered markers. Markers are set using the Timeline ruler in either the Timeline panel or the Effect Controls panel. The Timeline ruler in the Effect Controls panel allows you to view and edit markers.

Follow these steps to set a marker:

1. **Click a video clip in one of the Video tracks in the Timeline panel.**

2. **Move the CTI to the location where you want to set a marker.**

3. **Right-click in the Timeline ruler of either the Effect Controls panel or the Timeline panel.**

4. **In the drop-down menu that appears, choose Set Sequence Marker.** Then select a type of marker.

5. **If you made a mistake and want to delete a marker, right-click.** In the drop-down menu that appears, choose Clear Sequence Markers. Then choose the marker you want to delete.

NOTE To display a clip beyond its In and Out points, deselect the Pin to Clip option from the Effect Controls drop-down menu.

After you set markers, you can go to the markers and apply video effects to the location of a marker.

Follow these steps to go to a marker and apply an effect:

1. **Click a video clip in one of the Video tracks in the Timeline panel.**

2. **Right-click in the Timeline ruler of either the Effect Controls panel or the Timeline panel.**

3. **In the drop-down menu that appears, choose Go to Sequence Marker.** Then choose whether you want to go to the Next Marker, Previous, In, Out, or a Numbered marker. Note that the CTI moves to the location of the designated marker.

4. **To apply an effect to the location of the marker, click and drag an effect to the Effect Controls panel.** Then click the triangle in front of the name of the effect to display its controls. Make the necessary adjustments, and then click the Toggle Animation icon to set a keyframe at the location of the marker.

5. **After you are finished applying effects to the markers you set, you may want to delete them.** To do so, right-click the Timeline ruler. In the drop-down menu that appears, choose Clear Sequence Markers and click All Markers.

Using Video Effects with Keyframes

Premiere Pro's keyframe feature enables you to change video effects at specific points in the Timeline. With keyframes, you can have Premiere Pro use the settings of an effect at one point on the Timeline, gradually changing to the settings at another point on the Timeline. When Premiere Pro creates the preview, it interpolates the effect over time, rendering all of the frames that change in between the set points. You can use keyframing to make video clips or still clips more interesting. You can also import a still image of your logo and animate it using keyframes. If you want, you can use Premiere Pro's Titler to create a logo. To learn how to create a logo using Premiere Pro's Titler, see Chapter 10.

Figure 13.7 shows frames of the alpha channel file (trophy image) from the previous sections, animated over a polo match background video clip. The alpha channel file (Trophy image) is animated using the Basic 3D effect found in the Perspective folder. To make the alpha channel file (Trophy image) swivel and tilt to its original state, you must set keyframes.

The keyframe track

Premiere Pro's keyframe track makes creating, editing, and manipulating keyframes quick, logical, and precise. The keyframe track is found in both the Timeline panel and the Effect Controls panel. Figure 13.8 shows the Timeline panel with the keyframe track. Figure 13.9 shows the Effect Controls panel with the keyframe track. To view the keyframe track in the Timeline panel, expand the track by clicking the track's Expand button. To view the keyframe track in the Effect Controls panel, make sure that the Show/Hide Keyframes button is activated.

FIGURE 13.7

Frames from the alpha channel file (Trophy image), with the Basic 3D effect applied using keyframes, are seen over a polo match background.

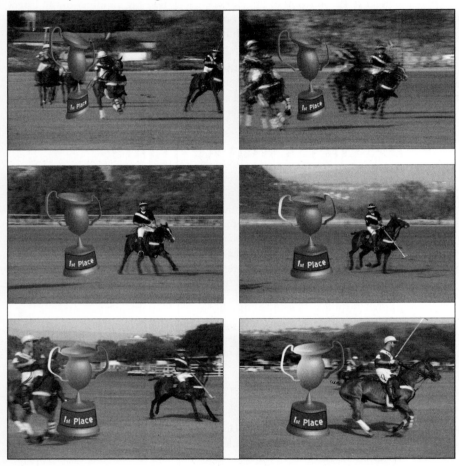

FIGURE 13.8

The Timeline panel with the Video 2 track expanded with keyframes

FIGURE 13.9

The Effect Controls panel with keyframes displayed for the Video 2 track

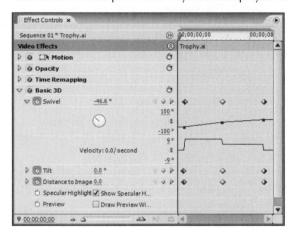

NOTE The keyframe track does not appear if you do not have a clip in the track.

To enable keyframing, click the tiny stopwatch icon next to one of the settings for an effect in the Effect Controls panel. You can also turn keyframing on and off by clicking the Show Keyframes icon in the Timeline panel and choosing an effect setting from the video clip's menu. In the keyframe track, a circle or diamond indicates that a keyframe exists at the current Timeline frame. Clicking the right-arrow icon (Go to Previous Keyframe) jumps the Timeline Marker (current-time indicator) from one keyframe to the next. Clicking the left-arrow icon (Go to Next Keyframe) moves the Timeline Marker backward from one keyframe to the next.

Follow these steps to apply an effect to a clip using keyframes:

1. **Before you start, load the video effects project from the previous section.** Alternatively, you can create a new project, import a background video clip (Artbeats LM229) for the Video 1 track, and import a still image (Trophy image) or logo (that has an alpha channel) for the Video 2 track.

ON the DVD If you want, you can use the Trophy image (alpha channel file) in the Video 2 track, and use Artbeats LM229 as the background (Polo match) in the Video 1 track. They are found in the MixedCuts folder and the Artbeats folder in the Tutorial Projects folder on the DVD that accompanies this book.

2. **Choose Window ⇨ Workspace ⇨ Effects to display all of the panels that you need.**

NOTE Using an image that has an alpha channel in the Video 2 track allows a background clip in the Video 1 track to show through when you preview it in the Program Monitor panel. To see a preview in the Program Monitor panel, click the Play button. To superimpose two video clips without alpha channels, you need to use the Keying Effects. The Keying Effects are briefly discussed in the next section. For a full description of these effects, see Chapter 14.

3. **Add an effect to the image in the Video 2 track by clicking an effect in the Effects panel and dragging it to the clip in the Timeline panel (or to the Effect Controls panel).** If you are animating a logo, for an unusual effect, you may want to try the Twirl effect. The Twirl effect is found in the Distort bin, in the Video Effects bin in the Effects panel. The examples in Figures 13.7, 13.8, and 13.9 use the Basic 3D effect.

4. **To create a keyframe for the effect that you applied in step 3 using the Timeline panel, move the Timeline Marker (edit line or CTI) over the first frame of the image in the Video 2 track.**

5. **In the Timeline panel, click the Expand/Collapse Track icon (a triangle icon that appears before the track name) to expand the track.** Then click the Show Keyframes icon to show the keyframe track.

6. **Click the clip's title bar menu, and choose an effects control.**

7. **Click the Add/Delete Keyframe icon to add a keyframe.** A circle appears on the keyframe track.

8. **To add another keyframe, move the Timeline Marker (edit line) to a new position.** Then click the Add Keyframe icon. Change the settings for the effect by clicking the keyframe in the Timeline panel and moving it up or down.

9. **To add more keyframes using the Timeline panel, repeat step 8 as many times as desired.** Figure 13.8 shows the Timeline panel with keyframes.

NOTE To delete a keyframe, click it and press Delete. You can move a keyframe by clicking and dragging it to a new location.

The keyframes that you created using the Timeline panel appear in the Effect Controls panel.

10. **You can also use the Effect Controls panel to adjust the settings for a keyframe.** In the Effect Controls panel, click the triangle in front of the effect to display the controls. Then move the Timeline Marker (edit line or CTI) over the keyframe that you want to edit. Make the necessary changes.

11. **To create a keyframe for the effect that you applied in step 3 using the Effect Controls panel, move the edit line in the Timeline of the Effect Controls panel to the beginning of the clip.** Then click the Toggle Animation icon in front of the effects control that you want to work with. A keyframe is added, and keyframing is enabled.

12. **Move the edit line in the Timeline of the Effect Controls panel to a new position.** Adjust the control's setting. As you adjust the control's setting, a keyframe is added.

13. **To add more keyframes using the Effect Controls panel, repeat step 12 as many times as desired.** Figure 13.9 shows the Effect Controls panel with keyframes.

NOTE When keyframing is enabled for an effect's control, you can click the Toggle Animation icon to delete all of the existing keyframes for that effect's control.

14. **To preview the video effect, choose Play from the Program Monitor panel.** You can also drag the Timeline Marker (CTI) as you view the preview in the Program Monitor panel.

15. **Choose File ⇨ Import to import a sound clip.** Then drag the sound clip to the Audio 1 track. This example uses SmartSound's No Borders sound clip. You can also choose File ⇨ New ⇨ SmartSound to import a SmartSound sound clip. To download SmartSound, go to www.smartsound.com/premiere/index.html.

If the sound clip is too long, click the left side of the clip and drag it inward. For more information on working with sound clips, see Chapter 7.

ON the DVD SmartSound's No Borders sound clip is found in the SmartSound folder in the Tutorial Projects folder on the DVD that accompanies this book.

16. **Choose Sequence ⇨ Render Work Area.** Choose File ⇨ Save to save your project.

Using Value and Velocity graphs to change keyframe property values

Premiere Pro's Value and Velocity graphs allow you to fine-tune the smoothness of an effect and increase or decrease the speed of an effect. Most effects can have various graphs, and each control (property) of an effect can have a Value and Velocity graph.

When you make adjustments to a control of an effect with the Toggle Animation icon turned on, you add keyframes and points to the graph, as shown in Figure 13.10. Before you make any adjustments to the controls for an effect, the graph is a straight line. After you make adjustments to the effect's control, you add keyframes and alter the graph.

FIGURE 13.10

The Effect Controls panel with keyframes and Value and Velocity graphs for the Strobe Light effect

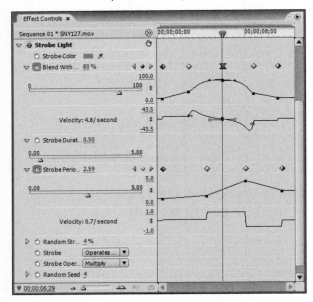

You can view and edit Value and Velocity graphs in the Effect Controls panel and the Timeline panel. You have limited ability to edit the graph in the Timeline panel. Unlike the Timeline panel, the Effect Controls panel allows you to view and edit more than one graph at a time. To do so, you simply create keyframes for a control (property) in an effect. Then click the triangle in front of the name of the control (property). In the Timeline of the Effect Controls panel, the Value graph appears above the Velocity graph. To view and edit a graph for an effect in the Timeline panel, click the Effect menu of a clip in a video track. Then select a property.

> **NOTE**   You can view the graphs for the properties of sound effects in either the Effect Controls panel or the Timeline panel. The graphs for sound effects work basically the same as they do for video effects.

Follow these steps to work with Value and Velocity graphs using the Effect Controls panel:

1. **Create a new project.**

2. **Import a video clip.** Drag the video clip from the Project panel to the Video 1 track of the Timeline panel.

ON the DVD The Artbeats SNY127 video clip is found in the Artbeats folder in the Tutorial Projects folder on the DVD that accompanies this book.

3. **Drag an effect to the video clip in the Timeline panel.** This example uses the Strobe Light effect found in the Stylize bin.

4. **Click the triangle in front of the video effect to view all of its properties.** Then click the triangle of the first property to view the controls. In the case of the Strobe Light effect, click the triangle in front of Blend with Original. The control is set to 0 (zero) percent.

5. **Move the CTI to the beginning of the Timeline.** Then click the Toggle Animation icon to create a keyframe and display the control's Value and Velocity graphs. Note that the graphs are straight horizontal lines. This means that there are no changes to the effect in the Timeline.

6. **To edit the graphs, move the CTI to the right.** Next, make adjustments to the control. This example moves the Blend with Original slider to the right. Note that another keyframe is created and a point is created on the graph, as shown in Figure 13.10.

7. **Continue editing the graph by creating new keyframes.** To create a new keyframe, move the CTI to the right and then make adjustments to the control. If you are using the Strobe Light video effect, you might also want to try to animate other Strobe Light controls, such as Strobe Duration and Strobe Period. You can also animate the Strobe Color.

After you create a graph, you can use the Selection tool to move the graph. Use one of these methods:

■ **To move the Value graph:** Place the cursor over the horizontal white line between the Value and Velocity graphs. When the cursor changes to an up-and-down arrow, click and drag either up or down.

■ **To move the Velocity graph:** Place the cursor over the horizontal white line below the Velocity graph. When the cursor changes to an up-and-down arrow, click and drag either up or down.

■ **To add a point on the Value graph:** Move the cursor over the place on the graph where you want to add a point. When the cursor changes to a Pen tool with a small plus sign, Ctrl-click/⌘-click. Note that a new keyframe is created above the new point on the graph.

■ **To change a sharp corner point on the graph to a smooth curve:** You can change the form of interpolation from Linear to Bezier. To change a Linear keyframe marker into a Bezier marker, either Ctrl-click/⌘-click and drag the point on the Value graph (below the Linear keyframe marker) or right-click the Linear keyframe marker. When a drop-down menu appears, choose Bezier.

This changes the mode of interpolation from Linear to Bezier and also changes the icon of the keyframe. The Linear keyframe marker icon changes from a diamond-shaped icon to an hourglass-shaped icon. The point on the graph now has directional handles and lines, which you can use to adjust the effect.

Superimposing Video Clips Using the Keying Video Effects

To superimpose two video clips that don't have alpha channels, you need to use the Keying video effects. (For more detailed information on Keying video effects, see Chapter 14.) Figure 13.10 shows the panels that are used to create a project using the Color Key effect in the previous section. To create the project, two video clips are superimposed: a polo match video clip in the Video 2 track and a NYC street background scene in the Video 1 track. In the Video 3 track, an alpha channel file (Trophy) is used so that when you superimpose the clips in the Video 1 and the Video 2 tracks, you can see the background through them. Figure 13.11 shows the Program Monitor panel with a frame of the final result of the three clips from the three video tracks superimposed onto one another.

The video project in Figure 13.11 uses the Polo match background clip and an alpha channel file (Trophy) from the section "The keyframe track." To superimpose a video clip over the Polo match background, you can move the alpha channel file (Trophy) from the Video 2 track to the Video 3 track. Then, import a new video clip of an NYC street scene (Artbeats SNY127) and drag it into the Video 2 track, as shown in Figure 13.11. To jazz up the project, you can add sound. The sound file used in this example is SmartSound's No Borders.

FIGURE 13.11

The panels used to create a project using the Color Key effect

ON the DVD The video clips used to create the project shown in Figure 13.11 include the following: Artbeats LM229 and Artbeats SNY127. The Artbeats video clips are in the Artbeats folder in the Tutorial Projects folder. The alpha channel file, Trophy, is found in the MoreClips folder in the Tutorial Projects folder. The sound clip is SmartSound's No Borders. The SmartSound folder is in the Tutorial Projects folder.

Follow these steps to superimpose two video clips using the Color Key video effects:

1. **Choose File ⇨ Open Project to open the project from the previous section.** Alternatively, choose File ⇨ New ⇨ Project to create a new project.

2. **Your onscreen project should have two video clips in the Video 1 and Video 2 tracks, and a third image with an alpha channel in the Video 3 track.** Choose File ⇨ Import to import the necessary clips. If you are using a new project, you need to import three files. If you are using the project from the previous sections, you need to import one new video clip. The video clips in the Video 1 and Video 2 tracks will be superimposed to create a background.

3. **Now you are ready to drag the clips from the Project panel to the Timeline panel.** If you are using a new project, you need to drag one video clip from the Project panel to the Video 1 track. Then drag another video clip into the Video 2 track and the clip with an alpha channel into the Video 3 track. This clip should have an alpha channel so that the background shows through.

   If you are using the project from the previous section, move the Trophy file with the alpha channel from the Video 2 track to the Video 3 track. Note that all of the effects remain with the video clip as you move it. Then drag the video clip from the Video 1 track to the Video 2 track. Drag the new video clip into the Video 1 track. The video clip in the Video 2 track should be directly above the video clip in the Video 1 track. If the video clip in the Video 2 track is not as long as the one in the Video 1 track, you may want to copy the video clip in the Video 2 track and paste the copy next to it or leave it the way it is, shorter than the clip in the Video 1 track.

4. **To superimpose the clips in the Video 1 and Video 2 tracks, you can use the Color Key effect from the Keying bin and the Color Balance (HLS) video effect from the Color Correct bin.** To apply the Color Key effect to the clip in the Video 2 track, select the Color Key effect from the Effects panel and drag it over the clip in the Video 2 track.

5. **Use the Effect Controls panel to adjust the settings of the video effect.** As you work, you can preview the video effect in the Program Monitor panel. To adjust the Color Key effect, click the triangle in front of the words *Color Key* to display the controls for the effect. Start by clicking the color swatch and picking a color that is similar to the color of the background clip in the Video 1 track. Then adjust the Color Tolerance, Edge Thin, and Edge Feather values.

   If you want to animate the controls over time, you need to set keyframes. To create a keyframe, move the CTI to the beginning of the video clip and click the stopwatch

(Toggle Animation) icon. The first keyframe is created. Next, move the CTI to a new location. As you adjust the control, a new keyframe is created. The keyframes are used to animate the control. To fine-tune the control, click the triangle in front of the control. This displays the graph for the control. Making adjustments to the graph changes the effect of the control.

CROSS-REF For more information on superimposing clips using the Video Keying effects and the Opacity option, see Chapter 14.

6. **To see more of the clip in the Video 1 track, reduce the opacity of the clip in the Video 2 track by using the Opacity option in either the Effect Controls panel or the Timeline panel.** To access the Opacity option in the Timeline panel, you need to expand the track, click the title bar of the track, and choose Opacity. A white line appears below the track's title bar. Drag this bar down to reduce the opacity.

7. **You can make further adjustments to the colors of the clip in the Video 2 track by applying the ProcAmp video effect from the Adjust bin.** To use the ProcAmp video effect, drag it over the clip in the Video 2 track. To lighten the clip, you may want to use the Levels video effect found in the Adjust bin.

8. **To have the colors of the clip in the Video 2 track change over time, you need to create keyframes for the ProcAmp Hue control.** Move the edit line (CTI) to the beginning of the clip. Then click the Toggle Animation icon in front of the Hue control to enable keyframing, and create your first keyframe. Move the edit line (CTI) to a new position, and adjust the Hue control to create another keyframe. Click the triangle in front of the word *Hue* to display the graph for this control. You can use the graph to fine-tune the effect.

9. **To jazz up your project, you can add a sound clip.** Choose File ➪ Import to import a sound clip. In the Import dialog box, locate a sound clip and click Open. This example uses SmartSound's No Borders sound clip, located on the DVD that accompanies this book. You can also choose File ➪ New ➪ SmartSound to import a SmartSound sound clip. To download SmartSound, go to www.smartsound.com/premiere/index.html.

10. **Drag the sound clip from the Project panel to the Audio 1 track.** If the sound clip is too long, click the left side of the clip and drag it inward. For more information on working with sound clips, see Chapter 7.

11. **Choose Sequence ➪ Render Work Area.**

12. **Click the Play button in the Program Monitor panel to preview your work.**

13. **Be sure to save your work.** If you want, you can export your project as a movie. Choose File ➪ Export ➪ Movie. In the Export Movie dialog box, name your movie. To change the settings, click the Settings button. Click Save to save the project as a movie.

Applying Effects to Different Image Areas Using the Image Matte Keying Effect

You can use an image matte to show an effect only in specific areas of a clip. When you apply a matte, Premiere Pro masks out the areas that you don't want shown.

An *image matte* is either a black-and-white image or a grayscale image. By default, Adobe Premiere Pro applies effects to the clip areas corresponding to white portions of the matte. (The effect does not appear in clip regions corresponding to black areas.) In gray areas, the effect is applied with some degree of transparency — which means that the areas where the effect is applied appear to be see-through to some extent.

You can use Adobe Photoshop, Adobe Illustrator, or even Adobe Premiere Pro's Titler to create an image matte. After you create an image matte, you need two clips, one for the Video 1 track and one for the Video 2 track. If you don't have an image matte or video clips, you can use any of the sample files found on the DVD that accompanies this book. Figure 13.12 shows the panels used to create an Image Matte project. The clips used in Figure 13.12 are called Queenstown and Waves. They are found in the MoreClips folder in the Tutorial Projects folder on the DVD.

FIGURE 13.12

The frames from the sample image matte project use the Emboss video effect only on a certain area of the clip (outside the Sun).

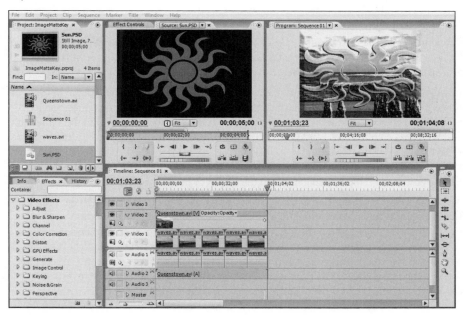

The image matte file (Sun) that is used in Figure 13.12 is created using Photoshop's Custom Shape Tool. You can load Photoshop CS from your Premiere Pro project. In Premiere Pro, select File ⇨ New ⇨ Photoshop File. In the Save Photoshop File As dialog box that appears, enter a filename, locate a folder where you want to save the file, and click Save. This places the Photoshop file in the Project panel in the Premiere Pro project, and it loads Photoshop CS. In Photoshop CS, select the Custom Shape Tool. Then pick a Shape. This example uses Sun 1. With the Sun 1 Shape selected, click and drag on the screen to create a sun. To add dimension to the sun, you can select Layer ⇨ Layer ⇨ Style ⇨ Blending Options, and then apply Drop Shadow, Inner Shadow, Outer Glow, and Bevel and Emboss effects. After making the changes, resave the file. You can then return to Premiere Pro to finish the Image Matte Key project.

Follow these steps to apply an effect using an image matte:

1. **Open an existing project, or create a new one.**

CROSS-REF   Refer to Chapter 3 for information on choosing a project preset.

2. **Choose Window ⇨ Workspace ⇨ Effects to display all of the panels that you need.**

3. **Import two video clips into the Project panel.**

ON the DVD   The video clips used to create the project in Figure 13.12 are in the MoreClips folder in the Tutorial Projects folder located on the DVD that accompanies this book. The matte image used in the project is called Sun and is in the MoreClips folder.

4. **Click and drag one of the video clips from the Project panel to the Video 1 track of the Timeline panel.** The video clip in the Video 1 track is the clip that appears inside the matte. This example uses the Waves video clip in the Video 1 track.

5. **Click and drag the other video clip to the Video 2 track.** The video clip in the Video 2 track is the clip that appears in the background of the matte. This example uses the Queenstown video clip in the Video 2 track.

   Because the video clip in the Video 1 (Waves) track is shorter than the video clip in the Video 2 (Queenstown) track, you can copy and paste the Video 1 clip to increase the length of the video clip in the Video 1 (Waves) track. Do this by selecting the clip in the Timeline, and then choosing Edit ⇨ Copy. Next, move the Edit line to the end of the clip and choose Edit ⇨ Paste Insert to paste another clip next to it. Do this until the length of the clip in the Video 1 track is as long as the clip in the Video 2 track. You may also have to use the Edit Line to edit the last clip to make it match the length of the clip in the Video 2 track.

6. **Apply an effect to the Video 2 track by dragging the effect from the Effects panel to the clip.** If you want, you can apply a different effect to the video clip in the Video 1 track. However, if you apply the effect to the Video 2 track, the effect can be seen only outside the matte image. If you apply the effect to the Video 1 track, the effect is seen only inside the matte image. This example applies the Color Emboss effect (found in the Stylize bin) to the Video 2 track and the Texturize effect (found in the Stylize bin) to the Video 1 track. In the Effect Controls panel, you can adjust the Texturize controls. Set the Texture Layer drop-down menu to Video 1, and increase the Texture Contrast and change the Light Direction.

7. **To superimpose the Video 2 track over the Video 1 track, select the Video 2 track.**

8. **Choose Image Matte from the Keying bin in the Effects panel.** Then click and drag it over the Video 2 track.

9. **In the Effect Controls panel, click the Setup icon.** When the Select a Matte Image dialog box appears, browse to and load the matte image. Click OK to apply the image matte. The properties for the Image Matte effect appear in the Effect Controls panel. They are Composite Using and Reverse. Set the Composite Using drop-down menu to Matte Alpha, and click the Reverse check box to reverse the effect.

10. **Drag the Alpha Glow effect from the Stylize bin to the Video 2 track.** This effect gives the Sun a three-dimensional look. If you want, you can also adjust the size and position of the clip in the Video 2 track by using the Motion effect. You can also reduce the Opacity effect to see more of the clip in the Video 1 track. This example applies the Bevel Edges effect (found in the Perspective bin) to the Video 1 track. If you need to make color or tonal adjustments, you can apply an effect from the Adjust, Color Correction, or Image Control bin.

11. **Click the Play button in the Program Monitor panel to preview the effect.**

12. **Choose File ⇨ Save to save your work.**

Touring Premiere Pro's Video Effects

Premiere Pro boasts over 100 video effects that are divided into 20 bins: Adjust, Blur & Sharpen, Channel, Color Correction, Distort, GPU, Generate, Image Control, Keying, Noise & Grain, Perspective, Pixelate, Presets, Render, Stylize, Time, Transform, Transition, Utility, and Video. Those are a lot of video effects to choose from, and so to help you deal with this overwhelming selection of video effects, this section includes a description of each effect according to its category folder.

CROSS-REF The Keying effects are discussed in detail in Chapter 14. The Color Correction effects are discussed in detail in Chapter 17.

NOTE Before undertaking a tour of the effects, remember that many effects provide previews in dialog boxes. If an effect provides a dialog box, you can click the Setup Dialog Box icon in the Effect Controls panel to see a preview.

TIP Although most effects can be controlled by sliders that you click and drag, you can also click underlined values at the center of the slider to set effects. When you click the underlined value, a dialog box appears showing the largest and smallest values that are allowed in the slider setting.

ON the DVD If you want, you can experiment with the different video effects by applying them to one of the video clips in the Tutorial Projects folder located on the DVD that accompanies this book. The figures within this section use various images that are located in the MoreClips folder.

Adjust

The Adjust effect enables you to adjust the color attributes of selected clips, such as the brightness and contrast of an image. (For more information on adjusting a color clip, see Chapter 17.) If you are familiar with Adobe Photoshop, you'll find that several Premiere Pro video effects — such as Auto Color, Auto Contrast, Auto Levels, Channel Mixer, Levels, and Posterize — are quite similar to filters found in Photoshop.

Auto Color, Auto Contrast, and Auto Levels

The Auto Color, Auto Contrast, and Auto Levels effects allow you to create quick, overall color corrections to a clip. These effects allow you to adjust the midtones, shadows, and highlights. The Auto Color effect focuses on adjusting the colors. The Auto Contrast effect focuses on adjusting the shadows and highlights along with the overall color. The Auto Levels effect focuses primarily on adjusting the shadows and highlights. You can fine-tune each of the effects by adjusting their controls. Each effect also allows you to adjust the result of the effect.

Each effect has five properties so that you can adjust its controls. They are Temporal Smoothing, Scene Detect, Black Clip, White Clip, and Blend with Original. The Auto Color effect also has a Snap Neutral Midtones control. Here's how these properties work:

- **You can adjust Temporal Smoothing to control how many surrounding frames are used to determine the amount of correction.** When you set Temporal Smoothing to 0 (zero), Premiere Pro analyzes each frame independent of the others. When you set Temporal Smoothing to 1, Premiere Pro analyzes frames 1 second before the frame on display.

- **When you enable Temporal Smoothing, Scene Detect displays.** When you select this option, Premiere Pro ignores changes in scenes.

- **Black Clip and White Clip controls adjust how much of the shadow and highlights are affected.**

- **The Blend with Original control can change how much of the effect is applied to the clip.** When the percentage amount is set to 0 (zero), 100 percent of the effect is seen on the clip. When the percentage amount is set to 100, 0 (zero) percent of the effect is seen on the clip.

- **The Snap Neutral Midtones control finds and adjusts the midtone (gray) colors.**

Brightness and Contrast

Using these effects is an easy way to adjust brightness and contrast in your image. Brightness controls how light or dark your image is. Contrast controls the difference between the brightest and darkest pixels in an image. In the Effect Controls panel, click and drag the Brightness slider to increase or reduce an image's brightness, and click and drag the Contrast slider to add or subtract contrast from an image.

Convolution Kernel

This effect uses mathematical *convolution* to change brightness values of a clip. You can use this effect to increase sharpness or enhance image edges. The matrix of numbers in the Convolution Kernel settings represents the pixels in the image. The center pixel text field is the pixel being analyzed. In the center box, enter the number that you want to use as the brightness multiplier. For example, if you enter 2, the pixel's brightness values are doubled. The same concept applies for neighboring text fields. You can enter a brightness multiplier in the surrounding boxes — you can also enter 0 (zero) to have no increase in the brightness value.

Values that you enter in the Scale box are used to divide the sum of the brightness values. If desired, enter a value in the Offset field, which is the same as the value that is added to the Scale field.

When using the Convolution Kernel filter, you can save settings by clicking the Save button; you can reload saved settings by clicking the Load button.

Extract

This effect removes the color from a clip to create a black-and-white effect. The Input and Output sliders in the Extract Settings dialog box, shown in Figure 13.13, enable you to control which image areas are affected. The Softness slider softens the effect. The preview area provides a good idea of the result of the effect.

FIGURE 13.13

The Extract Settings dialog box

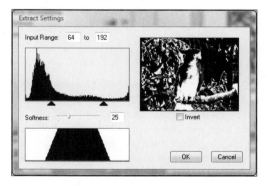

Levels

This effect enables you to correct highlights, midtones, and shadows in an image. To apply the same levels to all color channels, leave the drop-down menu in the Levels Settings dialog box, shown in Figure 13.14, set to RGB Channels. Otherwise, click to choose a red, green, or blue channel to which you want to apply the effect.

To complete your image correction, use the Input sliders to increase contrast. Drag the middle slider to raise or lower midtone values. Drag the Output sliders to decrease contrast.

Lighting Effects

These effects allow you to apply up to five light effects to a clip. There are three different types of lighting that you can apply: Spotlight, Omni, and Directional. You can also adjust each light's color, size, angle, and intensity, as well as the center of the light, and how far the light spreads. You can even apply a texture using the Bump controls. Figure 13.15 shows the Lighting Effects properties in the Effect Controls panel. Figure 13.16 shows the results of applying the Lighting Effects to a clip.

FIGURE 13.14

The Levels Settings dialog box

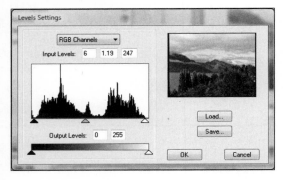

ProcAmp

The Brightness and Contrast options for the ProcAmp effect offer you an easy way to adjust brightness and contrast in your image. Brightness controls how light or dark your image is. Contrast controls the difference between the brightest and darkest pixels in an image. In the Effect Controls panel, click and drag the Brightness option to the right to increase an image's brightness; click and drag to the left to reduce an image's brightness. Click and drag the Contrast option right or left to add or subtract contrast from an image. Click and drag the Hue values to change the color of your image. Click and drag the Saturation option to the right to make the colors more vibrant. Drag the Saturation option to 0 (zero) to take all of the colors out of your image and make it a grayscale image. The Split Screen option allows you to apply the effect to only a portion of the image. The Split Percent value determines how much of the image is affected. Figure 13.17 shows a clip with the ProcAmp video effect. In the effect controls, the Split Percent value is set to 50 percent.

FIGURE 13.15

You can find the Lighting Effects properties in the Effect Controls panel

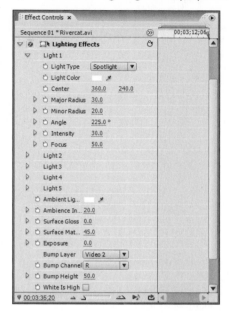

FIGURE 13.16

A preview of the Lighting Effects in the Program Monitor panel

FIGURE 13.17

A preview of the ProcAmp video effect in the Program Monitor panel

Shadow/Highlight

You can use this effect if your image has a backlighting effect problem. The effect is meant to brighten shadows and reduce highlights. To manually adjust the Shadow Amount and Highlight Amount, you must deselect the Auto Amount property (which is selected by default). When this property is selected, Premiere Pro automatically adjusts the shadow or highlight areas.

The Temporal Smoothing control is used to determine how many surrounding frames will be used to determine the amount of correction. The Blend with Original control can change how much of the effect is applied to the clip.

The controls in the More Options section allow you to fine-tune this effect.

Blur & Sharpen

The Blur effects contain options that allow you to blur images. Using Blur effects, you can create motion effects or blur out a video track as a background to emphasize the foreground. The Sharpen effects enable you to sharpen images. Sharpening helps bring out image edges when digitized images or graphics appear too soft.

Antialias

This effect reduces jagged lines by blending image edges of contrasting colors to create a smooth edge.

Camera Blur

By using this effect with keyframes, you can simulate an image going in or out of focus. You can also simulate a "camera blur" effect. Use the Blur slider in the Camera Blur Settings dialog box, shown in Figure 13.18, to control the effect.

FIGURE 13.18

The Camera Blur Settings dialog box

Channel Blur

This effect enables you to blur an image using the red, green, blue, or alpha channel. By default, the Blur Dimension drop-down menu is set to Horizontal and Vertical. At the default setting, any blurring that you apply affects the image horizontally and vertically. If you want to blur only in one dimension, set the drop-down menu to either Horizontal or Vertical. When you deselect the Edge Behavior/Repeat Edge Pixels option, the edges around the clip are blurred. When you select it, they are not.

Compound Blur

This effect blurs images based on luminance values. The effect gives the image a smudged appearance. The blur is based upon a Blur Layer. Click the Blur Layer drop-down menu to pick a video track. If you want, you can blur one video track with another to create a very interesting superimposed effect.

An example of an interesting effect is the superimposition of the Penguins and Highway video clips. These clips are found in the MoreClips folder on the DVD that accompanies this book. Place the Penguins file in the Video 2 track and the Highway file in the Video 1 track. Hide the Penguins clip by clicking the Eye icon in the Timeline panel. Drag the Compound Blur effect onto the Highway clip in the Video 1 track. In the Effect Controls panel, set the Blur Layer drop-down menu to the Video 2 track. Then move the Maximum Blur control to about 16. If you want, click the Invert Blur check box to invert the blur. If the layer sizes differ, you can click the Stretch Map to Fit check box to stretch the blur layer to the clip where the blur effect is applied.

If you want to increase the contrast between the layers, you can use the Unsharp Mask effect. You can find more information about this effect later in this chapter.

Directional Blur

This effect creates a motion effect by blurring an image in a specific direction. The sliders in the Effect Controls panel control the direction and the length of the blur.

Fast Blur

Use this effect to quickly blur a clip. Use the Blur Dimension drop-down menu in the Effect Controls panel to specify whether the blur should be vertical, horizontal, or both.

Gaussian Blur

This effect blurs video and reduces video signal noise. Similar to the Fast Blur effect, you can specify whether the blur should be vertical, horizontal, or both. The word *gaussian* is used because the filter uses a gaussian (bell-shaped) curve when removing contrast to create the blur effect.

Gaussian Sharpen

This effect creates strong, overall sharpening. You can obtain similar results by applying the Sharpen filter several times. This effect provides no controls.

Ghosting

This effect layers image areas from previous frames over one frame. Use this effect to show the path of a moving object — such as a speeding bullet or a pie thrown in the air.

Radial Blur

This effect creates a circular blurring effect. The Radial Blur controls allow you control the degree of blurring. For example, you can increase the value in the Amount field by dragging the Amount slider to the right. In the Blur Method area, choose Spin to create a spinning blur, or choose Zoom to create an outward blur. In the Quality section, choose Draft, Good, or Best. Keep in mind that the better the quality, the more processing time is needed to create the effect.

Sharpen

This effect includes a value that enables you to control sharpening within your clip. Click and drag the Sharpen Amount value in the Effect Controls panel to the right to increase sharpening. The slider permits values from 0 to 100; however, if you click the underlined sharpen amount onscreen, you can enter values up to 4000 into the Value field.

Sharpen Edges

This effect applies sharpening effects on image edges.

Unsharp Mask

This effect works like the Unsharp Mask filter in Photoshop. You can use this effect to increase detail in an image by increasing sharpness between colors. This effect has three controls that you can adjust: Amount, Radius, and Threshold. Increase the Amount value to increase the amount of the effect. Increase the Radius value to increase the amount of pixels that are affected. You can set the Threshold control from 0 to 255; a smaller value creates a more dramatic effect.

Channel

The Channel bin contains various effects that allow you to combine two clips, overlay a color on a clip, or adjust the red, green, and blue channels of a clip.

You can use the Calculations effect to blend channels from different clips. The Set Matte effect allows you to replace the channel (matte) of one clip with another. You can blend video clips based on color modes using the Blend effect. The Invert effect inverts the color values within a clip. The Solid Composite effect overlays a solid color over a clip.

3D Glasses

This effect allows you to create a left and right 3-D view effect. You can superimpose an image upon itself or superimpose two images. When using two different images, you may want to use images with the same dimensions.

To superimpose two different images, you can place one image in the Video 1 track and another image above it in the Video 2 track. Then apply the effect to the clip in the Video 2 track. In the Effect Controls panel, click the Left and Right View drop-down menus and set one to the Video 1 track and the other to the Video 2 track. Then click the 3D View drop-down menu to choose a 3D View option.

To view the 3-D effect, use either 3-D glasses with red and green lenses or 3-D glasses with red and blue lenses.

Arithmetic

This effect allows you to change the red, green, and blue values of a clip, based on a mathematical operation. The method used to change the color values is determined by the option that you select in the Operator drop-down menu. To use the Arithmetic effect, click the Operator drop-down menu and adjust the red, green, and blue values.

Blend

This effect allows you to blend video tracks using different modes: Crossfade, Color Only, Tint Only, Darken Only, and Lighten Only. The Blend with Original option is used to specify which clip you want to blend with. For example, if you apply the Blend effect to a clip in the Video 2 track and you want to blend it with a clip below it in the Video 1 track, set the Blend with Layer drop-down menu to Video 1. For both clips to appear translucent, set the Blend with Original value to 50 percent. In order to see both clips in the Program Monitor panel, they must be selected with the Timeline Marker.

If you apply the Blend effect to a clip in the Video 1 track and you want to blend it with a clip directly above it in the Video 2 track, set the Blend with Layer drop-down menu to the Video 2 track. Then hide the Video 2 track by clicking the Eye icon in the Timeline panel. In order to see both clips in the Program Monitor panel, they must be selected with the Timeline Marker, and the Blend with Original value should be set to less than 90 percent.

The best way to understand the Blend effect is to try it out. If you want, you can use the WhiteParrot and the Queenstown video clips found in the MoreClips folder in the Tutorial Projects folder of the DVD that accompanies this book. To create the Blend effect shown in Figure 13.19, you can place the Queenstown video clip in the Video 1 track. Directly above the Queenstown video clip, place the WhiteParrot video clip in the Video 2 track. You can apply the Blend effect to the WhiteParrot video clip in the Video 2 track. In the Effect Controls panel, set the Blend with Layer drop-down menu to the Video 1 track, set the Mode drop-down menu to Crossfade, and set the Blend with Original value to 60 percent. To achieve the transparency effect, you need to adjust the highlights, midtones, and shadows of the Highway video clip. Do this by using both the Levels video effect. Try using these Adjust video effects to alter the transparency of the cross fade.

Calculations

This effect allows you to combine two video clips in separate tracks using the clips channels and various Blending Modes. You can choose to overlay the clips using the composite channel (RGBA); the red, green, or blue channel; or the gray or alpha channel. The Blending Modes are Copy, Darken, Multiply, Color Burn, Classic Color Burn, Add, Lighten, Screen, Color Dodge, Classic Color Dodge, Overlay, Soft Light, Hard Light, Linear Light, Vivid Light, Pin Light, Difference, Classic Difference, Exclusion, Hue, Saturation, Color, Luminosity, Stencil Alpha, Stencil Luma, Silhouette Alpha, Silhouette Luma, Alpha Add, and Luminescent Add.

FIGURE 13.19

You can use the Blend effect to create interesting superimposition effects.

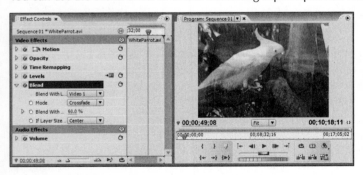

To create the effect shown in the Program Monitor panel in Figure 13.20, you can put the Penguins video clip in the Video 1 track and the Highway video clip in the Video 2 track. Then apply the Calculations effect to the Video 1 track. Hide the clip in the Video 2 track by clicking the Eye icon.

Figure 13.20 also shows the Effect Controls panel with the settings used for effect. In the Effect Controls panel, the Input Channel drop-down menu is set to RGBA, the Second Layer drop-down menu is set to Video 2, and the Second Layer Channel drop-down menu is set to RGBA. The Second Layer Opacity is set to 80 percent, and the Blending Mode drop-down menu is set to Overlay. To achieve the desired overlay, you may need to apply some Adjust, Color Correction, or Image Control video effects to adjust the color and gray levels of the clip.

FIGURE 13.20

The Calculations controls are shown in the Effect Controls panel, along with a preview of the effect in the Program Monitor panel.

Compound Arithmetic

This effect is designed to be used with After Effects projects that use the Compound Arithmetic effect. This effect mathematically uses layers to create a combined effect. The controls for this effect determine how the original layer and the second source layer are blended together. The Second Source Layer drop-down menu allows you to choose another video clip to use in the blending operation. The Operator drop-down menu allows you to pick from various modes to use as the blending method. Adjusting these two controls greatly changes the outcome of the effect. You can also click the Operate on Channels drop-down menu and make a selection. Use the Blend with Original Layer control to adjust the opacity of the original layer and the second source layer.

Invert

This effect inverts color values. You can turn black into white, white into black, and colors into their complements. The example in Figure 13.21 turns white to black.

The Invert effect has two properties that control the outcome of the effect. They are Channel and Blend with Original. The Channel drop-down menu (found in the Effect Controls panel) enables you to choose a color model: RGB, HLS, or YIQ. YIQ is the NTSC color space. Y refers to luminance, *I* refer to inphase chrominance, and *Q* refers to quadrature chrominance. The alpha choice enables you to invert the gray levels in an alpha channel. Use the Blend with Original slider if you want to blend the channel effect with the original image.

FIGURE 13.21

The Invert effect converts white to black.

Set Matte

This effect allows you to create traveling matte effects by combining two clips. However, the Track Matte effect is a better solution for creating traveling mattes. For more information on creating traveling mattes using the Track Matte effect, see Chapter 14.

To try out the Set Matte effect, place two video clips in the Timeline panel, one above the other. Then apply the effect to the clip in the first video track and hide the clip above it. The option that you choose in the Use For Matte drop-down menu (shown in the Effect Controls panel in Figure 13.22) controls the results of the effect. To invert the effect, click the Invert Matte check box.

Figure 13.22 shows the results of applying the Set Matte effect to a video clip of a white swan (WhiteSwan) in the Video 1 track. Directly above the clip in the Video 1 track is a video clip of the Sydney Opera House (Rivercat) in the Video 2 track. You can hide the clip in the Video 2 track by clicking the Eye icon. In the Effect Controls panel, set the Take Matte from Layer drop-down menu to the Video 2 track, and set the Use for Matte drop-down menu to Luminance. Because the layers differ in size, you need to select all of the If Layer Sizes Differ options. To make the clip in the Video 1 track stand out, you can adjust the tonal values (shadows, midtones, and highlights) using the Levels effect (found in the Adjust bin).

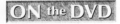 The WhiteSwan and Rivercat files are found in the MoreClips folder in the Tutorial Projects folder of the DVD that accompanies this book.

Solid Composite

This effect allows you to overlay a clip with a solid color. The way the color appears on the clip depends upon the Blending Mode that you select. You can adjust both the opacity of the original clip and the solid color.

FIGURE 13.22

The Set Matte controls are shown in the Effect Controls panel, and the result of the effect is shown in the Program Monitor panel.

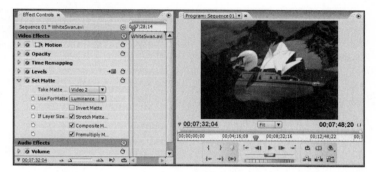

You can use the Solid Composite to create a sepia effect of a swan (WhiteSwan), as shown in Figure 13.23. To create the sepia effect, set the color swatch to a yellow-orange color and the Blending Mode to Luminosity. Then reduce the opacity of the source clip and the solid color. For further effect, you can also use the Levels effect to adjust the tonal values of the clips.

Color Correction

The Color Correction effects enable you to correct the colors in a clip. Some of these commands are similar to the color correction filters found in Adobe Photoshop. The Color Correction effects are Brightness & Contrast, Broadcast Colors, Change Color, Change to Color, Channel Mixer, Color Balance, Color Balance (HLS), Equalize, Fast Color Corrector, Leave Color, Luma Corrector, Luma Curve, RGB Color Corrector, RGB Curves, Three-Way Color Corrector, Tint, and Video Limiter. The Color Correction effects are discussed in detail in Chapter 17.

FIGURE 13.23

The Solid Composite controls are shown in the Effect Controls panel, and the result of the effect is shown in the Program Monitor panel.

401

Brightness & Contrast

The Brightness value affects the light areas in an image, while Contrast affects the difference between the brightest and darkest areas.

Broadcast Colors

If you are outputting your production to videotape, you may want to apply the Broadcast Colors effect to improve color output quality. As discussed in Chapters 10 and 17, the gamut, or range, of video colors is smaller than the color gamut of a computer monitor. To use the Broadcast Color effect, choose either NTSC for American television or PAL for European television in the Broadcast Locale drop-down menu. Then choose one of the following methods in the How to Make Colors Safe drop-down menu:

- **Reduce Luminance:** This option reduces pixels' brightness values, moving the pixel values toward black.

- **Reduce Saturation:** This option brings pixel values closer to gray, making the colors less intense.

- **Key out Unsafe:** Colors that fall beyond the TV gamut become transparent.

- **Key in Safe:** Colors that are within the TV gamut become transparent.

In the Maximum Signal Field, enter the IRE breakpoint value. (IRE measures image luminance.) Any levels above this value are altered. If you are unsure of what value to use, leave the default setting of 110.

 In some video cameras, black-and-white stripes appear in the viewfinder when an image's brightness surpasses 100 IRE. This indicates that the image luminance is too bright.

Field Interpolate and Reduce Interlace Flicker

Two other image-enhancing effects appear in the Video folder: Field Interpolate and Reduce Interlace Flicker.

- **Field Interpolate:** This effect creates missing scan lines from the average of other lines.

- **Reduce Interlace Flicker:** This effect softens horizontal lines in an attempt to reduce interlace flicker.

Timecode

This effect is not used to enhance colors. Instead, it is used to "burn" timecode into footage so that it is visible in the Program Monitor. When you apply this effect, you can choose position, size, and opacity options in the Effect Controls panel. You can also choose among timecode formats and apply a frame offset.

You can also use the Timecode effect to place timecode in transparent video in a track over your footage. This allows you to view timecode without affecting the actual program footage. To create transparent video, choose File ➪ New Transparent Video. Then drag the transparent video from the

Project panel into a track above your footage in the Timeline. Next, apply the Timecode effect by dragging it over the transparent video.

NOTE   Choosing the wrong field settings in the Project Settings dialog box can increase flicker. To access the Project Settings dialog box, choose Project ⇨ Project Settings ⇨ General. These settings are covered in more detail in Chapter 3.

Change Color

This effect adjusts a range of colors through its hue, saturation, and lightness.

ON the DVD   You may want to use the Rooster file found in the MoreClips folder of the DVD that accompanies this book to experiment with the Change Color effect. The file is full of a lot of colors for you to change.

After you apply the Change Color effect to a clip, you can get started.

1. **To start changing the colors of a clip, you first need to pick a color to change.** To do so, use either the color swatch or the Eyedropper tool in the Color to Change section.

2. **Click the View drop-down menu.** Choose whether you want to view the color changes in the Corrected Layer or the Color Correction Mask.

3. **Click the Match Colors drop-down menu to determine the method to match colors.** There are three methods of matching colors: RGB, Hue, and Chroma. The RGB chooses methods by using red, green, and blue colors. The Hue method uses hue colors to match the chosen color. The Chroma method uses saturation and hue but disregards lightness.

4. **Use the Hue Transform, Lightness Transform, and Saturation Transform controls to change the selected color.** Use the Matching Tolerance and Matching Softness to fine-tune the change of the selected color.

5. **To invert the selected color correction, click Invert Color Correction Mask.**

Change to Color

This effect allows you to change a color to another color by adjusting the color's Hue, Lightness, and Saturation (HLS) values.

After you apply the Change to Color effect to a clip, you can start changing colors. Here's how:

1. **In the From and To section, use either the color swatch or the Eyedropper tool to choose the color that you want to change.** Pick the color that you want to change it to.

2. **Use the Change and Change By drop-down menus to choose a method with which to change colors.**

3. **Click the triangle in front of the Tolerance section to display the Hue, Lightness, and Saturation controls.** Use these controls to change the set colors.

4. **Use the Softness control to determine the smoothness of the color change.**

5. **If you want, you can click the View Correction Matte check box.**

Channel Mixer

This effect enables you to create special effects by mixing colors from a clip's channels. With the Channel Mixer, you can create color effects and turn a color image into a grayscale image or into an image with a sepia tone or tint effect.

To use the Channel Mixer effect, click and drag any Source Channel slider in the Effect Controls panel to the left to decrease the amount of color that is supplied to the image. Click and drag to the right to increase it.

To convert an image to grayscale, click the Monochrome button and adjust the sliders.

Color Balance

This effect allows you to adjust the highlights, midtones, and shadows of the red, green, and blue colors. These controls allow you to create a unified color balance. Increasing the red, green, and blue color values increases the amount of that color in an image. Reducing these values increases the amount of that color's complement. Here's how the effect works:

- Increasing the red values increases the red colors in an image and reduces the cyan. Reducing the red values reduces the red colors in an image and increases the cyan.

- Increasing the green values increases the green colors in an image and reduces the magenta. Reducing the green values decreases the green colors in an image and increases the magenta.

- Increasing the blue values increases the blue color in an image and reduces the yellow. Reducing the blue values reduces the blue color in an image and increases the yellow.

Color Balance (HLS)

This effect enables you to change and adjust colors using Hue, Lightness, and Saturation sliders in the Effect Controls panel. Hue controls the color, Lightness controls how light and dark the color is, and Saturation controls the intensity of the color. For a full description of how to use this effect, see Chapter 17.

Equalize

You can use this effect to redistribute the brightness values in an image. To use the Equalize effect, first click the Equalize drop-down menu to pick an Equalize method. Then use the Amount to Equalize control to determine the amount to equalize.

Fast Color Corrector

This effect allows you to quickly adjust a clip's color and luminance. See Chapter 17 for more information.

Leave Color

This effect turns an entire color image into grayscale with the exception of one color. When you set the Tolerance and Edge Softness controls to 0 (zero) percent, and the Amount to Decolor control to 100 percent, an entire color image turns gray. To add color to the image, either reduce the percentage of the Amount to Decolor control or increase the Tolerance percentage value.

The Color to Leave swatch determines which color in your image will remain. Adjusting the Tolerance control determines how much of the swatch color is affected. For a smooth transition in color and gray areas, increase the Edge Softness control. Click the Match Colors drop-down menu to pick either the RGB or Hue color model.

Luma Corrector

This effect allows you to adjust a clip's luminance or brightness values. See Chapter 17 for more details.

Luma Curve

This effect allows you to make adjustments to a clip's luminance values by clicking and dragging a curve representing the clip's brightness values. See Chapter 17 for more details.

RGB Color Corrector

This effect allows you to make adjustments to color and luminance using RGB values. See Chapter 17 for more details.

RGB Curves

This effect allows you to adjust RGB Color values using curves. See Chapter 17 for more details.

Three-Way Color Corrector

This effect provides an assortment of controls for correcting colors as well as shadows (darkest image areas), midtones, and highlights (brightest image areas). See Chapter 17 for more details.

Tint

Use this effect to apply a color tint to your image. If desired, you can reassign the black-and-white portions of your clip with different colors by clicking the color swatch and choosing a color in the Color Picker panel. Choose color intensity by clicking and dragging the slider in the Color Picker panel.

Video Limiter

Use this effect after color correcting to ensure that the video falls within specific limits. See Chapter 17 for details.

Distort

The Distort commands, found in the Distort bin, enable you to distort an image by twirling, pinching, or spherizing it. Many of these commands are similar to the distort filters found in Adobe Photoshop.

Bend

This effect can bend your image in various directions. You can make adjustments either by clicking the triangle in front of the word Bend and adjusting the controls (as shown in Figure 13.24), or by clicking the Set Up icon next to the word Bend and making adjustments in the Bend Settings dialog box. In the Bend Settings dialog box, use the Intensity, Rate, and Width sliders to control effects for Horizontal and Vertical Bending. Intensity is the wave height, Rate is the frequency, and Width is the width of the wave. The Direction drop-down menu controls the direction of the effect. The Wave drop-down menu specifies the type of wave: sine, circle, triangle, or square. The example in Figure 13.24 applies the Bend effect to the Rooster file, which is found in the MoreClips folder on the DVD that accompanies this book.

FIGURE 13.24

The Bend controls in the Effect Controls panel and a preview of the effect in the Monitor panel

Corner Pin

This effect allows you to distort an image by adjusting the Upper Left, Upper Right, Lower Left, and Lower Right values (corners).

Figure 13.25 shows controls for the Corner Pin effect in the Effect Controls panel, and the result of the effect is shown in the Program Monitor panel. In the figure, note that the position of the clip is changed. The effect is applied to a clip in the Video 2 track. Another clip is below the clip in the Video 2 track. The clip in the background is the image from the Video 2 track, and the image in the foreground is the image from the Video 1 track. In the Video 2 track, this example uses the Rooster video clip, and in the Video 1 track, it uses the Maui video clip. You can find both clips in the MoreClips folder on the DVD that accompanies this book. The clip in the Video 2 track (Rooster) also has the Drop Shadow effect (found in the Perspective bin) applied to it.

The Video 3 track contains a Title clip that was created in Premiere Pro's Titler using the Path Type tool. To create a new title and display the Titler, choose File ➪ New ➪ Title. In the dialog box that appears, name the title and click Save. In the Titler, use the Path Type tool to create a curved path. Then type some text, and stylize it. When you are done, close the Titler and drag the Title clip from the Project panel to the Timeline panel. For more information on using the Titler, see Chapter 10. Figure 13.26 shows the Titler panel being used to create the Title clip in Figure 13.25.

FIGURE 13.25

The image after applying the Corner Pin effect

Lens Distortion

You can use this effect to simulate video being viewed through a distorted lens. You can make adjustments in one of two way: either by clicking the triangle in front of the word *Lens Distortion* and adjusting the controls (as shown in Figure 13.27); or by clicking the Set Up icon next to the word *Lens Distortion* and making adjustments in the Lens Distortion Settings dialog box.

You can use the Curvature slider in the Lens Distortion settings to change the lens curve. Negative values make the curvature more concave (inward); positive values make the curvature more convex (outward). Vertical and Horizontal Decentering sliders change the focal point of the lens.

The Vertical and Horizontal Prism FX settings create effects similar to changing Vertical and Horizontal Decentering. Use the Fill Color swatch to change the background color. Click the Fill Alpha Channel check box to make background areas transparent, based on the clip's alpha channel.

FIGURE 13.26

The Title clip used in the Corner Pin effect that appears in Figure 13.25

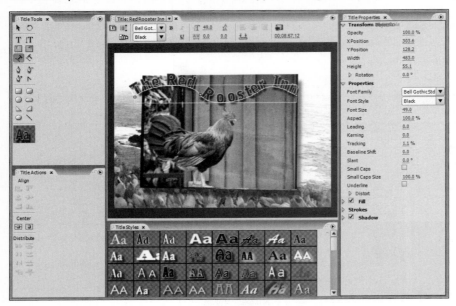

FIGURE 13.27

The Lens Distortion controls in the Effect Controls panel and a preview of the effect in the Monitor panel

Magnify

This effect allows you to magnify a certain portion of a clip or the entire clip.

Figure 13.28 shows the controls for the Magnify effect in the Effect Controls panel, and the result of the effect in the Program Monitor panel. In the figure, note that the Opacity of the magnified title clip is also changed. This example applies the Magnify effect over the Title clip (shown in Figure 13.26) that was used in the Corner Pin effect (shown in Figure 13.25). The Magnify effect is applied to a Title clip in the Video 3 track. Below the clip in the Video 2 track, is a video clip (Rooster).

The clip in the background is the (rooster) image from the Video 2 track, and the image in the foreground is the Title clip from the Video 3 track. The Video 2 track contains the video clip Rooster, and the Video 3 track contains a Title clip that was created using the Path Type tool in Premiere Pro's Titler. The (Title) clip in which you applied the Magnify effect can be animated by applying keyframes. To do so, move the Edit line to the beginning of the clip and then click the Stop Watch icon in front of both the Center and Magnification options. As you do so, a keyframe is created.

To create another keyframe, move the Edit line and then edit the Magnification controls. Continue doing this until you are satisfied with the animated effect.

FIGURE 13.28

The Magnify controls in the Effect Controls panel and a preview of the effect in the Program Monitor panel

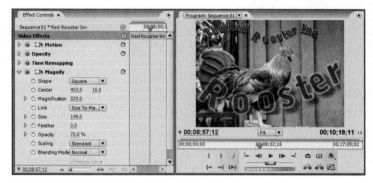

Mirror

This creates a mirrored effect. In the Effect Controls panel, click the Reflection Center values to designate the X and Y coordinates of the reflection line. The Reflection Angle option enables you to choose where the reflection appears. The following degree settings should give you an idea of how dragging the slider distorts the image:

- **0:** Left onto right side
- **90:** Right onto left side
- **180:** Top onto bottom
- **270:** Bottom onto top

Figure 13.29 shows the controls for the Mirror effect in the Effect Controls panel, and the results of the effect in the Program Monitor panel. Note that the Position, Scale, and Opacity of the clip have also been changed. The effect is applied to a video clip (Rooster) in the Video 2 track and a Title clip in the Video 3 track. Below the clip in the Video 2 track, another video clip (Maui) is added.

The video clips shown in Figure 13.29 are Maui in the Video 1 track, and Rooster in the Video 2 track. The (Title) clip in which you applied the Mirror effect can be animated by applying keyframes. To do so, move the Edit line to the beginning of the clip, and then click the Stop Watch icon in front of both the Reflection Center and Reflection Angle options. As you do so, a keyframe is created. To create another keyframe, move the Edit line and then edit the Reflection controls. Continue doing this until you are satisfied with the animated effect.

FIGURE 13.29

The Mirror controls in the Effect Controls panel and a preview of the effect in the Program Monitor panel

Offset

This effect allows you to shift a clip vertically and horizontally, creating a pan effect. Adjusting the Offset's Shift Center To controls can shift a clip vertically and/or horizontally. To blend some of the Offset effect with the original clip, you can adjust the Blend with Original Clip control.

Polar Coordinates

This can create a variety of unusual effects by changing the clip's X and Y coordinates to polar coordinates. In the polar coordinate system, the X and Y coordinates are distances radiating out from a focal point. By using this effect, you can transform a line into a half-circle or horseshoe shape.

In the Effect Controls panel, the Interpolation value controls the amount of the distortion — 0 (zero) percent provides no distortion, and 100 percent provides the most. In the Type of Conversion drop-down menu, Rect to Polar converts horizontal coordinates to polar Coordinates; Polar to Rect converts polar coordinates to rectangular ones.

Ripple

This effect turns a clip into rippled patterns. The Ripple Settings dialog box enables you to adjust the ripples on a horizontal and vertical plane and to control the intensity and frequency of the ripples.

Spherize

This effect can turn a flat image into a spherical one. Adjust the Radius property to control the spherizing effect. Dragging the slider to the right increases the value, providing a larger sphere. Adjusting the Center of Sphere values changes the location of the sphere.

Figure 13.30 shows the results of applying the Spherize effect to a video clip (Rooster) in the Video 2 track, and a Title clip (The Red Rooster Inn) in the Video 3 track. To animate the Spherize effect, you need to set keyframes for the Spherize controls. Below the clip in the Video 2 track is another video clip (Maui).

FIGURE 13.30

The Spherize controls are shown in the Effect Controls panel, and the effect is shown in the Program Monitor panel.

Transform

This effect allows you to move an image's position, scale its height and width, skew or rotate it, and change its opacity, as shown in Figure 13.31. You can also use the Transform effect to change the position of a clip. To change the position of a clip, click the box next to the word *Position* in the Effect Controls panel. Then click in the Program Monitor panel where you want the clip to move to. Use the Anchor Point setting to move a clip, based on its anchor point.

Figure 13.31 shows the results of applying the Transform effect to a video clip (Rooster) in the Video 2 track, and to a Title clip (The Red Rooster Inn) in the Video 3 track. To animate the Transform effect, you need to set keyframes for the Transform controls. Below the clip in the Video 2 track, the Video 1 track contains another video clip (Maui).

FIGURE 13.31

A preview of the Transform effect in the Program Monitor panel with the Transform properties in the Effect Controls panel

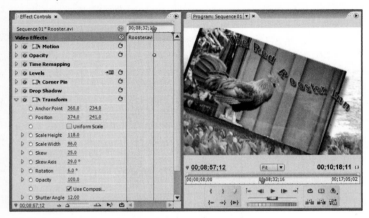

Turbulent Displace

This effect displaces a clip with the use of fractal noises. The effect can make an image feel like there is movement. The effect is sometimes used on waving flags or running water. Use the Displace drop-down menu to choose the type of displacement that you want to occur. Then adjust the Amount, Size, Offset, Complexity, and Evolution controls to make the proper adjustments to the distortion you want to create.

Twirl

This effect can turn an image into twirling digital soup. Use the Angle value to control the degree of twirling. Larger angle settings create more twirling.

Figure 13.32 shows the results of applying the Twirl effect to a video clip (Rooster) in the Video 2 track, and to a Title clip (The Red Rooster Inn) in the Video 3 track. To animate the Twirl effect, you need to set keyframes for the Twirl controls. Below the video clip in the Video 2 track, the Video 1 track contains another video clip (Maui).

Wave Warp

This creates wave-like effects that can make your clip look as if it were hit by a tidal wave. To control the effect, use the Wave settings found in the Effect Controls panel, shown in Figure 13.33. You can see the results of applying the Wave Warp effect to a video clip (RockyStream) in the Video 2 track. To animate the Wave Warp effect, you need to set keyframes for the Wave Warp controls. You can find the RockyStream video clip on the DVD that accompanies this book.

FIGURE 13.32

A preview of the Twirl effect in the Program Monitor panel with the Transform properties in the Effect Controls panel

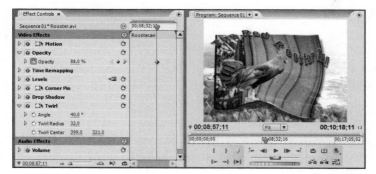

FIGURE 13.33

A preview of the Wave Warp effect in the Program Monitor panel with the Transform properties in the Effect Controls panel

Following is a brief description of the controls for the Wave Warp effect:

■ **Wave Type:** Controls the type of wave crests — Sine (waving), Square, Triangle, Sawtooth, Circle, Semicircle, Uncircle, Noise, or Smooth Noise.

■ **Wave Height:** Changes the distance between wave peaks. This allows you to control the amount of vertical distortion.

■ **Wave Width:** Changes the direction and wave length. This allows you to control the amount of horizontal distortion.

■ **Direction:** Controls the amount of horizontal and vertical distortion.

■ **Wave Speed:** Randomizes the wavelength and amplitude.

■ **Pinning:** Controls the amount of continuous waves, and selects image areas that will not have waves affect a certain area.

■ **Phase:** Determines the point at which a wave cycle begins.

■ **Antialiasing:** Determines the smoothness of the waves.

GPU

The GPU effects are Page Curl, Refraction, and Ripple (Circular). The GPU effects appear if you have a Graphics Processing Unit card that supports Direct 3D, PS 1.3+, and VS 1.1+.

Generate

The Generate bin features various interesting effects, some of which may be familiar to you. For example, the Lens Flare effect is similar to Adobe Photoshop's Lens Flare filter. Other effects may be new to you, such as the 4-Color Gradient, Cell Pattern, Checkerboard, Circle, Eyedropper Fill, Grid, Lens Flare, Lightning, Paint Bucket, Ramp, and Write-on.

4-Color Gradient

This effect can be applied over a solid black video to create a four-color gradient, or it can be applied to an image to create interesting blending effects.

Here's how to apply the 4-Color Gradient effect:

1. **Drag the effect over a video clip with an interesting image.** If you want, try using the 4-Color Gradient effect on the Highway.jpg file in the MoreClips folder on the DVD that accompanies this book.

2. **To blend the gradient and the video clip together, click the Blend drop-down menu and choose a Blending Mode (found in the Effect Controls panel).** Try experimenting with different modes.

3. **To move the position of the gradient, you can also click the words** *4-Color Gradient* **in the Effect Controls panel.** Notice that four circles with plus signs appear in the Program Monitor panel. Click one of the circle icons to move one of the gradients.

4. **If you want to reduce the opacity of the gradient, reduce the percentage value for the Opacity control.**

5. **To change the colors and the positions of the gradient, click the triangle in front of the Positions and Colors section.** Use these controls to create the desired effect.

6. **Use the Blend control to change the amount of blending between the gradients.** Use the Jitter control to adjust the amount of noise between the separate gradients.

Cell Pattern

This effect can be used to create interesting background effects, or it can be used as a matte. Figure 13.34 shows the Cell Pattern properties in the Effect Controls panel and a preview in the Program Monitor panel. This example applies the Cell Pattern effect to a black color matte that was created in Premiere Pro. You can also apply it to a solid color matte. To create a black video, select File ⇨ New ⇨ Color Matte. In the Color Picker dialog box, set the color to black. Then click OK. A black matte is automatically placed in the Project panel of your current project. To create a black video, select File ⇨ New ⇨ Black Video.

Drag the black matte (or black video) to the Video 2 track. In the Video 1 track, drag a video clip below the black matte. In this example, the BakerySign video clip is dragged to the Video 1 track. This video clip is on the DVD that accompanies this book. Apply the Cell Pattern effect to either a solid color matte or a black video. In order to blend the Color Matte clip and the BakerySign clip, apply the Difference Matte video effect (found in the Keying bin) to the Black Matte clip in the Video 2 track. The settings used to create the blending effect are shown in Figure 13.34.

Experimenting with the Cell Pattern controls in the Effect Controls panel changes the blending effect shown in Figure 13.34. Click the Cell Pattern drop-down menu and pick different cell patterns. To move the cell pattern, click the words *Cell Pattern* (in the Effect Controls panel). Then move the circle icon that appears in the Program Monitor panel to move the pattern. If you want, you can also click the word *Motion* and use the circle icon in the Program Monitor panel to move and change the size of both the pattern and the video clip.

You can change the look of the pattern by adjusting the Disperse, Size, and Offset controls. These controls only change the pattern; they do not affect the video clip. If you want, you can use the Motion controls to change both the pattern and the video clip. To do so, adjust the controls for the Position, Scale, Rotation, and Anchor Points options.

For more or less contrast within the pattern, use the Contrast control. If you want, you can invert the pattern by clicking the Invert check box. Remember that you can change a video effect over time by animating with keyframes.

FIGURE 13.34

The Difference Matte and Cell Pattern effect controls and a preview of their effect

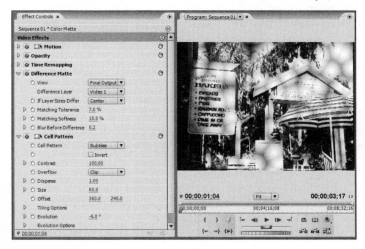

Checkerboard

You can apply this effect to a black video or a color matte to create a checkerboard background, or as a. The checkerboard pattern can also be applied to an image and blended together to create an interesting effect. Figure 13.35 shows a preview of the Checkerboard effect in the Program Monitor panel. The effect is applied to the BakerySign video clip on the DVD that accompanies this book.

Figure 13.35 shows the Checkerboard properties in the Effect Controls panel. To create the blending effect between the BakerySign scene and the checkerboard, choose Difference in the Blending Mode drop-down menu. Change the width of the checkerboard by increasing the value of the Width control. To change the Height, you first need to click the Size From drop-down menu and choose Width and Height Sliders. To blur the edges of the width and height, use the Width and Height Feather controls.

You can change the color and opacity of the checkerboard by clicking the Color Swatch icon and changing the color in the Color Picker dialog box, or by clicking one of the colors in the video clip with the Eyedropper tool. To move the pattern, use the Anchor control or click the word *Checkerboard* and move the circle icon in the Program Monitor panel. Remember that you can animate the Checkerboard video effect by setting keyframes for the effect controls.

FIGURE 13.35

The Checkerboard effect controls and a preview of its effect

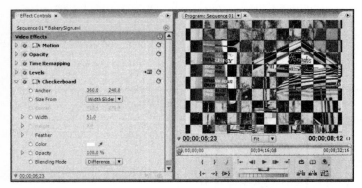

Circle

You can apply this effect to a black video or a solid color matte to create a circle or a ring. Try applying the Circle effect to the BakerySign video clip found in the MoreClips folder on the DVD that accompanies this book.

When you apply the Circle effect, the default settings are set to create a small white circle on a black background. To turn the circle into a ring, click the Edge drop-down menu and change the setting from None to Edge Radius. Then increase the Edge Radius value. If you want, you can also change the Edge drop-down menu setting to Thickness or Thickness * Radius and then adjust the Thickness control. To soften the outer and inner edges of the ring, set the Edge drop-down menu setting to Thickness & Feather * Radius. Then increase the values of the Feather Outer Edge and Feather Inner Edge controls. To change the color of the ring or circle, use the Color control. Increase the Feather Outer Edge value to feather the outer edge of the circle.

You can move the circle or ring by using the Center controls in the Effect Controls panel. You can also move the circle by clicking the word *Circle* and moving the circle icon in the Program Monitor panel. To increase the size of the circle or ring, increase the value of the Radius control.

Switching the Circle effect's Blending Mode from None to Normal allows you to see the video clip to which the effect has been applied. To make the ring or circle more translucent, reduce the value of the Opacity control. To invert the effect, click the Invert Circle check box.

To have the BakerySign file appear as if it is on a record, set the Edge drop-down menu to Edge Radius. Then set the Edge Radius to 57. Make sure that the Invert Circle check box is not selected. Set the Opacity value to 50 percent. Set the Blending Mode drop-down menu to Alpha Blending. Next, try using the Difference mode to create an interesting effect of blending the BakerySign clip onto itself. For the best results, first set the color swatch to white.

Figure 13.36 shows the Circle effect applied to the BakerySign video clip. It also shows the Circle properties in the Effect Controls panel that are used to create the effect shown in the Program Monitor panel. To create this effect, in the Effect Controls panel, set the Edge drop-down menu to Edge Radius and then adjust the Center, Radius, and Edge Radius controls. Next, feather the outer and inner edge radius. Then change the color swatch and set the Blending Mode drop-down menu to Exclusion.

You can also use the Circle effect to blend two video clips. You can experiment with video clips that are on the DVD that accompanies this book. First, apply the effect to a video clip in the Video 2 track. Then, add another video clip in the Video 1 track below. Blend the two images together by setting the Blending Mode drop-down menu to Stencil Alpha.

FIGURE 13.36

The Circle effect controls and a preview of their effect

Eyedropper Fill

This effect selects a color from the clip to which the effect has been applied. To change the sample color, use the Sample Point and Sample Radius controls in the Effect Controls panel. Click the Average Pixel Area drop-down menu to choose a method of choosing pixel colors. Increase the Blend with Original value to view more of the affected clip.

Grid

This effect creates a grid that can be used as a matte or that can be superimposed by using the Blending Mode options. Figure 13.37 shows the results of the Grid effect using the Overlay option in the Blending Mode drop-down menu. In this example, the effect is applied to the Highway video clip file, which you can find in the MoreClips folder of the DVD that accompanies this book.

Figure 13.37 also shows the Grid effect properties in the Effect Controls panel. You can adjust the width and height of the grid by using the Size From drop-down menu. When you click the drop-down menu, choose one of the three controls: Corner Point, Width, and Height. You can change the thickness of the lines in the grid by adjusting the Border control. The edges of the lines can be softened by increasing the Feather values. You can change the color of the lines in the grid by using the Color control. The grid can be inverted by clicking the Invert Grid check box. To blend the grid over the affected clip, click the Blending Mode drop-down menu and choose an option. To make the grid translucent, decrease the Opacity value.

FIGURE 13.37

The Grid effect controls and a preview of their effect

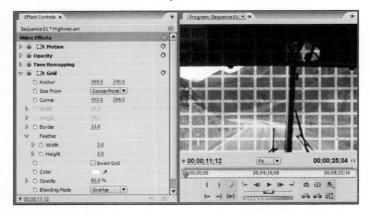

Lens Flare

This effect creates a flaring light effect in your image. The Lens Flare settings appear in the Effect Controls panel. Either click the rectangle that appears next to the word *Lens Flare* and pick a position for the lens flare in the Program Monitor panel, or click and drag the Flare Center controls to position the lens flare. Then pick a lens type: Zoom, 35mm, or 105mm. Next, click and drag the

Flare Brightness control to adjust flare brightness. Figure 13.38 shows the Lens Flare Settings controls and a preview of the effect.

FIGURE 13.38

The Lens Flare effect controls and a preview of their effect

Lightning

This effect enables you to add lightning to a clip. The Start point and End point controls allow you to choose starting and ending points for the lightning. Moving the Segments slider to the right increases the number of segments that the lightning contains, while moving the slider to the left decreases the number of segments. Conversely, moving the other Lightning effect sliders to the right increases the effect, while moving the slider to the left decreases it. You can stylize your lightning bolt by adjusting the Segments, Amplitude, Branching, Speed, Stability, Width, Pull Force, and Blending Mode options. Figure 13.39 shows a lightning bolt created using the Lightning effect.

Paint Bucket

You can use this effect to colorize an image or to apply a solid color to an area in an image. Note that the Paint Bucket effect works similarly to the Paint Bucket tool in Photoshop. Figure 13.40 shows the Paint Bucket properties in the Effect Controls panel and a preview of the effect in the Program Monitor panel. The effect is applied to the Highway video clip file. To blend the Paint Bucket color and the highway video clip, set the Blending Mode drop-down menu to Color. To create the effect in this example, you can invert the fill by selecting the Invert Fill check box.

You can select the color that is used to colorize the video clip by using the Color control. You control the amount of color applied to the image by changing the Tolerance value. The Threshold control can be used as a form of retouching and color-correcting. It allows you to preview the clip and fill color in a black-and-white state. When applying the Paint Bucket color to your clip, toggle this control on and off to view the results in black and white. This makes it easier to see the results of the Paint Bucket color.

The Fill Point and Fill Selector controls enable you to specify the area of the color effects. The Stroke drop-down menu determines how the edges of the color will work. To make the Paint Bucket color fill translucent, reduce the percent value for the Opacity control.

FIGURE 13.39

The image after applying the Lightning effect and Lightning options shown in the Effect Controls panel

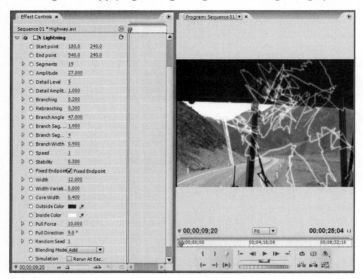

FIGURE 13.40

The Paint Bucket effect controls and a preview of its effect

Ramp

This effect allows you to create linear or radial blurs. Click the Ramp Shape drop-down menu to choose either Radial Ramp or Linear Ramp. You can set the start and end colors of the blur by clicking a color in your image and using the Eyedropper tool, or by clicking the color swatch and using the Color Picker dialog box. Moving the Ramp Scale slider to the left creates a smoother blend. When the Blend Witness slider is set to 50, both the blend and image clip to which you are applying the effect are set to 50 percent translucency. Moving the slider to the right makes the image clip more opaque; moving the slider to the left makes the blend less opaque.

Write-on

This effect can be used to animate a colored brush stroke on a video clip, or it can be used with the affected clip to create brush strokes on a clip beneath it. Here's how:

1. **Drag a clip into the Video 1 track.** This example uses the BakerySign video clip file, located on the DVD.

2. **Directly below the clip in the Video 1 track, drag another clip into the Video 2 track.** This example uses the Highway video clip file, located on the DVD.

3. **Apply the Write-on effect to the clip in the Video 2 track.** Use the controls in the Effect Controls panel to adjust the effect.

4. **Increase the Brush Size value to get a better look at the effect.** To change the color of the brush stroke, use the Color control. A small Brush Hardness percent value softens the edges of the brush stroke. To make the brush strokes translucent, reduce the percent value of the Brush Opacity.

5. **Use the Paint Style drop-down menu to determine where the brush strokes are applied.** If you set the drop-down menu to On Original Image, the brush strokes paint on the Video 2 track (the clip to which the effect was applied) with the color that is selected in the Color control. If you set the drop-down menu to On Transparent, the brush strokes paint on the Video 1 track (the clip below the clip to which the effect was applied) with the color that is selected in the Color control. If you set the Paint Style drop-down menu to Reveal Original Image, the brush strokes paint on the Video 1 Track, using the Video 2 track as the brush strokes.

6. **To move the brush stroke, use the Brush Position controls or click the word *Write-on* (in the Effect Controls panel) and move the circle icon that appears in the Program Monitor panel.** To animate the movement of the brush strokes, move the current-time indicator (CTI) to the beginning of the clip, and then click the Toggle animation icon in front of the Brush Position to create a keyframe. Continue moving the CTI and adjusting the Brush Position controls to create keyframes for your brush stroke animation.

7. **Use the Stroke Length and Stroke Spacing, Part Time Properties, and Brush Time Properties controls to adjust the way the brush strokes are applied.**

Image Control

The Image Control bin contains a variety of color special effects. They are Black & White, Color Balance (RGB), Color Match, Color Offset, Color Pass, Color Replace, Gamma Correction, and PS Arbitrary Map.

Black & White

This effect produces a grayscale version of a selected clip.

Color Balance (RGB)

This effect adds or subtracts red, green, or blue color values in a clip. You can easily add and subtract color values by clicking the Red, Green, or Blue color sliders in the Effect Controls panel. Dragging the sliders to the left reduces the amount of color; dragging the sliders to the right adds color. For a full description of how to use this effect, see Chapter 17.

Color Match

This effect allows you to match the colors of one clip to another. For a full description of how to use this effect, see Chapter 17.

Color Offset

This effect enables you to create 3-D images out of 2-D artwork by shifting the red, green, and blue color channels up, down, left, and right. Use the Offset slider to control the distance between color channels. You can use this effect to set up the image for viewing with 3-D glasses.

Color Pass

This effect converts all but one color in a clip to grayscale — or it can convert just one color in a clip to grayscale. You can use this effect to draw interest to specific items in a clip. For example, you may want to show a grayscale party scene in which a grayscale man or woman is wearing a colored hat or holding a colored balloon.

Follow these steps to set the Color Pass color and apply the effect:

1. **In the Color Pass Settings dialog box clip area, shown in Figure 13.41, click the color that you want to preserve.** Alternatively, you can click the color swatch and choose a color in the Color Picker panel.

2. **To increase or decrease the color range, drag the Similarity slider to the right or left.**

3. **To reverse the color effect (in other words, to make all colors normal and gray except for the selected color), click Reverse.**

Color Replace

This effect replaces one color or a range of colors with another color.

To choose a color or colors to replace, follow these steps:

1. **In the Color Replace Settings dialog box, shown in Figure 13.42, click the Target Color swatch and choose a color in the Color Picker panel.**

2. **To choose the replacement color, click the Replace Color swatch.** Choose a color in the Color Picker panel.

3. **To increase or decrease the color range of the replacement color, drag the Similarity slider right or left.**

4. **Choose the Solid Colors option to replace the color with a solid color.**

FIGURE 13.41

The Color Pass Settings dialog box

FIGURE 13.42

The Color Replace Settings dialog box

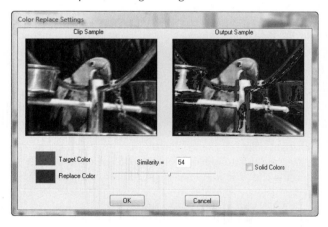

Gamma Correction

This effect enables you to adjust the midtone color levels of a clip. In the Gamma Correction Settings, click and drag the Gamma slider to make the adjustment. Dragging to the left lightens midtones; dragging to the right darkens them.

PS Arbitrary Map

This effect is primarily to be used with After Effects files that use the Arbitrary Map effect. The arbitrary map works by changing the brightness values.

Keying

The Keying effects allow you to create a variety of interesting superimposition effects. These effects consists of Alpha Adjust, Blue Screen Key, Chroma Key, Color Key, Difference Matte Key, Eight-Point Garbage Matte, Four-Point Garbage Matte, Green Screen Key, Image Matte Key, Luma Key, Multiply Matte, Non Red Key, RGB Difference Key, Remove Matte, Screen Key, Sixteen-Point Garbage Matte, Difference Matte Key, and Track Matte Key. The Keying effects are discussed in detailed in Chapter 14.

Noise & Grain

You can use the effects in the Noise & Grain bin to add noise to a clip.

Dust & Scratches

This effect changes pixels that are dissimilar and creates noise. Experiment with the Radius and Threshold controls for the desired effect. Click the Operate on Alpha Channel option to have the effect applied to the alpha channel.

Median

You can use this effect to reduce noise. It creates the effect by taking the median pixel value of neighboring pixels and applying this value to pixels within the radius pixel area specified in the Effect Controls panel. If you enter large values for the radius, your image begins to look as if it were painted. Click the Operate on Alpha Channel option to apply the effect to the image's alpha channel, as well as to the image.

Noise

This effect randomly changes colors in a video clip to give your clip a grainy appearance. In the Effect Controls panel, use the Amount of Noise slider to designate how much "noise," or graininess, you want to add to the clip. The more noise you add, the more your image disappears into the noise that you create.

If you choose the Color Noise option, the effect randomly changes the pixels in the image. If Color Noise is turned off, the same amount of noise is added to each red, green, and blue channel in the image.

Clipping is a mathematical stopgap that prevents noise from becoming larger than a set value. When the Clipping option is not selected, noise values start at lower values after reaching a certain point. If you turn Clipping off, you may find that your image completely disappears into the noise.

Noise Alpha

This effect creates noise by using the alpha channel of the affected clip.

Noise HLS and Noise HLS Auto

These effects allow you to create noise using Hue, Lightness, and Saturation. The noise can also be animated.

Perspective

You can use the effects in the Perspective bin to add depth to images, to create drop shadows, and to bevel image edges.

Basic 3D

This effect creates nice flipping and tilting effects. The Swivel slider in the Effect Controls panel controls rotation. The Tilt slider adjusts the tilt of the image. Dragging the Distance to Image slider creates an illusion of distance by reducing or enlarging the image. Click the Show Specular Highlight option to add a tiny flare of light to your image (indicated by a red plus [+] sign). Draw Preview enables you to view a wireframe simulation of the effect, which provides a good idea of how the effect will look without waiting for Premiere Pro to render it. The section "Using Video Effects with Keyframes" contains an example of the Basic 3D effect.

Bevel Alpha

This effect can make a two-dimensional image appear three-dimensional by beveling the image's alpha channel. This filter is especially handy for creating beveled effects with text. Sliders in the Effect Controls panel enable you to fine-tune the effect by changing bevel edge thickness, light angle, and light intensity. Change the light color by clicking the color swatch and choosing a color in the Color Picker panel. Try this effect on a Premiere Pro Title clip.

Bevel Edges

This effect bevels an image and adds lighting to give a clip a three-dimensional appearance. Image edges created with this effect are sharper than those created with the Bevel Alpha effect. To determine image edges, this filter also uses the clip's alpha channel. Similar to Bevel Alpha, sliders in the Effect Controls panel enable you to fine-tune the effect by changing bevel edge thickness, light angle, and light intensity. Change light color by clicking the color swatch and choosing a color in the Color Picker panel. Try this effect on a Premiere Pro Title clip.

Drop Shadow

This effect applies a drop shadow to a clip, using the clip's alpha channel to determine image edges. Sliders enable you to control the shadow's opacity, direction, and distance from the original clip. You can change the light color by clicking the color swatch in the panel and choosing a color from the Color Picker panel. Try this effect on a Premiere Pro Title clip.

Radial Shadow

You can use this effect to create a shadow on a clip with an alpha channel. Try using a Premiere Pro Title clip or a file from the DVD that accompanies this book to experiment with this effect. To import a Photoshop file with an alpha channel, click the Choose Layer option in the Import Layered File dialog box that appears. Then click OK to import the file into the Project panel. Drag the file to the Video 2 track. Create a color matte by using the File ⇨ New ⇨ Color Matte command. Drag the file to the Video 1 track. Apply the effect to the clip in the Video 2 track. When you apply the effect, a shadow is automatically created.

Use the controls in the Effect Controls panel to change the way the shadow appears. Use the Shadow Color control to change the color of the shadow. Use the Opacity control to make the shadow more or less translucent. To soften the edges of the shadow, increase the value of the Softness control.

You can move the shadow either by using the Light Source control or by clicking the words *Radial Shadow* (in the Effect Controls panel) and moving the circle icon that appears in the Program Monitor panel. Increase the Projection Distance to move the shadow farther away from the clip.

Click the Render drop-down menu to choose how the shadow will be rendered. The Color Influence control determines how much of the clip's color will appear in the shadow. To display only the shadow, click the Shadow Only check box.

Pixelate

The effects found in the Pixelate bin create special effects by shifting, moving, and remapping pixels and their color values. These effects can create dramatic color distortions in your image.

Facet

This effect creates a painterly appearance by grouping similarly colored pixels together within a clip.

Presets

You can save effects as presets so that they can be used on any clips in any project. When you save an effect as a preset, all of the customized settings are saved. To save an effect as a preset, select the effect from the Effect Controls panel. Then choose Save Preset from the Effect Controls drop-down menu. In the Save Preset dialog box, you can name your preset and give a description. The Type options determine how Premiere Pro will handle keyframes. When you click OK, the preset appears in the Preset bin, within the Effect Controls panel. If you want to organize all of your custom preset effects into a bin, you can create a new preset bin and drag them into the bin. To create a new preset bin, click the Effects drop-down menu and choose New Presets Bin. To rename the new preset bin folder, click and drag over the name and type a new name.

By default, the Presets bin consists of six bins with effects; Bevel Edges, Blurs, Mosaics, PIPS, Solarizes, and Twirls. The Blurs, Mosaics, Solarizes, and Twirls bins have In and Out effects in their bins. Try applying one of these effects to a clip. Drag the In and Out effect to a video clip. Note that the effect is applied to the beginning and end of the clip. The middle of the clip is left untouched. The Bevel Edges bin preset contains a Bevel Edges Thick effect and a Bevel Edges Thin effect. The Bevel Edges Thick effect creates a thick bevel around the edge of the clip that it is applied to, and the Bevel Edges Thin effect applies a thin bevel to the edge of the clip.

The PIPS preset bin contains a 25 percent PIPS bin. Within the 25 percent PIPS bin are five bins: 25 percent LL, 25 percent LR, 25 percent Motion, 25 percent UL, and 25 percent UR. The effects in the LL bin decrease the size of the clip and put the clip in the lower-left corner of the Program Monitor panel. The effects in the LR bin decrease the size of the clip and put the clip in the lower-right corner of the Program Monitor panel. The effects in the UL bin decrease the size of the clip and put the clip in the upper-left corner of the Program Monitor panel. The effects in the UR bin decrease the size of the clip and put the clip in the upper-right corner of the Program Monitor panel. Within the Motion bin are effects that decrease the size of the clip and use keyframes to move the clip from the lower-left corner to the upper-right corner, and vice versa, or from the upper-left corner to the lower-right corner, and vice versa.

Render

Ellipse

This effect makes ellipses in the form of a ring, with a hole in the center. The ellipse is created on a black background unless you have selected the Composite On Original check box. Figure 13.43 shows the Ellipse effect with the Composite On Original option selected. The effect is applied to the Highway.jpg file.

FIGURE 13.43

The Ellipse effect controls and a preview of its effect

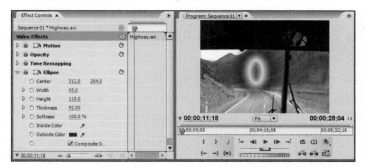

The controls for the Ellipse effect are found in the Effect Controls panel, as shown in Figure 13.43, and you can use them to move the ellipse or change the size and color of the ellipse. To adjust the size of the ellipse, use the Width and Height controls. To move the ellipse, use the Center control or click the word *Ellipse* (in the Effect Controls panel) and move the circle icon that appears in the Program Monitor panel. To increase the thickness of the ring of the ellipse, increase the value of the Thickness control. To soften the inner and outer edges of the ellipse, increase the Softness value. To change the color of the ellipse, use the Inside Color and Outside Color controls.

Stylize

The Stylize bin contains a variety of effects that change images without creating major distortions. For example, the Emboss effect adds depth throughout your image, while the Tiles effect divides your image into mosaic tiles.

Alpha Glow

This effect adds a glowing effect around alpha channel edges. In the Alpha Glow Settings, use the Glow slider to control how far the glow extends from the alpha channel. Use the Brightness slider to increase and decrease brightness.

The Start Color swatch represents the glow color. If you want to change the color, click the color swatch and choose a color from the Color Picker panel.

If you choose an End Color, Premiere Pro adds an extra color at the edge of the glow. To create an End color, select the End color check box and click the color swatch to pick the color in the Color Picker panel. To fade out the Start color, click the Fade Out check box.

Brush Strokes

This effect allows you to simulate the effect of adding brush strokes to a clip, as shown in Figure 13.44. The effect is applied to the BlueParrotPlaying video clip file.

FIGURE 13.44

The Brush Strokes effect controls and a preview of its effect

Figure 13.44 also shows the Brush Strokes properties in the Effect Controls panel. Start by picking a brush size and length using the Brush Size and Stroke Length controls. Adjust the angle of the strokes by changing the value of the Brush Angle. You can specify how the strokes are applied by using the Stroke Density and Stroke Randomness controls, as well as the Paint Surface drop-down menu. Use the Blend with Original control to determine how much of the original clip is viewed.

Color Emboss

This is the same as the Emboss effect, except that it doesn't remove color. Figure 13.45 shows the Color Emboss properties in the Effect Controls panel and a preview in the Program Monitor panel. The effect is applied to the BlueParrotPlaying video clip file.

FIGURE 13.45

The Color Emboss effect controls and a preview of its effect

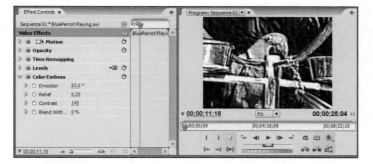

Emboss

This effect creates a raised 3-D effect from image edge areas in a clip. In the Effect Controls panel, use the Direction slider to control the angle of the embossing. Drag the Relief slider to raise the emboss level to create a greater emboss effect. To create a more pronounced effect, add more contrast by dragging the Contrast slider to the right. Use the Blend with Original slider to blend shading of the embossing with the clip's original image. Figure 13.46 shows the Emboss properties in the Effect Controls panel and a preview in the Program Monitor panel. The effect is applied to the BlueParrotPlaying video clip file.

Find Edges

This effect can make the image in a clip look like a black-and-white sketch. The effect seeks out image areas of high contrast and turns them into black lines that appear against a white background, or as colored lines with a black background. In the Effect Controls panel, use the Blend with Original slider to blend the lines with the original image. Figure 13.47 shows a preview of the Find Edges effect, applied to the BlueParrotPlaying video clip file.

Mosaic

This effect turns your image areas into rectangular tiles. In the Effect Controls panel, enter the number of mosaic blocks in the Horizontal and Vertical blocks fields. This effect can be animated for use as a transition, where the average of the colors in the other video track is normally used to pick the tile color. However, if you choose the Sharp Colors option, Premiere Pro uses the pixel color in the center of the corresponding region in the other video track. Figure 13.48 shows a preview of the Mosaic effect, applied to the BlueParrotPlaying video clip file.

The Emboss effect controls and a preview of its effect

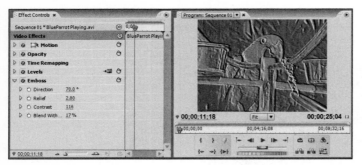

A preview of the Find Edges effect

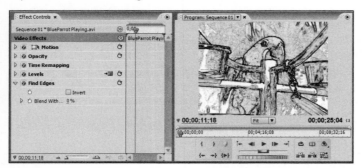

Posterize

This effect creates special color effects by reducing the tonal level in the red, green, and blue color channels. Click and drag the Levels amount in the Effect Controls panel to set how many levels of color are in an image. Figure 13.49 shows the Posterize effect, applied to the BlueParrotPlaying video clip file.

Replicate

This effect creates multiple versions of the clip within the frame. It produces this replication effect by creating tiles and placing multiple versions of the clip into the tiles. Dragging the Replicate Count slider in the Replicate settings (shown in Figure 13.50) to the right increases the number of tiles onscreen. The effect is applied to the BlueParrotPlaying video clip file.

FIGURE 13.48

A preview of the Mosaic effect

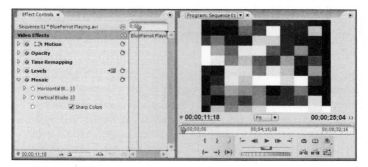

FIGURE 13.49

A preview of the Posterize effect

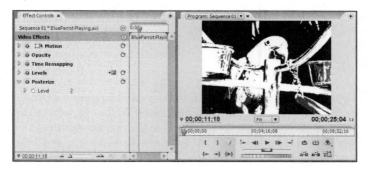

FIGURE 13.50

A preview of the Replicate effect

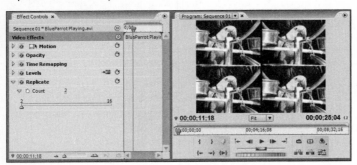

Roughen Edges

This effect gives the edges of an image a jagged look. Click the Edge Type drop-down menu to select a roughen style. If you choose a color option, you also need to select a color from the Edge Color control.

To customize the roughened edge, use the Border control to determine how large to make the roughened border. The Edge Sharpness control determines how sharp or soft the roughened edges appear. The Fractal Influence control determines how much of the roughening is controlled by fractal calculations. The Scale controls determine the size of the fractal used to create the roughened edges. The Stretch Width or Height control determines the width and height used to create the roughened edges. The Offset, Complexity, and Evolution controls are best used when animating the roughened edges.

Solarize

This effect creates a positive and a negative version of your image and then blends them together to create the solarizing effect. This can produce a lightened version of your image with darkened edges. In the Solarize settings shown in Figure 13.51, click and drag the Threshold slider to control the brightness level at which the Solarizing effect begins. The effect is applied to the BlueParrotPlaying video clip file.

Strobe Light

This effect creates the illusion of a strobe light flashing at regular or random intervals in your clip. In the Effect Controls panel, click the color swatch to choose a color for the strobe effect. Enter the duration of the strobe flash in the Duration field. In the Strobe Period field, enter the duration between strobe effects. (Duration is measured from the time the last strobe flashed — not when the flash ends.) If you want to create a random strobe effect, drag the Random Strobe Probability slider to the right. (The greater the probability setting, the more random the effect is.)

FIGURE 13.51

A preview of the Solarize effect

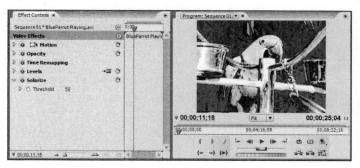

In the Strobe area of the Effect Controls panel, choose the Operates on Color option only if you want the strobe effect to be applied to all color channels. Choose Make Layer Transparent to make the track transparent when the strobe flashes. If you choose the Operates on Color option, you can select an arithmetic operator from the Strobe Operator drop-down menu that can further alter the strobe effect.

 If you set the strobe period longer than the strobe duration, the strobe is constant — not flashing.

Texturize

This effect can create texture in a clip by applying texture (such as sand or rocks) in one track to another track. To choose the video track supplying the texture, click in the Texture Layer drop-down menu in the Effect Controls panel and choose the track. Click and drag the Light Direction and Contrast sliders to create the best effect. In the Texture Placement drop-down menu, choose Tile Texture to repeat the texture over the clip. Choose Center Texture to place the texture in the clip's center, and then choose Stretch Texture to stretch the text over the entire frame area.

Figure 13.52 shows Texturize properties in the Effect Controls panel and a preview in the Program Monitor panel. To create the effect shown in the Program Monitor panel, the Texturize effect is applied to the BlueParrotPlaying video clip in the Video 2 track. The Video 1 track contains a graphic file called Sun.psd that was created earlier in this chapter (in the section "Applying Effects to Different Image Areas Using the Image Matte Keying Effect"). The Sun file graphic also appears in Figure 13.12. (Both clips are found in the MoreClips folder on the DVD that accompanies this book.) The Texture Layer drop-down menu is set to Video 1. For the full effect of the texture, the Texture Contrast value is set to 2.0. Adjusting the Light Direction control changes the result of the texture. Use the Texture Placement drop-down menu to change the placement of the texture.

The Texturize effect controls and a preview of its effect

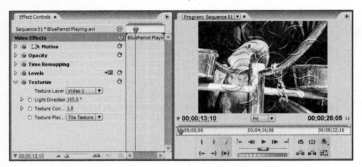

Threshold

This effect, shown in Figure 13.53, creates black-and-white images from color or grayscale images. You can adjust the amount of black or white in an image by changing the Level control. The Level control can be adjusted from 0 to 255. Move the Level control to the right to add more black to your image; setting the Level control to 255 turns the entire picture black. Move the Level control to the left to add more white to your image; setting the Level control to 0 (zero) turns the entire picture white.

The Threshold effect controls and a preview of its effect

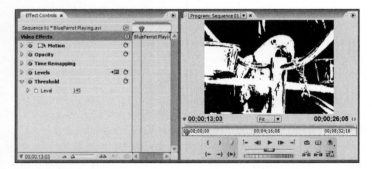

Time

The Time bin contains effects that specifically relate to different frames in the selected clip.

Echo

This effect creates a visual echo. In other words, frames from the selected clip are repeated again and again. This is effective only in clips that display motion. Depending on the clip, Echo can produce a repeated visual effect or possibly a streaking type of special effect. In the Effect Controls panel, use the Echo Time slider to control the time between the repetitions. Drag the Number of Echoes slider to designate how many frames to combine for the effect.

Use the Starting Intensity slider to control intensity of the first frame. A setting of 1 provides full intensity; .25 provides one-quarter intensity. The Decay slider controls how quickly the echo dissipates. If you set the Decay slider to .25, the first echo will be .25 of the starting intensity, the next echo will be .25 of the previous echo, and so on.

The Echo Operator drop-down menu creates effects by combining the pixel values of the echoes. These are the drop-down menu choices:

- **Add**: Adds pixel values
- **Maximum**: Uses maximum pixel value of echoes
- **Minimum**: Uses minimum pixel value of echoes
- **Screen**: Similar to Add, but less likely to produce white streaks
- **Composite in Back**: Uses the clip's alpha channels, and composites them starting at the back
- **Composite in Front**: Uses the clip's alpha channels, and composites them starting at the front

 **To combine an Echo effect with a Motion Settings effect, create a virtual clip and apply the effect to the virtual clip.**

Posterize Time

This effect grabs control of a clip's frame rate settings and substitutes the frame rate specified in the Effect Controls frame rate slider.

Time Warp

This effect is new to Premiere Pro. It allows you to change a clips speed and motion. Adjusting the controls of this effect allows you to either increase or decrease the speed of a video. The controls also allow you to adjust the frame rate of the motion of each clip.

Transform

The Transform bin is filled with Transformation effects from Adobe After Effects that enable you to flip, crop, and roll a video clip, as well as change the camera view.

Camera View

This effect simulates viewing the clip at a different camera angle. In the Camera View Settings dialog box, shown in Figure 13.54, you can use the sliders to control the effect. Click and drag the Latitude slider to flip the clip vertically.

FIGURE 13.54

The Camera View Settings dialog box

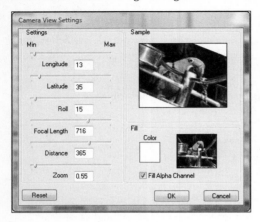

Use the Longitude slider to flip it horizontally. The Roll slider simulates rolling the camera by rotating the clip. Click and drag the Focal Length slider to make the view wider or narrower. The Distance slider enables you to change the distance between the imaginary camera and the clip. Use the Zoom slider to zoom in and out. To create a fill color to use as a background, click the color swatch and choose a color in the Color Picker panel. If you want the background area to be transparent, choose the Fill Alpha Channel option. (The clip must include an alpha channel to use this option.)

Clip

This effect hides the frame boundaries — similar to a Crop effect, except that the clip is not resized. You can use this effect to hide noise at image edges.

To use the Clip effect, drag the sliders in the Clipping Settings dialog box, to clip the top, left, bottom, and right sides of the clip. Choose whether you want to clip according to pixels or percent. Click the Fill Color swatch to open the Color Picker and choose a background color.

Crop

To use this effect, click and drag the Left, Top, Right, and Bottom controls. Premiere Pro resizes the clip according to these settings. If you have a clip below the cropped clip, you will be able to see it, as shown in Figure 13.55. Click the Zoom check box to zoom into the cropped area. The clips used in Figure 13.55 are the BlueParrotPlaying and BakerySign video clips. The BlueParrotPlaying clip is placed in the Video 2 track and the Crop effect is applied to it. The BakerySign clip is placed in the Video 1 track.

FIGURE 13.55

The results of the Crop effect

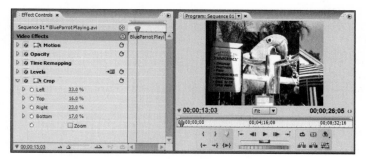

The Edge Feather

This effect allows you to create a 3-D feathered effect around the edge of the image clip that you are working with, as shown in Figure 13.56. To apply a feathered edge, move the Feather Value slider to the right to increase the size of the edge of the feather.

Horizontal Flip

This effect flips the frame from left to right.

Horizontal Hold

This effect is named after the horizontal hold knob found on a television set. As you might guess, the effect simulates turning the horizontal hold knob. In the Horizontal Hold Settings dialog box, shown in Figure 13.57, click and drag the slider to create the skewing effect.

FIGURE 13.56

The results of the Edge Feather effect

FIGURE 13.57

The Horizontal Hold Settings dialog box

Roll

This effect provides a rotating effect. The Roll Settings dialog box, shown in Figure 13.58, enables you to roll the image left, right, up, or down.

Vertical Flip

This effect flips your clip vertically. The result is an upside-down version of the original clip.

Vertical Hold

This effect simulates turning the vertical hold knob found on a television set. Use the slider in the Vertical Hold Settings dialog box to create the effect you want.

FIGURE 13.58

The Roll Settings dialog box

Transition

The effects found in the Transition bin are similar to those in the Video Transitions bin in the Effects panel.

Block Dissolve

You can use this effect to have a clip disappear using random blocks of pixels.

Gradient Wipe

This effect blends the clip with the effect onto another clip (called the gradient layer), based upon luminance values. To use the effect, place a clip in the Video 1 track and apply the effect to the clip. Then place another clip in the Video 2 track, and use this clip as the gradient layer. Hide the clip in the Video 2 track by clicking the Eye icon in the Timeline panel. In the Effect Controls panel, set the Gradient Layer drop-down menu to the Video 2 track. Use the Transition Completion and Transition Softness controls to determine how much of the gradient layer displays. Use the Gradient Placement drop-down menu to choose how to position the gradient. If you want, you can click the Invert Gradient check box to invert the gradient. Figure 13.59 shows the Effect Controls panel with the properties used to create the Gradient Wipe effect.

Linear Wipe

This effect allows you to wipe the affected clip away so that you can see the clip beneath it. Figure 13.60 shows the Linear Wipe properties in the Effect Controls panel and a preview of the effect in the Program Monitor panel. In this example, the effect is applied to a video clip file called BlueParrotPlaying. The BlueParrotPlaying file is placed in the Video 2 track, and a file called BakerySign is placed in the Video 1 track.

FIGURE 13.59

The Gradient Wipe effect controls and a preview of its effect

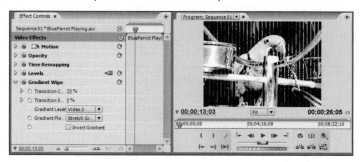

FIGURE 13.60

The Linear Wipe effect controls and a preview of its effect

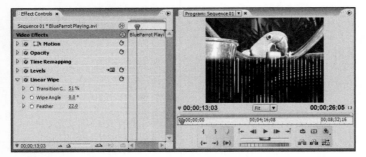

Follow these steps to use the Linear Wipe effect:

1. **Place a clip in the Video 1 track.** This example uses the BakerySign video clip file found in the MoreClips folder on the DVD that accompanies this book.

2. **Directly below the clip in the Video 1 track, place another clip in the Video 2 track.** This example uses the BlueParrotPlaying file found in the MoreClips folder on the DVD.

3. **Apply the Linear Wipe effect to the clip in the Video 2 track.**

4. **Use the controls for the effect in the Effect Controls panel to create the desired effect.** To wipe away the clip in the Video 2 track and see the clip below it in the Video 1 track, increase the Transition Completion percent value. To angle the linear wipe, adjust the Wipe Angle control. To create a smooth transition between the two clips, increase the Feather value.

Radial Wipe

You can use this effect to wipe away a clip, revealing a clip below it using a circular wipe. To create a radial wipe, either increase the Transition Completion percentage or click the words *Radial Wipe* (in the Effect Controls panel), and move the circle icon that appears in the Program Monitor panel. To change the angle of the radial wipe, adjust the Start Angle control. To increase the radial wipe from its center out, you need to adjust the Center Wipe controls. Click the Wipe drop-down menu to choose whether you want the radial wipe to be clockwise, counterclockwise, or both. Increasing the Feather value gives a smoother blend between the two clips.

Venetian Blinds

You can use this effect to wipe away the clip with the effect and display the clip below it using stripes. Figure 13.61 shows the Venetian Blinds properties in the Effect Controls panel and a preview of the effect in the Program Monitor panel.

The Venetian Blinds effect, shown in Figure 13.61, is applied to a Title clip (RocknRoll) that was created in the Premiere Pro project. To create the Title clip, use the Title Styles, Lithos Gold Strokes 52. Place the Title clip in the Video 2 track. In the Video 1 track, add a color matte clip, which you can create using the File ⇨ New ⇨ Color Matte command. Apply the Venetian Blinds effect to the Title clip in the Video 2 track. For a more dramatic effect, you can also apply the Radial Shadow effect, as shown in Figure 13.61.

To create Venetian blinds, increase the Transition Completion percent value. Adjust the Direction control to change the angle of the Venetian blinds. Use the Width control to determine how many Venetian blinds you want and how wide you want them to be. Increase the Feather value if you want the blinds to have a soft edge.

FIGURE 13.61

The Venetian Blind effect controls and a preview of its effect

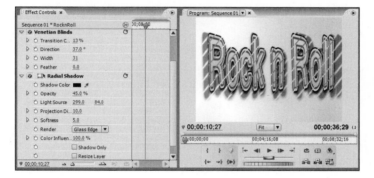

Utility

Cineon Converter

This effect allows you to convert the colors in a Cineon file. The Cineon file format is often used when converting motion-picture film to digital. To use this effect, import a Cineon file into your project and place it in a video track in the Timeline panel. The controls for the Cineon Converter allow you to control how the clip is converted. Click the Conversion Type drop-down menu to pick a conversion method. Then specify a black-and-white point for the clip using the 10 Bit Black Point, Internal Black Point, 10 Bit White Point, and Internal White Point. Then specify midtone values using the Gamma control. If the highlight areas need to be adjusted, try using the Highlight Rolloff control.

Video

The effects found in the Video bin simulate electronic changes to a video signal. You only need to apply these effects if you are outputting your production to videotape.

Timecode

This effect is not used to enhance colors. Instead, it is used to "burn" timecode into footage so that it is visible in the Program Monitor. When you apply this effect, you can choose position, size, and opacity options in the Effect Controls panel. You can also choose among timecode formats and apply a frame offset.

You can use the Timecode effect to place timecode in transparent video in a track over your footage. This allows you to view timecode without affecting the actual program footage. To create transparent video, choose File ➪ New Transparent Video. Then drag the transparent video from the Project panel into a track above your footage in the Timeline. Next, apply the Timecode effect by dragging it over the transparent video.

Summary

Premiere Pro's Video Effects provide dozens of special effects that can add interest to or correct video. This chapter covered the following topics:

- To add an effect to a clip, drag the effect from the Effects panel to the clip in the Timeline.
- Use the Effect Controls panel to specify settings for effects, to turn the preview on and off, and to enable and disable keyframing.
- Set keyframes where effect settings change in the Timeline.
- Use Value and Velocity graphs to fine-tune the results of an effect.

Chapter 14

Superimposing

By telling a story or providing information using innovative effects, you can ensure that your message is delivered more effectively. One of the best techniques for doing this creatively is to use superimposition. Premiere Pro helps you create sophisticated transparency effects by enabling you to overlay two or more video clips and then blend the two clips together as if you were creating a collage. For more sophisticated results, the Premiere Pro Video Effects Keying options provide a host of different effects that enable you to *key* out (hide) different parts of the image area in one track and fill them with the underlying video in the track beneath it.

This chapter provides a look at two powerful methods of creating transparency: the Premiere Pro Opacity option and the Premiere Pro Keying options found in the Video Effects bin (folder) of the Effects panel. The Opacity option enables you to create blending effects by changing the opacity of one video track. The Keying bin in the Effects panel is home to 18 different Keying options that enable you to create transparency based on color, alpha channels, or brightness levels. As you read through this chapter, think about all the different ways that you can apply the effects in your current or next project. Using transparency creatively will undoubtedly add to the success of your project.

If you put a video clip or still image in the Video 2 track and another in the Video 1 track, you see only the image that is in the top video track onscreen — in this case, the Video 2 track. To see both images, you need to either fade the Video 2 track or superimpose it.

Any video track higher than the Video 1 track can be faded using Premiere Pro's Opacity option or superimposed using the Keying options. Throughout this book, you find various examples of transparency effects. To review some

IN THIS CHAPTER

Fading video tracks

Superimposing tracks using the Keying effects

of these examples, see Chapters 10, 13, 16, and 29. You can also create fading and superimposing tracks with masks. Turn to Chapter 31 to learn how to work with masks using Adobe After Effects.

Fading Video Tracks

You can fade an entire video clip or still image over a video clip or another still image. The top video clip or still image is faded over the bottom one. When you fade a video clip or still image, you are changing the opacity of the clip or image. Any video track, except for the Video 1 track, can be used as a superimposed track and can be faded. Premiere Pro's fade Opacity option appears in the Timeline panel when you expand a video track. When a video track is expanded, you can display the opacity by clicking the Show Keyframes icon and choosing Show Opacity Handles. The Opacity graph line displays underneath a video clip when you expand the track. You can also see the opacity of a video clip in the Effects Control panel. When you select a clip in the Timeline panel, the Opacity option displays in the Effect Controls panel.

Figure 14.1 shows the results of fading two video clips. To create the effect in Figure 14.1, a video clip of a golfer (Artbeats GEL123) is placed in the Video 2 track, and a video clip of some flamingos (Flamingos) is placed in the Video 1 track. The golfer video track is faded so that you can see the flamingos in the track below. For this fade project, you can use SmartSound's Cold Metal sound clip.

FIGURE 14.1

The resulting video clips show a 45 percent, 40 percent, 35 percent, and 30 percent fade.

CROSS-REF Fading video tracks works similarly to fading sound tracks. For more information on fading sound tracks, see Chapter 7.

Follow these steps to fade a track using the Opacity graph line in the Timeline panel.

1. **Choose File ➪ New ➪ Project to create a new project.** Make sure that you use the proper preset. If you are creating a high-resolution project, you may want to use a DV preset. If not, use a Non-DV preset. Instead of creating a new project, you can also open a project that has two or more clips. If you do this, then you can skip to step 3 or 4.

2. **Choose File ➪ Import to import two files.** Locate either two video clips or a video clip and a still image. Press and hold the Ctrl/⌘ key to select more than one file. Click Open to import the files. If you want to have sound in your project, you can import it now.

ON the DVD If you want, you can use the two video clips that are used in the fade example, shown in Figure 14.1. On the DVD that accompanies this book, in the Tutorial Projects folder, you will find a video clip of a golfer (Artbeats GEL123) in the Artbeats folder. In the More Clips folder, you will find the Flamingos movie clip. The Cold Metal sound clip is found in the SmartSound folder.

3. **When the files appear in the Project panel, drag and drop one file to the Video 2 track and the other file to the Video 1 track in the Timeline panel, as shown in Figure 14.2.** You will change the opacity of the clip in the Video 2 track. Make sure that the files in the video tracks overlap each other. If you are adding sound to your project, drag the sound file to the Audio 1 track. If the imported sound clip is too long, use the Razor tool to edit it. For more information on working with sound, see Chapter 7.

FIGURE 14.2

The Opacity graph line enables you to change the opacity of a video clip.

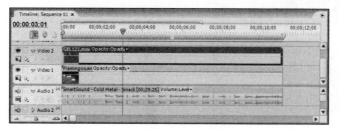

4. **To zoom into the Timeline, click and drag the time Zoom level slider to the right.** The time Zoom level slider is at the bottom of the Timeline panel. You can also click the Zoom In button or press the equal sign key on your keyboard.

5. **Select the clip in the Video 2 track. To expand the Video 2 track, click the Collapse/Expand Track icon to the left of the word *Video*.**

6. **Click the Show Keyframes icon**. Choose Show Opacity Handles to reveal the Opacity graph line, shown in the Timeline panel in Figure 14.2. Notice that yellow line displays beneath the video clip.

7. **To decrease the opacity of the file in the Video 2 track, use either the Pen tool or the Selection tool in the Tools panel to click and drag the white Opacity graph line down.** As you drag, the Opacity percent value displays. The Opacity percent value also displays in the Effect Controls panel. You can click the Collapse/Expand Track icon to display the Opacity percent value.

Follow these steps to fade a track using the Opacity graph line in the Effect Controls panel.

1. **You should have a new project onscreen with two video clips in the Timeline panel.** If you do not, follow the first three steps in the previous section.

2. **Select the top video clip in the Timeline panel.** Choose Window ➪ Effect Controls to display the Effect Controls panel. Notice that the Effect Controls panel displays the Opacity option for the selected clip.

3. **Click and drag the Opacity value to the right or left to fade the track.** Notice that the Opacity line moves to show the changes that you made.

4. **To view the Opacity graph line in the Effect Controls panel, shown in Figure 14.3, click the Collapse/Expand Track icon to the left of Opacity effect.** Then drag the current-time indicator (Edit line) along the Effect Controls Timeline to see the percent values. Figure 14.3 also shows the Value and Velocity graphs for the Opacity control. You can use the Value and Velocity graphs to adjust the Opacity control. For more information on using the Value and Velocity graphs, see Chapter 13.

FIGURE 14.3

The Effect Controls panel shows the Opacity percentage value for the selected clip.

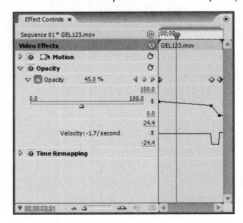

---

5. To preview the fade effect, click Play in the Program Monitor panel.

CROSS-REF You can also fade clips into one another using transitions. For more information on working with transitions, see Chapter 9.

6. Make sure to save your work.

Adding opacity handles (keyframes) using the Pen tool and Selection tool

To create more sophisticated fades, you may need to add a few handles (keyframes) to the Opacity graph line using either the Pen tool or the Selection tool. After you have a few handles (keyframes), as shown in Figure 14.4, you can then drag different segments of the Opacity graph line up or down, depending on the results you want.

FIGURE 14.4

The Opacity graph line in the Timeline panel displays a few opacity handles (keyframes).

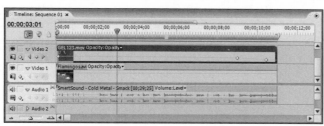

Here's how to use the Pen and Selection tools to add handles (keyframes) to the Opacity graph line.

NOTE To display the Opacity graph line, expand the video track by clicking the Collapse/Expand Track icon to the left of the word *Video*. Then click the Show Keyframes icon and choose Show Opacity Handles.

1. **With either the Pen or Selection tool selected, move the cursor over the Opacity graph line.** Move over to the area where you want to add a keyframe, and then press and hold Ctrl/⌘ as you click to create a keyframe. A keyframe appears as a yellow diamond on the Opacity graph line.

2. **To create a few keyframes, press and hold Ctrl/⌘ as you click the Opacity graph line a few times.**

3. **Now that you have a few handles (keyframes) on the Opacity graph line, you can move them.**

4. **If you have created too many keyframes and want to delete one, just click a keyframe in the Timeline panel and press Delete.** You can also click a keyframe in the Effect Controls panel and press Delete.

> **TIP** To delete all of the opacity keyframes from a Timeline, click the Toggle Animation icon in the Effect Controls panel. When the warning prompt appears, click OK to delete all existing keyframes.

5. **Click and drag the keyframe to move up and/or down, as shown in Figure 14.4.** When you click the handle, you should see a yellow diamond at the bottom of the Pen icon. A plus sign (+) indicates that you are going to add a handle when you click the Opacity graph line. Make sure that you see the white diamond, and reposition the mouse more accurately over the keyframe that you want to move.

> **TIP** Use the Go to Previous Keyframe and the Go to Next Keyframe buttons in the Timeline panel to move quickly from one keyframe to another.

6. **Use the Effect Controls panel to display the fade level percentage.** To display the Effect Controls panel, choose Window ⇨ Effect Controls. Notice all of the Opacity keyframes. Click a keyframe to view its percentage, or click and drag the Timeline to scroll through the different percentages. The Effect Controls panel also shows the Value and Velocity graphs for the Opacity control. You can use the Value and Velocity graphs to adjust the Opacity control. For more information on using the Value and Velocity graphs, see Chapter 13.

   For a quick preview, click and drag the Edit line through the Timeline (from either the Timeline panel or the Effect Controls panel) to preview the fade effect in the Program Monitor panel. To display the Program Monitor panel, choose Window ⇨ Program Monitor. You can also preview an effect by clicking the Play button in the Program Monitor.

7. **Choose File ⇨ Save to save your work.**

> **TIP** If desired, you can fade more video tracks. Just import more video clips and/or still images into the Project panel. Create new video tracks and drag the video clips and/or images into the new video tracks. Then use the Opacity graph line to fade the video tracks.

Adjusting the Opacity graph line using the Pen tool and Selection tool

The Pen tool or Selection tool enables you to either move an entire Opacity graph line as a unit or to move two handles (keyframes) simultaneously. Follow these steps to use either the Pen tool or the Selection tool to move two handles (keyframes) simultaneously.

> **NOTE** Before you proceed to step 1, you should have a Premiere Pro project with a clip in the Video 2 track. The Video 2 track should be selected and expanded, and the Opacity graph line should be displayed. These steps are covered in the "Fading Video Tracks" section, earlier in this chapter.

1. **Use either the Selection tool or the Pen tool to create two handles (keyframes) on the Opacity graph line.** Position the handles (keyframes) so that they appear at the beginning and end of the Opacity graph line. With either the Pen tool or Selection tool, press and hold the Ctrl/⌘ key as you click the Opacity graph line.

2. **Use either the Selection tool or Pen tool while pressing the Ctrl/⌘ key to click the Opacity graph line to add two more handles (keyframes).** Place the handles (keyframes) in the middle of the clip. Try to spread all of the handles (keyframes) equally apart from each other.

3. **Move either the Selection tool or the Pen tool between the two middle handles (keyframes).** When an up-and-down-arrow icon appears next to the tool, click the Opacity graph line and drag down. When you click and drag between the two keyframes, the keyframes and the Opacity graph line between the two keyframes move as a unit. The Opacity graph line outside the keyframes gradually moves.

The Selection tool or the Pen tool also enables you to move just a section of the Opacity graph line completely separate from the rest. Here's how:

1. **Start with an Opacity graph line that has two handles (keyframes) — one at the beginning of the Opacity graph line and another at the end.**

2. **Create two more handles (keyframes).** They should be side by side in the middle of the Opacity graph line.

3. **Select either the Selection tool or Pen tool, if it is not selected.**

4. **Use either the Selection tool or the Pen tool to select the first keyframe.** Then press and hold the Shift key as you select the second keyframe.

5. **Click and drag the Opacity graph line down.** Notice that only the line between the first keyframe on the Opacity graph line and the second keyframe moves. The line moves at a constant percentage.

6. **Deselect the first and second keyframes.** Then use either the Selection tool or Pen tool to select the third keyframe. Press and hold the Shift key as you select the fourth keyframe.

7. **Click and drag the Opacity graph line down.** Notice that only the Opacity graph line between the third and fourth keyframes moves. The line moves at a constant percentage.

8. **Move either the Selection tool or the Pen tool to the right of the third keyframe and to the left of the last keyframe.** Then press the Ctrl/⌘ key as you click the Opacity graph line. As you click, notice that you create a keyframe between the third and fourth keyframes. With this new keyframe selected, click and drag the Opacity graph line down in the shape of a V.

Setting opacity keyframes using the Effect Controls panel and the Timeline panel

You can use either the Effect Controls panel or the Timeline panel to set keyframes. Here's how to add keyframes using the Timeline panel:

 Before you proceed to step 1, you should have a Premiere Pro project with a clip in the Video 2 track, and the track should be selected.

1. Click the Collapse/Expand Track icon to expand the Video 2 track.

2. Click the Show Keyframes icon, and choose Show Keyframes.

3. Click the drop-down menu from the title bar of the clip in the Video 2 track. Choose Opacity.

4. Move the current-time indicator (Edit line) to where you want to set a keyframe. Click the Add/Remove Keyframe icon to add a keyframe.

5. Repeat step 4 as many times as you need.

6. Use either the Pen tool or the Selection tool to set the opacity for each keyframe. With the Selection tool selected, click a keyframe and drag it either up or down on the Opacity graph line to where you want the opacity value to be.

Notice that the keyframes that you created using the Timeline panel now appear in the Effect Controls panel. You can continue editing the keyframes in either the Timeline panel or the Effect Controls panel. You can also preview the effect of the opacity keyframes by moving the current-time indicator on the Timeline of either the Timeline panel or the Effect Controls panel.

Here's how to add keyframes using the Effect Controls panel.

 Before you proceed to step 1, you should have a Premiere Pro project with a clip in the Video 2 track, and the track should be expanded.

1. Click the Collapse/Expand Opacity icon to display the Opacity options.

2. Move the current-time indicator (Edit line) in the Effect Controls panel to where you want to set a keyframe.

3. Adjust the Opacity percent value.

4. Click the Toggle Animation icon to set a keyframe. The keyframe is set with the current Opacity value at the location of the current-time indicator.

5. To set another keyframe, move the current-time indicator to the desired location.

6. Click the Add/Remove Keyframe button to create a keyframe at the position of the current-time indicator (Edit line). Then adjust the Opacity value.

7. Another way to create a keyframe on the Timeline in the Effect Controls panel is to move the current-time indicator (Edit line) to where you want to set a keyframe. Then adjust the Opacity value. Notice that, as you adjust the Opacity value, a keyframe is created. As long as the Toggle Animation icon is on, Premiere Pro continues to record

your actions. Every time you move the current-time indicator (Edit line) and adjust the Opacity value, Premiere Pro adds a keyframe to the Opacity Timeline.

8. **If you decide you want to delete all of the keyframes and start all over again, just click the Toggle Animation icon.** When the warning prompt appears, click OK.

Superimposing Tracks Using the Keying Effects

You can superimpose a video clip and/or still image over another one using the Keying effects; these effects are found under Keying, which is in the Video Effects bin in the Effects panel. Using the Keying effects — or *keying* — makes part of the image transparent. The following sections cover how to use the different Keying effects.

Displaying the Keying effects

To display and experiment with the Keying effects, shown in Figure 14.5, you first need to have a Premiere Pro project onscreen. Either load an existing Premiere Pro project or create a new one by choosing File ➪ New ➪ Project. Import two video clips into the new project.

FIGURE 14.5

The Keying effects are in the Keying bin, which is in the Video Effects bin in the Effects panel.

ON the DVD If you want, you can use one of the video clips found in the Tutorial Projects folder on the DVD that accompanies this book. Most of the images shown in this chapter are located on the DVD.

To display the Keying bin, follow these steps:

1. **Drag a clip from the Project panel to the Video 1 track.**

2. **Drag a clip from the Project panel to the Video 2 track.**

3. **Click and drag the clip in the Video 2 track so that it overlaps the clip in the Video 1 track.**

4. **Select the clip in the Video 2 track.** This is the clip to which you apply a Keying effect.

5. **Choose Window ⇨ Effects.** In the Effects panel, click the Collapse/Expand triangle to the left of the Video Effects bin. To display the Keying effects, click the Collapse/Expand triangle in front of the Keying bin.

   In the Keying bin, you have several Keying effects to choose from: Alpha Adjust, Blue Screen, Chroma, Color, Difference Matte, Garbage Matte, Image Matte, Luma Key, Multiply, Non Red Key, RGB Difference, Remove Matte, Track Matte.

6. **To apply a Keying effect, click and drag it onto the clip in the Video 2 track or into the Effect Controls panel.**

   Each Keying effect has it own set of controls that you can adjust. To learn about keying effects and their controls, see the following sections.

7. **To preview the Keying effect, you can move the current-time indicator in the Timeline panel or the Effect Controls panel.** You can also click the Play button in the Monitor panel. By default, the preview quality is set to Automatic Quality. To change the preview quality, click the Program Monitor menu and choose Highest Quality or Draft Quality. To render the work area, choose Sequence ⇨ Render Work Area.

8. **To preview the clip without the Keying effect, you can choose Effect Enabled from the Effect Controls panel menu.** Alternatively, you can click the Toggle the Effect On or Off button to the left the Keying effect.

Apply Keying effects using keyframes

Premiere Pro allows you to animate a Keying effect control over time using keyframes. You can add keyframes using either the Effect Controls panel or the Timeline panel.

Follow these steps to animate a Keying effect control using the Effect Controls panel.

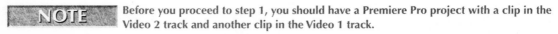 **Before you proceed to step 1, you should have a Premiere Pro project with a clip in the Video 2 track and another clip in the Video 1 track.**

1. **Click and drag a Keying effect to the clip in the Video 2 track.**

2. **Select the clip in the Video 2 track if it is not already selected.**

3. **Click the Collapse/Expand triangle to the left of the Keying effect to display its controls.**

4. **To animate a Keying effect control over time, move the current-time indicator (Edit line) to where you want to add your first keyframe.**

5. **Click the Toggle Animation icon to the left of the control to add a keyframe.**

6. **Make the desired adjustments to the control.**

7. **To create a second keyframe, move the current-time indicator (Edit line) to a new location and adjust the control.** As you adjust the control, a keyframe is added to the control's Timeline. While the Toggle Animation icon is turned on, every time you move the current-time indicator and adjust the control, a keyframe is added to the control's Timeline.

NOTE In the Effect Controls panel, you can click the Toggle Keyframe button to add keyframes. You can also move among keyframes by clicking the Next Keyframe and Previous Keyframe buttons.

8. **To move a keyframe, click and drag it to its new location.**

9. **To edit a keyframe, move the current-time indicator (Edit line) over the keyframe and adjust the control.**

10. **To delete a keyframe, click the keyframe and press Delete.**

11. **To delete all of the keyframes for a control and start all over again, click the Toggle Animation icon.** When the warning prompt appears, click OK.

Follow these steps to animate a Keying effect control using the Timeline panel.

NOTE Before you proceed to step 1, you should have a Premiere Pro project with a clip in the Video 2 track and another clip in the Video 1 track. The clip in the Video 2 track should have a Keying effect applied to it, and the track should be selected in the Timeline panel.

1. **Click the Collapse/Expand triangle to the left of the Video 2 track to expand the track.**

2. **Click the Show Keyframes icon.** Choose Show Keyframes.

3. **Click the video clip's drop-down menu in the title bar.** Choose a Keying effect control.

4. **Move the current-time indicator (Edit line) to where you want to add a keyframe.** Click the Add/Remove Keyframe button to add a keyframe.

5. **In the Effect Controls panel, make the adjustments to the control.**

6. **To add a second keyframe, move the current-time indicator (Edit line) to a new location.** Adjust the control. As you adjust, a second keyframe is applied.

7. **To edit keyframes, select the desired keyframe you want to edit by clicking either the Go to Next Keyframe or the Go to Previous Keyframe button.** Then edit the keyframe.

Alpha Adjust

You can use the Alpha Adjust effect to create transparency from imported images that contain an alpha channel. An alpha channel is an image layer that represents a mask with shades of gray, including black and white, to indicate transparency levels. Premiere Pro reads alpha channels from such programs as Adobe Photoshop and 3-D graphics software, and also translates nontransparent areas of Adobe Illustrator files as alpha channels.

TIP Click a file with an alpha channel in the Project panel. Then choose File ⇨ Interpret Footage. In the Interpret Footage dialog box, you can select the Ignore Alpha Channel option to have Premiere Pro ignore the alpha channel of that file, or you can select the Invert Alpha Channel option to have Premiere Pro invert that file's alpha channel.

Figure 14.6 shows a few frames of an Alpha Adjust project. The project creates the illusion that the type is moving, when in reality the type is not moving — the background video clip is moving. To create the project, you can import a file with three-dimensional type that is created in Adobe Illustrator CS3. To make the type 3-D, you can use Illustrator's Extrude & Bevel 3D Effect. Save the 3-D type in Illustrator format, import it into your Premiere Pro project, and place it into the Video 2 track. You can then apply the Alpha Adjust Key effect to the clip in the Video 2 track. The Video 1 track has a video clip of a swan (WhiteSwan). The Audio 1 track contain SmartSound's Island Party sound clip. Figure 14.7 shows the Timeline panel used to create the Alpha Adjust project, as well as the Alpha Adjust Key effect settings in the Effect Controls panel.

FIGURE 14.6

Frames from the Alpha Adjust Key project

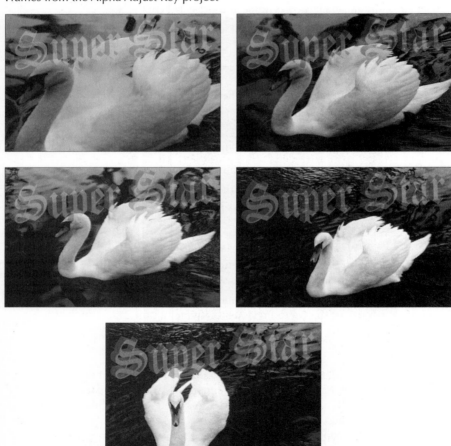

The Alpha Adjust options in the Effect Controls panel allow you to adjust how the alpha channel appears. Here is how the controls work:

- **Opacity:** Reducing the opacity makes the image in the alpha channel more transparent.
- **Ignore Alpha:** When you select the Ignore Alpha option, Premiere Pro ignores the alpha channel.
- **Invert Alpha:** Selecting the Invert Alpha option causes Premiere Pro to invert the alpha channel.
- **Mask Only:** Selecting the Mask Only option displays only the mask of the alpha channel without the image.

ON the DVD You can load the 3-D type (SuperStar) and the WhiteSwan clip from the MoreClips folder. The SmartSound's Island Party sound clip can be found in the SmartSound folder. These folders can be found in the Tutorial Projects folder on the DVD that accompanies this book.

FIGURE 14.7

The Timeline and Effect Controls panels from the Alpha Adjust Key project

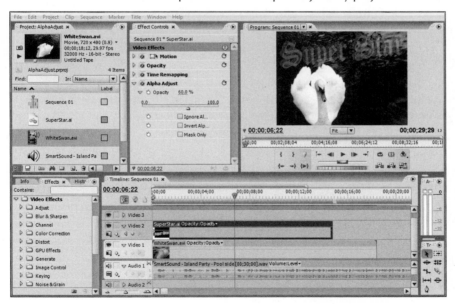

Blue Screen and Green Screen

Blue and green are traditional keys used in broadcast television where announcers are often shown in front of a blue or green background. The Blue Screen keys out well-lit blue backgrounds, and the Green Screen keys out well-lit green areas. Both keys have the following options:

- **Threshold:** Start by dragging to the left to key out more green and blue areas.
- **Cutoff:** Click and drag to the right to fine-tune the Keying effect.
- **Smoothing:** This control sets antialiasing, which blends pixel colors to create smoother edges. Choose High for the most smoothing, Low for some smoothing, or None for no smoothing. Choosing None is often the best choice when keying titles.
- **Mask Only:** This control allows you to choose whether to display the clip's alpha channel.

Normally when using the Blue Screen Key or Green Screen Key effects, you would videotape a person or object against either a properly lit blue or green background. This way, you can import the video clip into Premiere Pro and use either the Blue Screen Key or Green Screen Key effect to remove the background and replace it with any image you want.

The following example of a Blue Screen Key effect uses the video and sound clips from the RGB Difference Key example. In the RGB Difference Key example, you can see moving cabs (FilmDisc's clip cm0105) through a silhouette on a blue background (FilmDisc's clip bc0115). When you apply the Blue Screen Key effect to the silhouette clip (FilmDisc bc0115), you can see the moving cabs through the blue background, and the silhouette is black.

Figure 14.8 shows a few frames from the Blue Screen Key project. Figure 14.9 shows the Effect Controls panel with the Blue Screen Key options. In the Timeline panel used to create the Blue Screen Key project (shown in Figure 14.9), you can see that FilmDisc's clip cm0105 is in the Video 1 track, and FilmDisc's clip bc0115 is in the Video 2 track.

The clip in the Video 1 track is longer than the clip in the Video 2 track. To fade out the clip in the Video 1 track, you can set an Opacity keyframe at the 12-second mark. At the 16-second mark, you can set a second Opacity keyframe to 60 percent. At the 20-second mark, you can set a third Opacity keyframe to 22 percent. The sound clip used in the Blue Screen Key project is SmartSound's New Vistas.

When you finish a project using keyframes and video effects, you should render it by choosing Sequence ➪ Render Work Area. Always save your work.

ON the DVD If you want, you can load the clips used to create the Blue Screen Key and the Green Screen Key effects project from the Tutorial Projects folder on the DVD that accompanies this book. The clips used to create the Blue Screen Key project are FilmDisc's bc0115 and FilmDisc's cm0105. The sound clip is SmartSound's New Vistas. The clips used in the Green Screen key project are Artbeats GEL123, FilmDisc's ny0114, and SmartSound's No Borders sound clip.

FIGURE 14.8

A few frames from a project created using the Blue Screen Key effect with FilmDisc's clips bc0115 and cm0105

FIGURE 14.9

The Timeline and Effect Controls panels used in the Blue Screen Key project (shown in Figure 14.8)

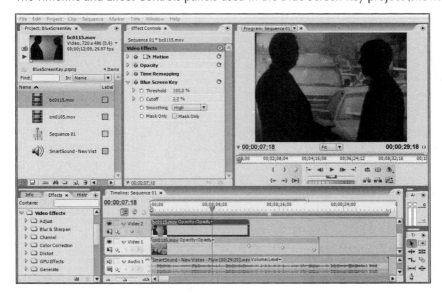

If you want to create the Green Screen Key effect project, try using Artbeats GEL123 with FilmDisc's ny0114. Place the golfer clip in the Video 2 track and the NYC clip in the Video 1 track. Apply the Green Screen Key effect to the golfer clip in the Video 2 track. Key out the green grass so that you can see the NYC scene.

Chroma

The Chroma Key effect in the Keying bin enables you to key out a specific color or a range of colors. This key is often planned during preproduction so that the video is shot against a one-colored background. To select the color to key out, use the Eyedropper tool to click the background area of the image thumbnail. Alternatively, you can click in the color swatch (under the word *Color*) and choose a key color from the Premiere Pro color picker.

To fine-tune the key, click and drag the sliders and make adjustments to the following options:

- **Similarity:** Click and drag to the left or right to increase or decrease the range of colors that will be made transparent.

- **Blend:** Click and drag to the right to create more of a blend between the two clips. Dragging to the left produces the opposite effect.

- **Threshold:** Clicking and dragging to the right keeps more shadow areas in the clip. Dragging to the left produces the opposite effect.

- **Cutoff:** Clicking and dragging to the right darkens shadow areas. Dragging to the right lightens shadow areas. Note that if you drag beyond the level set in the Threshold slider, gray and transparent areas become inverted.

- **Smoothing:** This control sets antialiasing, which blends pixel colors to create smoother edges. Choose High for the most smoothing, Low for some smoothing, or None for no smoothing. Choosing None is often the best choice when keying titles.

- **Mask Only:** Selecting the Mask Only option causes only the alpha channel of the clip to display.

Figure 14.10 shows a few frames from a project using the Chroma Key effect. The frames show a black horse galloping around an Indian tent. The two video clips are from FilmDisc. The black horse clip is FilmDisc's cl0113. The Indian tent clip is FilmDisc's na0110. These clips are on the DVD that accompanies this book.

To create the project, you can import the video clip of the Indian tent into the Video 1 track and import the video clip of the black horse galloping into the Video 2 track. In this example, you want the project to start with the black horse clip (cl0113) and then gradually have the Indian tent clip (na0110) appear. To make this happen, you place the ending points of both clips at the same location on the Timeline. As a result, the extra frames of the black horse clip appear at the beginning of the project rather than the end of the project. At the end of the Indian tent clip, you reduce the opacity so that the clip slowly fades out. The Timeline panel for the project is shown in Figure 14.11.

In the Audio 1 track, you can place SmartSound's American Sunset sound clip. In this example, you need to shorten the length of the sound clip to just under 20 seconds but still leave the length of the audio clip longer than the video clips, for a special effect. You also need to fade out the sound clip so that it gradually ends.

To apply the Keying effect, select the black horse clip in the Video 2 track and drag the Chroma Key effect over it. In the Chroma Key settings, you can use the Eyedropper tool to select the green grass, setting the color to green. Adjust the Similarity, Blend, Threshold, and Cutoff values so that you can see the Indian tent that is in the Video 1 track. Now set keyframes for the Chroma Key effect in the Effect Controls panel, so that the green grass in the black horse clip slowly fades away and reveals the Indian tent, as if the Indian tent were being painted. Set a keyframe at the beginning of the black horse clip for Similarity, Blend, Threshold, and Cutoff values. Set the values to zero percent. Then, for these four values, set a keyframe just below the nine-second mark and adjust the keyframe value accordingly.

The controls that you will use to create the project are shown in Figure 14.11. When you finish a project using keyframes and video effects, you should render it by choosing Sequence ⇨ Render Work Area. Always save your work.

FIGURE 14.10

A black horse clip (FilmDisc cl0113) superimposed onto an Indian tent clip (FilmDisc na0110), in a project using the Chroma Key effect

ON the DVD You can create the Chroma Key project using files from the DVD. The black horse clip is FilmDisc's cl0113.The Indian tent clip is FilmDisc's na0110. The sound clip is SmartSound's American Sunrise. The clips are located in the FilmDisc and SmartSound folders that are found in the Tutorial Projects folder on the DVD that accompanies this book.

FIGURE 14.11

The Timeline and Effect Controls panels used to create a project using the Chroma Key effect (shown in Figure 14.10)

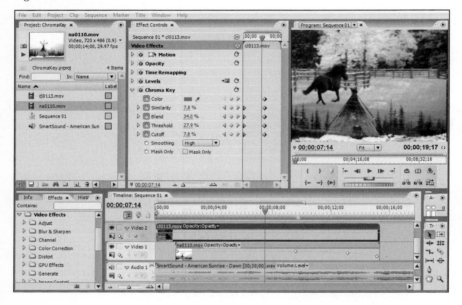

Color

The Color Key effect does a similar job to the Chroma Key effect. You can use both effects to key out a specific color or a range of colors. When you key out a color, it becomes translucent. You can choose a color by using the Key Color swatch, and specify the amount of transparency with the Color Tolerance control. You can adjust the edge size and smoothness of a color by using the Edge Thin and Edge Feather controls. Figure 14.13 shows the Color Key controls in the Effect Controls panel. You can use the clips from the previous sections to experiment with the Color Key controls.

In the following example of a Color Key effect, you can give the golfer (Artbeats GEL123) a very interesting golf experience. To do this, replace the greens with NYC buildings (FilmDisc's ny0114). You can see frames from the Color Key project in Figure 14.12.

Place the video clip of NYC buildings in the Video 1 track. Then place the golfer clip in the Video 2 track. Because the golfer clip is shorter than the NYC building clip, you can drag another copy of the golfer clip from the Project panel and place it next to the golfer clip that is already in the Video 2 track of the Timeline panel. This makes the length of the video clip in the Video 2 track 22 seconds. The video clip in the Video 1 track is 24½ seconds. To have the video clip in the Video 1 track slowly fade out, you can set an Opacity keyframe at the 22-second mark to 100 percent, and at the 24-second mark, set another Opacity keyframe to 20 percent.

In order to see the NYC building scene in the Video 1 track through the golfer clip in the Video 2 track, you can apply the Color Key effect to the golfer clip in the Video 2 track. In the Effect Controls panel, you can use the Eyedropper tool to click the green grass to set the Color Key swatch to green. Then you can set the Color Tolerance to 56, Edge Thin to 2, and Edge Feather to 4.0. Now place SmartSound's No Borders in the Audio 1 track.

Figure 14.13 shows the Timeline and Effect Controls panels that are used to create the Color Key project. When you finish a project using keyframes and video effects, you should render it by choosing Sequence ➪ Render Work Area. Always save your work.

FIGURE 14.12

A few frames from a project created using the Color Key effect to superimpose a golfer clip (Artbeats GEL123) in the Video 2 track over a clip of NYC buildings (FilmDisc's ny0114) in the Video 1 track

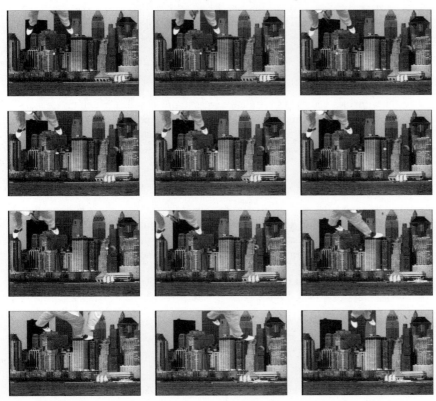

FIGURE 14.13

The Timeline and Effect Controls panels for the Color Key project

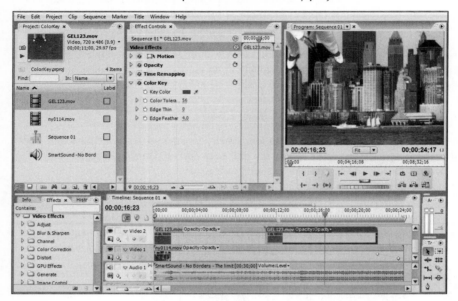

Difference Matte

The Difference Matte effect enables you to key out image areas in one clip that match image areas in another clip. Whether you use the Difference Matte effect depends upon the clips that you use in your project. If your project has a background without motion over a clip that contains motion, you may want to use Difference Matte to key out image areas from the static clip.

Garbage Matte

A video clip may contain an object that you don't want to appear in your project. When this happens, you can create a Garbage Matte to eliminate (mask out) the unwanted object. Usually, the video clip in which you want to mask out an item goes on the Video 2 track in the Timeline panel. Another clip that you want to use as a composite goes in the Video 1 track.

The Keying bin has three different types of Garbage Mattes: Four-Point Garbage Matte, Eight-Point Garbage Matte, and Sixteen-Point Garbage Matte.

> **NOTE**   Sometimes, you may need to create a more sophisticated mask. In this case, you can use Adobe After Effects. For more information on how to create a mask using Adobe After Effects, see Chapter 31.

You can use a Garbage Matte effect to create a split-screen effect that splits the screen between a clip in one track and a clip in another track, as shown in Figure 14.14. You can also use a Garbage

Matte effect to create a mask, as shown in Figure 14.15. Notice that in Figure 14.14 the video clip from the Video 1 track displays on the left side of the preview, and the video clip from the Video 2 track displays on the right side. Note also that in Figure 14.15 the same video clips (FilmDisc's kd0402) are used in the Video 1 and Video 2 tracks. In this example, the Four-Point Garbage Matte effect is applied in the Video 2 track, and the settings are adjusted so that you can see the video clip in the Video 1 track on the left side of the Monitor panel. The Change Color video effect is applied to the clip in the Video 1 track to change the color of the video clip. The Color Emboss and Replicate video effects are also applied. The Audio 1 track contains SmartSound's Piano Sonata sound clip.

FIGURE 14.14

The Effect Controls panel with the Four-Point Garbage Matte settings used to create the split-screen project, and the Program Monitor panel with an example of a split screen

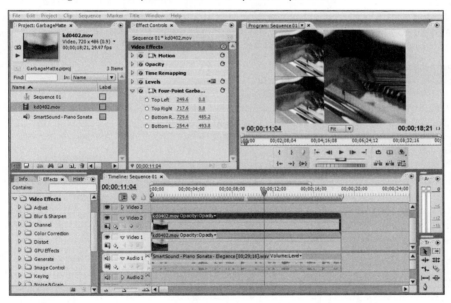

The example in Figure 14.15 uses two different video clips, but again, if you want, you can use the same video clip. The video clip of a piano keyboard in the Video 1 track is FilmDisc's kd0402. The video clip of a clock in the Video 2 track is FilmDisc's bc0104. The example applies the Sixteen-Point Garbage Matte effect to the clock clip in the Video 2 track. You can use the Garbage Matte to mask out the background so that you only see the clock. The Timeline used to create the mask effect is shown in Figure 14.15. The Audio 1 track contains SmartSound's Piano Sonata.

To create a split screen or mask effect using the Garbage Matte effect, follow these steps:

1. **Choose File ➪ New ➪ Project to create a new project.**

2. **Choose File ➪ Import to import two video clips.** Import a video clip in which you want to mask out an item, and import another clip (or a still image) that you want to use to composite. If you want, you can use the same video clip twice.

ON the DVD   You can load the video clips used to create the split-screen and mask project from the FilmDisc folder in the Tutorial Projects folder on the DVD that accompanies this book. The sound clip is found in the SmartSound folder.

3. **Drag the video clip that you want to split or mask from the Project panel into the Video 2 track of the Timeline panel.**

4. **Drag the video clip that you want to use to composite from the Project panel into the Video 1 track of the Timeline panel.**

5. **Select the video clip in the Video 2 track.** Then click and drag the Four-Point Garbage Matte, the Eight-Point Garbage Matte, or the Sixteen-Point Garbage Matte effect from the Effects panel to the video clip in the Video 2 track in the Timeline panel or to the Effect Controls panel. The example in Figure 14.14 uses the Four-Point Garbage Matte effect. The example in Figure 14.15 uses the Sixteen-Point Garbage Matte effect.

FIGURE 14.15

The Effect Controls panel with the Sixteen-Point Garbage Matte settings used to create the mask project, and the Program Monitor panel with an example of a mask

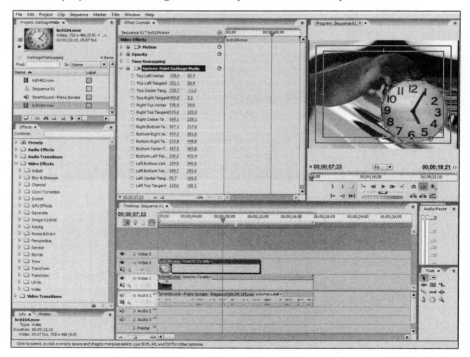

6. **Click the Expand/Collapse triangle in the Effect Controls panel to display the Garbage Matte controls.** You can enter numbers in the fields to adjust the matte (by adjusting the first numbers in the left fields), or you can click the words *Garbage Matte* in the Effect Controls panel to display an outline around the clip, which appears in the Program Monitor panel. Click one of the left points on the outline to adjust the matte. In the example in Figure 14.15, you can drag the left center and corners to the middle of the clip's preview.

7. **Choose Sequence ⇨ Render Work Area, to render your work.**

8. **Click the Play button in the Program Monitor panel to preview the effect.** Then choose File ⇨ Save to save your project.

Image Matte

The Image Matte Key (the controls for which are shown in Figure 14.16) is used to create transparency in still images, especially graphics. Image areas that correspond to black portions of the matte are transparent; areas corresponding to white areas of the matte are opaque. Gray areas create blending effects.

FIGURE 14.16

The Image Matte Key options in the Effect Controls panel and the Timeline panel used to create the Image Matte Key project

When using the Image Matte Key, click the Setup button (next to the Reset button in the Effect Controls panel) to choose an image. The final result depends upon the image you choose. You can create a composite using the alpha channel or the luminance of the clip. You can reverse the Keying effect, to make areas that correspond to white transparent and areas corresponding to black opaque.

Figure 14.17 shows a frame from a project that you can create using an Image Matte Key effect. To create the project, import a video clip of a glacier and a highway (GlacierHighway) to the Video 1 track. In the Video 2 track, import a video clip of waves (Waves). Select the Video 2 track and drag the Image Matte Key effect over the clip. Next, click the Setup icon in the Effect Controls panel. In the Select a Matte Image dialog box, select an Adobe Photoshop file (Smile), which you can find on the DVD. When the Photoshop file was created, the Presets in the New dialog box were set to match the Premiere Pro project. In Photoshop, the Preset was set to Film & Video to set the width and height to 720 x 480 pixels. To display the text in Premiere Pro without a background, in the New dialog box, you can set the Background contents to None rather than White.

FIGURE 14.17

A frame from the Image Matte Key project

You can use the Type tool in Photoshop to create the Smile text (shown in Figure 14.18). This example uses the Blackoak font with a font size of 60 points. Next, you can apply the Warp text command using the Bulge style. For the finishing touches, you can use various Layer Styles (Drop Shadow, Inner Shadow, Outer Glow, Inner Glow, and Bevel & Emboss).

The Timeline panel is shown in Figure 14.16. You can place SmartSound's Blues To Go sound clip in the Audio 1 track. For another Image Matte example, see Chapter 13 and Chapter 29.

ON the DVD You can load the video clips used to create the Image Matte Key project in Figure 14.17 from the MoreClips folder in the Tutorial folder of the DVD that accompanies this book. The files used are GlacierHighway, Waves, and Smile. The sound clip is SmartSound's Blues To Go; the SmartSound clips are in the Tutorial Files folder on the DVD.

FIGURE 14.18

The Photoshop Smile file was created with a transparent background.

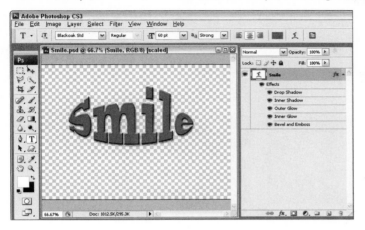

Luma

The Luma Key effect keys out darker image areas in a clip. Use the Threshold and Cutoff sliders to fine-tune the effect, as follows:

- **Threshold:** Click and drag to the right to increase the range of darker values that will be keyed out.

- **Cutoff:** This key controls the opacity of the Threshold range. Click and drag to the right to produce more transparency.

Figure 14.19 shows a few frames from a project using a Luma Key effect. The frames show football players, superimposed onto a video clip of a football. Both clips are from Artbeats. The football players video clip is Artbeats SP127, and the football video clip is Artbeats SP123.

To create the Luma Key project, you can import the football video clip into the Video 1 track and import the football players video clip into the Video 2 track. Select the video clip in the Video 2 track and apply the Luma Key effect. Adjust the Threshold and Cutoff values so that you can see the football through the football players. The football video clip in the Video 1 track is longer than the video clip of the football players. Because you want to start the project with a few frames of just the football and not the football players, you can place the football players video clip at about the three-second mark. This way, your project will end with just a few frames of the football players clip. Because the sound clip is a lot longer than both video clips, you need to shorten its length.

Figure 14.20 shows the Timeline used to create the project shown in Figure 14.19. You can place SmartSound's Movie Logos in the Audio 1 track. The Luma Key settings used to create the project appear in Figure 14.20. When you finish a project using video effects, you should render it by choosing Sequence ➪ Render Work Area. Remember to always save your work.

FIGURE 14.19

A few frames from the Luma Key effect project. The two superimposed clips are Artbeats SP123 and SP127.

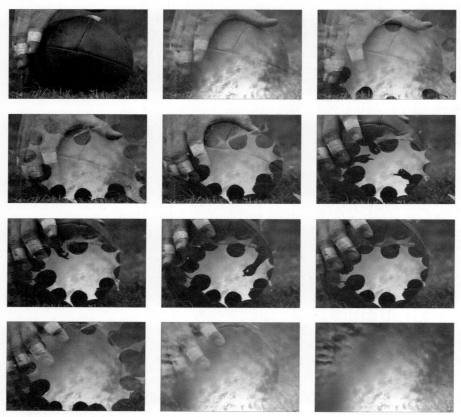

ON the DVD You can load the clips used to create the Luma Key project (shown in Figure 14.19) from the Artbeats and SmartSound folders in the Tutorial Projects folder on the DVD that accompanies this book. The video clips used to create the project are Artbeats SP127 and Artbeats SP123. The sound clip is SmartSound's Movie Logos.

Multiply and Screen

The Multiply and Screen Key effects are transparency effects in which the image in the lower video track exhibits a high degree of contrast. You can use the Multiply Key effect to create transparency in areas that correspond to bright image areas in the lower video track. Use the Screen Key effect to create transparency in areas that correspond to dark image areas in the lower video track. For both key effects, you can adjust the Opacity and Cutoff percent values to fine-tune the effect.

FIGURE 14.20

The Timeline panel and the Effect Controls panel used to create the Luma Key effect project

If you want to experiment with the Multiply and Screen Key effects, you can use these clips: FilmDisc's bc0104 in the Video 1 track, FilmDisc's kd0402 in the Video 2 track, and SmartSound's Piano Sonata sound clip in the Audio 1 track.

Non Red

As with the blue and green screens, the Non Red Key is used to key out blue and green backgrounds, but it does both at once. This key also includes a blending slider that enables you to blend two clips together. Figure 14.21 shows a frame of the Non Red Key effect in the Monitor panel. To create the effect, a video clip, NYC buildings (FilmDisc's ny0114) is placed in the Video 2 track and a video clip of moving cabs (FilmDisc's ny0114) is placed in the Video 1 track, as shown in the Timeline panel in Figure 14.21. The Non Red Key effect is applied to the NYC buildings clip in the Video 2 track. The Non Red Key options are shown in the Effect Controls panel in Figure 14.21. The sound clip used for the Non Red Key project is SmartSound's New Vistas. These clips can be found on the DVD that accompanies this book.

FIGURE 14.21

A frame from a project created using the Non Red Key effect to superimpose moving cabs (FilmDisc's cm0105) in the Video 1 track over NYC buildings (FilmDisc's ny0114) in the Video 2 track

RGB Difference

The RGB Difference Key is an easy-to-use version of the Chroma Key effect. Use this key when precise keying is not required or when the image being keyed appears in front of a bright background. As with the Chroma Key, the RGB Difference Key provides Similarity and Smoothing options but does not provide Blend, Threshold, or Cutoff controls.

Figure 14.22 shows frames from an RGB Difference Key project, called the Working Hard project. The frames show a video clip of a silhouette of two people shaking hands (FilmDisc's bc0115), which is placed in the Video 2 track. The Video 1 track contains a video clip of moving cabs (FilmDisc's cm0105). The Video 3 track contains the Working Hard Title clip, which you can create in Premiere Pro. To create the Working Hard Title clip, use the CaslonPro Slant Blue 70 Style and set the font size to 100 points. The sound clip is SmartSound's New Vistas, and runs for the entire length of the project.

The Working Hard project (shown in Figure 14.22) is divided up into three parts: the introduction, main scene, and conclusion. Figure 14.23 shows the Timeline for the RGB Difference Key for the Working Hard project. The introduction comprises the first eight-and-one-half seconds of the project. For this duration, you want to see just the moving cabs clip with the Working Hard Title clip superimposed over it. To superimpose the Working Hard Title clip (in the Video 3 track) over the moving cabs clip (in the Video 1 track), you can set the opacity of the Title clip to 40 percent.

FIGURE 14.22

Frames from the RGB Difference key, the Working Hard project. The video clips used are FilmDisc's clips bc0115 and cm0105.

The Main scene of the project starts at the 8.5-second mark and ends at the 21-second mark. At the 8.5-second mark, you can place the hand-shaking video clip in the Video 2 track, directly over the moving cabs clip in the Video 1 track. Both clips end at about the 21-second mark. To create the blending effect of the two video clips (shown in Figure 14.23), the RGB Difference Key is applied to the hand-shaking video clip in the Video 2 track. By applying the RGB Difference Key, you can see the moving cabs through the silhouette. To show the moving cab video clip through the shaking hands (which is a solid-black silhouette), you can set the Color swatch control for the RGB Difference effect in the Effect Controls to black.

FIGURE 14.23

The Timeline and the Effect Controls panels used in the RGB Difference Key, for the Working Hard project (shown in Figure 14.22)

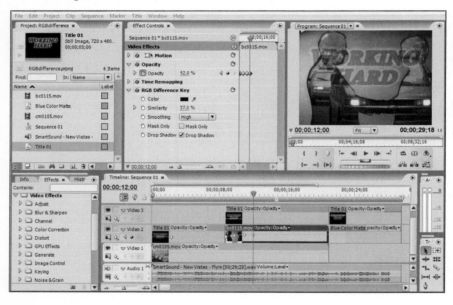

Figure 14.23 shows the Effect Controls panel with the RGB Difference Key settings used in Figure 14.22. At the beginning of the shaking hands clip, you want to see part of the moving cabs clip in the blue background area, and so you must reduce the opacity for the shaking hands clip. Set keyframes for the Opacity control to gradually fade in the shaking hands clip. Start by setting the first Opacity keyframe to 50 percent, the second keyframe to 70 percent, the third keyframe to 86 percent, and the fourth keyframe to 92 percent. In this Main scene area, you can superimpose the Working Hard Title clip over the video clips by placing a copy of the Title clip in the Video 3 track and setting the opacity for the Title clip to 30 percent.

For the conclusion of the Working Hard project, you can place a copy of the Title clip in the Video 3 track and place a yellow Color Matte clip in the Video 2 track. To create a Color Matte clip, choose

File ⇨ New ⇨ Color Matte. In the Color Picker dialog box that appears, choose a color, and then click OK. In the Choose Name dialog box, name your color, and then click OK. To make the Color Matte clip more interesting, you can apply the Noise effect (in the Noise&Grain bin). When you finish a project using keyframes and video effects, you should render it by choosing Sequence ⇨ Render Work Area. Always save your work.

ON the DVD You can use files from the DVD to create the RGB Difference Key project (shown in Figure 14.22). The shaking hands clip is FilmDisc's bc0115. The moving cabs clip is FilmDisc's cm0105. The sound clip is SmartSound's New Vistas. The clips are located in the FilmDisc and SmartSound folders in the Tutorial Projects folder on the DVD that accompanies this book.

Remove Matte

The Keying effects create transparency from alpha channels created from red, green, and blue channels, as well as the alpha channel. Normally, the Remove Matte effect is used to key out the black or white backgrounds. This is useful for graphics with solid white or black backgrounds.

Track Matte

The Track Matte Key enables you to create a moving or traveling matte effect. Often, the matte is a black-and-white image that is set in motion onscreen. Image areas corresponding to black in the matte are transparent; image areas corresponding to white are opaque. Gray areas create blending effects. To create the Track Matte Key effect, shown in Figure 14.24, you can import two video clips and create some type using Premiere Pro's Title panel. For this example, you need to import a clip of waterfalls (TwoWaterfalls) into the Video 1 track. Now import a clip of waves (Waves) into the Video 2 track. In the Video 3 track, place the title clip, which you can create using Premiere Pro's Title panel (shown in Figure 14.25).

FIGURE 14.24

A frame of the Track Matte Key project

When creating the title, you can click the Show Background Video icon in the Title panel so that you can see the video clip in the Video 2 track (as shown in Figure 14.26). The video clip in the Video 2 track appears in the Title clip after you apply the Track Matte Key effect to the Video 2 track. Figure 14.27 shows the Track Matte Key options in the Effect Controls panel. In order for the Title clip in the Video 3 track to be used as a matte for the waves video clip in the Video 2 track, you can set the Matte pop-up menu to the Video 3 track. The Composite pop-up menu should be set to Matte Alpha. To reverse the effect, click the Reverse option.

FIGURE 14.25

A title created in Premiere Pro's Title panel, which is then imported into the Video 3 track

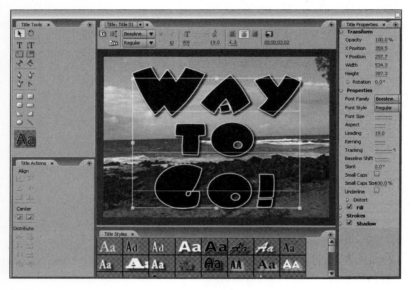

Figure 14.26 shows the Timeline panel used to create the Track Matte Key project. In the Timeline panel, you can see two video clips in the Video 1 and 2 tracks. The Video 3 track contains the Title clip that is used as a matte. The Audio 1 track contains SmartSound's The Great Escape sound clip.

CROSS-REF   The example at the end of Chapter 16 uses the Track Matte Key effect.

FIGURE 14.26

The Timeline panel for the Track Matte Key project

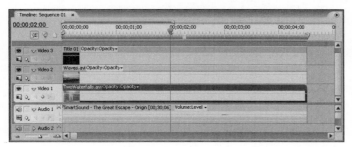

FIGURE 14.27

The Effect Controls panel for the Track Matte Key project

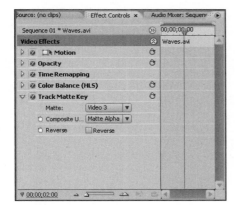

Summary

Premiere Pro's superimposition options create interesting and attractive effects that blend video tracks together or make various areas of one track transparent. This chapter covered the following topics:

- Use the Premiere Pro Opacity options to blend a video track with the one beneath it.
- Click and drag the Opacity handles in the Opacity graph line to adjust the fading effect.
- To create Keying effects that make portions of a video track transparent, open Premiere Pro's Effects bin by choosing Window ➪ Effects. Then open the Video Effects bins so that you can open the Keying bin.

- Premiere Pro provides several Keying effects to choose from: Alpha Adjust, Blue Screen, Chroma, Color, Difference Matte, Garbage Matte, Image Matte, Luma Key, Non Red Key, RGB Difference, Remove Matte, Track Matte.

- Use the Color Key, Blue Screen Key, and Green Screen Key effects to key out background image areas based on color.

- Use the Alpha Adjust Key effect to key out images based on an imported image's alpha channel.

- Use the Track Matte Key effect to create traveling matte effects.

Chapter 15

Using Color Mattes and Backdrops

During the course of a video production, you may need to create a simple, colored, background video track. You may want the track to be a solid-color background for text, or a background for transparency effects. This chapter looks at how to use colored background mattes and still-frame background images in Adobe Premiere Pro. You learn how to create a color background in Premiere Pro and how to export a still frame from a clip to use as a backdrop. This chapter also has tutorials on creating backdrops in two popular digital imaging programs — Adobe Photoshop and Adobe Illustrator.

NOTE You can copy and paste a layer from a Premiere Pro video track to Adobe After Effects and then animate it in After Effects' 3-D space. To turn a layer in After Effects' Timeline to a 3-D layer, either click the layer's 3-D layer toggle button switch icon (a 3-D cube icon) or choose Layer ⇨ 3D Layer. To animate a layer's orientation, first move the current-time indicator (CTI) to the start of the layer. Then click the Orientation stopwatch in the Transform section of the layer to create a keyframe. To create more keyframes, move the CTI to the right, and then adjust the layer's orientation by using the Rotation tool on the layer in the Composition panel. This creates another keyframe. Continue this procedure until you have created the orientation animation that you want.

Creating a Color Matte

If you need to create a colored background for text or graphics, you can use a Premiere Pro *color matte*. Unlike many of the Premiere Pro video mattes, a color matte is a solid matte that comprises the entire video frame. You can use a color matte as a background or as a temporary track placeholder until you shoot or create the final track.

> **NOTE** You may want to use a black video as a background matte. To create a black video, choose File ▷ New ▷ Black Video.

An advantage of using a colored background is its versatility. After you create the color matte, you can easily change its color with a few clicks of the mouse. Follow these steps to create a color matte in Premiere Pro:

1. **With a project onscreen, choose File ▷ New ▷ Color Matte.** The Color Picker dialog box appears.

2. **Select a matte color.** If an exclamation mark icon appears next to the color swatches in the upper-right corner of the dialog box, as shown in Figure 15.1, you've chosen a color that is out of the NTSC color gamut. This color cannot be reproduced correctly in NTSC video. Click the exclamation mark icon to have Premiere Pro choose the next-closest color.

FIGURE 15.1

The Premiere Pro Color Picker dialog box

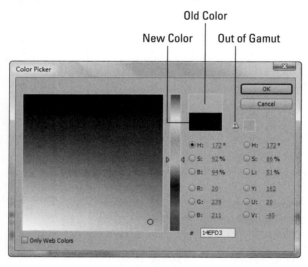

> **CROSS-REF** For more information on color gamuts, see Chapter 17.

3. Click OK to close the Color Picker dialog box.

4. In the Choose Name dialog box that appears, type a name for the color matte in the name field, as shown in Figure 15.2.

5. Click OK to place the color matte in the Project panel.

6. To use the color matte, simply drag it from the Project panel into a video track.

 The default duration of a color matte is determined by the Still Frame setting in the General Preferences dialog box. To change the default setting, choose Edit ⇨ Preferences ⇨ General. In the Still Image Default Duration area, enter the number of frames that you want to use as the still image default.

FIGURE 15.2

The Choose Name dialog box

Creating a color matte from the Project panel

Follow these steps to use the Project panel to create a background matte in Premiere Pro:

 Before you begin, you must have a project onscreen.

1. **In the Project panel, click the New Item icon, which is located between the New Bin icon and the trash icon.** Choose Color Matte.

2. **When the Color Picker dialog box appears, select a color matte.**

3. **Click OK to close the Color Picker dialog box.** The Choose Name dialog box appears.

4. **Type a name for the color matte.**

5. **Click OK.** The color matte appears instantly in the Project panel, as shown in Figure 15.3, ready for you to drag it to the Timeline panel.

 To change the duration of a color matte, click it in the Project panel and choose Clip ⇨ Speed/Duration. In the Clip Speed/Duration dialog box, click the Duration values to change them. Then click OK.

FIGURE 15.3

The Project panel with a color matte

New Item

Editing a color matte

The Premiere Pro color mattes have a distinct advantage over simply creating a colored background in the Title panel or creating a colored background in another program. If you are using a Premiere Pro color matte, you can quickly change colors if the original matte color proves unsuitable or unattractive. Follow these steps to change the color of a color matte in Premiere Pro:

 Before you begin, you must have a project onscreen with a color matte in the Project panel.

1. In the Project panel, double-click the Color Matte icon.

2. **When the Color Picker dialog box appears, select a new color matte.** Click OK to close the Color Picker dialog box.

3. **To change the colors of a color matte after you place it in the Timeline, simply double-click the matte clip in the Timeline panel.** When Premiere Pro's Color Picker dialog box appears, select a new color and then click OK. After you click OK, the color changes, not only in the selected clip but also in all of the clips in the tracks that use that color matte.

Follow these steps to change the color of a color matte in Premiere Pro by using a video effect:

 Before you begin, you must have a project onscreen with a color matte in the Project panel.

1. **Drag the Color Matte icon from the Project panel to a video track in the Timeline panel.**

2. **In the Effects panel, open the Video Effects bin.** Open the Generate bin.

3. **Click one of the Generate video effects and drag it over the color matte in the Timeline panel.** To create a 4-Color Gradient, use the 4-Color Gradient effect. Use the video effect controls in the Effect Controls panel to adjust how the effect displays.

4. **Click one of the Stylize video effects and drag it over the color matte in the Timeline panel.** Try applying different Stylize video effects to a 4-Color Gradient. For some interesting results, you might want to try Posterize, Replicate, Solarize, Threshold, and Brush Strokes. Use the video effect controls in the Effect Controls panel to adjust how the effect displays.

5. **Use video effects to enhance the color matte in the Timeline panel.** For some more interesting effects, try using the Twirl or Wave Warp Distort video effects. You can also adjust the color of the color matte by using the video effects in the Adjust bin, Color Correction bin, and Image Control bin.

 CROSS-REF You can create a color matte in Premiere Pro and then animate and incorporate it into a project. This chapter's section "Creating a Color Matte" provides examples of creating color mattes and incorporating them into projects.

Using the Title Designer to Create a Background

The Title Designer can be used to create backgrounds. You can either use the various tools to create a piece of artwork as the background or you can use the Rectangle tool to create a background. Turn to Chapter 10 to learn how to use the tools in the Title Designer to create artwork for a background. Follow these steps to create a background using the Rectangle tool in Premiere Pro's Title Designer:

NOTE Before you begin, you must have a Premiere Pro project onscreen.

1. **Choose File ➪ New ➪ Title.** In the New Title dialog box that appears, name your title and click OK. The Title Designer appears onscreen.

2. **In Title Tools panel, click the Rectangle tool.** Then click and drag in the drawing area of the Title panel to create a rectangle that is the entire size of the drawing area.

3. **Click the Fill Type drop-down menu in the Title Properties panel and select a Solid or Gradient fill type.** Then select the color or colors that you want to use. The example in Figure 15.4 uses the Linear Gradient fill type.

 You can apply video effects to a title in a video track in the Timeline panel. Video effects can change the color or distort a title clip.

FIGURE 15.4

You can use the Title Designer to create either a solid or gradient color matte.

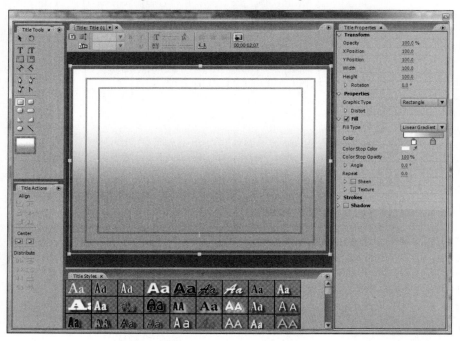

If you want to use a texture, click the Texture check box. Then click the Texture swatch and select a texture from the Texture folder. The example in Figure 15.5 uses the 1080music_fullbkg.png texture.

FIGURE 15.5

You can also use the Title Designer to create a textured color matte.

Creating a Backdrop from a Still Frame

As you work in Premiere Pro, you may want to export a still frame from a video clip and save it in a TIFF or BMP format so that you can bring it into Photoshop or Illustrator and enhance it to use as a background matte. Figure 15.6 shows the results of using Photoshop to paint over a still frame that was exported from Premiere Pro to give it the look of a painting. Follow these steps:

1. **To create the backdrop shown in Figure 15.6, import a video clip into a Premiere Pro project.** The example in Figure 15.6 uses the Queenstown video clip.

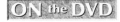 **The Queenstown video clip is in the MoreClips folder on the DVD that accompanies this book.**

2. Drag the clip from the Project panel to the Video 1 track in the Timeline panel.

NOTE   You can either use Premiere Pro's color-correcting video effects or use Photoshop's Image Adjust color-correcting commands to color-correct the frame that you want to use as a backdrop. This example uses Premiere Pro's Color Balance (HLS), Levels, Brightness & Contrast, and Unsharp Mask video effects to color-correct the frame.

3. Move the current-time indicator to find a frame to export.

4. With the current-time indicator on the frame that you want to export, choose File ⇨ Export ⇨ Frame. In the Export Frame dialog box, click the Settings button. In the Export Frame Settings dialog box, click the File Type drop-down menu and choose whether you want to export the frame in BMP, GIF, or TIFF format. (This example exports the frame in TIFF format.) Click OK to close the Export Frame Settings dialog box. Back in the Export Frame dialog box, enter a name for the frame. Locate a place to save your frame, and then click Save.

FIGURE 15.6

A backdrop created by exporting a frame from a video clip in Premiere Pro into Photoshop.

5. **Launch Photoshop.** Choose File ⇨ Open. Locate the frame file and click Open.

6. **To apply a brush stroke effect, choose Filter ⇨ Filter Gallery.** In the Filter Gallery dialog box, open the Brush Strokes folder and select a filter. The example in Figure 15.6 uses the Spatter filter.

   To add more of a painted look to your backdrop, you can paint in a new layer. By painting in a layer above the background, you don't affect the background. If you make a mistake, you can use the Eraser tool to erase the brushstrokes without erasing the background.

7. **Choose Layer ➪ New ➪ Layer.** In the New Layer dialog box that appears, you can name the layer. Click OK to create a new layer above the Background layer.

8. **Click the Eyedropper tool and pick a color from the background to paint with.** In this example, a light-green color is first selected to paint with, followed by a dark-green color. Next, some yellow and orange are added to the green areas. Some light-pink and purple colors are then added to the mountains. A turquoise color is added to the water.

9. **Click the Brush tool.** Choose Window ➪ Brushes. Select a brush to paint with and start painting. This example uses the Dry Brush to paint with because it adds texture as you paint.

10. **When you are done, you can flatten the layers if you want by choosing Layer ➪ Flatten Image.** Save your file. Choose File ➪ Save As to save a copy of the original background. You can now import the painted background file into a Premiere Pro project to use as a backdrop. You can use the backdrop behind opening or ending titles, behind the title credits, or even as a backdrop for a silhouette of a person.

Follow these steps to export and save a portion of a video clip and use the still frame as a backdrop:

> **NOTE** Before you begin, open or create a project containing a video clip in one of the Timeline panel's video tracks.

1. **Double-click the clip from which you want to create a backdrop in the Project panel.** The clip opens in the Source panel.

2. **Use the Scrubbing tool or the Frame Advance icon to move to the frame that you want to export.**

> **CROSS-REF** For more information on using the Source panel, see Chapter 6.

3. **Choose File ➪ Export ➪ Frame.** The Export Frame dialog box appears.

4. **In the Export Frame dialog box, click the Settings button.** The Export Frame Settings dialog box appears.

5. **In the Export Frame Settings dialog box, choose Windows Bitmap, GIF, Targa, or TIFF from the File Type format drop-down menu.** If you choose GIF, your image can contain a maximum of 256 colors. If you want, you can have the frame imported into the Project panel onscreen by selecting the Add to Project When Finished option. Click OK to apply the settings and close the Export Frame Settings dialog box.

6. **In the Export Frame dialog box, click Save to save the file.** You can now import the image into Photoshop by launching the program and choosing File ➪ Open. Photoshop enables you to enhance or manipulate your image. If you want, you can create a collage, inform the painted landscape image seen in Figure 15.6, by dragging and dropping all of the files into one file. You may also want to import the final Photoshop image into Premiere Pro. To import the final Photoshop file into a Premiere Pro project, choose File ➪ Import. Locate and select the file, and then click Open.

Creating Background Mattes in Photoshop

Adobe Photoshop is an extremely versatile program for creating full-screen background mattes, or backdrops. Not only can you edit and manipulate photographs in Photoshop, but you can also create black-and-white, grayscale, or color images to use as background mattes. In this section, you create various Photoshop projects. First, you learn how to create a simple textured backdrop. Then you create more complicated backdrop examples that illustrate more of Photoshop's digital imaging power.

Start by creating a new Photoshop file. You can create a new Photoshop document in two different ways: from within a Premiere Pro project or from Photoshop. The advantage of creating a Photoshop file from within your Premiere Pro project is that you don't have to import the file into Premiere Pro — it is automatically placed in your Premiere Pro project. Here's how to create a Photoshop background file from within a Premiere Pro project:

 Before you begin, you must have a Premiere Pro project onscreen.

1. **Choose File ⇨ New ⇨ Photoshop File.** In the New Photoshop File dialog box, click the Name drop-down menu and name your file. Make sure that the Add to Project (Merged Layers) check box is selected. That way, when you save the file, it is automatically saved in the Project panel of the current Premiere Pro project. Click the Save button to save the file. Premiere Pro launches Photoshop with the saved Photoshop file onscreen. The Photoshop file (shown in Figure 15.7) appears with the Safe Action margins and the Safe Title margins. The Photoshop file also appears in the Project panel of the Premiere Pro project you are working on.

2. **In Photoshop, select the Gradient tool from the Tools palette.** Then click and drag in the drawing area of your document to create a gradient (as shown in Figure 15.7). If you want, you can adjust the Gradient tool options and recreate the gradient until you have the desired effect. To jazz up the background, you can apply a filter to it. Remember to resave your file, so that the changes are updated in your Premiere Pro project.

3. **Choose File ⇨ Save.** Every time you save the Photoshop file, it is automatically updated in the Premiere Pro project. If you continue making changes to the file in Photoshop, be sure to save the changes so that the Photoshop file is updated in the Premiere Pro project.

4. **To view the changes made to the Photoshop file in Premiere Pro, activate the Premiere Pro project.** Notice that the Photoshop file is updated in the Project panel of the Premiere Pro project.

5. **To use the Photoshop file as a background for the Premiere Pro project that you are working on, drag the Photoshop file from the Project panel to the Video 1 track of the Timeline panel.** In the Timeline panel, you can click the left side of the Photoshop file and drag right to extend its duration. You can also choose Clip ⇨ Speed/Duration. In the Clip/Speed Duration dialog box, enter the desired duration and click OK.

6. **Choose File ⇨ Save to save your Premiere Pro project.** Continue to make the necessary additions and changes to your project and save it. Choose File ⇨ Export ⇨ Movie to save your Premiere Pro project in a movie format.

FIGURE 15.7

When you create a Photoshop file from within a Premiere Pro project, the changes to the Photoshop file are automatically applied to the Photoshop file in the Project panel of Premiere Pro.

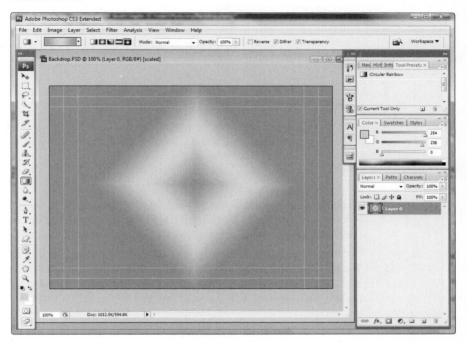

Here's how to create a background file using Photoshop:

1. **Launch Photoshop.**

2. **Choose File ⇨ New.** In the New dialog box, click the Name drop-down menu and name your file. Click the Preset drop-down menu and choose Film & Video. Click the Background Contents drop-down menu and choose White, Background Color, or Transparent. A new Photoshop document appears with Safe Action margins and Safe Title margins.

3. **Select the Brush tool from the Tools palette.**

4. **Choose Windows ⇨ Brushes to display the Brushes palette.** In the Brushes palette, select a brush style and size. This example uses the Rough Round Bristle Brush.

5. **Click either the Swatches or Color palette to select a painting color.**

NOTE To give you more room for drawing, double-click a palette's tab to minimize it. When you need to use the palette, double-click its tab to expand it.

6. **Click and drag in the drawing area of your document to create brush strokes.** Continue painting in the drawing area until the area is entirely painted, as shown in Figure 15.8.

7. **To start all over again, choose Edit ⇨ Fill.** In the Fill dialog box, click the Contents drop-down menu and select a color to use. Set the Blending Mode to Normal and the opacity to 100 percent.

   If you want to experiment, you can change the mode and opacity settings. Click OK to fill the document with the information from the Fill dialog box. Now use the Brush tool to paint.

8. **After you are finished editing the Photoshop background file, choose File ⇨ Save.** In the Save dialog box, save the file in Photoshop format.

9. **To import the Photoshop file into Premiere Pro, launch Premiere Pro.** Choose File ⇨ Import. In the Import dialog box, locate the Photoshop file that you want to import, click it, and choose Open. The Photoshop background file appears in the Project panel. To apply the Photoshop background to your movie, click and drag it to the Video 1 track in the Timeline panel.

10. **To change the duration of the Photoshop background file in the Timeline panel, click the left side of the Photoshop file and drag right.** You can also choose Clip ⇨ Speed/Duration. In the Clip/Speed Duration dialog box, enter the desired duration and click OK.

11. **Choose File ⇨ Save to save your Premiere Pro project.** Continue to make the necessary additions and changes to your project and save it. Choose File ⇨ Export ⇨ Movie to save your Premiere Pro project in a movie format.

Creating simple backgrounds with the Gradient tool

In this section, you create several Photoshop gradient backgrounds. In Premiere Pro, you can use the File ⇨ New ⇨ Photoshop File command to create the Photoshop files. Start by launching Premiere Pro and creating a new project. Then choose File ⇨ New ⇨ Photoshop File. In the Save Photoshop File As dialog box, click the File Name drop-down menu and name your file. Then click Save. You are now ready to create a Photoshop background file to use in your Premiere Pro project.

NOTE   Photoshop launches with the new Photoshop file ready for you to work on. The changes you make to the Photoshop file are updated in Premiere Pro. The Photoshop file appears in the Project panel of your Premiere Pro project.

You can create a background Photoshop file with the Brush tool.

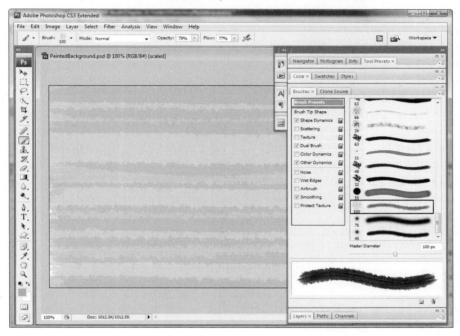

Creating a Photoshop background with the Gradient tool and image-editing tools

In this section you create a custom gradient with the Gradient Editor and then use the image-editing tools to give it a painted effect. Start by creating a new project in Premiere Pro by choosing File ➪ New ➪ Photoshop File. In the Save Photoshop File As dialog box, click the File Name drop-down menu and name your file. Then click Save to display a new Photoshop document. After you have created, applied, and edited a Photoshop gradient, be sure to save your work so the changes automatically update in your Premiere Pro project. To add the Photoshop background gradient to your Premiere Pro project, activate Premiere Pro and drag the Photoshop gradient file from the Project panel to the Video 1 track of the Timeline panel.

NOTE If you prefer to only have one program open at a time, you can create a new Photoshop document with only Photoshop open. After you are done working, save your file. Next, load a Premiere Pro project or create a new one. Then import the Photoshop file into the project and drag the imported file from the Project panel to the Timeline panel.

Follow these steps to create a custom gradient in Photoshop:

1. **Select the Gradient tool from the Tools palette.**

2. **To display the Gradient Editor, double-click the gradient swatch in the Gradient toolbar (at the top of the document, right below the menus).**

3. **In the Gradient Editor, select a preset to work with (see Figure 15.9).** To display more gradient presets, click the Presets drop-down menu and make a selection.

4. **To customize your gradient, click the boxes below the gradient bar at the bottom of the dialog box.** You can click a Color Stop box and move it. Double-click a Color Stop box to display the Color Picker and choose a new color. You can add more colors by creating new Color Stops. Just click an area of the gradient bar to add a new Color Stop.

5. **Type a name for your gradient in the Name field.** Click the New button to save your custom gradient at the bottom of the Presets list.

6. **When you are done creating a custom gradient, click OK to close the Gradient Editor.**

FIGURE 15.9

Photoshop's Gradient Editor allows you to create custom gradients.

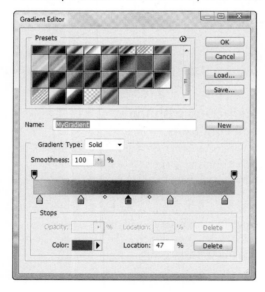

7. **There are five different types of gradients you can create: Linear, Radial, Angle, Reflected, and Diamond.** Click one of these gradient icons in the Gradient toolbar. The example in Figure 15.10 uses the Angle gradient.

8. **To fill your document with the custom gradient, click in the area where you want your gradient to start.** Drag to where you want it to end. Typically, you drag from the center of the drawing area to the edge of the drawing area.

9. **You can overlay one gradient over another by reducing the opacity and changing the mode.** You can then use the Gradient tool to create various gradients on top of each other. Figure 15.11 shows the effects of applying various gradients on top of each other with the opacity set to 50 percent and the mode set to Overlay.

FIGURE 15.10

A custom Angle gradient created in Photoshop

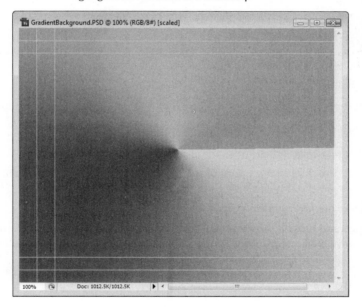

FIGURE 15.11

Various Angle gradients (shown in Figure 15.10) are created on top of each other with the Gradient tool's mode set to Overlay and the opacity set to 50 percent.

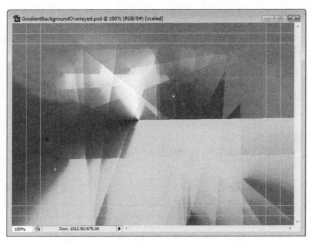

Follow these steps to use the Smudge and Blur tools to give a gradient a painted look:

1. **Select the Smudge tool from the Tools palette.**

2. **Choose a large brush.**

3. **Click and drag in the colors of your gradient to blend them together.** Figure 15.12 shows the effects of applying the Smudge tool to a gradient.

4. **Select the Blur tool from the Tools palette.**

5. **Click and drag in the areas that have been blended together to soften the edges and create a watercolor effect.** Figure 15.13 shows the effects of applying the Blur tool to a smudged gradient.

Follow these steps to use the Dodge and Burn tools to give a gradient dimension:

1. **Select either the Dodge or Burn tool from the Tools palette.**

2. **Use the Dodge tool to lighten color areas and the Burn tool to darken color areas.** Click the Range drop-down menu in the toolbar to specify whether you want to affect the highlights, midtones, or shadows.

3. **Choose a brush size and exposure.** Then click and drag over the areas you want to change.

FIGURE 15.12

The Smudge tool is used on a Photoshop gradient to give it a painted effect.

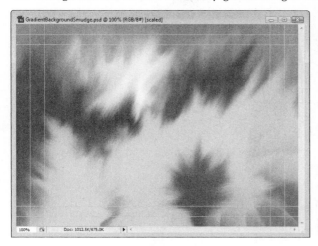

Creating a Photoshop background with the Gradient tool and the Liquify filter

In Photoshop, use the Gradient tool to create a gradient. Then choose Filter ➪ Liquify. In the Liquify dialog box, click and drag over the areas you want to liquefy. Select a brush size and pressure from the Tool Options area of the dialog box. You can experiment with the other settings for different results. Figure 15.14 shows an interesting background being created with the Liquify filter.

FIGURE 15.13

The Blur tool is used on a smudged gradient to give it a watercolor effect.

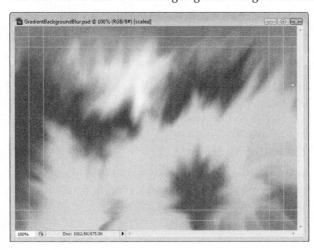

FIGURE 15.14

A Photoshop gradient background file created with the Photoshop Liquify filter

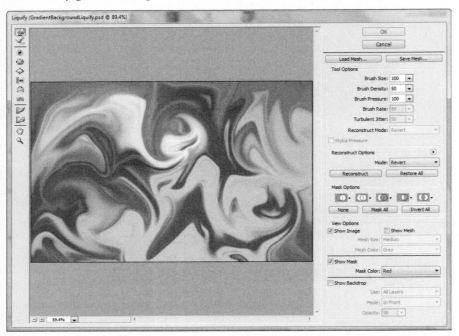

Creating a Photoshop background with the Gradient tool and the Elliptical Marquee tool

In Photoshop, use the Elliptical Marquee tool to make a selection. The Elliptical Marquee tool is in the same location as the Rectangle Marquee tool. Click the Rectangle Marquee tool in the toolbar and drag to the right to select the Elliptical Marquee tool. Then use the Gradient tool with a Radial gradient to create a radial gradient in the selection. This example uses the Orange, Yellow, Orange gradient. Continue to create various elliptical selections and fill them with radial gradients with the Gradient tool until you have a background that looks similar to the one shown on the left side of Figure 15.15.

To give the background a more painted effect, you can apply a filter from the Filter Gallery. The right side of Figure 15.15 shows the radial gradients after applying a filter from the Filter Gallery. You can also use a filter from the Filter Gallery to distort or create other interesting effects in your background. Choose Filter ➪ Filter Gallery to display the Filter Gallery dialog box (shown in Figure 15.16). Click an effect in one of the folders. Then adjust the filter's controls.

To create the effect in Figure 15.15 (on the left side), you can apply the Plastic Warp filter. If you want to conserve the Photoshop background file with the elliptical gradients before applying the Filter Gallery, you need to use the File ➪ Save As command to create a duplicate file. Do this before applying any filters to your background.

FIGURE 15.15

A Photoshop gradient background file created with Photoshop's Elliptical Marquee tool and Gradient tool (left), and after applying the Plastic Wrap filter (right)

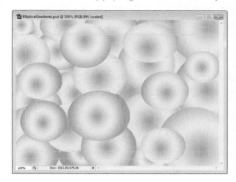 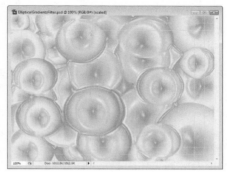

FIGURE 15.16

The Plastic Wrap filter dialog box, showing the applied filter

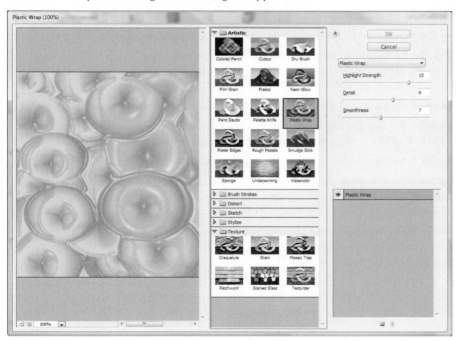

Animating a Photoshop background using layers, the Gradient tool, and the Pencil tool

In a Premiere Pro project, you may want to use an animated background rather than just a still backdrop. In this section you use a rainbow-colored gradient as a background. You duplicate the background and create white arrows with the Pencil tool in separate layers. This animation slowly builds upon one layer to the next. To create the arrow animation, you can use the Make Frames from Layers command, found in the Animation palette.

Follow these steps to create a radial, rainbow-colored gradient background with white arrows, and then animate it using Photoshop CS3 Extended for use in a Premiere Pro project:

1. **In Photoshop, create a new Film & Video document.**

2. **Use the Gradient tool to create a rainbow-colored radial gradient, as shown in Figure 15.17.** The rainbow gradient is used as the background of an arrow animation.

3. **Select the Pencil tool from the Tools palette.** Choose Window ➪ Brushes. Pick a brush style and size. The example in Figure 15.17 uses the Watercolor Small Round Tip brush.

4. **Set the Foreground color to white.**

5. **Click the Background layer in the Layers palette.** Drag it over the New Layer icon at the bottom of the palette to duplicate the Background layer. Photoshop creates a layer called Background copy.

6. **Use the Pencil tool to create a white arrow at the bottom-left side of the gradient.**

7. **Click the Background copy layer in the Layers palette.** Drag it over the New Layer icon at the bottom of the palette to duplicate the Background copy **layer.** Photoshop creates a layer called Background copy 2.

8. **Use the Pencil tool to create a white arrow at the bottom-right side of the gradient.**

9. **Continue duplicating the layer you are on and adding new arrows until you have created all of the arrows you want in your animation (see Figure 15.18).**

10. Choose Window ➪ Animation to display the Animation palette.

11. **The Animation palette should be set to Frame Animation rather than Timeline animation.** Choose Convert to Frame Animation from the Animation palette menu to work in this mode.

12. **Choose Make Frames from Layers in the Animation palette menu.** The layers from the Layers palette now appear in frames in the Animation palette. Each frame should have a time delay of at least .5 seconds. To set the time delay, click it and enter a new figure.

FIGURE 15.17

A Photoshop gradient background file created with layers using the Paintbrush tool, and then animated in Premiere Pro

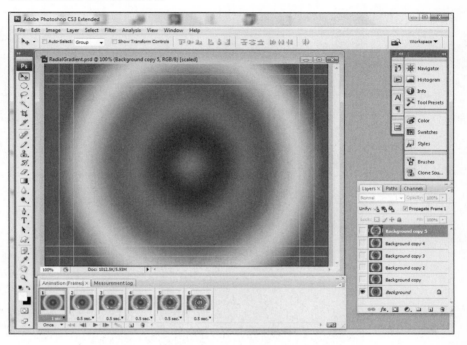

13. **Choose File ⇨ Save to save your document in Photoshop format.** Choose File ⇨ Export ⇨ Render Video to export your document as a movie. In the Render Video dialog box, you can choose either the QuickTime or Image Sequence options; both options can be imported into Premiere Pro. For this example, click the QuickTime Export drop-down menu and choose AVI. Click Render.

14. **Launch Premiere Pro.** Create a new project. Choose File ⇨ Import, locate the AVI movie, and open it. To use the AVI movie in the background of the project, drag it from the Project panel to the Video 1 track of the Timeline panel. Continue creating the rest of the Premiere Pro project, by creating a title to use in the Video 2 track. If you want, you can add more elements to the project.

FIGURE 15.18

The frames from the Radial gradient and arrow animation created in Photoshop CS3 Extended

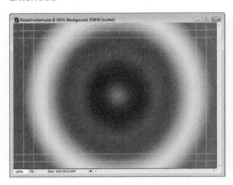 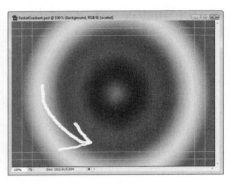

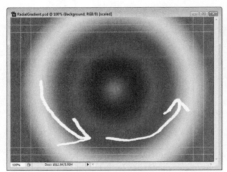 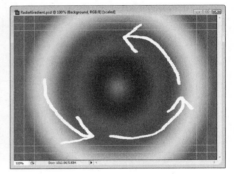

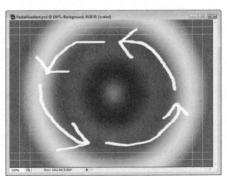

Defining and Applying a Pattern

You can use all of Photoshop's tools and commands to create a design. Then you can define the design as a pattern and fill an area with the pattern. Here's how:

1. **Use Photoshop's tools and commands to create a design.**

2. **Select the design with the Rectangular Marquee tool, as shown in Figure 15.19.** To create the design in Figure 15.19, you can use the Gradient tool with the Radial Gradient option and the Transparent Stripes gradient. This example applies a gradient twice — once with the foreground set to black and the second time with the foreground set to lavender.

3. **Choose Edit ▷ Define Pattern.**

4. **In the Pattern Name dialog box (shown in Figure 15.19), you can name your pattern.** Click OK to define the design as a pattern.

FIGURE 15.19

A rectangular selection is made in a design so that it can be defined as a pattern.

5. **Create a new Photoshop file in which to apply the pattern that you have just created.**

6. **Choose Edit ➪ Fill.** In the Fill dialog box (shown in Figure 15.20), click the Use dropdown menu and choose Pattern. Set the mode to Normal and the opacity to 100 percent. Click OK. Photoshop fills the document with the pattern.

FIGURE 15.20

The Fill dialog box allows you to fill with a solid color, gradient, or a pattern.

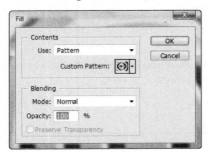

Creating a pattern with the Pattern Maker filter

You can open a photograph in Photoshop, and then use the Pattern Maker filter to create a pattern from a section of the photograph. Here's how:

1. **Open a photograph in Photoshop.**

2. **Choose Filter ➪ Save As to save your file with a different name.** This prevents you from accidentally saving over the photograph file.

3. **Choose Filter ➪ Pattern Maker.** The photograph appears in the Pattern Maker dialog box, shown in Figure 15.21.

4. **In the Pattern Maker dialog box, select an area to use as a pattern.** Click Generate to have Photoshop create a pattern from the selected area, as shown in Figure 15.22. If you are not satisfied with the pattern Photoshop has made, press Alt/Option to activate the Reset button. Click Reset to start over.

5. **When you are satisfied with your pattern, click OK.** Photoshop fills the file with the pattern.

In the Pattern Maker dialog box, a selection is made within a photograph of Seaglass jewelry so that it can be used to create a pattern (shown in Figure 15.22).

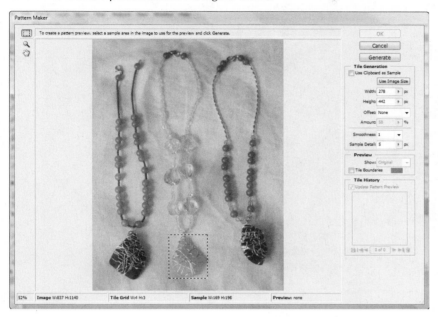

Creating background patterns with the Pattern command

You can create a background pattern matte using the Pattern command in Photoshop, as shown in Figure 15.23. Using the Pattern command, you can quickly choose preset patterns and add 3-D effects. The Pattern command creates a pattern on a new layer. After you save the pattern background in Photoshop, you can load it directly into Premiere Pro.

FIGURE 15.22

A pattern is made from a selection made in a photograph of Seaglass jewelry (shown in Figure 15.21).

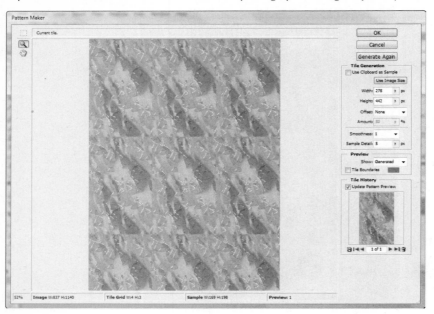

Follow these steps to create a background pattern in Photoshop using the Pattern command:

1. **Create a new file in Photoshop by choosing File ➪ New.** In the New dialog box, click the Presets drop-down menu and choose Video & Film. When you create the file, set the background contents to Transparent.

2. **To create the pattern in a layer, choose Layer ➪ New Fill Layer ➪ Pattern.** The New Layer dialog box appears, as shown in Figure 15.24.

3. **In the New Layer dialog box, click OK.** The Pattern Fill dialog box opens, as shown in Figure 15.25. In the Pattern Fill dialog box, you can choose a pattern by clicking the pattern preview. When the drop-down menu of pattern thumbnails appears, make a selection. If you want, you can use the Scale option to scale the pattern.

4. **Click OK to create the pattern.**

FIGURE 15.23

A background pattern matte created using Photoshop's Pattern command

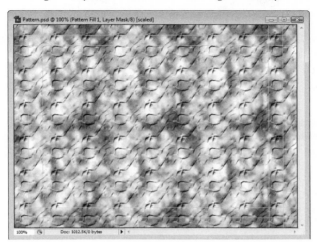

FIGURE 15.24

Photoshop's New Layer dialog box

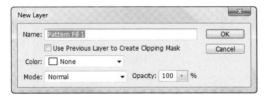

5. **To add 3-D or additional special effects to your pattern, choose Layer ⇨ Layer Style ⇨ Bevel and Emboss.** The Layer Style dialog box appears, as shown in Figure 15.26. To add more variation to the pattern, click the Contour check box and experiment with the contours. Notice that the layer style changes when you click Contour. You can also click the Texture check box to add a texture to your image. Select a pattern and experiment with the Scale and Depth sliders. Use the Depth, Size, and Soften sliders to fine-tune the effect. Click OK to apply the Bevel and Emboss settings. The pattern is created with a mask. The layer mask thumbnail displays in the Layers panel.

FIGURE 15.25

Photoshop's Pattern Fill dialog box

FIGURE 15.26

Photoshop's Layer Style dialog box

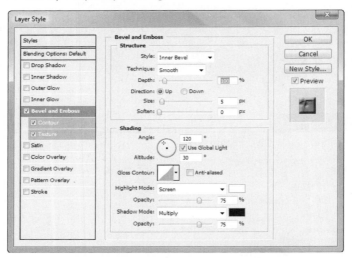

6. **Choose Window ➪ Layers to display the Layers panel.** The layer mask thumbnail appears next to the word *Pattern.*

7. **To use the pattern's mask to create special effects, select the Brush tool and then select a brush size.** Set the painting color to black, and reduce the opacity to 40 percent. Then start drawing in the pattern. To erase your brushstrokes and start over, choose Edit ➪ Fill. In the Fill dialog box, set the Use drop-down menu to White, the mode to Normal, and the opacity to 100 percent. Click OK. The example in Figure 15.27 uses the Gradient tool with the Radial Gradient option and the Transparent Stripes gradient. The gradient is applied with the foreground set to black and the background set to white.

> **NOTE** To remove the mask, choose Layer ➪ Layer Mask ➪ Delete. This removes the mask and discards any changes you may have made to the mask.

8. **When you complete your background pattern, choose Layer ➪ Flatten Image.**

9. **Save the file in Photoshop format.** You can then import it into any Premiere Pro project.

FIGURE 15.27

The background pattern matte from Figure 15.23 edited with the Gradient tool

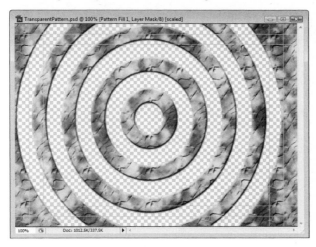

Sample Book Cover Project

In this section, you create a project called the Superhero book cover project. You use the Photoshop Gradient tool and several filters to create a background. You use Photoshop to create a graphic that you animate in Premiere Pro using the Motion effect. In Premiere Pro, you create a title for the project. To make your project more interesting, you also add a sound clip. You can see a frame from the book cover project in Figure 15.28.

FIGURE 15.28

A frame from the Superhero book cover project shown in the Program Monitor panel

To create the animated Superhero book cover project, you need four items:

- **A background image:** Create an image using the Title Designer, or using Photoshop or Illustrator. You can start from a photograph.

- **A title:** You can create a title in Premiere Pro's Title Designer, which is described in Chapter 10.

- **A graphic with an alpha channel:** The graphic needs to be on a transparent background because you animate it in Premiere Pro. Again, you can create the Superhero character graphic using the Title Designer, or using Photoshop or Illustrator.

- **A sound clip:** This can make your project more exciting.

Follow these steps to create the Superhero book cover project:

1. **In Premiere Pro, choose File ⇨ New Project to create a new project.**

2. **In the New Project dialog box, set the preset to DV – NTSC Standard 48 kHz.**

3. **Name your project.** Click OK to create the new project.

4. **Choose File ⇨ New ⇨ Photoshop File.** In the Save Photoshop File As dialog box, click the File Name drop-down menu and name your file. Then click Save.

5. **Create a simple background in Photoshop (as shown in Figure 15.29).** Here's how:

FIGURE 15.29

A simple background image created in Photoshop

a. **Set the background color to a light color, and set the foreground color to a darker shade of the same color.** To change the foreground and background colors, click the foreground and background swatches in the toolbox. In the Color Picker dialog box that appears, pick a color. The example in Figure 15.29 uses a foreground color of peach and a background color of white.

b. **Click the Gradient tool in the toolbox.** Set the Gradient tool to use a Radial gradient. The mode should be Normal, and the opacity set to 100 percent.

c. **With the Gradient tool selected, click and drag outward from the center of your image to create a gradient.**

d. **With the radial gradient onscreen, choose Filter ➪ Noise ➪ Add Noise to add color to the gradient.** The Add Noise dialog box is shown in Figure 15.30.

e. **Choose Filter ➪ Render ➪ Lighting Effects to add more depth and lighting variations.** Figure 15.31 shows the Lighting Effects dialog box.

f. **Choose File ➪ Save to save your file.** Save your file in Photoshop format. Then close the file.

6. **After you save your Photoshop background file, it automatically updates in the Project panel of your Premiere Pro project.** Activate your Premiere Pro project. Then drag and drop the Photoshop background image from the Project panel to the Video 1 track in the Timeline panel.

> **TIP**
>
> If you are not familiar with Photoshop's tools, you can use the Eraser tool to erase any unwanted items. If you make a mistake, choose either Edit ⇨ Undo, or File ⇨ Revert. If you are familiar with Photoshop's tools, you may want to use the Pen tool to outline the character and then select it. If you use the Pen tool, you need to convert the path into a selection by choosing Make Selection from the Path drop-down menu.

FIGURE 15.30

You can use the Add Noise filter to add texture to a background.

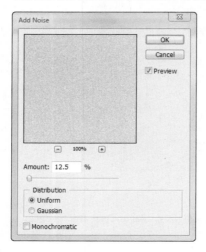

FIGURE 15.31

You can use Photoshop's Lighting Effects filter to create a background.

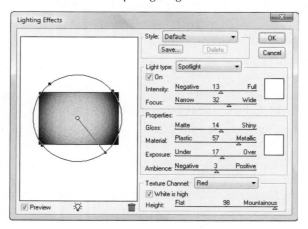

7. **Create a graphic character in Photoshop, as shown in Figure 15.32.** In your Premiere Pro project, choose File ➪ New ➪ Photoshop File. In the Save Photoshop File As dialog box, click the File Name drop-down menu and name your file. Then click Save.

   a. **Choose Window ➪ Layers to display the Layers palette.** Click the Layers palette menu and choose New Layer. Create at least four layers in which to draw the graphic character. This allows you to keep the separate parts of the body in separate layers, which makes it easier to edit individual parts. You can always create more layers. Create a new layer before drawing so that the item is created in the new layer. To rename a layer, double-click its name in the Layers palette. To move items forward or backward, move the layers up and down in the Layers palette.

   b. **Select the Brush tool from the Tools palette.** Choose Window ➪ Brushes. Select a brush style and size. The example in Figure 15.32 uses the Oil Medium Wet Flow brush. When drawing this image, the brush size was reduced and the foreground color set to black. When you draw, be sure to enclose your strokes so that it is easy to fill the separate areas.

FIGURE 15.32

A superhero created in Photoshop using the Brush, Gradient, Paint Bucket, and Magic Wand tools

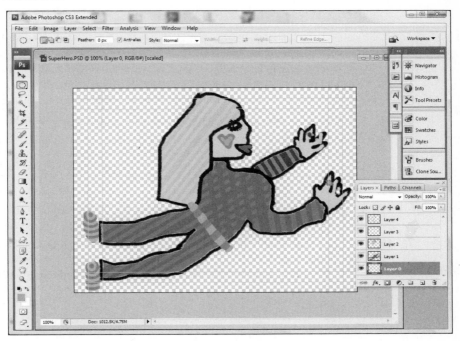

    c. Use the Magic Wand tool to click an area that you want to fill. Increasing the Tolerance amount in the Magic Wand Toolbar area results in a larger selection. Once the entire area is selected, you can fill the area with a gradient using the Gradient tool, a solid color with the Paint Bucket tool, or a pattern using the Fill command. If the area is not properly selected, you might need to change the Tolerance amount or you might need to use the Brush tool to paint the outline of the area you want to select.

    d. For the finishing touches, use the Brush tool with different colors to add some details. To pick colors, you may want to use the Colors or Swatches palettes.

    e. Choose File ➪ Save to save your file. Then save your file in Photoshop format with the Layers option selected. This keeps the graphic isolated from the background. Click Save, and then close the file.

  8. Activate Premiere Pro. Notice that the graphic file appears in the Project panel. Drag the file to the Video 2 track in the Timeline panel.

  9. Choose Window ➪ Effect Controls. The Motion controls appear in the Effect Controls panel, as shown in Figure 15.28.

 10. To create motion manually using the Program Monitor panel, first click the Transform icon that appears next to the word *Motion* in the Effect Controls panel. In the Program Monitor panel, drag the graphic character to the left.

 11. To create motion from left to right, you need to create two keyframes. First, click the Expand/Collapse icon to display the Motion controls. Then move the edit line to the beginning of the clip, and click the Position Toggle Animation icon to create the first keyframe. To create the last keyframe, move the edit line to the end of the clip. Then move the graphic character all the way to the right of the Program Monitor panel. The last (second) keyframe is created. You can create more keyframes to create a more interesting animation. The example in Figure 15.28 also animates the scale of the character. For more information on working with Motion controls, turn to Chapter 16.

 12. Click the Play button in the Program Monitor panel to preview the animation.

 13. Choose File ➪ New ➪ Title. In the New Title dialog box that appears, name your title and click OK. The Adobe Title Designer panel opens, as shown in Figure 15.33.

 14. Create some text with the Type tool. Then close the Title Designer panel to have the title appear in the Project panel.

 15. Drag the title clip from the Project panel to the Video 3 track in the Timeline panel, as shown in Figure 15.28.

 16. Use the Motion and Opacity controls in the Effect Controls panel to animate the title. In the example in Figure 15.28, the text slowly fades in and moves from the center down. To do this, you can set keyframes for the Position and Opacity effects, as shown in Figure 15.34.

 17. Choose File ➪ Save to save the project.

 18. Choose File ➪ Import to import a sound file. The project in this example uses SmartSound's New Vistas sound clip. This sound clip is on the DVD that accompanies this book.

19. **Make the entire project have the same time duration.** Because the sound clip has a longer time duration than the video clips, increase the duration of the video clips. To do so, select the left side of a video clip and drag to the right to extend its duration.

 To extend the duration of either of the Photoshop clips that are in the Timeline panel, click the end of the clip and drag to the right.

20. **Preview the file by clicking the Play button in the Program Monitor panel.** When the preview plays, you should see the text and superhero visible over the background you created in Photoshop. To change the quality of the preview, click the Program Monitor menu and choose Highest Quality, Draft Quality, or Automatic Quality. By default, Premiere Pro sets the preview to Automatic Quality. To render the work area, choose Sequence ➪ Render Work Area.

21. **Choose File ➪ Save to save your project in Premiere Pro format.** Choose File ➪ Export ➪ Movie to export your project as a movie.

FIGURE 15.33

Superhero text created in Premiere Pro's Title Designer

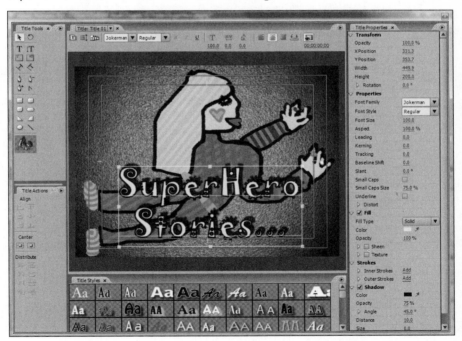

511

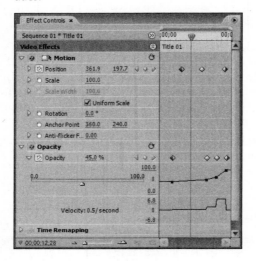

FIGURE 15.34

The Motion and Opacity settings in the Effect Controls panel allow you to add motion to titles.

Creating Background Mattes in Illustrator

In this section, you learn how to create a Premiere Pro project called the Coffee Bean presentation, shown in Figure 15.35. To create this project, you use Adobe Illustrator to create a simple background matte, a chart, and a graphic. You then import these items into a Premiere Pro project so that they can be animated. You also create a title and animate it in Premiere Pro.

Preparing a background matte to import

Follow these steps to create a background matte in Illustrator:

NOTE   As you work, you may find that you like different versions of your background. Use the Save As command to save these different versions. This allows you to import them all into Premiere Pro and experiment with the different backgrounds.

1. **Launch Illustrator.**
2. **Choose File ⇨ New to create a new file.** Select a document type. For a Premiere Pro project, select either Video and Film or Basic RGB Document (CMYK color is for print work). Click OK to create a new document.
3. **Select the Rectangle tool.**

FIGURE 15.35

The Coffee Bean presentation project in Premiere Pro

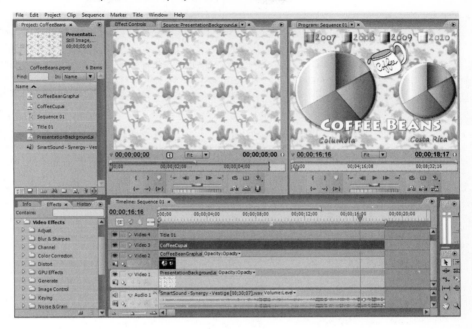

4. **With the Rectangle tool selected, move your mouse to the top-left corner of the screen.** Then click and drag to the bottom-right corner of the screen. Be sure to create a rectangle that is the entire size of the document. If you need to enlarge the rectangle, click a corner and drag outward.

5. **Choose Window ➪ Swatches.** Click a swatch to fill the rectangle.

6. **You can access more swatches from other libraries.** Choose Window ➪ Swatch Libraries, and then select a library. In the library that you selected, pick a swatch. You can also access swatch libraries by choosing Open Swatch Library from the Swatches panel menu.

7. **To select a pattern library, choose Window ➪ Swatch Libraries ➪ Pattern, or from the Swatches panel menu.** Choose Swatch Libraries ➪ Pattern. Then make a selection.

To create the background for the Coffee Bean presentation, this example uses the Wild Flowers Color pattern (shown in Figure 15.36), which is found in the Nature_Foliage library. To match the results in Figure 15.36, you need to scale and move the pattern, and then use the Filter Gallery to apply the Accented Edges Brush Stroke filter. Proceed to step 11 to use a filter from the Filter Gallery on a pattern.

NOTE   To move a pattern within an object, press the tilde (~) key while dragging with the Selection tool. To scale a pattern within an object, Tilde-drag with the Scale tool. To rotate a pattern within an object, Tilde-drag with the Rotate tool.

8. **To create your own pattern, use the tools in the Tools palette to create some objects.** Fill the objects with a solid color or a gradient. (You cannot fill a pattern design with a pattern.) Then select the pattern with the Selection tool and choose Edit ➪ Define Pattern. In the New Swatch dialog box, name your pattern, and then click OK. The pattern now appears in the Swatches palette. Click the pattern to apply it to an object. Figure 15.37 shows a pattern design created with the Rectangle and Brush tools.

FIGURE 15.36

A rectangle filled with the Wild Flowers Color pattern found in the Nature_Foliage library

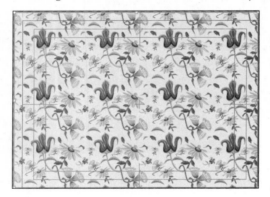

FIGURE 15.37

A pattern design created with the Rectangle and Brush tools, and a rectangle filled with the pattern

 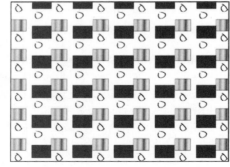

9. **To select a gradient library, choose Window ⇨ Swatch Libraries ⇨ Gradient, or from the Swatches panel menu, choose Swatch Libraries ⇨ Gradients.** Make a selection.

10. **To edit a gradient in an object, use the Gradient tool to click and drag inside the object.** You can also edit a gradient by using the Gradient palette. Either double-click the Gradient tool or choose Window ⇨ Gradient to display the Gradient palette (shown in Figure 15.38). In the Gradient palette, you can choose whether you want the gradient to be linear or radial. You can also click the Gradient sliders and change the colors of the gradient, as well as move the Gradient sliders to change the look of the gradient.

> **NOTE** To save custom swatch libraries, place the swatches you want in your library in the Swatches palette. Then choose Save Swatches from the Swatches panel menu. In the dialog box that appears, name the library. Then locate a place to save the new library and click Save.

FIGURE 15.38

The Gradient palette allows you to customize a gradient.

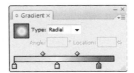

11. **Choose Effect ⇨ Filter Gallery to display the Filter Gallery dialog box (shown in Figure 15.39).** Here you can choose a filter to apply to the rectangle's fill. Click OK when you find an effect that you are happy with. Figure 15.39 shows the Accented Edges Brush Strokes filter applied to the Wild Flowers Color pattern (shown in Figure 15.36).

12. **Click the Ellipse tool in the Tools palette.**

13. **Create a circle or ellipse in the middle of the document.** To create an ellipse, press and hold Alt/Option as you click and drag from the center out. To create a perfect circle, press and hold the Shift key as you click and drag to create the ellipse.

14. **Fill the circle or ellipse with a gradient.**

15. **Continue making circles.** The circles are filled with the gradient that you selected in step 9 (shown in Figure 15.40). If you need to move or change the size of a circle, use the Selection tool.

FIGURE 15.39

The Filter Gallery dialog box is used to apply the Accented Edges Brush Strokes filter to the Wild Flowers Color pattern (shown in Figure 15.36).

FIGURE 15.40

You can use the Ellipse tool with a gradient to create a background.

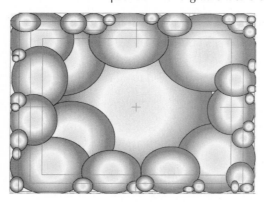

16. **Use the Pen tool to create a mountain shape.** Add a fill. In this example, the shape is filled with the Fall Leaves pattern (shown in Figure 15.41) from the Nature_Foliage Pattern library.

FIGURE 15.41

The Pen tool creates a mountain shape over the circles in Figure 15.40.

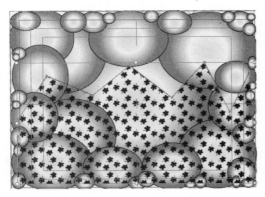

17. **Now that you have created some different backgrounds, you can choose one or use them all in the Premiere Pro Coffee Bean presentation.** Be sure to save your file. Choose File ➪ Save to save the file in Illustrator format.

18. **Launch Premiere Pro.** Create or open a project. Choose File ➪ Import to import the Illustrator files into the Premiere Pro project.

Creating a chart for a presentation

Follow these steps to create a chart using Illustrator:

1. **Launch Illustrator.** Create a new RGB or Film and Video document.

2. **Click the Graph tool in the Tools palette.** Press and hold to select a graph type — Column Graph, Stacked Column Graph, Bar Graph, Stacked Bar Graph, Line Graph, Area Graph, Scatter Graph, Pie Graph, or Radar Graph. Choose a basic Column or Stacked Column graph (shown in Figure 15.42) to start out. You can always change the graph type in the Graph Type dialog box (shown in Figure 15.43) by choosing Object ➪ Graph ➪ Type.

FIGURE 15.42

A Stacked Column graph

Graph tool

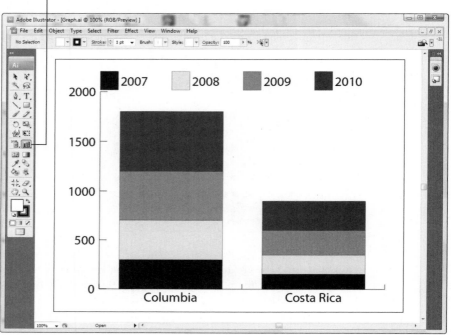

FIGURE 15.43

The Graph Type dialog box allows you to select a graph style.

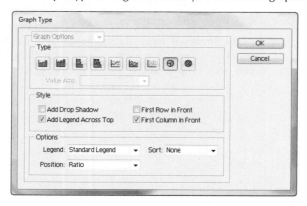

3. Click and drag in the document area to create a graph.

4. In the Data dialog box that appears, enter graph data. If you want, you can import the data by clicking the Import Data button. Figure 15.44 shows the Data dialog box used to create the graph shown in Figure 15.42.

FIGURE 15.44

Graph data used to create the graph shown in Figure 15.42

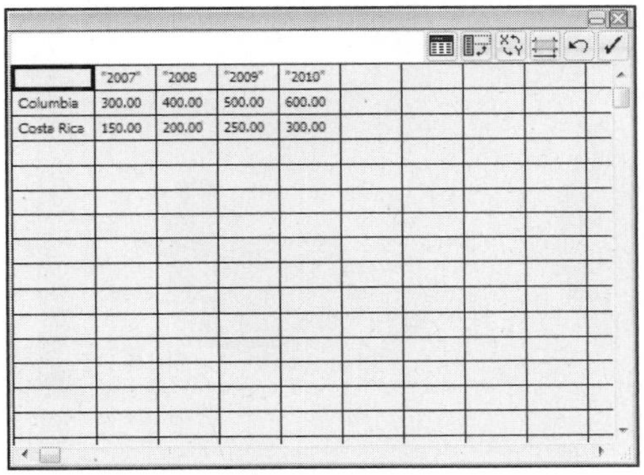

5. Click the Checkmark button in the Data dialog box to create the graph. Click the Transpose Row/Column button or Switch X/Y button, and then click the Checkmark button to change the way the graph appears.

6. Click the Close button to close the Data dialog box.

7. To reopen the Data dialog box, choose Object ⇨ Graph ⇨ Data.

8. Stylize the graph. Change the graph type. Change the fill of the items in the graph. Change the font style, size, and color, as shown in Figure 15.45.

9. To select an item and its group, double-click the item with the Group Selection tool. The item and its group are selected. Pick a color, gradient, or pattern to fill. You can also use commands, such as Drop Shadow, from the Effect menu to jazz up the graph.

10. Use the Selection tool to select all of the text in the graph. Use the Group Selection tool to select individual words. Then change the font style, size, and fill of the selected words.

11. If you want, you can create designs for your graph. Create a design as you would a pattern. Select it and choose Object ⇨ Graph ⇨ Data. To apply a design to a graph, first select it. Then choose either Object ⇨ Graph ⇨ Column, or Object ⇨ Graph ⇨ Row.

12. When you are done creating and stylizing your chart, choose File ⇨ Save to save the file in Illustrator format. You are now ready to load the chart into a Premiere Pro project. In Premiere Pro, choose File ⇨ Import.

FIGURE 15.45

A pie graph is used in the Premiere Pro Coffee Bean presentation.

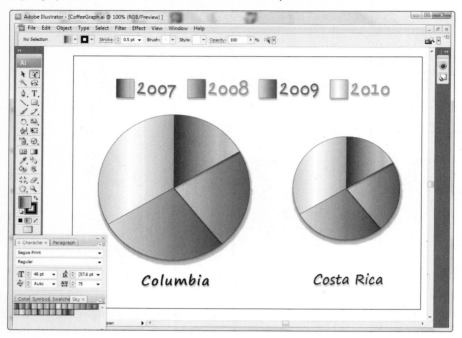

Creating a graphic item for a presentation

In the Premiere Pro Coffee Bean presentation (shown in Figure 15.35), a coffee cup is created using the Brush tool in Illustrator (shown in Figure 15.46). The coffee cup is then imported into the Premiere Pro project and placed in a video track over the chart and below the title clip that was created in Premiere Pro. The coffee cup is then animated in the Premiere Pro Coffee Bean presentation so that it moves.

Here's how to use the Brush tool to create a graphic in Illustrator for use in Premiere Pro:

1. **Launch Illustrator.** Create a new RGB or Film and Video document.
2. **Select the Brush tool.**
3. **Choose Window ⇨ Brushes.** In the Brushes palette, select a brush style and size.
4. **Set the foreground color to black.**

FIGURE 15.46

The coffee cup used in the Premiere Pro Coffee Bean presentation

5. **Start drawing.** Draw the cup and the word *Coffee*. If you make a mistake, you can select the area and delete it. Use the Direct Selection tool to edit the area. The Selection tool can also be used to select and change the size of an item.

6. **In order to fill the separate segments of the cup, you need to join the beginning and ending points of all segments.** If you have some points that are not joined, use the Direct Selection tool, with the Shift click activated to select the beginning and ending points. Then click the Connect Selected Endpoints icon (shown in Figure 15.47), located in the Anchor Point toolbar at the top of the document (below the menus).

FIGURE 15.47

You can join a beginning and ending point using the Connect Selected Endpoints icon located in the Anchor Point toolbar.

7. Use the Selection tool to select different parts of the cup and add a fill.

8. Save your file so that you can import it into Premiere Pro.

Pulling together the Coffee Bean presentation project

A great feature of using Illustrator with Premiere Pro is that Premiere Pro translates the blank areas of the Illustrator file as an alpha channel mask. In this example, you import the chart and coffee cup files that you created using Illustrator into the Premiere Pro Coffee Bean project. When you import these items, they appear on a transparent background. In this project, a background matte is created in Illustrator, imported into Premiere Pro, and placed in the Video 1 track to be used in the background. In Premiere Pro a title is created and placed in the Video 4 track, which is added to the Timeline panel. The Project panel for the project is shown in Figure 15.48. Figure 15.49 shows the Timeline panel used to create the project. Figure 15.50 shows frames from the Coffee Bean project.

FIGURE 15.48

The Project panel used in the Coffee Bean presentation project

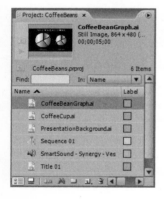

FIGURE 15.49

The Timeline panel used in the Coffee Bean presentation project

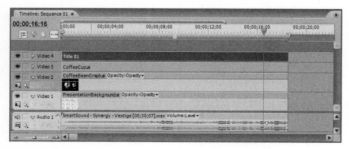

FIGURE 15.50

Frames from the Coffee Bean presentation project

Follow these steps to create the Coffee Bean presentation project:

1. **Launch Premiere Pro.**

2. **Choose File ➪ New ➪ Project to create a new project.**

3. **In the New Project dialog box, choose a preset.**

4. **Click OK to apply the settings to the new project.** The new project opens.

5. **Choose Window ➪ Workspace ➪ Effects.** The Effects and Effect Controls panels display.

6. **Choose File ➪ Import.**

ON the DVD If you want, you can load the images from the Coffee Bean presentation. They are found in the MoreClips folder on the DVD that accompanies this book.

7. **In the Import dialog box, locate and select the Background Presentation file, the Coffee Bean Chart file, and the Coffee Cup files.** Press and hold the Ctrl key to select more than one file.

8. **Click Open.** Premiere Pro imports the files into the Project panel.

9. **Drag the Background Presentation file and Coffee Bean Chart file to the Video 1 and Video 2 tracks, respectively.** Drag the Coffee Cup file to the Video 3 track.

10. **Choose File ➪ New ➪ Title.** In the New Title dialog box that appears, name your title and click OK. The Adobe Title Designer panel opens, as shown in Figure 15.51.

11. **Create some text with the Type tool.** Click a style in the Style panel to stylize the text.

12. **Close the Title Designer panel.** Notice that it appears in the Project panel.

13. **Choose Sequence ➪ Add Tracks.** In the Add Track dialog box, click the Video Tracks Placement drop-down menu and choose After Last Track. Click OK to create the Video 4 track. Drag the title clip to the Video 4 track.

NOTE If you want, you can create two titles and set them side by side in the same video track. You can then add a transition, such as the Cross Dissolve, to create a smooth transition between the two titles.

14. **Import a sound clip into Premiere Pro.** Drag the sound clip from the Project panel to the Audio 1 track of the Timeline panel. This example uses SmartSound's Synergy sound clip, which is on the DVD that accompanies this book. Because the sound clip is longer than necessary, you can cut the end of it and slowly fade it out. For more information on working with sound, turn to Chapter 7.

15. **To add dimension to the chart and the title, the Bevel Edges video effect is added.** To add depth to the coffee cup, you can add the Radial Shadow video effect. In the Effects panel, open the Video Effects bin (folder) to display the video effects folders. Then open the Perspective bin. Drag the Bevel Alpha effect to the Chart clip that is in the Video 2 track. Drag the Bevel Alpha effect to the title clip that is in the Video 4 track. Drag the Radial Shadow effect to the coffee cup that is in the Video 3 track. The controls for these video effects are found in the Effect Controls panel.

FIGURE 15.51

FIGURE 15.51

The title for the Coffee Bean presentation project is shown in the Title Designer panel.

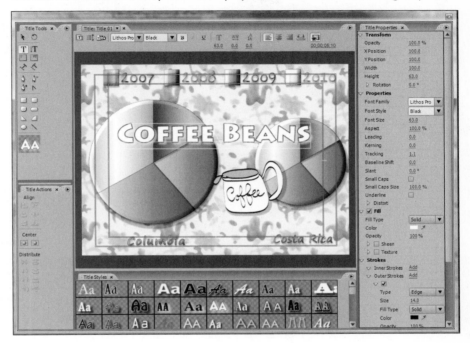

CROSS-REF   See Chapter 13 to learn about working with video effects.

16. **To animate the coffee cup and the title, you can set keyframes for the controls of the Motion effect in the Effect Controls panel.** Figure 15.52 shows the Position keyframes used to make the title move down. Figure 15.53 shows the Position, Scale, and Rotate keyframes used to move the cup up.

CROSS-REF   See Chapter 16 to learn about animating motion effects.

17. **Click the Play button in the Program Monitor panel to preview the project.**

18. **Choose File ⇨ Save to save the file in a Premiere Pro project format.** Choose File ⇨ Export ⇨ Movie to output the project in a movie format.

FIGURE 15.52

The keyframes in the Effect Controls panel, used to create the title animation

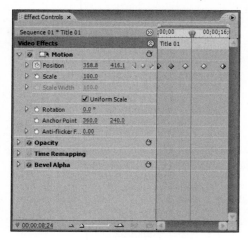

FIGURE 15.53

The keyframes in the Effect Controls panel, used to create the coffee cup animation

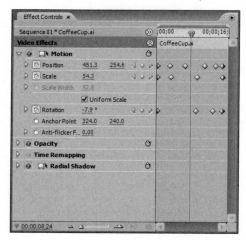

Summary

You can use Premiere Pro's Color Matte command to easily create solid-color backgrounds for text and graphics. This chapter covered these topics:

- You can use Adobe Photoshop or Adobe Illustrator to create your own backgrounds to use as background mattes in a Premiere Pro project.

- Photoshop and Illustrator files can be imported directly into Premiere Pro. All you need to do is save the Photoshop files in Photoshop format and the Illustrator files in Illustrator format.

Chapter 16

Creating Motion Effects

Motion creates interest and adds to the power of just about any presentation. In Adobe Premiere Pro, you can jazz up presentations by sending a title or logo spinning across the screen or bouncing a clip off the borders of the frame area. You can animate books by using a graphic with an alpha channel, or you can superimpose one moving object over another. You can also use Traveling Matte effects to create movies for the Web. A Traveling Matte effect has one image within a shape that moves across the screen over another image. This chapter not only shows you how to create traveling mattes, but also how to set titles and graphics in motion, including how to make them bend and rotate onscreen.

To create these motion effects, you use Premiere Pro's Motion controls, found in the Effect Controls panel.

Touring the Motion Effect Controls in the Effect Controls Panel

Premiere Pro's Motion effect controls allow you to scale, rotate, and move a clip. By animating the motion controls, you can wake up an otherwise boring image by setting it in motion over time using keyframes. You can make a clip move and jiggle, or make a still frame move across the screen. When you select a clip in the Timeline panel, the Motion effects display in the Effect Controls panel, which is shown in Figure 16.1.

FIGURE 16.1

The Effect Controls panel and the Motion effect controls

Figure 16.2 shows frames of the Greetings from San Francisco project that was created using the Motion, Opacity, Time Remapping, and Levels video effect in the Effect Controls panel. The Greetings from San Francisco project consists of a moving Greetings Photoshop clip and a moving Trolley video clip. The moving Greetings clip and Trolley video clip are seen over a video clip of the Golden Gate Bridge. The project consists of two video clips (a Trolley and the Golden Gate Bridge), a Greetings Photoshop clip, and a sound clip.

The Greetings from San Francisco project is divided up into three parts: the introduction, main scene, and conclusion. The background video clip of the Golden Gate Bridge and the sound clip appear throughout the entire length of the project. The Greetings Photoshop clip appears in the introduction and conclusion of the project. The Trolley video clip appears in the main scene of the project. The Timeline panel used to create the Greetings from San Francisco project shows the clips that are used to create the project (see Figure 16.3). You can find these clips on the DVD that accompanies this book.

In the Timeline panel shown in Figure 16.3, you can see that the video clip of the Golden Gate Bridge is in the Video 1 track. It is used as the background scene for the project. The Golden Gate Bridge clip runs from the zero-second mark to the 26½-second mark. The sound clip is SmartSound's The Great Escape, which runs from the zero-second mark to the 28-second mark.

FIGURE 16.2

Frames from the Greetings from San Francisco project. To create the frames (seen in Figure 16.2), video clips sf0116 and tr0107 from FilmDisc were used.

This clip is placed in the Video 2 track two separate times in the main scene section of the project. The first time you see the Trolley video clip, you only see the end of the clip, as the first part of the clip is cut out. You can apply the Position, Scale, and Rotation effects to this clip using keyframes. Keyframes allow the effect to be applied over time. Figure 16.4 shows the Effect Controls panel with the keyframes for the first Trolley clip. The Position effect is used to move the clip so that it starts moving from the top-right-hand corner down toward the center of the screen. The Scale effect is used to reduce the clip to 50 percent and then slowly enlarge it. The Rotation effect is used to rotate the clip slightly and then slowly reverse the rotation.

FIGURE 16.3

The panels used to create the Greetings from San Francisco project. The project is created using the Motion, Opacity, Time Remapping, and Levels video effects.

FIGURE 16.4

The Effect Controls panel with the keyframes used to move, scale, and rotate the Trolley clip

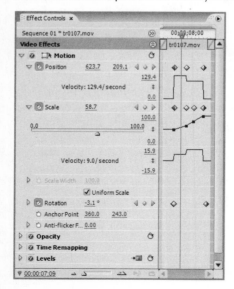

In the main scene there is a second Trolley video clip in the Video 2 track. You can set keyframes for the Opacity effect to this video clip. This example sets the keyframes from 75 percent to 5 percent, so that the Trolley slowly fades out and you can see the Golden Gate Bridge in the background. You can see the Opacity keyframes for the Trolley clip in the Effect Controls panel in Figure 16.5.

FIGURE 16.5

The Effect Controls panel with the keyframes used to change the opacity of the Trolley clip

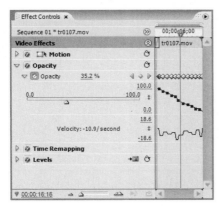

In the introduction and conclusion of the project, you have a Greetings Photoshop file in the Video 2 track over the Golden Gate Bridge clip in the Video 1 track. You can apply the Position and Scale effects to the Greetings Photoshop file in the introduction of the project. The Effect Controls panel shown in Figure 16.6 contains the settings for the Greetings file for the introduction. At the Greetings conclusion, this example uses the Opacity keyframes from 0 percent to 100 percent to slowly fade the Greetings Photoshop file into view. It also uses the Position, Scale, and Rotation effects on the Greetings Photoshop file at the conclusion of the project. The Opacity keyframes for the Greetings clip in the conclusion of the project are shown in the Effect Controls panel in Figure 16.7.

To create the Greetings Photoshop file, choose File ➪ New ➪ Photoshop File. In the Save Photoshop File As dialog box, enter a filename (Greetings), and then click Save. This loads Photoshop and places the Photoshop file in the Project panel of the project. In Photoshop, you can use the Shape tool to create a Balloon shape. You can then use the Type tool to create some text. This example uses the Kristen ITC font with a font size of 48 points. You can now apply the Drop Shadow, Inner Shadow, and Outer Shadow Blending Options (Layer ➪ Style ➪ Blending Options). Figure 16.8 shows the Greetings file in Photoshop. Note that the Photoshop file has two layers: the Shape layer and the Type layer.

FIGURE 16.6

The Effect Controls panel with the settings used to change the position and scale of the Greetings Photoshop clip

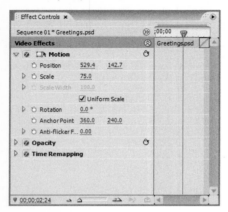

FIGURE 16.7

The Effect Controls panel with the keyframes used to change the opacity of the Greetings Photoshop clip

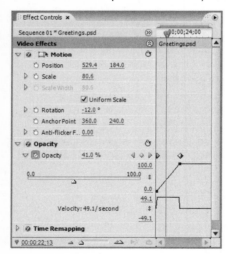

The last thing you can do to the project is to apply the Page Peel transition between the Greetings introduction file and the first video clip in the main scene of the Greetings project. This example also applies the Additive Dissolve transition between the two video clips in the main scene section.

FIGURE 16.8

The Greetings Photoshop file has two layers: a Shape layer and a Type layer.

Working with the Motion Controls

To use Premiere Pro's Motion controls, you need to have a project onscreen with a video clip selected in the Timeline panel. Follow these steps to create a new project, import two video clips, and display the Motion effect controls:

1. **Create a new project by choosing File ➪ New ➪ Project.** In the New Project dialog box, choose a preset, name the project, and click OK.

2. **Load two video clips by choosing File ➪ Import.** You can use your own video, or you can use FilmDisc's sf0116 and tr01017. After you import a file into your project, it appears in the Project panel.

3. **If you want, you can load a sound clip by choosing File ➪ Import.** Locate a sound, and click Open. (This example uses SmartSound's The Great Escape file.) Then drag the sound clip from the Project panel to Audio track 1 in the Timeline panel. You can also choose File ➪ New ➪ SmartSound to import a SmartSound sound clip.

To download SmartSound's QuickTracks, go to: `www.smartsound.com/ premiere/index.html`.

If the sound clip is too long, click the left side of the clip and drag it inward. For more information on working with sound clips, see Chapter 7.

ON the DVD FilmDisc's sf0116 and tr01017 video clips, and SmartSound's The Great Escape sound clip, are found in the Tutorial Projects folder on the DVD that accompanies this book.

4. **Click one of the video clips in the Project panel and drag it to the Video 1 track in the Timeline panel.** Drag the other video clip to the Video 2 track in the Timeline panel. In this example, you would drag FilmDisc's sf0116 to the Video 1 track and tr01017 to the Video 2 track. The Timeline panel should now contain two video clips.

 You can choose how a clip displays on the Timeline by clicking the Set Display Style icon and then clicking one of the options. To view the Set Display Style icon, you need to expand a video track by clicking the triangle to the left of the word *Video*.

5. **With the clip in the Video 2 track selected, choose Window ⇨ Effect Controls.** To display the Motion controls, click the triangle to the left of the word *Motion*.

6. **To scale a clip's height and width in proportion, make sure the Uniform Scale option is selected.** Then click and drag over the value in the Scale section, or click the value, type a new value, and press Enter. Acceptable ranges are from 0 to 700. Type **0** to make the clip invisible; type **600** to enlarge the clip to seven times its normal size. In this example, the clip is scaled down to 50 percent (as shown in Figure 16.9).

FIGURE 16.9

The Effect Controls and Program Monitor panels allow you to adjust the Motion effects Scale option.

TIP To scale the height of a clip separately from the width, deselect the Uniform Scale option in the Effect Controls panel.

7. **Use the Rotation option to rotate a clip around its center point.** To rotate, click and drag the Rotation degree value or enter a value in the Rotation degree field. To create one complete rotation, type **360** degrees. Then rotate the clip 90 degrees. If you rotate the clip –90 degrees, the clip rotates counter-clockwise. In the example in Figure 16.3, the clip only rotates –4 degrees.

8. **To see a preview of how the Scale and Rotation effects have changed the clip in the Video 2 track, open the Program Monitor panel by choosing Window ➪ Program Monitor.** Then either click the Play button in the Program Monitor panel or click and drag the shuttle or jog slider. You can also see a preview by moving the current-time indicator in the Effect Controls panel or the Timeline panel. Notice that the clip has been scaled and rotated and that it remains scaled and rotated throughout the duration of the clip.

 To go back to the default motion settings, click the Reset icon to the left of the word *Motion* in the Effect Controls panel.

9. **To move the position of a clip, click and drag the Position values to change the values and move the clip on its X-axis and Y-axis.** To move the clip from its center point, click and drag the Anchor Point values.

10. **To move a clip manually, click the Transform icon, which is in front of the word *Motion* in the Effect Controls panel.** Notice that in the Program Monitor panel, a wireframe appears around the clip, as shown in Figure 16.10. Click inside the wireframe, and move the clip. As you move the clip, the Position values change. You can also manually rotate and scale a clip. To scale a clip, click and drag either a corner or side handle. To keep the clip's proportions, press and hold the Shift key as you scale. To rotate a clip manually, move the cursor just outside of either a corner or side handle, and then click and drag in the direction you want to rotate.

FIGURE 16.10

A wireframe appears around the active clip in the Program Monitor panel when you manually adjust the clip.

11. **Click the Play button in the Program Monitor panel to preview the effects of the Position settings.** To render a work area, choose Sequence ➪ Render Work Area. Notice that the clip starts at the new position and remains there throughout the duration of the clip. To move the clip's position to different places throughout the duration of the clip, you need to set keyframes. The next section explains more about working with keyframes.

 By default, Premiere Pro displays a preview in Automatic Quality. To change the preview display, click the Monitor panel menu and choose Highest Quality or Draft Quality.

Setting Keyframes to Create Motion Effects Using the Effect Controls Panel

To create motion that moves in more than one direction or that changes size or rotation throughout the duration of a clip, you need to add keyframes. You can use keyframes to create effects at specific points in time — for example, to create an effect using a graphic or video clip in motion simultaneously with another video clip. Using keyframes, the effect can occur at a specific point in your narration, and you can also add music to the effect. The motion path displays when you select the Transform icon (next to the word *Motion*) in the Effect Controls panel. When the motion path displays, keyframes appear as points in the motion path and designate a change in position.

 You can also add keyframes to the motion path at specific points by clicking the Timeline. (The Timeline is described in the next section.)

Here's how to add keyframes to a motion path to create the effect of a clip moving diagonally from top left to bottom right:

1. **Create a new project by choosing File ⇨ New ⇨ Project.** In the New Project dialog box, choose a preset, name the project, and click OK.

2. **Choose File ⇨ Import.** In the Import dialog box, locate and select a clip. Then choose Open to import the clip into the Project panel.

ON the DVD If you want, you can use FilmDisc's tr01017 video clip, which is found in the FilmDisc folder in the Tutorial Projects folder on the DVD that accompanies this book.

3. **Drag the clip from the Project panel to the Video 2 track of the Timeline.** This is the clip to which you will apply motion effects.

NOTE At any time, you can import another clip into this project and use it as the background. After you import the clip, drag it into the Video 1 track of the Timeline. This example uses FilmDisc's sf0116 video clip in the Video 1 track. You can also import a sound clip. After you import a sound, drag it into the Audio 1 track. This example uses SmartSound's The Great Escape clip.

4. **Click the clip in the Video 2 track to select it.**

5. **Choose Window ⇨ Workspace ⇨ Effects to display both the Effect Controls panel and the Program Monitor panel.** Then click the Effect Controls tab to display it.

6. In the Effect Controls panel, click the triangle to the left of the word *Motion* to display the Motion effects properties.

7. Move the current-time indicator in the Timeline of the Effect Controls panel to the beginning of the clip.

 You can set the Timeline to show clips in one-second intervals by clicking and dragging the Time Zoom Level slider at the bottom of the panel.

8. **Reduce the size of the clip to 50 percent by using the Motion effects Scale property.** The clip is scaled to 50 percent throughout its duration. If you want to rotate the clip, change the value for the Rotation property.

9. **In the Effect Controls panel, click the Transform icon, next to the word *Motion,* so that you can see the motion path as it is created.** Notice that the clip is selected with an outline around it.

10. **To create a starting point, move the clip in the Program Monitor panel to the top-right corner of the panel.**

11. **To create the first keyframe, click the Toggle Animation icon to the left of the word *Position* in the Effect Controls panel.**

12. **To set a second keyframe, move the current-time indicator in the Effect Controls panel to the right.** Then click in the middle of the clip, and move it to the center of the Program Monitor panel. Notice that a second keyframe is automatically created and that a motion path displays from keyframe one to keyframe two, as shown in Figure 16.11. Also notice that Value and Velocity graphs are created for the Position control. You can adjust the Position control by using these graphs. To view the Position graph, click the triangle to the left of the word *Position*.

FIGURE 16.11

The motion path is between keyframes one and two.

13. **To set a third keyframe (the last keyframe), move the current-time indicator in the Effect Controls panel to the right (toward the end of the clip).** Then, in the Program Monitor panel, click in the middle of the clip and move it to the top-left side. Notice that a third keyframe is automatically created and that the motion path is showing a specific point for each keyframe, as shown in Figure 16.12. Notice also the change to the graphs.

FIGURE 16.12

The motion path is between keyframes two and three.

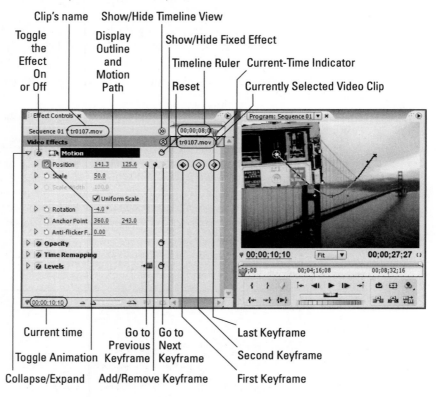

14. **Move the current-time indicator to the beginning of the clip, and click the Play button in the Program Monitor panel to preview the motion effect.** To preview specific segments of the motion effect, click and drag the current-time indicator in the Timeline of the Effect Controls panel.

CROSS-REF For more motion path controls, you may want to try using Adobe After Effects. For more information on using After Effects, see Chapters 30, 31, and 32.

Using the Timeline Panel to Preview and Add Keyframes

The Timeline panel allows you to view, add, and edit motion keyframes similar to how you use the Effect Controls panel.

Follow these steps to preview keyframes in the Timeline panel:

1. **You should have a project onscreen with a video clip in the Timeline panel.**

2. **Click the Collapse/Expand Track triangle next to the name of the video track with the video clip.** Then click the Show Keyframes icon, and click Show Keyframes. Notice that a line appears in the area below the clip's name. If the video clip has any motion effect keyframes applied to it, you see white diamonds representing the keyframes on the line, as shown in Figure 16.13. To the right of the clip's name is a drop-down menu displaying the Motion effect controls.

FIGURE 16.13

A preview of motion keyframes in the Timeline panel

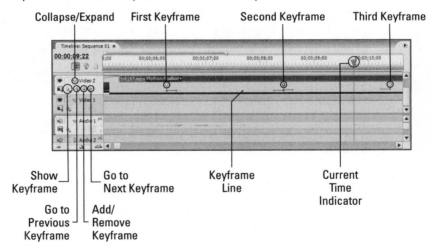

3. **Click and drag the current-time indicator in the Timeline panel to see a preview of the motion path in the Program Monitor panel.** To see a preview of the motion path, make sure that the Transform icon is selected in the Effect Controls panel (it is next to the word *Motion*).

541

Adding keyframes using the Timeline panel is the same as adding keyframes using the Timeline in the Effect Controls panel. Here's how to add keyframes in the Timeline panel:

1. **Move the current-time indicator in the Timeline panel to where you want to add a keyframe.**

2. **Click the Motion drop-down menu, and choose the control you want to affect.**

3. **Either enter a number in one of the Motion effect controls to change the Motion effect that you choose, or manually adjust the clip in the Program Monitor panel.**

4. **Click the Add/Remove Keyframe icon in the Timeline panel to add a keyframe.**

For more information on editing keyframes, see the next section.

Editing Motion Paths

To edit motion paths, you can move, delete, or add keyframes, or even copy and paste them. You can sometimes create smoother motion paths by adding keyframes.

Follow these steps to add a keyframe:

1. **Select the clip that you want to animate.**

2. **Move the current-time indicator to where you want to add a keyframe.**

3. **To add a keyframe, use the Effect Controls panel or the Timeline panel.**

   ■ To add a keyframe using the Effect Controls panel, turn on the Toggle Animation stopwatch. If the Toggle Animation stopwatch is already activated, click the Add/Remove Keyframe icon to add another keyframe.

   ■ To add a keyframe using the Timeline panel, click the Add/Remove Keyframe icon, or press and hold the Ctrl/⌘ key as you use the Pen tool or the Selection tool to add a keyframe to the motion line.

Moving a keyframe point

After you add a motion keyframe, you can return to it at any time to move it. You can move a motion keyframe point using either the Effect Controls panel or the Timeline panel. You can also move a keyframe point using the motion path that displays in the Program Monitor panel. When you move the keyframe point in the Effect Controls or Timeline panel, you change when the motion effect occurs on the Timeline. When you move the keyframe point in the motion path, you affect the shape of the motion path.

Follow these steps to move a keyframe point using the Effect Controls or Timeline panel:

1. **Move the current-time indicator to where you want to move the keyframe.** As you move the current-time indicator, use the Info panel to find the correct location.

2. **Select the keyframe point that you want to move by clicking it with the mouse.** When you click a keyframe point in the Timeline panel, the cursor displays its position on the Timeline.

 To select more than one keyframe at a time, press and hold the Shift key as you select the keyframe point.

3. **Click and drag the selected keyframe point to the new location.**

Follow these steps to move a keyframe point using the motion path that displays in the Program Monitor panel:

1. **To display the motion path in the Program Monitor panel, select the Transform icon, which is next to the word _Motion_ in the Effect Controls panel.**

2. **Select the keyframe point that you want to move by clicking it with the mouse.**

3. **Click and drag the selected keyframe point to the new location.**

   These tips help you make intricate edits on the motion path:

   ■ To move a keyframe on the motion path one pixel at a time, press one of the directional arrow keys on your keyboard.

   ■ To move the motion path five pixels at a time, hold down the Shift key and press a directional arrow key on your keyboard.

   ■ Click in the Info box below the Timeline, and enter a specific coordinate for the point on the path. When you select a point, the point number appears in the Info box. For example, if you want to center the clip in the middle of the screen, type **0,0** in the box. If you enter a positive number in the first box, the clip moves to the right. If you enter a negative number, the clip moves to the left. If you enter a positive number in the right box, the clip moves down; entering a negative number makes the clip move up. For example, if you type **−10,10**, the clip moves ten pixels to the left and ten pixels down from the middle of the screen.

Deleting keyframe points

As you edit, you may want to delete a keyframe point. To do this, simply select the point or points and press the Delete key. If you want to delete all of the keyframe points for a Motion effect option, click the Toggle Animation icon in the Effect Controls panel. A warning prompt appears, asking whether you want to delete all existing keyframes; if so, click OK.

Copying and pasting keyframe points

Follow these steps to copy a keyframe point and paste it in another place in the Timeline:

1. **To copy a keyframe point, first select it by clicking it.**

2. **Choose Edit ⇨ Copy.**

3. Move the current-time indicator to the new location.

4. Choose Edit ⇨ Paste.

Adding keyframes to change a motion path's speed

Premiere Pro determines motion speed by the distance between keyframes. To increase the speed of motion, set keyframes farther apart. To slow the speed of motion, create keyframes that are closer together.

 You can also adjust the characteristics of a motion by moving the handles of a keyframe using a Bezier interpolation. See the next section for details.

Follow these steps to change the speed of motion:

1. **If you don't already have keyframes, create keyframes on the Timeline by using either the Effect Controls panel or Timeline panel (see the steps earlier in this chapter).**

2. **To increase motion speed, drag keyframes farther apart.** To decrease motion speed, drag keyframes closer together. To move a keyframe, click the keyframe to select it, and then click and drag the keyframe point and move it on the Timeline.

 You can also use the Clip ⇨ Speed/Duration command to change the speed and/or duration of a clip. You can also use the Time Remapping control in the Effect Controls panel.

Changing a keyframe's interpolation method

Premiere Pro interpolates the data between one keyframe and another. The interpolation method that you use has a dramatic effect on how the motion effect displays. By changing the interpolation method, you can change the speed, smoothness, and shape of a motion path. The most common keyframe interpolation methods used are Linear interpolation and Bezier interpolation. To view the different interpolation methods for a keyframe, right-click the keyframe in the Timeline panel. When the Interpolation menu appears, as shown in Figure 16.14, you can pick a new interpolation method.

FIGURE 16.14

Right-click a keyframe in the Timeline panel to display the Interpolation menu.

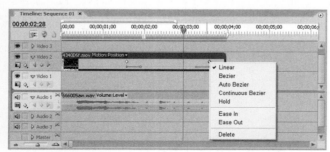

Following are different interpolation methods:

- Linear interpolation creates a uniform rate of motion change.
- The Bezier interpolation methods (Bezier, Auto Bezier, and Continuous Bezier) allow for smoother motion changes.
- Hold interpolation creates abrupt motion changes. You can use it to create a strobe effect.
- Ease In and Ease Out interpolation allows you to have a slow motion change or a fast motion change. It also allows a gradual start and finish.

Linear interpolation versus Bezier interpolation

The motion effect results of animating the Motion's Position property controls are determined by various factors. The effect that a Position motion path has is determined by how many keyframes are used, what type of interpolation method a keyframe uses, and the shape of the Position motion path. Both the number of keyframes used and the interpolation method greatly affect a motion path's speed and smoothness. Figure 16.15 shows a Position motion path in the shape of a V, and Figure 16.16 shows a Position motion path in the shape of a U. Both paths were created using three keyframes. The three keyframes were created by animating the Motion Position's property. The V shape was created by applying the Linear interpolation method on the second keyframe in Figure 16.15. The U shape was created by applying the Bezier interpolation method on the second keyframe in Figure 16.16.

A motion path displays in the Program Monitor panel, as shown in Figures 16.15 and 16.16. The motion path is made up of tiny white dots, with each dot representing a frame in the clip. Each X on the white path represents a keyframe. The spacing between the dots determines how fast or slow the motion occurs. The farther apart the dots are spaced, the faster the rate of motion; the closer together the dots are, the slower the rate of motion. If the dots vary in spacing, the motion rate also varies. The dots represent temporal interpolation because it has to do with how fast or slow a motion path works over time. The shape of the motion path indicates spatial interpolation because it has to do with how the shape of the motion path displays in its spatial surroundings.

In the Effect Controls panel, the motion path is displayed by a graph, as shown in Figures 16.15 and 16.16, and the keyframes are different icons, depending upon the interpolation method that you use. Notice that in Figures 16.15 and 16.16, the second keyframe icons in the Effect Controls panel are different. The keyframe icon in Figure 16.15 looks like a diamond, which indicates that it is using Linear interpolation. The second keyframe icon in Figure 16.16 looks like an hourglass, which indicates that it is using Bezier interpolation. An Auto Bezier interpolation icon is represented by a circle icon. Also notice in Figures 16.15 and 16.16 that the graph in the Effect Controls panel is different for a keyframe with a Linear interpolation and a keyframe with a Bezier interpolation.

TIP To view or change interpolation methods, right-click a keyframe in the Timeline panel, Program Monitor panel, or Effect Controls panel. Ctrl-click/⌘-click a keyframe in the Timeline panel to automatically change from one interpolation method to another.

FIGURE 16.15

The Program Monitor panel and Effect Controls panel show the middle keyframe of the Position Motion path using Linear interpolation.

FIGURE 16.16

The Program Monitor panel and the Effect Controls panel show the middle keyframe of the Position Motion path using Bezier interpolation.

Using Bezier interpolation to adjust the smoothness of a motion path

You can use Bezier handles to adjust the smoothness of a Bezier curve. Bezier handles are two-directional lines that control the shape of the Bezier curve. The directional lines for both the Bezier and Continuous interpolation can be adjusted. For Auto Bezier, the Bezier curve is created automatically, although the Auto Bezier option does not allow you to adjust the curve's shape. The advantage of using Bezier interpolation is that the two Bezier handles can be manipulated independently of one another. This means that the incoming handle and the outgoing handle can have different settings.

Dragging the Bezier handles up accelerates the change of motion. Dragging the handles down decelerates the change of motion. Increasing the length of the directional lines (dragging away from the center point) increases the size of the curve and spreads the tiny white dots farther apart, making the motion effect faster. Decreasing the length of the directional lines (dragging toward the center point) decreases the size of the curve and brings the tiny white dots closer together, making the motion effect slower. You can make more dramatic motion effects by varying the angle and length of directional lines. You can adjust the Bezier handles in the Program Monitor panel or by using the Effect Controls panel.

Using the interpolation method

The best way to understand how the interpolation method works is to try it! Here's how:

1. **Create a new project.**

2. **With the project onscreen, drag a clip from the Project panel to a video track in the Timeline panel.**

3. **In the Effect Controls panel, click the triangle in front of the word *Motion* to display the Position, Scale, Rotation, and Anchor Point properties.**

4. **Set the Motion Scale property to 50 percent.**

5. **Use the Timeline panel or the Effect Controls panel to move the current-time indicator to the beginning of the clip.**

6. **In the Program Monitor panel, click the clip and move it to the top-left corner of the panel.**

7. **Click the Position Toggle Animation icon to create a Position keyframe.**

8. **Using the Effect Controls panel, move the current-time indicator to the middle of the clip.** Then move the clip in the Program Monitor panel to the bottom-middle of the panel to create a second keyframe.

9. **Using the Effect Controls panel, move the current-time indicator to the end of the clip.** Then move the clip in the Program Monitor panel to the top-right corner of the panel to create a third keyframe. Notice the motion path in the Program Monitor panel.

10. **In the Effect Controls panel, click the triangle to the left of the word *Position* to display the Position graph.**

11. **Try different interpolation methods.** To change interpolation methods for the second keyframe, Ctrl-click/⌘-click it in the Timeline panel, the Program Monitor panel, or the Effect Controls panel. You can also try adjusting the Bezier handles to change the shape of the Bezier curve. Alternate from Bezier to Linear interpolation, and vice versa. Slowly ease in and out keyframes. Use the Hold interpolation to animate the clip rotating at a specific point in time.

12. **Try experimenting with the effects by changing the shape of the motion path.**

Adding Effects to Motion Paths

After you have animated an object, title, or clip, you may want to apply some other effects to it. You can change the moving object's opacity to make it translucent. You can apply one of the Image Control video effects or one of the Color Correcting video effects if you want to color-correct the moving object. You can also try some of the other video effects to create some interesting special effects.

Changing opacity

The Fixed Effects section of the Effect Controls panel contains the Motion effect controls and the Opacity controls. By reducing the opacity of a clip, you make the clip more translucent. To change the opacity of a clip throughout its duration, click and drag to the left on the Opacity percent value. You can also change the Opacity percent field by clicking in the field, typing a number, and pressing Enter. Alternatively, you can expand the Opacity controls by clicking the triangle to the left of the Opacity name and then clicking and dragging the Opacity slider.

To set keyframes for opacity using the Effect Controls panel, follow these steps:

1. **Activate the Toggle Animation icon.**
2. **Change the Opacity percent field.** Click the Toggle Keyframe icon to set a keyframe.

To set keyframes for opacity using the Timeline panel, follow these steps:

1. **Click the Show Keyframes icon.**
2. **Choose Opacity from the clip's title drop-down menu.** Click the Add/Remove Keyframe icon to add a keyframe.

To change the Opacity percent field, use the white line below the clip's name. Click and drag down on the white line to reduce the opacity of the clip. For more information on using the Opacity controls, see Chapter 14.

Adjusting speed using Time Remapping

The Time Remapping control allows you to adjust the speed of a clip over time using keyframes. With Time Remapping you can set keyframes to increase and/or decrease the speed of a clip at different intervals. You can also freeze a clip in time or have a clip go backwards. The Time Remapping controls are available in the Effect Controls panel and can display in the Timeline panel. To view Time Remapping in the Effect Controls panel, make sure the Effect Controls panel is displayed, and then click a video clip in the Timeline panel. To display Time Remapping in the Timeline panel, click the menu on the video clip in the Timeline. When the pop-up menu appears, choose Time Remapping Speed.

To change the speed of a video clip using the Timeline panel, drag the Speed line up or down. To change the speed of a video clip using the Effect Controls panel, click the triangle to the left of Time Remapping to display the Speed percent value. Then drag over the Speed percent value to change the speed.

To change the speed of a video clip in different places in the clip, you need to set keyframes. To add keyframes to a video clip, move the current-time indicator line in either the Effect Controls panel or the Timeline panel, and then click the Add/Remove Keyframe icon to add a keyframe. To add a second keyframe, move the current-time indicator line to the place in the clip that you want to adjust the speed, and then make the adjustments. As you make the adjustments, another keyframe is added. If you want the speed of a clip to keep changing, you have to keep adding keyframes. Figure 16.17 shows the Effect Controls panel and the Timeline panel with Time Remapping keyframes.

FIGURE 16.17

Setting keyframes for Time Remapping in either the Effect Controls panel or the Timeline panel can change the speed of a clip over time and at different intervals.

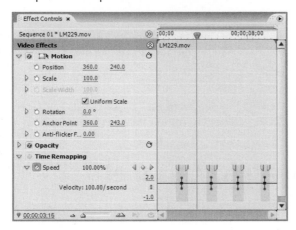

Applying special effects

After you have animated a clip using the Fixed Effect controls (Motion and Opacity) in the Effect Controls panel, you may find that you want to add a few more effects to your clip. You can find various effects in the Video Effects bin (folder) of the Effects panel. To adjust an image's color, try using one of the Image Control video effects or one of the Color Correcting video effects. For more information on adjusting color using video effects, see Chapter 17. If you want to distort a clip, try using one of the Distort video effects. For more information on using the video effects, see Chapter 13. Follow these steps to add effects to a clip:

What is an alpha channel?

Essentially, an alpha channel is an extra grayscale image layer that Premiere Pro translates into different levels of transparency.

Alpha channels are typically used to define the transparent areas of a graphic or title. They enable you to combine a logo or text in one video track with a background video clip in another track. The background track surrounds the logo or text and is seen through the letters in the text. If you view an alpha channel of text, it might appear as pure-white text on a black background. When Premiere Pro uses the alpha channel to create transparency, it can place colored text in the white area of the alpha channel, and a background video track in the black area.

You can create alpha channels in programs such as Adobe Photoshop or Adobe Illustrator. Most 3-D programs also create alpha channels. When you create titles in the Title Designer, Premiere Pro automatically creates an alpha channel for the text. (For more information about alpha channels, see Chapter 15. Chapter 28 provides detailed instructions for creating alpha channels in Photoshop. For more information on Adobe Illustrator, turn to Chapter 29.)

1. **Start by moving the current-time indicator on the Timeline in the Effect Controls panel or in the Timeline panel to the place where you want to add an effect.**

2. **Choose an effect from the Effects panel.** Drag it to the Effect Controls panel or the Timeline panel.

3. **Adjust the settings for the effect.** Click the Toggle Animation icon to create a keyframe. If you want the effect to change over time, you need to create various keyframes.

Using a Clip with an Alpha Channel

If you create motion effects with text or logos, you may want the text or logo to appear as though it were on a sheet of clear acetate to enable a background video track to show through. The standard digital method of creating this effect is to use an alpha channel.

If the image that you set in motion includes an alpha channel, Premiere Pro can mask out the background and substitute the background area with visuals from another video track.

The following steps explain how to apply the Motion effect to a clip with an alpha channel (or layer with transparency). Figure 16.18 shows the Greetings Photoshop file that was used to create the Greetings from San Francisco project (shown in Figures 16.3 and 16.4).

FIGURE 16.18

The Greetings Photoshop file that was used to create the Greetings from San Francisco project in Figures 16.3 and 16.4

Follow these steps to apply motion to a clip with an alpha channel:

1. **Create a new project by choosing File ⇨ New ⇨ Project.** In the New Project dialog box, choose a preset, name the project, and click OK to create the new project.

2. **Import two clips into the Project panel by choosing File ⇨ Import.** To see the transparency effects of an alpha channel (or layer with transparency), you need two images in two different video tracks, one on top of the other. One image should be a file that has an alpha channel; the other clip is used as the background. If you want, you can use the Greetings Photoshop file and the Golden Gate Bridge file (FilmDisc's Destinations — San Francisco 1: SF0116). Figure 16.19 shows the Greetings Photoshop file over the Golden Gate Bridge file. Figure 16.20 shows the Greetings Photoshop file's alpha channel in the Source panel. You can also use the text tools in the Title panel to create a title with an alpha channel (transparent background). You can also use the graphic tools in the Title panel to create a shape or a background.

NOTE When you import a file with an alpha channel (layer) into Premiere Pro, the Import Layered File dialog box appears, as shown in Figure 16.21. In this dialog box, you have two options: You can choose a layer to import, or you can merge the layers. Select Footage from the Import As pop-up menu. To merge the layers, click the Merged Layers option from the Layer Options section. To choose a layer to import, click Choose Layer from the Layer Options section. Then click the Choose Layer menu, and select the layer with the alpha channel. Click OK to import the file. For the Greetings Photoshop file, you can merge the Shape and text layers.

The Greetings Photoshop file over the Golden Gate Bridge file

Cloud shape created from alpha channel (right-hand image)

ON the DVD The Greetings Photoshop file and the background file (FilmDisc's sf0116) are found in the Tutorial Projects folder on the DVD that accompanies this book.

CROSS-REF To review how to create titles and graphics using the Title panel, see Chapter 10.

552

FIGURE 16.21

The Import Layered File dialog box allows you to import a Photoshop file with layers and then merge the layers or choose a layer.

3. **Drag the background image to the Video 1 track in the Timeline panel.**

4. **Drag the file with the alpha channel (either the title clip or graphic file) from the Project panel to the Video 2 track in the Timeline panel.**

5. **Change the duration of the image in the Video 2 track to match the background clip in the Video 1 track.** The clip in the Video 2 track should be selected. If it isn't, select it now.

6. **To apply motion effects to the clip in the Video 2 track, use the Effect Controls panel or the Timeline panel.**

7. **Press Enter to render the project.** To preview the motion effects in the Program Monitor panel, click the Play button.

8. **To add a sound clip, choose File ➪ Import.** In the Import dialog box, select a sound clip and click Open. This example uses SmartSound's The Great Escape, located in the SmartSound folder in the Tutorial Projects folder on the DVD.

9. **Choose File ➪ Save to save the project.**

Creating Traveling Mattes

A traveling matte (or mask) is a special effect that combines motion and masking. Typically, the matte is a shape that moves across the screen. Within the matte is one image; outside the mask is a background image.

Figure 16.22 shows a frame of the Traveling Matte effect in the Program Monitor panel. Notice that one image is seen through a puzzle-shaped graphic, which is the mask. The matte is simply a puzzle shape on a transparent layer that was created in Photoshop using Photoshop's Shape tool. To create the shape in this example, you can use Puzzle 4 from the Shapes Object palette.

FIGURE 16.22

A frame for a Traveling Matte effect displays in the Program Monitor panel.

To create a Traveling Matte effect, you need two video clips: one for the background and another to travel within the matte. You also need a graphic image for the actual matte. Figure 16.22 shows the clips in the Timeline that are used to create the Traveling Matte effect, as well as the resulting effect. The Video 3 track contains a puzzle image. The Video 2 track contains a moving cabs video clip, and the Video 1 track contains a video clip of the Golden Gate Bridge.

Follow these steps to create a Traveling Matte effect:

1. **Create a new project by choosing File ⇨ New ⇨ Project.** In the New Project dialog box, choose a preset. If you are using the images from the DVD, choose the DV-NTSC Standard 48 kHz preset. Name the project, and click OK to create the new project.

2. **Choose File ⇨ Import to import two clips: one to use in the background and one to use as the element to appear in the mask.** The example in Figure 16.22 uses a Golden Gate Bridge video clip as the background, and a clip of moving cabs to appear in the mask. Both clips that are shown in Figure 16.22 are from FilmDisc. The Golden Gate Bridge clip is file sf0116, and the moving cabs clip is file cm0105.

3. Drag the image that you want to use as your background to the Video 1 track.

4. Drag the image that you want to appear within the matte to the Video 2 track.

5. **Import a graphic image to use as a matte by choosing File ⇨ Import.** This example uses the Puzzle image, which is on the DVD. In the Import Layered File dialog box, leave the Import As drop-down menu set to Footage and select the Choose Layer option. In the Choose Layer drop-down menu, choose the appropriate layer; this example uses Shape 1. Click OK to import the star shape into the Project panel.

NOTE If you want, you can use Photoshop to create your own image to use as a matte. To activate Photoshop from within your Premiere Pro project, choose File ⇨ New ⇨ Photoshop file. (You can use Photoshop's Shape tool to create the puzzle piece. When creating the file, set the pixel dimensions to be the same as those you want to use for your project. For more information on using Adobe Photoshop, see Chapter 28. For more information on using Adobe Illustrator, see Chapter 29.) You can also use the tools in the Title panel to create a matte shape. To use the Title panel, choose File ⇨ New ⇨ Title. (For more information on creating shapes in the Title panel, see Chapter 10.) Remember that after the traveling matte is complete, one clip appears within the white area. A background image appears in the black area.

6. **Drag the graphic image that you want to use as a matte from the Project panel into the Video 3 track.** The example in Figure 16.19 uses the puzzle graphic as the matte graphic.

7. **Extend the duration of the image in the Video 3 track by clicking and dragging the left side of the clip.** Extend the duration so that it is the same as the clip in the Video 1 and Video 2 tracks.

8. **Select the matte in the Video 3 track by clicking it with the Selection tool.**

9. **To apply motion to the matte graphic, use the Motion controls in the Effect Controls panel or Timeline panel.**

10. **Select the Video 2 track, which is the track sandwiched between the matte and the background image.**

11. **Choose Window ⇨ Effects to display the Effects panel.**

12. **Click the triangle in front of the Video Effects bin (folder) to display the video effects.** Then click the triangle in front of the Keying bin (folder). Select the Track Matte key option, and drag it over the clip in the Video 2 track. The Track Matte Key controls display in the Effect Controls panel. Set the Matte drop-down menu to Video 3 track. (For a detailed discussion of the Keying effects, see Chapter 14.)

13. **If you want, you can add sound to your project.** This example uses SmartSound's Movie Logos sound clip.

14. **Press Enter to render the project.** Preview the project in the Program Monitor panel by clicking the Play button.

15. **If you want, you can add a sound clip to the project.** Make sure to save your file by choosing File ⇨ Save.

Summary

Premiere Pro enables you to create motion effects from graphics and video clips. This chapter covered the following topics:

■ You can change motion speed and direction with the Motion properties.

■ You can rotate and scale images with the Motion properties.

■ You can use the Motion control with clips that have alpha channels to create motion effects where image backgrounds are transparent.

■ You can use the Track Matte Key effect to create a Traveling Matte effect.

Chapter 17

Enhancing Video

When shooting video, you may sometimes have little control over the locale or lighting conditions. This can result in video clips that are too dark or too bright or that display a color cast onscreen. Fortunately, Premiere Pro's Video Effects panel provides a number of effects specifically designed to coax rich colors out of stubbornly dull or poorly lit video. Using Premiere Pro's color effects, you can adjust image brightness, contrast, and colors. All of the effects can be previewed onscreen in the Program Monitor or in Premiere Pro's Reference Monitor while you adjust controls in the Effect Controls panel. Although there is no substitute for high-quality video shot with well-planned lighting, Premiere Pro's Video Effects may be able to boost the overall tonal and color quality of your production.

This chapter looks at the Premiere Pro effects that you can use to enhance colors. It starts with an overview of the RGB color model and then proceeds to review the color enhancement effects in the Color Correction, Adjust, and Image Control bins of the Video Effects panel.

> **TIP** You may also be able to enhance a scene by using a matte, and then keying one scene behind another. See Chapter 14 for information about using key effects.

The RGB Color Model

Before you begin to correct color, lightness, brightness, and contrast in Premiere Pro, you should review a few important concepts about computer color theory. As you will soon see, most of Premiere Pro's image-enhancement effects are not based on the mechanics of color in the video world. Instead, they're based on the fundamentals of how a computer creates color.

When you view images on a computer display, colors are created from different combinations of red, green, and blue light. When you need to choose or edit colors, most computer applications allow you to choose from 256 levels of red, 256 levels of green, and 256 levels of blue. This results in over 17.6 million possible colors (256 × 256 × 256). In both Premiere Pro and Photoshop, each red, green, and blue color component of an image is called a *channel*.

Premiere Pro's Color Picker provides an example of how red, green, and blue channels create color. Using the Color Picker, you can choose colors by specifying red, green, and blue values. To open Premiere Pro's Color Picker, you must first have a project onscreen and then choose File ⇨ New ⇨ Color Matte. In the Color Picker dialog box, shown in Figure 17.1, notice the Red, Green, and Blue entry fields. If you click a color in the color area, the numbers in the entry fields change to show how many levels of red, green, and blue are used to create that color. To change colors, you can also enter a value from 0 to 255 into each of the Red, Green, and Blue fields.

FIGURE 17.1

Premiere Pro's Color Picker enables you to choose colors by specifying red, green, and blue color values.

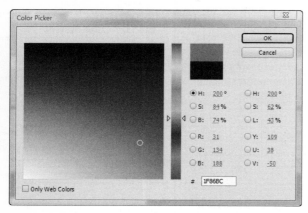

If you want to use Premiere Pro to correct color, it's helpful to have a basic understanding of how the red, green, and blue color channels interact to create red, green, and blue color, and their complements (or opposites), cyan, magenta, and yellow. The following list of color combinations can help you understand how different channels create colors. Note that the lower numbers are darker and the higher numbers are lighter. The combination 0 red, 0 green, 0 blue creates black — the absence of light. If you set the red, green, and blue values to 255, white is created — the greatest amount of light. If you add equal values of red, green, and blue, you produce a shade of gray, with lower red, green, and blue values producing dark gray, and higher values producing lighter gray.

0 red + 0 green + 0 blue	black
255 red + 255 green + 255 blue	white
255 green + 255 blue	cyan
255 red + 255 blue	magenta
255 red + 255 green	yellow

Notice that adding two of the RGB color components produces cyan, magenta, or yellow. These are the complements of red, green, and blue. Understanding this relationship is helpful, because it can provide some direction as you work. From the preceding color calculations, you can see that adding more green and blue to an image produces more cyan; adding more red and blue produces more magenta; adding more red and green produces more yellow.

The preceding calculations also provide a basis for the results of adding or subtracting one of the red, green, or blue channels from an image:

Adding red	less cyan
Reducing red	more cyan
Adding green	less magenta
Reducing green	more magenta
Adding blue	less yellow
Reducing blue	more yellow

The HLS Color Model

As you will see from the examples in this chapter, many of Premiere Pro's image enhancement effects use controls that adjust red, green, and blue color channels. Those effects that don't use the RGB color model use Hue, Saturation, and Lightness controls. If you are new to color correcting, you may wonder why you would use HLS (also known as HSL) instead of RGB — as RGB is the computer's native method of creating colors. The answer is that many artists find creating and adjusting colors using HLS to be more intuitive than using RGB. In the HLS color model, colors are created in much the same way as color is perceived. *Hue* is the color, *lightness* is the brightness or darkness of the color, and *saturation* is the color intensity.

Using HLS, you can quickly start your correction work by choosing a color on a color wheel (or a slider representing a 360-degree wheel) and adjusting its intensity and lightness. This technique is generally quicker than trying to add and subtract red, green, and blue values to fine-tune colors.

The YUV Color System

If you are exporting to videotape, keep in mind that the color gamut (the range of colors that make up an image) that displays on a computer screen is greater than the color gamut of a television screen. Your computer monitor creates colors using red, green, and blue phosphors. American broadcast television uses the YCbCr standard (often abbreviated as YCC). YCbCr uses one luminance channel and two chroma or chrominance channels.

> **NOTE**   *Luminance* values are the brightness values of an image. If you view the luminance values of an image, you see it as a grayscale image. *Chrominance* is often described as the combination of hue and saturation, or color subtracted from luminance.

YCbCr is based upon the YUV color system (although the term is often used synonymously with YUV). YUV is the color model used by Premiere Pro and PAL analog television systems. The YUV system is composed of a luminance channel (Y) and two color chroma channels: U and V. The luminance channel was, and still is, based on the luminance value used for black-and-white television. This value was kept so that viewers with black-and-white television could view the television signal when color was adapted.

Like RGB and HLS, YUV color values are displayed in the Adobe Color Picker. YUV color can be derived from RGB color values. For example, the Y (luminance) component is derived from percentages of red, green, and blue. The U component is derived by subtracting the Y luminance value from the blue RGB value and multiplying it by a constant. The V component is derived by subtracting the Y luminance value from the red RGB value and multiplying it by another constant. This is why the term *chrominance* essentially means a signal based upon color subtracted from a luminance value.

If you are working on a high-definition project, you can choose between 8-bit and 16-bit YUV color in the Video Rendering section of the Project Settings dialog box (Project ➪ Project Settings ➪ Video Rendering). Most project presets also allow you to access a Maximum Bit Depth check box, which allows a color bit depth up to 32 bits, depending upon the project's preset Compressor setting. Selecting the Maximum Bit Depth option can improve the quality of video effects but is more taxing on your computer system.

> **NOTE**   The term *YUV 4:2:2* appears as a choice for Video Rendering when using a High Definition preset. The 4:2:2 ratio is a color down-sampling ratio from analog to digital. The value 4 represents Y (luminance), and 2:2 indicates that the chroma values are sampled at half the rate of luminance. This process is called *chroma subsampling*. This subsampling of color is possible because the human eye is much less sensitive to changes in color than luminance.

Color Correcting Basics

Before color correcting a clip, you first need to decide whether your clip needs an overall adjustment to the shadows, midtones, and highlights, or the color of the clip needs to be enhanced or possibly changed. Your clip might need a variety of adjustments. The best way to decide what changes your clip needs is to view its color and luminance distribution. You can do this by displaying the Vectorscope, YC Waveform, YCbCr Parade, and RGB Parade. These options, which are located in the Monitor's menu, are discussed in detail in this chapter. Once you are familiar with your image's composition, it is easier to use the Color Correction, Adjust, or Image Control video effects to make color luminance adjustments to your clip.

If you have used Adobe Photoshop, you know how important it is to view your clip's histogram. Try using the Levels video clip (in the Adjust bin) to become familiar with reading a clip's histogram. The histogram displays, and allows you to make overall adjustments to, your clip's shadows, midtones, highlights, and separate color channels. If this seems a little overwhelming at first, you might want to have Premiere Pro make the color corrections for you — that is, until you are more familiar with all of this new jargon. If so, try using the Auto Color, Auto Contrast, and Auto Levels video effects (in the Adjust bin). If your clip needs just a subtle adjustment, but you want it to stand out more, you might want to use the Brightness & Contrast video effect (found in the Color Correction bin). You can also use the Sharpen or Unsharp Mask effects (in the Blur & Sharpen bin).

The following sections discuss some of the color correcting basics in more detail. Before you start your color correction project, make sure that you are familiar with Premiere Pro's color options that allow you to view your clip's color and luminance distribution. You can then begin using video effects to make color corrections. You might need to experiment a few times with different video effects before you achieve the desired results. Don't be afraid to try new video effects; remember that you can always hide a video effect by clicking the toggle effect icon next to the video effect's name in the Effect Controls panel. You can also remove a video effect by clicking it in the Effect Controls panel and pressing the Delete key.

NOTE Adobe After Effects includes many of the same color-correcting techniques as Adobe Premiere Pro. However, After Effects enables you to mask or isolate areas onscreen. After you mask an area, you can choose to color correct the masked area only. For more information on using After Effects and masking, turn to Chapters 30, 31, and 32.

Start a Color Correcting Session

Before you start correcting video, you can improve the results with a few minor workspace changes. You may want to start by setting your workspace to Premiere Pro's Color Correction workspace (Window ➪ Workspace ➪ Color Correction).

- **Use a Reference Monitor.** Using a Reference Monitor is similar to working with another Program Monitor onscreen. Thus, you can view two different scenes from a video sequence simultaneously: one in the Reference Monitor and one in the Program Monitor. You can also view Premiere Pro's video scopes in the Reference Monitor while viewing the actual video that the scopes represent in the Program Monitor.

  If you choose to use the Color Correction workspace, the Reference Monitor opens automatically. If the Reference Monitor is not open, you can display it by choosing Reference

Monitor from the Program Monitor panel menu. By default, the Reference Monitor is *ganged* to play in sync with your Program Monitor. You can also *ungang* the Reference Monitor (so that you can view one scene in the Reference Monitor and another in the Program Monitor) by deselecting Gang to Program Monitor in the Reference Monitor panel menu. Another way to ungang the Reference Monitor is to click the Gang to Program Monitor button in the Reference Monitor.

- **View the highest-quality output.** You can change the output quality of Premiere Pro's Source, Program, and Reference Monitors. When making color adjustments, you want to view the highest-quality output so that you can accurately judge colors. To set a monitor to highest quality, click the Monitor's panel menu, and choose Highest Quality.

- **Use the maximum bit depth.** To obtain the highest-quality output, you can set Premiere Pro's video rendering to the maximum color depth allowed by the project's preset Compressor. Choose Project ➪ Project Settings ➪ General ➪ Video Rendering. In the Video Rendering section, select Maximum Bit Depth.

- **Use Premiere Pro's video scopes.** If your project will be viewed on a video monitor, you can use Premiere Pro's video scopes to help ensure that your video levels don't stray beyond target levels for professional video. The next section discusses video scopes.

Using the Video Scopes

Premiere Pro's video scopes provide a graphic representation of color information. They simulate video scopes used in professional broadcast studios and are most important to Premiere Pro users who are outputting NTSC or PAL video. Several of the scopes output graphic representations of a video signal's chroma (the color and intensity) and luminance (brightness values — essentially black, white, and gray values).

To view a scope readout for a clip, double-click the clip in the Project panel or move the current-time indicator to the clip in a sequence on the Timeline. Then pick the scope or group of scopes from the Source, Program, or Reference Monitor's menu.

The Vectorscope

The Vectorscope displays a graphic representation of a clip's chroma in relation to hue. The Vectorscope, shown in Figure 17.2, displays hues along a color wheel with Red, Magenta, Blue, Cyan, Green, and Yellow (R, MG, B, Cy, G, YL) markers. Thus, the angle of the readout indicates hue properties. Readings toward the outer edges of the Vectorscope indicate highly saturated colors. Moderately saturated colors appear between the center of the circle and its outer edges. Black and white portions of the video appear at the center.

The tiny target boxes in the Vectorscope indicate upper levels of saturation. NTSC video levels should not go beyond these boxes.

The top of the scope displays controls allowing you to change the intensity of the Vectorscope display. You can click a different intensity, or you can click and drag to change the intensity percentage. These intensity options do not change chroma levels in the video; they only change the scope's display. The 75 percent option above the Vectorscope changes the display to approximate analog chrominance; the 100-percent option displays digital video chrominance.

FIGURE 17.2

The Vectorscope charts video chroma.

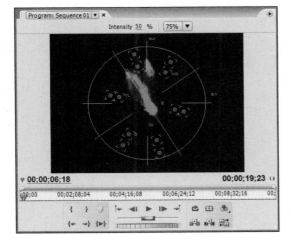

YC Waveform

The YC Waveform scope, shown in Figure 17.3, provides a waveform representation of video signal intensity. (Y represents luminance, and C represents chrominance.) In the YC Waveform, the horizontal axis represents the actual video clip, while the vertical axis charts signal intensity measured in IRE (for Institute of Radio Engineers).

The green waveform pattern in the scope represents video luminance. The waveform for brighter video appears at the top of the chart; the waveform for darker video appears at the bottom of the chart. Chroma is indicated by a blue waveform. (In general, luminance and chroma overlap, and their IRE values should be about the same level.)

In the United States, acceptable luminance levels for NTSC video range from 7.5 IRE (black level, referred to as *pedestal* level) to 100 IRE (white level); for Japan, the values range from 0 IRE to 100 IRE.

To aid you in interpreting the scope, you can turn the Chroma display on and off by clicking the Chroma check box. Like the Vectorscope, you can click and drag over the Intensity percentage to change the intensity of the scope display. By default, the YC Waveform attempts to display waveforms as they would appear if output to analog video. To view the waveform for digital video, deselect the Setup (7.5 IRE) check box.

FIGURE 17.3

The YC Waveform Scope displays luminance and chrominance.

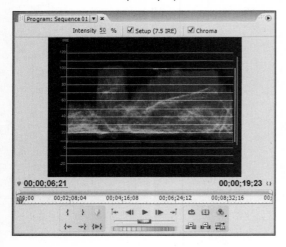

YCbCr Parade

The YCbCr Parade scopes, shown in Figure 17.4, provide a "parade" of waveforms that indicate the luminance and color differences in a video signal.

The order of the parade is as follows:

- **Y:** The first waveform is the Y or luminance level.
- **Cb:** The second waveform is Cb (blue minus luma).
- **Cr:** The third waveform is Cr (red minus luma).
- The vertical bars at the end of the chart indicate the range of signal of the Y, Cb, and Cr waveforms.

You can control the intensity of the display by clicking and dragging over the intensity readout.

FIGURE 17.4

The YCbCr Parade displays luminance and color differences.

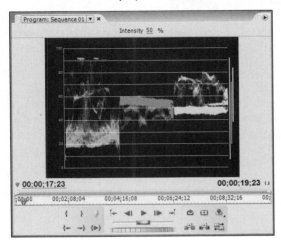

RGB Parade

The RGB Parade, shown in Figure 17.5, displays waveforms for red, green, and blue levels in a video clip. The RGB Parade scope can help you determine how color is distributed throughout a clip. In the scope, red is the first waveform, green is the second, and blue is the last. The vertical bars at the right of the RGB Parade scope represent the range of each RGB signal.

FIGURE 17.5

The RGB Parade shows waveforms for red, green, and blue levels.

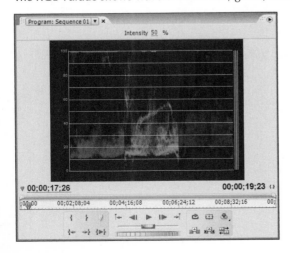

Color Enhancement Effects

Premiere Pro's color enhancement tools are dispersed among three bins in the Video Effects panel — Color Correction, Adjust, and Image Control. Not surprisingly, you can find the most powerful effects in the Color Correction bin. The Color Correction effects provide the most precise and quickest options for correcting color.

Color Correction effects are applied in the same manner as other video effects. As discussed in Chapter 13, to apply an effect, you can simply click and drag the effect over a video clip in the Timeline. After you apply the effect, you can adjust it using controls in the Effect Controls panel. As with other video effects, you can click the Show/Hide Timeline button to view a Timeline in the panel. To create keyframes, you can click the Toggle Animation button before moving the current-time indicator and making adjustments. You can also click the Reset button to cancel the effect. See Chapter 13 for detailed instructions on using the Video Effects panel and applying keyframes.

ON the DVD   Before you begin exploring Premiere Pro's color enhancement commands, you must start by creating a new project. Import a color clip into Premiere Pro, and drag it into the Video 1 track. If you don't have a video clip to use, you can use one of the clips found in the Tutorial Projects folder on the DVD that accompanies this book.

The Primary Color Correction tools

Premiere Pro's most powerful color correcting tools reside in the Color Correction bin (folder) in the Effects panel. You can use these effects to fine-tune chroma (color) and luminance (brightness values) in your video. As you make adjustments, you can view the effects in the Program Monitor, in the video scopes, or in Premiere Pro's Reference Monitor. The effects in this section are grouped according to similarity, to make it easier for you to compare the different features.

When using the color correcting effects, you may notice that many share similar features. For example, each effect option allows you to choose how you want to view the scene that you are correcting in the Program or Reference Monitor. These commands include the following:

- **Output:** The Output drop-down menu controls what displays in the Program or Reference Monitor. The menu displays the following choices:
  - **Composite:** Displays the composite image as it normally displays in the Program or Reference Monitor.
  - **Luma:** Displays luminance values (a grayscale image displaying lightness and darkness values).

■ **Mask:** When correcting using the Secondary Color Correction controls, the Mask option displays a black-and-white version of the image. White areas indicate image areas that will be affected by color adjustments; black areas will not be affected.

■ **Tonal Range:** Several Color Correction effects include the Tonal Range Definition bar, which allows you to specify a tonal range of shadows, midtones, and highlights to correct. When you choose Tonal Range in the Output drop-down menu, the target tonal range displays in the Program or Reference Monitor.

■ **Show Split View:** This option splits the screen so that you can compare the original (uncorrected) video and live adjustments.

■ **Layout:** Choose between a vertical or horizontal split view. This option allows you to view corrected and uncorrected areas as a vertical split screen or horizontal split screen.

■ **Split View Percent:** Choose the percentage of corrected video that you want to display in the split screen view.

Fast Color Corrector

The Fast Color Corrector, shown in Figure 17.6, allows you to quickly adjust a clip's color and luminance. You can also remove color casts from white areas using the Fast Color Corrector's White Balance control. To use the Fast Color Corrector, start by setting the Output options (described above), and then begin correcting color using the Hue Balance and Angle color wheel. To correct brightness and contrast, use the Levels sliders located below the color wheel.

 Because the controls described above appear in most of the Color Correction effects, they are not repeated in the individual effect descriptions.

ON the DVD The Green Parrot video clip on the DVD needs color correction. Use the Eyedropper tools in the image to control the color cast, and then use the Gamma control to help adjust color in the midtones. To practice changing hues, use the Hue settings.

White Balance

Use the White Balance controls to help remove color casts. Select the White Balance Eyedropper tool and click an image area that should be white. When you click, Premiere Pro adjusts the colors throughout the image.

Hue Balance and Angle color wheel

The Hue Balance and Angle color wheel allows you to quickly choose hue and adjust hue intensity. You can click and drag the outer wheel to change hue — which changes the Hue Angle values — and then click and drag the circle in the middle of the wheel to control color intensity — which changes the Balance Magnitude values. Changing angles alters the color toward the direction in which you point it; clicking and dragging the bar or handle in the middle fine-tunes the adjustment.

FIGURE 17.6

The Fast Color Corrector controls

Show/Hide Timeline

Balance Gain   Toggle Effect On/Off

Hue Angle   Balance Angle

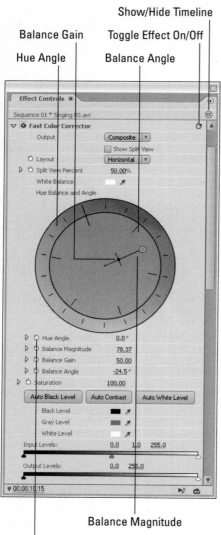

Balance Magnitude

Toggle Animation (for Keyframes)

To see a graphic representation of using the wheel, view the Vectorscope in the Reference Monitor. The following list describes the color wheel controls. For most of these adjustments, you can click and drag within the color wheel or click and drag the sliders beneath the wheel:

- **Hue Angle:** Click and drag the outer wheel to adjust the hue. Clicking and dragging the outer wheel left spins to green colors, while clicking and dragging right spins to red colors. As you drag, the Hue Angle readout indicates the degree on the wheel.

- **Balance Magnitude:** Click and drag the circle in the middle of the wheel toward a hue to control the intensity of the color. As you drag outward, the color becomes more intense (you can easily see this in Premiere Pro's Vectorscope).

- **Balance Gain:** Use this handle to fine-tune the Balance Gain and Balance Angle controls. Dragging the handle outward creates a coarser effect; keeping the handle near the center creates a more subtle effect.

- **Balance Angle:** Clicking and dragging the Balance Angle alters the color in the direction in which you point the handle.

- **Saturation:** Click and drag the Saturation slider to adjust color intensity. Dragging the slider left toward 0.0 removes, or desaturates, colors (turning it into a grayscale version displaying luminance values). Dragging to the right intensifies saturation.

- **Auto Black Level:** Click the Auto Black Level button to increase black levels above 7.5 IRE. This effectively clips, or cuts off, darker levels and proportionally redistributes pixel values, which usually lightens shadow areas.

- **Auto Contrast:** Clicking the Auto Contrast button has the same effect as applying both Auto Black Level and Auto White Level. The shadow areas are lightened, and highlight areas are darkened. This may help to add contrast to some clips.

- **Auto White Levels:** Click the Auto White Levels button to lower white levels so that no highlight areas are above 100 IRE. This effectively clips, or cuts off, white levels. When the pixel values are redistributed proportionally, the effect usually darkens highlight areas.

- **Black Level, White Level, Gray Level:** These controls provide similar adjustments to the Auto Contrast, Auto White Level, and Auto Black Level, except that you can choose the level by clicking in your image or by clicking the swatch and choosing a color from the Adobe Color Picker. By setting black and white points, you can specify which areas should be the brightest and darkest image areas; thus, you can expand an image's tonal range. When you set a white or black point, you should click the lightest or darkest area that you want to maintain in the image. After you click, Premiere Pro adjusts the tonal range of the image based upon the new white point. For example, if you click a white area in your image, Premiere Pro makes all areas lighter than the white point white and then remaps the pixels proportionally.

NOTE In the United States, acceptable luminance levels for NTSC Video range from 7.5 IRE to 100 IRE; for Japan, the range is 0 IRE to 100 IRE. As discussed earlier, the YC Waveform scope measures luminance using an IRE scale.

- **Levels:** Use the Levels controls to adjust contrast and brightness. The outer markers on the Input and Output sliders indicate black and white points. The Input sliders designate white and black points in relation to the Output levels. Input and Output levels range from 0 (black) to 255 (white). You can use the two sliders together to increase or decrease contrast in an image. For example, if you drag the white Input slider left to 230, pixels that were 230 become 255 (white); highlights are brightened and the number of highlighted pixels increases. However, if you drag the white Output slider to the left to 230, you remap the image so that 230 is the lightest value in the image (Premiere Pro also remaps other pixel values in the image accordingly).

  As you might expect, dragging the black Input and Output sliders reverses the effects of the white Input and Output sliders. Dragging the black Input slider to the right darkens the image. If you drag the black Output slider to the right, you lighten it.

  To change midtones with little effect on the highlights and shadows, click and drag the gamma Input slider. Drag to the right to lighten midtones; drag to the left to darken midtones.

NOTE Premiere Pro's Adjust bin includes a Levels effect. This effect also provides a histogram — a graphic chart of pixel values in your image. To learn more about levels, see the Levels effect in the Adjust Effects section later in this chapter.

Three-Way Color Corrector

The Three-Way Color Corrector is Premiere Pro's Swiss Army knife of color adjustment. The Three-Way Color Corrector provides an assortment of controls for correcting colors as well as shadows (darkest image areas), midtones, and highlights (brightest image areas). As you can see from Figure 17.7, in many respects, the Three-Way Color Corrector is an extended version of the Fast Color Corrector. It extends the functionality of the Fast Color Corrector because it allows you to target specific color ranges and provides a Secondary Color Correction group, which allows you to further specify a tonal range for your adjustments. Following is a review of the options.

The Balance commands can remove color casts from an image by neutralizing white, black, and gray. They can also be used to add a color cast. For example, you may want a warm, red color cast in a scene that takes place around a burning fire in a fireplace. If you do not want neutral blacks, whites, or grays and you *do* want a color cast, you can set the color in the Adobe Color Picker by clicking the white, black, or gray tile adjacent to the eyedropper icon. Note that the balance commands can affect all colors in a clip.

- **White Balance:** Select the White Balance Eyedropper tool, and click an image area that is supposed to be white.
- **Gray Balance:** Select the Gray Balance Eyedropper tool, and click an image area that is supposed to be gray.
- **Black Balance:** Select the Black Balance Eyedropper tool, and click an image area that is supposed to be black.

FIGURE 17.7

The Three-Way Color Corrector controls

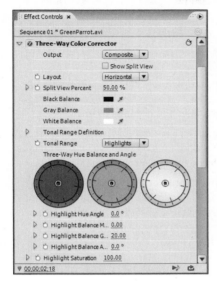

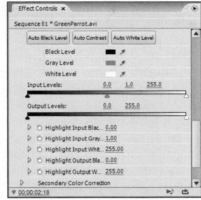

Hue Balance and Angle color wheels

The Three-Way Color Corrector's Hue Balance and Angle color function is similar to the wheel in the Fast Color Corrector. However, the Three-Way Color Corrector allows you to use either a master wheel (one wheel) or three wheels. To view the three wheels, as shown in Figure 17.7, choose Shadows, Midtones, or Highlights from the Tonal Range drop-down menu. The first wheel represents shadows, the second wheel represents midtones, and the third wheel represents highlights.

The following list describes the color wheel controls. For most of these adjustments, you can click and drag on or within the color wheel (see the descriptions on the wheel in Figure 17.6), or click and drag the sliders beneath the wheel.

- **Hue Angle:** Click and drag the outer wheel to adjust the hue. Clicking and dragging the outer wheel left rotates the wheel toward green; clicking and dragging right rotates the wheel toward red. As you drag, the Hue Angle readout indicates the degree on the wheel.

- **Balance Magnitude:** Click and drag the circle in the middle of the wheel toward a hue to control the intensity of the color. As you drag outward, the color becomes more intense (you can easily see this in Premiere Pro's Vectorscope).

- **Balance Gain:** Using this handle, you can fine-tune the Balance Gain and Balance Angle controls. Dragging the handle outward creates a less subtle, coarser effect; keeping the handle near the center creates a more subtle effect.

- **Balance Angle:** Clicking and dragging the control alters the color in the direction in which you point the handle.

- **Saturation slider:** Click and drag the Saturation slider to adjust color intensity for the overall image, or for the shadows, midtones, and highlights. Dragging the slider left toward 0.0 removes, or desaturates, colors (turning it into a grayscale version displaying luminance values). Dragging to the right intensifies saturation.

- **Auto Black Level:** Click the Auto Black Level button to increase black levels to above 7.5 IRE. This effectively clips, or cuts off, darker levels and proportionally redistributes pixel values, which usually lightens shadow areas.

- **Auto Contrast:** Clicking the Auto Contrast button has the same effect as applying both Auto Black Level and Auto White Level. In general, shadow areas are lightened and highlight areas are darkened. Clicking Auto Contrast can help add contrast to image areas.

- **Auto White Level:** Click the Auto White Level button to lower white levels so that no highlight areas are above 100 IRE. This effectively clips, or cuts off, white levels. When the pixel values are redistributed proportionally, the effect usually darkens highlight areas.

- **Black Level, White Level, Gray Level:** These controls provide adjustments similar to Auto Contrast, Auto White Level, and Auto Black Level, except that you can choose the level by clicking in your image or by clicking the swatch and choosing a color from the Adobe Color Picker. By setting black and white points, you can specify which areas should be the brightest and darkest image areas; thus, you can expand an image's tonal range. When you set a white or black point, you should click the lightest or darkest area that you want to maintain in the image. After you click, Premiere Pro adjusts the tonal range of the image based upon the new white point. For example, if you click a white area in your image, Premiere Pro makes all areas lighter than the white point white, and then remaps the pixels proportionally.

- **Levels:** Use the Levels controls to adjust contrast and brightness. Levels change the overall image, or the shadows, midtones, and highlights, depending upon which tonal range you select in the Tonal Range drop-down menu.

To change middle areas with little effect on the brightest and darkest image areas, click and drag the gamma Input slider. Drag to the left to darken the middle range area; drag to the right to lighten it.

As discussed in the Fast Color Corrector section, the Input and Output sliders indicate black and white points. The Input sliders designate white and black points in relation to the Output levels, which can range between 0 and 255. You can use the two sliders together to increase or decrease contrast in an image. For example, you can darken your image by dragging the black point Input slider to the right. If you reset the black point Input slider to 25, pixels that were 25 become 0 (black), shadows are darkened, and the number of shadow pixels increases. However, if you drag the black Output slider to the right to 25 or higher, you remap the image so that the new Output value is the darkest value in the image, thereby lightening it, as Premiere Pro remaps the pixels in the image accordingly.

Secondary Color Correction tools

The Secondary Color Correction tools provide controls to restrict color correction to a specific range or specific color in a clip. These controls, shown in Figure 17.8, allow you to pinpoint a specific color or tonal range to correct, without worrying that other ranges will be affected. Using the Secondary

Color Corrector, you can restrict color correction by specifying a hue, saturation, and luminance range. The Secondary Color Correction option appears in the Three-Way Color Corrector, Luma Correct, Luma Curve, RGB Color Corrector, RGB Curves, and Video Limiter effects.

FIGURE 17.8

The Secondary Color Correction controls

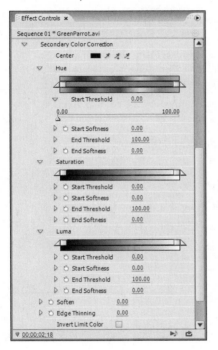

Follow these steps for using the Secondary Color Correction controls:

1. **Click the eyedropper icon, and select the color area in the image in the Program or Reference Monitor that you want to change.** You can also pick a color by clicking the color swatch and choosing a color in the Adobe Color Picker.

2. **Adjust the color range using one of the following techniques:**

   ▪ To extend the color range, click the eyedropper icon with the plus (+) sign.

   ▪ To subtract from the color range, click the eyedropper icon with the minus (-) sign.

   ▪ To expand the Hue control, start by clicking the Hue triangle to open the Hue slider. Then click the square Start and End Threshold sliders to specify the color range. Note that you can add to the colors that are visible in the Hue slider by clicking and dragging the colored area.

3. **To soften the difference between the color range that you want to correct and the adjacent areas, click and drag the Start and End Softness sliders.** You can also click and drag the triangles in the Hue slider.

4. **Adjust saturation and luminance ranges by clicking and dragging the Saturation and Luma controls.**

5. **Use Edge Thinning to fine-tune the effect.** Edge thinning can thin the edges of the color from a thin −100 to a very thin 100.

6. **If you want to adjust all colors except for the color range that you selected, choose Invert Limit Color.**

7. **To view a mask (flat black, white, and gray area) representing the color change, choose Mask in the Output drop-down menu.** A mask can make it easier to see just what image areas you are adjusting. When you choose Mask, the following occurs:

   - Black represents image areas that are completely changed by the color correction.

   - Gray represents partially changed image areas.

   - White represents the area that is not changed (masked out).

Luma Corrector

The Luma Corrector allows you to adjust a clip's luminance or brightness values. The Luma Corrector is shown in Figure 17.9. When using the Luma Corrector, you start by isolating the tonal range that you want to correct. You can then use the Luma Corrector's Definition controls to adjust brightness and contrast.

FIGURE 17.9

Use the Luma Corrector to adjust luminance values.

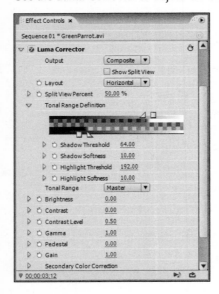

TIP To help you see the tonal range, you can click Tonal Range in the Output drop-down menu. This causes the Program or Reference Monitor to display the tonal range that will be affected by the Luma Corrector. After you establish the tonal range to correct, you can then switch the Output drop-down menu to either Composite or Luma.

These are the controls in the Luma Corrector:

- **Tonal Range Definition:** Click the triangle to view the Tonal Range Definition bar, and then click and drag to set the range of shadows, midtones, and highlights that you want to adjust. Clicking the squares controls shadow and highlight thresholds — the upper and lower limits of shadow and highlight areas. Clicking the triangles controls shadow and highlight softness — the drop-off between the affected and nonaffected areas. The softness sliders essentially allow a softer adjustment range. You can also use the sliders (described below) to set the tonal range for the correction.

  The following slider controls can be used to adjust the tonal range if you do not want to click and drag in the Tonal Range Definition bar to adjust the image areas to be affected by the Luma Corrector:

  - **Shadow Threshold:** Specifies the tonal range of shadows (darker areas).
  - **Shadow Softness:** Specifies the shadow tonal range with a soft edge.
  - **Highlight Threshold:** Adjusts the tonal range of highlights (bright image areas).
  - **Highlight Softness:** Determines the highlight's tonal range with a soft edge.

- **Tonal Range drop-down menu:** You can choose whether to apply the correction to the composite master image, highlights, midtones, or shadows.

The Definition controls allow you to set brightness and contrast, as follows:

- **Brightness:** Sets the black level in the clip. If blacks do not appear as black, try raising contrast.
- **Contrast:** Adjusts contrast based on the contrast level.
- **Contrast Level:** Sets the contrast level for adjusting Contrast control.
- **Gamma:** Primarily adjusts midtone levels. Thus, if an image is too dark or too light, but shadows and highlights are not too dark or too light, you should use the Gamma control.
- **Pedestal:** Adds a specific offset pixel value. Combined with Gain, the Pedestal can be used to brighten an image.
- **Gain:** Adjusts brightness values by multiplying pixel values. The result is to change the ratio of lighter to darker pixels; this has more of an effect on lighter pixels.

Luma Curve

Luma Curve allows you to make adjustments to a clip's luminance values by clicking and dragging a curve representing the clip's brightness values. The curve's x-axis represents the original image values, and the y-axis represents the values that are changed. Because all points are equal when you begin, the Luma Curve opens by displaying a straight diagonal line. The left end of the horizontal axis represents darker areas of the original image; brighter areas are represented on the right side of the horizontal axis.

To adjust midtones, click and drag in the middle of the curve. Click and drag up to lighten the image; click and drag down to darken it. To darken highlight areas, drag down on the top-right area of the curve. Dragging up the bottom-left area of the curve lightens shadows. Creating an S-shaped curve, as shown in Figure 17.10, can add contrast to an image.

FIGURE 17.10

Use the Luma Curve to adjust luminance values by clicking and dragging a curve.

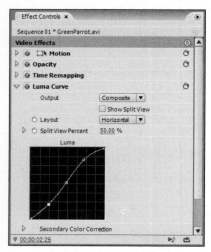

To fine-tune adjustments, you can click to create up to 16 anchor points on the curve by clicking it. You can then click and drag the anchor points or click and drag the area between anchor points. To remove an anchor point, click and drag it off the curve.

RGB Color Corrector

The RGB Color Corrector allows you to make adjustments to color and luminance using RGB values. As you can see from Figure 17.11, the RGB Color Corrector provides many of the same controls as the Luma Corrector, but adds RGB color controls:

- **Tonal Range Definition:** Click the triangle to view the Tonal Range Definition bar, and then click and drag to set the range for shadows, midtones, and highlights that you want to adjust. Clicking the squares controls shadow and highlight thresholds — the upper and lower limits of shadow and highlight areas. Clicking the triangles controls shadow and highlight softness — the drop-off between the affected and nonaffected areas. The softness sliders essentially allow a softer adjustment range. You can also use the slider controls (described below) to set the tonal range for the correction.

  The following slider controls can be used to adjust the tonal range if you do not want to click and drag in the Tonal Range Definition bar to adjust the image areas to be affected by the RGB Corrector:

  - **Shadow Threshold:** Specifies the tonal range of shadows (darker areas).
  - **Shadow Softness:** Specifies the shadow tonal range with a soft edge.
  - **Highlight Threshold:** Adjusts the tonal range of highlights (bright image areas).
  - **Highlight Softness:** Determines the highlight's tonal range with a soft edge.

- **Tonal Range:** Click in the Tonal Range drop-down menu to specify whether you want to apply the correction to the composite master image, highlights, midtones, or shadows.

The Definition controls allow you to set brightness and contrast:

- **Brightness:** Sets the black level in the clip. If blacks do not appear as black, try raising the contrast.
- **Contrast:** Adjusts contrast based on the contrast level.
- **Contrast Level:** Sets the contrast level for adjusting the Contrast control.
- **Gamma:** Primarily adjusts the midtone levels. For example, if an image is too dark or too light, but shadows and highlights are not too dark or too light, you can use the Gamma control.
- **Pedestal:** Adds a specific offset pixel value. Combined with Gain, the Pedestal can be used to brighten an image.
- **Gain:** Adjusts brightness values by multiplying pixel values. The result is to change the ratio of lighter to darker pixels, although it has more of an effect on lighter pixels.
- **RGB:** Click the RGB triangle to expand and view the RGB sliders. These sliders control Gamma, Pedestal, and Gain for the red, green, and blue color channels in the clip.

Use the RGB Color Corrector to specify a tonal range and correct color using RGB controls.

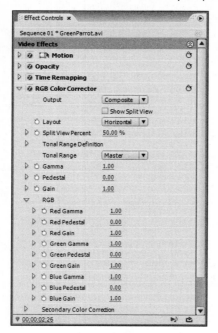

RGB Curves

The RGB Curves effect allows you to adjust RGB Color values using curves. In the Curves effect, shown in Figure 17.12, the x-axis of the dialog box represents the original image values, and the y-axis represents the values that are changed. Because all points are equal when you begin, the Curves dialog box opens by displaying four diagonal lines.

The left side of the horizontal axis of each curve represents darker areas of the original image; brighter areas are represented on the right side of the horizontal axis.

To lighten an image area, click and drag up on a curve; to darken an area, click and drag down. As you drag, the curve shows how the rest of the pixels in the image change. To prevent part of the curve from changing, you can click the curve to establish anchor points. As you click and drag, the anchor points lock down the curve. If you want to delete an anchor point, drag it off the curve.

If you click and drag a curve representing a channel, dragging upward increases that channel's color in the image, whereas dragging downward reduces it and adds that color's complement. For example, dragging up on the green channel adds more green, and dragging down on the curve adds more magenta.

FIGURE 17.12

Use the RGB Curves effect to adjust RGB values by clicking and dragging a curve.

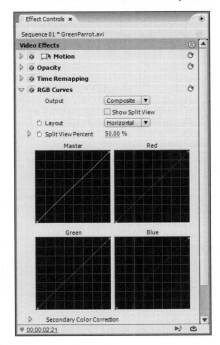

Video Limiter

Use the Video Limiter effect after color correcting to ensure that the video falls within specific limits. You can set limits for a clip's overall signal, chroma, or both luminance and chroma. Like the Luma Corrector and RGB Color Corrector, the Video Limiter effect allows you to target the effect to a specific tonal range. The Video Limiter, shown in Figure 17.13, provides the following options:

- **Reduction Axis:** Use the reduction axis to choose which part of the video signal to limit: Luminance, Chroma, Chroma and Luminance, or overall video Signal (Smart Limit).

- **Signal Min and Signal Max:** After you choose a reduction axis, the Signal Min and Signal Max sliders change based upon the reduction axis. Thus, if you choose Luminance in the reduction axis, you can set minimum and maximum values for luminance.

- **Reduction Method:** Use Reduction Method to choose a specific tonal range to compress: Highlights, Midtones, Shadows, or Compress All. Choosing a reduction method can help keep images sharp in specific image areas.

- **Tonal Range Definition:** Click the triangle to view the Tonal Range Definition bar, and then click and drag to set the range for shadows, midtones, and highlights that you want to adjust. Clicking the squares controls shadow and highlight thresholds–the upper and lower limits of shadow and highlight areas. Clicking the triangles controls shadow and highlight softness — the drop-off between the affected and nonaffected areas. The softness sliders essentially allow a softer adjustment range. You can also use the slider controls (described below) to set the tonal range for the correction.

The following slider controls can be used to adjust the tonal range if you do not want to click and drag in the Tonal Range Definition bar to adjust the image areas to be affected by the Luma Corrector:

- **Shadow Threshold:** Specifies the tonal range of shadows (darker areas).
- **Shadow Softness:** Specifies the shadow tonal range with a soft edge.
- **Highlight Threshold:** Adjusts the tonal range of highlights (bright image areas).
- **Highlight Softness:** Determines the highlight's tonal range with a soft edge.

FIGURE 17.13

Use the Video Limiter to set limits for a clip's overall signal, chroma, or both luminance and chroma.

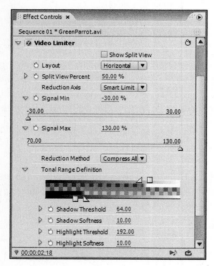

More Color Correction tools

This section covers some of the other video effects in the Color Correction bin (folder).

Balancing colors with the Color Balance (RGB) effect

The Color Balance effect allows you to change the shadows, midtones, and highlights of a clip's red, green, and blue color channels. When you work with red, green, and blue channels, RGB color theory applies. This means that when you increase a color's value, you add more of its color to the clip; when you decrease the color's value, you reduce the color and add more of its complement color. Remember that red's complement color is cyan, green's complement color is magenta, and blue's complement color is yellow.

Using HLS Color Balance

Although the RGB color model is used by computer displays to create colors, it's not very intuitive. Many users find the HLS color model to be more intuitive. As discussed earlier, *hue* is the color, *saturation* is the color intensity, and *lightness* is the brightness or darkness of the color.

To use the HLS Color Balance effect, start by clicking and dragging the Hue circular control (or drag over the numerical readout) to choose a color, as shown in Figure 17.14.

FIGURE 17.14

The HLS Color Balance effect enables you to adjust color balance using Hue, Saturation, and Lightness controls.

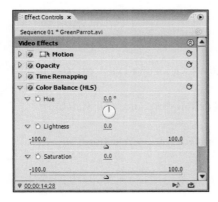

 If you want to enter a precise number for a slider, click any numerical value above the slider. Doing so opens a dialog box in which you can enter a specific value.

The best way to see the effect of the changing hues is to add saturation to your image. Click and drag the Saturation slider to the right. To see the effect of the Lightness slider, click and drag to the right to add more light to the image, and then drag to the left to reduce the amount of light.

The Change Color effect

The Change Color effect, shown in Figure 17.15, allows you to change the hue, saturation, and lightness of a specific color or color area. You can follow these general steps to correct a clip using the Change Color effect:

FIGURE 17.15

The Change Color effect changes colors in a specific area.

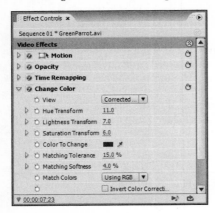

1. **Select the Color To Change eyedropper icon.** Click in the image to take a sample of the color area that you want to change.

2. **Choose Color Correction Mask in the View drop-down menu to view the area that will be affected when you adjust colors.**

3. **Adjust the color range in the mask using the Matching Tolerance and Matching Softness sliders.**

4. **Use the Hue Transform, Lightness Transform, and Saturation Transform sliders to adjust the colors in your clip.**

Here is an overview of the Change Color controls:

- **View:** Choose either Corrected Layer or Color Correction Mask. Corrected Layer displays your image as you correct it. Color Correction Mask displays a black-and-white mask representing the area to be corrected. White areas are the areas that will be affected by color adjustments. Figure 17.16 shows the mask.

- **Hue Transform:** Click and drag to adjust the hue of the colors to be applied. The degree slider simulates a color wheel.

- **Lightness Transform:** This control increases or decreases color lightness. Use positive values to brighten the image, and negative values to darken it.

- **Saturation Transform:** This control increases and decreases color intensity. You can achieve some interesting effects by desaturating only a specific image area (drag the Saturation slider to the left), which can make a portion of your image gray and the rest color.

■ **Color To Change:** Use the Eyedropper tool to click in your image to choose the color that you want to change, or click the swatch to pick a color using the Adobe Color Picker.

The Color Correction Mask displays image areas that will be altered by the Change Color effect.

■ **Matching Tolerance:** This item controls the similarity of colors (based on the Color To Change) that will be adjusted. Choose a low tolerance to affect colors that are similar to the Color To Change. If you choose a high tolerance value, larger areas of the image will be affected.

■ **Matching Softness:** Clicking and dragging to the right generally softens the color correction mask. This control can also soften the look of the actual correction.

■ **Match Colors:** Choose a method for matching colors in this drop-down menu. The choices are Using RGB, Using Hue, and Using Chroma. RGB matches RGB values; Hue matches Hue, which means that shades of a specific color are affected; Chroma matches using saturation and hue, and thus ignores lightness.

■ **Invert Color Correction Mask:** Click this check box to reverse the mask. When the mask is reversed, black areas in the mask are affected by the color correction, rather than the lighter areas of the mask.

The Change to Color effect

The Change to Color effect allows you to quickly change a selected color to another using hue, saturation, and lightness. When you change a color, other colors are not affected. Here is an overview of the Change to Color options, shown in Figure 17.17:

- **From:** Click the From eyedropper icon to select the color area that you want to change, or click the swatch to choose a color using the Adobe Color Picker.

- **To:** Click the area in the image that you want to use as the final, corrected color, or click the swatch to choose a color using the Adobe Color Picker.

- **Change:** Choose which combination of HLS values you want to affect. Your choices include the following: Hue; Hue and Lightness; Hue and Saturation; and Hue, Lightness, and Saturation.

- **Change By:** The Change By choices are Setting to Color or Transforming to Color. Choose Setting to Color to change the color directly without any interpolation. Choose Transforming to Color to base the color change on the difference between the From and To pixel values, as well as the Tolerance value.

- **Tolerance:** Expanding the Tolerance slider allows you to control the color range that will be changed based upon hue, lightness, and saturation values. Higher values expand the image range that will be changed, and lower values reduce the range. You can see the range to be changed by clicking View Color Correction Matte.

- **Softness:** Click and drag to the right to create smoother transitions between the From and To colors.

- **View Correction Matte:** Click to display a black-and-white mask in the Program or Reference Monitor. This allows you to clearly see which image areas will be affected by the Change to Color effect. White areas are affected, black areas are not, and gray areas are partially affected.

FIGURE 17.17

Use the Change to Color effect to change a selected color to another color.

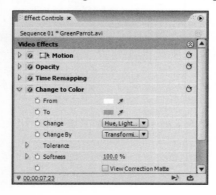

Changing brightness and contrast

The Brightness and Contrast effect is one of the easiest image effects to use. Brightness controls the light levels in your image, while contrast is the difference between the brightest and darkest levels. As with other effects, to use Brightness and Contrast, you must drag the effect from the Video

Effects panel over the clip that you want to adjust. Take a moment to experiment with each of the Brightness and Contrast settings:

- **Brightness:** To increase overall brightness in your clip, click and drag the Brightness slider to the right. As you drag, the entire image lightens. To decrease brightness, click and drag to the left. As you drag, the entire clip becomes darker.

- **Contrast:** To see the effect of the Contrast slider, first click and drag the slider to the right. As you drag, you add contrast, increasing the difference between the lightest and darkest areas of your image. This also tends to create a sharper image. To decrease sharpness, click and drag to the left. As you drag, the entire clip begins to fade out.

Using other Color Correction effects

These other effects in the Color Correction bin affect a video clip's color:

- **Broadcast Colors:** If you are outputting your production to videotape, you may want to run the Broadcast Colors effect to improve color output quality.
- **Channel Mixer:** This effect allows you to create sepia tone or tint effects.
- **Equalize:** This effect redistributes brightness values in an image.
- **Leave Color:** This effect turns an entire color image into grayscale with the exception of one color.
- **Tint:** This effect allows you to add a tint color to your image.

 **For more information about these effects, see Chapter 13.**

The Adjust effects

The video effects in the Adjust bin (folder) are Auto Color, Auto Contrast, Auto Levels, Convolution Kernel, Extract, Levels, Lighting Effects, ProAmp, and Shadow/Highlight.

Changing levels

The Levels effect can be used for fine-tuning shadows (dark image areas), midtones (mid-level image areas), and highlights (light image areas). Using levels, you can correct the red, green, and blue channels simultaneously or individually. The Levels effect in the Adjust bin is virtually identical to the Levels command found in Adobe Photoshop. To display the Levels Settings dialog box, shown in Figure 17.18, click the Setup button in the Effect Controls panel (the Setup button looks like a tiny dialog box).

In the Levels Settings dialog box, Premiere Pro displays a histogram of the image. The histogram is a chart that provides a graphical representation of the brightness levels of the pixels in your image. Darker pixel levels are represented at the left side of the histogram, and brighter levels are represented at the right side of the histogram. The taller the level line is in the histogram, the larger the number of pixels that occur at that brightness level. The lower the level line is, the fewer the number of pixels that occur at that brightness level.

FIGURE 17.18

Premiere Pro's Levels Settings dialog box enables you to adjust shadows, midtones, and highlights.

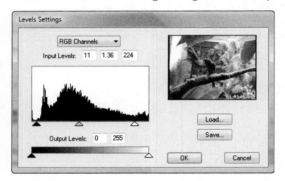

Use the Levels controls to adjust contrast and brightness. The outer markers on the Input and Output sliders indicate black and white points. The Input sliders designate white and black points in relation to the Output levels. The Input and Output range is from 0 to 255. You can use the two sliders together to increase or decrease contrast in an image. If you want to lighten a dark image, click and drag the white Input slider to the left. Here's how it works: If you reset the white Input slider to 230, pixels that were 230 (as well as those lighter than 230) become 255 (white); highlights are brightened, and the number of highlight pixels increases. However, if you drag the white Output slider to the left, you darken the image. If you drag this slider to 230, any pixels that were white (255) are now 230 and the image is remapped accordingly. Thus, any pixels that were 230 are darker, as well.

If you drag the black Input slider right to 25, pixels that were 25 become 0 (black); shadows are darkened, and the number of shadow pixels increases. If you drag the black Output slider to the right to 25 or higher, you remap the image so that the new Output value is the darkest value in the image, thereby lightening it, and Premiere Pro remaps the pixels in the image accordingly.

To change midtones with little effect on the highlights and shadows, click and drag the gamma Input slider. In general, it's often best to start correcting using the Midtone slider — drag to the right to lighten midtones, and drag to the left to darken midtones.

Changing channel levels

The Levels Settings dialog box also enables you to change levels for individual red, green, and blue channels. For example, to add contrast to the red channel, choose Red from the drop-down menu in the Levels Settings dialog box. When you pick a channel, the histogram displays changes to show you the pixel distribution of colors for only that channel. As you click and drag the highlight slider, you can increase contrast in the red channel. By clicking and dragging the Output slider, you can reduce contrast in the red channel.

TIP If you frequently use the same Levels settings, you can save them to disk by clicking the Save button in the Levels Settings dialog box. You can reload your settings by clicking the Load button.

Using other Adjust effects

These other effects in the Adjust bin affect a video clip's color:

- **Auto Color, Auto Contrast, Auto Levels:** Use these effects to have Premiere Pro perform a quick overall color correction.

- **Convolution Kernel:** Use this effect to change the brightness and sharpness of your image.

- **Extract:** This effect enables you to convert your color clip to black and white.

- **Lighting Effects:** This effect allows you to add lighting to your image.

- **ProAmp:** This effect enables you to adjust the hue, saturation, and luminance of a clip.

- **Shadow/Highlight:** You can use this effect on images with backlighting problems. It brightens shadows and reduces highlights.

CROSS-REF For more information about these effects, see Chapter 13.

The Image Control effects

Premiere Pro provides even more color effects in the Image Control bin (folder). The effects in the Image Control bin are Black & White, Change to Color HLSColor Balance (RGB), Color Match, Color Pass, Color Replace, and Gamma Correction. This section covers the Image Control effects used for correcting colors. (For more information on other Image Control effects, see Chapter 13.)

Balancing colors with the Color Balance (RGB) effect

The Color Balance (RGB) effect enables you to change the balance of a clip's red, green, and blue color channels. As you work with this effect, you put RGB color theory into practice. Here's how the red, green, and blue sliders work:

- **Click and drag the red slider to the right.** As you drag, you gradually increase red in your image. Drag the slider to the left to decrease red. Note that as you reduce red, you increase cyan. Cyan is added because you now have more green and blue in your image. To increase cyan, you can also click and drag both the green and blue sliders to the right.

- **Click and drag the green slider to the right.** As you drag, you increase green in your image. Drag to the left to decrease green. As you reduce green, you add magenta. Magenta is added because you have more red and blue in your image than green. To add more magenta, click and drag both the red and blue sliders to the right.

- **Click and drag the blue slider to the right.** As you drag, you increase blue in your image. Drag to the left to decrease blue. As you reduce blue, you add yellow. Yellow is added because you have more red and green in your image. You can add even more yellow by clicking and dragging both the red and green sliders to the right.

Color Match

The Color Match effect, shown in Figure 17.19, allows you to match colors, highlights, midtones, or shadows in one clip with the color in another. This effect allows you to copy the color or color tones in one clip to another so that the two clips match when edited together. You can match two colors within the Program Monitor or match a color in the Source Monitor with a color in the Program Monitor. Before applying the effect, select the clip that you want to adjust in the Timeline, and then drag the Color Match effect over it. If you are matching a color in a Source clip, display it in the Source Monitor.

FIGURE 17.19

Premiere Pro's Color Match effect allows you to match the colors in one clip with colors in another.

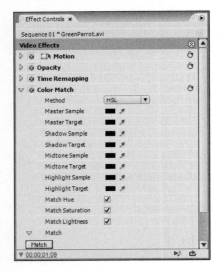

Follow these steps for using Color Match in the Effect Controls panel:

1. **Start by choosing a selection in the Method drop-down menu.** The choices include HLS, RGB, and Curves. HLS allows you to apply the effect to different HLS values, RGB allows you to apply the effect to one or a combination of color channels, and Curves allows you to match color using brightness and contrast.

2. **Select the Sample color (the color you want to match) by choosing a Sample eye-dropper and clicking in the Source or Program Monitor.** You can pick a Master Sample, or you can choose to match shadows, midtones, highlights, hue, saturation, or lightness.

3. **Select the Target color (the color you want to change or correct) by selecting a Target eyedropper and clicking in the Source or Program Monitor.** You can pick a

Master Target, or you can choose to match shadows, midtones, highlights, hue, saturation, or lightness. Note that the Target control you select should correspond with the Sample control. For example, if you pick a Highlight Sample, you should pick a Highlight Target.

4. **You can also choose to include or exclude any combination of HLS or RGB values by selecting or deselecting the HLS and RGB check boxes.**

5. **When you are ready to match colors or color components, display the Match button by clicking the triangle in the Match section.** Click the Match button.

Gamma Correction

The Gamma Correction effect changes midtones with little or no effect on shadows and highlights. In the Gamma Correction Settings dialog box, simply click and drag the slider. As you click and drag to the right, you increase gamma, thereby darkening your image. By clicking and dragging to the left, you decrease gamma, thereby lightening the midtones.

Using other Image Control effects

You can use these other Image Control effects to affect a video clip's color:

■ **Black & White:** This effect turns a color image into a grayscale image.

■ **Color Pass:** You can use this effect to convert all but one color of a clip to grayscale.

■ **Color Replace:** This effect replaces one color range with another.

 For more information about these effects, see Chapter 13.

Using Stylize effects

These effects in the Stylize bin affect a video clip's color:

■ **Color Emboss, Emboss:** Embossing a clip creates a raised 3-D effect from image edge areas.

■ **Find Edges:** This effect can make the image in a clip look as if it is a black-and-white sketch.

■ **Mosaic:** This effect turns your image areas into rectangular tiles.

■ **Posterize:** This effect enables you to reduce the number of gray levels in your image.

■ **Solarize:** This effect creates a positive and negative version of your image and then blends them together.

■ **Threshold:** This effect creates a black-and-white image.

CROSS-REF For more information about these effects, see Chapter 13.

Retouch Using After Effects and Photoshop

Sometimes in a video clip, you may want to remove from or add to image areas. You can use either Photoshop CS3 or After Effects CS3 to do this. Both applications have a powerful Clone Stamp tool that allows you to easily and seamlessly remove unwanted items from your video. The Rubber Stamp tool allows you to choose image areas where you want to cover up or replace unwanted items. Both applications also have some powerful painting tools that allow you to paint out image areas or add to your image.

Which program you use depends on your final output. If you are going to output your final product onto paper, such as a photograph, you probably want to use Photoshop. If you want to do more video editing, you probably want to use After Effects. In either case, you can start in Premiere Pro, and then work your way to Photoshop or After Effects.

Figure 17.20 shows a frame of a video clip of a mother and father with their little girl (FilmDisc FA0106 video clip). The mother wants herself and her little girl to be the stars of the show, so you can use the Rubber Stamp tool in After Effects and in Photoshop to remove Dad.

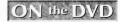 The video clip used in this example is from FilmDisc fa0106). It is in the FilmDisc folder in the Tutorial Projects folder on the DVD that accompanies this book.

FIGURE 17.20

A frame from a video clip to be retouched

Trimming out unwanted areas in Premiere Pro

Before you start retouching in either Photoshop or After Effects, you might first want to trim out unwanted areas of your video clip using Premiere Pro. Premiere Pro's Razor tool is a quick and easy way to trim a clip. For more information on editing clips, turn to Chapters 6 and 12.

In this example, the Razor tool is used to trim the beginning and end of the video clip (shown in Figure 17.20) while you keep the middle part. Figure 17.21 shows the two places where the video clip is cut. To trim the beginning of the clip, move the Timeline marker (current-time indicator) to the six-second mark and then make an incision with the Razor tool. To trim the end of the clip, move the Timeline marker (current-time indicator) to the 14.5-second mark and then make an incision with the Razor tool. Next, use the Selection tool to select the beginning and ending, and then press the Delete key to delete them. You are now left with only the middle part of the video clip to work with (shown in Figure 17.22).

FIGURE 17.21

You can use the Razor tool to cut the video clip in the Timeline panel.

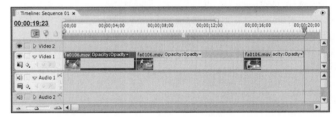

FIGURE 17.22

You can retouch the trimmed video clip in After Effects and Photoshop.

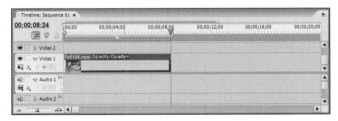

Exporting Premiere Pro clips to After Effects and Photoshop

Once you have trimmed your video clip in Premiere Pro, you can export it to After Effects or Photoshop for retouching. You need to export your trimmed clip as a movie to import it into Photoshop CS3. To import your trimmed video clip into After Effects CS3, all you need to do is copy and paste it.

Here are the steps to copying and pasting a video clip from Premiere Pro to After Effects:

1. **In Premiere Pro, select the video clip in the Timeline panel.** Then choose Edit ➪ Copy.

2. **Launch After Effects.** Create a new composition, by choosing Composition ➪ New Composition. In the Composition Settings dialog box, ensure that the preset matches that of the Premiere Pro video clip. In this example, it is NSTC DV.

3. **Select the Timeline panel in After Effects, and then choose Edit ➪ Paste.** The Premiere Pro video clip appears in the Timeline panel of After Effects, as shown in Figure 17.23.

 You can import a Premiere Pro project into After Effects, and vice versa, by using the File ➪ Import command.

FIGURE 17.23

The After Effects Timeline panel with a video clip from Premiere Pro

Here are the steps to export a video clip from Premiere Pro to Photoshop:

1. **In Premiere Pro, select the video clip in the Timeline panel.** Then choose File ➪ Export ➪ Movie. In the dialog box that appears, name your movie. By default, the movie is named Sequence 01.avi. To change the movie type, click the Settings button to load the Export Movie Settings dialog box. Click the File Type drop-down menu to change the file type.

Then click the Range drop-down menu and choose Work Area Bar rather than Entire Sequence. Deselect the Export Audio option if you have no audio to export. Then click OK.

Locate a place to store your movie, and then click Save. Wait a minute while Premiere Pro renders your movie. After the movie is rendered, it is saved to your hard drive and placed in the Project panel of the Premiere Pro project that you are working on, as shown in Figure 17.24. To view and play the Premiere Pro movie in the Source panel, double-click it in the Project panel.

FIGURE 17.24

You can edit the Premiere Pro movie in Photoshop.

2. **To import the Premiere Pro movie into Photoshop, first launch Photoshop.** Then choose File ➪ Import ➪ Video Frames To Layers. In the Load dialog box that appears, locate the Premiere Pro video clip that you want to import into Photoshop. Then click Load.

3. **In the Import Video To Layers dialog box (shown in Figure 17.25), you can choose the range of video frames you want to import.** Click the Selected Range Only option and hold the Shift key while you choose the range of frames you want to import. Then click OK to import the Premiere Pro video frames into Photoshop's Animation and Layers panels, as shown in Figure 17.26.

4. **In Photoshop, you can display all the panels that you need to work in Video mode.** Set the workspace to video and film by choosing Window ➪ Workspace ➪ Video&Film.

FIGURE 17.25

Photoshop's Import Video To Layers dialog box allows you to choose the number of frames you want to import.

FIGURE 17.26

When Premiere Pro's video frames are imported into Photoshop, they appear in the Animation and Layers panels.

Retouch using the After Effects Clone Stamp tool

To use the After Effects Clone Stamp tool for retouching, double-click the video clip that needs retouching in the Timeline panel. This displays the video clip in the Layer panel. With the Workspace set to Standard, you should find the tools below the menus. Click the Clone Stamp tool, located between the Paintbrush and Eraser tools. Then move it next to the unwanted item. Find an area that you can click and use to cover up the unwanted item. In this example, an area in the water is selected next to dad. You can use the adjoining water area to paint water over dad's image in order to remove him from the clip.

Now that you have found the area that you want to use with your Clone Stamp tool, Alt/Option-click this area. Before you start using the Clone Stamp tool, pick a brush from the Brush Tips panel and an opacity and flow percentage from the Paint panel. Then start cloning over the unwanted item. You may need to click a few different times in different areas to get the desired look. You also may need to change brush size and opacity. In the clip in this example, you need to click different water areas to properly remove dad from the scene. You also need to click the pink floating device to use it to cover up dad's hands. Figure 17.27 shows a frame before, while, and after being retouched.

Remember that when you are retouching, it is a good idea to have a backup of your original file so that if you make a mistake you can always go back to the original file. The Undo command only gets you so far. In this example, the original clip is called *Retouching* and the retouched clip is named *Retouched*. That way, you can always go back to your original clip if you make a mistake that you cannot undo. As you work, don't forget to save your file. You can preview your work by moving the Timeline marker or by choosing Composition ➪ Preview ➪ Ram Preview. To render your movie, choose Composition ➪ Make Movie. Choose the settings you want, and then click Render.

When you are done retouching, you may decide to add some text to your clip. For information on working with type in After Effects, turn to Chapter 32.

CROSS-REF You might also want to try using the After Effects masking tools to mask out unwanted areas from a video clip. For information on using masking tools in After Effects, turn to Chapter 31.

Retouch with the Photoshop Selection and Clone Stamp tool

After you have loaded the movie that you want to retouch into Photoshop CS3, choose Window ➪ Workspace ➪ Video&Film. Before you begin retouching in Photoshop, you should always make a copy of the original file. That way, if you make a mistake that cannot be reverted, you can always go to the original source file. To create a backup of your original file, choose File ➪ Save As and change the name of the file to a name such as *FinalRetouched*. Remember to save your work as you make changes.

FIGURE 17.27

A frame in After Effects before, during, and after retouching. The video clip is FilmDisc fa0106.

It is now time to use the Selection tools or the Quick Mask option to create a selection around the area that you want to retouch. This way, only that area is affected. In Figure 17.28, the Polygonal Lasso tool is used to create a selection around dad in Frame 1.

After the selection is created, you can save it by choosing Select ➪ Save Selection. In the Save Selection dialog box, set the Channel option to New and then click OK. Any time you want to load the selection, simply select Load ➪ Selection. In the Load Selection dialog box, click the Channel drop-down menu and choose Alpha 1.

With the selection onscreen, you can use the Clone Stamp tool to clone over dad using adjacent water pixels. Alt/Option-click to select the adjacent area that you want to work with. Then pick a brush size, opacity, and flow, and start cloning. When you are done cloning, copy the selection by choosing Edit ➪ Copy. This stores the copied area into the Clipboard. The copied area can be used on the following frames to save time in retouching.

The Polygonal Lasso tool is used to make a selection around dad. The video clip is FilmDisc FA0106.

Here's how to use a copied selection on frames to save time when retouching:

1. **First make a selection of the area that you need to retouch in Frame 1.** Then use the Clone Stamp tool to retouch within the selection in Frame 1. When you are done retouching, choose Edit ➪ Copy.

2. **With the copied and retouched selection from Frame 1 in the Clipboard, move to Frame 2.** Do this by clicking Frame 2 in the Animation panel and clicking Layer 2 in the Layers panel.

3. **Choose Edit ⇨ Paste.** Use the Move tool to move the selection into its desired location. Then choose Merge Down from the Layers panel menu to merge the pasted layer onto the frame you are working on. Now use the Clone Stamp tool to fine-tune the selection.

4. **Continue to the next frame by clicking it in the Animation panel and by clicking the matching layer in the Layers panel.** Then repeat step 3. Continue this procedure until you are done retouching your animation. Figure 17.29 shows the results of the retouched project.

FIGURE 17.29

The results of the retouched project. The video clip is FilmDisc FA0106.

5. **To export your retouched movie project, choose File ⇨ Export ⇨ Render Video.** In the Render Video dialog box, shown in Figure 17.30, choose your settings and then click Render.

FIGURE 17.30

Photoshop's Render Video dialog box allows you to output your animation as a movie.

Summary

If your video clips need color correction or if they need brightness or contrast enhanced, you can use Adobe Premiere Pro's Video Effects. The Color Correction, Adjust, and Image Control bins (folders) all contain effects that can enhance video. This chapter covered these topics:

- You can view Premiere Pro scopes in a Reference Monitor while you correct video clips.
- To quickly adjust hue and luminance, you can use the Fast Color Corrector in the Color Correction bin.
- To correct luminance, you can use the Luma Corrector or Luma Curves in the Color Correction bin.
- You can use the Video Limiter effect to ensure that the video falls within specific limits.
- To match a color in one clip with another, you can use the Color Match effect.
- You can retouch a video clip to add and enhance the video or to remove unwanted image areas.

Part V

Outputting Digital Video

Chapter 18

Exporting to DVD, MPEG, AVI, and QuickTime

After you complete the finishing touches on your Adobe Premiere Pro project, you're ready to export the production as a digital file. When you export the file, you can output it to DVD, CD, or videotape, or you can export it to disk for viewing on another computer system. If you export your Premiere Pro project as a QuickTime, Video for Windows (AVI), or MPEG file, you can easily view it on most Macs and PCs by simply double-clicking the exported video movie.

Movies saved in QuickTime or Video for Windows can be integrated into other multimedia programs, such as Adobe After Effects, Macromedia Director, or Adobe Flash. MPEG1 files can be used on the Web. The Hollywood movies and music videos you see on DVD are encoded in MPEG2 format before the DVD is burned. Because DVD is becoming the most popular vehicle for viewing film and video productions, video producers and editors will undoubtedly be most interested in using Premiere Pro's DVD-creation capabilities — particularly because Adobe Encore CS3, a sophisticated DVD-authoring program, is now included as part of the Adobe Premier Pro CS3 package (Chapters 26 and 27 cover how to create DVDs using Adobe Encore).

This chapter explains how to export Premiere Pro projects to Encore, MPEG format, QuickTime, and Video for Windows. It covers the simple steps you need to follow to begin the export process, and then focuses on export settings, such as choosing a compressor, keyframes, and data rates.

CROSS-REF In this book, exporting Premiere Pro project is divided into different chapters. This chapter covers exporting DVD, MPEG, QuickTime, and Video for Windows. Chapter 19 covers Web file formats. Chapter 20 discusses how to export your Premiere Pro project using the Advanced Windows Media and RealVideo Export plug-ins. Chapter 21 covers exporting to videotape.

IN THIS CHAPTER

Using DVD markers

Exporting to Adobe Encore

Exporting in AVI and QuickTime

Changing export settings

Changing video settings

Changing audio settings

Using DVD Markers

Premiere Pro's Encore chapter markers streamline the process of authoring interactive DVDs. Premiere Pro's Encore markers appear as chapter markers in Encore, and can be used as the destination for navigational links. Thus, Premiere Pro's Encore chapter markers can help you organize a DVD project while you're developing it.

Creating DVD chapter markers

To create DVD chapter markers in Premiere Pro, you set Encore chapter markers along the Timeline of your project. Because you don't want to keep resetting your DVD markers, it is most efficient to create DVD markers when you have completed your production. As you create markers, they can be easily edited, and Encore allows you to preview your production before you burn a DVD.

Follow these steps for creating Encore chapter markers:

1. **Open the Timeline panel.**

 2. **In the Timeline, move the current-time indicator to where you want to create an Encore chapter marker.** Then click the DVD icon in the Timeline. This opens the Encore Chapter Marker dialog box, shown in Figure 18.1.

FIGURE 18.1

Use the Encore Chapter Marker dialog box to create chapter markers in Encore.

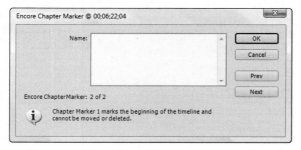

> **NOTE** Premiere Pro automatically creates a Chapter Marker 1 to indicate the beginning of the Encore Timeline. This marker cannot be edited. In Encore, the Play button on the menu template automatically starts at Chapter 1.

> **TIP** You can also quickly create a DVD marker at the current-time indicator by choosing Marker ⇨ Set DVD Marker, or by right-clicking/Control-clicking the Timeline and choosing Set Encore Marker from the drop-down menu that appears. This creates a DVD marker without opening the Encore Chapter Marker dialog box, so it's a quick technique for adding markers.

3. **Enter a short name for your marker.**

Moving, editing, and deleting markers

If you want to move an Encore chapter marker, simply click and drag it to the position where you want it on the Timeline. To quickly move to an Encore chapter marker, right-click/Control-click at the top of the Timeline (on the time tick marks), choose Go To Encore Chapter Marker from the drop-down menu that appears, then choose Next or Previous from the drop-down menu that appears. Alternatively, you can choose Marker ⇨ Go to Encore Chapter Marker (from Premiere Pros menu bar), and then choose Next or Previous from the drop-down menu that appears.

If you want to edit the button, double-click the marker on the Timeline. This opens the Encore Chapter Marker dialog box. You can also move to an Encore chapter marker and choose Marker ⇨ Edit Encore Chapter Marker.

If you want to delete a marker, you have several options. Perhaps the easiest is to right-click/Control-click the marker and choose Clear Encore Chapter Marker, or Clear All Encore Chapter Markers from the menu that appears. Alternatively, you can choose Marker ⇨ Clear Encore Chapter Marker, and then choose either Encore Chapter Marker at Current Time Indicator, or All Chapter Markers.

Exporting to Adobe Encore

If you want to export your Premiere Pro project to DVD, you can export it to Encore either for authoring or to burn it. If you export for authoring in Encore, Premiere Pro exports MPEG2 files for audio and video, places the audio and video MPEG files into the Encore Project panel, and creates a Timeline for your project in Encore with the MPEG files in it. If you export the file to Encore for burning only, Encore creates an auto-play DVD that automatically plays without a menu.

When you export, you can choose from among several DVD format types. For example, you can export to a single-sided 4.7GB disc, or a double-layer disc, which stores more data but requires a double-layer DVD disc. You can also export to one of two Blu-ray single-disc layer formats: MPEG2 or H.264. If your DVD recorder is not compatible with Encore, you can use one of Encore's Burn options to save to a disc folder, and then use your DVD recorder's software to burn the DVD.

What Is Blu-ray?

Blu-ray is a new high-definition DVD disc format that was developed by the Blu-ray Disc association, which is composed of companies such as Sony, Panasonic, Pioneer, Samsung, Sharp, TDK, JVC, Apple, and Dell. The format provides more than five times the storage capacity of the standard 4.7GB single-layer DVD. (A dual-layer Blu-ray disc can store 50GB, which can provide up to 9 hours of high-definition content, or 23 hours of standard-definition content.) The format is called Blu-ray because it reads and writes data using a blue-violet laser instead of the traditional red laser. Blu-ray supports an enhanced MPEG2 standard for high definition as well as MPEG4 and H.264. It supports all of the audio codes of traditional DVDs as well as Dolby TrueHD.

 DVD+R and DVD-R are competing DVD recording formats. DVD+RW and DVD-RW are competing rewritable DVD formats.

Follow these steps for exporting to Encore from Premiere Pro:

1. **Select the Timeline panel that includes the sequence that you want to export to Encore.**

2. **Choose File ⇨ Export to Encore.**

3. **In the Export to Encore dialog box, shown in Figure 18.2, select the options for creating your DVD.**

   ▦ Enter a name for your disc in the Name field (not required).

   ▦ Choose a DVD format in the Type drop-down menu:

   DVD Single layer stores 4.7GB

   DVD Double layer stores 8.5GB

   Blu-ray Disc Single-layer MPEG2 stores 25GB

   Blu-ray Disc Single-layer H.264 stores 25GB

   ▦ If you want to burn the disc in Encore, select Direct Burn without Menus. This creates an auto-play disc without menus. If you choose this option, you need to place a DVD disc in your DVD burner. To export your Premiere Pro files and open Encore, select Author with Menus.

   ▦ If you are burning a disc, enter the number of copies you want to burn.

   ▦ In the Export Range drop-down menu, choose whether you want to export the entire sequence or the work area.

   ▦ To loop playback, so that the DVD continually repeats, click Loop Playback.

   ▦ If you want to change the encoding settings, click Settings (DVD encoding settings are discussed in the next section).

4. **Click OK.** Premiere Pro opens the Save As dialog box.

5. **Enter a name for the MPEG files in the Save As dialog box. Click Save.**

After rendering the files, Premiere Pro opens Encore. If you chose the Author with Menus option, it places your Premiere Pro files in the Project panel, and places the files in a Timeline in the Timeline panel.

 Adobe provides an excellent primer on the DVD format. To view it, go to www.adobe.com/go/learn_dv_primer_dvd.

FIGURE 18.2

Use the Export to Encore dialog box to export a Premiere Pro sequence to Encore for DVD burning or authoring.

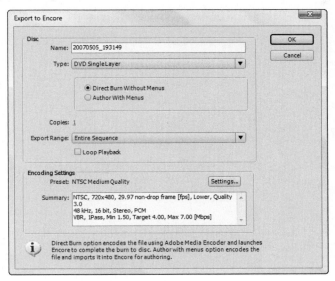

Using the Adobe Media Encoder

Adobe's Media Encoder provides an efficient means of choosing MPEG2 settings before burning a DVD or creating MPEG files. Although most Premiere Pro users choose the MPEG2-DVD format to prepare files for DVD creation, other MPEG formats exist. The different MPEG formats described in this section are options that are available in software that burns DVDs. The different formats allow for different screen sizes and different data rates. Some enable subtitles, links, and menus to be integrated into the DVD production.

Using the Adobe Media Encoder is quite simple: Follow these steps to set options in the Media Encoder before creating an MPEG file or burning a DVD from the Burn DVD dialog box:

1. **If you did not click the Settings button in the Export to Encore dialog box, click the sequence in the Timeline panel that you want to export.** Choose File ⇨ Export ⇨ Adobe Media Encoder. This opens the Export Settings dialog box, shown in Figure 18.3.

FIGURE 18.3

Use the Export Settings dialog box to export in MPEG format.

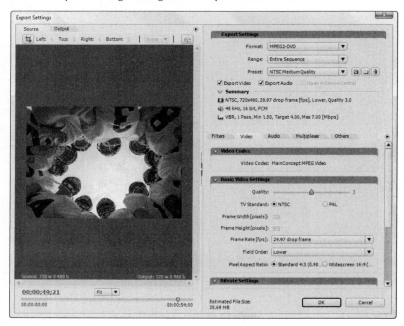

2. **If you are creating an MPEG file, choose an MPEG format from the Format drop-down menu.** (If you opened the Export Settings dialog box from the Burn DVD dialog box, the MPEG2-DVD format is chosen automatically.) When you select a format, the presets and audio and video codecs are automatically chosen for you. The following list describes the format choices:

- **MPEG1:** This option creates a generic MPEG1 file at 720 x 480 pixels with a frame rate of 29.97 frames per second. The default bit rate is 1.7MB per second.

- **MPEG1-VCD:** This format uses MPEG1 encoding and provides a frame size of 352 x 240 pixels (NTSC). VCD discs can be played in standard CD drives, and they can play as much as 74 minutes of audio and video.

- **MPEG2:** This option creates a generic MPEG2 file. The default bit rate for the generic MPEG2 file is 4.2MB per second — more than twice the rate of an MPEG1 file. If you click in the Basic Video Settings section, you can change a variety of settings for the generic file.

- **MPEG2 Blu-ray:** This option is used for creating a disc using the Blu-ray High Definition format. Blu-ray discs store 25GB on a single layer. This option allows frame size presets of 1440 x 1080 pixels at frame rates of 23.97, 24, 25, and 29.97, and HDTV frame presets of 1920 x 1080 pixels interlaced and progressive, as well as 1280 x 720 pixels at frame rates of 23.97, 24, 25, 29.97, 50, and 59.94.

■ **H.264 Blu-ray:** This option is used for creating a disc using the Blu-ray High Definition format with the H.264 standard and extension of MPEG4. Blu-ray discs store 25GB on a single layer. The H.264 Blu-ray option allows frame-size presets of 1440 x 1080 pixels at frame rates of 23.97, 24, 25, and 29.97, and HDTV frame presets of 1920 x 1080 pixels interlaced and progressive, as well as 1280 x 720 pixels at frame rates of 23.97, 24, 25, and 29.97.

■ **MPEG2-DVD:** This option is the Hollywood standard for creating DVDs. This format uses a full frame of 720 x 480 pixels. When the file is exported, audio and video are separated into two MPEG2 files. The video file extension is .m2v; the audio file extension is .wav (NTSC) or .mpa (for PAL systems).

■ **MPEG2-SVCD:** This format uses MPEG2 encoding and provides a frame size of 480 x 480 pixels. This format can provide titles and links. It's supported by major electronics companies such as Sony, Phillips, Matsushita, and JVC.

3. **Click the Range menu to choose what portion of the Premiere Pro project you want to export — either the work area from the Timeline panel or the entire sequence.**

4. **Change the preset if desired.** These presets provide different bit rates and types of encoding: two-pass encoding or one-pass encoding. Although the preset chosen by the format should be suitable for most work, you may want to experiment to see which presets provide the best results. Note that there are presets for Progressive Scan DVDs. If you are working with progressive scan footage and the DVD will be viewed on a progressive scan DVD player, you will obtain high-quality results with one of these presets. The default calls for high-quality variable bit rate and two passes. Figure 18.4 shows many of the presets that are available when you choose the MPEG2-DVD option. Keep in mind that some are low quality and others high quality, and that the choices provide different aspect ratios.

FIGURE 18.4

MPEG2-DVD presets available in the Export Settings dialog box

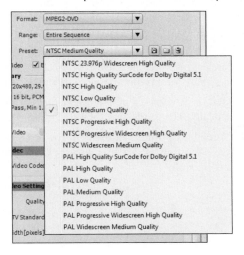

5. **Deselect Export Video or Export Audio if you do not want to export either video or audio.**

6. **If you want to change audio settings, click the Audio tab.** You can choose from Dolby Digital, MPEG, and PCM (Pulse Code Modulation is an uncompressed format that can produce CD audio quality). Note that Premiere Pro allows you to export three times using Dolby Surround Sound before you must pay a license fee. Figure 18.5 displays MPEG2-DVD audio options.

FIGURE 18.5

MPEG2-DVD audio options

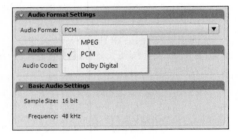

7. **Change quality settings if desired.** To lower video quality, click and drag the Quality slider to the left. When you lower the quality, the MPEG compresses faster. Thus, if you're testing or viewing rough edits only, you can save yourself time by lowering the quality.

8. **Choose either NTSC or PAL.** The NTSC standard is used in North America and Japan. Europe uses PAL.

9. **If desired, change the frame rate and field order.** The Field Order drop-down menu does not appear if you are using the Progressive Scan preset, which does not use video fields. For more information about progressive scanning, see Chapter 3.

10. **If desired, apply a noise reduction filter.** The noise reduction filter is applied before the file is encoded. Noise reduction can reduce file size and video noise. To apply the filter, click the Filters tab and then select the Video Noise Reduction check box. Click and drag the Noise Reduction slider to specify the amount of noise reduction.

11. **Switch aspect ratios if needed.** If you chose a preset, then either Standard or Widescreen is chosen automatically. As a result, you shouldn't need to change this setting.

12. **Review the "Adobe Media Encoder optional features" in the next section.** Then finish the DVD-burning or MPEG-exporting process by following the instructions in the "Completing the MPEG export" section.

Understanding Encoding and Bit Rates

The Adobe Media Encoder's presets include a variety of technical encoding terms. Although many Premiere Pro users prefer not to change MPEG settings, here is a review of some of the encoding terms you may encounter if you choose to change settings:

- **Variable bit rate (VBR)** varies the bit rate of a clip as it plays back. When a high-action scene needs more bits or bandwidth, the encoding process delivers the extra bits; in areas that don't require high bandwidth, it lowers the bit rate. Thus, for clips that vary in action, VBR can provide better quality than constant bit rate (CBR), which does not vary the bit rate of the clip as it plays back. Although VBR generally provides higher quality, it requires more processing power than CBR. Because the MPEG file may be played back on different systems, keep in mind that a file exported at a constant bit rate may play back more reliably on older computers and playback systems.

  If you select CBR, you can select the bit rate (in megabits per second) for the file. If you select VBR, you can select a target, maximum, and minimum bit rate. You also specify the number of passes used to analyze the file.

- **Two-pass encoding** increases the digital quality of exported video. When two-pass encoding is used, the video is processed twice. The first time, the encoder analyzes the video to determine the best way to encode it. On the second pass, the encoder uses the information gathered in the first pass to encode the video. As you might guess, two-pass encoding takes longer than one-pass, but it increases the quality of the encoded video.

  If you are exporting using MPEG2 format, you can also change several intra-frame compression options. When MPEG2 files are compressed, Groups of Pictures (GOP) are analyzed and compressed into one frame. For example, in MPEG2, as many as 15 frames may be grouped together (12 frames in PAL). The GOP consists of I frames, B frames, and P frames. An *I frame* is a keyframe of the entire frame data, and a *P frame* is a predictive frame that can be a small percentage of the size of the I frame. A *B frame* is a frame that can use a portion of the I frame and the P frame. When exporting to MPEG2, Adobe Media Encoder provides these options. Most users do not need to change the default settings for these options:

  - **M Frames:** Choose the number of B frames (between consecutive I and P frames) in the drop-down menu. The default setting is 2.

  - **N Frames:** Choose the number of frames between I frames in the drop-down menu. The N frames value must be a multiple of M Frames. The default setting is 12.

  - **Closed GOP Every:** Enter the number of repeated Closed Group of Pictures. The Closed GOP does not process frames outside of the Group of Pictures. (This option does not appear in the MPEG2-DVD preset.)

  - **Automatic GOP Placement**: Leave this option selected to allow Automatic GOP placement. (This option does not appear in MPEG2-DVD preset.)

Adobe Encoder optional features

During the export process, the Adobe Media Encoder allows you to create custom presets and to crop, preview, and deinterlace video.

Previewing

The Media Encoder provides a preview of your source file and a preview of the final video output. The following list describes options for previewing source and output video:

- To preview the source file, click the Source tab.
- To preview the video based upon the settings in the Media Encoder, click the Output tab.
- To scrub through video in either the Source or Output tab, click and drag in the Time Ruler at the bottom of the preview area.

Cropping and scaling

Before you export your file, you can crop the source video. Cropped areas appear as black in the final video. Follow these steps to crop your video:

1. **Click the Source tab.** This opens the Source view of your video.
2. **Select the Crop tool, shown in Figure 18.6.**
3. **To crop precisely using pixel dimensions, click and drag over the Left, Top, Right, or Bottom numerical fields.** Clicking and dragging right reduces the cropping area. As you click and drag, the cropping area is displayed onscreen. Alternatively, you can click and drag a corner over the area of the video that you want to retain. As you click and drag, a readout appears, displaying the frame size in pixels.
4. **If you want to change the aspect ratio of the crop to 4:3 or 16:9, click in the Crop Proportions drop-down menu.** Choose the aspect ratio.
5. **To preview the cropped video, click the Output tab.**
6. **If you want to scale your video frame to fit within the crop borders, select the Scale to Fit check box (next to the Interlace check box).**

Deinterlacing video

To deinterlace video, click the Output tab and then click the Deinterlace check box. Deinterlacing removes one field from a video frame to prevent blurring artifacts, which can occur when video is output on a computer. This blurring is most likely to occur during scenes that exhibit motion. The blurring results from the difference in frame information between the odd, or upper, video field and the even, or lower, video field that comprise a video frame.

FIGURE 18.6

Use the Crop tool to crop the video frame.

Saving metadata

If you are creating an MPEG file, you can embed metadata with the file by choosing XMP Info in the Export Settings panel menu. This opens the XMP dialog box where you can enter copyright information and descriptive information about the file. XMP is Adobe's Extensible Metadata Platform. XMP data can be shared with other applications that support this format.

Saving, importing, and deleting presets

If you make changes to a preset, you can save your custom preset to disk so that you can use it later. After you save presets, you can import or delete them. Here are the options:

- **Saving presets:** If you edit a preset and want to save it to use later, or use as a basis for comparing export quality, click the Save Preset button (the disk icon). Then enter a name in the Choose Name dialog box. If you want to save the Filter tab settings, click the Save Filter Settings check box. To save cropping and deinterlace settings, select the Save Other Tasks check box.

- **Importing presets:** The easiest way to import a custom preset is to click the Preset drop-down menu and choose it from the top portion of the list. Alternatively, you can click the Import Preset button (the folder icon) and then load the presets from disk. Presets have a .vpr file extension.

- **Deleting presets:** To delete a preset, load the preset and then click the Delete Preset button (the trash icon). An alert appears, warning you that the deletion process cannot be undone.

Completing the MPEG export

After you choose and fine-tune settings in the Export Settings dialog box, you can simply click OK to return to the Burn DVD screen or to start the process of creating an MPEG file. After clicking OK, click Burn if you are returning to the DVD Layout screen, or name your file in the Save File dialog box and choose a folder and drive location.

Exporting in AVI and QuickTime

If you don't choose to export your movie as a DVD or in MPEG format, you may want to export in either Windows AVI or QuickTime format. If you export a movie in Video for Windows (called Microsoft AVI in the Export Movie Settings dialog box) format, your movie can be viewed on systems running Microsoft Windows. Mac users can also view AVI movies by importing them into the latest version of Apple's QuickTime Movie player. On the Web, Microsoft has switched from AVI format to Advanced Windows Media format (covered in Chapter 21). However, AVI format is still accepted as a format that can be imported into many multimedia software programs. Video-editing programs such as Premiere Pro capture movies using Microsoft's DV AVI format.

After you edit your work and preview your production, you can export your project by selecting the sequence you want to export in the Timeline and choosing File ➪ Export ➪ Movie. This opens the Export Movie dialog box. At the bottom of the dialog box (shown in Figure 18.7), Premiere Pro displays the current video and audio settings. If you want to export using these settings, simply name the file and click Save. The length of time Premiere Pro takes to render the final movie depends on the size of your production, its frame rate, frame size, and compression settings.

FIGURE 18.7

The Export Movie dialog box displays the current video and audio settings for your Premiere Pro project and allows you to change settings.

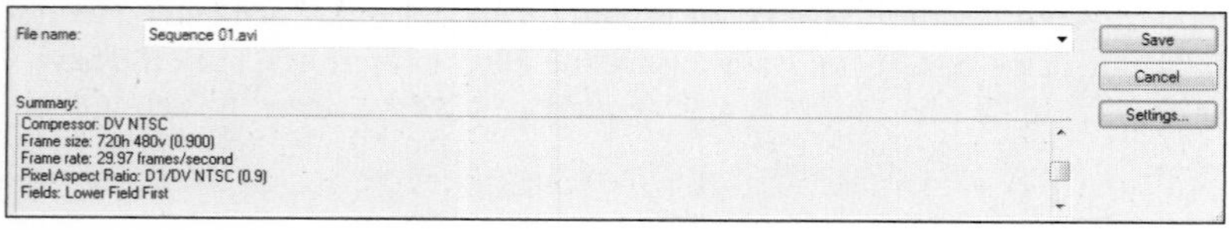

 You can export a frame by moving the current-time indicator to the frame and choosing File ⇨ Export ⇨ Frame.

 Video for Windows files are saved with an .avi (audio video interleave) file extension. These files are often referred to as AVI files.

Changing Export Settings

Although the video and audio settings used during the creation of a Premiere Pro project may be perfect during editing, they may not produce the best quality for specific viewing environments. For example, a digital movie with a large frame size and high frame-per-second rate may stutter when playing back in a multimedia program or on the Web. Thus, you may want to change several configuration settings before exporting your Premiere Pro project to disk. To change export settings, click the Settings button in the Export Movie dialog box. (If the Export Movie dialog box is not onscreen, you can display it by selecting a sequence in the Timeline panel and choosing File ⇨ Export ⇨ Movie.)

After you click Settings, the Export Movie Settings dialog box appears, as shown in Figure 18.8. When this dialog box appears, it automatically opens to the General settings.

FIGURE 18.8

The Export Movie Settings dialog box

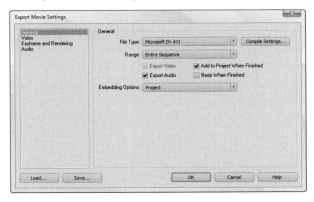

Following is a description of the choices available in the Export Movie Settings dialog box:

- **File Type:** If you want to switch file types, you can use this menu. Apart from selecting a QuickTime or AVI format, you can also choose to save your digital movie as a series of still frames in different file formats, such as GIF, TIFF, or Windows Bitmap.

- **Range:** You can choose to export the entire sequence or the work area specified in the Timeline.

- **Export Video:** Deselect this option if you do not want to export the video.

- **Export Audio:** Deselect this option if you do not want to export the audio.

- **Add to Project When Finished:** This option adds the exported movie to the Project panel.

- **Beep When Finished:** This option causes your computer to beep when the project is finished.

- **Embedding Options:** This option allows you to create a link between Premiere Pro and the exported movie. To create the link, choose Project in the Embedding Options drop-down menu. After the link is created, you can open the original project by choosing Edit ➪ Edit Original in another Adobe Application. Keep in mind that this option isn't available for all export choices.

Changing Video Settings

To review or change video settings, choose Video in the Export Movie Settings dialog box. The video settings reflect the currently used project settings. When choosing settings, you must understand that choices you make may affect quality. For example, if you are exporting to the Web, you want to reduce the frame size of DV projects and change from non-square to square pixels. Consider the following options when exporting to the Web or multimedia applications:

- If you change the frame size, make sure that the aspect ratio matches that of your project. For example, you can change a DV image from 720 x 480 to either 320 x 240 or 160 x 120 pixels, and the pixel aspect ratio changes from 4:3 to 3:2. Switching the pixel aspect ratio to square pixels before exporting maintains the 4:3 image aspect ratio.

- Reducing the frame rate for Web and multimedia export usually produces smoother playback. Several codecs provide better quality if the exported frame rate is a multiple of the original frame rate. Thus, you can choose 15 frames per second for footage recorded at 30 frames per second.

Choosing a QuickTime compressor

When creating a project, capturing video, or exporting a Premiere Pro project, one of the most important decisions you can make is to choose the correct compression settings. A compressor, or *codec* (COmpressor/DECompressor), determines exactly how the computer restructures or removes data to make the digital video file smaller. Although most compression settings are designed to compress files, not all of these settings are suitable for all types of projects. The trick is to choose the best codec for your Premiere Pro project to produce the best quality with the smallest file size. One codec may be better for Web digital video, and another may be best suited to a project that contains animation created in a painting program.

The settings that appear in the Compressor drop-down menu are based upon the file type chosen in the Export Movie Settings dialog box. The QuickTime codecs, shown in Figure 18.9, are different from the Video for Windows codecs. Furthermore, depending on the compressor, the options in the Video section of the Export Movie Settings dialog box may change.

Here is a brief review of some of the QuickTime codec choices that are available in the Export Movie Settings dialog box:

■ **Animation:** This setting can be useful for storing two-dimensional animation, particularly animated titles with flat colors. Using this compressor, you can set the bit depth to Millions+ (of colors), which enables exporting an alpha channel with the movie. If you choose the 100 percent option, animation provides lossless compression, which can produce large file sizes. This codec is generally not suitable for "real-life video" footage. It is generally considered to be useful for storage and authoring, rather than as a delivery codec.

■ **Cinepak:** This format was one of the most popular for Web and multimedia work. Although it can still be used for playback on slower computer systems, this codec has largely become a relic of the past, supplanted by the Sorenson codec. When exporting, you can also set the data rate using Cinepak, but be aware that setting the data rate below 30 Kbps can lower the quality of the video.

FIGURE 18.9

The QuickTime compressors, also known as codecs

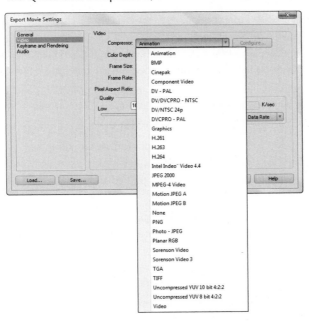

- **MJPEG-A, MJPEG-B:** These formats are used for editing and capturing video. They can provide very good results when quality is set to 100 percent. Both codecs use spatial compression, and so keyframe control is not available. MJPEG also usually requires a hardware board for playback.

- **Sorenson 3:** This format is used for high-quality desktop video for the Web and for CD. This codec provides better compression than Cinepak, reducing file sizes by three to four times as much as Cinepak does. Keep in mind that when exporting from a DV project to Web or multimedia, this codec allows you to change the pixel aspect ratio to square pixels. Sorenson 3 provides better quality and is the successor to Sorenson 2; it should thus be used instead of Sorenson 2.

NOTE Sorenson also sells a high-end version of the Sorenson codec that provides better quality and more features. For example, Sorenson Pro provides temporal stability, which allows the video frame rate to slow down for slower systems.

- **Planar RGB:** This is a lossless codec that is good for animation created in painting and 3-D programs; it is an alternative to the Animation codec.

- **Video:** This is an outdated codec and generally should not be used.

- **Component Video:** This is generally used for capturing analog video. When you capture video, this may be your only choice, depending on the video capture board that is installed in your computer.

- **Graphics:** Used for graphics with 256 colors or less, this codec is generally not used in desktop video.

- **Photo-JPEG:** Although this codec can create good image quality, slow decompression makes it unsuitable for desktop video.

- **H.263:** This option is used for video conferencing and provides better quality than the H.261 codec. This codec is not recommended for video editing.

- **PNG:** This option generally is not used for motion graphics. This codec is included in QuickTime as a means of saving still graphics in PNG Web format or flat RGB animation.

- **TIFF:** Short for Tagged Information File Format, this is a printing format for still images.

- **BMP:** This is a Windows-compatible graphics format for still images.

- **DV-PAL and DV-NTSC:** These are DV formats for PAL and NTSC (choose the format that applies to the geographic region for your intended audience).

NOTE The QuickTime codecs list may contain hardware-specific codecs supplied by computer and board manufacturers. For example, Sony Vaio computer owners see a Sony DV format in the QuickTime codec list. Follow the instructions provided with your capture board or computer when choosing one of these codecs.

Choosing a Video for Windows compressor

If you are exporting a Video for Windows file, the compressor choices are different from the QuickTime choices. Here is a brief review of several AVI codecs:

- **Cinepak:** Originally created by Radius, this option provides the same features as QuickTime's Cinepak. This codec is primarily used for multimedia output on older systems. Compression can be time-consuming, but image quality is generally good.

- **Indeo Video 5.10:** Created by Intel (makers of the Pentium computer chip), this codec provides good image quality. It's often used for capturing raw data, and the quality is similar to desktop video produced using the Cinepak codec.

- **Microsoft RLE (Run Length Encoding):** The bit depth for this codec is limited to 256 colors, making it suitable only for animation created in painting programs with 256 colors or images that have been reduced to 256 colors. When the Quality slider is set to High, this codec produces lossless compression.

Changing bit depth

After you choose a codec, the dialog box changes to show the different options provided by that codec. If your codec enables you to change bit depth, you can choose another setting in the Bit Depth drop-down menu. For example, while the Sorenson codec does not enable you to switch bit depths, the Cinepak codec enables you to choose 256 colors. Because the Cinepak codec allows 256 colors, clicking the Palette button enables you to load a palette or have Premiere Pro create a 256-color palette from the clips in the movie. However, be aware that reducing the palette to 256 colors can result in poor picture quality. Unless you are working with an animation created in a painting program, you probably don't want to reduce the colors in your video project to 256.

Choosing quality

The next option controlled by the selected codec is the Quality slider. Most codecs enable you to click and drag to choose a quality setting. The higher the quality is, the larger the file size of the exported movie.

Choosing a data rate

Many codecs enable you to specify an output data rate. The *data rate* is the amount of data per second that must be processed during playback of the exported video file. The data rate changes, depending on which system plays your production. For example, the data rate of CD playback on a slow computer is far less than the data rate of a hard drive. If the data rate of the video file is too high, the system cannot handle the playback. If this is the case, playback may be garbled as frames are dropped. Here are a few suggestions for different playback scenarios:

- **World Wide Web:** Choose a data rate that accounts for Web connection speeds. For slower Web connections, remember that even though a modem may be capable of 56 Kbps (kilobits per second), the actual connection speed is probably slower. Also remember that the data rate field accepts data in kilobits per second, rather than bits per second. For Sorenson and Cinepak codecs, try a data rate of 50 Kbps. Adobe recommends trying a data rate of 150 Kbps for movies with a frame size of 240 x 180 pixels. Keep in mind that when uploading to the Web, a smaller file size is more important than the data rate.

See Chapter 19 for more information about exporting video to the Web, especially if you are using a streaming media server.

- **Videotape editing:** If you are exporting video files for further editing, the data rate should be set so that the computer editing system can handle it. To export for further editing, use a codec that does not compress video and therefore does not reduce video quality.

- **CD-ROM:** For CD playback, specify a data rate that is consistent with the data rate of the CD drive. The data rate setting is especially important for older CD drives. For example, a double-speed CD has a data rate at 300 Kbps. Typical data rates for double-speed CDs are between 200 Kbps and 250 Kbps. For older compressors, such as Cinepak, Adobe recommends data rates for a 12-speed (12X) CD drive to be 1.8MB per second; for a 24X CD drive, 3–3.6MB per second. If you are using the Sorenson 3 codec, you can set the data rate at 200 Kbps or below. Sorenson recommends this formula as a starting point: height × width × frames per second ÷ 48000. Thus, if exporting a 320 x 240 video at 15 frames per second, you can limit the data rate to 24 Kbps as a starting point; at 30 frames per second, you can limit the data rate to 48 Kbps. (For high-action clips, you generally need a higher data rate.)

- **Intranets:** The data rate speed depends upon the actual speed of the network. Because most intranets use high-speed connections, you can generally set the playback to 100 Kbps more.

- **Hard disk:** If you are creating a production for playback on a computer system, try to ascertain the data rate of the audience's hard drive. The data rates for most modern hard drives are in excess of 33 million bits per second.

Setting recompression

If you specify a data rate, select the Recompress check box. This option helps to guarantee that Premiere Pro keeps the data rate beneath the one specified in the data rate field. If you want Premiere Pro to recompress every frame, whether or not it is below the data rate, choose Always in the Recompress drop-down menu. However, better quality is produced if you choose the Maintain Data Rate setting. This recompresses only the frames that are higher than the specified data rate.

Changing frame rates and frame size

Before exporting video, you may want to reduce the frame rate or the frame size to reduce the file size of your production. The frame rate is the number of frames that Premiere Pro exports per second. If you change the frame size, be sure to specify the horizontal and vertical dimensions in pixels. If your video was captured at a 4:3 aspect ratio, be sure to maintain this ratio to avoid distorting clips. As noted earlier, to maintain the aspect ratio, you may need to change the pixel aspect ratio.

Specifying keyframes

Another video export setting that can control export file size is the Keyframe setting in the Keyframe and Rendering section of the Export Movie Settings dialog box, shown in Figure 18.10.

The Keyframe and Rendering section of the Export Movie Settings dialog box

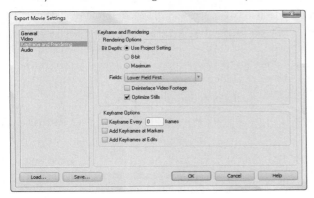

You can change keyframe settings when choosing codecs, such as Cinepak and Sorenson video, with temporal compression. The keyframe setting specifies how many times to save the complete video frame. (Typically, the more keyframes created, the better the video quality; but this results in large file sizes.) If the keyframe setting for the codec is specified in frames, a setting of 60 creates a keyframe every two seconds at 30 frames per second. As the codec compresses, it compares each subsequent frame and saves only the information that changes in each frame. Thus, using keyframes efficiently can significantly reduce the file size of your video.

Before creating keyframes, you should research the selected codec, if possible. For example, the Sorensen 3 codec creates keyframes automatically every 50 frames. Sorenson documentation recommends setting a keyframe every 35 to 65 frames. When experimenting, try to keep as few keyframes as possible. However, note that images displaying motion generally require more keyframes than those without much motion.

To help ensure smooth transitions, you may want to force Premiere Pro to create a keyframe at transitions and edits. To set keyframes at edit points, select the Add Keyframes at Edits option in the Export Movie Settings dialog box. To set keyframes at specific points in your production, set markers at points where you want Premiere Pro to create a keyframe, and then select the Add Keyframe at Markers option in the Export Movie Settings dialog box.

 To view compression information about a clip, select the clip in the Project panel and choose File ⇨ Get Properties for Selection.

Changing Audio Settings

When you export your final project, you may want to change the audio settings. To access the audio options, choose Audio in the Export Movie Settings dialog box. The settings in the Audio section of the Export Movie Settings dialog box, shown in Figure 18.11, are as follows:

- **Compressor:** In the Compressor drop-down menu, choose a compressor if desired. (The audio codecs are reviewed at the end of this section.)

- **Sample Rate:** Lower the rate setting to reduce file size and to speed up the rendering of the final production. Higher rates produce better quality and increase processing time. For example, CD quality is 44 kHz.

- **Sample Type:** Stereo 16-bit is the highest setting; 8-bit mono is the lowest setting. Lower bit depths produce smaller files and reduce rendering times.

- **Channels:** Choose either Stereo (two channels) or Mono (one channel).

- **Interleave:** This option determines how frequently audio is inserted into the video frames.

Choosing 1 frame in the drop-down menu tells Premiere Pro to load the audio for the frame into RAM until the next frame is processed. However, this can cause the sound to break up if the computer cannot handle a lot of audio data quickly. If you increase the time interval, Premiere Pro uses longer audio sequences, which require less processing but more RAM. Adobe recommends ½ to 1 second interleave values for most hard disks.

FIGURE 18.11

The Audio section of the Export Movie Settings dialog box

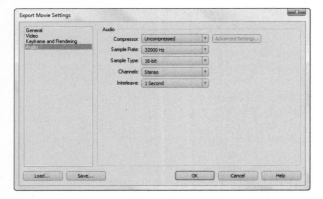

Choosing QuickTime audio codecs

Following is a brief review of several QuickTime audio codecs. You must specify a codec only if you want to add compression to sound. For each codec, the compression ratio appears next to its name:

- **ULaw 2:1:** Used as a common audio format on Unix platforms, ULaw is used for digital telephony in both North America and Japan.

- **16-bit Endian and 16-bit Little Endian:** This format is not used for video editing, but it is used by hardware engineers and software developers.

- **24-bit integer and 32-bit integer soft:** This format is not used for video editing, but it is used by hardware engineers and software developers.

- **IMA Designed by the Interactive Multimedia Association:** This cross-platform format can be used to compress audio for multimedia.

- **32-bit floating point and 64-bit floating point:** This format is not used for video editing, but it is used by hardware engineers and software developers.

- **Alaw:** This format is used for European digital telephony.

- **Qdesign Music codec:** This format can be used for high-quality Web output and can provide CD quality over a modem.

- **Qualcomm Pure Voice:** This speech format shouldn't be used at an audio rate higher than 8 kHz.

- **MACE 3:1 and MACE 6:1:** This Macintosh audio codec can be used for QuickTime movies for PCs and Macs. MACE 3:1 provides better quality because it uses less compression.

Choosing Video for Windows audio codecs

Premiere Pro offers the following audio compression options when exporting a project as a Video for Windows file:

- **Indeo audio software:** This option is good for Web output of music and speech. It was created for use with Indeo video codecs.

- **Truespeech:** This option is used for speech over the Internet. It works best at low data rates.

- **Microsoft GSM 6.10:** This option is for speech only and is used for telephony compression in Europe.

- **MS-ADPCM:** Microsoft's version of an Adaptive Differential Pulse Code Modulation compressor, this option can be used for CD-quality sound.

- **Microsoft IMA ADPCM:** This option, used for cross-platform multimedia, was developed by the Interactive Multimedia Association.

- **Voxware codecs:** This option can be used for speech output on the Web. Quality is best when exporting at low data rates.

Summary

Premiere Pro movies can be output to DVD directly from Premiere Pro. If you want to create an interactive DVD, you can set DVD markers that will be used to create menus and buttons in Premiere Pro DVD templates.

To view a Premiere Pro project on a CD or the Web, or to view it on a computer system that does not have Premiere Pro installed, you can export the Premiere Pro file in QuickTime, AVI, or MPEG format.

This chapter covered the following topics:

- You can place Encore chapter markers on the Timeline if you want to create interactive DVDs using Encore.

- To export your movie as an MPEG file, you can choose File ➪ Export ➪ Adobe Media Encoder.

- To burn a DVD directly from Premiere Pro, you can choose File ➪ Export ➪ Export to Encore.

- To change export settings when exporting to AVI or QuickTime, you can click the Settings button in the Export Movie dialog box.

- When exporting, you can change video, keyframe and rendering, and audio settings.

- Choosing the correct codec and reducing frame rates and frame size reduces the file size of the exported production.

Chapter 19

Outputting to the Web and Intranets

I f you're a video producer or Web designer, you may want to showcase your Premiere Pro video productions on a Web page, or on a company intranet. Before you start creating digital movies for the Web, it can be helpful to know exactly how a Web browser loads a digital movie onto a Web page and what options are available to you. For example, when a QuickTime movie displays on a Web page, you can have it play immediately or you can add controls for starting and stopping the movie. This chapter provides an overview of the movie file formats for the Web. It also discusses how to add a digital movie to the Web, and the QuickTime HTML options that are available.

Understanding Your Web Delivery Options

You don't need to be a Webmaster or Java programmer to play a Premiere Pro movie on a Web or intranet page. To get started, all you need to know is a little HTML. As you'll discover from reading this chapter, movies can be displayed by using a simple HTML *embed* tag, as illustrated in this example:

```
<EMBED SRC="mypremiere.mov", WIDTH=320,
    HEIGHT=240>
```

In this case, the name of the movie is my mypremiere.mov. Its frame size is 320 x 240 pixels. The embed command tells the browser to load the movie from a Web server and use a plug-in to play the movie. Although this technique works, it can lead to poor playback. Unless the movie is saved so that it can stream or use progressive playback, viewers need to wait until the entire movie is downloaded to their hard drives before they can view it. It's almost like having to wait for a VCR to play the entire program from start to finish before you can view it. If you want to display digital movies on a Web or intranet page, you should investigate two delivery choices that are designed to enhance playback quality: *streaming video* and *progressive download*.

Streaming video

If you can afford it, streaming is the best vehicle for delivering digital video over the Web or an intranet. In many ways, streaming is similar to cable TV. You see the program as it arrives at your home or office, and no portion of the file is downloaded to your hard drive before or during playback. Instead, it is *buffered* to memory first and then displays onscreen. Typically, the video is streamed at different data rates: a data rate for modems (narrow-band connections) as well as data rates for faster connections (broadband).

NOTE Streaming video does not use the Web standard Hypertext Transfer Protocol (HTTP). HTTP determines the formatting, transmittal method, and responses that Web servers and browsers use when responding to commands issued over the Internet. Instead of HTTP, streaming media uses Real Time Streaming Protocol (RTSP), which not only allows streaming media but can also provide users with the power to interact with the streaming server. For example, RTSP allows viewers to rewind video and jump to different chapters in QuickTime movies. (To take advantage of streaming, users need a high-speed Internet connection, such as DSL, cable modem or T1.)

Furthermore, special server software is needed to stream the video. Often, the server software and video content are on a separate computer that just handles video streaming.

The three primary producers of streaming media software are Apple, Microsoft, and Real Networks. Apple's QuickTime streaming software (www.quicktime.com) is part of its OS X server package. Apple also provides QuickTime streaming software for Linux and Windows NT. Microsoft provides Windows Media server software (www.microsoft.com/windows/windowsmedia) with its Windows 2003 server package. Real Networks server software must be purchased from RealMedia (www.realnetworks.com).

Progressive download

For short video clips, progressive download can often provide a suitable alternative to streaming media. Although progressive download doesn't provide video and audio quality as high as that in streaming media, it allows the beginning of the video clip to play before it finishes downloading. For most producers, this is the key to preventing viewers from surfing away while the video downloads. However, unlike streaming media, the video actually downloads to the viewer's hard drive. A further drawback is that playback can become distorted if the data rate of the Web connection slows. In contrast, streaming media removes portions of the video to keep the playback consistent (often, the viewer doesn't notice).

NOTE For an in-depth discussion of streaming media, see Adobe's Streaming Media Primer at www.adobe.com/motion/primers. For the latest on streaming media as well as a few streaming media tutorials, check out www.streamingmedia.com. If you're looking for a job in the streaming media industry, click the careers link on the aforementioned Web page.

Choosing the Right Web File Format

Before you begin planning to output your digital movies to the Web or an intranet, you should be familiar with the different movie file formats that can be viewed in a browser. The file formats listed here all require a plug-in to be installed in the browser software. Saving QuickTime Windows Media and RealVideo files for the Web is covered in Chapter 20.

- **QuickTime (MOV):** Apple's QuickTime format is a most popular Web video file format. It is cross-platform and provides good quality. QuickTime provides numerous HTML options that can change how the movie appears on a Web page. Different QuickTime tracks can also be added to Web-based movies.

  Although not a requirement for Web playback, for best results, QuickTime movies should be streamed by Apple's QuickTime streaming software. This software is included with Apple's Mac OS X server package. As mentioned earlier, Apple Inc. has created QuickTime Streaming Server versions for Windows NT and Linux. Premiere Pro users can quickly create QuickTime streaming-ready movies by exporting their movies using Adobe's Media Encoder (File ➪ Export ➪ Adobe Media Encoder).

- **Windows Media Format (WMV):** Video created in Windows Media Format is loaded on a Web page into Microsoft's Windows Media Player. In Premiere Pro, you can output projects in Windows Media Format by choosing File ➪ Export ➪ Adobe Media Encoder. The current version of Windows Media Player provides compression improvements from 15 to 50 percent over previous versions. Microsoft's Web site claims that it provides the "highest fidelity audio and best quality video at any bit rate from dial-up to broadband."

- **RealVideo (RM):** RealNetworks' streaming video format is one of the most popular formats available. For true high-quality video, RealVideo encoded movies must be created with RealNetworks RealVideo format. Premiere Pro's File ➪ Export ➪ Adobe Media Encoder command enables you to export Premiere Pro movies in RealVideo format.

- **Flash Video (FLV):** Flash Video is rapidly becoming one of the most popular formats for displaying video on the Web. Movies saved in FLV format can be viewed in Adobe's Flash player. FLV files can be loaded from a Web server for progressive downloading, or streamed using Flash Media Server. The combination of Flash Video and Flash Media Server has grown in popularity, largely because the Flash player is used in over 90 percent of the world's browsers. When video is played within Flash, it can be controlled by Actionscript, Flash's versatile scripting language that provides powerful interactive features. Premiere Pro's Export Timeline ➪ Adobe Media Encoder command enables you to export Premiere Pro movies in FLV format for use in Flash Video. Using Flash Video is covered in Chapter 22.

- **Audio Video Interleave (AVI):** All Windows computers are equipped to read Microsoft AVI files; however, because AVI is not cross-platform, it is not often used on the Web. For Web use, Microsoft has dropped the format and replaced it with the more sophisticated Windows Media Format.

Understanding HTML

If you plan to output digital video to the Web, you should have an understanding of how digital movies are loaded onto a Web page. With this knowledge, you can control how your movie displays and when it begins to play. Your first step is to understand how you can use Hypertext Markup Language (HTML) to load text and images on a Web page.

How a movie is loaded onto a Web page

When you see a digital movie on a Web page, it appears because the HTML code instructs the browser to load the movie from a Web server. HTML is a series of text codes, or *tags*, that tell the browser what to do. Although numerous programs exist that can automatically write HTML code for you, you can construct an entire Web page using a simple text editor. For example, the following HTML code snippet tells the Web browser to put the words **Premiere on the Web** on a Web page in bold type:

```
<b>Premiere on the Web</b>
```

The following example is a simple Web page displaying in Windows Media Format (see Figure 19.1). To create the Windows Media page, this example used Adobe GoLive, which created most of the following HTML instructions. (Loading a movie into GoLive is covered later in this chapter.)

```
<html xmlns="http://www.w3.org/1999/xhtml">
 <head>
 <meta http-equiv="content-type" content="text/html;charset=utf-
   8" />
 <meta name="generator" content="Adobe GoLive" />
 <title>Web Movie Center</title>
 </head>
 <body>
 <div align="center">
 <h1>WEB MOVIES</h1>
 <object id="MediaPlayer" classid="clsid:6BF52A52-394A-11D3-
   B153-00C04F79FAA6" type="application/x-oleobject"
   standby="Loading Microsoft Windows Media Player components..."
   height="240" width="320">
 <param name="enabled" value="true" />
 <param name="fullscreen" value="false" />
 <param name="url" value="PremiereMovie.wmv" />
 <param name="autostart" value="false" />
 <param name="uimode" value="full" />
 </object></p>
 </body>
</html>
```

If you are using QuickTime, you could use the following snippet of HTML to load a QuickTime movie into a Web page without the QuickTime controller.

```
<embed src="mymovie.mov" width="320" height="240"
    type="video/QuickTime" controller="false" autoplay="true">
```

FIGURE 19.1

A sample Web page that contains a Windows Media movie

To those unfamiliar with HTML, it may look complicated. However, after you become familiar with the syntax, HTML coding becomes quite easy. If you scan through the code, you see several HTML tags, such as <head> and <body>. Each tag designates a specific area or formatting section in the page. Most tags begin with a word, such as <title>. At the end of the section, the tag is repeated with a forward slash (/) in front of it. For example, the end tag of <title> is </title>.

Here's a review of the some of the more important elements in HTML code:

- <html>: This tag simply tells the browser that the HTML coding system will be used.

- <head>: The "head" area of the page provides the browser with information concerning the character set that is used (within the meta tag). If scripting languages such as JavaScript will be used, this information also normally appears in the "head" area.

- <title>: The window title of the browser page appears within the title tag.

- <body>: The main elements of a Web page are found within the "body" area. In the previous example, notice that the </body> tag ends just above the ending </html> tag. Within the body is the information that loads the QuickTime movie.

- `<object>`: In the Windows Media example, the `<object>` tag is used to load the player and the movie. The ID option's player name allows you to assign a word to the player so that it can be referred to in a Web scripting language. The CLASSID is a unique hexadecimal code for the ActiveX control defining the Windows Media player. The URL attribute specifies the path and filename of the movie to be loaded. The `height` and `width` sections show the height and width of the movie on the page.

> **NOTE**   *ActiveX* **is a term that Microsoft created to describe reusable components that can be used in Web pages.**

- `<embed>`: In the QuickTime example, the `<embed>` tag loads the digital movie plug-in. The `src` section provides the name of the digital movie that will be loaded from the Web server. The `height` and `width` sections show the height and width of the movie on the page. The `type` attribute tells the browser that a QuickTime movie is being loaded. The `controller="false"` code tells the browser not to place the QuickTime controller. The `autoplay="true"` code tells the browser to start playing the movie as soon as the page loads.

To enable the movie to be seen on the Web, you must name the page. If you name the page `Index.htm`, most Web servers will load this as the home page for a Web site. For the page and movie to appear, both must be copied to the Web server that hosts the Web site.

QuickTime settings for Web pages

QuickTime is one of the more popular digital video Web formats. Below is a list of HTML tags that enable you to customize how a QuickTime movie appears on a Web page. Many of the tags are simple true/false statements, such as `Loop=True` or `Loop=False`. You can easily insert these tags using a word processor that can save files in standard text format. However, it's easier to insert these tags using a Web-page layout program, such as Adobe Dreamweaver or GoLive.

- `Bg color`: Specifies the background color for the movie. Colors are specified in hexadecimal code when assigned in HTML. (For example, in the code, `bg color="#FF0000"`, FF0000 displays red.)

- `Cache=True/False`: Caches the movie. This allows the movie to load faster if the user returns to the page. (Netscape browsers read the cache setting; Internet Explorer does not.)

- `Controller=True/False`: Adds the QuickTime controller, which enables the user to start and stop the movie.

- `Hidden=True/False`: Hides the QuickTime movie but plays the audio.

- `HREF`: Enables you to enter a clickable link. When the user clicks the QuickTime movie, the browser jumps to the specified Universal Resource Locator (URL), or Web address. (For example: `HREF=http://myhomepage.com/Page-3.com`)

- `Target=`: Related to the `HREF` tag. When the movie jumps to a URL, it tells the movie which frame to play in. (Note that the frame is an HTML frame, not a digital video frame.) You can include a frame name or common frame tags, such as `_self`, `_parent`, `_top`, or `_blank`. (For example: `target = _ top`)

- `Loop=True/False`: Plays the movie nonstop. You can also choose `Loop=Palindrome`, which plays the move from beginning to end, then from end to beginning.

- `Play every frame=True/False`: Forces every frame to be played. If this option is activated, every frame of the movie plays. This option is usually not turned on, primarily because it could slow movie playback and throw the soundtrack out of sync or turn it off entirely.

- `Scale`: Enables you to resize the movie. (For example: `Scale=2` doubles the movie size.)

- `Volume`: Enables you to control the volume. This tag uses values from 0 (zero) to 256. By default, the value is set to 256. To turn off the sound, use `Volume=0`.

Loading Streaming Video onto a Web Page

Setting up video to be streamed over a Web page is slightly more involved than setting up a digital movie to progressively download from a Web page. Although differences exist for setting up files in Windows Media Server, RealNetworks' Helix Server, and Apple's QuickTime Streaming Server, they all require the creation of a pointer or *metafile*. Typically, the pointer or metafile is a small file that is saved on a Web server. When a user clicks a link on a Web page, the metafile causes the streaming media plug-in to load and provides instructions as to which movie to load off the streaming media server.

The following sections provide brief, general summaries of the steps involved for setting up streaming files for Windows Media Server, RealMedia Helix Server, and QuickTime Media Server. For specific instructions, consult user documentation.

In all cases, you save your video clip to a directory on your streaming media server. The Web server will contain HTML code that points to the streaming media server.

Windows Media

Windows Media Server requires you to set up a metafile on your Web server. This is a file that the browser uses to load the Windows Media Player plug-in, which in turn instructs the streaming media server to play the movie. General steps for setting up the process are described next. For more information, go to `www.microsoft.com/windows/windowsmedia/forpros/server/server.aspx`.

1. **Export your Premiere Pro project as a Windows Media file using Adobe Media Encoder (File ⇨ Export ⇨ Adobe Media Encoder).** In this example, the name of this movie is MyWindowsMovie.wmv.

2. **Upload the exported movie to the correct directory on your media server.**

3. **Create an asx metafile in a text editor. The metafile includes instructions specifying the location of the actual movie file on the Windows Media Server.** The text of the metafile could be as simple as this:

```
<asx version="3.0">
<entry>
<title>My Movie Title</title>
<ref href="mms://ServerName/Path/MyWindowsMovie.wmv>
</entry>
</asx>
```

4. **Name the file *MyWindowsMovie.asx*. Note that the filename of the movie is the same as the actual exported Windows media file, but it uses an** `.asx` **(Advanced Streaming Redirector) file extension.** Save the file on your Web server.

5. **On your Web page, write HTML that creates a link to the ASX file created in step 3.** When the user clicks on the link, Internet Explorer is instructed to open up the Windows Media player. The HTML might look something like this:

```
<a href="http://webserverpath/myWindowsMovie.asx">Click to play
    movie</a>
```

RealVideo streaming

RealNetworks Helix streaming server can stream not only RealMedia files, but Windows Media and QuickTime files, as well. The process of loading a RealMedia streaming movie for a RealNetworks streaming media server requires setting up a metafile, or *ram* file, on your Web server that includes the path to the digital movie. When a user clicks a link, the browser instructs the RealMedia plug-in to load and sends the URL of the movie to the plug-in. Below is one simple technique for using a metafile. For more information about RealNetworks streaming products, see `www.realnet works.com`. You can download an evaluation copy of the Helix Server at `www.realnet works.com/products/media_delivery.html`.

1. **Export your Premiere project as a RealMedia file using the Adobe Media Encoder (File ⇨ Export ⇨ Adobe Media Encoder).** In this example, the name of the movie is MyRealMovie.rm.

2. **Upload the exported movie to the correct directory on your media server.**

3. **Create a metafile in a text editor.** The metafile includes instructions as to the location and name of the actual media file. The text of the metafile could be as simple as this:

```
rtsp://servername/path/MyRealmovie.rm
```

4. **Name the file *MyRealMovie.ram*. Note that the filename includes the name of the exported RealMedia file but uses the** `.rm` **file extension.** Save the file on your Web server.

5. **On your Web page, write HTML that creates a link to the RAM file.** If your `ram` file is in the same directory as your web page, the HTML might look something like this:

```
<a href =myRealMovie.ram">Click to view movie</a>
```

QuickTime streaming

When setting up a movie for QuickTime streaming, you must create a "reference movie" on your Web server. The reference movie is a small file that contains reference information about the movie or movies to be loaded from the QuickTime Streaming Media Server. Within the reference movie is the URL of the QuickTime movie that must be loaded. If the media stream contains alternate files for different connection speeds, the URLs of those movies are also included in the reference movie. For detailed information, see Apple's QuickTime Web site, which provides detailed, step-by-step information:

1. **Export a QuickTime streaming movie file using the Adobe Media Encoder (File ⇨ Export ⇨ Adobe Media Encoder).** By default, this movie seeks a *hinted track*. The hinted track contains information about the server, packet size, and the protocol needed for streaming. If you are not using the Adobe Media Encoder, but you are using QuickTime Pro, make sure that you create the movie as a hinted movie. In this example, the name of the movie is MyQTmovie.mov.

2. **Create a reference movie for the clip and its alternatives.** A reference movie is a movie on the Web server that points to the actual movie. The easiest way to create a reference movie is to use Apple's MakeRef movie, which you can download from Apple's QuickTime Web site. When creating the reference movie, you name the URLs of the Web server. You must also do this for all alternate movies that might be loaded at different connection speeds. The URL in the movie might be something like this:

   `rtsp://qtmedia.`*mywebsite.com*`/MyQTmovie.mov`

3. **Save the movie using a filename such as refMyQTMovie.mov.**

4. **Create a link for your movie, such as the following:**

   `<a href="refMoviemypremieremovie.mov">my movie</a>`

   You could also embed the movie with a command such as this:

   ```
   <embed src="ref.mov" width="pixels" height="pixels"
       autoplay="true" controller="true" loop="false"
       pluginspace="http://www.apple.com/quicktime/download/">
   ```

Placing a Windows Media Movie on a Web Page with Adobe GoLive

If you want to add video movies to your Web page, your best bet is to use a Web-page layout program such as Adobe GoLive or Dreamweaver.

Adobe GoLive is one of the best Web-page layout programs for QuickTime movie producers. GoLive even features a QuickTime tab, which enables you to edit the tracks of a QuickTime movie and add special effects. GoLive's panels allow you to quickly and easily place a QuickTime movie on a page.

Follow these steps to add a QuickTime, Flash, Windows Media, or Real movie to a Web page and edit its attributes with Adobe GoLive:

1. **Create a new window in GoLive for the Web page by choosing File ⇨ New.**

2. **In the New dialog box, click Web ⇨ Pages ⇨ HTML Page.** Click OK.

3. **If the Objects panel is not open, open it by choosing Window ⇨ Objects.**

4. **Click the QuickTime, Windows Media, or Real icon in the panel, shown in Figure 19.2.** Drag it to the Web page. GoLive provides a placeholder for the digital movie. The position of the placeholder determines where the movie appears on the page. You can click and drag the placeholder to specify the size of the movie when it appears on the page.

FIGURE 19.2

The Adobe GoLive Objects panel includes icons for different Web movie formats.

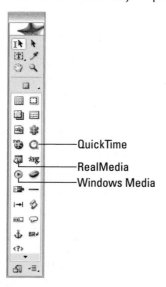

5. **To specify the filename and attributes, open the Inspector panel (if it isn't already open) by choosing Window ⇨ Inspector.**

6. **In the Inspector panel, click the Basic tab, shown in Figure 19.3.**

7. **To select the QuickTime, Windows Media, or RealMedia movie that you want to load, click the folder icon in the Basic tab section.** This opens a dialog box in which you can choose the movie from your hard drive. (Alternatively, if you have a Web site already designed, you can drag the Point-and-Shoot icon directly to the file in your Adobe GoLive site window on your computer's desktop.)

After you place the movie in a Web page, you can adjust its frame size in the width and height fields to match your movie's frame size.

8. **Click the More tab in the Inspector panel, shown in Figure 19.4.**

9. **If you want to enter a name for your movie (for Web scripting use only), type a name in the Name field.** The QuickTime version of this page also enables you to designate a page from which to download the QuickTime plug-in. If you want to add padding between the movie and surrounding text, enter a value in pixels in HSpace, for horizontal space, and/or VSpace, for vertical space. To hide the movie and play back audio only, QuickTime users can select the Is Hidden check box in the QuickTime More tab.

FIGURE 19.3

The Inspector panel's Windows Media Basic tab

10. **To view or change attributes for the HTML object tab, click Attribs.** Here you can enter a name for the player, change the URL of the source media, and specify whether you want the user interface windows controller and buttons to appear (`uimode="full"`). If you don't want the Windows Media controls to appear, you can set uimode to "none."

11. **To specify more HTML attributes, click the QuickTime Windows Media or RealMedia tab, shown in Figure 19.5.** For example, you can specify whether the movie automatically plays upon opening or whether you can right-click to access a context menu to control the movie. After you click the Windows Media tab, you can also click the Windows Media URL button, which allows you to reset the URL and reset the uimode attribute by selecting from a drop-down menu. For QuickTime users, clicking check boxes in the QuickTime movie tab automatically creates the attributes described in the section "QuickTime settings for Web pages."

FIGURE 19.4

The Inspector panel's Windows Attributes tab

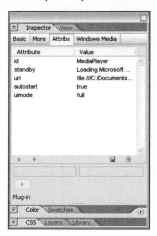

FIGURE 19.5

The Inspector panel's Windows Media tab

12. **If you want to preview a QuickTime movie while in GoLive, click the Open Movie button at the bottom of the QuickTime tab.** When the movie appears, the Basic tab provides track, size, and data rate information about the movie.

Placing a QuickTime Movie on a Web Page with Adobe Dreamweaver

Now that Dreamweaver is part of the Adobe family, more and more Premiere Pro users will probably start using Dreamweaver as their Web layout program. Placing a video movie on a Web page in Dreamweaver is a fairly simple task. Unlike GoLive, Dreamweaver does not have specific tools for importing different movie formats. In Dreamweaver, you import a movie by inserting an ActiveX media element into the Web page. Here are the steps for loading a QuickTime movie into Dreamweaver:

1. **If your movie isn't in your Web site's production folder, copy it into the folder.**

2. **If you didn't already create a new HTML page, choose File ⇨ New.** Create the page and save it.

3. **In Dreamweaver, move the cursor to where you want to insert the movie.** Click the mouse. Choose Insert ⇨ Media ⇨ ActiveX, as shown in Figure 19.6. This places an ActiveX area on your HTML page.

4. **Set the properties for your movie in the Properties palette, shown in Figure 19.7.** Click the Embed check box. This tells Dreamweaver to use the Embed HTML tag and allows you to load the movie filename into the Properties palette. In the Src (source) field, click the folder icon and then locate your movie. After you click OK, the movie filename appears. Enter the width and height in the W and H fields. Onscreen, the ActiveX box grows to match your movie's size. In the ClassID field, you must choose the ClassID for QuickTime: clsid:02BF25D5-8C17-4B23-BC80-D3488ABDDC6B. If it doesn't appear in the drop-down menu, type it in.

FIGURE 19.6

You can insert an ActiveX media element into your Web page.

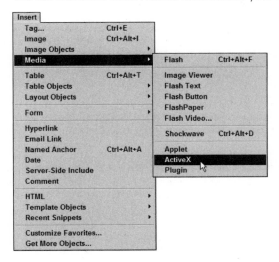

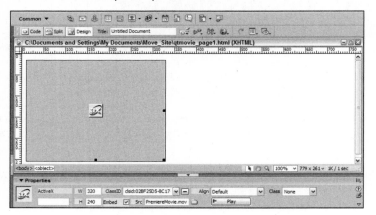

FIGURE 19.7

The ActiveX and Properties palette in Dreamweaver

Creating a Web Link in Premiere Pro

Adobe Premiere Pro enables you to add an HREF track in a QuickTime movie. Using the HREF track, you can make the user's browser jump to another Web location while the movie plays. In Premiere Pro, this feature is called a *Web link*.

You set up a Web link in Premiere Pro using markers. A marker adds a visual clue on the Timeline for specific important points in a movie. Follow these steps for adding a marker to the Timeline. (Before following these steps, you should have at least one clip in the Timeline.)

1. **Activate the Timeline panel by clicking it.**

2. **If a clip is selected in the Timeline, deselect it.**

3. **Click and drag the current-time indicator in the Timeline panel to move to the frame where you want to set the Web link.**

4. **Choose Marker ⇨ Set Sequence Marker ⇨ Unnumbered.** The marker appears on the Timeline.

 You can also create a marker by clicking and dragging a Marker icon in the Timeline to a specific frame in the current sequence or by double-clicking the Marker icon in the Timeline.

5. **Now that you've created a marker, double-click it in the Timeline window to open the Marker dialog box, shown in Figure 19.8.** Specify the URL that you want to jump to.

6. **In the Marker dialog box, enter a URL in the URL field, such as** `http://myhome-page.com/page_2.htm`. You can enter a frame in the Frame Target field if you are using HTML framesets. Frames are handy tools if you want to create an effect in which the QuickTime movie opens a frame in a Web page. To create this effect, you need to enter the name of the URL and the filename for the frame in the Frame Target area.

 **NOTE** Web links can be created only from Timeline sequence markers. You cannot create a Web link from a clip marker.

FIGURE 19.8

Premiere Pro's Marker dialog box allows the movie to open a Web page at a specific point in the movie.

```
Marker @ 00;00;01;04

           Comments: [                    ]        [   OK    ]
                     [                    ]        [ Cancel  ]

           Duration: 00;00;00;01                   [ Previous ]
    Marker Options                                 [   Next  ]
            Chapter: [                    ]
       Web Links                                   [  Delete ]
               URL: [                    ]
       Frame Target: [                    ]

    (i) Marker Options will only work with compatible
        output types.
```

Summary

If you will be exporting a movie to the Web or an intranet, knowing the HTML options that are available to you can help you add features to your movies. A program such as Adobe GoLive or Dreamweaver can simplify the task of loading a digital movie onto a Web page, as well as the task of writing the HTML code. QuickTime movies enable you to add many features that can be used on the Web. This chapter covered these topics:

■ Streaming and progressive downloading are two common techniques for displaying video on Web pages.

■ Common Web video file formats include Flash Video, QuickTime, RealMedia, and Windows Media.

■ You can add a clickable HREF track to a QuickTime movie.

Chapter 20

Exporting to the Web and Mobile Devices

N ow that Internet users are flocking to Web video sites such as YouTube, and downloading everything from podcasts to the latest episode of their favorite TV shows, Premiere Pro users will undoubtedly want to turn their creative efforts into video podcasts and streaming video productions.

Streaming media enables users to view a video program as it is delivered from a special streaming server. The clip starts playing before the entire video is streamed, and the video is not saved to the user's hard drive. Before the advent of streaming media, Web users had to wait for an entire clip to download before the video actually started to play. When media is streamed, information packets are sent by the streaming server applications such as RealNetworks' Helix server, Microsoft's Windows media server, or Apple's QuickTime streaming media server.

Fortunately, Premiere Pro users can easily export video for Web streaming and for handheld video devices such as iPods and cell phones. Premiere Pro's Adobe Media Encoder provides a consistent and straightforward tool for outputting video files in streaming and non-streaming formats. This exporting module, installed within Premiere Pro, takes the guesswork out of choosing the appropriate output settings for Web and mobile video viewing. You can export your Premiere Pro projects in Windows Media, RealMedia, QuickTime, or mobile device formats. The H.264 standard can be used for mobile devices such as iPods and cell phones. Furthermore, presets built into the Media Encoder enable you to easily export a video sequence that is optimized for multiple bandwidths. In other words, you can export a high-quality file to the Web or an intranet and have the Media Encoder create versions for users with either high- or low-bandwidth connections. When you output to an intranet or the Web, the Media Encoder presets can save you time and help ensure quality playback for users who view your videos.

If you are outputting to a mobile device, you can set an option in the Media Encoder to preview your video in Adobe Device Central. This allows you to view your video as a user would on a cell phone or other mobile device.

 Exporting movies in FLV format for Flash is covered in Chapter 22.

Encoding Terms

This chapter provides an overview of how to choose Web encoding formats using the Media Encoder. As you choose different formats, you will see a variety of arcane encoding terms such as two-pass encoding, variable bit rate, and constant bit rate. These terms appear, regardless of whether you are exporting to Windows Media, QuickTime, or mobile device format. Fortunately, the Media Encoder provides exporting presets, and you may never have to change the encoding settings. Nevertheless, before continuing, you may want to review some brief definitions of these terms:

- **Two-pass encoding:** Two-pass encoding can improve the digital quality of exported video. When you use two-pass encoding, the video is actually processed twice. The first time, the encoder analyzes the video to determine the best manner to encode it. On the second pass, it uses the information gathered in the first pass to encode it. As you might guess, two-pass encoding takes longer than single-pass encoding.

- **Variable bit rate:** Bit rate defines how much data is transferred per second. Variable bit rate (VBR) varies the bit rate of a clip as it plays back. When a high-action scene needs more bits or bandwidth, the encoding process delivers the extra bits; in areas that don't require high bandwidth, it lowers the bit rate. Thus, for clips that vary in action, VBR can provide better quality than constant bit rate (CBR), which does not vary the bit rate of the clip as it plays back. For Windows Media, the Media Encoder's Bit rate Mode drop-down menu allows you to choose between Constrained and Unconstrained VBR.

  - **Unconstrained VBR** encoding allows you to specify an average value for the bit rate. This encoding process attempts to provide the highest quality while still trying to sustain the average bit rate. Despite its attempts, the bit rate may vary widely from the specified average. Thus, unconstrained VBR tries to provide high quality within the confines of bandwidth constraints.

  - **Constrained VBR** is similar to unconstrained VBR, except that it adds peak video bit rate values and a peak buffer size to the equation. Controls for maximum buffer rate are in the Advanced Settings section, visible by scrolling down in the Export Settings dialog box.

- **Keyframe:** When some codecs compress video, they can compare each frame with subsequent frames and can save only the information that changes. When the information changes, the codec saves a full frame of video only when it needs to. This frame is often called a *keyframe*. As a result, codecs that use keyframes can reduce the file size of exported video. The number of keyframes needed depends upon the codec and the amount of motion in the video. For Web work, the fewer keyframes the better, because fewer keyframes result in smaller file sizes. Presets for Windows Media and RealMedia specify keyframe distance in seconds; presets for QuickTime are in frames.

- **Deinterlace:** Deinterlacing removes one field from a video frame to prevent blurring artifacts that can occur when video is output on a computer. This blurring is most likely to occur during scenes that contain motion. The blurring results from the difference in frame information between the odd, or upper, video field and the even, or lower, video field that comprise a video frame.

- **Video Noise Reduction:** All formats include a Filters tab that allows you to apply a video noise reduction filter. This filter is applied before compression and can reduce file size by removing noise artifacts from source video.

- **Metadata:** Metadata for Web video clips is text data about the clip that can be searched for on the World Wide Web or read by computer applications. Often, metadata information includes information such as title, date, and creator. The Media Encoder allows you to add metadata to MPEG and QuickTime files.

The following additional encoding options appear when exporting to H.264 format for mobile devices:

- **Profile:** You can choose the profile used for the video stream. Choices include Baseline, Main, and High. Baseline is considered the best choice for mobile devices that require less computing power. The Main profile was originally created as a high-end broadcast profile, but it has been superseded by High, which should be used for high-definition video.

- **Level:** Constrains the parameters or the encoding process. These settings control maximum macroblocks per section, maximum frame size, and maximum video bit rates. The higher the level specified, the higher all maximum settings used.

 The H.264 format was created to provide high-quality video at lower bit rates.

Using the Adobe Media Encoder

Premiere Pro's Adobe Media Encoder provides a consistent interface for exporting to the major streaming media formats. Whether you are exporting to Windows Media, RealMedia, QuickTime, or H.264 format, the basic steps for exporting are the same. All exporting starts in the Media Encoder's Export Settings dialog box, which provides video and audio settings, as well as presets and options for exporting multiple streams with one file. Follow these basic steps for exporting:

1. **Select the Timeline or Program Monitor panel that includes the footage to be exported.** If you want to export a clip, select the clip in the Project panel.

2. **Choose File ➪ Export ➪ Adobe Media Encoder.** This opens the Export Settings dialog box.

3. **To preview in Output mode, click the Output tab, shown in Figure 20.1.**

FIGURE 20.1

Use the Export Settings dialog box to export video for the Web.

4. **In the Export Settings section, click the Export drop-down menu to choose an export format such as Windows Media, RealMedia, QuickTime, or H.264.**

5. **In the Range drop-down menu, choose whether you want to export the entire sequence (or clip) or the Work area.** If you are exporting a clip, you can choose Entire Clip or choose to export from the clip's In to Out point.

6. **Choose a preset in the Preset drop-down menu.** Choose the best preset for your intended audience. The presets are descriptions of the type of Web connection that you expect your audience to be using. Figure 20.2 shows the Windows Media NTSC Source to Download 256 Kbps preset. This choice indicates the approximate amount of data that is sent each second, measured in kilobits per second.

7. **Choose whether you want to include video or audio in the export by deselecting or selecting the Export Video or Export Audio options.**

8. **Review the video settings in the Video tab.** Make changes if needed. For example, you may want to change the frame size or frame rate. Because you are exporting to the Web, you should leave the pixel aspect ratio set to square pixels (available in Windows Media and QuickTime formats). Because you are exporting to a computer screen and not a video screen that uses interlacing, the field order settings should be set to Progressive.

FIGURE 20.2

The Source tab with the Crop tool

9. **Review the audio settings by clicking the Audio tab.** Make changes if needed.

10. **Review the different streams — shown later in Figure 20.6 — that are associated with the preset by clicking the panel menu in the middle of the Export Settings dialog box.** If desired, add or subtract video streams (called *Audiences* when exporting in Windows Media or RealMedia format, and *Alternates* when exporting in QuickTime format). Note that not all presets include more than one video stream.

11. **If you want to add a filter to reduce video noise before the file is compressed, click the Filters tab.** In the Filters tab, select the Video Noise Reduction option, and then drag the slider to set the Noise Reduction value.

12. **If you want to send the exported file to an FTP site, click the Others tab.** Enter FTP server and log-in information.

13. **To start the Export process, click OK.** A Save dialog box appears, allowing you to name and save your file.

Adobe Media Encoder Optional Features

During the export process, the Adobe Media Encoder allows you to create custom presets and to crop, preview, and deinterlace video.

Previewing

The Media Encoder provides a preview of both your source file and of the final video output. The following list describes options for previewing source and output video:

- To preview the source file, click the Source tab.

- To preview the video based upon the settings in the Media Encoder, click the Output tab.

NOTE The Source and Output panel menu allows you choose to display the source and output screens either with pixel aspect ratio correction or in square pixels. The Aspect Ratio Corrected option adjusts the display so that source pixels display properly on a computer monitor. The 1:1 Pixel Preview option displays the source image with square pixels, which can result in image distortion.

- To scrub through video in either the Source or Output tab, click and drag in the Time Ruler at the bottom of the preview area.

Cropping and scaling

Before you export your file, you can crop the source video. Cropped areas appear black in the final video. Follow these steps:

1. **Click the Source tab.** This opens the source view of your video, as shown previously in Figure 20.2.

2. **Select the Crop tool.**

3. **To crop precisely using pixel dimensions, click and drag over the Left, Top, Right, or Bottom numerical fields.** Clicking and dragging right reduces the cropping area. As you click and drag, the cropping area displays on-screen. Alternatively, click and drag a corner over the area of the video that you want to retain. As you click and drag, a readout displays the frame size in pixels.

4. **If you want to change the aspect ratio of the crop to 4:3 or 16:9, click in the Crop Proportions drop-down menu.** Choose the aspect ratio.

5. **To preview the cropped video, click the Output tab.**

6. **If you want to scale your video frame to fit within the crop borders, select the Scale To Fit option (next to the Deinterlace option).**

 **TIP** To deinterlace video, click the Output tab and then select the Deinterlace option.

Saving, importing, and deleting presets

If you make changes to a preset, you can save your custom preset to your hard drive so that you can use it at a later time. After you save presets, you can import or delete them.

- **Saving presets:** If you edit a preset and want to save it to use at a later time or use it as a basis for comparing export quality, click the Save Preset button (disk icon). Then enter a name in the Choose Name dialog box, shown in Figure 20.3. If you want to save settings in the Filters tab, select the Save Filter Settings option. To save cropping and deinterlace settings, select the Save Other Tasks option.

FIGURE 20.3

Choose a name for a preset in the Choose Name dialog box.

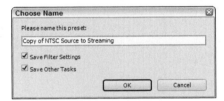

- **Importing presets:** The easiest way to import a custom preset is to click the Preset drop-down menu and choose it from the top portion of the list. Alternatively, you can click the Import Preset button (folder icon) and then load the presets from your hard drive. Presets have a .vpr file extension.
- **Deleting presets:** To delete a preset, load the preset and then click the Delete Preset button (trash icon). An alert appears, warning you that the deletion process cannot be undone.

Viewing help on-screen

Brief information messages describe the different fields in the Media Encoder. For example, to view an information statement about the bit rate field, move your mouse over that field. In the information line (toward the bottom of the screen), the following message appears: "Data Rate for Video in Kilobits per Second."

Exporting to Windows Media Format

The Media Encoder allows you to export movies in Windows Media format, Microsoft's audio and video format. Windows Media movies can play in Internet Explorer and can be streamed from Microsoft's streaming media server. Windows media files are recognizable by their .wmv file extension. WMV files can be read by Windows Media Player version 7 and higher.

 You can output files in previous versions of Windows Media by selecting older codecs (such as Windows Media 7 or 8) in the Video Codec drop-down menu.

To export in Windows Media format, open the Media Encoder and then choose a Windows Media preset. Many of the presets are shown in Figure 20.4.

FIGURE 20.4

Windows Media presets

Custom
Audio Download 128Kbps
Audio Download 32kbps
Audio Download 64kbps
Audio Streaming
Creative ZEN Vision 25fps
Creative ZEN Vision 30fps
HDTV 1080p 24 High Quality 5.1
HDTV 1080p 24 High Quality
HDTV 1080p 25 High Quality
HDTV 720p 24 High Quality
HDTV 720p 25 High Quality
Microsoft Zune Audio
Microsoft Zune Video 25fps
Microsoft Zune Video 30fps
NTSC Source to Download 1024kbps
NTSC Source to Download 128kbps
NTSC Source to Download 256kbps
NTSC Source to Download 512kbps
NTSC Source to Download 56kbps
✔ NTSC Source to Streaming
NTSC Widescreen Source to Download 1024kbps
NTSC Widescreen Source to Download 256kbps
NTSC Widescreen Source to Streaming
PAL Source to Download 1024kbps
PAL Source to Download 128kbps
PAL Source to Download 256kbps
PAL Source to Download 512kbps
PAL Source to Download 56kbps
PAL Source to Streaming
PAL Widescreen Source to Download 1024kbps
PAL Widescreen Source to Download 256kbps
PAL Widescreen Source to Streaming
Palm Treo or LifeDrive series
Palm Tungsten series

The options for Windows Media files allow for multiple bit rate encoding, in which one file provides multiple streams at different bit rates. Thus, the file includes streams for different "audiences." When a browser sends the signal to start streaming the video, the Windows media server uses "intelligent streaming" to decide which bit rate to use. The server can choose this bit rate when the stream starts, or it can choose a slower bit rate if the bandwidth decreases. (Keep in mind that, even though you can connect to the Internet at a specific bit rate, you may not be able to connect at this bandwidth all the time.)

Viewing audience settings

To use a preset with multiple bit rates for different audiences, you can choose the NTSC Source to Streaming. To view the multiple streams, click the panel menu icon in the middle-right side of the Export Settings dialog box, as shown in Figure 20.5. Note that the bit rates range from a 28.8 Kbps modem to a stream for broadband and cable modems. The frame sizes for the different streams begin at 128 x 96 and jump to 510 x 384. To see the video and audio settings for any stream, click it in the drop-down menu. After you click a stream, the video and audio settings for the stream appear in their respective tabs.

FIGURE 20.5

Multiple streams are available for different audiences.

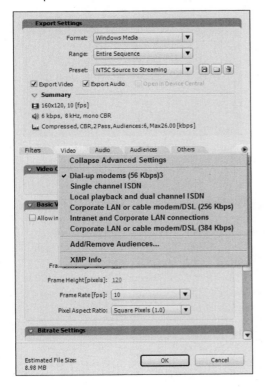

Adding and removing audiences

If you want to change the number of streams in a preset, you can add or remove preset bit rates for different target audiences. To add an audience, choose Add/Remove Audiences from the Video panel drop-down menu. In the Target Audience dialog box, click Add. This opens the System

Audiences dialog box, shown in Figure 20.6. Here, you can see the list of target audience streams and the data rates in kilobits per second. To add an audience, simply click the check box for the stream that you want to add. Then click OK.

If you want to remove a target audience from a preset, click Delete in the Target Audience dialog box.

FIGURE 20.6

Select a stream to add to the target audience.

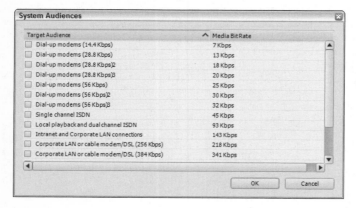

Using QuickTime Streaming

The Media Encoder provides exporting options for creating QuickTime streaming media files. As discussed in Chapter 19, QuickTime is Apple's cross-platform digital media format. QuickTime streaming files can be streamed from both Apple's streaming media server and RealNetworks RealMedia streaming media server. Not only are QuickTime files cross-platform, but Apple's streaming media server is also available on Windows NT and UNIX platforms. The Media Encoder also includes presets for progressive downloading of files. In a progressive download, the entire video clip is downloaded before it can be viewed.

> **TIP**   You can also prepare a QuickTime movie for streaming by exporting a Premiere Pro movie. Choose File ⇨ Export Movie and then choose QuickTime as a setting. You can then use Apple's QuickTime Pro to export the file for Apple's QuickTime streaming media server.

When you choose a QuickTime preset, the standard video codec that is selected is H.264.

> **NOTE**   The H.264 codec, also referred to as MPEG-4 part 10, provides very high quality video at low data rates. Apple asserts that the H.264 codec can match MPEG-2 quality at half the data rate.

If you wish to choose a preset with multiple streams, you can choose NTSC Source to Streaming Alternate Present. To view the streams (called Alternates), click the panel menu, as shown in Figure 20.7. The alternate streams range from a 56 Kbs modem to another for a 1 Mbps cable modem. To view the specific video and audio settings of a stream, simply click the Alternate stream name in the panel drop-down menu. After you click the stream, the video and audio options update to reflect your choice.

Unlike Windows Media, which packs its audience streams into one file, QuickTime exports a separate file for each stream. QuickTime streaming also requires a "hint" track which can be contained in the target stream. (The hint track instructs the QuickTime Streaming Server how to package the video as a stream. It contains information about the server, packet size, and the protocol needed for streaming.) If desired, you can set a prefix for all of the stream files and a separate file location. These options are shown in Figure 20.7 in the Alternates tab, which also allows you to specify that the file is for a streaming server and/or that the streams automatically loop or autoplay when loading. Figure 20.7 also shows the XMP Info menu option. This option allows you to add metadata to your QuickTime files using Adobe's Extensible Metadata Platform. The MetaDeta fields include Author, Description, and Copyright information.

FIGURE 20.7

QuickTime streaming alternate choices

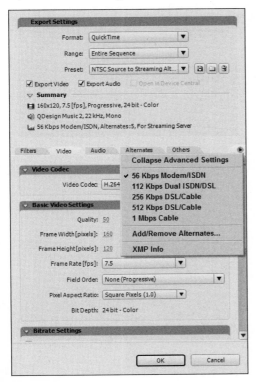

Exporting to Advanced RealMedia Format

The Media Encoder's RealMedia export formats enable you to create digital movies in RealMedia format, one of the most popular streaming video formats used on the Web. RealMedia quickly became popular because it was one of the first true streaming video formats. As the data streams, the RealPlayer (or newer RealOne Player) software and the RealMedia server communicate to ensure that the data is sent at the best data rate. The RealMedia options in the Export Settings dialog box enable you to create one video clip for multiple audiences. When the clip is downloaded, RealMedia switches to either the faster stream for faster connection users or the slower stream for slower dial-up modem users.

When you choose a RealMedia preset, the Export Settings section of the Export Settings dialog box allows you to pick a bit rate setting. You can choose Frame rate and Keyframe Interval settings in the Video tab. Unlike Windows Media or QuickTime, RealMedia also provides video content options, as shown in Figure 20.8.

FIGURE 20.8

A RealMedia preset with video content options

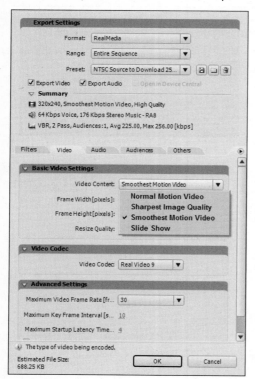

- **Normal Motion Video:** Use this option for clips that include some motion and stills.
- **Sharpest Image Quality:** Use this option for sporting events and other action clips.
- **Smoothest Motion Video:** Use this option for clips that feature limited motion.
- **Slide Show:** This option makes your video appear as a series of still frames.

Like the Windows Media format, RealMedia allows you to add or subtract target audiences by clicking Add/Remove Audiences in the panel menu to the right of the Others tab. (See the "Adding and removing audiences" section earlier in this chapter.)

Exporting to Mobile Devices

With over eight million video iPods already sold and millions of cell phones capable of download-ing video, it is obvious that the viewing venue of many future video productions will be mobile devices. If you want to output your Premiere Pro production for viewing on a mobile device such as a cell phone or an iPod, the Media Encoder makes the process simple and straightforward. Once you choose a mobile preset, the Media Encoder automatically chooses the correct frame size and pixel aspect ratio, as well as choosing default settings for other options such as frame rate and audio codec. To export for a mobile device, follow these steps:

1. **Select the Timeline or Program Monitor panel that includes the footage to be exported.** If you want to export a clip, select the clip in the Project panel.

2. **Choose File ⇨ Export ⇨ Adobe Media Encoder.** This opens the Export Settings dialog box.

3. **Click the Format drop-down menu and choose H.264 as the export format.** (Note that the H.264 Blu-ray format is for high-definition DVDs that use the Blu-ray format.)

4. **In the Range drop-down menu, choose whether to export the entire sequence or the work area.** If you are exporting a clip, you can choose Entire Clip or choose to export from the clip's In to Out point

5. **Click the Preset drop-down menu and choose a mobile preset, as shown in Figure 20.9.** If you are exporting to create a podcast, choose one of the iPod video settings. If you are exporting for a mobile phone, choose one of the 3GPP (Third-Generation Partnership Project) settings.

6. **Choose whether you want to exclude video or audio in the export by deselecting the Export Video or Export Audio options.** If either the Export Video or Export Audio options are deselected, and you want to include audio or video, select the appropriate choice.

7. **Review the video settings in the Video tab.** Make changes if needed. See the Encoding Terms section at the beginning of this chapter for a discussion of many of the options.

8. **If you chose a 3GPP preset, select the Open in Device Central option to preview how your footage will look on a mobile phone.** Note that the preview will only appear if QuickTime is installed on PC systems.

9. **Review the Audio settings by clicking the Audio tab.** Make changes if needed.

10. **Review the Multiplexer settings by clicking the Audio tab.** The correct options here are chosen automatically by the Media Encoder. For example, if you choose an iPod preset, the iPod stream setting is chosen with MP4 (MPEG-4) as the Multiplexing choice. If you choose a 3GPP preset, the Media Encoder sets the Multiplexing choice to 3GPP.

FIGURE 20.9

You can choose the Mobile Video H.264 format for mobile device output.

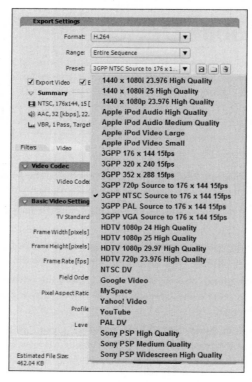

11. **If you want to add a filter to reduce video noise before the file is compressed, click the Filters tab.** In the Filters tab, select the Video Noise Reduction option, and then drag the slider to set the Noise Reduction value.

12. **If you want to send the exported file to an FTP site, click the Others tab, and then enter FTP server and log-in information.**

13. **To start the Export process, click OK.** A Save dialog box appears, allowing you to name and save your file.

If you choose a 3GPP preset, and you selected the Open in Device Central option, the Device Central window opens with a preview of your video in a cell phone skin.

Previewing in Device Central

Device Central provides a visual testing simulator for previewing mobile content on a variety of different mobile devices. Device Central also includes previews for Flash Lite format, a format developed for mobile phones and electronic devices. To preview your video in Device Central, follow the steps in the previous section. Choose a 3GPP preset, and make sure that the Open in Device Central option is selected (PC users must also have QuickTime installed). After your video is rendered, the Adobe Device Central CS3 window opens.

Your video displays in a default mobile device in the Emulator tab. To view your video on a specific device, select the manufacturer, and then double-click the model. For example, to preview your video on a Motorola RAZR phone, click the plus sign to the left of Motorola, and then double-click one of the RAZR phone options, as shown in Figure 20.10. Once you select the phone, its name and frame size appear at the bottom of the screen. Click the Play button to play the video. The button controls at the bottom of the screen also allow you to zoom in and rotate the phone.

FIGURE 20.10

Device Central allows you to preview videos on different mobile devices.

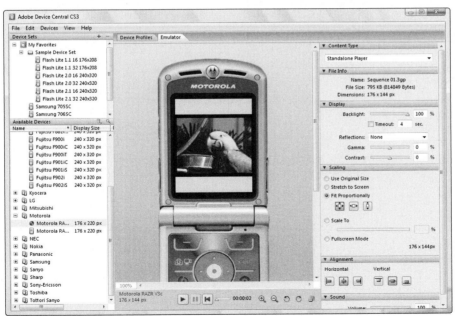

The controls along the right side of the Device Central window allow you change screen brightness and contrast, scale, alignment, and volume. You can also click the Fullscreen Mode option to stretch your video out sideways across the length of the screen. You can then click the rotate button to rotate the phone. Although you can adjust different controls to change how your video appears, it's important to realize that Device Central does not change the video. It's really a showcase of phone skins that allows developers to see how their content looks on different devices.

Viewing device profiles

Apart from showing live previews of mobile devices, Device Central also provides in-depth listings of mobile phone specifications. To view specifications for a selected phone, click the Device Profiles tab, shown in Figure 20.11. The Device Profiles tab lists a phone's general specification and includes specific information on Flash, Bitmap, Video, and Web Formats and browsers that the phone uses.

FIGURE 20.11

The Device Profiles tab for the Motorola RAZR V3c

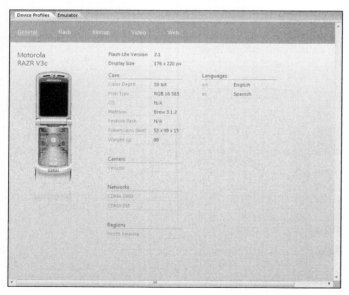

Summary

Slow Web connection speeds can make downloading digital video a time-consuming task. Premiere Pro's Adobe Media Encoder takes advantage of video streaming and helps to optimize download times. This chapter covered these topics:

- You can use the Adobe Media Encoder to export files in different file formats suitable for viewing on the Web or on Mobile devices.

- You can use the Media Encoder's QuickTime format to export QuickTime movie files for progressive download and for the Web Streaming Media server.

- You can use the Media Encoder to export files in Windows Media or RealNetwork's RealMedia format.

- You can use the H.264 format to export video for mobile devices. If you export using one of the 3GPP presets, you can preview your video in Adobe Device Central.

Chapter 21

Exporting to Videotape, Hi-8 Tape, and Film

D espite the excitement generated by outputting video to the World Wide Web, videotape still remains one of the most common media for distributing and showing high-quality video productions. Provided you have the right hardware, Adobe Premiere Pro enables you to export clips and complete projects to videotape.

Professionals who demand high-quality output can also have Premiere Pro export their projects to an Advanced Authoring Format (AAF) file. An AAF file is a multimedia file format that allows Premiere Pro users to send data to other digital video editing systems.

This chapter discusses the steps you need to take to output your Premiere Pro files to videotape or to an AAF file.

Preparing to Export Video

In order to precisely export your Premiere Pro project to videotape, your system must support device control, which enables you to start and stop a videotape recorder or camcorder directly from Premiere Pro. If you have a DV camcorder and your computer has an IEEE 1394 port, chances are good that you can use device control. If you have professional videotape recording equipment and a capture board in your computer, you may be able to export video to your videotape recorder using serial device control. Before you get started, you may want to add black video or bars and tone to the beginning of your project.

Adding black video, color bars, and tone

If you are sending your Premiere Pro project to a video production facility, you may want to add black video to the beginning of your project. The black video provides the production facility more time to get its equipment rolling before your project begins. Follow these steps to create black video:

1. **Click the New Item button at the bottom of the Project panel.**

2. **In the pop-up menu, shown in Figure 21.1, choose Black Video.** This adds five seconds of black video to the Project panel.

FIGURE 21.1

Click the New Item button to add Black Video, as well as bars and tone.

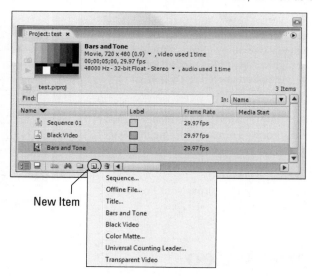

New Item

3. **To add the black video to the Source Monitor, double-click Black Video in the Project panel.** You can then insert the black video into a sequence by moving the CTI to the front of the time ruler in the Timeline panel and then clicking the Insert button in the Source Monitor panel.

In order to calibrate color and audio, production facilities set their electronic equipment to color bars and a 1 kHz tone. If you are working with a video production facility, you can easily add bars and tone to your Premiere Pro project. Follow these steps:

1. **Click the New Item button at the bottom of the Project panel.**

2. **In the drop-down menu, shown in Figure 21.1, choose Bars and Tone.** This adds five seconds of color bars and a tone to the Project panel.

3. **To increase the duration of the bars and tone, select Bars and Tone in the Project panel (or right-click Bars and Tone in the Project panel) and then choose Speed/Duration in the drop-down menu.** In the Clip Speed/Duration dialog box, add the desired time in frames.

4. **To add the bars and tone to the Source Monitor panel, double-click Bars and Tone in the Project panel.** You can then insert the bars and tone into a sequence by moving the CTI to the front of the time ruler in the Timeline panel and then clicking the Insert button in the Source Monitor panel.

Checking project settings

Before exporting to videotape, review your production's project settings by choosing Project ⇨ Project Settings ⇨ General. Review the Video, Audio, and Keyframe and Rendering sections. As you view the settings in these dialog boxes, make sure that they are set to the highest-quality output, because Premiere Pro uses these settings when exporting to videotape.

NOTE The video settings in Premiere Pro are explained in several chapters in this book (including Chapters 3 and 18). However, you may want to review the Fields setting in the General options of the Project Settings dialog box, as shown in Figure 21.2.

FIGURE 21.2

The General options in the Project Settings dialog box

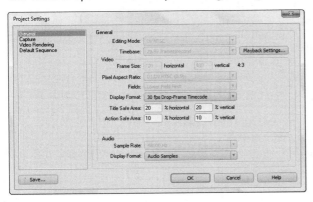

Fields are relevant only when exporting to videotape or importing into another application, such as Adobe After Effects. The NTSC, PAL, and Secam standards divide each frame into two fields. In NTSC video, where the frame rate is approximately 29.97 frames per second, approximately 30 video frames appear each second. Each frame is divided into two fields that appear for $1/50$ of a second. PAL and Secam display a video frame every 25 frames, and each field displays for 1/60 of a second.

When the field displays, it displays alternating scan lines. For example, the first frame may scan lines 1, 3, 5, 7, and so on. After the first field is scanned, the frame then scans lines 2, 4, 6, 8, and so on. As a result, in some respects, a video frame is like a child's puzzle, with the video fields being two zigzagging, interlocking pieces. If you view only one of the pieces, you don't get a sharp picture. In fact, if you could freeze a field onscreen, you would see an image with blurry lines.

When specifying export settings, you can choose Upper Field First or Lower Field First, depending on which field your system expects to receive first. If this setting is incorrect, jerky and jumpy video may result. The default setting for a DV project is Lower Field First.

TIP   If you don't know the order in which your equipment expects fields, run a quick export of a project that includes motion. Export the project set to Upper Field First, and then export it set to Lower Field First. The correct field setting should provide the best playback. Use this setting when you export your video project.

Checking device control settings

Before you begin exporting your project to videotape, ensure that your device control options are properly installed. These settings appear in Premiere Pro's Preferences dialog box. To open the Preferences dialog box and access the Device Control section directly, choose Edit ⇨ Preferences ⇨ Device Control.

Click the Device pop-up menu, and choose the device control option for your equipment. Next, click the Options button. This opens the DV Device Control Options dialog box, where you can choose your output device, as shown in Figure 21.3.

In the DV/HDV Device Control Settings dialog box, choose the correct video standard (NTSC or PAL). Choose a device brand and a device type. Next, pick the timecode format you want to use in the Timecode Format menu. If your camcorder is off, turn it on and click the Check Status button. If all connections are properly set, the Offline readout should change to Online. If you are connected to the Internet, to check the compatibility of your camcorder with Premiere Pro, click Go Online for Device Info. This command brings you to a Web page that lists camcorders and their compatibility with Premiere Pro.

FIGURE 21.3

Choose your camcorder in the Device Brand drop-down menu.

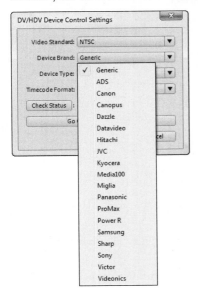

Setting digital video playback options

After you check your video and device control settings, your next step is to establish playback options. The choices that are available depend upon the hardware you are using.

If you are using digital video equipment, start by connecting the IEEE 1394 cable from your camcorder or tape deck to your computer.

Now, set the playback to your camcorder by following these steps:

1. **Turn on your camcorder or recording device.** If you are using a camcorder, make sure it is set to the VCR or VTR setting.

2. **To set the playback to a digital video recording device, choose Project ⇨ Project Settings ⇨ General.** (The Editing mode was set when you created the project.)

3. **Click the Playback Settings button.**

If you choose DV Playback in the Editing Mode field, the Playback Settings dialog box appears, as shown in Figure 21.4.

Playback Settings options for a DV camcorder or VCR

These are the options in the DV Playback Settings dialog box:

- In the Realtime Playback section:
  - **Desktop Video Display During Playback:** Select this option to view your video on your desktop computer system.
  - **External Device:** If you want to view playback on an external device such as a camcorder, select it in the External Device drop-down menu.
  - **Aspect Ratio Conversion:** This option allows you to choose whether pixel aspect ratio conversion is handled by hardware or software. In the Aspect Ratio Conversion drop-down menu, choose None for no conversion, choose Hardware if your hardware supports aspect ratio conversion, or choose Software to allow Premiere Pro to handle the aspect ratio conversion.
  - **Desktop Audio** and **External Device Audio:** Choose whether you want to playback audio on your desktop computer system or on an external device such as a camcorder.
- In the Export section, choose your external device in the External Device drop-down menu.

Exporting with Device Control

This section describes how to export to videotape with device control for DV hardware.

Before starting the export session, make sure that you have set the control options in the Playback Settings dialog box and that you have reviewed your video settings. To export to videotape using DV device control, follow these steps:

1. **Turn on your videotape deck.** Load the tape you want to record onto. To record using device control, insert a tape into your tape deck; then write down the timecode location at which you want to begin recording.

 To pre-stripe videotape, place an unused tape (without any timecode) in your camcorder. Place the lens cap on and begin recording until the tape runs out.

2. **Select the Sequence that you want to export by clicking it in the Project panel.**

3. **Choose File ⇨ Export ⇨ Export to Tape.**

4. **In the Export to Tape dialog box, shown in Figure 21.5, select Activate Recording Device.** This tells Premiere Pro to take control of the recording device.

5. **If you don't want the recording to begin at the current location, choose Assemble at Timecode.** Enter the timecode where you want recording to begin.

6. **In the Delay Movie Start field, enter a delay in quarter-frames.** (Some devices need this delay to sync the recording device with the movie after starting the recording process.)

7. **In the Preroll field, enter the number of frames you want to back up before the specified timecode.** This enables the tape to attain the proper speed before recording. Five seconds (150 frames) is usually sufficient.

8. **In the Option section, choose whether you want Premiere Pro to abort after dropped frames, report dropped frames in a text report, or render audio before export.** This last option can help prevent dropped frames due to complicated audio.

9. **Click Record.**

FIGURE 21.5

The Export to Tape dialog box instructs Premiere Pro to take control of the recording device.

Exporting without Device Control

If your hardware setup does not allow device control, you can still record to videotape by manually controlling your video recording device. Before you start, make sure that you can play back video on your recording device or camcorder. If not, review the playback settings. Follow these steps:

1. **Make sure that your camcorder or recording device is connected properly.**

2. **Turn on your videotape deck.** Load the tape onto which you are recording into your tape deck.

3. **Select the sequence that you want to export by clicking it in the Project window.** You should be able to see the sequence on your video display.

4. **Cue the tape recorder to the position where you want to begin recording.**

5. **Move the CTI to the start of your Premiere Pro movie.**

6. **Press the Record button on your recording device.**

7. **Press the Play button in the Program Monitor panel.**

8. **After you are finished recording, click the Stop button in the Program Monitor panel.** Press the Stop button on your recording device.

Exporting with Serial Device Control (Windows only)

Adobe Premiere allows you to control professional VTR equipment through your PC's serial communications (COM) port. The computer's serial port is often used for modem communication and printing. Serial control allows transport and timecode information to be sent over the computer's serial port. Using serial device control, you can capture, playback, and record video. Because serial control exports only timecode and transport signals, you need a hardware capture card to send the video and audio signals to tape. Premiere supports the following standards: nine-pin serial port, Sony RS-422, Sony RS-232, Sony RS-232 UVW, Panasonic RS-422, Panasonic RS-232, and JVC-232.

Serial device control setup

Before you can export using serial device control, you must set up Premiere Pro's Serial Device Control preferences. First, read your equipment manuals and connect your recording equipment to your computer's COM port. Then follow these steps in Premiere Pro:

1. **Open the Device Control Preferences dialog box by choosing Edit ⇨ Preferences ⇨ Device Control.**

2. In the Device Control Preferences dialog box, choose Serial Device Control in the Control Device drop-down menu.

3. In the Options dialog box, shown in Figure 21.6, choose from the following options:

FIGURE 21.6

Set serial device options in this dialog box.

- **Protocol:** In the Protocol drop-down menu, choose the serial protocol specified by your recording equipment manufacturer.

- **Port:** Choose your COM port from the Port drop-down menu.

- **Use VTRs Internal Cue:** This may be necessary if your equipment cannot properly cue to specific timecode numbers. (It should not be necessary if you are using high-end equipment.)

- **Use 19.2K Baud for RS-232:** This is a high-speed communication option that can improve editing accuracy. This option is available only for RS-232 mode equipment.

- **Time Source:** Choose the time source used by your source videotape. If you want your equipment to choose the time source, select the LTC+VITC option. Otherwise, choose LTC (Longitudinal Timecode) or VITC (Vertical Interval Timecode).

- **Timebase:** In the Timebase drop-down menu, select the Timebase that matches your source videotape.

Calibrating for serial export

To help ensure accuracy when exporting with serial control, you may want to use Premiere Pro's Time Code video effect to help calibrate your VTR. This effect allows you to superimpose a time-code over a video effect. You can use the superimposed timecode to match the desired in point of the exported video with the in point on the tape.

To calibrate, follow these steps:

1. **Start by applying the Timecode video effect to a short video sequence.** The Timecode video effect is in the Video bin within the Video Effects bin in the Effects panel.

2. **Insert a timecode-striped videotape into your videotape recorder.**

3. **Export the tape using an Assemble or Insert edit.**

4. **Use the controls in the Export to Tape dialog box to move to the in point of the sequence.**

5. **Use the Play and Frame Forward buttons to move to the tape's in point.** Look for black or duplicate frames. If black or duplicate frames appear before the desired in point, count the frames.

6. **Click Options in the Export to Tape dialog box.** Enter the number of black or duplicate frames in the Delay Start Movie field.

7. **Export again.** Repeat step 5 until the first frame of the exported video matches the in point of the tape.

Exporting using serial device control

When you export to tape using serial device control, you set the in and out points in the Export to Tape dialog box. Before you begin, make sure that you have correctly set the preferences in the Serial Device Control Preferences dialog box (see the section "Serial device control setup" earlier in this chapter). You should also have a good understanding of the capabilities of your videotape recorder. Before you get started, your VTR must be powered up and a tape must be in the VTR. Follow these steps to export using serial device control:

1. **Select the sequence to be exported in the Timeline panel.**

2. **Choose File ⇨ Export ⇨ Export to Tape.**

3. **In the Export to Tape dialog box, click Options.** Set options that are specific to your videotape recorder. You may also want to change the following options:

   ▪ **Sync Record:** Use this option to set the tape timecode to the in point entered in the Set In field in the Export to Tape dialog box. This option is dependent upon the VTR's capabilities.

   ▪ **Delay Movie Start:** This option allows you to delay starting the export so that you can sync up properly with your tape machine. This allows you to delay exporting after the Record command is sent to the VTR. In the Delay Movie Start field, enter the number of frames to use to create the delay duration.

   ▪ **Preroll:** Preroll backs up the videotape recorder so that it is up to speed when recording starts. Enter the time in seconds to preroll before the designated timecode starting point.

   ▪ **Hard Record Frame Control:** Choose either Drop-Frame or Non-Drop-Frame. This setting is used only when you export using Hard Record.

4. **In the Export to Tape dialog box, choose Assemble or Insert.** Note that when executing an Assemble or Insert edit, if you are not recording to striped tape, you must have 15 seconds of black and timecode on the tape to which you are recording.

 If you plan to execute a Hard or Crash edit, you must choose the Assemble or Insert option in step 7.

5. **Set the in and out points on the tape using the transport controls in the Export to Tape dialog box.** Cue the tape using the transport controls, and click the In Point and Out Point buttons at the desired frame locations. The transport control icons are similar to those in the Source Monitor window.

6. **If you are executing an Insert edit with VTRs that support RSS-422 or RSS-232, click the Preview button to preview the export to tape.**

7. **To begin exporting to tape, choose one of the following options, depending upon whether you are executing an Assemble, Insert edit, or Hard Record:**

   ▧ For Assemble and Insert edits, click Auto Edit. This sends a signal for the VTR to begin its preroll and start recording at the in point specified in the Export to Tape dialog box.

   ▧ To execute a Hard Record, click the Record button. The VTR immediately begins recording.

Exporting an EDL File

Rather than export to tape, some video producers may want to export an Edit Decision List (EDL) so that their Premiere Pro edits can be reconstructed on high-end video editing systems. An EDL file is a text-based file that contains the names of clips, reel numbers, and transitions, as well as the in and out points of all edits. Premiere Pro allows you to create an EDL file for CMD 3600 format. To create an EDL, first select the video sequence in the Timeline panel and then choose File ⇨ Export ⇨ Export to EDL to open the EDL Export Settings dialog box. The EDL Export Settings dialog box, shown in Figure 21.7, provides the following options, which you may edit. After you change settings, simply click OK. You can then choose a name and location for the file. You can view the file in a text editor or word processor.

- **EDL Title:** Enter the title that appears in the first line of the EDL file.
- **Start Timecode:** Enter the starting timecode for the first edit.
- **Drop Frame:** Specify whether you want drop-frame or non-drop-frame on the master tape.
- **Include Video Levels:** Leave the check box selected to include Video Level comments.
- **Include Audio Levels:** Leave the check box selected to include Audio Level comments.
- **Audio Processing:** This option allows you to choose whether you want audio processing to occur. Choices are Audio Follows Video, Audio Separately, and Audio at the End.

■ **Tracks to Export:** This option allows you to choose which tracks to export to the EDL file. One video track and four mono tracks are allowed. If you have a track above the video track, EDL uses this track as a track for superimposing key effects.

FIGURE 21.7

Use the EDL Export Settings dialog box to export an EDL file.

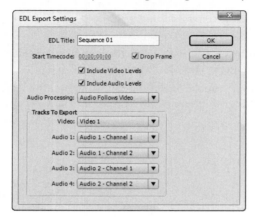

Exporting to AAF

In your day-to-day work as a digital video editor or producer, you may need to re-create your Premiere Pro project on another video system, perhaps a high-end system. This could prove to be costly and time-consuming. Fortunately, you can export your Premiere Pro project in Advanced Authoring Format (AAF). This standard industry format, which was created in the late 1990s, has been embraced by a variety of high-end video systems. Theoretically, you should be able to export your Premiere Pro project in AAF and later import the file into another system. After the import, you should be able to work with all of your files and footage. However, in reality, how accurately the high-end system reads the AAF file may vary from system to system.

Exporting to AAF is quite easy. Simply select the Project window and choose Project ➪ Export Project as AAF. In the Save As dialog box that appears, enter a name for the AAF file. After you save, a dialog box appears, allowing you to specify whether you want to save the file as Legacy AAF or Embed audio. If you choose Legacy AAF, you cannot embed audio information in the file. Click OK to complete the export.

Summary

Premiere Pro allows you to output your movies directly to videotape. You can output with or without device control. This chapter covered these topics:

- To export to videotape, you can choose File ⇨ Export ⇨ Export to Tape.
- Settings in the Project Settings dialog box provide setup controls for outputting to videotape.
- To create an AAF file, you can choose Project ⇨ Export Project as AAF.

Chapter 22

Using Flash and Flash Video

IN THIS CHAPTER

Creating cue points for Flash in Premiere Pro

Creating Flash video files

Integrating digital video into Flash

A dobe Flash is responsible for enlivening more Web pages than any other computer application. Flash is an interactive Web animation program that you can use for virtually everything that moves on the Web: animated logos, full-featured cartoons, advertisements, interactive games, and video. Flash can display video on the Web, and you can use it to start, stop, and navigate video. Using Flash's ActionScript programming language, you can even have the video trigger events such as slide shows, or have it open up other video clips.

With the advent of Flash video, Premiere Pro users can take full advantage of Flash's Web interactivity.

This chapter shows you how to output your Premiere Pro video projects to the Web using the Flash Video (FLV) format. This chapter starts with how to create Flash video navigational cue points in Premiere Pro, and then covers how to export your Premiere Pro projects in FLV format. You will also learn how to output the video that you create in Premiere Pro to the Web in a Flash player.

Yahoo, YouTube, and many other Web sites have turned to Flash video as one of their most commonly used Web video formats. If you want to work with video on the Web, you'll probably be using Flash video, as well.

Adobe Flash is a multimedia program originally designed to provide efficient delivery of animated graphics over the Web. Unlike images created in graphics programs such as Photoshop, those created in Flash are not based on pixels; they are based on vectors. *Vector images* are based on mathematical coordinates, and they are the foundation of programs such as Adobe Illustrator and Macromedia Freehand. In Illustrator and Freehand, you can click and drag the mouse to create an image, and move it and bend it with ease. The image transformations are quickly processed by mathematical computations. To display the image on a computer screen, Flash renders the vector-based data to a screen image.

Flash features a rich set of drawing tools, but if you need graphics created in other programs, such as Photoshop or Illustrator, you can easily import them. Images are animated in a timeline interface, somewhat similar to Premiere Pro's. However, instead of video tracks, Flash supports a multitude of superimposition effects using layers. Interactivity is provided by Flash's powerful scripting language, ActionScript. Using ActionScript, you can program navigation and interactive buttons and use Premiere Pro markers to trigger events.

When you finish creating graphics, animation, and interactivity, you can publish the Flash movie as an SWF file that can be saved to a Web server, or stored on Flash's streaming media server.

During the publishing process, Flash can create an HTML file containing the scripting code that loads Flash onto a Web page. The movie appears in a Web browser courtesy of a Flash plug-in that must be installed in the user's Web browser. Fortunately for Flash developers, the Flash plug-in is one of the most popular in the world. According to Adobe, it is installed in over 90 percent of the computers that can access the Internet. This means that millions of computers can view video over the Web in Flash's FLV format.

Creating Cue Points for Flash in Premiere Pro

If you plan to export a Premiere Pro video project to Flash, it can be very helpful to understand how to use Premiere Pro markers to create navigation cue points for Flash. These cue points are embedded in Flash video. Using ActionScript, a Flash designer or programmer can create buttons that enable a user to quickly move from one part of a video clip to another. ActionScript also enables the designer to use the cue points to open up images, or jump Flash's playback head to another section of a presentation.

To create a cue point in Premiere Pro for Flash, you need to create unnumbered event markers before exporting your project to FLV format. Markers are covered in Chapter 6, but here is a brief review of how to create a marker to use as a Flash cue point:

1. **Move the current-time indicator to the frame where you want the marker to appear.**
2. **Double-click the Set Unnumbered Marker button in the Timeline.** This opens the Marker dialog box.
3. **In the Chapter field, enter a descriptive name, as shown in Figure 22.1.** Click OK.

Navigation, Event, and ActionScript Cue Points

Apart from navigation cue points, Flash provides ActionScript programmers two other types of cue points: *event* cue points and *ActionScript* cue points.

You can use event cue points to trigger events. For example, if you have a narrator and you want to have Flash playback images or slides at specific points in the video, you can use event cue points to trigger slide changes. Cue points can also trigger subtitles or even another movie to play. For example, you can have a character in one movie answer a character in another movie. The cue points send the information for the other movie to start at just the right place.

For Creative Suite 3, the easiest way to create event navigation cue points is to load the audio and video into Adobe Soundbooth. Using Soundbooth's Marker panel, you can create markers on an audio timeline that can be exported as an XML file with Flash cue points. The cue points can be loaded into the Flash Video encoder (included with Flash) or they can be used to create cue points from ActionScript.

FIGURE 22.1

You can use markers in Premiere Pro to create cue points for Adobe Flash.

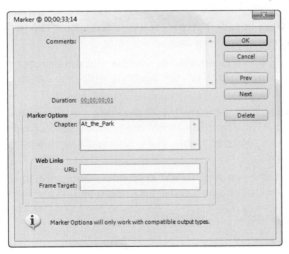

When you export your Premiere Pro file in Flash video format, the marker name, its type (Navigation), and its time are embedded in the video. As mentioned earlier, you can use Flash's ActionScript programming language to access the cue points.

Creating Flash Video Files

Flash allows you to play video for progressive downloading or streaming video from Adobe's Flash Media Server. In order to use either progressive downloading or streaming video in Flash, you first need to convert your video into a Flash video (FLV) file. You can create an FLV file directly from Premiere Pro using the Adobe Media Encoder. If you want to use progressive or streaming video in Flash, it's important to understand that Flash does not use the QuickTime or Windows Media formats. For playing video in Flash 8 or Flash 9 players, Flash uses On2 Technology's On2VP6 codec, which provides higher-quality video with smaller file sizes than the Sorensen Spark codec (used for Flash 7). Note that FLV files created with the On2VP6 codec cannot be viewed in Web browsers with the Flash 6 or Flash 7 player installed.

NOTE On2Technology also sells Flx Exporter, a stand-alone video exporter that can export video in FLV format. See www.on2.com for more details. Sorenson Media sells Sorenson Squeeze for Flash, a stand-alone video exporter that can export video for Flash 7, 8, and 9 players. See www.sorensonmedia.com for more information.

To export a Flash video file from Premiere Pro, follow these steps:

1. **Select the sequence in the Timeline panel that includes the footage you want to export.** If you wish to export a clip, select the clip in the Project panel

2. **Choose File ⇨ Export ⇨ Adobe Media Encoder.**

3. **In the Adobe Media Encoder's Export Settings dialog box, choose Adobe Flash Video in the Format drop-down menu.**

4. **In the Range drop-down menu, choose whether you want to export the entire Sequence or the Work Area.** If you are exporting a clip, you can choose Entire Clip or the clip's In to Out point.

5. **Choose a Flash video preset in the Preset drop-down menu, as shown in Figure 22.2.** The default preset is 256 Kbps. This should provide adequate quality for most high-speed Internet connections. However, higher-quality settings for high-speed connections are 512 Kbps and 768 Kbps.

6. **Click the Video tab if you want to add keyframes, change the frame width or bit rate, set key frames, or choose a codec for Flash 6 or 7.** If you want to export the video so it can be used in Flash 6 and 7 players, set the video codec to Sorenson Spark. The Video tab is shown in Figure 22.3.

NOTE Flash allows you to create keyframes by choosing the distance between keyframes. If the keyframe distance is 30, at a frame rate of 29.97, Flash creates one key frame each second. If you created markers in Premiere Pro, Flash creates a keyframe at the marker location to be used as a cue point. You can increase video quality by adding keyframes, but this can increase file size and decrease playback performance. If you increase keyframes, you may also need to increase the data rate.

7. **If you do not want to export video with audio, deselect Export Audio in the Export Settings section.**

FIGURE 22.2

Exporting in Adobe Flash Video format

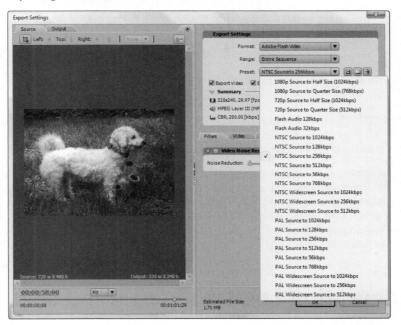

FIGURE 22.3

Video settings options for Flash video

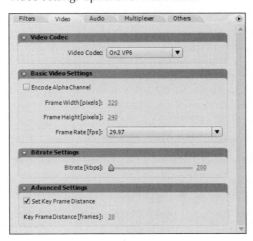

8. **If you want to apply a video noise reduction filter before exporting, click the Filters tab.** Then select the Video Noise Reduction filter. Adjust the slider to control the amount of noise reduction. Reducing noise can improve quality and reduce file size.

9. **If you do want to change frame size, click in the Frame Width and Frame Height area.**

10. **To start the export process, click OK.** Name your file, and then click Save.

After you create an FLV file, you can save it to your Web server and have Flash download it progressively, or you can stream the video using Flash Media Server.

NOTE Flash Professional 9 also provides a stand-alone Flash Video Exporter, which is an application that allows you to export multiple files to FLV format. You can also use the Flash Video Encoder to import cue points from Adobe Soundbooth.

NOTE In early versions of Flash, multimedia producers sometimes embedded a video into a Flash movie, rather than load it from a Web server or streaming media server. Embedded video provides poorer playback than streaming or progressive video, and the frame rate of the video always plays at the frame rate of the animation, which provides further constraints on using video in Flash. When video is streamed, it is loaded in sections into a Web browser and thus consumes less memory than video embedded in a Flash movie.

Integrating Digital Video into Flash

After you create a Flash video (FLV) file, you can easily set it up to playback in Flash using the Flash CS3's FLV component. This component allows you to quickly display and control video from within Flash. It also allows you to drag objects onstage to speed up your production work.

Using the MediaPlayback component

The fastest way to set up and play external video from Flash is to use the FLVPlayback Component, which allows the viewer to start, stop, and pause video that displays onscreen. To use the FLVPlayback Component and link it to a Flash video file, follow these steps:

1. **Create a new document in Flash.** Specify a document size that is appropriate for your project. Choose the ActionScript 3 option, and click the Templates tab to choose an appropriate size for your Flash project.

2. **If you don't see the components onscreen, choose Window ➪ Components.**

3. **In the Components panel, click the plus sign to open the Video section.**

4 **Click and drag the FLVPlayback Component into the Flash main screen.** Figure 22.4 shows the Components panel open with the FLVPlayback Component onscreen.

5. **Now use the Component Inspector to tell Flash where to find your video file.** Choose Window ➪ Panels ➪ Component Inspector.

FIGURE 22.4

Use the FLVPlayback Component to display and control video in Flash.

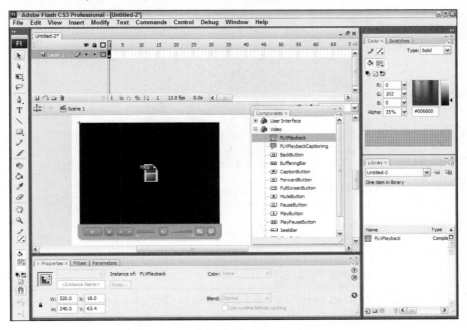

6. **In the Component Inspector, set options for video in the Parameters tab.** In the Source field, enter the location of your video, such as `http://mystreaming.com/flv/mymovie.flv`. If the video is in the same directory as your movie, you can simply enter a relative path. You can also click the Magnifying Glass icon, and then the folder icon, which automatically enters the path to the file after you navigate to it on disk, as shown in Figure 22.5. The Content Path dialog box allows you to match the component's dimensions to the source video dimensions.

7. **If you want to change "skins" for the video player, click the Skin field.** Choose a different skin.

8. **Test your movie by choosing Control ⇨ Test Movie.**

9. **If you will be using ActionScript to work with the component, click in the Properties panel.** Enter an instance name.

10. **When you complete all of your design work, publish the movie by choosing File ⇨ Publish.** This creates the SWF file that can be stored on your Web server. Figure 22.6 shows an FLV file playing in a Flash movie in Internet Explorer using the FLVPlayback Component.

FIGURE 22.5

Choosing the content path in the Component Inspector

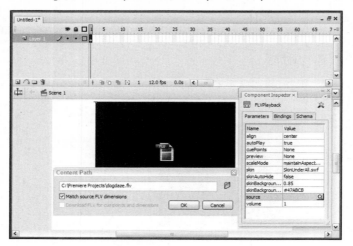

FIGURE 22.6

A video from Premiere Pro playing in Flash player in Internet Explorer

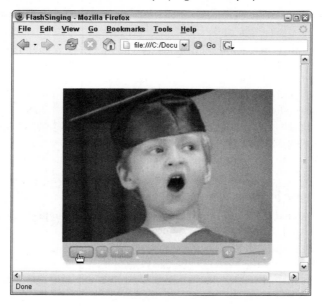

Using ActionScript with cue points

If you want to truly take advantage of Flash's many interactive features, your best bet is to learn as much ActionScript as possible. The latest version of ActionScript, ActionScript 3, is more akin to a full-featured programming language, such as Java, than it is to a simple scripting language. As discussed earlier, you can use ActionScript to program buttons that move from one navigation point to another, or trigger events based upon cue points.

This section provides a brief look at some ActionScript commands that you can use with cue points. Each of the following steps uses ActionScript 3, and they do not work with video components designed to work with ActionScript 2. Note that, even though the examples could be programmed in a more sophisticated manner, they are presented in the fewest steps possible. However, even though they are quite simple, they do require a basic knowledge of how to create simple ActionScript commands.

> **TIP** More information about using Flash video and ActionScript is available on the Web at the Flash Developer center: www.adobe.com/devnet/flash. Dan Carr's article, *Controlling Flash Video with FLV Playback Programming,* is especially valuable to Premiere Pro users (www.adobe.com/devnet/flash/articles/flvplayback_programming.html).

Using navigational cue points

This example shows you how to use a button to jump to a navigational cue point in a video. It creates a button that jumps the video to the embedded navigational cue point named *interview*. In the ActionScript, an EventListener *listens* for the button click and sends the video playback head to the interview section using the seekToNavCuePoint command. The command is placed in a custom function called myNavCueFinder. Here are the steps to get started:

1. **Create a new ActionScript 3.0 Flash file.**

2. **Open the Components panel.** From the Video section, drag an FLVPlayback Component to the main window.

3. **Name the instance of the FLVPlayback VideoHolder.**

4. **Use the Component Inspector to set the source for the video.** (Note that this could easily be done with ActionScript, but this example is keeping the ActionScript code at a minimum.)

5. **Drag an instance of a button from the library onscreen.** Name the button instance button_interview.

6. **Click in Frame 1 of the Flash Timeline.** Open the Actions window to create your ActionScript. Note that the script starts by loading the Flash video package (`import fl.video.*`). This command loads a package of classes specifically designed to add video control features to Flash. Here is the ActionScript:

```
import fl.video.*;
videoholder.autoPlay=false;

function myNavCueFinder(event:MouseEvent); void
{
    videoholder.SeektoNavCuePoint("interview");
}
button_interview.addEventListener(MouseEvent.CLICK.
    myNavCueFinder);
```

7. **Test the movie by choosing Control ⇨ Test.** Try out the button.

Listening for cue points

This example shows you how you can access cue points from a Flash video movie. The example displays the name and time of the cue point as the video plays. You can use the custom function `myCuepointDisplayer` to load the name of a cue point into memory. Once you have the cue point name, you can load an image with the same name as the cue point, or you can send Flash's Timeline to a specific point in the Flash production with the Flash actions `gotoAndStop()` or `gotoAndPlay()`. In this example, the cue point name and cue point time are displayed in Flash's Trace panel.

1. **Create a new ActionScript 3.0 Flash file.**

2. **Open the Components panel.** From the Video section, drag an FLVPlayback Component to the main window.

3. **Name the instance of the FLVPlayback VideoHolder.**

4. **Use the Component Inspector to set the source for the video.** (Note that you can easily do this with ActionScript, but this example is keeping the ActionScript code at a minimum.)

5. **Click in Frame 1 of the Flash Timeline and open the Actions window to create your ActionScript.** Here is the ActionScript:

```
import fl.video.*;

function myCuepointDisplayer(event:MetaDataEvent); void
{
    trace("cuepoint name:"+event.info.name);
trace("cuepoint time:"+event.info.time);
}
videoholder.addEventListener(MetaDatEvent.CUE_POINT.
    myCuepointDisplayer);
```

Using ActionScript to stream an FLV movie

If you want to stream video using Flash, you need to use Flash Media Server. When you set up Flash Communication Server, you create an application folder for your Flash project. In order to stream video, you need to connect to "register" the application's location on the Flash Video Server with ActionScript. You can do this by using the ActionScript connect command, which connects to the server using Real Time Messaging Protocol (RTMP) communications protocol. The following script provides the basics of connecting to Flash Media Server and playing the Flash movie. This script attaches a NetStream object to the video object in the Flash main window. Note also that when issuing the Play command, you do not use the .flv file extension.

```
Mync=new NetConnection();
Mync.connect("rtmp://mydomain/myappfolder");
MyNetStream=new NetStream(my_nc);
MyonscreenvideoObject.attachVideo(MyNetStream);
MyNetStream.play("myflvfile");
```

 If you don't want to set up a streaming media server, you can still use Flash Media Server by paying a monthly hosting charge to an Internet Service Provider such as Vitalstream (www.vitalstream.com).

Summary

Adobe Flash is the most widely used program to display animation on the Web. Premiere Pro users can take advantage of Flash's interactivity by outputting video in Flash's FLV format:

- To create navigation cue points for Flash video, you can use unnumbered sequence markers in Premiere Pro.
- You can output Premiere Pro files to FLV format using the Adobe Media Encoder.
- You can use the FLVPlayback Component to quickly place video in Flash.
- You can use ActionScript in Flash to trigger events based upon cue points that are embedded in an FLV file.

Chapter 23

Outputting to CD-ROM and Macromedia Director

Although more and more video continues to appear on the Web, one of the oldest media for distributing digital movies is CD-ROM. Virtually every computer sold today can play CD-ROMs. A standard CD-ROM holds 650MB of data, usually enough space for at least 30 minutes of compressed digital video. CD-ROMs are among the cheapest digital media available and are still widely used for distributing interactive and educational content geared toward young children.

Many multimedia producers who distribute their work on CD-ROM find that to truly take advantage of the medium, they need to add interactivity to their Adobe Premiere Pro presentations. A popular interactive multimedia program is Macromedia Director. If you import a Premiere Pro movie into Director, you can create buttons that start, stop, and rewind your Premiere Pro movie. You can also put several movies made with Premiere Pro into different Director frames and create buttons that enable the viewer to move from one movie to another.

This chapter guides you through the steps for exporting your Premiere Pro movie to CD-ROM. It also includes an overview of how to use Macromedia Director to create interactive behaviors that control digital movies.

IN THIS CHAPTER

Exporting Premiere Pro movies to CD-ROM

Using Macromedia Director

Exporting Premiere Pro Movies to CD-ROM

Before Premiere Pro turned "pro," earlier versions of the program actually provided multimedia project presets for both QuickTime and AVI movies. The presets created a square pixel project at 320 x 280 pixels at 15 frames per second, with audio set at 16-bit mono and a sampling rate of 22050 Hz. Today's multimedia producer is more likely to work in a digital video project at 720 x 480 pixels at 29.97 frames per second. In order to use the file for multimedia purposes, the producer would then export the video at a smaller frame size, a lower frame rate, and with square pixels. Follow these steps to export to CD-ROM:

1. **Complete your editing.**

2. **Select the Timeline panel that you want to export, and choose File ➪ Export ➪ Movie.** Click the Settings button in the Export Movie dialog box. If you want to export using RealMedia, Windows Media, or an MPEG format (MPEG1 is suitable for CD-ROM), select the sequence to export in the Timeline panel and choose File ➪ Export ➪ Adobe Media Encoder, instead.

3. **Change settings as desired in the General, Video, Keyframe and Rendering, and Audio sections.** One of the most common formats for CD-ROMs is QuickTime. If you want to export a QuickTime movie, choose QuickTime as the file type. If you're exporting QuickTime movies, you may want to choose Sorensen Video 3 as your compressor (in the Video settings section). Sorensen can provide higher-quality movies in smaller file sizes. Figure 23.1 shows the Sorenson Video settings in the Export Movie Settings dialog box.

FIGURE 23.1

The Sorenson Video settings in the Export Movie Settings dialog box

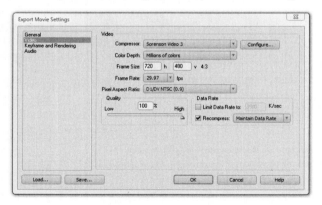

One of the most important settings in this dialog box is the data rate. The value that you enter in the Data Rate section limits the flow of data so that the video doesn't pour out at a rate that the CD drive can't handle. Typical data rates for double-speed (2×) CD-ROMs are between 200 Kbps and 250 Kbps. For older compressors, such as Cinepak, Adobe recommends data rates for a 12-speed (12×) CD drive to be 1.8MB per second; for a 24× CD-ROM, 3 to 3.6MB. (See `www.adobe.com/cfusion/knowledgebase/index.cfm?id=315097` for more details.)

However, if you are using the Sorenson 3 codec, you can set the data rate at 200KB per second or lower. Sorenson recommends this formula as a starting point: height × width × frames per second ÷ 48000. Thus, if exporting a 320 x 240 pixel video at 15 frames per second, you could limit the data rate to 24KB per second as a starting point. At 30 frames per second, you could limit the data rate to 48KB per second. (Of course, for high-action clips, you generally need a higher data rate.)

4. **After editing settings in the Export Movie Settings dialog box, click OK.**

5. **In the Export Movie dialog box, name your file.**

6. **Click Save.** The codec starts compressing your movie.

7. **If you are importing your Premiere Pro movie into Director or another multimedia program, such as Macromedia Authorware, import the Premiere Pro movie into the program.** Then complete the final production in Director or Authorware.

8. **Save the final production to a CD-ROM using a CD recorder.** Most Mac CD-recording software enables you to partition the CD-ROM to create a Mac version and a Windows version.

Using Macromedia Director

Although Macromedia Director has not been updated in several years, it remains one of the most powerful and widely used multimedia CD authoring tools. Like Premiere Pro, Director enables you to import graphics files from such programs as Adobe Photoshop and Adobe ImageReady. It also enables you to import source images from Macromedia FireWorks and Macromedia Flash.

Although Director is often used for creating animated sequences, for Premiere Pro users it offers the power of adding interactivity to digital movies. Unlike Premiere Pro, Director features a powerful programming language called Lingo. Using Lingo, you can create scripts or behaviors that enable the user to jump from frame to frame or to start and stop digital movies imported into Director. For example, using both Premiere Pro and Director, you can create educational productions that enable users to choose what areas they want to learn and what video segments they want to see.

NOTE Director can import AVI, QuickTime, RealMedia, and Windows Media files. Thus, you need to export your Premiere Pro movie in one of these formats in order to use it in Director. You can export in AVI and QuickTime formats, using the File ⇨ Export ⇨ Movie command. To export in RealMedia or Windows Media format, choose File ⇨ Export ⇨ Adobe Media Encoder.

Director overview

To understand how Premiere Pro movies can be integrated into a Director presentation, you should become familiar with the various elements of the Director interface. Director uses three primary screen areas: the Stage, the Score, and the Cast windows, as shown in Figure 23.2. The *stage* is where all animation and activity take place. You may view this as equivalent to Premiere Pro's

Program Monitor. The *score* is somewhat similar to Premiere Pro's Timeline. In the Director score, each frame is represented by a tiny rectangle. Each track in Director is called a *channel*. All program elements imported or created in Director are automatically added to its *cast*. To start the process of creating a production, cast members are dragged from the cast window to the stage. Cast members can include graphics such as buttons, digital movies, text, audio, and behaviors.

FIGURE 23.2

The Director Stage, Score, and Cast windows

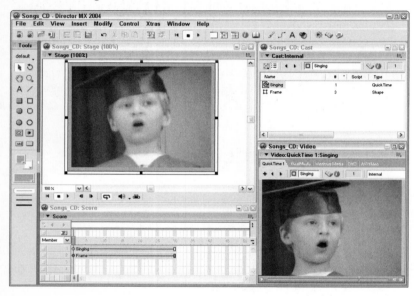

Importing Premiere Pro movies into Director

For Premiere Pro users, one of Director's most valuable features is that it enables you to import and control video files. Before you can use a Premiere Pro movie in Director, you must first import it into the program. To import a movie into Director, follow these steps:

1. **If you have multiple casts in Director, start by selecting the cast into which you want to import the digital movie.** Choose File ➪ Import.

2. **In the Import Files dialog box, select the digital movie that you want to import.**

3. **If you are importing only one file, click the Import button.** Otherwise, select another digital movie and click Add.

4. **When you are finished adding movies, click Import.** After the movie is imported, it is loaded as a cast member in the Cast window.

Changing movie properties

Although you will most likely control digital movies in Director using Lingo, you can easily change settings that affect playback in the Cast Member properties windows. To open the Property Inspector window shown in Figure 23.3, select the digital movie in the Cast tab and then click the Info button. The digital movie's properties window (in the Property Inspector) enables you to choose to playback both video and sound, or one or the other. Perhaps the most important setting in the dialog box is the Paused check box. This enables you to prevent the movie from playing as soon as the viewer enters the frame that contains the video. If you select the Paused button, you can use Lingo to have the user start and stop the movie. If you select Loop, the digital video movie plays continuously.

FIGURE 23.3

The Property Inspector window

QuickTime movies enable the QuickTime controller to appear onscreen as a device for starting and stopping QuickTime movies. Many multimedia producers choose not to show the controller, preferring to create their own interface and controlling it with Lingo.

Usually, the Sync to Soundtrack option is selected. The other choice in the drop-down menu — Play Every Frame — can result in video playing without audio. If the Director to Stage option is selected, you can place other cast members over QuickTime movies.

Placing the movie onstage

For a digital movie to be viewed in Director, it must be positioned in Director's Stage window. Before dragging the movie from the Cast window to the Stage window, most Director users select the frame where the QuickTime, RealMedia, and Windows Media will reside. Typically, the background and buttons are created in Director or Photoshop. After you select the frame in the Score window, you can click and drag the movie from the Cast window to the Score window to place the movie on that frame.

At this point, you must decide whether you want the movie to play in one Director frame or whether the movie should play over multiple Director frames. Projects are often easier to manage if the movie plays in one Director frame. When movies play in one frame, Director must stop its own playback head and turn the processing over to the video movie.

Pausing the playback head with the Tempo channel

If you set up Director to play a QuickTime movie in one frame, you must tell Director to halt and wait for the end of the movie or wait for a button to tell it to move off the frame. The easiest way to tell Director to wait for the end of a movie is to specify this in Director's Tempo channel.

To access the Tempo channel controls for the movie, simply double-click the Tempo channel frame directly above the movie frame. In the Frame Properties: Tempo dialog box, shown in Figure 23.4, select Wait for Cue Point and then click {End} in the Cue Point drop-down menu.

FIGURE 23.4

Director's Frame Properties: Tempo dialog box enables you to pause the playback head while a digital video movie plays.

Pausing the playback with a behavior

Although the Tempo channel provides a quick way of stopping Director's playback head, most experienced Director users don't use it because it does not provide as much control as Lingo. To pause the playback head while a digital movie plays, you can use a Lingo behavior instead of the Tempo channel. Fortunately for nonprogrammers, Director comes packaged with prewritten behaviors. You can use a prewritten behavior to pause the playback head by dragging the Hold on Current Frame behavior from Director's Behavior library (in the Navigation section) into the Score channel frame that appears directly above the digital movie frame. (The Score channel appears above channel 1.)

Using Lingo

Although playing QuickTime and AVI windows from within Director is quite easy, it is helpful to learn a few Lingo commands to control navigation and start and stop QuickTime movies. Director provides a simple interface to get you started creating Lingo scripts. The following section shows you how to create a simple navigational script using Director's Behavior Inspector. After you learn how to use the Behavior Inspector, you can create scripts that control QuickTime movies.

Creating behaviors

Director *behaviors* are Lingo scripts that you can use to control navigation and to control QuickTime movies. After you create a behavior, you can click and drag it over an onscreen object such as a button. If the behavior includes commands for mouse events, you can program the behavior to execute when the user clicks the mouse on the object that contains the behavior. Follow these steps for creating a simple navigational behavior:

1. **Choose Window ➪ Inspectors ➪ Behavior.**

2. **To create a new behavior, click the plus sign (+) button.** Choose New Behavior.

3. **In the New Behavior dialog box, enter a name for your behavior.** Click OK.

4. **To use the Behavior Inspector's automatic scripting features, click the arrow at the far left of the Behavior Inspector window to expand it.** The Behavior Inspector is shown in Figure 23.5.

FIGURE 23.5

Create behaviors in the Behavior Inspector

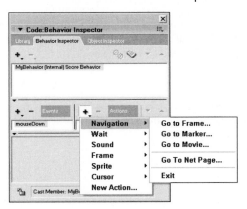

5. **In the Events section in the Behavior Inspector, click the plus sign (+) button.** Choose an event to trigger your behavior. For most button-triggered programs, choose Mouse Up or Mouse Enter. Choose Mouse Up instead of Mouse Down to enable the user to release the mouse. If a Mouse Down triggers the event, the user cannot cancel after clicking the mouse. If you use a Mouse Up event, the user can cancel the event by moving the mouse off the button before releasing the mouse.

6. **In the Actions section, select an action category.** For example, if you are creating a navigational button, choose Navigation.

7. **In the menu that appears, choose a specific action, such as Go To Frame.** If you choose Go To Frame, enter the frame number you want to go to.

8. **Click OK.**

9. **If you want to see the Lingo script that was created, click the Script window icon.**

10. **Close the Behavior Inspector by clicking the Close icon.**

11. **To use your behavior, drag it from the Cast window.** Release it over an object such as a button graphic in the Stage window.

Creating your own Lingo

When you know the basics of creating behaviors, you can begin using Lingo to control QuickTime and AVI movies. Most of the Lingo that controls QuickTime and AVI movies refers to the movie by the channel the movie is in or by its cast-member name or number. When you drag a movie from the Cast window to the stage, the movie becomes known as a *sprite*. Lingo addresses different sprites according to the channel the sprite is in. Thus, if you drag a digital video movie into channel 1, you refer to it as *Sprite 1*.

To create your own behaviors that control QuickTime movies, you can use the Behavior Inspector to get you started, and then enter the Lingo commands that control digital video movies by opening the Script Window dialog box and entering them there. The following sections review some commonly used Lingo commands that control digital video movies.

Playing movies with Lingo

If you want to create Lingo buttons that start, stop, and reverse QuickTime movies, you can set and change the sprite's `movieRate` property and the `movieRate` function. The following are common movie rate values:

Play	1
Stop	0
Reverse	−1

 You can slow down the movie by setting the movie rate to .5.

Below is a simple script that starts a QuickTime movie in channel 3 when the user clicks the mouse on an object containing the following behavior:

```
On mouseUp
Set the movieRate of sprite 3 to 1
End mouseUp
```

You can also use *dot syntax*:

```
On mouseUp
sprite(3).movieRate=1
End mouseUp
```

Checking movie duration

Director's movieTime and duration commands are more helpful Lingo code. Use movieTime to check how much of a QuickTime movie has played. Duration measures the length of a QuickTime movie. Both duration and movieTime are measured in *ticks* (one tick equals one-sixtieth of a second), not frames. By constantly comparing the movieTime property of a QuickTime movie to its duration, you can tell when the movie actually stops playing. When the movie stops playing, you can then send Director's playback head to another frame. The following Lingo code is an example. A movie script that is executed when the production starts puts the duration of a QuickTime movie into a *variable* called gmovduration. In this example, the QuickTime movie is in Director's third channel (like a video track). In Lingo, this is designated as Sprite 3.

```
Global gmovduration
Put the duration of sprite 3 into gmovduration
```

Another script, executed when the playback head exits a frame, compares the current movieTime of the QuickTime movie to its duration. If the movieTime is less than the duration, then the movie hasn't ended yet. Thus, the Lingo script keeps Director playback on the current Director frame. The Lingo command, go to the frame, keeps the playback head in the current frame. When the QuickTime movie finishes, its movieTime is no longer less than its duration. At this point, the "go to the frame" section of the code is not executed, and so Director's playback moves on to the next frame in the Director production.

```
Global gmovduration
On Exit Frame
Put the movieTime of sprite 3 into myMovieTime
If myMovieTime < gmovduration then go to the frame
End
```

You can also change the movieTime of a digital movie with a script like this:

```
Set the movieTime of sprite 3 to 360
```

The dot syntax version would be as follows:

```
sprite(3).movieTime=360
```

The preceding Lingo code results in the playback of the QuickTime movie jumping to the new time position you have assigned.

Changing digital movie settings

You can use Lingo commands to control the movie settings. You can do this in the Cast Properties window that controls looping and whether the movie pauses when the playback head enters the frame. For example, at the beginning of a movie or at a certain point in a movie, you can turn off looping with the following line of Lingo code:

```
Set the loop of member "Mymovie" =True
```

You can also stop the movie from playing when the playback head enters the frame with this Lingo code:

```
Set the pausedAtStart of member "Mymovie"=TRUE
```

Playing a portion of a digital movie

Director also enables you to start and stop a digital video movie from any point in the movie using its startTime and stopTime commands. Using these Lingo commands, you can create a button labeled Show intro or Show interview. When the user clicks the button, only the specified segment is played. and stopTime are measured in ticks (a tick is ⅟₆₀ of a second). For example, this snippet of Lingo code tells Director to start playing the digital movie not at its beginning, but one minute into it.

```
Set the startTime of sprite 1=360
```

Or

```
sprite(1).startTime=360
```

To set the stop point of the movie, you can use this Lingo snippet:

```
Set the stopTime of sprite 10=720
```

Or

```
sprite(10).stopTime=720
```

Other Lingo commands

Director includes numerous Lingo commands that work with QuickTime movies. For example, Lingo includes commands that can turn QuickTime soundtracks on and off. Lingo can determine whether QuickTime or Video for Windows is installed on a computer, and it can tell the video producer when keyframes occur. Lingo commands are well documented in Director's Lingo dictionary. However, if you are a Director beginner, be forewarned: You won't become a Lingo expert overnight.

Summary

The most widely used medium for distributing digital movies is on CD-ROM. Many Premiere Pro movies are imported into interactive multimedia programs such as Macromedia Director before the project is saved to CD-ROM. When exporting a movie that will play on CD-ROM, you should base your export settings on the system that will be playing your movie. This chapter covered the following topics:

- If you want to add interactivity to a Premiere Pro movie, you can export your movie into Macromedia Director.

- The Sorenson Video codec is commonly used for exporting movies to CD-ROM.

- Macromedia Director's programming language, Lingo, features many commands that enable onscreen clickable buttons that can start and stop digital video movies.

Part VI

Premiere Pro and Beyond

Chapter 24

Editing Audio with Adobe Audition

lthough Premiere Pro includes audio-editing, mixing, and recording tools, it does not include tools for intricate audio editing. Premiere Pro users who need more audio-editing power than either Premiere Pro or Adobe Soundbooth offer should examine the features provided by Audition, Adobe's professional audio production application. Audition's tools allow you to precisely zoom in, pinpoint, and select audio data, and then cut, copy, and paste it. Audition also features tools that can extend, search for, and remove silence from an entire audio clip. It can automatically recognize and select beats in an audio rhythm, and when copying and pasting in Audition, you can even mix the audio as you paste.

If you own Audition, or if you're considering purchasing it, this chapter provides a basic overview of its audio-editing capabilities. As you read through this chapter, you will see how Audition's selection, zooming, and editing controls can enhance the sound of music and narration in Premiere Pro.

> **NOTE** This chapter focuses on audio-editing features not found in Premiere Pro, particularly in regard to audio waveform editing. Because Premiere Pro provides mixing and audio effects (covered in Chapters 7 and 8), those areas of Audition are not discussed in detail.

> **NOTE** There is no Macintosh version of Audition.

Understanding Audition

To work efficiently with Adobe Audition, you should first become familiar with the program's menus and panels. Although Audition's interface is quite different from Premiere Pro's, there are several similarities. Like Premiere Pro, Audition's workspace, shown in Figure 24.1, is divided into different panels that you can resize, move, dock, and separate. Furthermore, you can choose different workspaces and save workspaces using options in the Window menu. Figure 24.1 shows the Editing workspace. When the Editing workspace opens, it switches the Main panel and menus to Edit view, with this view set to display an audio waveform. The following sections provide an overview of the different panels that you can use to edit audio in Audition.

Audition in Edit view

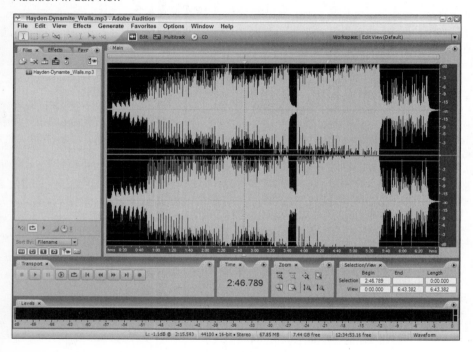

Becoming Familiar with the Main Panel

The Main panel is Audition's Timeline work area for audio production. The contents of the Main panel change according to whether you are working in Edit view, Multitrack view, or CD view. You can switch from one view to another by choosing one of these views in the View menu. When you change views, Audition changes the tools and menu commands to correspond with the chosen view. For example, you can import video with audio into Multitrack view, but you cannot import video into Edit view, which displays only one audio track at a time.

- **Edit View:** This view provides editing options and menus for cutting, copying, and electronically splicing audio data together. If you need to remove narration flubs or extraneous noise, or add silence to a clip, you can use Edit view. In Edit view, you can view and edit the waveform of an audio clip. You can also view audio data in a spectral frequency display, which allows you to cut, copy, and paste according to audio frequency. You can also select a portion of the audio and apply an audio effect from Audition's Effects or Favorites menus.

  In Edit view, the default vertical scale format is decibels, and the default horizontal scale format is beats per minutes. To change either of these options, choose View ➪ Vertical Scale Format. After you have completed editing in Edit view, you can save your file in standard audio formats such as WAV, AIF, WMA, or MP3Pro.

- **Multitrack View:** Shown in Figure 24.2, this view is primarily used as a multi-timeline view for mixing. In this view, you can drag audio clips from the File panel and drop them into different tracks. Using this view, you can also sequence one audio clip after another. Like Premiere Pro's Audio Mixer panel, Multitrack view provides volume, panning, and automation controls. (Audition's Mixer window provides even more sophisticated mixing options.) While in Multitrack view, you can also apply audio effects to tracks by clicking the FX button. If you need to edit a clip while in Multitrack view, you can quickly switch to Edit view by double-clicking the clip in one of the tracks.

FIGURE 24.2

The Audition Main panel in Multitrack view

> **TIP**   After you switch to Edit view, the View menu contents change to provide you with different Edit view options. For example, to change to waveform or spectral frequency display, you can choose View ➪ Waveform Display or View ➪ Spectral Frequency Display.

In Multitrack view, you can use a session as SMPTE (Society of Motion Pictures and Television Engineers) master or slave. This allows you to synchronize Audition's MultiTrack transport controls with a MIDI sequencing application or hardware device.

By using sessions as SMPTE masters or slaves, you can synchronize the transport controls of Multitrack view with a MIDI sequencing. A session that generates SMPTE timecode is a SMPTE master; a session that receives time code is a SMPTE slave.

While working in Multitrack view, you save your work in a session file. When you are finished mixing, you can then export your file into a stereo or mono track in a variety of standard audio formats.

- **CD View:** Use this view for producing audio CDs. In CD view, you can change track order and burn a CD.

Transport panel

You can use this panel to play, stop, and rewind audio. Figure 24.3 shows the different buttons and their functions. Unlike Premiere Pro, Audition does not provide a scrubbing transport control. To scrub audio in Audition, you must activate the Scrub tool and then click and drag forward or backwards over an audio clip. In Multitrack view, click and drag over the track. Note that you can also play audio from the current cursor position by pressing the Spacebar.

FIGURE 24.3

Transport panel controls

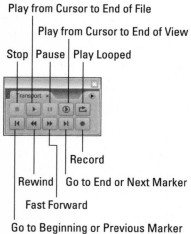

Play from Cursor to End of File

Play from Cursor to End of View

Stop | Pause | Play Looped

Record

Rewind | Go to End or Next Marker

Fast Forward

Go to Beginning or Previous Marker

Zoom panel

When editing audio, you can use this panel to zoom into waveforms so that you can edit more precisely. As shown in Figure 24.4, Audition's zoom tools allow you to zoom horizontally, vertically, and to the edges of selections. When you zoom in horizontally to a waveform, the waveform becomes stretched out, which allows you to work more precisely.

FIGURE 24.4

Audition provides several zoom tools for zooming into audio data.

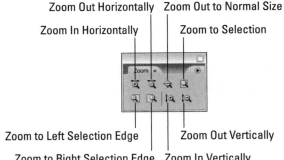

Time panel

This panel provides a time readout of the currently selected audio sequence. Time can be viewed in different audio formats, such as SMPTE drop-frame, non-drop-frame, audio samples, and bars and beats. As audio plays, the time readout displays the sample or frame that is being played. If you click within an audio clip, the Time panel readout changes to show the point in the audio sequence that you clicked. You can change display formats by selecting View ⇨ Display Time Format.

Selection/View panel

This panel is divided into two sections: the Selection area displays the start and length of a selection; the View area displays what portion of the audio clip appears in the Main panel. As you click and drag to create a selection, the selection area of this panel automatically changes to reflect the selection.

Levels panel

This panel displays audio levels in dbfs (decibels below full scale). Stereo clips display two bars, while mono clips display one bar. When you play audio, vertical lines at the far right of the panel indicate peak levels. If the amplitude level peaks above zero, clipping or distortion can occur. Clipping is indicated by red lights to the right of the levels gauge.

Tools panel

This panel, shown in Figure 24.5, provides tools for selecting and scrubbing audio. Activation of tools depends upon whether you are in Edit view or Multitrack view. For example, you can create a selection by clicking and dragging the Time Selection tool in Edit view, but in Multitrack view, you must click and drag with the Multitrack's Time Selection tool. To use the Marquee and Lasso tools while in Edit view, choose View ➪ Spectral Frequency Display. You can use the Marquee tool to create rectangular selections and the Lasso tool to create polygonal and rounded selections.

In both Edit view and Multitrack view, you can scrub audio by clicking and dragging with the Scrub tool. If you click and drag slowly, you hear the sound in slow motion; if you click and drag more quickly, Audition plays the selected sound at a faster rate.

In Multitrack view, you can select and move audio blocks by clicking in the middle of a clip and dragging with the Move/Copy tool. In Multitrack view, the Hybrid tool can often be used as a selection tool or in place of the Move/Copy tool.

FIGURE 24.5

The Tools panel for Edit view and Multitrack view

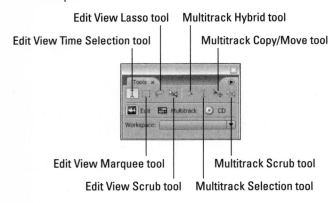

Edit View Lasso tool   Multitrack Hybrid tool

Edit View Time Selection tool   Multitrack Copy/Move tool

Edit View Marquee tool   Multitrack Scrub tool

Edit View Scrub tool   Multitrack Selection tool

Files panel

This panel displays files that have been opened in Audition. In both Edit view and Multitrack view, you can drag audio clips directly into the Main panel. Icons at the bottom of the panel allow you to restrict the display in the panel to audio, loop, video, MIDI files, or markers.

Effects panel

Audition's Effects panel provides access to a variety of audio effects, many similar to those found in Premiere Pro. However, unlike Premiere Pro, Audition's effects are grouped according to category, such as Amplitude, Delay Effects, and Restoration. In Audition, you can apply effects to audio by selecting audio data and by clicking and dragging the effect over the audio in Multitrack view. You can also apply effects from Edit view by selecting audio data and choosing an effect from the Effects menu. You store effects and settings for effects in the Favorites menu, where you can quickly access them when needed. (Using the effects in the Favorites menu is covered later in this chapter, in the section "Applying and Creating Custom Effects.")

Importing Audio and Video

After you become familiar with Audition's panels and workspace, you can import audio and video and then begin editing. Audio and video files can be imported into Audition in several ways. You can load an audio file directly into Audition, or you can load an audio clip into Audition directly from Premiere Pro. If you create a mix in Audition, you can also link the file so that you can return to Audition and edit the mix, if necessary.

Opening audio files

Audition can read all major audio file formats, such as WAV, AIF, and MP3. The steps are quite similar to opening a file in Premiere Pro:

1. **In Edit view, choose File ➪ Open.**

2. **In the Open dialog box, navigate to the file you want to open.** To open more than one file, press Ctrl and then click the files you want to open.

3. **To preview the audio before opening, click Play.**

4. **To open the audio file, click Open.**

> **TIP** Audition also allows you to easily append one audio file to another. To append an audio clip to the clip onscreen, choose File ➪ Open Append. After locating the file on your hard drive, click Append.

> **TIP** If you choose File ➪ Open As instead of File ➪ Open, Audition allows you to convert the file from stereo to mono (and vice versa) and to change its sample rate and resolution. If you want to change audio attributes of a file that is already loaded, choose Edit ➪ Adjust Sample Rate or Edit ➪ Adjust Sample Type.

Importing audio with or without video

Audition allows you to import audio from Premiere Pro, separate audio from a video clip, and import video. Here are some techniques for importing audio when working on a video project:

- **Importing Audio from Video:** In Audition's Edit view, you can import audio from a video clip, without the video. To import audio from a video clip, choose File ⇨ Open Audio From Video. Navigate to the video file, and then click Open to open the audio file.

- **Importing Video with Audio:** Like Premiere Pro, Audition allows you to view video with audio so that you can synchronize the sound with the picture. To load a video file into Audition, switch to Multitrack view by choosing View ⇨ Multitrack View. Next, click in a track to establish a starting time for the video and audio. To import the video and audio into the track, choose Insert ⇨ Video. Navigate to an AVI, MOV, WMV, or MPG file, and then click Open.

The video loads into a video track and the audio into an audio track, with a video monitor window displaying the video, as shown in Figure 24.6. You can use the Move/Copy tool to move the video and audio in sync. To separate audio from video, select the audio or video and choose Clip ⇨ Group Clips. (After you choose Group Clips, the check mark in the menu disappears, indicating that the clips are no longer grouped.)

FIGURE 24.6

A video with audio, inserted into Audition

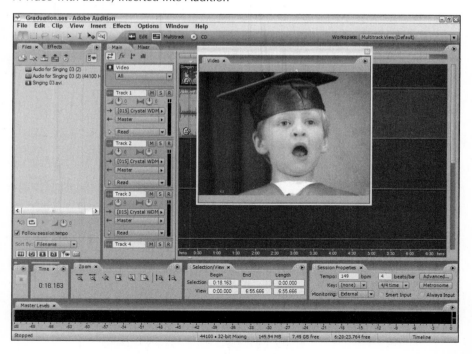

Linking an Audition Mix with Premiere Pro

If you prefer to mix audio in Audition rather than Premiere Pro, you can create a link between the two programs. This allows you to easily return and edit the audio in Audition. In Audition, follow these steps:

1. **Choose View ⇨ Multitrack.**

2. **After you are finished mixing, choose File ⇨ Export Audio Mix Down to export the mix-down file.**

3. **In the Export Audio Mix Down dialog box, select Embed Edit Original link data.**

If you need to return to Audition after importing the file into Premiere Pro, follow these steps in Premiere Pro:

1. **Select the audio clip in the Timeline or Project panel.**

2. **Choose Edit ⇨ Edit Original.**

Playing Audio and Scrolling

To play an audio clip that you have opened in Audition, simply press the Spacebar or click the Play button in the Transport panel. (The transport controls are shown in Figure 24.3.) When you need to jump to another area of an audio clip, you can click and drag Audition's current-time indicator (also referred to as a cursor). To scroll, click and drag the scrolling control in the horizontal colored bar above the time display in Edit view or Multitrack view.

As mentioned earlier, unlike Premiere Pro, Audition provides no scrubbing transport control. To scrub, you must use the Scrub tool. To select the Scrub tool, click it in the Tools panel. Then click and drag slowly in the waveform in Edit view or over an audio clip in Multitrack view. As you click and drag, the audio plays.

Selecting Audio

Before you can apply most of Audition's audio-editing options, you must first select the audio data that you want to edit. Because pinpointing the precise sound that you want to edit can sometimes be difficult with a mouse, Audition provides numerous utilities to help you select audio. For example, Audition can find silence and beats, and it can extend or reduce a selection based on the audio waveform.

 You can extend a selection by clicking and dragging the yellow triangles at the top of the selection area at the top of the waveform.

Here are the most common ways to select audio in Audition:

- **Range Selection:** Click and drag with the Selection tool over the audio waveform. If you did not select the area you want, press Shift and click in the waveform to extend or reduce the selection. Figure 24.7 shows a waveform selection in Edit view.

- **Visible Range:** To select only the visible portion of the waveform that appears onscreen, double-click the waveform.

- **Channel Selection:** You can select only one channel by dragging the mouse near the top of the upper channel or bottom of the lower channel. As you drag, the cursor changes either to an R or an L, indicating whether you are selecting the Right or Left channel.

FIGURE 24.7

A waveform selected in Edit view

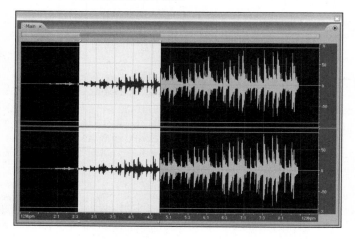

- **Spectral Selection:** Audition allows you to edit audio by selecting a frequency range. For example, if you want to edit high frequencies from an audio clip, you can click and drag over a spectral frequency display with the mouse. (To view audio frequencies, choose View ⇨ Spectral Frequency Display.) To create a rectangular selection, click and drag with the Marquee tool. To create a polygonal or rounded selection, click and drag with the Lasso tool. When you release the mouse, the Lasso tool closes the selection. After you create a selection, you can then resize the selection by clicking and dragging an edge. To move the selection, position the cursor over the selection and then click and drag to move it.

 To restrict editing to a specific channel, choose Edit ⇨ Edit Channel and then choose the channel in the submenu.

Using zero crossing points

When editing audio, the best point to edit is often where the waveform crosses zero on the wave-form display, at the *zero crossing point*. By selecting and editing at zero crossing points, you avoid hearing a click or pop when Audition automatically splices audio edits together. (Selecting a zero crossing point is somewhat similar to selecting the blank space between words in a text document.) To edit using a zero crossing point, start by selecting the audio with one of the selection tools. Then choose Edit ➪ Zero Crossing. In the Zero Crossing submenu, choose one of the following options:

- **Adjust Selection Inward:** Adjusts inward to the closest zero point

- **Adjust Selection Outward:** Adjusts outward to the closest zero point

- **Adjust Left Side To Left:** Adjusts the left selection border to the closest zero point to the left

- **Adjust Left Side To Right:** Adjusts the left selection border to the closest zero point to the right

- **Adjust Right Side To Left:** Adjusts the right selection border to the closest zero point to the left

- **Adjust Right Side to Right:** Adjusts the right selection border to the closest zero point to the right

Snapping selections

Like Premiere Pro, Audition provides an invisible magnetic-like force that can help you work more precisely. Audition's Snapping option can make selections snap to the current-time indicator, mark-ers, ruler ticks, and zero crossing points. By default, Snapping is enabled, although you can easily disable it, if you want.

To activate or deactivate Snapping, choose Edit ➪ Snapping and then choose from the following options:

- **Snap To Markers:** This option enables the cursor to snap to markers.

- **Snap To Ruler (Coarse):** This option enables the cursor to snap to major ruler divisions or to snap only to the major numeric divisions.

- **Snap To Ruler (Fine):** This option enables the cursor to snap to each ruler subdivision.

- **Snap To Zero Crossings:** This option allows the cursor to snap to zero crossings (where the waveform crosses zero on the waveform display).

- **Snap To Frames:** When Audition's time format is set to frames, this option allows snap-ping to frames.

Finding beats

As you edit music, you may want to select between one beat and another. Often, a beat is indicated by a regular peak in the waveform display. However, you may be able to save yourself editing time by having Audition find or select the beat.

To automatically find the beginning of the beat, click in the waveform and then choose Edit ➪ Find Beats ➪ Find Next Beat (Left Side). If you want to find the next beat after that, choose Edit ➪ Find Beats ➪ Find Next Beat (Right Side).

Deleting, Trimming, Copying, and Pasting

After you have selected the audio data that you want to edit, you may want to delete or copy the selection. Before making a selection, you need to decide whether you want to edit the audio data in Waveform or Spectral Frequency Display. If you want to edit an audio clip's waveform, choose View ➪ Waveform Display in Edit View. If you want to edit by selecting a frequency, choose View ➪ Spectral Frequency Display in Edit View.

In Edit view, you can cut, copy, and paste in Waveform Display or Spectral Frequency. When pasting in Audition, you can choose to simply paste audio data at the current-time indicator, or you can paste and mix. Follow these steps:

1. **Select the data that you want to cut.** Using one of the zoom tools can help you make your selection more precise.

2. **To cut the data, choose Edit ➪ Cut or Edit ➪ Delete Selection.** After executing the Cut or Delete Selection command, the selection is removed and the surrounding audio is spliced together.

 The Cut command places the cut selection in the Clipboard, while the Delete Selection command does not.

 You can delete audio in Multitrack view by selecting audio in a track and choosing Edit ➪ Insert/Delete Time.

TIP When you cut, copy, or paste, Audition allows you to use up to five Clipboards. To use one of the Audition Clipboards, choose Edit ➪ Set Current Clipboard. In the submenu that appears, select one of the five Audition Clipboards, or select the Windows Clipboard and then proceed to cut, copy, or paste.

To copy audio, follow these steps:

1. **Select the data that you want to copy.**

2. **Choose Edit ➪ Copy.**

Trimming audio removes everything but the selected area. To trim audio, follow these steps:

1. **Select the audio data that you want to retain.**

2. **Choose Edit ➪ Trim.**

When pasting audio, you can choose to paste it into the current time area, or you can paste and mix audio at the same time. The Mix Paste command allows you to blend audio levels and modulate sound for special effects. Follow these steps:

1. **Copy or cut the data that you want to move.**

2. **Click or click and drag in the waveform area where you want to paste.**

3. **Choose Edit ➪ Paste or Edit ➪ Mix Paste.** If you choose Mix Paste, the Mix Paste dialog box opens, as shown in Figure 24.8. Choose among these options when pasting, and then click OK:

   ▪ **Volume:** This option allows you to change volume levels before pasting.

   ▪ **Invert:** This option inverts the pasted waveform, pasting in an upside-down version.

   ▪ **Lock Left/Right:** This option locks the volume sliders in the dialog box so that they move simultaneously.

   ▪ **Insert:** This option inserts audio at the current-time indicator. If you have made a selection, then pasted audio replaces the selection.

   ▪ **Overlap:** This option mixes the audio data at the current volume level while pasting.

   ▪ **Modulate:** This option creates a special effect by multiplying waveform values together when pasting.

   ▪ **Crossfade:** This option fades in audio when pasting. Enter a value in milliseconds for the fade duration.

   ▪ **From Clipboard:** This option pastes from the specified Clipboard number.

   ▪ **From Windows Clipboard:** This option pastes from the standard Windows Clipboard. This feature becomes activated if you select Edit ➪ Copy after choosing Edit ➪ Set Clipboard and set the Clipboard to the Windows Clipboard option.

   ▪ **From File:** This option allows pasting from an audio file on disk.

   ▪ **Loop Paste:** This option pastes audio based upon the number that you specified in the Loop Paste field.

FIGURE 24.8

The Mix Paste command provides several options for pasting audio clips.

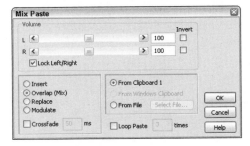

Deleting silence

When editing, you may want to delete silence to remove dull spots from your narration or to make the narration move more quickly. Audition's Delete Silence command provides a fast and easy method of deleting silence. When you apply the Delete Silence command, Audition removes the silences and shortens the audio clip.

To remove silence from a selected area, select it first with a selection tool. If you do not make a selection, the Delete Silence command deletes silence from the entire audio clip. To delete silence, follow these steps:

1. **Choose Edit ⇨ Delete Silence.**
2. **In the Delete Silence dialog box, shown in Figure 24.9, set options for deleting silence.** If desired, change the values in the "Silence is defined as" and "Audio is defined as" sections. You can also change the duration of continuous silence in milliseconds. To scan for silence, click Scan for Silence Now. To automatically set levels for the Signal fields, click Find Levels. This causes Audition to analyze the waveform or selected range and set an appropriate starting dB level.
3. **To remove the silence, click OK.**

FIGURE 24.9

The Delete Silence dialog box options

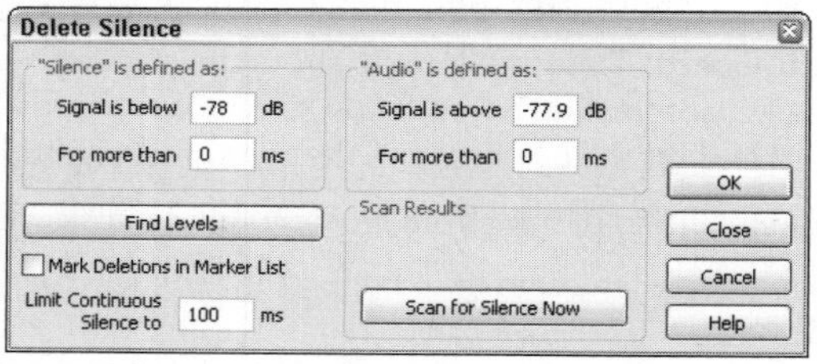

Creating silence

When editing, you may find that you need to create silence in order to add a little breathing room in a narration or between audio clips. Adobe Audition provides two methods for creating silence in Edit view: the Mute command, which mutes or turns sound into silence in a selected area, and the Silence command, which inserts silence.

To mute audio, follow these steps:

1. **Select the range that you want to mute.**

2. **Choose Effects ⇨ Mute.**

To insert silence into an audio clip, follow these steps:

1. **Click the point in the waveform where you want to create silence.** If you want to replace audio with silence, select the area with a selection tool.

2. **Choose Generate ⇨ Silence.**

3. **Enter the number of seconds of silence that you want to create.** You can use decimal numbers (for example, .5 for one-half second).

4. **Click OK to insert the silence.** This extends the audio clip's duration.

Applying and Creating Custom Effects

Although Audition users can apply effects in Multitrack view or in the Mixer window, you can apply, edit, and create your own audio effects in Edit view. To apply an effect, simply click and drag over a clip area and choose an effect from the Effects menu. You can also customize and store selected effects using Audition's Favorites menu.

You can apply effects such as fade-ins and fade-outs to the selected area of a waveform by simply clicking Favorites ⇨ Fade In or Effects ⇨ Favorites Fade Out. You can use the Favorites ⇨ Vocal Remove effect to remove male or female voice frequencies from audio data.

If you want to add an audio effect to the Favorites menu, choose Favorites ⇨ Edit Effects. In the Favorites dialog box, click New, and then name your effect. In the Audition Effect drop-down menu, choose an effect, as shown in Figure 24.10. After you choose the effect, click Edit Settings to adjust the settings for the effect. When you return to the Favorites dialog box, click Save to save your effect.

To view settings for a favorite effect or to edit Favorites, choose Edit ⇨ Favorites. In the Favorites dialog box (shown in Figure 24.10), select an effect and then click Edit. Next, click Edit Settings to open the settings for the effect that you want to edit. The settings for the Smooth Fade In effect are shown in Figure 24.11. After you edit the settings, click OK. Then click Save in the Favorites dialog box.

FIGURE 24.10

You can choose from Audition effects to create a new favorite effect.

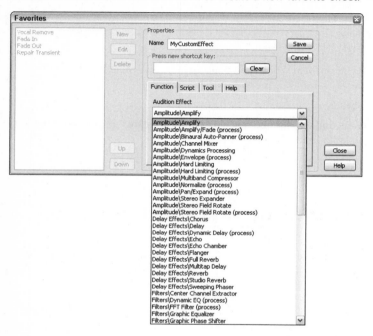

FIGURE 24.11

Editing Fade In settings

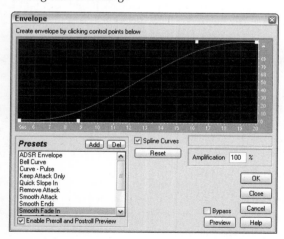

Generating Audio

Although you primarily use Audition for editing audio, you can also use it to generate sound effects or background tones. For example, Audition's Generate command allows you to create noise that could be used as a waterfall sound, and you can use Audition's Generate Tones command to create different electronic sounds.

Generating noise

Audition's Generate Noise command allows you to create Brown, Pink, or White noise. The categories provide noise at different frequencies: Brown noise is low-frequency noise, such as thunder; Pink noise is noise at frequencies often found in nature, such as rainfall; White noise is a higher-frequency noise that can create hissing sounds. It is easy to create noise and experiment with the results by following these steps:

1. **Click in the waveform area where you want the noise to appear.** If you want noise to replace audio, select the audio.

2. **In Edit view, choose Generate ➪ Noise.**

3. **In the Generate Noise dialog box, shown in Figure 24.12, choose a noise option: Brown, Pink, or White.** Choose values for intensity and duration, and select a style; for example, the Spatial Stereo option creates a surround-sound effect.

4. **Click OK to generate the noise.** Add it to the waveform.

FIGURE 24.12

The Generate Noise dialog box

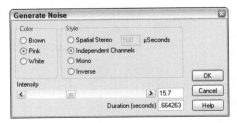

Generating tones

Audition's Generate Tones command allows you to generate tones by controlling frequency, phase options, and wave shapes. You can use the Generate Tones command to create a variety of tones. The dialog box provides a few presets, such as Bell, Chord, and Out of Control.

Follow these steps to generate tones:

1. **In Edit view, click in the waveform area where you want the noise to appear.** If you want noise to replace audio, select the audio.

2. **Choose Generate ⇨ Tones.**

3. **In the Generate Tones dialog box, click a preset, if desired.** You can change settings in the Initial Settings tab, then click the Final Settings, and change settings again. Click OK to create the tones.

Saving Audio Files

After you have finished editing audio in Edit view, you can choose to save your file, rename it, or revert to the last saved version using standard commands in Audition's File menu. As mentioned earlier, Audition saves in all standard audio application formats. If you are working in Multitrack view, you can save work as a session file by choosing File ⇨ Session. If you want to export the session in an audio format that can be read by Premiere Pro, choose File ⇨ Export.

Summary

Adobe Audition provides more extensive audio-recording and audio-editing features than Premiere Pro. To edit audio clips, use Audition's Edit view, where you can edit an audio clip's waveform, or use Audition's Spectral Frequency Display. If you want to layer audio into different tracks to create a mix, use Audition's Multitrack view and its Mixer window (Window ⇨ Mixer). This chapter covered these topics:

■ To export audio from Premiere Pro for editing in Audition, you can choose Edit ⇨ Edit in Audition.

■ To import video into Audition, you can choose Import ⇨ Video in Multitrack View.

■ To create silence, you can choose Effects ⇨ Mute or Generate ⇨ Silence.

■ To apply an effect in Edit view, you can select the audio waveform, and then choose an effect from Audition's Effects or Favorites menu.

Chapter 25

Using Adobe Soundbooth with Premiere Pro

IN THIS CHAPTER

Introduction to the Soundbooth workspace

Loading audio

Editing audio

Exporting audio from Premiere Pro

Working with video and audio in Soundbooth

Using the AutoComposer

Adobe Soundbooth is an audio editing program designed for Premiere Pro and Flash users who need to edit and correct audio, but don't need to delve too deeply into technical details. Using Soundbooth, you can quickly edit audio files and clips, create fade-ins and fade-outs, and improve audio quality. As part of the Adobe Creative Suite 3 Production Premium suite, Soundbooth is nicely integrated into the video production workflow. Premiere Pro users can send an audio track to Soundbooth for editing. When editing is complete, the updated changes appear in Premiere Pro. Soundbooth also provides a video monitor channel so that you can edit audio while viewing video. It even includes an AutoCompose Score task that allows you to create your own custom music scores.

This chapter provides an introduction to the audio editing features provided by Soundbooth. As you read the chapter, you'll see how Soundbooth conveniently transforms many complex audio tasks into simple procedures that only require a few mouse clicks. Apart from the basics of audio editing, this chapter shows you how you can create fade-ins and fade-outs with one mouse click, and choose presets for standard audio effects, which eliminates the need to choose among numerous levels and slider controls to create the right effect. It also provides an overview of how to use the AutoCompose score-editing feature.

Introduction to the Soundbooth Workspace

The best way to learn how to edit audio in Soundbooth is to first become familiar with the program's workspace. Like Premiere Pro, Soundbooth's interface, shown in Figure 25.1, is divided into separate panels that you can resize, dock, and undock. Figure 25.1 shows the default audio editing view, with the Editor panel consuming most of the screen space. Soundbooth also provides two other panel arrangements: Edit Audio to Video and Edit Score to Video. These views open a video monitor onscreen so that you can work with audio while viewing video. You can change workspaces by choosing from the Workspace drop-down menu at the top-right corner of the screen or by choosing one from the Window ⇨ Workspace submenu.

FIGURE 25.1

The Soundbooth audio editing workspace

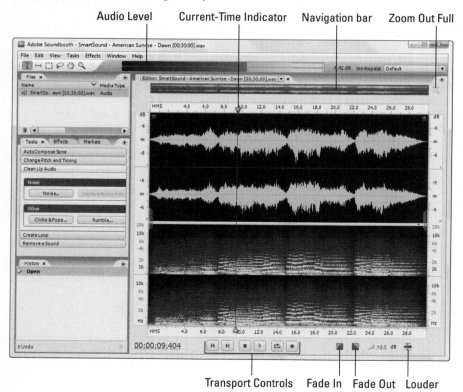

Editor panel

The Editor panel is the focal point for editing in Soundbooth. Undoubtedly its most important component is the audio Timeline where you can edit audio by clicking and dragging, or cutting and pasting either the wavelength or spectral display. You can view the spectral frequency by choosing View ⇨ Spectral Frequency Display. Across the top of the Editor panel is the Navigation bar. If the audio wavelength or spectral frequency display doesn't fit within the edit panel, you can scroll the audio by clicking and dragging here. If you want to view all of the audio within the Editor panel, click the Zoom Out Full Magnifying icon to the right of the Navigation bar.

Like Premiere Pro, Soundbooth features a current-time indicator (CTI). To move, or scrub, through audio while playing back the audio, click and drag the CTI. To quickly move the CTI to a specific point, click anywhere in the wavelength or spectral frequency. You can also move the CTI by clicking and dragging the time readout of hours, minutes, and seconds at the bottom-left corner of the panel.

As you can see from Figure 25.1, sound levels in dB are arranged vertically in the panel. Time is displayed horizontally. You can control where the time and audio levels appear by choosing View ⇨ Vertical Ruler and then choosing Left, Right, or Both. You can choose to have the time readout at the bottom of the screen by choosing View ⇨ Bottom Timeline Ruler. You can control how audio channels display by choosing View ⇨ Channels Separated or Layered. If you choose separated, you can view each track as a separate channel across the Timeline, as shown in Figure 25.1. Note that as audio plays, sound levels appear above the Editor panel.

At the bottom of the Editor panel is a time readout indicating the current position of the CTI. You can click and drag over this readout to change the time readout, which in turn changes the position of the CTI. To the right of the time readout are the Transport controls. From left to right, the Transport controls are Go to Next Marker, Go to Previous Marker, Stop, Play, Loop Playback, and Record. To the right of the Transport controls are Fade buttons that are used to quickly fade in and fade out audio. Next on the right is a dB control that allows you to raise or lower overall audio up or down by clicking over the dB readout. The Louder button allows you to quickly raise audio levels with a mouse click. The Louder button is discussed in the Normalizing and Hard Limiting Audio section later in this chapter.

Finally, if you have opened several audio files in Soundbooth, you can quickly change views from one to another by clicking the down arrow in the Editor panel and choosing the audio file by name.

Files panel

The Files panel lists files that are loaded into Soundbooth. You can quickly view a file's waveform in the Editor panel by double-clicking it in the Files panel. You can sort by clicking the Name column at the top of the file list, and you can close the file by clicking the trash icon.

Tools panel

The Tools panel allows you to switch from one editing tool to another. You can choose from the following tools, as shown in Figure 25.2:

- **Time Selection:** Click and drag with this tool to select audio on the audio wavelength or spectral frequency display.

- **Frequency Selection:** Click and drag with this tool to select audio by frequency. The display must be set to spectral display (View ⇨ Spectral Frequency Display).

- **Rectangular Marquee:** This tool allows you to make a rectangular selection in the spectral frequency display.

- **Lasso:** Use this tool to create freehand closed selections in the Spectral Frequency Display. When you click and drag in a circular motion, the Lasso tool automatically closes the selection, Thus you don't need to close the selection by returning to your original starting point.

- **Hand:** Use this tool to scroll through audio without changing the CTI.

- **Zoom:** Use this tool to zoom into the wavelength or spectral frequency display to fine-tune edits.

FIGURE 25.2

Tools panel selection tools

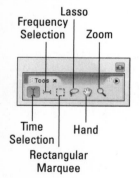

Tasks panel

The Tasks panel allows you to quickly apply a variety of audio editing tasks. Using the Tasks panel, you can quickly change pitch and time, clean up audio, create loops, remove sounds, and create your own score. Creating a score using the AutoCompose Score task is covered later in this chapter in the section "Using the AutoComposer."

Effects panel

The Effects panel provides a quick and non-technical way of applying audio effects without the need for tweaking knobs, sliders, and other controls. You choose effects by choosing presets such as Reverb Large Room and Reverb Small Room. To apply an effect, first select an area in the wavelength or spectral frequency display. Next, choose an effect from the Effect Preset drop-down menu. You can choose from the following effects:

Fix: Remove Hiss

Loudness: Everything the Same Level

EQ: Fix Muddy Low End

Once you select a preset, more presets appear in the Tasks panel. These allow you to fine-tune the effect. For example, if you choose Reverb Large Room, the Convolution Reverb is added to the Effects Rack, as shown in Figure 25.3. It includes choices such as A Cold House, Judges Chamber, Under The Bridge, and Smokey Bar. As a test, try changing a Smokey Bar into a Judges Chamber, or vice versa.

FIGURE 25.3

In the Effects panel you can choose effects from a list of presets.

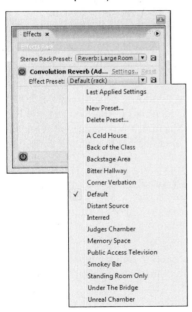

Markers panel

In Soundbooth, markers are used as navigational points or cue points to be exported to Adobe Flash. The Markers panel provides an efficient interface for adding, subtracting, and managing markers. To add a marker, move to an area in the audio Timeline, and then click the plus sign. The marker appears listed in the panel, where you can name it, edit its position, or delete it. To edit a marker, first select it in the panel, and then name it by entering a name in the name field. You can change a marker position in the Timeline by simply clicking and dragging the time read-out in the Markers panel. To delete the selected marker, simply click the minus sign.

History panel

Like Premiere Pro, Soundbooth has a History panel that allows you to undo a step or jump back in audio-editing history. To return to a previous step, simply click it in the History panel. You can also select an individual action in the History panel and remove it by clicking Delete in the History panel's menu.

Loading Audio

Before you can start editing audio, you need to load an audio file into the program. You can load audio in three ways: by opening it from the File menu, recording it directly in Soundbooth, or loading a template from the AudioCompose Score task in the Tasks panel. This section covers opening an audio file and recording audio.

Opening a file

Soundbooth supports virtually all major audio formats, including Windows WAV, Macintosh AIFF, and MP3. It also allows you to load QuickTime, MPEG, and AVI video files so that you can edit the audio that is linked to the video. Like most other Windows and Macintosh programs, you can load a file by choosing File ➪ Open. As a shortcut, you can also open an audio file by clicking in the blank area under the word Name in the Files panel.

 In Soundbooth, the File ➪ Import command loads Adobe Flash cue points. It does not load audio files.

Recording audio

Apart from opening audio files from disk, Soundbooth also allows you to quickly record audio. Once the audio is recorded, it is automatically loaded into Soundbooth's Editor panel. To record audio directly into Soundbooth, follow these steps:

1. **Attach your microphone or audio playback device to your computer's audio input/microphone jack.**

2. **Choose File ➪ Record.** This opens the Record dialog box, shown in Figure 25.4.

FIGURE 25.4

Set options for recording audio in the Record dialog box.

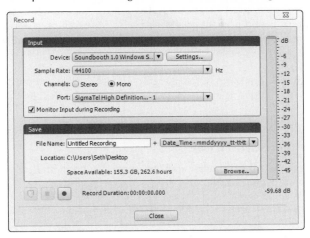

3. **In the Record dialog box, choose a sample rate and whether you want to record using stereo or mono.** You can choose the input port in the Port drop-down menu and access your audio card by clicking the Settings button.

4. **To play audio while recording, click the Monitor Input during Recording option.**

5. **Name your file in the File Name field.**

6. **If desired, change the location where you want to save your scan by clicking the Browse button.**

7. **To start recording, click the red recording button.** As you record, Soundbooth shows the recording levels, with colors indicating safe and warning ranges. Green shows audio in the safe recording range, while yellow is in the warning range.

8. **After you finish recording, click the Stop button.** Click Close. Your audio appears in the Editor panel.

Editing Audio

For most Premiere Pro users, Soundbooth's chief attraction is how easily it allows you to edit Premiere Pro audio files. This section covers the basics of editing audio: cutting and pasting audio as well as creating fade-ins and fade-outs. As you'll soon see, editing in Soundbooth rarely requires more than a few mouse clicks.

Playing and selecting audio

Before you edit a sound file or sound clip in Soundbooth, you often need to locate the section you want to edit, and then select it. To locate an edit point, you can click and drag the current-time indicator to scrub through sound near the area you want to edit. You can also use the Transport controls, or you can press J to play audio, press K to play backward, and press the Spacebar to start and stop audio.

Once you find that area, you can zoom in using the Zoom tool to help you precisely select the area you want to edit. Your next step is using the mouse to select in the audio clip's waveform.

Follow these steps to create a selection in a waveform in the Editor panel:

1. **Activate the Time Selection tool.**

2. **Click and drag over the area you want to select.** Soundbooth lightens the selected area, as shown in Figure 25.5.

You can use these techniques to select a section of an audio clip or the entire audio file:

■ If you want to select the entire file, choose Edit ➪ Select All, or triple-click in the Editor panel.

■ If you want to select the area that is visible in the Editor panel, choose Edit ➪ Select View or double-click in the Editor panel.

 **If you want to change the length of a selection, press and hold Shift, and click where you want the edit to end.**

 **Once you create a selection, you can move the selection to another area of the Timeline. To do this, move the mouse pointer to the Timeline ruler where the dotted line indicates the middle of the selection. When the mouse pointer changes to a hand, click and drag.**

Follow these steps to select in the Spectral Frequency Display to view the spectral display (choose View ➪ Spectral Frequency Display):

1. **Select the Frequency Selection, Marquee, or Lasso tool.**

2. **Click and drag in the spectral display.** If you are using the Lasso tool, click and drag in a circular motion. If you do not return to the starting point of the selection, Soundbooth completes and closes the selection path.

FIGURE 25.5

A selection in the audio waveform

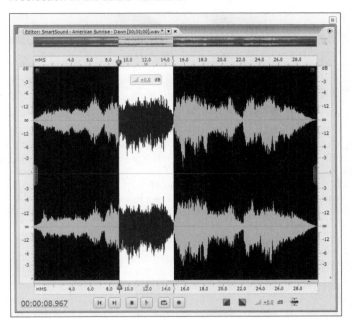

Cutting, copying, and pasting audio

Soundbooth conforms to the standard Windows and Macintosh cut, copy, and paste procedures. However, if you simply want to delete a section of audio so that the selected area is removed and the audio is shortened, you can select the area and choose Edit ⇨ Delete.

To cut, copy, and paste audio, follow these steps:

1. **Select the audio that you want to cut, copy, or paste.**
2. **Choose either Edit ⇨ Copy, or Edit ⇨ Cut.**
3. **Move the current-time indicator where you want to paste.** Then click Edit ⇨ Paste. If you want to replace audio with the copied selection, click and drag where you want the pasted clip to appear, and then click Edit ⇨ Paste.

 You can paste and mix audio at the same time. After copying, pasting, and selecting the area where you want to paste and mix audio, choose Edit ⇨ Mix Paste. Before executing the command, the Mix Paste dialog box allows you to set volume levels for both the copied audio and the existing audio.

 To insert silence, select the area where you want the silence to appear. Then click Edit ⇨ Silence.

Trimming audio

Soundbooth allows you to quickly shorten the duration of an audio file by trimming its beginning or ending. To do this, first display the entire audio file in the Editor panel, by clicking the Zoom Out Full button in the top-right corner of the Editor panel. This displays the trim beginning and trim editing handles, as shown in Figure 25.5. To trim from either side, simply click and drag the handles at either end of the waveform.

NOTE If you cut or trim audio that is linked to a video file, Soundbooth creates silence in the selection area, instead of removing the audio and making the audio file shorter. This keeps audio and video in sync.

Changing volume

Soundbooth allows you to quickly raise or lower the volume of a selection. First select the area that you want to edit, and then click and drag in the audio dB display that appears in the middle of the selection (shown in Figure 25.5). Drag right to raise volume, and drag left to lower volume.

Normalizing and hard limiting audio

 Normalizing audio boosts or lowers the audio wavelength to its maximum safe level without introducing distortion. Typically normalizing boosts audio to a target level of –3 dB. Although you can normalize audio in Premiere Pro, it's certainly easier in Soundbooth. To normalize audio, simply click the Louder button once in the Editor panel. This normalizes the entire file (if you select only a portion of the file, Soundbooth normalizes the selection). If you click the Louder button again, Soundbooth increases the volume by 3 dB with each click, but prevents clipping. This process is known as *hard limiting*.

Creating fade-ins and fade-outs

 Soundbooth's ability to quickly create audio fades exemplifies the program's ease of use. In Soundbooth you can create a fade-in or fade-out with one mouse click. To fade in, simply click the Fade-In button in the Editor panel. To fade out, click the Fade-Out button. By default, Soundbooth provides a linear-curve fade-out, which is represented by a straight line that indicates the audio level gradually increasing or decreasing. To choose a different fade curve, right-click/⌘-click the fade button and choose the curve. Once the fade appears in the Editor panel, you can adjust the curve by clicking and dragging the fade icon in the wavelength area. The two other curves represent logarithmic and exponential fades. The logarithmic curve arcs upward, showing that the fade begins quickly, and then slows as it ends. An exponential curve arcs downward, starting slowly and gradually speeding up.

Exporting Audio from Premiere Pro

For Premiere Pro users, the Soundbooth workflow is typically a roundtrip from Premiere Pro to Soundbooth and back. Premiere Pro can send an audio file directly to Soundbooth. Once you save the file in Soundbooth, the file is automatically updated in Premiere Pro. How you send a file to Soundbooth depends upon whether or not the audio is linked to video.

Audio-only roundtrip

To send an audio-only clip from Premiere Pro to Soundbooth, select a master audio clip, sub-clip, or instance of a clip in the Premiere Pro Timeline panel, and then choose Edit ➪ Edit in Soundbooth. Premiere Pro creates a copy of the clip in the Premiere Pro Project panel and opens up the clip in Soundbooth for editing. When you save the file in Soundbooth, the file is automatically updated in Premiere Pro.

Linked audio roundtrip

If you want to edit a linked audio file, select the audio file in Premiere Pro's Timeline panel. Then choose Edit ➪ Edit in Soundbooth ➪ Render and Replace. Premiere Pro creates a copy of the file in the Project panel (the filename is appended with the word *extract*) and then opens the file in Soundbooth. All edits in Soundbooth are saved back to the extract file in Premiere Pro, which replaces the original audio track in the Premiere Pro Timeline.

Project panel roundtrip

If you want to send an audio clip sitting in the Project panel to Soundbooth, simply click the clip, and choose Edit ➪ Edit in Soundbooth ➪ Extract Audio. Premiere Pro makes a copy of the sound clip in its Project panel and then opens the clip in Soundbooth for editing. Changes saved in Soundbooth are saved to the audio file in Premiere Pro's Project panel.

Working with Video and Audio in Soundbooth

As mentioned earlier, Soundbooth allows you to import video with audio files. This allows you to sync up the audio with the video. To use this workflow, simply choose File ➪ Open to load your video into Soundbooth. To set up your workspace to view both audio and video, choose Window ➪ Workspace ➪ Edit Audio to Video. If you are editing a score to video, you can also choose Window ➪ Workspace ➪ Edit Score to Video. This workspace opens the Video panel as well as the Tasks panel. The Tasks panel is opened to the AutoCompose Score task, described in the section "Using the AutoComposer."

 **TIP** You can view the audio waveform of a clip in Premiere Pro's Source monitor by choosing Audio Waveform in the Source monitor menu.

Once you finish editing audio, saving an audio file in Soundbooth is as simple as choosing File ⇨ Save, or File ⇨ Save As. Soundbooth saves in all standard audio formats, including WAV, AIFF, and MPA.

Using the AutoComposer

If you need music to accompany your video project, Soundbooth may be able to provide you with a custom musical score. Soundbooth's AutoCompose Score task allows you to load a musical template from disk and customize it by changing the tempo and intensity. You can make changes throughout the entire score or change specific sections by using keyframes.

Creating the score

If you want to view a reference video clip in Soundbooth so that you can make score changes while viewing video, first change workspaces by choosing Window ⇨ Workspace ⇨ Edit Score to Video. Load the video into Soundbooth by choosing File ⇨ Open. Later, you can load the reference video using the AutoCompose Score task.

The following steps describe how to load a music template and edit it to create your own custom score:

1. **If the Tasks panel is not open, choose Window ⇨ Tasks.**

2. **In the Tasks panel, click AutoCompose Score.** The AutoCompose Score task opens, as shown in Figure 25.6.

3. **In the AutoCompose Score task, load a score template by clicking the Browse Scores button.** This opens Adobe Bridge. Soundbooth score templates are designated with an .sbst file extension. Locate an SBST file, and then double-click the file to load it into Soundbooth.

4. **When the score appears in the Editor panel, press the Spacebar to play it.**

NOTE You can purchase addition scores from the Web using Soundbooth's Resource Central Panel. To open Resource Central, choose Window ⇨ Resource Central. Choose a music style from the Genre drop-down menu, then select a score that you wish to purchase. Next click the Show Bundle button. On the Bundle screen, click the Buy button which directs you to the Adobe Store where you can purchase the score. Note that you can also use Resource Central to download sound effects.

FIGURE 25.6

Use the AutoCompose Score task to customize a score for your Premiere Pro project.

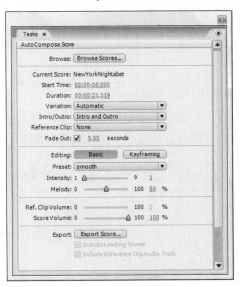

Once a score is loaded, AutoCompose provides a variety of features for editing and adjusting the music. Use the following steps as a guide:

1. **If you loaded a reference video clip into Soundbooth, load it into the video track by choosing it in the Reference Clip drop-down menu.**

2. **If you have a video clip in the video channel, you may want to adjust the start time of the music to sync with the video.** To change the start time, click and drag over the Start Time readout in the AutoCompose Score task panel. As you drag, the score moves in the Timeline. Set the start time to the specific time you want it to begin playing with the video. To set the start time precisely, enter the time in the Start Time entry field.

3. **Set the duration of the score.** You can do this by changing the time readout in the Duration field. You can also choose a time in the Variation drop-down menu. The lengths specified in the Variation drop-down menu are arranged in an order created by the template's composer.

4. **Choose whether you want an intro or outro in the Intro/Outro drop-down menu.** An intro keeps an introductory segment in the score, and an outro keeps a concluding segment in the score. If you make a change, you can see it reflected in the Timeline in the Editor panel.

5. **Set the fade-out time in seconds.** If you do not want a fade-out, deselect the Fade Out option.

6. **Choose an editing mode, either Basic or Keyframing.** Basic allows you to make changes to the overall score; Keyframing allows you change specific areas of the score using keyframes. Keyframe changes can be gradual (linear keyframes) or more abrupt (hold keyframes). Figure 25.7 shows the Editor panel with a score, video reference clip, and linear and hold keyframes.

FIGURE 25.7

Editing a score with keyframes and a reference video

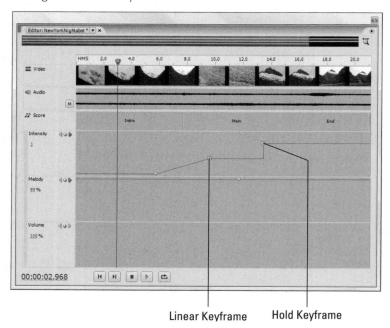

Linear Keyframe   Hold Keyframe

If you select Basic, you can make the following adjustments:

a. **Choose Smooth, Medium, or High in the Preset menu.** Each choice sets the Intensity and the other sliders (the names of the sliders depends upon the score that is loaded). Adjust the Intensity and other sliders as desired.

b. **Adjust the volume level using the Score volume slider.** If you want to adjust the volume of the video clip (if you loaded one), click and drag the Reference Clip volume slider.

If you select Keyframes, you can adjust the Intensity and other musical components in the Editor panel:

a. **To create keyframes for Intensity, move the current-time indicator to where you want to make an adjustment.** Click and drag the Intensity blue graph line or enter a number in the Intensity field (in the Editor panel, not the Task panel). To add other keyframes, move the CTI to where you want to create the keyframe, then click the Add/Remove Keyframe button. If you want to move the keyframe, click and drag it. Be aware that some scores may not allow you to make major adjustments to the blue graph line.

b. **To create keyframes for other components, move the current-time indicator to where you want to make an adjustment.** Click and drag the Melody blue graph line or enter a number in the field to the left of the graph line. To add other keyframes, move the CTI to where you want to create the keyframe. If you want to move the keyframe, click and drag it.

c. **Once you create a keyframe, you can adjust it to be a linear or hold keyframe, by right-clicking/control-clicking the keyframe.** A linear keyframe makes a gradual change, while a hold keyframe makes an abrupt change.

d. **If you want to remove a keyframe, click the Go to Next Keyframe or Go to Previous Keyframe button.** Click Add/Remove Keyframe.

7. **As you work and continue to make adjustments, you can press the Spacebar to play your score.**

8. **To save your file in SBST format, click File ⇨ Save Soundbooth Score Document As.** Name your file, choose a location, and then click Save.

Exporting the score

Once you finish editing a score, you can export it so that you can include it in a Premiere Pro project. Here are the steps for exporting the score:

1. **If you are working with reference video and you offset the start time from the start of the Timeline, select Include Leading Silence.** This causes Soundbooth to insert silence for the offset duration, allowing you to match your audio to the proper video frame.

2. **To include the audio track from the reference video, click Include Reference Clip Audio.**

3. **Click Export Score.**

4. **In the Export Soundbooth Score dialog box, choose a file format and destination.** Enter a filename, and click Save.

Summary

Soundbooth allows you to edit, enhance, and record audio for your Premiere Pro projects.

- To edit a Premiere Pro audio clip in Soundbooth, select it in the Project panel, and then choose Edit ➪ Edit in Soundbooth.

- To edit a Premiere Pro audio track in a Premiere Pro Timeline, select it and then choose Edit ➪ Edit in Soundbooth ➪ Render and Replace.

- To normalize audio in Soundbooth, click the Louder button in Soundbooth's Editor panel.

- You can edit an audio file by selecting its waveform in Soundbooth's Editor panel, and then cut and paste it.

- If you want to create a custom score for your Premiere Pro project, you can use Soundbooth's AutoCompose Score task.

Chapter 26

Using Adobe Encore to Create DVDs

A dobe Encore CS3 is a high-end DVD authoring program that allows you to create interactive DVDs. As part of the Adobe Video Collection, Encore allows you to import audio and video that is exported from Premiere Pro. Using Encore, you can create menus and navigational buttons that add sophisticated interactivity to your Premiere Pro projects. You can even use your Encore project to create an interactive Flash movie. Because many of Encore's navigational links are created automatically by dragging and dropping graphics onscreen, it probably won't take Premiere Pro users long to get up and running in Encore. Although the interface is different from Premiere Pro's, most users will probably find themselves right at home in Encore's Project and Timelines panels. This chapter provides an overview of the basics of DVD authoring in Encore. So follow along, and you'll see how to integrate Premiere Pro footage into a DVD-authoring program that provides more graphics and navigational features than those provided by Premiere Pro.

CROSS-REF This chapter leads you through the steps of creating a simple interactive DVD in which Encore automatically creates links to multiple video files. Chapter 27 shows you how to create DVD chapters and link to chapter files.

NOTE A trial downloadable version of Adobe Encore is available at www.adobe.com. If you want to create a DVD project using this chapter as a guide, you can use a Premiere Pro project as your video source footage. However, in order to import it into Encore, you must export the project in one of these formats: AVI, DV-AVI (Mac OS), H.264, MPEG-2, QuickTime, WMV. Note that Encore supports the following audio formats as well: AC3 (Dolby Digital), AIF, AIFF (not AIFF-C), mp3, MPG, M2P, QuickTime, WMA.

Creating a New Project

To start working in Encore, you must specify whether your new project will be NTSC or PAL, and whether the project is formatted as Blu-ray or standard DVD. Blu-ray provides a high-definition format.

If you choose to create a Blu-ray project, you can choose from the following frame sizes: 740 x 480, 1280 x 820, 1440 x 1080, 1920 x 1080. You can choose different frame rates, depending upon whether the project is NTSC or PAL. You can also choose to use the MPEG-2 or H.264 codec. After you create a project, you can then use Encore panel utilities to begin the DVD authoring process. To create a new project, follow these steps:

1. **Click New Project in the Encore opening splash screen, or choose File ⇨ New Project.** The New Project dialog box appears, as shown Figure 26.1.

2. **Choose whether you want to use the NTSC (U.S. Standard) or the PAL (European) video standard.**

3. **If you want to create a project in Blu-ray format, click the Blu-ray option, and change the dimensions, frame rate, or codec, if desired.**

FIGURE 26.1

You can choose a video standard in the New Project dialog box.

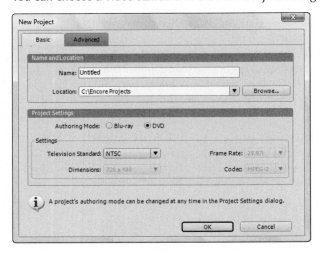

Navigating the Encore panels

The following sections provide a brief overview of the Encore panels. The process of opening, closing, and docking panels in Encore is virtually identical to working with panels in Premiere Pro. Like Premiere Pro, you can also choose a workspace from the Window menu.

After you create a new project, you're ready to start examining Encore's most important panels: Project, Menu, Timelines, and Disc. These four panels allow you to perform most major tasks related to a project. To access any of the panels, click its tab or choose a panel name from the Encore Window menu. Like the Premiere Pro Project panel, the Encore Project panel allows you to view the project assets (video, audio, and graphics) that comprise your project. The Menus panel allows you to manage menus where you'll place navigational buttons. The Timelines panel lists timelines, and the Timeline Viewer provides a bird's-eye overview of your project, as well as allowing you to set chapter markers. The Disc tab is used for burning DVDs.

After you open a project onscreen, Encore's other panels provide options for DVD navigation and graphics. As mentioned earlier, like Premiere Pro's panels, you can drag the Encore panels apart and reunite them in different combinations. The following sections describe panels that help you create buttons, menus, and navigational structure.

The Properties panel

This is a multipurpose information panel that provides details about what is selected in other panels. Figure 26.2 shows the Properties panel displaying information about an Encore menu. The information in the panel changes to reflect different items that you click in the Project panel or in the Menu Viewer. For example, if you click a video clip in the Project tab, the Properties panel displays information about the clip's location and duration.

FIGURE 26.2

The Properties panel provides information about different Encore production elements.

The Layers panel

This panel allows you to manipulate layers used in menus. You can select, show, hide, and change the stacking order of objects on menu screens. The Layers panel is shown in Figure 26.3. Typically, layers displayed in Encore are created in Adobe Photoshop. Encore reads Photoshop layer sets that are preceded with a (+) as menu button sets. Layers with button graphics and colors in the button set for a sub-picture (used to highlight buttons) are named with a (=1), (=2), or (=3) prefix. (Each of these special layers can be used to create a different color, or they can include different shapes that appear as part of the button. The button colors that display when the DVD plays are based upon a color set within Encore.)

FIGURE 26.3

The Layers panel displays information about graphic elements on a menu page.

The Character panel

Use this panel to specify font-related options for characters that are created for buttons and menus. The Character panel drop-down menus access choices for changing typefaces, type size, and style. The Character panel is shown in Figure 26.4.

The Library panel

Encore's Library comes stocked with templates for menus, buttons, and various backgrounds. You can use the Library panel to quickly load graphics from the Library or to add graphics to the Library. The section "Using menu templates" later in this chapter, tells you how to use a menu screen from the Library panel as the basis for an interactive menu. The icons in the middle of the panel allow you to change views so that you can see Only Menus, Only Buttons, or Only Backgrounds.

Menus panel and Menu Viewer

Encore's Menus panel displays menus and their buttons. You can drag a menu from the Library directly into the Menus panel. Double-clicking a menu in the Menus panel opens it in the Menu Viewer, where you can edit the graphics and the links to the menu's buttons.

FIGURE 26.4

You can use the Character panel to change type settings.

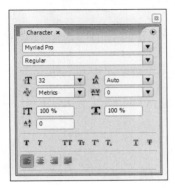

Timelines panel

This panel provides an overview of your DVD media sources in sequential order. You can also use the Timeline window to divide your DVD into chapters, add subtitles to tracks, and choose the language for subtitles. As you will see later in this chapter, you can place video into different Timelines and link the Timelines to buttons on DVD menus.

Importing source video and audio

Encore allows you to import audio, video, and graphics files. In Encore, source material such as video clips, graphics, and sound files are called *assets*. Adobe Photoshop users will be happy to learn that Encore is fully compatible with Photoshop; you can load Photoshop layers in as separate buttons in a menu. To load an asset into Encore, choose File ➪ Import as Asset. In the Import as Asset dialog box, select the file that you want to import and click Open.

If you want to create a practice project, load an AVI, MPEG-2, or other file supported by Encore (DV-AVI [Mac OS], H.264, QuickTime, WMV) using the File ➪ Import as Asset. Then continue following the sections to choose a menu, link buttons, and burn or preview a DVD.

Like Premiere Pro, all imported source material appears in the Project panel, as shown in Figure 26.5.

NOTE Encore can import MPEG-2 files, which are considered DVD-compliant (meaning that they meet DVD recording standards). Encore can also import some non-DVD-compliant files, such as NTSC AVI and QuickTime files — which must have a frame size of 720 x 480, 720 x 486, or 704 x 480 with a frame rate of 23.976, 23.978, 24 frames per second or 29.97 frames per second. PAL files must have a frame size of 720 x 576 or 704 x 576 with a frame rate of 25 frames per second. Encore also supports high-definition video frame sizes at and interlaced and progressive frame rates of 23.976p, 29.97i, 59.94p. High-definition interlaced and progressive frame rates for PAL are 25i and 50p. Files that are not DVD-compliant are transcoded by Encore to make them DVD-compliant. Working with DVD-compliant files saves time, because Encore does not need to transcode them when you burn a DVD or import files. Also note that when you import AVI files, Encore automatically imports audio. If you import MPEG files, you need to import the audio separately.

FIGURE 26.5

Encore's Project panel with video and graphics files

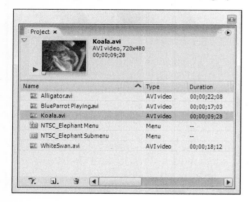

Using menu templates

To most computer users, the term *menu* refers to a drop-down menu of choices that appear at the top of a computer application. In the world of DVD development, a menu is a screen with interactive buttons. Typically, the first screen that you see when viewing a DVD production is a menu screen. Clicking a button on the menu typically moves you to another menu or to the start of the production. In this section, you choose a menu from a list of predesigned templates to use for your project.

You can use the Encore Library panel to load a background and preset buttons to start creating your opening DVD screen. Follow these steps:

1. **Click the Library panel to access it.** Figure 26.6 shows the Library panel with a list of templates.

2. **In the Set drop-down menu, choose a category, such as General, Corporate, or Education.**

3. **From the buttons in the middle of the window, click the first one on the left to display the menus.**

4. **Choose a menu from the list by clicking it.** Note that the submenus in the list can be used to link additional menus to the main menu.

The Library panel with predesigned templates

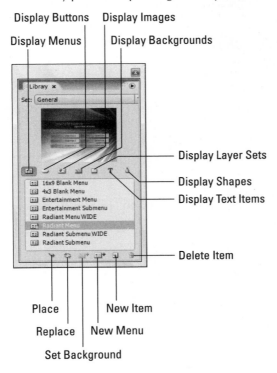

Display Buttons   Display Images

Display Menus   Display Backgrounds

Display Layer Sets

Display Shapes
Display Text Items

Delete Item

Place   New Item

Replace   New Menu

Set Background

5. **Create a new menu based on the template by clicking the New Menu button (not the New Item button).** Alternatively, you can double-click the menu or drag it from the Library into the Menus panel. The new menu appears onscreen in the Menu Viewer, as shown in Figure 26.7. The menu is now listed in the Project and Menus panels.

6. **Click the Menus panel to display your new menu's name in the panel.**

7. **Select the menu in the Menus panel.** After you select the menu, its buttons appear in the bottom portion of the Menus panel.

FIGURE 26.7

You can use the Menu Viewer screen to edit text and buttons on the menu.

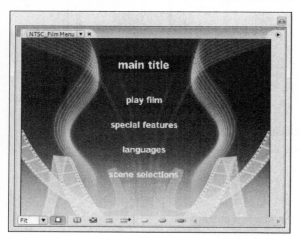

Editing the menu

Now you can customize the menu by changing the text and placement of buttons. You can edit the menu using the menu-editing tools shown in Figure 26.8.

FIGURE 26.8

Menu-editing tools

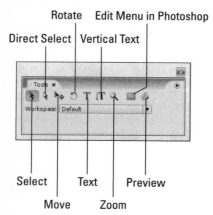

The menu contains the following tools:

- **Selection tool:** Use to select a button set, which can include the button, its text, and its sub-pictures. Once you select a button set with the Selection tool, you can click and drag to move it.
- **Direct Select tool:** Use to select, move, and resize individual objects on a menu screen.
- **Move tool:** Use to move objects that you select in the Layers panel. After you select an object in the Layers panel, the object is selected in the Menu Viewer. You can then click and drag it with the Move tool.

TIP To move an object among stacked objects in layers, right-click the object with a selection tool. In the drop-down menu that appears, choose Select. In the Select drop-down menu, choose the object that you want to move. You can then move the object with the Move tool.

- **Rotate tool:** Use to rotate text and graphics. Click and drag in a circular motion. You can also rotate using the Selection or Direct Select tool by clicking and dragging the corner handle of an object. To rotate at 45-degree angles, press Shift while rotating.
- **Text tool:** Use to create and edit text.
- **Vertical Text tool:** Use to create and edit vertical text.
- **Zoom tool:** Use to zoom in and out.
- **Edit Menu in Photoshop:** Use to open the selected menu in Photoshop.
- **Preview:** Use to preview the DVD in the Preview panel.

Along with the Encore layout tools, you can also use the Arrange, Align, and Distribute commands found in the Object menu. These commands allow you to quickly move and align objects onscreen. Figure 26.9 shows an expanded view of this menu.

FIGURE 26.9

You can use the Arrange, Align, and Distribute commands as you edit a menu.

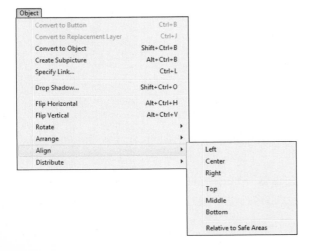

Creating Button Links and Timelines

In this section, you link the video files to buttons on your menu page. These links trigger the video to play when the user clicks a button. Set up the Encore window so that you can see the Project panel and the Menu Viewer. (If you don't have a video file in the Project panel, you can import one by choosing File ⇨ Import as Asset.) To create a link to a button, follow these steps:

1. **Click a video file in the Project panel.** Drag it over the button to which you want to link. When the cursor is correctly positioned over the button, a rectangle appears over the button. Release the mouse after the rectangle appears; the button name changes to indicate Chapter 1 or the name of the video file.

>  If you don't release the mouse over a button, Encore creates a new button on the menu page.

2. **With the Selection tool activated, click the linked button.** Observe the Properties panel. Note that the Link field displays the link to the button, as shown in Figure 26.10.

3. **If desired, you can type a new name for the button in the Name field in the Basic tab of the Properties panel.**

4. **Click the Timelines tab.** You can see that Encore created a Timeline listing for the video file.

FIGURE 26.10

A linked button displayed in the Properties panel

> **NOTE** If you want to view the Timeline in the Timeline Viewer, double-click the Timeline in the Timelines panel.

5. **Repeat steps 1 and 2 to create more links to buttons to different video files, as needed.**

> **NOTE** You can also create a Timeline by choosing Timeline ⇨ New Timeline and then dragging video files to the Timeline.

Examining the Timeline

Encore's Timeline Viewer provides a graphic display of the video and audio in your project. The Timeline Viewer can display a track for video as well as for audio and subtitles. (As discussed earlier, to view a Timeline in the Timeline Viewer, you can double-click the Timeline listing in the Timelines panel.) As in Premiere Pro, you can place different video clips into the Timeline. Figure 26.11 shows a Timeline in the Timeline Viewer with a video file and its audio file.

 If you import a DV AVI or QuickTime DV file with audio, the audio file is imported automatically with it. If you import MPEG-2 files, you need to import the audio separately.

Click the Timeline in the Project panel, and then view the Properties panel. The End Action field in the Properties panel displays Return to Last Menu, which indicates that, after the video is over, the original menu will display.

FIGURE 26.11

Encore's Timeline provides a graphical representation of audio and video files.

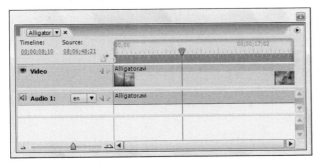

Viewing the Flowchart

As the links to your DVD become more complicated, you may want to refer to Encore's Flowchart panel, which provides you with a graphical view of your project workflow. To view a flowchart, shown in Figure 26.12, simply click the Flowchart tab. (If the tab isn't open onscreen, choose Window ➪ Flowchart.) When viewing the flowchart, you can use the Selection tool to create links. You can also create links by right-clicking/control-clicking on an item in the Flowchart and choosing Specify Link; then pick links from list of objects in your project.

Use the Direct Select tool to drag objects onto the flowchart and the Move tool to move objects. Unlinked objects appear at the bottom of the flowchart. You can drag these objects into the main area of the flowchart and link them using the Selection tool. To create a link, simply click and drag from one object to another.

 You can also create links using the properties palettes. The flowchart updates to reflect the links.

FIGURE 26.12

The flowchart provides a graphical representation of your DVD project.

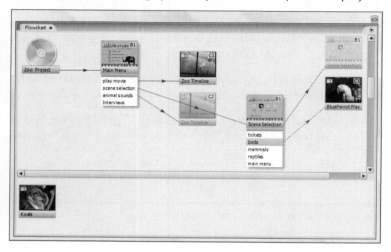

Completing Your Project

After you create your menus and button links, you're ready for the finishing steps of your DVD project.

Previewing the DVD

When you run the preview, Encore creates a simulation mode where you can test the button links. Follow these steps to preview your DVD:

1. **Choose File ⇨ Preview.**

2. **When the project switches to Preview mode, click the menu screen buttons to check that all of the links work properly.**

3. **If you need to fix a link, click the button in the Project tab.** Correct the link in the Properties panel.

Burning the DVD

After you preview your work and test the button links, you're ready to burn a single-layer or dual-layer DVD. You'll find burning options for the DVD on the Disc tab. Here are the steps:

1. **Insert a blank DVD into your DVD burner.**

2. **Choose Window ⇨ Build.** The Build panel appears. You can also choose File ⇨ Build, and then a destination such as Disc, Image, DVD Master, or Flash.

3. Choose DVD or Blu-ray or Flash in the Format menu.

4. In the Output submenu, specify one of the following options:

    ▪ **DVD Disc or Blu-ray Disc.**

    ▪ **DVD Folder or Blu-ray Folder:** This option allows you to create Blu-ray or DVD file structure on your hard drive which allows you to play the project back using a DVD or Blu-ray software player. This option is often used for quality assurance purposes.

    ▪ **DVD Image or Blu-ray Image:** This option creates a Blu-ray or DVD image on your hard drive, which is by third-party mastering application.

    ▪ **DVD Master (not available for Blu-ray Discs):** Write to a digital linear tape (DLT) connected to a computer. This option is commonly used for mass duplication.

5. **Choose the current project as your source, and choose your destination, such as your disc recorder.** Then choose settings appropriate for your destination.

6. **Click Build.** If the Save alert appears, save your project.

7. **When the process is complete, click OK.**

FIGURE 26.13

Use the Build panel to start the process of burning a DVD.

Summary

Encore is a DVD production application. Using Encore, you can design DVD menus with interactive buttons, and preview and burn DVDs. This chapter covered these topics:

- Use File ➪ Import as Asset to load source material into Encore.
- The Library panel provides numerous predesigned buttons and menus.
- You can create linked buttons by dragging a video file from the Project panel onto a button in the Menu Viewer.
- Preview your DVD by choosing File ➪ Preview.

Chapter 27

Customizing DVD Screens and Navigation in Adobe Encore DVD

This chapter takes you into the world of DVD creation with Adobe Encore CS3. The previous chapter covered how to quickly create a DVD project with a menu screen and interactive buttons. This chapter focuses on customization. It covers how to create menus and buttons using your own graphic images and how to customize links from buttons to menus, from buttons to DVD chapters, and from buttons to the Timeline.

This chapter provides a step-by-step look at how to create a custom DVD presentation in Encore. After you read through this chapter, you will be ready to enter the world of DVD production.

ON the DVD A sample graphic button and background menu are included in the MoreClips folder in this book's DVD.

Creating Menus and Buttons from Still Images

Although Encore DVD's menu templates provide a quick way to make menus and buttons, multimedia and design professionals may want to create their own, based upon digitized images or backgrounds. This section shows you how to create completely new menus. Before you begin, you should plan your entire menu structure. Design your menu on paper, and use flowcharts to plan navigation. After you create all of your source material or assets, you are ready to start.

Custom DVD Presentation

These are the general steps for creating a custom DVD presentation (many of these steps are covered in this chapter):

1. **Create the video and audio in Premiere Pro.**

   Note that Encore Chapter markers from Premiere Pro can be used as chapters in Adobe Encore CS3. Create markers by moving the current-time indicator (CTI) in Premiere Pro and then double-clicking the Encore Chapter marker icon in the Timeline panel. Enter text into the Chapter field in the Marker dialog box. Encore uses this text to name chapters in its Timeline. Export the Premiere Pro project file using the File ➪ Export ➪ Export to Encore command. In the Export to Encore dialog box, select Author with Menus. Premiere Pro creates one MPEG2 file for video and one for audio and opens the project as a Timeline within Encore.

2. **Plan the navigation for the DVD production.**

3. **Create the buttons and background screen for the menus in Photoshop or another graphics application.**

4. **Import audio, graphics, and other assets into Encore DVD.**

5. **Create a custom menu in Encore DVD.**

6. **Place the background screen and buttons into Encore DVD.**

7. **Create a Timeline or Timelines.**

8. **Create chapters in the Timelines.**

9. **Link buttons to the chapters.**

10. **Create disc navigation.**

11. **Preview the DVD project, and burn it to disc.**

Creating custom menus

Encore integrates well with Adobe Photoshop. Although Encore can read TIFF, JPEG, and BMP graphics, your best option is to create images in Photoshop and import them directly into Encore DVD, particularly because Encore can interpret a Photoshop layer as a button.

NOTE   In order for Encore DVD to correctly interpret Photoshop layers as DVD highlight elements, layer-naming prefixes are required in Photoshop. For example, a layer set for buttons requires a "(+)" prefix. Subpicture colors must be named with prefixes such as (=1), (=2), and (=3). (Subpictures can be used to highlight buttons. All colored shapes in subpicture layers in Photoshop appear in the button, but the final color and opacity seen in the DVD are controlled by menu color sets in Encore DVD.)

If you want to create a completely new menu, the steps are quite simple. For the standard DVD 4:3 aspect ratio, you can create an image in Photoshop or you can use one of the NTSC or PAL presets. If you are using square pixels, create the image at 720 x 534 pixels (PAL 768 x 576). The default aspect ratio in Encore is 4:3. (You can change this to the DVD Widescreen format of 16:9.) To create a new menu, follow these steps:

1. **If you haven't created a new project, create the project by choosing File ⇨ New Project.** In the New Project dialog box, enter a name for your project. In the Television Standard drop-down menu, choose either NTSC or PAL. Specify whether you want the Authoring Mode to be either Blu-ray or DVD. Click OK.

2. **Import the Photoshop background screen that you want to use for your menu by choosing File ⇨ Import as Menu.** In the Import as Menu dialog box, select your file and click Open.

   The menu now appears in the Menus panel and in the Menu Viewer, as shown in Figure 27.1.

3. **To rename the menu, right-click/Ctrl-click the menu listing in the Project panel or Menus panel.** Enter a new name in the Rename Menu dialog box. Alternatively, you can rename the menu in the Name field of the Properties panel.

FIGURE 27.1

A custom background loaded into the Menu Viewer

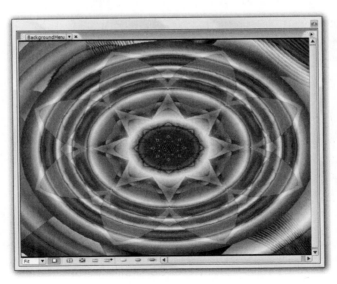

Adding buttons to the menu

After you create your custom menu, you may want to add buttons that you have created in Photoshop or another graphic application to your DVD screen. If you didn't create buttons in Photoshop, you can add a graphic as a button by following these steps:

1. **Import graphic elements into your project by choosing File ⇨ Import as Asset.**

2. **Drag the button graphic or button graphics to the Menu Viewer panel.** (If your menu doesn't appear in the Menu Viewer, double click it in the Project panel.)

3. **Select the graphic with the Direct Select tool.** Choose Object ⇨ Convert to Button.

4. **If you want all of the buttons on the menu to be similar, drag the same button object to the menu screen as many times as you want.** Repeat step 3 so that Encore recognizes them as different buttons. Figure 27.2 shows button graphics that were created in Photoshop being added to a menu.

FIGURE 27.2

Buttons created in Photoshop and imported into Encore DVD

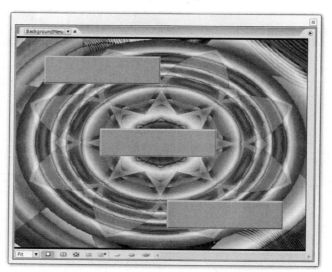

 If you wish to edit Photoshop graphics that are already imported in Encore, select the graphic, then choose Edit ⇨ Edit in Photoshop.

Menu Viewer controls

When working in the Menu Viewer, you can use the Object menu to align and distribute your buttons. You can also press the arrow keys to move selected objects right, left, up, and down. In the Menu Viewer, the buttons at the bottom of the screen provide the following functions:

- **Correct Menu Pixels for TV Display:** This option rescales the menu to the proper height and width for video display.

- **Show Safe Area:** This option displays the title- and action-safe zones, which help ensure that text and graphics are not cut off from the television monitor. If your production will be viewed on a television monitor, don't place text beyond the inner title-safe zone and don't place crucial visual objects outside of the outer action-safe zone.

- **Show Button Routing:** Routing buttons are menu buttons that can be used as DVD remote control buttons. If you do not turn on the Automatically Route Button option in the Menu Viewer, remote control routings for buttons are displayed in the menus.

- **Show Guides:** This option displays guides to help you design the menu screen.

- **New Guide:** This option creates a new vertical or horizontal guide.

- **Show Normal Subpicture Highlight:** Subpictures allow you to create different-colored button states for activated buttons. This option displays the unselected state for buttons.

- **Show Selected Subpicture Highlight:** This option displays the selected or highlighted state for buttons.

- **Show Activated Subpicture Highlight:** This option displays the activated state for buttons. Activation requires selecting a button with the remote control and pressing Enter. However, buttons can be set to Auto Activate when simply clicked by the mouse. To set a button to Auto Activate, select the button and choose Auto Activate from the Properties panel.

Using Color Sets for Menus and Buttons

When you click a DVD button in a menu or move the mouse over the button, it typically changes colors. In order to help you maintain a consistent color scheme in your production, Encore stores menu highlight colors in a color set. When you import a menu into Encore DVD, it creates a color set from subpictures in Photoshop layers. (As mentioned earlier, subpictures are used for highlighting buttons.) Fifteen colors comprise each color set, and each menu can use only one specific color set. Because you can have many different menus in a DVD production, you can use multiple color sets. However, to help ensure a consistent look throughout a project, you may want to use only one color set or Encore DVD's default color set.

By default, Encore creates one predefined default color set. If you import a menu from Photoshop, Encore creates a color set named Automatic. (If you want to alter the colors and opacities of this color set, you must duplicate it and rename it.) If desired, you can switch from one color set to another, or you can create your own color set. You can save color sets and use them in other projects. To view the color set for a menu, select the menu in the Menu Viewer and choose Menu ⇨ Edit Menu Color Set. This opens the Menu Color Set dialog box, shown in Figure 27.3.

At first, the layout of the Menu Color Set dialog box may look confusing. The grouping in the dialog box shows three different colors for normal states, three different colors for selected states, and three different colors for activated states. Each set of three colors is called a *highlight group*. For example, you can use one highlight group for buttons labeled *part 1*, *part 2*, and so on, and another highlight group for buttons labeled *next chapter* or *previous chapter*. If you want to change colors for any color set, simply click the color swatch and adjust the colors in the Color Picker dialog box that appears. If you want to create a new color set, click the New Color Set button (the page icon to the left of the disc icon).

FIGURE 27.3

The Menu Color Set dialog box controls the highlight color for buttons.

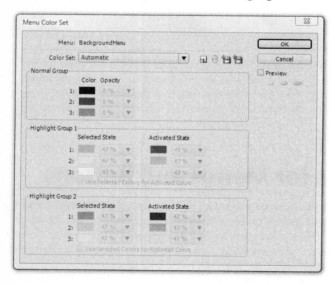

You can also change the opacity for colors in the Menu Color Set dialog box to create rollover effects. For example, suppose you created a menu with a button set in Photoshop. The button set includes a colored shape in the (=2) layer, and you want this shape to appear in the button when it is activated. To do this, import the menu with the button set into Encore DVD. In order to adjust opacity for the automatic menu color set created from this menu, duplicate the menu color set and rename it (by clicking the New Color Set button in the Menu Color Set dialog box). Now you can create a rollover effect by adjusting opacity in the Menu Color Set dialog box. If your button uses Highlight Group 1, you can set the opacity for color 2 to 0 percent for the Selected State in this highlight group. You can then raise color 2's opacity to 100 percent for the Activated State in Highlight Group 1. The result: When the button is activated in the DVD menu, the subpicture shape, originally created in the Photoshop (=2) layer, appears.

Changing Menu Color Sets

You can easily change color for a menu using the Menus panel and Properties panel. Follow these steps:

1. **Select the menu whose color set you want to select or change.** Shift-click to add other menus to the selection.

2. **If the Properties panel isn't open, choose Window ⇨ Properties to open it.**

3. **Click the Color Set drop-down menu.** Select a color set. Choose Automatic to keep the menu's color set, or choose Menu Default to switch to the default color set for your project.

Creating and Using Timelines

After you plan your navigation and create your menus and buttons, you need to create a Timeline for your DVD production. Like Premiere Pro's Timeline, Encore's Timeline provides a visual representation of source footage and sound. Figure 27.4 shows a Timeline with the CTI and a chapter marker. For standard NTSC productions, the Timeline frame rate is 29.97 frames per second; for PAL, the frame rate is 25 frames per second. If you don't have a video file in your Encore project, you can add one by choosing File ⇨ Import as Asset. Encore can import MPEG-2, QuickTime, and AVI files (NTSC: 720 x 480 or 720 x 486; PAL: 720 x 576 or 704 x 576), as well as DV-AVI (Mac OS), H.264, WMV (Windows Media).

FIGURE 27.4

The Encore Timeline with video and audio tracks and chapter points

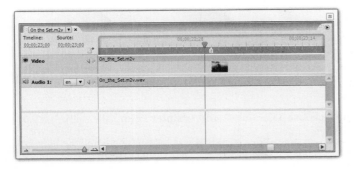

 The default length in the Timeline for still images is six seconds. To change the default length, choose Edit ➪ Preferences ➪ Timelines.

After you've imported a video file into Encore, follow these steps to create a timeline in and place video or still images in it:

1. **Create a new Timeline by choosing Timeline ➪ New Timeline.** This creates an untitled Timeline in the Project panel.

2. **Drag the video or still image from the Project panel into the video track in the Timeline.** Video clips are automatically positioned at the start of the Timeline and assigned to be Chapter 1. If you place still images on the Timeline instead, chapter entries are created at the beginning of each still image.

3. **Now assign a name to the Timeline.** Right-click/Ctrl-click the untitled Timeline in the Project panel. Choose Rename in the pop-up menu to assign a name to the Timeline. The Rename Timeline dialog box opens, where you can enter a name for the Timeline. You can also rename the Timeline by editing the name in the Properties panel.

TIP You can create a Timeline automatically and place video on it by selecting the video in the Project panel and choosing Timeline ➪ New Timeline. You can also import a video file directly into a timeline by choosing File ➪ Import As Timeline.

Adding a chapter point to the Timeline

In DVD movie productions, chapter points are typically used to jump to specific scenes. In Encore, you can mark a frame on the Timeline as a chapter point and then link menus, buttons, or other Timelines to it. To keep organized, you can assign names to chapter points and even write notes about specific chapter points. (You can write descriptive notes in the Properties panel when creating chapter points.)

Follow these steps to create chapter points on the Timeline:

1. **If the Timeline panel is not onscreen, open it by choosing Window ➪ Timelines.**

2. **If you want to preview the video as you add chapter points, open the Monitor panel by choosing Window ➪ Monitor.**

3. **Click and drag the CTI to the frame where you want to create the chapter point.**

NOTE If you have placed an MPEG-2 video in the Timeline, you can click the Skip Forward or Skip Backward button to move to a GOP header, which is indicated by the white vertical lines at the bottom of the ruler. (A *GOP* is a collection of frames based upon a single keyframe and is usually 13 frames long.) Chapter points for MPEG-2 files must start at the nearest prior GOP header. If you are working with AVI videos, Adobe recommends that chapter points be at least 15 frames apart to ensure best quality.

4. **To create a chapter point, choose Timeline ➪ Add Chapter Point.** Alternatively, click the Add Chapter button in the Timeline panel.

Naming chapter points

After you create a chapter point, you can assign it a descriptive name and provide a description of the chapter point in the chapter point's Properties panel. Follow these steps to create chapter point names and chapter point descriptions:

1. **If the Timeline panel isn't open, open it by choosing Window ⇨ Timelines.**

2. **In the Timelines panel, select the desired Timeline.** At the bottom of the frame, Encore DVD displays the chapter points, as shown in Figure 27.5.

3. **Select the desired chapter point in the Timeline panel.**

4. **If the Properties panel is not open, choose Window ⇨ Properties.** The Properties panel displays the chapter point's attributes.

5. **In the Properties panel, edit the Name field for the chapter.**

6. **To add a description, click in the Description text box.** Type a description of the chapter point.

FIGURE 27.5

Chapter points appear in the Timeline panel.

Customizing Navigation

After you assemble your buttons in the Menu Viewer, pick your subpicture colors, and add chapters, your next step is to ensure that the buttons lead your viewers in the right direction. The following sections provide details about looping menu buttons, menu navigation, first-play options, how long the menu stays onscreen, and button navigation.

Setting First Play disc links

By default, your completed DVD begins to play when it displays the first menu you create. From this menu, you can direct navigation to go to any menu or chapter. Follow these steps to set First Play options for the disc:

1. **Choose Window ⇨ Build to open the Build panel.**

2. **Choose Window ⇨ Properties to open the Properties panel.** Alternatively, click the Properties panel tab to activate it.

3. **Activate the First Play pop-up menu by clicking the Arrow icon.** Choices for First Play appear in the submenus, as shown in Figure 27.6. Choose the chapter or the menu you want to use as your First Play location. You can also click and drag the Pick Whip icon (the curlicue icon in the pop-up menu) to the chapter or menu.

4. **If you want to use the Pick Whip icon (the curlicue icon), make sure that the Project tab is visible onscreen.** Drag the First Play Pick Whip icon to any of the following destinations:

   ▪ To a menu or Timeline in the Project tab

   ▪ To the chapter in the Timeline

   ▪ To the menu or button in the Menus tab

NOTE   The Override options in the Properties panel specify the end action for the First Play link, overriding the default end action of the menu or Timeline. In the Override field, you can designate a menu and the button to highlight or a Timeline and starting chapter point.

FIGURE 27.6

Changing the First Play setting

Setting menu display time and looping

If you are planning to display your DVD at a kiosk or at a public locale such as a museum, you may want to use Encore DVD's menu display settings to control navigation if nobody clicks a button. Menu-timing choices are controlled in the Menus panel. Activate the menu by first clicking the menu name in the Menus panel and then clicking the Motion tab in the Properties panel. These are the timing choices:

- **Hold Forever:** The menu displays until an action is taken. This is the default setting.
- **Duration:** Set the duration in time. For a motion menu, the duration should be the time multiplied by the Loop setting.
- **Loop #:** Use the Loop setting to choose how many times the menu repeats itself.
- **Loop Point:** Use the Loop Point setting for animated buttons. Click the Animate Button check box, and enter the time in the Loop Point field.

Setting button navigation

Without question, the most common interactive navigational tool in DVD productions is the button. When linking buttons in Encore, you must link to another menu or to a chapter point in a Timeline. When linking a button, the most versatile method is to use the button's Property panel.

These steps explain how to create a link from a menu button to a menu or chapter point. When creating the link, you can link directly from the button in the Menu Viewer or you can create a link from the button through the Menus tab.

1. If the Menus panel isn't activated, choose Window ⇨ Menus.
2. In the Menus panel, click the menu that contains the buttons that you want to link or double-click the menu, which opens the menu in the Menu Viewer.
3. Select the button from which you want to create a link. If you are working in the Menu Viewer, select a button with the Selection tool, which selects the button set.
4. If the Properties panel isn't open, choose Window ⇨ Properties.
5. Click the Link drop-down menu. Choose the button or chapter point from the submenu, as shown in Figure 27.7. Alternatively, click the Pick Whip icon, and drag it to a Timeline, menu in the Project panel, or a chapter point in the Timeline Viewer. Note that if you are linking to a Timeline, you link to a chapter point within the Timeline, setting a specific point where the video should begin to play.

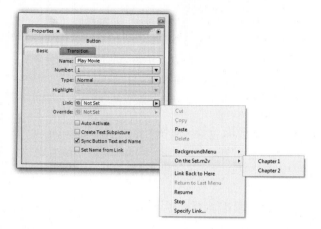

FIGURE 27.7

Creating a navigation link for a button

Setting Timeline Navigation

When you select a Timeline in the Project panel, Encore provides two navigation choices: you can set an end action for the Timeline, or you can set a menu remote link. An end action specifies where the navigation takes the user when the Timeline finishes playing. The menu remote choice creates a destination for the DVD navigation when the user clicks or otherwise uses the remote control. Normally, when the user clicks the remote control, navigation returns to the last menu used. Follow these steps for setting these Timeline navigation choices:

1. **Select a Timeline in the Project panel.**

2. **If the Properties panel isn't open, choose Window ⇨ Properties.** The Properties panel now shows properties for the selected Timeline.

3. **In the Properties panel, select a destination for End Action by clicking the pop-up menu down arrow and choosing an option from the submenu, as shown in Figure 27.8.** Notice that Figure 27.8 shows another Timeline as a possible navigational link. If doing so is more convenient, you can also create the link by clicking and dragging the Pick Whip icon to an asset in the Project panel.

4. **In the Properties panel, select a destination for Menu Remote by clicking the drop-down menu arrow and choosing an option from the submenu.** If it is more convenient, you can also create the link by clicking and dragging the Pick Whip icon to an asset in the Project panel.

FIGURE 27.8

Setting end action navigation

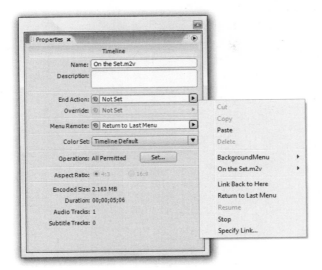

Summary

Encore DVD enables you to import custom-made graphics and buttons to use for a DVD production. You can also customize button links. This chapter covered these topics:

- You can import a menu into Encore by choosing File ➾ Import as Menu.
- You can use Object ➾ Convert to Button to designate a graphic object as a button.
- You can change color settings for activated buttons by setting the highlight group in the Properties panel.
- You can create new chapters in the Timeline tab of the Project panel.
- You can use the Properties panel to set links for buttons.

Chapter 28

The Photoshop Connection

During video production, you may want to export still frames from your Adobe Premiere Pro project for use on a Web page or in a print document, such as a brochure or a flyer. If you export the still frames to Adobe Photoshop, you can prepare them for print and optimize them for the Web. You can even export an entire Premiere Pro project with all of its video tracks, into Adobe After Effects. Once in After Effects, each track appears as a separate layer. A frame exported from After Effects to Photoshop retains its layers. A frame exported from Premiere Pro to Photoshop does not.

You can also use Photoshop as an image data source. You can use Photoshop to create backgrounds, titles, or images with alpha channels. These images can then be integrated into a Premiere Pro project.

Exporting a Premiere Pro Frame to Photoshop

Although Premiere Pro is primarily used for creating desktop video projects, you can easily export a video frame from your project to use as a still image. The frame can be any individual frame from a clip, or it can display a frame from a transition or video effect.

In addition to using the still frame for print purposes, you can use the still frame to create or enhance a Web site or to create a background scene in an interactive presentation. After the frame is in Photoshop, you can edit the clip's colors, convert the clip to grayscale or black and white, and even add or delete items or people from the clip.

CROSS-REF To learn how to export an entire video clip as a QuickTime or AVI movie, see Chapter 18.

Follow these steps to export a frame from Premiere Pro:

1. **Open or create a Premiere Pro project.** Figure 28.1 shows the Premiere Pro project that is used to create the frame shown in Figure 28.3. To create the project, you can import two video clips (GoldFishes and Kuai) into a Premiere Pro project. These video clips are on the DVD that accompanies this book. Place the Kuai video clip (used as the background) in the Video 1 track and the GoldFishes clip in the Video 2 track. Place a title in the Video 3 track; this example uses the Tekton Pro Yellow 93 Style for the title.

FIGURE 28.1

The Premiere Pro panels used to create the frames shown in Figure 28.2

To make the background video clip (in the Video 1 track) more interesting, you can apply the Brush Strokes and Replicate video effects. To superimpose the GoldFishes clip over the background, you can use the Color Key video effect. However, before applying this effect, you need to use the Levels and RGB Curves video effects to increase the contrast of the clip. For the finishing touch, you can animate the title by setting keyframes for the Motion's Position effect in the Effect Controls panel. Frames from this Premiere Pro project are shown in Figure 28.2.

2. **Locate the project frame that you want to export.** Start by opening the Program Monitor panel. To display the Program Monitor panel, choose Window ⇨ Program Monitors ⇨ Sequence 01. Use the Frame Forward and Frame Back buttons in the Program Monitor panel to locate the frame you want to export. Figure 28.3 shows a frame that is selected to export in the Program Monitor panel.

FIGURE 28.2

Frames from the Premiere Pro project

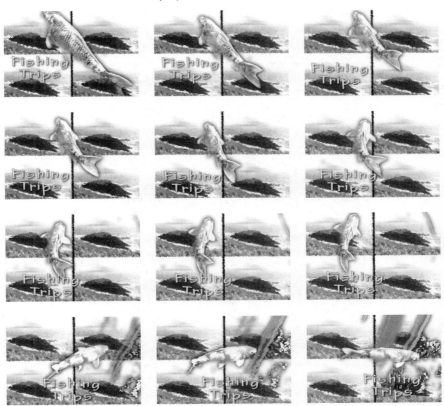

3. **After you choose the frame you want to export, choose File ⇨ Export ⇨ Frame.**

4. **In the Export Frame dialog box, name your frame.** Also notice that below the File Name field, the frame's file type and video settings appear. Click the Settings button if you need to change the file format and image size.

5. **In the Export Frame Settings dialog box, click the File Type drop-down menu in the General area.** You can choose Windows Bitmap, GIF, Targa, or TIFF. If you are going to use the still frame for print, you probably want to save your file in TIFF format. Use the Targa format if you are going to import this frame into a 3-D program. If you are going to use this frame for multimedia purposes, choose Windows Bitmap.

If you are going to use the frame for the Web and want to reduce the number of colors in the image to 256, use the GIF format. When you select the GIF format, a Compile Settings button appears. You can click this button and choose whether you want your GIF file to be dithered and whether you want the image to contain a transparent background.

The Video settings in the Export Frame Settings dialog box enable you to change the color depth and choose a compressor and frame size for the exported still frame.

FIGURE 28.3

A frame to be exported as a still frame

> **NOTE** If you are going to use this frame for multimedia purposes, you may want to import the still frame into Director. To learn more about using Premiere Pro and Director, see Chapter 23.

6. **When you finish adjusting the General and Video settings, click OK to return to the Export Frame dialog box.**

7. **In the Export Frame dialog box, click Save to save the frame in the chosen format.** The frame that you just saved appears onscreen. If this is the right frame, you can close the file and export another frame, or quit Premiere Pro and launch Photoshop to import the frame.

Importing a Still Frame from Premiere Pro into Photoshop

After you export a still frame from Premiere Pro, you can import it into Photoshop to color-correct it or incorporate it into a collage or other project. Follow these steps to import a still frame from Premiere Pro into Photoshop:

1. **Launch Photoshop.**

2. **Choose File ⇨ Open.**

3. **In the Open dialog box, locate and select the Premiere Pro file you saved as a still image.** Then click the Open button to import the Premiere Pro file into Photoshop.

4. **When the Premiere Pro still image file opens in Photoshop, you see all of the tracks from that frame flattened into one layer called Background.**

5. **To add information to your document, as shown in Figure 28.4, you can create a new layer.** Click the New Layer icon at the bottom of the Layers palette to create a new layer in which to work.

FIGURE 28.4

The Premiere Pro still frame from Figure 28.3 after editing it in Photoshop

6. **To create a shape object in the new layer, select the Shape tool from the Tools palette.** In the Shapes toolbar, click the Shape Layers icon rather than the Paths icon. Then click the Shape drop-down menu and select a shape. Once you select a shape, click and drag in the drawing area of the document. The example in Figure 28.4 uses the Fish

shape, filled with a light-blue color. For a more interesting look, in the Layers palette, the layer mode is set to Difference.

7. **Use the Type tool to create some text.** You don't have to create a new layer; the type is automatically created on a new layer. Both horizontal and vertical type are created in the example shown in Figure 28.4. The Earwig Factory font is used for both. The Layer Style Blending option is applied to the text to add a drop shadow, inner shadow, and glow to one and a bevel to the other. The horizontal type is warped using the Warp Text option.

The Warp Text icon is at the far-right side of the Type toolbar. Click the icon to display the Warp Text dialog box (shown in Figure 28.5). Click the Style drop-down menu and select an option. This example selects the Fish option to make the text look like a fish. Click OK to apply the style.

FIGURE 28.5

The Warp Text dialog box allows you to warp your text into the shape of a fish.

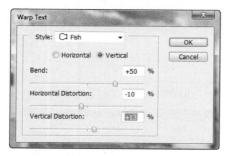

8. **You can use the Illustrator Symbols library to add items to your Photoshop file.** To do so, launch Illustrator and create a new Basic RGB file. Next, choose Window ⇨ Symbols. Click the Symbols library menu and choose Open Symbol Library. Then make a selection. This example uses the Nature Symbol library (shown in Figure 28.6). Select a symbol, and then click and drag in the drawing area of the document. With the Selection tool, select the symbol in the drawing area and choose Edit ⇨ Copy.

Now activate the Photoshop document that you are working on and choose Edit ⇨ Paste. When the Paste dialog box appears, choose Smart Object and click OK. The symbol appears with a bounding box around it. Click a corner to resize, rotate, or move the item. Then double-click inside the bounding box. The item appears in its own separate Vector Smart Object layer. To add a drop shadow to the symbol, choose Layer ⇨ Layer Style ⇨ Drop Shadow. Figure 28.7 shows the still frame from Figure 28.4 after applying Illustrator symbols.

FIGURE 28.6

Illustrator Symbol libraries allow you to quickly and easily add items to your document.

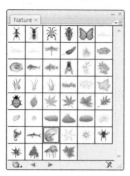

9. **Choose File ➪ Save As to create a copy of the original still frame.** You also might want to create a copy of the Photoshop file with layers, and one after flattening the layers. That way, you can always go back to the separate items and move them without affecting the rest of the document. To flatten the file, choose Layer ➪ Flatten Image.

FIGURE 28.7

The still frame from Figure 28.4 after applying Illustrator symbols

If you want to load a Premiere Pro frame into Photoshop and have the tracks appear as separate layers, you must export the frame from Premiere Pro to After Effects first, and then to Photoshop. This technique is discussed in the following section.

Exporting a Frame to After Effects and Then to Photoshop

You can use After Effects to export a frame from a Premiere Pro project to Photoshop. If you want to export a frame (containing all of its video tracks) from a Premiere Pro project, you need to first import the Premiere Pro project into After Effects. In After Effects, the video tracks from a Premiere Pro project appear as separate layers. Then, in After Effects, you can export the frame with all of its video layers into Photoshop. Each video layer appears as a Photoshop layer.

Follow these steps to import a frame from a Premiere Pro project into After Effects and then export the frame from After Effects to Photoshop:

1. **Launch After Effects.**

2. **Choose File ➪ New ➪ New Project.**

3. **Choose File ➪ Import ➪ File.** In the Import File dialog box that appears, locate the Premiere Pro project you want to import. Then set the Import As drop-down menu to Composition. Click Open. In the Premiere Pro Importer dialog box that appears, click the Select Sequence drop-down menu and choose All Sequences (shown in Figure 28.8). Click OK to import the Premiere Pro project into the After Effects project.

FIGURE 28.8

The Premiere Pro Importer dialog box allows you to import an entire Premiere Pro project into After Effects.

4. **Double-click the Sequence file in the Project panel to display the Timeline panel and Composition panel.** In the Timeline panel, all Premiere Pro tracks appear as layers. In the Composition panel, you see the layers as a composite (with the exception of the Title layer, which appears with the motion path, but with no text). Presently, titles cannot be imported to and from Premiere Pro and After Effects. Click the Title layer in the Timeline panel and delete it, or click the eye icon to hide the layer.

 Titles from Premiere Pro and from After Effects cannot be imported into one another. You can only export a frame with a title in it.

5. **To create text in After Effects, choose Layer ⇨ New ⇨ Text.** Use the Type tool to create some text. Use the Character panel to stylize the text. If you would rather create the text on a curve, choose Effect ⇨ Text ⇨ Path Text. In the Path Text dialog that appears, select a font and then type in the field. Click OK to have the text appear in the Composition panel. Click and drag the handles that appear at either end of the text to adjust the curved path. Notice that the text moves with the path. To change the type size or fill, use the Effect Controls panel. For more information about text on a path, turn to Chapter 32.

6. **Move the current-time indicator in the Timeline panel to the frame you want to export.** Figure 28.9 shows the After Effects project with the frame that is to be exported to Photoshop.

7. **Choose Composition ⇨ Save Frame As ⇨ Photoshop Layers to save the still frame with all of its layers.** To save a still frame as a composite without the layers, choose Composition ⇨ Save Frame As ⇨ File.

8. **To open the After Effects frame in Photoshop, choose File ⇨ Open.** When the file opens, the video tracks from Premiere Pro appear in different Photoshop layers, as shown in Figure 28.10. Even the Blank Title layer that is hidden appears in the Photoshop Layers palette, although it remains hidden. To view it, click the eye icon next to its layer. To delete it, drag the layer icon in the Layers palette to the trash icon at the bottom of the palette.

FIGURE 28.9

The Premiere Pro project from Figure 28.1, imported into After Effects. All of the video tracks appear as layers.

9. **In Photoshop you can apply filters to the layers, or you can add new layers and new items to the document.** The example in Figure 28.11 uses the Rotate, Scale, and Distort commands (Edit ➪ Transform) on the type layer that is imported from After Effects. For a more unusual effect, you can use the Edit ➪ Transform ➪ Distort, and Edit ➪ Transform ➪ Warp commands. This example also applies the Filter ➪ Distort ➪ Twist command (shown in Figure 28.12) to the text.

Now add three layers. In the first layer, apply a black-and-white radial gradient. To have the layer work as a layer mask, set the layer mode to Lighten. This causes the white areas of the gradient to apply a fade effect to the layers below it. In the second layer, use the Shape tool to create a seal shape. A third layer is automatically created when you use the Type tool to create some text. This example uses the Mistral font for the text.

NOTE   You can use Illustrator to create 3-D shapes, and then copy and paste them into Photoshop. To convert a 2-D object into a 3-D object, use Illustrator's Effect ➪ 3D command. The stroke color is used to create the depth of the 3-D object.

FIGURE 28.10

The still frame from After Effects, shown in Figure 28.9, after exporting it to Photoshop

FIGURE 28.11

The still frame from After Effects, shown in Figure 28.10, after editing it in Photoshop

10. **In Photoshop, choose File ⇨ Save As to create a copy of the file.** You can use this file as a background in Premiere Pro, or leave it in Photoshop and output it as a flyer.

FIGURE 28.12

Using Photoshop filters can create some interesting effects.

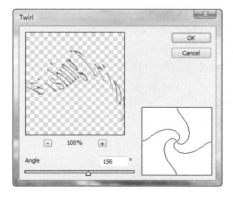

Creating a Photoshop Layer File and Animating It in Photoshop

In this section, you learn how to create two presentations by using the Layers and Animation palettes. The first example is a simple graphic presentation. It consists of three layers: a type layer, a layer with a shape, and a Background layer.

In Photoshop, the Animation palette is used to animate the type and graphic shape by setting keyframes for the Position option. The second example is a little more sophisticated. It consists of working with a type layer and video layers. Again, the type is animated using the Position option, and the video layers are faded out using the Opacity option. Afterward, the Photoshop layers are exported as either a movie or a sequence file, which can be imported into Premiere Pro where you can add sound to create a presentation. Figure 28.13 shows a frame of the first Photoshop animation project, and Figure 28.14 shows a few frames from the second one.

CROSS-REF Turn to Chapter 32 for information on importing and animating Photoshop files in After Effects.

To create and animate a Photoshop layer project using a simple graphic (shown in Figure 28.13), follow these steps:

1. **Launch Photoshop.** Create a new Film & Video Photoshop file, name it, and click OK.
2. **Choose Window ⇨ Layers, and Window ⇨ Animation.** You need these palettes to create this project. The mode in the Animation palette should be set to Timeline rather than Frame Animation. The mode appears next to the word Animation in the Animation palette. To change the mode of the Animation palette, click the Animation menu. The Layers and Animation palettes for this Photoshop animation project appear in Figure 28.15.

FIGURE 28.13

A frame from a Photoshop animation project using a simple graphic

3. **Use the Gradient tool to create a gradient in the Background layer.** To create the background in Figure 28.13, you can use two different gradients on top of each other. This example applies a Blue, Yellow, Blue linear gradient, and then the Transparent Stripes linear gradient. Before applying this gradient, set the foreground color to violet, so that the gradient applied is violet and transparent. In the transparent areas, the colors from the previous gradient show through.

4. **Apply a filter to the background to jazz it up.** The example in Figure 28.13 applies the Filter ➪ Distort ➪ Polar Coordinates command to the background gradient. In the Polar Coordinates dialog box, the Rectangular to Polar option is selected. Applying the filter more than once can sometimes produce interesting results. You may want to apply various filters to arrive at the desired result.

FIGURE 28.14

A few frames from a Photoshop animation project consisting of a type layer and video layers

ON the DVD The video clips shown in Figure 28.14 are Artbeats SUR111, BG117, and BG113. They are found in the Artbeats folder on the DVD that accompanies this book.

5. **Use adjustment layers to change the colors of the Background layer.** After you apply a filter to the background, you may want to change the colors in the Background layer. The example in Figure 28.13 uses two adjustment layers: Curves and Hue/Saturation. Curves is used to lighten or darken an image, and Hue/Saturation is used to change colors. Adjustment layers allow you to apply an effect and still make changes to the effect after you apply it. To add an adjustment layer to the Background layer, either choose Layer ➪ New Adjustment Layer or click the Create Adjustment layer icon at the bottom of the Layers palette. Then make a selection and make the necessary changes.

6. **Click the New Layer icon at the bottom of the Layers palette to create a new layer in which to create a shape.** The new layer appears in the Layers palette, as well as in the Timeline of the Animation palette.

FIGURE 28.15

The Layers and Animation palettes for the Photoshop animation project using a simple graphic

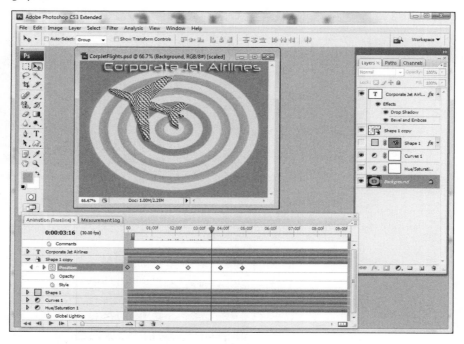

7. **Select the Shape tool from the Tools palette.** In the Shapes toolbar, select the Shape Layers icon, click the Shape drop-down menu, and select a shape. The example in Figure 28.13 uses the Airplane shape in the Symbols Shape library. Click the Shapes menu to reveal the Shapes libraries.

8. **With the Shape tool, click and drag in the new layer to create a shape in the new layer.**

 You can copy a shape from Photoshop to After Effects. In Photoshop, select the shape, and then choose Edit ⇨ Copy to copy the shape. In After Effects, choose Composition ⇨ New Composition. Then choose Layer ⇨ New ⇨ Shape Layer. With the shape layer selected in the Timeline panel, choose Edit ⇨ Paste. For more information on working with After Effects, turn to Chapters 31, 32, and 33.

9. **Choose Layer ⇨ Layer Style ⇨ Blending Options.** Then choose a style. The example shown in Figure 29.13 applies the Drop Shadow, Inner Shadow, Outer Glow, Inner Glow, and Bevel and Emboss styles to the airplane. For the Bevel and Emboss style, the Contour and Texture options are also selected.

10. **Select the Horizontal Type tool from the Tools palette.** Move the mouse to the place on the image where you want the text to appear, and click the mouse once. Begin typing. Notice that as you type, a new Type layer is automatically created in the Layers palette and in the Timeline of the Animation palette. The example in Figure 28.13 places the text at the bottom of the document and then animates it so that it moves up the document. You'll animate the text in step 14.

In Photoshop, you can arc your text by using the Warp Text command.

11. **With the text selected, choose a font, size, and color.** You can also add tracking (spacing between the letters) using the Character palette. Choose Window ⇨ Character to display the Character palette.

12. **To add interesting effects to your text, choose Layer ⇨ Layer Style and then choose an effect.** To create the text effect shown in Figure 28.13, you can use the Drop Shadow, Inner Shadow, Outer Shadow, Color Overlay, and Pattern Overlay Layer Style options. After you apply the effects, they appear in the Layers palette. This example also uses the Warp Text option on the text. The Warp Text option is found just below the menu bar.

13. **To move the text onscreen, drag it with the Move tool.**

14. **Now that you've created some text and stylized it, you are ready to animate it.** To do so, follow these steps:

    a. Click the icon in front of the Type layer in the Timeline to display the options.

    b. Move the current-time indicator to the beginning of the Timeline in the Animation palette.

    c. Click the stopwatch icon in front of the Position option to create a keyframe.

    d. Move the current edit line to the right. Use the Move tool to move the type up slightly to create a second keyframe.

    e. Repeat step d to create more keyframes.

    f. To view the type animation, click the Play button at the bottom of the Animation palette.

15. **Before you can animate the shape item, you first have to rasterize it.** To do so, choose Layer ⇨ Rasterize ⇨ Shape. In the example in Figure 28.13, the airplane shape moves from the bottom-right side to the top-left side of the document. To do so, follow these steps:

    a. **Click the icon in front of the rasterized shape layer in the Timeline to display the options.**

    b. **Move the current-time indicator to the beginning of the Timeline in the Animation palette.**

    c. **Click the stopwatch icon in front of the Position option to create a keyframe.**

    d. **Move the current edit line to the right.** Use the Move tool to move the rasterized shape diagonally to the left to create a second keyframe.

    e. **Repeat step d to create more keyframes.**

    f. **To view the rasterized shape animation, click the Play button at the bottom of the Animation palette.**

16. **Choose File ⇨ Save.** Be sure to save your work in Photoshop format with all of its layers. Choose File ⇨ Export ⇨ Render Video. To export the Photoshop project as a sequence, in the Render Video dialog box, click the Image Sequence radio button. Then click an option in the Range section. To export the Photoshop project as a movie, click the QuickTime Export. Then click the drop-down menu to select a movie type, and click Render to export your Photoshop project.

17. **To import the Photoshop project into Premiere Pro and add sound, open or create a Premiere Pro project.** Choose File ⇨ Import. Drag it to a video track in the Timeline panel.

To create and animate a Photoshop layer project with video layers and a type layer (shown in Figures 28.16 and 28.17), follow these steps:

1. **Launch Photoshop.** Create a new Film & Video Photoshop file, name it, and click OK.

2. **Choose Window ⇨ Layers, and Window ⇨ Animation.** You need these palettes to create this project. The mode in the Animation palette should be set to Timeline rather than Frame Animation.

3. **Choose Layer ⇨ Video Layers ⇨ New Video Layer from File.** Then locate the video that you want to import. The video appears in the Layers palette, as well as in the Timeline of the Animation palette. To create the frames shown in Figure 28.17, you need to import three video clips. This example uses one of the video clips in the opening; the other two are composed together by using the Darken mode and reducing the Opacity value in the Layers palette (shown in Figure 28.16). The second video clip is faded out so that only the third video clip is visible at the end of the project. The Type layer is visible throughout the project. Figure 28.16 shows the Animation and Project panels used to create the Photoshop video and text animation project.

4. **Use the Move tool to move the video clips in the Timeline panel so that one clip is at the beginning of the Timeline and the other two are overlapping at the end of the Timeline.** The end of the first clip (in Layer 3) should overlap the beginning of the

second clip (in Layer 2). The end of the second clip should overlap the beginning of the third clip (in Layer 1). The first video clip (a surfer) is in Layer 3 of the Layers palette. The second video clip (a woman) is in Layer 2 of the Layers palette and the third video clip (a man) is in Layer 1 of the Layers palette.

5. **To view the overlapping areas of the second and third video clips, set the mode for the second clip (in Layer 2) to Darken.** This reveals the dark areas of the second video clip (in Layer 2) over the third video clip (in Layer 1). Next, click the drop-down menu next to the Opacity value and choose a mode. Then click the Opacity value and decrease the opacity.

6. **Use adjustment layers to change the colors of the video clips.** After you apply an effect to a video clip, you may decide that you want to change the effect. You can do so with adjustment layers. In Figure 28.16, to lighten and change the color of the second video clip in Layer 2, use two adjustment layers: Brightness/Contrast and Photo Filter.

7. **Use the Filter Gallery to give the video clips a painterly effect.** Use Smart Filters so that you can undo the filter and apply a new one to change the effect. To apply a filter to a video clip, select the video clip. Then choose Filter ⇨ Convert to Smart Filters. Next, choose Filter ⇨ Filter Gallery. In the dialog box that appears, select a filter. This example uses the Dry Brush, Poster Edges, and Crosshatch filters.

FIGURE 28.16

The Animation and Layers palette used to create the Photoshop animation project consisting of a type layer and video layers

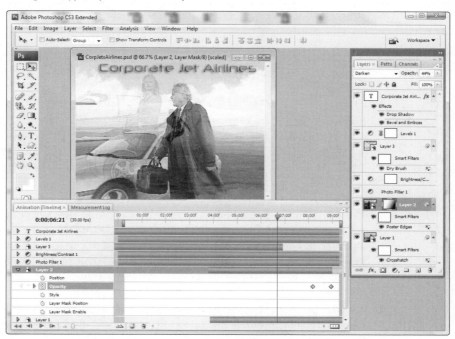

FIGURE 28.17

Frames from the Photoshop animation project consisting of a type layer and video layers

8. **Use a layer mask to fade portions of a video clip into the video clip below it.** The example in Figure 28.16 uses a layer mask on the second video clip so that you can fade a portion of it into the third video clip. Click the video clip (Layer 2) in the Layers palette. Then click the Add Layer Mask icon at the bottom of the Layers palette. Now use the Gradient tool to create a black-and-white linear gradient on the layer mask. The black areas of the gradient are the area of the clip that is faded.

9. **To fade the first video clip into the second, you need to set two Opacity keyframes.** Click the first video clip in the Timeline (Layer 3) and display the Opacity option. Move the current-time indicator toward the end of the clip and click the Opacity stopwatch

Preventing Distorted Graphics

If you create a graphic at 720 x 480 pixels (or 720 x 486 pixels) in a square pixel program such as Adobe Photoshop 7 and import it into a Premiere Pro NTSC DV project, the graphic may appear distorted in Premiere Pro. The graphic is distorted because Premiere Pro automatically converts it to a non-square 0.9-pixel aspect ratio. You can convert the imported Photoshop graphic file back to square pixels. First, select the graphic in the Project panel. Then choose File ➪ Interpret Footage. In the Pixel Aspect Ratio section of the Interpret Footage dialog box, click Conform to, choose Square Pixels (1.0) in the drop-down menu, and click OK. Although this technique works, it may reduce graphic quality. If you are using Photoshop 7, your best bet is to create full-screen graphics for DV projects at 720 x 534 pixels or 720 x 540 pixels (768 x 576 pixels for PAL). After creating your graphics, choose Edit ➪ Preferences ➪ General. In the dialog box, select the default Scale to Frame Size option before you import the graphics into Premiere Pro. You can also choose to import a graphic, then select it in the Project panel, and choose Clip ➪ Video Options ➪ Scale to Frame Size. This squeezes the graphic to fit into your DV project frame size.

If you are creating full-screen graphic files in Photoshop CS for a Premiere Pro DV project, create them in Photoshop CS using the Film & Video 720 x 480 DV preset. This preset (which sets the Photoshop pixel aspect ratio to 0.9) can help you prevent distortion because you can preview graphics in Photoshop before importing them into a Premiere Pro DV project.

---

icon to create a keyframe. Then move the current-time indicator to the end of the clip and reduce the opacity some more so that it fades out into the second video clip.

10. **To fade the second video clip into the third video clip, you need to set two Opacity keyframes as you did in step 9.**

11. **To finish the project, use the Type tool to create some type.** Place the type at the bottom of the frame. Stylize the text by selecting a font, color, and size. You can also click the Add Layer Style icon at the bottom of the Layers palette to select a Blending option.

12. **The Type layer should be at the top of the Layers palette so that you can see it throughout the project.** If it is not, move it there.

13. **To have the type move, you need to set Position keyframes.** Click the Type layer in the Animation palette. Display the Position option for the Type layer. Move the current-time indicator to the beginning of the Type layer, and then click the stopwatch icon in front of the Position icon to create a keyframe. To create a second keyframe, move the current-time indicator to the right. Then move the text in the frame window to create a second keyframe. Continue creating keyframes until you have made a type animation.

14. **To view the project, click the Play button at the bottom of the Animation palette.**

15. **Choose File ➪ Save.** Be sure to save your work in Photoshop format with all of its layers. Choose File ➪ Export ➪ Render Video.

16. **To import the Photoshop project into Premiere Pro and add sound, open or create a Premiere Pro project.** Choose File ➪ Import. Drag the project to a video track in the Timeline panel.

Creating a Photoshop File with an Alpha Channel

To display a Photoshop file in Premiere Pro without its background, you must isolate the item in the foreground from the background to create an alpha channel, or mask (as shown in Figure 28.18). In Photoshop you can select an item in a few different ways. You can use either a Selection tool (such as the Lasso, Polygonal Lasso, Magnetic Lasso, Magic Wand, or Quick Selection tool) or the Pen tool to create a path and then convert the path to a selection. You can also use the Color Range command and the Quick Mask mode to create a selection. Once you have a selection onscreen, you can save the selection to an alpha channel. When you save a file with a background and an alpha channel in Photoshop format, the file is then imported into Premiere Pro with a transparent background. When you load the Photoshop file into Premiere Pro, the alpha channel enables you to use the Motion effect on the selected item, without its background appearing.

FIGURE 28.18

A Photoshop file of kids after selecting them and creating an alpha channel

This all works fine when you are working with a Background layer (shown in Figure 28.19). However, when the background is converted to a layer with transparencies, things work a little differently. If you double-click the Background layer in the Layers palette, the New Layer dialog box appears, allowing you to convert the Background layer to a regular layer.

ON the DVD To use the cat image (shown in Figure 28.19), load the SnowWhite.psd file found in the MoreClips folder on the DVD that accompanies this book.

NOTE To convert a Background layer to a regular layer, double-click it in the Layers palette. To turn a regular layer to a Background layer, choose Layer ➪ New ➪ Background from Layer.

Now, when you use the Eraser tool to erase away the background, the background is converted to transparent areas (as shown in Figure 28.20). If you use the Eraser tool on a Background layer rather than a regular layer, you erase to white, not transparency. In the Layer mode, you can also select an area with a Selection tool, and then press Delete to delete the background and leave the area transparent. When a Photoshop file has a transparent background, you don't have to save the selection to an alpha channel. Photoshop reads the transparent areas as transparent and makes an alpha channel of the items in the document. Just save the file in Photoshop format, and Photoshop does the rest.

FIGURE 28.19

A Photoshop file of a cat with a Background layer

Follow these steps to select an image and save the selection to an alpha channel:

1. **Launch Photoshop.** Open the file with the image you want to isolate (mask).

2. **Create a selection with a Selection tool (Lasso, Polygonal Lasso, Magnetic Lasso, or Magic Wand) to select the image you want to isolate from the background.** This example uses the Polygonal Lasso tool to select the cat. For a soft-edged selection, you can set the Lasso tool to have a feather radius of 2. After you make your selection, you can add to the selection by pressing and holding the Shift key as you use a Selection tool to select the area you want to add. To subtract from your selection, press and hold Alt/Option as you use a Selection tool to subtract from the selected area.

FIGURE 28.20

A Photoshop file of a cat with a transparent layer

3. **To make a selection with the Pen tool, first use the Pen tool to make a closed path.** Select the Pen tool from the Tools palette. In the Toolbar, click the Paths icon rather than the Shapes Layer icon. Then click around the item. Make sure the ending point of the path meets the starting point; a tiny circle appears next to the Pen icon when it does.

When the path is finished, choose Window ⇨ Paths to display the path in the Paths palette. Double-click the path in the Paths palette to rename it. To convert the path into a selection, choose Make Selection from the Paths palette menu. In the Make Selection dialog box, enter a feather radius to soften the edges of the selection. If you enter a very large feather radius, the selection has a vignette appearance. Click OK to convert the path to a selection.

4. **To make a quick selection using the Color Range command, choose Select ⇨ Color Range.** In the Color Range dialog box (shown in Figure 28.21), click the Eyedropper icon and click in the document in the area you want to select. Click the Eyedropper icon with the plus sign to add to the selection, and click the Eyedropper icon with the minus sign to subtract from the selection.

NOTE A path created with the Pen tool or the Shape tool can be copied and pasted into After Effects to be used as a mask. For more information on importing masks into After Effects from Photoshop and Illustrator, turn to the end of Chapter 31.

Increasing the Fuzziness value increases the feather of the selection, so don't use too much. Click OK to make a selection. To add to the selection, you can use the Brush tool in Quick Mask mode. Double-click the Quick Mask Mode icon at the bottom of the Tools palette. In the Quick Mask Options dialog box, the Masked Areas radio button should be selected. If not, do so. This way, a color overlay appears over the non-selected areas, leaving the selected areas unaffected.

FIGURE 28.21

The Color Range dialog box allows you to quickly make a selection.

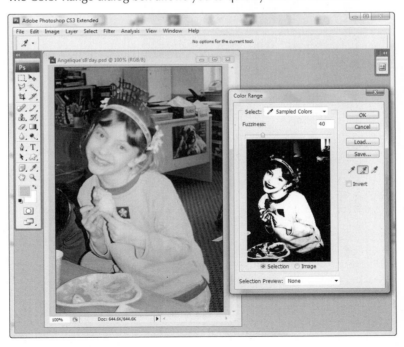

Clicking the Selected Areas radio button gives you the opposite result. You can experiment with these options. Next, choose a color for the overlay. By default, it is set to red at 50 percent opacity. Click OK to view and work in Quick Mask mode. In Quick Mask mode, the non-selected areas are covered with a tint (as shown in Figure 28.22).

Before you start painting, select a brush size. If you prefer, you can use the Pencil tool. Next, click the Default Foreground and Background Colors icon to set the foreground to black and the background to white. When you paint with black, you subtract from the selection. Click the Switch Foreground and Background Colors icon to change the foreground color to white and the background color to black.

Now, as you paint with white, you add to the selection. To see the selection, click the Quick Mask Mode icon to exit Quick Mask mode. To return to Quick Mask mode, click the Quick Mask Mode icon. Quick Mask mode is very useful when selecting difficult areas such as hair. When you are done making the selection, click the Quick Mask Mode icon to exit Quick Mask mode and view the selection.

FIGURE 28.22

Quick Mask mode allows you to use either the Pencil or Brush tools to add or subtract to or from a selection.

5. **With the selection onscreen, choose Select ⇨ Save Selection.** In the Save Selection dialog box, you can name the alpha channel in the Name field. Click OK to save the selection to an alpha channel.

 To load a saved selection, choose Select ⇨ Load Selection. To load a selection using the Channels palette, drag the alpha channel over the Load Channel As Selection icon.

6. **To see the alpha channel, choose Window ⇨ Channels.** In the Channels palette, you see a Red, Green, Blue, and alpha channel, as shown in Figure 28.23. Click Alpha Channel in the Channels palette to display the alpha channel. The alpha channel, shown in Figure 28.24, displays the white area as the selected area. The white area is the only area that Premiere Pro reads. The black area represents the area that Premiere Pro doesn't read. This happens only if the Color Indicates option is set to the default setting, Masked Areas, in the Channel Options dialog box. To display the Channel Options dialog box, double-click the alpha channel in the Channels palette.

FIGURE 28.23

The Channels palette displaying the Red, Green, Blue, and alpha channels

7. **To import this file into Premiere Pro with the alpha channel, save the alpha channel with the file by choosing File ⇨ Save As.** In the Save As dialog box, click the Format drop-down menu and choose Photoshop format. In the Save section, only the Alpha Channel option should be selected. Click Save to save the file.

FIGURE 28.24

A Photoshop file of a cat with the alpha channel displayed

Placing a Photoshop Alpha Channel File into a Premiere Pro Project

Now that you've created a Photoshop file with an alpha channel, you are ready to import it into a Premiere Pro project. After it's in Premiere Pro, you can import an image to go behind it, and you can also use the Motion Effects to animate the image without the background. Figure 28.25 shows the Peace&Love Premiere Pro project that is created with a Photoshop alpha channel file, an Illustrator graphic file, and a background created using black video and Premiere Pro's 4-Color Gradient video effect. You can also add a SmartSound sound clip.

To create the Peace&Love project in this example, you can use a Photoshop alpha channel file (SnowWhite.psd or WhiteCat.psd) and a graphic Illustrator file (Peace&Love.ai) behind the Photoshop alpha channel file. In Premiere Pro, create a background using black video and Premiere Pro's 4-Color Gradient video effect.

FIGURE 28.25

The Premiere Pro Peace&Love project uses a Photoshop alpha channel file and an Illustrator graphic file.

Follow these steps to import a Photoshop file with an alpha channel into a Premiere Pro project:

1. **Launch Premiere Pro, and then choose File ⇨ New ⇨ Project to create a new project.** In the New Project dialog box, select a preset, name your project, and click OK.

2. **In the new Premiere Pro project, choose File ⇨ Import.**

3. **In the Import dialog box, locate a Photoshop file with an alpha channel (for example, WhiteCat.psd or SnowWhite.psd).** Click Open. When you open a Photoshop file with a transparent layer, the Import Layered File dialog box appears. In the dialog box, set the Import As drop-down menu to Footage. In the Layer Options sections, click the Choose Layer drop-down menu and choose the Photoshop Layer. Click OK. Premiere Pro stores the Photoshop file in the Project panel, as shown in Figure 28.26. Double-click the Photoshop file in the Project panel to see it in the Source panel, as shown in Figure 28.27.

 The cat image (SnowWhite.psd or WhiteCat.psd) and the graphic background image (Peace&Love.ai) are located in the MoreClips folder on the DVD that accompanies this book.

FIGURE 28.26

The Project panel with a Photoshop alpha channel file

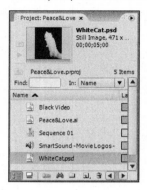

4. **Choose File ➪ Import to import a video clip or graphic image to place behind the Photoshop alpha channel file.** This example uses the Peace&Love file, which is created in Illustrator using the Effect 3D command.

5. **Drag the cat file from the Project panel to the Video 3 track in the Timeline panel.** To give the Photoshop alpha channel more depth, you can apply the Drop Shadow video effect, found in the Perspective bin.

6. **Drag the graphic background file (Peace&Love.ai) from the Project panel to the Video 2 track in the Timeline panel.** In the Video 1 track, place a 4-color gradient created using Premiere Pro's 4-Color Gradient video effect. Figure 28.25 shows the Timeline panel for the Peace&Love project.

7. **Choose File ➪ New ➪ Black Video or Color Matte.** If you choose Color Matte, pick a color in the Color Picker. Then give the color matte a name and click OK. Next, drag the black video or the color matte to the Video 1 track in the Timeline panel. Then, in the Effects panel, open the Video Effects folder and locate the Generate bin. In the Generate bin, select the 4-Color Gradient video effect and drag it over the black video or color matte in the Video 1 track. In the Effect Controls panel, click the controls to make your gradient.

   To animate the cat image, you can use Premiere Pro's Motion settings. The Motion controls are found in the Effect Controls panel (shown in Figure 28.25). In this example, the cat in the Peace&Love project moves from the bottom-left corner up to the top-right corner.

8. **To start the cat animation, first select the clip in the Video 3 track of the Timeline panel.** Then move the edit line to the beginning of the clip. Click the word *Motion* in the Effect Controls panel. Move the cat to the bottom-right corner. Now click the triangle next to the Motion effect to display the effect controls. Click the Position Toggle Animation icon to create a Position keyframe. Also click the Rotate Toggle Animation icon to create a Rotate keyframe. Keep moving the edit line and the cat to create more Position and Rotate keyframes.

FIGURE 28.27

The Photoshop alpha channel file seen in the Source panel

9. **To preview the Peace&Love project, click the Play button in the Program Monitor panel.** By creating an alpha channel for the cat file, you can have the cat image move without having the background move with it. In order to create the alpha channel, you need to create and save a selection around the cat (refer to the previous section to learn how). When you save a selection, Photoshop saves the selection as a mask in an alpha channel. Because the cat image is in the Video 3 track, you can see the graphic background in the Video 2 track and the 4-color gradient background in the Video 1 track. When you add motion to the cat, the cat moves above the background clips in the Video 1 and 2 tracks.

10. **Choose File ⇨ Import to import a sound clip.** This example uses SmartSound's Movie Logos sound clip. The sound is trimmed and slowly fades out. To have the other clips match the length of the sound clip, you can extend the length of the other clips by clicking the right end of the clip in the Timeline panel and extending it to the right.

11. **Choose File ⇨ Save to save your work.** Choose File ⇨ Export ⇨ Movie to save your project in a movie format.

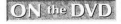 SmartSound's Movie Logo sound clip is found in the SmartSound folder on the DVD that accompanies this book.

Summary

You can easily export a frame from Premiere Pro to Photoshop or export Photoshop files into Premiere Pro. This chapter covered these topics:

- If you want to load a Premiere Pro frame into Photoshop and have a Premiere Pro frame appear as layers, you can export the Premiere Pro project to After Effects first, and then to Photoshop.

- Premiere Pro automatically reads the background transparency of Photoshop layers. It does not convert Photoshop transparency into a white background.

- Premiere Pro can use Photoshop alpha channels to create transparency effects.

Chapter 29

Using Adobe Premiere Pro and Adobe Illustrator

dobe Illustrator is one of the most powerful desktop illustration programs available for personal computers. Using Adobe Illustrator, graphic designers can place text on a curve or bend and reshape the letters in a word. Illustrator, which is a vector-based program, provides designers with the power they need to create virtually any shape that can be drawn. In *vector-based* programs, shapes are defined mathematically, and you can easily move and reshape them. In Illustrator, shapes appear as paths that are filled or outlined with color. Onscreen, a *path* resembles a wireframe outline with tiny squares called *anchor points*. Editing the anchor points edits the path.

For Adobe Premiere Pro users, Illustrator opens up a new world of possibilities. You can import Illustrator type and shapes directly into Premiere Pro. When Premiere Pro opens an Illustrator file, it automatically converts it from Illustrator's vector format to Premiere Pro's raster format (pixel based), and the file appears with a transparent background. This conversion enables you not only to use the Illustrator text but also to use shapes created in Illustrator as masks.

IN THIS CHAPTER

Working with Illustrator type

Using an Illustrator text shape in a Premiere Pro project

Working with Illustrator graphics

Creating Illustrator shapes

Using Illustrator shapes as masks in Premiere Pro

Creating a mask using Photoshop and Illustrator

Working with Illustrator Type

You can create type effects in Illustrator and then import them into Premiere Pro for use as title effects, logos, and credits. You can also import Illustrator type into Premiere Pro, use the type as a mask, and have a video clip run through the shape of the text, as described later in this chapter. With Adobe Photoshop CS3 Extended, you can also import or copy and paste Illustrator type and graphics, and animate them in Photoshop's Animation palette.

CROSS-REF For more information on animating in Photoshop, turn to Chapter 28.

Illustrator features six tools with which you can create type: the Type tool, Area Type tool, Type on a Path tool, Vertical Type tool, Vertical Area Type tool, and Vertical Type on a Path tool.

The Type tool enables you to create text that reads horizontally, from left to right. To create horizontal text, click the Type tool in the toolbox, click in the document where you want the type to appear, and then start typing. The Area Type tool is used to create type inside a path shape. The Type on a Path tool creates text on a path. The Vertical Type tool flows text from top to bottom (vertically), rather than from left to right (horizontally) as the Type tool does. To create vertical text, click the Vertical Type tool in the toolbox, click in the document where you want the type to appear, and then start typing.

The Vertical Area Type tool works like the Area Type tool. Both type tools create type within a path. When you type using the Vertical Area Type tool, the type appears from top to bottom (vertically) inside the path rather than from left to right (horizontally) as it does when using the Path Area Type tool.

The Vertical Type on a Path tool works similarly to the Type on a Path tool; both type tools create type on a path. However, instead of the type appearing left to right (horizontally) as it does when using the Type on a Path tool, it appears top to bottom (vertically).

Using Illustrator type tools

Follow these steps to create text using Illustrator's type tools:

1. **Launch Illustrator, if it is not already open.**
2. **Choose File ➪ New to create a new document.** In the New Document dialog box, click the New Document Profile drop-down menu and make a selection, depending on how you are going to output your document. Choose Basic RGB, Video & Film, Web, Mobile and Devices, or Basic CMYK.
3. **Choose Window ➪ Type ➪ Character, or Window ➪ Type ➪ Paragraph to display the Character or Paragraph palette.**
4. **Select either the Type tool or the Vertical Type tool.**
5. **Move the cursor to the middle of the document.**
6. **Click the document, and type a few words.** To have the text continue onto another line (as shown in Figure 29.1), press Enter. To center the text (as shown in Figure 29.1), use the alignment in either the Paragraph palette or the Type toolbar.

FIGURE 29.1

Illustrator's Type tool allows you to create horizontal type.

Follow these steps to apply a fill and stroke to text with a solid color:

1. **Click and drag over the text you want to stylize.** You can stylize an entire word or just a letter or two in the word. You can change the font and font size from the Character palette or from the Character bar at the top of the document.

 By default, Illustrator uses the fill color as the type color. If you set the fill color to the color you want the text to be, you do not need to change it later.

2. **Choose Window ⇨ Color to display the Color palette.**

3. **To set the text fill color to the desired type color, use the color swatch in either the Tools palette or the Color palette.** Double-click the Fill color swatch in the Tools palette (the top, overlapping square toward the bottom of the Tools palette) or the Fill color swatch in the Color palette (the top, overlapping square in the top-left corner of the Color palette). The Color Picker dialog box appears.

4. **In the Color Picker dialog box, click a color in the Select Color area or on the color slider next to it.** If you are creating a project for the Web, be sure to select the Only Web Colors option.

5. **In the Color Picker dialog box, click OK.** The fill color changes to the newly selected color. If you decide to change the fill color, the easiest way to pick a new color is to use the color bar in the Color palette. To display the Color palette, choose Window ⇨ Color. In the Color palette, click a color in the color bar at the bottom of the palette to change the fill color. To create a new color, move the sliders in the middle of the palette.

6. **To apply a stroke to the text, click the Stroke color swatch (which is below the Fill color swatch) and pick a color.** Select a color either by using the Color Picker dialog box — which you can access by double-clicking the Stroke color swatch in the Tools or Color palette — or by dragging the sliders or color bar in the Color palette. To set the size of the stroke, click the Weight drop-down menu in the Stroke palette and select a size. To display the Stroke palette, choose Window ⇨ Stroke.

7. **Set the stroke fill color to black.** Click the Default Fill and Stroke Color button, which is below the overlapping Fill and Stroke color swatch in the Tools palette. This sets the Stroke color swatch to black and the Fill color swatch to white. Next, click the Swap Fill and Stroke button (the curved arrow next to the Fill and Stroke color swatch) to set the fill to black and the stroke to white. To use the Illustrator text as a mask with a video clip running through the shape of the text, you must set the fill color to black. Now you are ready to use a type tool to start creating some type.

Follow these steps to fill text with a pattern:

1. **Click and drag over the text you want to stylize.** You can stylize an entire word or just a letter or two in the word. You can change the font and font size from the Character palette or from the Character bar at the top of the document.

2. **Choose Window ⇨ Swatch to display the Swatch palette.** Click a pattern swatch to fill with a pattern. To display different Swatch libraries, click Window ⇨ Swatch Libraries ⇨ Patterns, and then make a selection. This example uses the Decorative library with the Decorative_Ornament swatch, shown in Figure 29.1.

3. **Add a drop shadow with the SVG filters.** Choose Effect ⇨ SVG Filters and then select a shadow option to add a drop shadow. This example uses AI_Shadow_1, as shown in Figure 29.1.

4. **Fill with a wood grain.** Choose Effect ⇨ SVG Filters ⇨ AI_Woodgrain to fill with a wood grain. Figure 29.2 shows the effects of applying the Woodgrain filter to text. You can apply the SVG filters to both text and graphic paths. Try using some of the other SVG filters for other special effects, such as Dilate, Cool Breeze, Erode, Gaussian Blur, Static, Turbulence, and PixelPlay.

FIGURE 29.2

You can fill a path with the SVG Woodgrain filter to give the path the appearance of a wood grain.

Transforming and distorting using the Effect commands

You can use the Effect commands to alter paths that you created using Illustrator's type tools, Pen tool, Paintbrush tool, Pencil tool, or other graphic path-creation tools (such as Rectangle, Ellipse, Polygon, Star, and Flare). For interesting text effects, you can use one of the Effect commands to alter a text path.

The Effect ⇨ Warp commands work like Photoshop's Warp Text option, except that Illustrator's Warp commands can be applied to any path, not just a text path. In Figure 29.3, the Effect ⇨ Warp ⇨ Shell Upper command is applied to both text and graphic paths. To preview the effect in the Warp Options dialog box, click the Preview check box.

The graphics shown in Figure 29.3 were made with the Star tool. With the Star tool selected, Alt-click/Option-click the drawing area. In the Star dialog box that appears, you can choose how many points you want your star path to have. In Figure 29.3, the three different graphics have different points; the first one has four, the second one has nine, and the third one has three. After you enter the amount of points you want, click OK to create the graphic path. The paths in Figure 29.3 are filled using the Window ⇨ Swatch Libraries ⇨ Patterns ⇨ Basic Graphics ⇨ Basic Graphics_Dots command.

You can use the Photoshop Effect Gallery commands to create interesting fills for text and graphic paths. Choose Effect ⇨ Effect Gallery or select one of the Effect Gallery options. Then click the folders and controls in the dialog box to create the fill you are looking for, as shown in Figure 29.4.

FIGURE 29.3

You can apply the Effect Warp commands to text and graphic paths.

FIGURE 29.4

The Effect Gallery can create interesting fills for graphic and text paths.

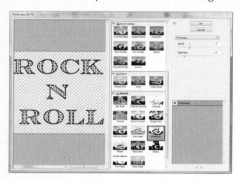

The Effect ➪ Distort & Transform ➪ Transform command allows you to scale, move, and rotate text, as shown in Figure 29.5. Figure 29.6 shows the Effect ➪ Distort & Transform ➪ Free Distort command when it is applied to text. Figure 29.7 shows the Effect ➪ Distort & Transform ➪ Twist command when it is applied to text. The other Distort & Transform commands are Pucker & Bloat, Roughen, Tweak, and Zig Zag. To preview the Distort & Transform effect in the dialog box, click the Preview check box.

FIGURE 29.5

You can use the Transform Effect dialog box to scale, move, and rotate text paths.

FIGURE 29.6

You can use the Free Distort dialog box to distort text paths.

FIGURE 29.7

The Twist dialog box allows you to twist text paths.

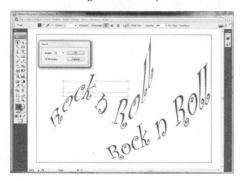

The Effect Stylize commands allow you to add an arrow, rounded corners, a drop shadow, a feather, and an inner and outer glow. You can use the Scribble Options dialog box (Effect ⇨ Stylize ⇨ Scribble) to give a path a scribbled look, as shown in Figure 29.8. To preview the effect in the Stylize dialog box, click the Preview check box.

FIGURE 29.8

The Scribble Options dialog box allows you to create scribble effects.

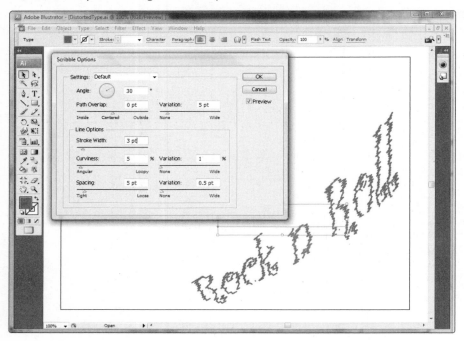

To create a 3-D effect, you can use Illustrator's 3D Effect commands. Figure 29.9 shows the 3D Extrude & Bevel Options dialog box (Effect ➪ 3D ➪ Extrude & Bevel), with the command applied to a text path. To preview the effect in the Extrude & Bevel dialog box, click the Preview check box.

Using the Area Type tool inside a path shape

Before you can use the Area Type tool, you first need to create a path shape. To create a path shape, you can use the Ellipse, Polygon, Star, or Rectangle tool. Select one of these tools, and then click and drag in the drawing area to create a path shape. To distort or to create more elaborate path shapes, you can apply one of Illustrator's Distort & Transform commands to a shape. In Figure 29.10, the Distort & Transform Pucker & Bloat command is used to convert a rectangle to a flower. In the Pucker & Bloat dialog box, dragging the slider to the right bloats the path and turns it into a flower shape. Dragging the slider to the left *puckers* the path (collapses the path toward its center) and makes the path a star shape.

 The Pucker & Bloat filter was known as the Punk & Bloat filter in older versions of Illustrator.

FIGURE 29.9

The Extrude & Bevel command can create a 3-D effect.

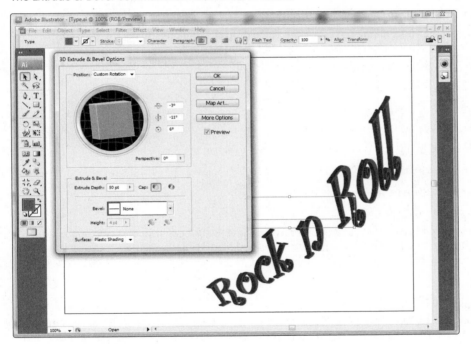

Export a Path from Photoshop to Illustrator

You can create a path using a Photoshop shape tool:

1. **Click the shape tool in the Tools panel.**
2. **Click the Path mode on the toolbar.** Select a shape from the Shape drop-down menu.
3. **Click and drag in the drawing area to make a path shape.** Once you've done this, a path shape appears in the Paths panel.

Export a path from Photoshop to Illustrator by following these steps:

1. **Choose File ⇨ Export ⇨ Paths to Illustrator.**
2. **In the Export Paths dialog box, click the Paths drop-down menu.** Select the path you want to export, or choose All Paths to export all of the paths.
3. **Click Save to export the path as an Illustrator file.**

Open the exported path in Illustrator:

1. **Choose File ⇨ Open.**
2. **Locate the file in the Open dialog box.**
3. **Click Open.** In Illustrator, use the Selection tool to select the path.

You can fill the path with text:

1. **Select the Area Type tool.**
2. **Click inside the path.**
3. **Start typing.** Keep in mind that in order to have text fit correctly inside a path, you may need to experiment with different fonts, font sizes, leading, and spacing.

When making your shape, ensure that there is plenty of space inside the shape so that you can use the Area Type tool to add text inside it. Once you create the path shape, you can click inside it with the Area Type tool and start typing. Your text appears onscreen in the shape of the path, and reads from left to right.

If you want, you can use the Pen tool to create a closed path. For example, to use the Pen tool to create a diamond path, first select the Pen tool, and then click in the drawing area of your document five different times in the shape of a diamond. The fifth time that you click, the last point should meet the first point. There should be a tiny circle below the Pen tool when the last point has met the first point. Click to close the path. For more information on using the Pen tool and working with Bezier paths, see Chapter 10.

You can also use Photoshop to create paths with a shape tool, and then export the path to Illustrator. Figure 29.11 shows a path shape with text inside of it. The path shape is created in Photoshop using a shape tool with the Path option. The path is then exported from Photoshop and imported into Illustrator. In Illustrator, the Area Type tool is used to create the type inside the path shape.

FIGURE 29.10

A simple rectangle path shape converts into a more elaborate path by using the Distort & Transform Pucker & Bloat command.

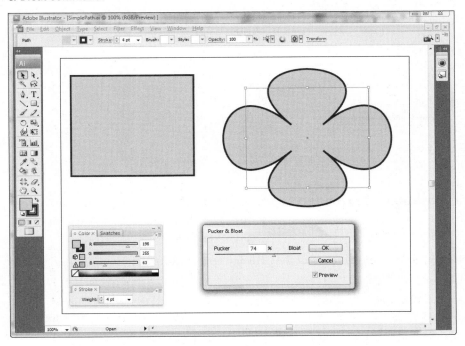

A path shape created with a Photoshop shape tool, and then imported into Illustrator, where text is typed inside the path with the Area Type tool

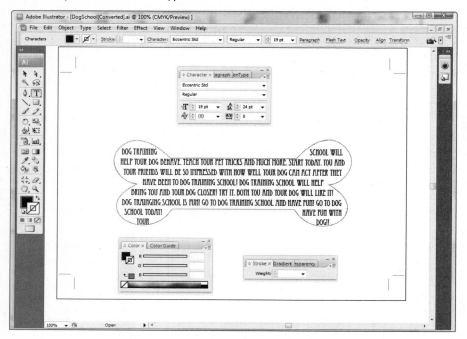

Using Photoshop CS3 Extended to animate text shapes

When you have a path shape with text inside of it, you can copy the path and the text from Illustrator and paste it into Photoshop for animating. Follow these steps:

1. **Use the Selection tool to select the path and text in Illustrator.**

2. **Choose Edit ⇨ Copy.**

3. **Launch Photoshop.** Choose File ⇨ New. In the New dialog box (shown in Figure 29.12), choose Film & Video from the Preset drop-down menu. Click OK to create a new document.

4. **Choose Edit ⇨ Paste.** In the Paste dialog box that appears (shown in Figure 29.13), choose Smart Object. Click OK.

5. **Click and drag one of the corners of the pasted object to scale it.** Double-click the object to paste it into the document onscreen. You can see the pasted object in Figure 29.14.

FIGURE 29.12

Photoshop's New dialog box allows you to choose a Film & Video preset.

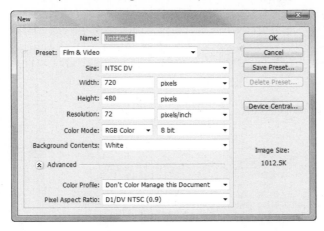

6. **Choose Layer ⇨ Layer Style ⇨ Drop Shadow to add a drop shadow to the pasted shape.** You can adjust the controls in the Layer Style dialog box.

FIGURE 29.13

When copying an Illustrator path to Photoshop, a Paste dialog box appears, allowing you to specify how you want to paste the path.

7. **Click OK.**

8. **To create a background in the background layer, select the background layer in the Layers palette.** Use the Gradient tool, the Brush tool, or a filter. In this example, shown in Figure 29.15, the Clouds filter is used for the background. Select a foreground and background color to use as clouds, and then Choose Filter ⇨ Render ⇨ Clouds.

CROSS-REF For more information on making background mattes in Photoshop, turn to Chapter 15.

FIGURE 29.14

A Photoshop background is created for our type that is within a path shape.

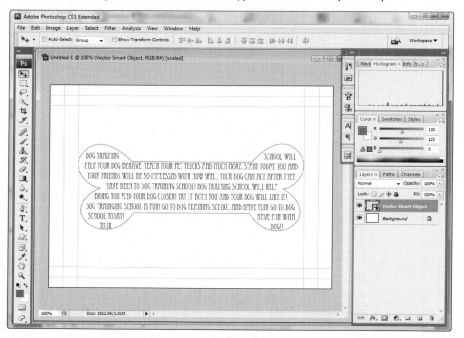

9. **To animate the Smart Object (graphic shape and text) in Photoshop CS3 Extended, use the Animation palette.** Choose Window ➪ Animation. Click the Vector Smart Object Layer in the Layers palette to activate it. In Figure 29.15, the position of the Smart Object (the bone and text) is animated. Keyframes are set for the Vector Smart Object position to have the bone and text move up and down.

    ▨ **To create a Position keyframe, move the current-time indicator to the beginning of the clip.**

    ▨ **Click the stopwatch icon next to the word *Position* to create a keyframe.** If the Position option is not visible, click the triangle next to the Vector Smart Object to display it.

    ▨ **To set a second keyframe, move the current-time indicator to the right.**

    ▨ **Click the Vector Smart Object in the drawing area and move it up.** A second keyframe is created.

    ▨ **To create a third keyframe, move the current-time indicator to the right again.**

    ▨ **Click the Vector Smart Object in the drawing area and move it down.** A third keyframe is created.

FIGURE 29.15

A background created in Photoshop for animating a layer containing a bone path and text. The animation is created using the Photoshop CS3 Extended Animation palette.

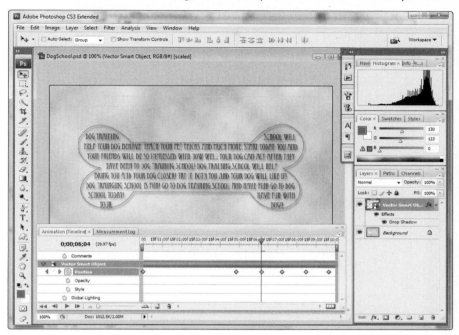

CROSS-REF For more information on working with Photoshop, see Chapters 11, 15, and 28.

10. **Click Play in the Animation palette to play the animation.**

11. **To save your file in Photoshop format, choose File ⇨ Save.** Choose File ⇨ Export ⇨ Render Video to export the movie. In the Render Video dialog box, you can choose to export the Photoshop file as a sequence file or as a QuickTime or AVI movie file. Then you can import it into Premiere Pro to add sound or to create more video effects for a more elaborate movie, animation, or presentation.

Using the Path Type tool

The Path Type tool creates text on a path. To use the Path Type tool, you first need to create a path. You can create a path using the Pen, Pencil, Paintbrush, or Ellipse tool. You can also use the Arc or Spiral tool to create an arc or spiral path on which the text can appear, as shown in Figure 29.16.

FIGURE 29.16

A spiral and an arc path with text

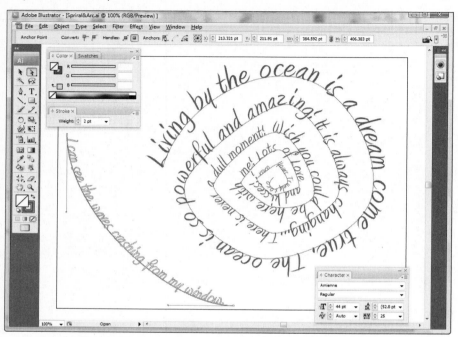

The Arc and Spiral tools are found in the same place as the Line tool in the toolbox. Click and hold the mouse down as you click the Line tool in the toolbox. With the mouse still pressed, click and drag down to select either the Spiral tool or the Arc tool. Then release the mouse. Now move the Spiral or Arc tool to the center of the drawing area of your document. Alt-click/Option-click to display the Spiral or Arc dialog box. In the Spiral or Arc dialog box, make your selections, and then click OK to create a spiral or arc. You may need to adjust the spiral or arc with the Scale and Rotate tools.

After you create a path, select it with the Selection tool. Then click it with the Path Type tool and start typing. The text appears on the path as you type (refer to Figure 29.16). In some cases, the font size may be too big to appear on the path, and so you may need to scale down the font size. To do so, click and drag over the text with the Path Type tool to select it. Then choose Type ➪ Size and select a size, or click the Font Size drop-down menu in the Character palette. To display the Character palette, choose Window ➪ Type ➪ Character.

After you add some type to your path, you may find that you want to edit the path. To edit the path, click it with the Direct Selection tool. Click the separate points and directional lines to adjust the path. Notice that the text moves with the path. To stroke the path, select it with the Direct Selection tool, click the Stroke color swatch, and pick a fill color. Use the Stroke palette to select a stroke width. More on adjusting path in the "Editing with anchor points" section of this chapter.

Converting Illustrator type to path outlines

You may want to convert your Illustrator type into path outlines so that you can manipulate it further. Illustrator type path outlines can be manipulated just like graphic path outlines. To manipulate path outlines, click the type path's anchor points using the Direct Selection tool (the white arrow), and move the anchor points to alter the type path and the type. This enables you to create your own type designs, as shown in Figure 29.17, to use as titles in a Premiere Pro project.

NOTE When you convert text to outline format, it is no longer considered a font. The outline paths now appear as art, not text. As a result, if you send an Illustrator file to another person, that person does not need to have the font on their machine.

Follow these steps to convert your type into outline type paths:

1. **In Illustrator, choose a font and then create text using either the Type tool or the Vertical Type tool.** You can also create a path and use either the Area Type or Path Type tool.

2. **Use the Selection tool to select the type.**

3. **Choose Type ➪ Create Outlines to convert the text from type to an outline path.**

4. **Fill the path outlines with gradients.** To fill with a gradient, you can click a gradient swatch in the Swatch palette. Choose Window ➪ Swatch Libraries ➪ Gradients and then make a selection to display a gradient swatch library. The example in Figure 29.17 uses the Blue/Yellow/Pink swatch from the Color Combinations Gradient Swatch library.

5. **Use the Selection tool to click one of the corners to scale or rotate the outline path.** You can also use the Selection tool to move the outline path, or click away from the path on the drawing area to deselect the path.

6. **Use the Group Selection tool to select individual letters that you want to edit.** Click inside the path to select the entire letter. After you select a letter path, you can use the Free Transform tool (in the Tools palette) to transform the path. You can also use any of the Effect commands in the Effect menu, or the other transformational tools in the Tools palette, to edit individual letter paths. Use the Direct Selection tool to select a portion of a path that you want to edit. Then click and drag a path, path point, or directional line to make the necessary adjustments. For more information on editing path outlines, proceed to the next section.

TIP Click inside a path with the Group Selection tool to select the entire path. Double-click with the Group Selection tool to select the entire group path.

FIGURE 29.17

A path type outline with anchor points and directional lines

Editing path outlines

After you convert your text into outlines, Illustrator views the text as art (a graphic path that is in the shape of text). You no longer need the font to display the text because it is considered a graphic; you can select and manipulate the entire selection, an individual letter, or just a section of the path outline. Use the Selection tool (the black arrow) to select the entire path. Use the Group Selection tool to select an individual letter. Use the Direct Selection tool to select just a portion of a path.

With the Direct Selection tool, you can click and drag a point, path, or directional line to transform the path. Use the Group Selection tool to select a part of a path group, and then use either the Free Transform tool or the Effect ➪ Distort & Transform ➪ Transform command to transform the path. With the Selection tool, you can click and drag a corner point to scale or rotate a path. The paths can be manipulated using the commands in the Effect menu, as well as the transformation and distort tools.

You may want to manipulate, distort, or enlarge the text and paths so that when you import them into Premiere Pro, you can run a video clip through some interesting shapes, as shown later in this chapter. You can resize type path outlines with the Scale tool, rotate them with the Rotate tool, and move them with the Selection tool. You can manipulate them using the Reflect, Shear, and Free Transform tools. You can also distort them using the Warp, Reshape, and Twist tools — the sky is the limit!

> **TIP** To select an entire path, use the Selection tool. To select a portion of a path, use the Group Selection tool. To select a point on a path, use the Direct Selection tool. The Group Selection and Direct Selection tools reside in the same location in the Tools palette.

Here's how to scale, rotate, and move path outlines:

- **Scaling path outlines:** Select the part of the path outline that you want to scale. To use the Scale dialog box, double-click the Scale tool in the toolbox. When the Scale dialog box appears, make the adjustments you want, and click OK to scale the text.

- **Scaling a single path outline:** Click the outline path with the Group Selection tool (the white arrow with the plus sign). Next, select the Scale tool in the toolbox, and click once in your document. Now, with the Scale tool selected, click and drag the letter to scale it.

- **Rotating type:** Select the path outline of the letter you want to select. Next, click the Rotate tool (next to the Scale tool in the toolbox) and click in your document. Click and drag the letter to rotate it. If you want to display the Rotate dialog box, press and hold the Alt/Opt key while you click the text with the Rotate tool.

- **Moving path outlines:** Click inside the path using the Group Selection tool and drag the path to where you want to move it. You can also use the arrow keys to move the letter onscreen. By default, the arrow keys are set to move in one-pixel increments. You can change the increments in the Keyboard Increment section of the General Preferences dialog box. To access this dialog box, choose Edit ⇨ Preferences ⇨ General.

Editing with anchor points

Type path outlines can be manipulated so that you can create new typefaces. You manipulate type path outlines by moving either anchor points or directional lines. Figure 29.17 shows a type path outline with anchor points and directional lines.

To move an anchor point, click it with the Direct Selection tool (the white arrow) and then drag. Illustrator also enables you to move multiple anchor points at one time. To select more than one anchor point, press and hold the Shift key as you select anchor points. You can also click and drag over the anchor points you want to select.

> **TIP** You can also press the arrow keys to move a selected anchor point. Anchor points move in keyboard increments that you set in the General Preferences dialog box. To display the General Preferences dialog box, choose Edit ⇨ Preferences ⇨ General.

Editing with directional lines

Curves on a path are created from a curve anchor point. Curve anchor points have *directional lines*, which determine the size and arc of your curve. Clicking and dragging a directional line changes the form of the curve.

Other ways to adjust the type path outline include using the Pen+ tool, the Pen– tool, and the Convert tool. Use the Pen+ tool to click the path to add an anchor point. This anchor point can then be manipulated. Clicking an anchor point with the Pen– tool deletes it. Use the Convert tool to click a corner anchor point to convert it to a curve anchor point, and vice versa.

To distort your path, you can use the Warp tool. Illustrator enables you to create some interesting distortions with the Warp tool, so that you can convert plain path outlines into interesting and unusual ones.

Using an Illustrator Text Shape in a Premiere Pro Project

Earlier in this chapter, you learned how to use Illustrator to create type and then convert the type into type shapes. This section shows you how to use Illustrator's Type tool to create text, convert it into a type shape, and then import it into a Premiere Pro project that uses the text shape as a mask. The Premiere Pro project in this section features a video clip playing through and behind an Illustrator text shape. Figure 29.18 shows the panels from the project, called San Francisco.

> **TIP** You can copy and paste text from Illustrator into After Effects. To do this, copy the text object in Illustrator, launch After Effects, and create a new project. Choose Composition ⇨ New Composition to create a new composition. Choose Layer ⇨ New ⇨ Text to create a new text layer. Then click the Timeline panel and choose Paste. To learn about working with After Effects, turn to Chapters 30, 31, and 32.

Follow these steps to create an Illustrator text shape, import it into a Premiere Pro project, and then use it as a mask:

> **ON the DVD** The images shown in Figure 29.18 are on the DVD that accompanies this book. The images are a "Welcome to: San Francisco California" text shape created in Illustrator, a video clip of the Golden Gate bridge in California from FilmDisc sf0116), and a sound clip from SmartSound (American Sunrise — Dawn).

1. **Launch Adobe Illustrator.** Choose File ⇨ New to create a new document. In the New Document dialog box, click the New Document Profile and choose Video and Film. The document size should be the same as the Premiere Pro project. Click OK to create a new document. If you don't have access to Adobe Illustrator, skip steps 1 to 7.

FIGURE 29.18

An Illustrator text shape is used in the Premiere Pro San Francisco project.

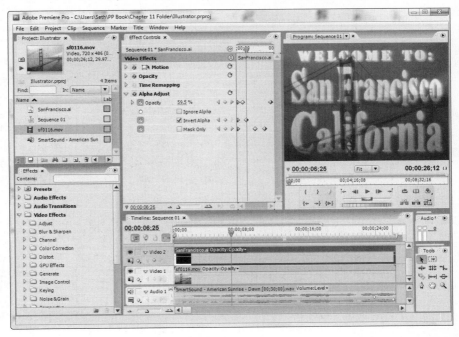

2. In Illustrator, select either the Type tool or the Vertical Type tool.

3. Choose a font and type size.

4. **Set the foreground color to black so that the text you create is black.** The black text is used later as a mask in Premiere Pro.

5. **Create some text, as shown in Figure 29.19.**

CROSS-REF   To learn about using the different Illustrator type tools, see the section "Working with Illustrator Type," earlier in this chapter.

6. **To convert the type into outlines, select it with the Selection tool and choose Type ⇨ Create Outlines.** Manipulate the text using the Free Transform tool. Choose Effect ⇨ Distort & Transform, or convert the type into outlines using the Direct Selection tool. This example converts the "Welcome to: San Francisco California" text into outlines and then manipulates the text by using the Direct Selection tool, as shown in Figure 29.20.

FIGURE 29.19

Text created in Illustrator for a Premiere Pro project

7. **After you create an Illustrator text path shape, save your file in Illustrator format.** Premiere Pro can then read the Illustrator file information. If you want, you can quit Illustrator.

8. **Launch Premiere Pro and create a new project.** The Illustrator and Premiere Pro files should be the same file size.

9. **Import an Illustrator text shape, a video clip, and a sound clip.** Choose File ➪ Import to import the files needed for this project. If you want, you can import the files that are used to create the frames shown in Figure 29.10. You can find the Illustrator file in the MoreClips folder (which is in the Tutorial Projects folder) on the DVD that accompanies this book. The video clip of the Golden Gate Bridge in San Francisco is from FilmDisc (sf0116). The sound clip, America Sunrise, is found in the SmartSound folder on the DVD.

FIGURE 29.20

The Illustrator text is converted to outline paths and then edited with the Direct Selection tool.

10. **Drag the video clip to the Video 1 track, the Illustrator text shape to the Video 2 track, and the sound clip to the Audio 1 track.** If the text shape is not as long as the video clip, you can click the end of the text shape in the Timeline panel and drag to the right until it is the same duration as the video clip. (For more information on basic editing, refer to Chapter 6.) If the sound clip is longer than the video clip, you can edit it by dragging the end of the clip to the left to match the size of the video clip. Because the sound clip in this project is longer than the video track, it is shortened and then a fade is added to slowly fade the sound out. Fading a sound clip is similar to fading a video track. To fade a sound clip, move the current-time indicator to the end of the sound clip and click the Add/Remove Keyframe button to add a keyframe at the end of the clip. Then move the current-time indicator in slightly, and add another keyframe. Drag the last keyframe down to fade the sound clip. (For more information on editing sound clips, turn to Chapter 7.)

11. **Select the text shape in the Video 2 track.**

12. **Choose Window ⇨ Workspace ⇨ Effects.** In the Effects panel, open the Video Effects bin (folder).

13. **In the Effects panel, open the Keying bin and drag the Alpha Adjust Key effect over the text shape in the Video 2 track**.

14. **In the Effect Controls panel, use the Alpha Adjust settings to create transparency with the clip in the Video 1 track.** Use the Alpha Adjust Opacity setting to reduce the opacity of the text shape so that you can see more of the video clip in the Video 1 track. Drag the Opacity slider to the left to make the text shape in the Video 2 track more transparent and to see more of the background. Drag the Opacity slider to the right to make the text shape in the Video 1 track more opaque. Click the Invert Alpha or Mask Only option, or both, to alter the effect.

If you want, you can animate the Alpha Adjust settings by moving the current-time indicator, and then click the Toggle Animation button (a stopwatch icon) to set keyframes and change the option settings over time. The results vary, depending upon which Alpha Adjust option you are using. If you want, you can choose to have the different Alpha Adjust controls turned on and off using keyframe animation.

Figure 29.21 shows the Illustrator text over a video clip with no changes made to the Alpha Adjust controls.

FIGURE 29.21

The Alpha Adjust video effect is applied to the text. No changes are made to any of the Alpha Adjust controls.

Figure 29.22 shows the Illustrator text over a video clip with the Alpha Adjust Invert Alpha option selected.

Figure 29.23 shows the Illustrator text over a video clip with the Alpha Adjust Invert Alpha option selected and the opacity set to 45 percent. Figure 29.24 shows the Illustrator text over a video clip with the Alpha Adjust Invert Alpha and Mask Only options selected and the opacity set to 100 percent. Figure 29.25 shows the Illustrator text over a video clip with the Mask Only option selected and the opacity set to 100 percent.

FIGURE 29.22

The Alpha Adjust video effect is applied to the text. The Invert Alpha option is selected, and opacity is set to 100 percent.

FIGURE 29.23

The Alpha Adjust video effect is applied to the text. The Invert Alpha option is selected, and opacity is set to 45 percent.

FIGURE 29.24

The Alpha Adjust video effect is applied to the text. The Invert Alpha and the Mask Only options are selected, and opacity is set to 100 percent.

FIGURE 29.25

The Alpha Adjust video effect is applied to the text. The Mask Only option is selected, and opacity is set to 100 percent.

Choosing the Keying video options results in different effects. Using the Keying video effects and options enables you to run video clips inside or behind text and graphic shapes. For more information on using Keying video effects, refer to Chapter 13.

15. **To soften the edges of the text shape, you may want to blur it by using the Gaussian Blur video effect.** To do so, select the text shape in the Video 2 track. In the Effects panel, open the Blur & Sharpen bin and drag the Gaussian Blur video effect over the text shape in the Video 2 track. The Effect Controls panel appears onscreen if it is not there already. Drag the Blurriness slider slightly to the right.

16. **Choose File ➪ Save to save your project.**

17. **Press Enter to render the project.** Click the Play button in the Program Monitor panel to preview the project. If you want, you can make a movie by choosing File ➪ Export ➪ Movie. Click the Settings button if you want to change the settings of your movie. For more information on outputting your Premiere Pro projects to movies, turn to Chapter 18.

Working with Illustrator Graphics

Illustrator graphic shapes can be used in the same way as Illustrator text shapes for creating logos, special effects, and masks. You can then import these graphics into Premiere Pro for use in your movie project. Figure 29.26 shows a variety of different types of graphics that you can create in Illustrator CS3, using the Brush, Graphic Style, Swatch, and Symbol libraries. To create the 3-D shapes, you can use the Graphic Style Libraries ➪ 3D Effects, and the Symbol Libraries ➪ 3D Symbols commands.

CROSS-REF To learn about working with After Effects, turn to Chapters 30, 31, and 32.

To create a 3-D shape using the 3D Effects library, you first need to create a graphic path using a tool from the Tools palette. Then click a 3D Effects style to apply it to the graphic path. To create a graphic path, you can use one of the basic shape tools: the Rectangle tool, Rounded Rectangle tool, Ellipse tool, Polygon tool, or Star tool. Many graphic style libraries can be used to apply interesting fills to graphics. To create button and rollover graphics, use the Buttons and Rollovers library (Window ➪ Graphic Style Libraries ➪ Buttons and Rollovers). To use the Graphic Styles palette, choose Window ➪ Graphic Style Libraries and then select the palette that you want to display. You can also choose Window ➪ Graphic Styles to display the Graphic Styles library. Then click the Graphic Styles menu and choose Open Graphic Style Library and make a selection.

FIGURE 29.26

Illustrator allows you to easily create interesting symbols and graphics.

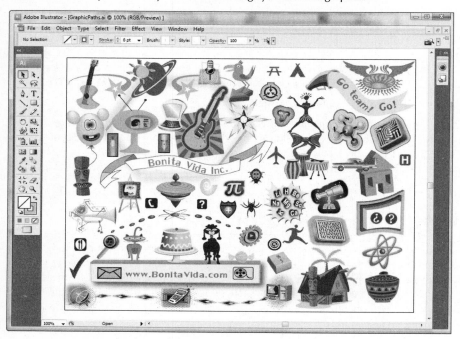

To create a 3-D shape using the 3D Symbols library, just click a 3-D symbol and drag it to the drawing area of your document. The example in Figure 29.26 uses the Celebration, Communication, Logo Elements, Mad Science, Maps, Mobile, Nature, Primitive, Retro, and Tiki libraries to create some of the graphics. You can access the symbol libraries by choosing Window ⇨ Symbol Libraries, and then selecting the library that you want. You can also choose Window ⇨ Symbols, click the Symbols menu, choose Open Symbol Library, and make your selection. Illustrator CS3 includes other interesting graphic style and symbol libraries.

 To move an object in front of or behind another object, select the object you want to move, and choose Object ⇨ Arrange. Then, choose either Bring to Front or Send to Back.

Another way to create interesting graphic effects is by drawing brush strokes using styles from the Brush Stroke libraries. To create a brush stroke, use either the Paintbrush or the Pencil tool to create a stroke in your document. Then choose Window ⇨ Brush Libraries and make a selection. The example in Figure 29.26 uses the Decorative_Banner and Seals strokes. You can also create a basic shape with either the Rectangle or Ellipse tool and stroke it with a brush stroke.

Copying a Shape from Illustrator

You can copy and paste a graphic shape from Illustrator to Photoshop. When you paste in Photoshop, a Paste dialog box appears, allowing you to choose how you want to paste the graphic shape. Choose Smart Object to have the object appear with all of its attributes, then click OK. The object appears with small boxes on each corner.

You can click and drag these boxes to scale or rotate the object. To flatten the object into a layer, double-click inside the object. You can copy filled selections from Photoshop and paste them into Illustrator as filled paths. When you copy an object created with the Shape or Pen tool in Photoshop, and paste it in Illustrator, a Paste Options dialog box appears, allowing you to specify that the compound shape is fully editable. Click OK. To have a Photoshop object appear in Illustrator as a path, fill or stroke the path with the desired option.

You can also copy and paste graphic objects from Illustrator into After Effects. To do this, copy the graphic object in Illustrator, launch After Effects, and create a new project. Choose Composition ➪ New Composition to create a new composition. Choose Layer ➪ New ➪ Solid to create a new solid. Then click the Timeline panel and choose Paste.

Creating Illustrator Shapes

Illustrator's drawing capabilities make it the perfect application to create intricate masks for Premiere Pro. The following example shows you how to create a simple graphic shape in Illustrator that you can use as a mask in Premiere Pro (see Figure 29.29).

Follow these steps to create a simple mask:

1. **Launch Illustrator, if it isn't running already.**
2. **Choose File ➪ New to create a new document.** In the New Document dialog box, click the New Document Profile drop-down menu and select Video & Film. Click OK to create a new document.
3. **Select the Rectangle, Ellipse, Polygon, or Star tool from the toolbox, as shown in Figure 29.27.**

FIGURE 29.27

Illustrator's Rectangle, Ellipse, Polygon, and Star tools

4. **Click and drag to create a shape, or Alt-click/Option-click to display the tool's dialog box.** In the dialog box that appears, make your adjustments.

5. **Click OK to create the shape.** Create at least one rectangle, ellipse, polygon, and star shape. Figure 29.28 shows a star shape, and the Star dialog box for the star shape. The shapes that you create are filled with whatever fill and stroke colors are selected in the toolbox. If you want, you can change the fill and stroke colors by double-clicking the Fill or Stroke color swatch in the toolbox. When the Color Picker appears, make your selection and click OK.

FIGURE 29.28

The Star dialog box allows you to specify the inner and outer radii, as well as the number of points you want your star shape to have.

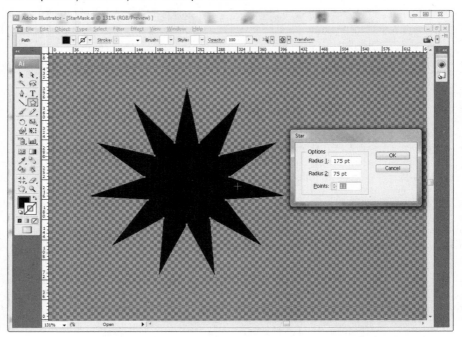

NOTE   You should experiment with different fill shades. Filling with black, white, and different shades of gray and colors will result in different effects in Premiere Pro. You should also try experimenting with a stroke and no fill. In the examples shown in Figures 29.29 and 29.30, the fill color is set to black.

6. **When you have a shape onscreen, experiment with a few of the Effect ➪ Distort &**
   Transform commands. These commands create interesting transformations, such as the
   following:

   ▪ To transform the star shape into a flower shape, use the Pucker & Bloat command.

   ▪ To transform the star shape into a blob shape, use the Roughen command.

   ▪ To transform the star shape into abstract art, use the Tweak command.

   ▪ To twirl the star shape, use the Twist command, as shown in Figure 29.29.

   ▪ To transform the star shape into a snowflake, use the Zig Zag command.

FIGURE 29.29

Use the Twist command to twist objects.

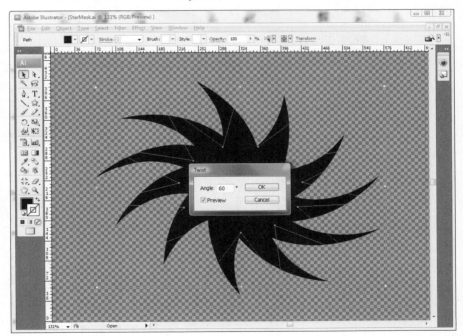

7. **Convert the star shape to a rectangle, rounded rectangle, or an ellipse.** Try using the
   Effect ➪ Convert to Shape ➪ Ellipse command to convert the star into an ellipse.

8. **You can also transform simple shapes created in Illustrator into more elaborate**
   shapes by bending and distorting them using the Arc command. With a graphic
   selected, choose Effect ➪ Warp ➪ Arc. By using the options in the Style drop-down menu
   in the Warp Options dialog box, you can apply an arch, bulge, shell, flag, wave, fish, rise,
   fisheye, inflate, squeeze, or twist distortion to a graphic.

9. **The Effect ⇨ Stylize commands (Drop Shadow, Inner Glow, Outer Glow, and Feather) allow you to add drop shadows, glows, or feathers to your graphic.** The Effect ⇨ Stylize ⇨ Round Corners command allows you to make round corners. The Effect ⇨ Stylize ⇨ Scribble command creates a scribble effect inside your graphic. Try experimenting with these styles.

10. **You can turn a polygon into a blob (as shown in Figure 29.30) using the Polygon tool and the Zig Zag command.** Click the Polygon tool in the Tools palette. Then Alt-click/Option-click the drawing area of your document to display the tool's dialog box. In the dialog box that appears, make your adjustments. Click OK to create a polygon. With the polygon selected, choose Effect ⇨ Distort & Transform ⇨ Zig Zag. In the Zig Zag dialog box, increase the size and reduce the amount of ridges. Then click the Absolute option below the Size slider, and the Smooth option in the Points section. Click the Preview check box to preview your blob. Make any additional changes you want, and then click OK to create the blob.

FIGURE 29.30

You can create a blob shape in Illustrator using the Polygon tool and the Zig Zag command.

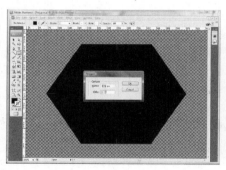

Using Illustrator Shapes as Masks in Premiere Pro

After you create graphic shapes and manipulate the shapes in Illustrator, you can import the shapes into Premiere Pro and use them as masks using the Track Matte Key effect. Figure 29.31 shows a Premiere Pro project using a twisted star shape (created in Illustrator) as a mask (matte). Follow these steps to create a Premiere Pro mask project using the Track Matte Key effect:

ON the DVD The Artbeats LM229 video clip is located in the Artbeats folder on the DVD that accompanies this book. You can find the StarTwistedMask.ai file in the MoreClips folder on the DVD that accompanies this book.

FIGURE 29.31

A Premiere Pro project using the Track Matte Key effect to display a video clip through a twirled star shape on an Illustrator background

1. **Launch Premiere Pro.** Choose File ➪ New ➪ Project.

2. **Choose Window ➪ Workspace ➪ Effects to display the Effects panel and the Effect Controls panel.** This displays all of the necessary panels for these steps.

3. **Choose File ➪ Import, locate a video clip to use with the mask, and click Open.** This example uses the Artbeats LM229 video clip.

4. **Drag the video clip from the Project panel to the Video 2 track in the Timeline panel.**

5. **Choose File ➪ Import, locate a file to use as the mask (matte), and click Open.** To extend the mask to the length of the video clip, click the end of the clip and drag right. This example uses the StarTwistedMask file that was created in Illustrator in the previous section.

6. **Drag the mask file from the Project panel to the Video 3 track in the Timeline panel.**

7. **Drag the Track Matte Key effect (located in the Keying bin) from the Effects panel to the video clip in the Video 2 track.** Click the triangle next to the Track Matte Key in the Effect Controls panel to display the options. Click the Matte drop-down menu and select Video 3. The Composite drop-down menu should be set to Matte Alpha and the Reverse check box should not be selected, as shown in Figure 29.31.

 You can find the Scribble.ai file that is used as the background in Figure 29.31 in the MoreClips folder on the DVD that accompanies this book.

8. **Choose File ⇨ Import to import a clip to appear in the background.** Drag the clip from the Project panel to the Video 1 track. Import a video clip, a Photoshop file, or an Illustrator file. (To extend the mask to the length of the video clip, click the end of the clip and drag right.) The example in Figure 29.31 imports an Illustrator file that was created to use as a background. This file (Scribble.ai) is on the DVD that accompanies this book. To create the Illustrator background file, create a new file with a rectangle. Then fill the rectangle with Graphic Style Scribble 22 (Scribble 22 is in the Scribble Effects Graphic Styles library). Illustrator has many wonderful graphic styles that you can use to create backgrounds. Try experimenting with them. Have fun! For more information on working with background mattes, turn to Chapter 15.

9. **Choose File ⇨ Import to import a sound clip.** Drag the sound clip from the Project panel to the Audio 1 track. The example in Figure 29.31 uses the SmartSound New Vista sound clip. This sound clip is in the SmartSound folder on the DVD that accompanies this book. If you need to shorten the sound clip, click the end of the sound clip and drag to the left. For more information on editing sound, turn to Chapter 7.

10. **Choose Sequence ⇨ Render Work Area or press Enter to render your movie.** Then press Play in the Program Monitor panel to view the movie.

11. **The mask (matte) file in the Video 3 track can be animated over time by setting keyframes for the Position, Scale, and Rotation effects, as shown in Figure 29.32.** Figure 29.33 shows a few frames from animating the mask file in the Video 3 track. For more information on using Motion video effects and setting keyframes, turn to Chapter 16.

12. **Choose File ⇨ Save to save your work in Premiere Pro format, and File ⇨ Export ⇨ Movie to save your file in a movie format.**

FIGURE 29.32

Setting keyframes for the Position, Scale, and Rotation effects in the Effect Controls panel can make for an interesting animation, as shown in Figure 29.33.

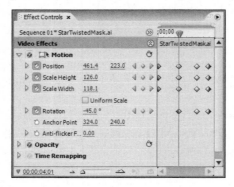

FIGURE 29.33

The results of animating the position, scale, and rotation of the mask file in the Video 3 track

Follow these steps to create a Premiere Pro mask project using the Image Matte Key effect (shown in Figure 29.34):

ON the DVD The Artbeats LM229 video clip is located in the Artbeats folder on the DVD that accompanies this book.

1. **Choose File ➪ Import, locate a file to use as the background, and click Open.** This example uses the Kuai video clip in the MoreClips folder in the DVD that accompanies this book.

2. **Drag the background video clip from the Project panel to the Video 1 track in the Timeline panel.**

FIGURE 29.34

This Premiere Pro project uses the Image Matte Key effect to display a video clip through a twirled Illustrator text shape on a video clip background.

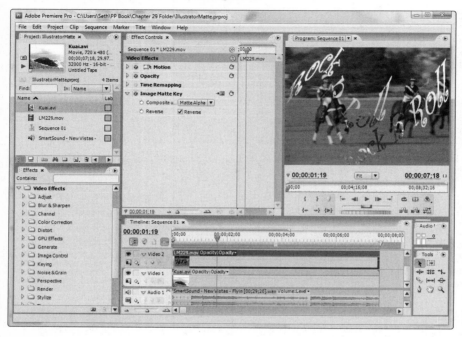

3. **Choose File ⇨ Import, locate a video clip to use with the mask, and click Open.** This example uses the Artbeats LM229 video clip.

4. **Drag the video clip from the Project panel to the Video 2 track in the Timeline panel.** If this video clip is longer than the background video clip, you can shorten it by clicking the end of the clip and dragging left.

5. **Choose File ⇨ Import, locate a sound file to use, and click Open.** This example uses the SmartSound New Vista sound clip. This sound clip is in the SmartSound folder on the DVD that accompanies this book.

6. **Drag the Image Matte Key effect (located in the Keying bin) from the Effects panel to the video clip in the Video 2 track.** The Image Matte Key option is a good choice to use when you would like a video clip to show through an Illustrator shape.

7. **Click the Image Matte Key Setup button in the Effect Controls panel.** When the Select a Matte Image dialog box appears, choose a mask file. This example uses the TwistedType.ai file (which was created in the section "Transforming and distorting using

the Effect commands," earlier in this chapter). Click Open to view the twisted type in the Monitor panel. Notice that the white areas on the outside of the text don't show up in the preview; only the black areas show through. The video clip shows through the black areas. If you want, you can reverse the effect (shown in Figure 29.34) by clicking the Reverse check box or by changing the Composite Using option. These options are found in the Image Matte key in the Effect Controls panel.

8. **Choose Sequence ⇨ Render Work Area or press Enter to render your movie.** Then press Play in the Program Monitor panel to view the movie.

9. **Choose File ⇨ Save to save your work in Premiere Pro format, and File ⇨ Export ⇨ Movie to save your file in a movie format.**

Creating a Mask Using Photoshop and Illustrator

You can create elaborate masks by combining the strengths of Adobe Photoshop and Adobe Illustrator. Start by digitizing a photograph with a scanner, or by capturing a photograph with a digital camera or camcorder, or by using a digital stock image. Many photo-finishing labs can develop your film, as well as archive the pictures on a DVD, CD, or floppy disk. Load the photograph into Photoshop for retouching and color correcting. Use the Photoshop brush tools and the Clone Stamp tool to retouch the image. Use the Image ⇨ Adjust command to color correct the image. Then load the file into Illustrator, and use one of the path-creation tools to create a path around the image area that you want to import into Premiere Pro. The example in Figure 29.35 uses Illustrator's Paintbrush tool with a Calligraphic brush to create paths. After the paths are created, you can import them into a Premiere Pro project. The Premiere Pro project in Figure 29.35 has a video clip running in the background.

Follow these steps to create a complex mask using both Photoshop and Illustrator:

1. **Digitize a photograph and open it in Photoshop.**

2. **Retouch and color correct the photograph, and then save the file in Photoshop format.**

3. **Choose Select ⇨ All, and then Edit ⇨ Copy.**

4. **Launch Adobe Illustrator and create a new Film & Video document.**

5. **Choose Edit ⇨ Paste to paste the copied Photoshop file into Illustrator.** (You can also choose File ⇨ Place.) Locate the digitized Photoshop image, and click Place to place the Photoshop file in Illustrator. Figure 29.36 shows the sample image used in this section.

6. **If the Layers palette is not onscreen, choose Window ⇨ Show Layers.**

ON the DVD If you want, you can load the sample image shown in Figure 29.36 (SeaglassNecklaces.psd) from the MoreClips folder on the DVD that accompanies this book.

FIGURE 29.35

A Premiere Pro project created by using a Photoshop photograph file and an Illustrator file

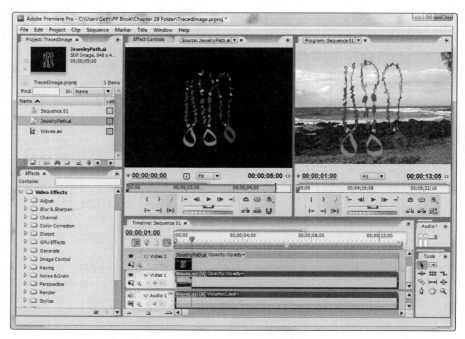

7. **In the Layers palette, double-click the layer.** The Layer Options dialog box appears, as shown in Figure 29.37.

8. **Click both the Lock and Dim image options to lock and dim the layer.** Make sure that the Dim option is set to 75 percent.

9. **Click OK for the effects to take place.**

10. **Click New Layer from the Layers palette menu to create a new layer.** In the Layer Options dialog box that appears, name the layer Image Mask. Do not click the Lock or Dim Images check boxes. Click OK.

11. **Select the Pen, Pencil, or Paintbrush tool.**

12. **Trace the dimmed image's outline.** When you are tracing the image, you might want to use various layers for different parts of the image. In Figure 29.35, an Image Mask layer was created for the basic information. Another layer was used for drawing beads, and another layer for drawing pendants. Figure 29.38 shows the Layers palette with the photograph dimmed in Layer 1, and a few path strokes created with the Paintbrush tool in other layers. To create the brush strokes, you can use the Calligraphic brush stroke, located in the Artistic Brush library (Window ➪ Artistic ➪ Artistic_Calligraphic).

FIGURE 29.36

A sample Photoshop file used to create a mask in Illustrator

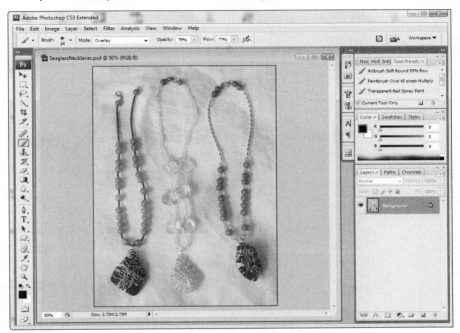

FIGURE 29.37

The Layer Options dialog box enables you to lock and dim a layer.

If you use the Pen tool for tracing, a small circle appears next to the tool when the starting and finishing points meet. When this happens, you can click to close the path.

When you are drawing, it's easier to see the image you are tracing if you trace with a stroke and no fill, as shown in Figure 29.38. If you draw with a fill, you won't see the image in the layer below, and in Premiere Pro you won't see the video in the track below the Illustrator file. To set the fill to None, click the Fill color swatch (the top overlapping square) in the toolbox and then click the third small square from the left (the one with the diagonal line) below the Fill color swatch. Click the Stroke color swatch (behind the Fill color swatch), and then click the first small square to set the stroke color to black. Choose Window ➪ Stroke to display the Stroke palette. The Stroke palette enables you to choose the width of your stroke.

The Layers palette with the dimmed image on one layer and the Paintbrush paths in other layers

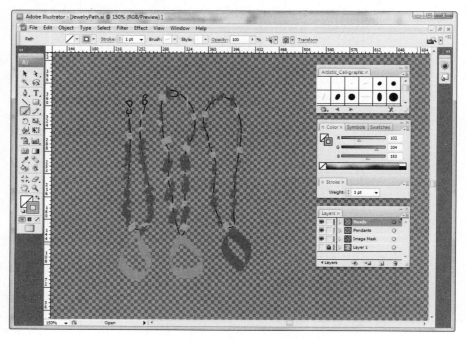

13. **After you create a few black strokes, you may want to hide the bottom layer with the image in it to see how your path strokes look.** Click the eye icon next to the layer you want to hide.

14. **When you finish tracing over the dimmed image, you can either hide it (as shown in Figure 29.39) or delete it.** If you delete it, you may first want to use the File ➪ Save As command to duplicate the file.

15. **Save your final file in Illustrator format.**

16. **Launch Premiere Pro, and create a new project.**

17. **Choose File ➪ Import.** Locate the Illustrator file you want to import, and click Open. This example uses the JewelryPath.ai file.

18. **Drag the Illustrator file from the Project panel to the Video 2 track in the Timeline panel.**

19. **Choose File ⇨ Import.** Locate a video clip, and click Open. This example uses the Waves video clip in the MoreClips folder on the DVD that accompanies this book. If you want, you can use an Illustrator or Photoshop background file and then use video effects with keyframes to animate the Illustrator file in the Video 2 track.

FIGURE 29.39

The traced image created in Illustrator

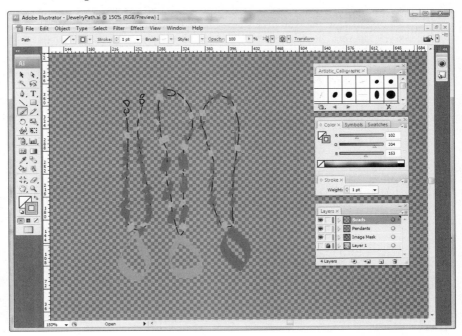

20. **Drag the video clip from the Project panel to the Video 1 track in the Timeline panel.** You should now have a background clip in the Video 1 track and an Illustrator file in the Video 2 track. To make the background more interesting, you can apply the Color Balance (HLS) effect and animate the effect over time by changing the hue. Press Enter to render the project.

21. **Click the Play button in the Program Monitor panel to preview the project.**

22. **Choose File ⇨ Save to save the Premiere Pro project in Premiere Pro format.** Choose File ⇨ Export ⇨ Movie to save the Premiere Pro project in a movie format.

ON the DVD If you want, you can load the JewelryPath.ai file from the MoreClips folder on the DVD that accompanies this book. You can find the Waves video clip in the MoreClips folder on the DVD that accompanies this book.

Summary

You can use Adobe Illustrator to create text and masks for Premiere Pro projects. This chapter covered the following topics:

- Illustrator features six type tools: the Type tool, Area Type tool, Path Type tool, Vertical Type tool, Vertical Area Type tool, and Vertical Type on a Path tool. You can convert Illustrator text into art to create your own custom text to use in a Premiere Pro project.

- You can create shapes in Illustrator using the Rectangle, Ellipse, Polygon, and Star tools. You can then alter the shapes using some of the Effect commands. You can convert these shapes into backgrounds and import them into Premiere Pro, and then animate them using Motion, Opacity, and other video effects.

- When creating masks using Illustrator, you can use the Alpha Adjust option when you only want the black or colored areas of the mask to appear.

- The Track Matte and the Image Matte Key effects options are useful when you want a video clip to show through an Illustrator image.

- You can create complex masks by using both Photoshop and Premiere Pro.

Chapter 30

Introduction to After Effects

Adobe Premiere Pro features a complete set of video-editing tools. However, from time to time, you may need to make a few quick edits in Adobe After Effects. After Effects is another digital-video-editing application created by Adobe Systems. It provides certain functionality that Premiere Pro does not, such as creating Bezier masks in the Composition panel (see Chapter 31), creating motion paths, and creating composite projects (see Chapter 32). If you want to create masks or special effects in After Effects, you may find it more convenient to import the video clips into After Effects and trim the clips (change the clips' in and out points) while you work in After Effects.

CROSS-REF See Chapter 31 to learn how to create masks in After Effects. Chapter 32 covers creating special effects in After Effects.

AVI movies, QuickTime movies, and Premiere Pro projects can be imported into After Effects for more video editing and compositing. After editing in After Effects, the work can be exported and saved as a Premiere Pro project. You can re-import it into Premiere Pro or export it from After Effects and save it in some other format. After Effects allows you to export your work and save it as an AVI or QuickTime movie; in MPEG-4, DV Stream, 3G, or Adobe Flash (SWF) format; or as a Premiere Pro project. You can also export your After Effects work as a sequence of separate graphic files. Later, you can import the sequence folder into Premiere Pro.

Many digital video producers use both Premiere Pro and After Effects to create a project. This chapter introduces you to trimming a video clip in After Effects using the Layer panel, as well as trimming in the Timeline panel. This chapter also shows you how to export clips from After Effects as Premiere Pro projects, AVI movies, QuickTime movies, and graphic sequences.

 For information on editing video clips using Premiere Pro, refer to Chapters 6 and 12.

Trimming in After Effects: What's It All About?

In After Effects, you can use either the Layer panel or the Timeline panel to trim a video clip. If you want, you can trim a clip from a Premiere Pro project. You can also trim a video clip at the beginning or the end. When you trim at the beginning of the video clip, you change the clip's *in point*. When you trim at the end, you change the clip's *out point*. As in Premiere Pro, even though the in and out points change after editing, the original in and out points are always accessible, and you can re-edit the clip at any time.

NOTE When you trim the in point in the Layer panel, the clip is edited in the Timeline panel, but its starting time in the composition doesn't change. Also, when you trim a still image, only the duration of the still image changes, not the actual still image.

Creating a new After Effects project

Trimming video clips in the After Effects Timeline panel is easy. To trim a video clip using the After Effects Timeline panel, you need to have an After Effects project onscreen with at least one video clip in the Timeline panel.

Follow these steps to create a new After Effects project and import video clips:

1. **Launch After Effects.** Choose File ⇨ New ⇨ New Project to create a new project.

2. **Choose Composition ⇨ New Composition.** The Composition Settings dialog box appears, as shown in Figure 30.1.

3. **In the Composition Settings dialog box, you can set the frame size to the same size as that of the project.** Choose a preset, and notice that the Width and Height values automatically change. If you want, you can change the Frame Rate and Resolution settings. If you are working with a project that uses a non-DV preset, select the appropriate non-DV preset from the Preset drop-down menu in the Composition Settings dialog box. For DVD output, choose a DV preset.

4. **Click OK to close the Composition Settings dialog box.**

5. **Choose File ⇨ Import ⇨ File.** Locate a video clip to use, and click Open. If you need to select more than one file, press and hold the Ctrl/⌘ key. To import various files, choose File ⇨ Import ⇨ Multiple Files. Locate clips and select them. When you have selected all of the video clips, still images, and sound clips you are going to use in the project, click the Done button.

FIGURE 30.1

The Composition Settings dialog box enables you to set the frame size of your project.

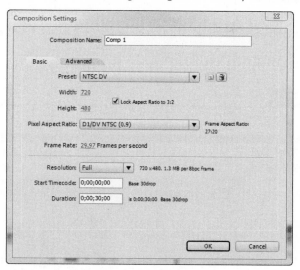

ON the DVD If you want, you can follow along using the video clips found in the FilmDisc folder on the DVD that accompanies this book. The video clips are FilmDisc cl0113 and FilmDisc na0110.

6. **Drag the video clips from the Project panel to the Composition panel.** The items appear in layers in the Timeline panel. To change the order of the clips, just drag one layer above another. Figure 30.2 shows the After Effects panels.

Importing Photoshop Files into After Effects

You can also load an Adobe Photoshop layered file into After Effects by choosing File ➪ Import ➪ File. In the Import File dialog box, to import the Photoshop file with all of its layers, choose Composition from the Import Kind drop-down menu. Then select a footage dimension and click OK. A folder appears in the After Effects Project panel with all of the layers. You can also import a Photoshop layered file with just one layer. In the Layer Options section of the Import dialog box, you can select the Merged Layers option to have the Photoshop layers merged together, or you can select the Choose Layer option to choose which Photoshop layer you would like to import. After you make your selection, choose a footage dimension and click OK. Only one layer is imported into the Project panel in After Effects. For more information on working with Adobe Photoshop, turn to Chapter 28, which also shows you how to export a frame from After Effects as a Photoshop file with layers.

7. **Choose File ⇨ Import ⇨ File.** Locate a sound clip to use. Click Open. Drag the sound clip from the Project panel to the Timeline panel. This example uses SmartSound's American Sunrise sound clip. This clip is in the SmartSound folder on the DVD that accompanies this book.

8. **Choose Composition ⇨ Preview.** Make a preview selection to preview your work.

9. **Choose File ⇨ Save to save your project in the After Effects format.**

FIGURE 30.2

The After Effects panels

Creating a new After Effects project and importing a Premiere Pro project

A Premiere Pro project can be imported into After Effects and then trimmed in After Effects. Afterwards, the Premiere Pro project can be re-imported into Premiere Pro or exported as a movie.

Follow these steps to import a Premiere Pro project into an After Effects project:

1. **Launch After Effects.** Choose File ⇨ New ⇨ New Project to create a new project. Then choose Composition ⇨ New Composition to choose the settings for the project.

2. **To load a Premiere Pro project into After Effects, choose File ⇨ Import ⇨ File.**

3. **In the Import File dialog box, locate the Premiere Pro project you want to import and click Open.**

4. **In the Premiere Pro Importer dialog box, shown in Figure 30.3, click the Select Sequence drop-down menu.** Make a selection. Leave the Import Audio check box selected to import audio.

FIGURE 30.3

The Premiere Pro Importer dialog box allows you to choose which Premiere Pro sequence you want to import into After Effects.

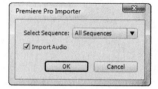

5. **In the Premiere Pro Importer dialog box, click OK.** After Effects imports the Premiere Pro project, which appears in the After Effects Project panel.

6. **Double-click the Premiere Pro project Sequence file to have all of the Premiere Pro files displayed in the Timeline panel and Composition panel.** The Timeline panel appears with layers. The layers are the video and sound tracks from the Premiere Pro project. The items in the layers can be viewed in the Composition panel.

Trimming Using the Timeline Panel

When you have an After Effects project with the items you need in the Timeline panel, you can trim them using the Timeline panel. After Effects makes this an easy task, where you can trim either by dragging the in and out points in the layer duration bar or by using the current-time indicator.

Trimming with the layer duration bar

A video clip's duration in the Timeline panel displays as a layer duration bar. Figure 30.4 shows the layer duration bar before trimming. Figure 30.5 shows the layer duration bar after trimming. Also notice that the changes are updated in the Info panel.

Here's how to trim a video clip using the layer duration bar:

- **To trim the in point:** Click at the beginning of a clip and drag to the right to change the in point and trim the video clip.

- **To trim the out point:** Click at the end of a clip and drag to the left to change the out point and trim the video clip.

FIGURE 30.4

The layer duration bar of a video clip before trimming

FIGURE 30.5

Trimming the in point and out point using the Timeline panel

Trimming with the current-time indicator

Follow these steps to trim a clip at the current-time indicator:

1. **Click the layer in which your video clip resides.**

2. **Move the current-time indicator to the point you want to trim.**

3. **Trim the in or out point as follows:**

   - To trim the in point, press Alt+[/Option+[.

   - To trim the out point, press Alt+]/Option+].

Trimming Using the Layer Panel

Trimming in the After Effects Layer panel is similar to trimming in Premiere Pro's Monitor panel, except that trimming a clip's in point in the After Effect's Layer panel doesn't affect the clip's relative starting position in the Timeline panel. In other words, no gap appears in front of it when you remove frames from the clip's in point. Follow these steps to trim using the Layer panel:

1. **Choose File ➪ New ➪ New Project to create a new project.** You also can choose to load a project.

2. **Choose Composition ➪ New Composition.** The Composition Settings dialog box appears.

3. **Set the frame size to be the same as the size of the project.** Choose a preset, and notice that the Width and Height values automatically change. If you want, you can change the Frame Rate and Resolution values.

4. **If you want to import a Premiere Pro project into After Effects, skip to step 7.** You can also copy and paste a video clip from Premiere Pro's Timeline panel into After Effects' Timeline panel, and vice versa.

5. **To import multiple clips into After Effects, choose File ➪ Import ➪ Multiple Files.** When the Import Multiple Files dialog box appears, select a file. Click Open to import the selected file. Continue selecting files and choosing Open until you import all of the files you need. To close the dialog box, click Done.

> **TIP** You can choose File ➪ Import ➪ Capture in Adobe Premiere Pro to capture, save, and then import some new footage into your After Effects project. To import the captured video from Premiere Pro to After Effects, select the clip from the Project panel in Premiere Pro and then copy it. After you copy the clip, activate the Project panel in After Effects and paste the captured clip into the Project panel. To use the clip in your After Effects project, just drag it from the Project panel to the Timeline panel.

6. **Drag the imported items from the Project panel to the Composition panel.** The items appear in the Timeline panel.

7. **To import a Premiere Pro project into After Effects, choose File ➪ Import ➪ File.** When the Import File dialog box appears, select a Premiere Pro file. In the Import Project dialog box that appears, select a Premiere Pro sequence to import and then click OK. The Premiere Pro project appears in the After Effects Project panel.

8. **Double-click the Premiere Pro Sequence file in the Project panel to display the Premiere Pro project Sequence files in the Composition panel and the Timeline panel.** The Timeline panel appears with layers representing the video and sound tracks from the Premiere Pro project.

9. **To display the Layer panel, shown in Figure 30.6, either double-click the layer in the Timeline panel or select the layer and choose Layer ➪ Open Layer.** The Layer panel opens.

10. **Click the In and Out buttons, shown in Figure 30.6, to trim the clip.** Just move the current-time indicator to where you want to set the in or out point, and then click the In or Out button in the Layer panel.

The trimmed portion of your video footage appears in the Timeline panel as outlines, as shown in Figure 30.7.

FIGURE 30.6

Trimming a clip using the In and Out buttons in the Layer panel in After Effects

FIGURE 30.7

A trimmed clip appears in the Timeline panel.

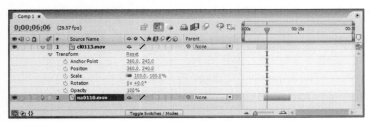

Exporting Your After Effects Files

If you want to export your After Effects work so that you import it into Premiere Pro, you can save the After Effects file in Adobe Premiere Pro Project format, as an AVI movie or QuickTime movie, or as an *image sequence,* which is a series of separate graphic files, rather than a stream of video frames.

To export your After Effects projects and save them in Adobe Premiere Pro Project format, choose File ➪ Export ➪ Adobe Premiere Pro Project. In the Export As Adobe Premiere Pro Project dialog box that appears, name your file and click Save.

To export your After Effects projects and save them in a movie format, choose the File ➪ Export command, or the Composition ➪ Make Movie command.

NOTE   You can choose to export the entire After Effects project, or you can just export a section of the project. To export a portion of your After Effects project, click the Timeline panel and move the work area bar over the area you want to save (the work area bar appears where the current-time indicator is located).

Exporting an AVI movie and a QuickTime movie from After Effects

Almost any computer can read QuickTime and AVI movies. To quickly save your After Effects project as either an AVI or QuickTime movie, follow these steps:

1. **Click the Timeline panel to activate it, if necessary.**

2. **Choose File ➪ Export ➪ AVI, or File ➪ Export ➪ QuickTime Movie.** When exporting an AVI movie, the AVI Settings dialog box appears, as shown in Figure 30.8. When exporting a QuickTime movie, the Movie Settings dialog box appears, as shown in Figure 30.9.

FIGURE 30.8

The AVI Settings dialog box allows you to choose compression settings for an AVI movie.

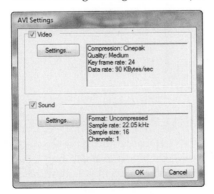

 The File ⇄ Export command also allows you to export your After Effects project as a Flash video.

3. **In the settings dialog box, click the Settings button in the Video section.** The Compression Settings dialog box appears.

4. **In the Compression Settings dialog box, click the top drop-down menu to choose a type of compression.**

5. **Set any desired options in the Movie Settings dialog box that appears when exporting a QuickTime movie.**

   ▦ Click the Filter button to apply a filter (video effect) to your work.

   ▦ Click the Size button to apply a custom size to your work.

   ▦ Click the Sound Settings button to change the sound settings.

6. **Click OK to set the compression settings.** Close the dialog box.

7. **In the Save As dialog box, name your movie.** Click Save.

FIGURE 30.9

The Movie Settings dialog box allows you to choose compression settings for a QuickTime movie.

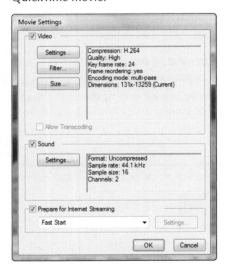

Exporting an image sequence from After Effects

A quick way to save your After Effects work in a sequence format is to use the File ⇄ Export command. You can save your sequence file in Photoshop format. A Photoshop sequence file can be imported into Premiere Pro or Adobe Photoshop for more editing. Follow these steps to save your work as an image sequence using the File ⇄ Export command:

Before you begin, create a new folder on your hard drive and name it. You can use this folder to save your sequence files.

1. **Click the Timeline panel to activate it, if necessary.**

2. **Choose File ⇨ Export ⇨ Image Sequence.** The Save As dialog box appears.

3. **Save your sequence image in the new folder you created.** All of the sequence files are saved in the folder.

4. **Click Save.** The Export Image Sequence Settings dialog box appears, as shown in Figure 30.10.

5. **Select a format option type (BMP, JPEG, MacPaint, Photoshop, PICT, PNG, QuickTime Image, SGI, TGA, or TIFF).** You can also set the frames per second. By default, the Frames per Second option is set to Best. If you want to use a different option, click the menu.

 For best results, save your image sequence in Photoshop format if you want to import it into Premiere Pro.

FIGURE 30.10

The Export Image Sequence Settings dialog box

6. **Click the Options button in the Export Image Sequence Settings dialog box to view and set the compression and color options.** Click OK to exit compression and color options and return to the Export Image Sequence Settings dialog box.

7. **In the Export Image Sequence Settings dialog box, click OK to create a sequence.** The Export dialog box displays how long the sequence will be and how many frames will be created in the sequence.

 Turn to the end of this chapter to learn how to import the sequence into Premiere Pro.

The Make Movie command

The Make Movie command offers precise control over your rendering options. For better-quality files, use this command to save your After Effects project as a movie file or an image sequence file. Follow these steps to save your work using the Make Movie command.

 If you are outputting to a sequence, create a new folder in which to save your sequence frames before naming and saving your file.

 You can choose to export either the entire After Effects project or just a section of the After Effects project. To export a portion of your After Effects work, click the Timeline panel and move the work area bar over the area you want to save (the work area bar appears where the current-time indicator is located).

1. Click the Timeline panel to activate it.

2. **Choose Composition ⇨ Make Movie, or Composition ⇨ Pre-Render.** The Render Queue panel appears, as shown in Figure 30.11, and enables you to change the Render settings and the output module.

FIGURE 30.11

The Render Queue panel allows you to adjust the render output settings.

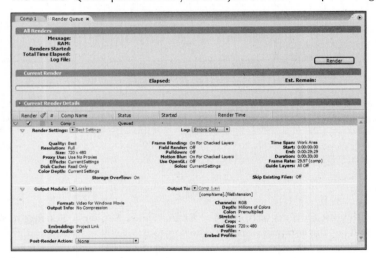

3. **To view and change the render settings, click the current render settings to display the Render Settings dialog box.**

4. **In the Render Settings dialog box, choose the resolution with which you want your work to be saved by clicking the Resolution menu.** Be careful not to use a resolution higher than what you are working with, because your work will appear blurry. You can choose a resolution lower than what you are working with. You may want to reduce the resolution of your work if you want to reduce the file size of the final movie, which may be an issue if you are outputting to the Web or e-mailing your movie to someone.

5. **In the Render Settings dialog box, click the Time Span drop-down menu to specify whether you want to output a designated work area, an entire composition, or a custom area.**

6. Click OK to close the Render Settings dialog box.

7. **Double-click Output Module to view.** Change the Output Module settings.

8. In the Output Module Settings dialog box, click the Format drop-down menu to select a format in which to save your work.

9. In the Output Module Settings dialog box, click the Channels and Depth drop-down menus to select how many colors you want your movie to be saved with.

10. In the Output Module Settings dialog box, click the Audio Output section to select the audio output you want.

11. In the Output Module Settings dialog box, click OK to close the dialog box.

12. When you are ready to output your After Effects work, click the Render button in the Render Queue panel.

Importing After Effects Files into Premiere Pro

To import an After Effects file that was saved in Premiere Pro Project format into Premiere Pro, simply choose File ⇨ Open.

To load a movie created in After Effects or an image sequence file into Premiere Pro, you need to create a new Premiere Pro project and import the file. Follow these steps to import a file:

1. **In Premiere Pro, choose File ⇨ New ⇨ New Project to create a new Premiere Pro project.**

2. **Choose File ⇨ Import.**

3. **Locate the AVI file or QuickTime file.**

4. **Click Open.** The file appears in the Project panel, ready for you to drag it to a video track in the Timeline panel.

Follow these steps to import a Photoshop sequence file (that was created in After Effects) into Premiere Pro:

1. **In Premiere Pro, choose File ⇨ New ⇨ New Project to create a new Premiere Pro project.**

2. **Choose File ⇨ Import.**

3. **In the Import dialog box, locate the Sequence folder.**

4. **Click the Import Folder button.** The Sequence folder appears in the Project panel. You can now drag it to a video track in the Timeline panel.

Summary

If you import clips into After Effects to create special effects, you may also want to edit the in and out points of the clips while you are in After Effects. Later, you can import the clips into Premiere Pro as AVI movies, QuickTime movies, or a sequence of separate graphic files. This chapter covered the following topics:

- In After Effects, you can trim clips in the Timeline panel or the Layer panel.

- Clips can be trimmed by clicking the edge of a clip and then dragging, or pressing a keyboard command. To trim the in point, press Alt+[/Opt+[. To trim the out point, press Alt+]/Option+].

- To import a sequence of graphics created in After Effects into Premiere Pro, you can choose File ➪ Import. In the Import dialog box, you can locate the file and click the Import Folder button.

Chapter 31

Working with Masks in Adobe After Effects

Matte effects are undoubtedly one of the more interesting special effects provided by Adobe Premiere Pro. In Chapters 14 and 15, you learned how to use mattes to hide portions of one video clip in a track behind the masked area of a shape in another video track.

If you want to create a matte effect in Premiere Pro, one technique is to create a shape in another program to use as a mask and import it into Premiere Pro. Although this is a rather straightforward and simple process, it does not enable you to create the mask at the same time as previewing the clip with which it will be used. Nor does it enable you to change the matte's shape as the clip runs.

If you need to create sophisticated matte effects, you can turn to Adobe After Effects. In After Effects, you can create masks using the After Effects Pen tool, edit them, and animate them over time. You can also import Adobe Illustrator and Adobe Photoshop files into After Effects to be used as masks. After Effects also enables you to import Illustrator and Photoshop paths or Photoshop alpha channels to be used as masks.

This chapter looks at After Effects' masking options. It also discusses the features that Premiere Pro lacks but which you still may want to use to add interesting and unusual matte effects to Premiere Pro. To do this, you can import a Premiere Pro project into After Effects and use After Effects' masking capabilities to add pizzazz to your clips.

Understanding After Effects Masks

You can load a video clip or an entire Premiere Pro project into After Effects and isolate an area by using a mask so that the viewer sees only a portion of the video clip or project. In After Effects, masks can be created using *paths*. A path is similar to a wireframe line onscreen that can be used to create anything from shapes with sharp corners to flowing waves created from perfect curves. After Effects allows you to create three types of masks: Rectangular, Elliptical, and RotoBezier. To create a rectangular-shaped mask, use the Rectangular Mask tool in the Tools palette. To create an elliptical-shaped mask, use the Elliptical Mask tool in the Tools panel. If you are creating any other shaped mask, you can work with either a Bezier or RotoBezier mask. To create a Bezier mask, you can use the Pen tool, which is found in the Tools panel. Note that when you use the Pen tool in After Effects, you can also select the RotoBezier option. The RotoBezier option enables you to more easily create curves.

The Pen tool in After Effects is quite similar to the Pen tool in Illustrator and Photoshop. You can edit the path using the Pen +, Pen –, and Convert tools. These tools reside in the same location in the Toolbox as the Pen tool. You can use the Selection tool (arrow icon) in the Tools panel to edit a point on the path by clicking the point and dragging it to the position you want. If you double-click the path with the Selection tool, you can move, scale, or rotate the path as a whole. The effects of a mask display in the Composition panel. You can edit masks in either the Composition panel or the Layer panel. Masks can be altered over time by using the Timeline panel.

Creating Oval and Rectangular Masks

You can have a lot of fun creating interesting effects with masks. A quick way to create a mask in After Effects is to use either the mask tools (the Elliptical Mask tool or the Rectangular Mask tool) in the toolbar or the Layer ➪ Mask ➪ New Mask command.

Figure 31.1 shows a frame that includes a video clip with an oval mask that is used on the video clip's perimeter. The mask in Figure 31.1 is created using the Layer ➪ Mask ➪ New Mask command. In Figure 31.1, a still Photoshop image is placed in the background. For an added effect, the Liquify command (Effect ➪ Distort ➪ Liquify) is applied to the background still image.

ON the DVD When creating a mask in After Effects for the first time, you may want to use a video clip for the mask and a still image as the background. If you want, you can use the video clip of the snowboarder and the Crystal background image used in this section. The snowboarder video clip is Artbeats RL113. It is found in the Artbeats folder on the DVD that accompanies this book. The Crystal background still image is found in the MoreClips folder on the DVD.

Here's how to create an oval or rectangular mask in After Effects using the Layer ➪ Mask ➪ New Mask command:

1. **Launch After Effects.**
2. **Choose File ⇨ New ⇨ New Project to create a new project.**
3. **Choose Composition ⇨ New Composition to create a new composition.**
4. **In the New Composition dialog box, set the frame size.** Click OK.

FIGURE 31.1

This After Effects frame is created using an oval mask. You can see the mask options in the Timeline panel.

5. **Choose File ⇨ Import ⇨ File.**
6. **Choose File ⇨ Import ⇨ File to import a clip to use in the background.** Alternatively, import a still image to use as the background (shown in Figure 31.2). When creating a mask, it is easier to view the effects of the mask if you have a background that you can see through the transparent areas of the mask. Locate the still image or video clip that you want to import. In this example, when importing the CrystalBackground.psd file, select Footage from the Import As drop-down menu. Do not select the Photoshop Sequence check box. Click Open.

NOTE   If you want, you can copy a clip from the Project or Timeline panel in Premiere Pro and paste it into either the Project or Timeline panel of After Effects.

FIGURE 31.2

The Photoshop still image imported to use as a background

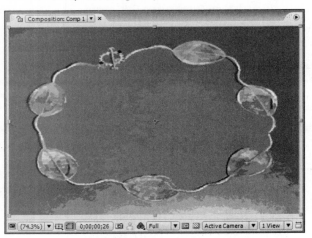

7. **When the imported background clip appears in the Project panel, drag it to the Timeline panel.**

8. **To apply an effect to the background clip, choose a command from the Effect menu.** In Figure 31.3, the Effect ⇨ Distort ⇨ Liquify command is applied to the Photoshop still image. In this example, you can click and drag the image areas you want to distort using the Liquify effect. The controls for the Liquify effect appear in the Effect Controls panel. You can adjust the controls to change the effect. Figure 31.4 shows the Effect Controls panel. After you apply an effect to the background, click the lock column to the left of the triangle next to the background clip, so that the background clip is not accidentally affected when you begin working with the video clip you are masking.

NOTE   If you want, you can create your own background using the commands in the Effect menu.

ON the DVD   You can use one of the video clips found on the DVD that accompanies this book. The snowboarder video clip used in Figure 31.1 is Artbeats RL113. It is found in the Artbeats folder on the DVD. You can also use a video clip of a skydiver from the Artbeats folder on the DVD. The skydiver video clip is Artbeats RL104.

9. **Choose File ⇨ Import ⇨ File to import a video clip you want to mask.**

10. **In the Import File dialog box, select a file that you want to mask.** Set the Import As menu to Footage. Click Open. The imported video clip appears in the Project panel.

The Photoshop still image (shown in Figure 31.2) after distorting it with the Liquify effect

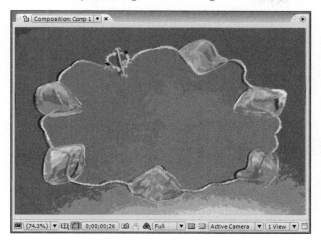

Adjusting the controls in the Effect Controls panel changes the way an effect appears.

11. **Click and drag the imported video clip that you will mask to the middle of the Composition panel.** Not only does the video clip appear in the Composition panel, but it also appears in the Timeline panel. This clip should appear on top of the background clip.

12. **In the Timeline panel, click the triangle next to the name of the video clip to display its options.** Notice that the Mask option is not currently available.

13. **To add a mask in the shape of the selected video clip, choose Layer ⇨ Mask ⇨ New Mask.** Notice that in the Timeline panel, the selected video clip now has a Masks option.

NOTE   You can use the Rectangular Mask tool in the toolbar to create a rectangular-shaped mask. To create an elliptical-shaped mask, use the Elliptical Mask tool in the Tools panel. See the following step-by-step instructions to learn how.

14. **Click the triangle next to the word *Masks* in the Timeline panel.** Then click the triangle next to the word *Mask 1* to reveal the Mask 1 options. The options are Mask Path, Mask Feather, Mask Opacity, and Mask Expansion.

15. **To change the shape of the mask, click Shape (next to Mask Path in the Timeline panel).** Alternatively, choose Layer ⇨ Mask ⇨ Mask Shape. The Mask Shape dialog box appears, as shown in Figure 31.5.

FIGURE 31.5

The Mask Shape dialog box enables you to select a shape for your mask.

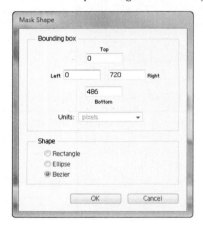

16. **To convert the mask to an ellipse, select the Ellipse option in the Mask Shape dialog box.** Don't change the Bounding box values, and leave the Units menu set to pixels. Click OK to see the effects of the mask in the Composition panel.

17. **To feather the mask (to soften the edges of the mask), enter a value in the Mask Feather section in the Timeline panel.** Alternatively choose Layer ⇨ Mask ⇨ Mask Feather. In the Mask Feather dialog box (shown in Figure 31.6), enter a feather value and click OK. Figure 31.7 shows the oval mask after applying a very large feather of 405 pixels. Notice how translucent the video clip has become, so that you can even see the background through the mask.

18. **To preview the effect of the mask over time, move the current-time indicator along the Timeline.**

19. **Save your file by choosing File ⇨ Save.**

    If you want, you can continue editing the mask using the Mask 1 options. For more information on editing a mask, proceed to the next section.

FIGURE 31.6

The Mask Feather dialog box allows you to enter a feather value so that the edges of the mask are softer. The larger the feather, the more transparent the mask becomes.

FIGURE 31.7

The video clip with a mask from Figure 31.1 after applying a feather of 405 pixels

Creating a Star Mask and Other Masks

Here's how to create a star mask in After Effects using the Star tool:

1. **Launch After Effects.**
2. **Choose File ⇨ New ⇨ New Project to create a new project.**
3. **Choose Composition ⇨ New Composition to create a new composition.**
4. **In the New Composition dialog box, set the frame size.** Click OK.
5. **Choose File ⇨ Import ⇨ File to import a video clip you want to mask.**

6. **In the Import File dialog box, select a file that you want to mask.** Set the Import As menu to Footage. Click Open. The imported video clip appears in the Project panel.

7. **Drag the clip from the Project panel to either the Composition panel or the Timeline panel.**

8. **Choose File ⇨ Import ⇨ File to import a video clip to use in the background.** Import a still image to use as the background. After you import the background clip, remember to drag it from the Project panel to the Timeline panel. The background clip must be below the mask clip in order for you to view the mask.

> **TIP** If desired, you can create your own background using the After Effects Brush tool. To use the Brush tool, start by choosing Layer ⇨ New ⇨ Solid. In the Solid Footage Settings dialog box, name the solid and set the presets. Then click OK. When the solid appears in the Timeline panel, double-click it to display the solid in the Layer panel. Then select the brush from the Tools panel and begin painting. Use the Paint panel to change the painting color and brush size.

9. **To create a star mask (shown in Figure 31.8), click the Star tool in the Tools panel.** Click and drag the clip in the Composition panel. To edit the mask, click the points on the edge of the mask with the Selection tool. To feather the mask, either enter a value in the Mask Feather section in the Timeline panel or choose Layer ⇨ Mask ⇨ Mask Feather. For more information on editing a mask, go to the next section.

FIGURE 31.8

After Effects has a Star tool that allows you to create masks in the shape of a star.

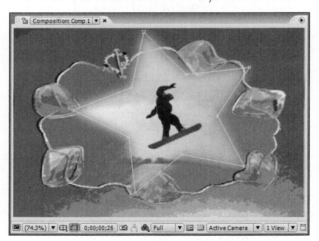

10. **To create an ellipse mask, click the Ellipse tool.** Click and drag the clip in the Composition panel. To create a rectangle mask, click the Rectangle tool instead.

 Not only can you create masks with After Effects tools, but you can also copy shapes and paths from Photoshop and Illustrator into After Effects to use as a mask.

11. **After you create a path or a shape in Illustrator or Photoshop, choose Edit ⇨ Copy.** In After Effects, you should have a background and a video clip to mask in the Timeline panel. The example in Figure 31.9 uses Photoshop's Shape tool with a tree shape to create a mask for After Effects.

You can copy a shape from Photoshop and paste it into After Effects to use as a mask.

Editing a Mask

After you create a mask, you can edit the mask by using the Layer menu and either the Layer panel or the Composition panel, along with the Selection tool in the Tools panel. You can also edit a mask by using the Mask options in the Timeline panel. (See the preceding section to review creating simple elliptical and rectangular masks.) Here are a few mask-editing tips:

- **To edit the mask, you must first select it.** If the mask isn't selected, you can select it by double-clicking the name of the clip you are working on in the Timeline panel. In the Layer panel that appears, click the path to select it. You can also select a mask by clicking it in the Timeline panel.

- **You can edit the mask in the Layer panel or the Composition panel.** If you change the path in the Layer panel, you can see the effect of the mask on the video clip in the Composition panel. Figure 31.10 shows the path and the mask in the Layer panel.

■ **You can edit a mask by using the Mask options in the Timeline panel.** In the Timeline panel, click the triangle next to the clip with the mask that you want to edit. When the masks for that clip appear, click the triangle next to the mask that you want to edit. The mask options allow you to invert the mask, edit the shape, change the opacity, or expand the mask. They also allow you to soften the edges of the mask.

FIGURE 31.10

The Layer panel shows the mask as a path.

Directional Line   Anchor Point

Here's how to edit a mask:

1. **Start by selecting in the Timeline panel the mask that you want to edit.** The mask should be displayed in the Composition panel.

2. **With the mask selected in the Timeline panel, you can choose Layer ➪ Mask ➪ Free Transform Points to transform the mask.** Notice that in the Composition panel, the mask appears with a bounding box with handles around it. In the Composition panel, click and drag one of the handles to increase or decrease the size of the mask. Move the mouse over one of the handles, and wait for the cursor to change to a curved line with arrows at either end. Then drag in the direction you want to rotate the mask. To activate the changes, double-click inside the mask shape in the Composition panel.

TIP   If you want to cancel the changes you made to your mask, choose Layer ➪ Mask ➪ Reset Mask to reset the mask to its original state. If desired, you can remove the mask by choosing Layer ➪ Mask ➪ Remove Mask and then choosing Layer ➪ Mask ➪ New Mask to create a new mask and start over again.

3. **To resize a mask using the Selection tool, choose the Selection tool from the toolbar.** Then click and drag one of the four corners of the mask in either the Composition panel or Layer panel. To display the mask in the Layer panel, double-click the clip in the Timeline panel. To keep the proportions of the mask as you change the size of the mask, press and hold the Shift key as you drag.

4. **To increase or decrease the expansion of a mask, click and drag the Mask Expansion values.** The Mask Expansion values are found in the Timeline panel in the Mask section of the selected video clip.

5. **To change the shape of a mask, use the Layer ⇨ Mask ⇨ Mask Shape command or the Mask Shape option in the Timeline panel.**

6. **To display the mask's path in the Layer panel, double-click the video clip's name in the Timeline panel or double-click inside the mask.** The mask appears as a path in the Layer panel. To display the anchor points, you may need to click the path with the Selection tool found in the Tools panel.

7. **To edit the path, click an anchor point, shown in Figure 31.11, using the Selection tool.** Then press an arrow key on your keyboard to move the anchor point up, down, right, or left. As you edit the path, the mask in the Composition panel is affected. Clicking and moving the directional line in the oval path changes the shape of the curve.

FIGURE 31.11

You can edit an oval path by moving anchor points and directional lines.

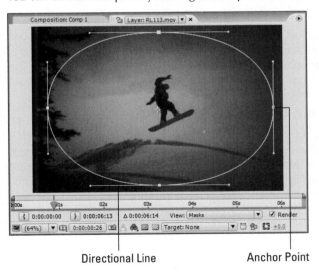

Directional Line   Anchor Point

8. **To display the mask's path in the Composition panel, double-click Comp 1 in the Project panel.** Click the mask with the Selection tool to select it.

9. **Click and drag inside the mask with the Selection tool to move the mask.** Click the edge of the mask to display the path of the mask.

10. **With the Selection tool, click either an anchor point or directional line to edit the path.**

11. **Click and hold the Pen tool in the Tools palette to display the Add Vertex tool, Delete Vertex tool, and Convert Vertex tool.** Use the Add Vertex tool to add an anchor point to the path. Use the Delete Vertex tool to delete an anchor point. Use the Convert Vertex tool to convert a curved anchor point to a straight anchor point and vice versa.

12. **With the mask in the Timeline panel, change the opacity of the mask by choosing Layer ⇨ Mask ⇨ Opacity.** In the Opacity dialog box, set the opacity you want. Click OK, and notice the change in the Composition panel. You can also change the opacity of a mask by using the Mask Opacity option in the Timeline panel.

13. **To soften your mask's edges, you can apply a feather by choosing Layer ⇨ Mask ⇨ Mask Feather.** In the Feather Mask dialog box, type a small value to create a small feather. A large value results in a large feather. You can also feather a mask by using the Mask Feather option in the Timeline panel.

14. **To adjust the colors of the clip, you can use any of the Effect ⇨ Color Correction commands.** After you apply a command, use the Effect Controls panel to adjust the controls for that effect.

15. **To stroke the mask, choose Effect ⇨ Generate ⇨ Stroke.** Use the Effect Controls panel to set the stroke color, width, and opacity. You can also set a fill color by choosing Effect ⇨ Generate ⇨ Fill. Again, use the Effect Controls panel to set the fill color and opacity, and use a fill mask.

16. **Choose Effect ⇨ Perspective ⇨ Basic 3D to swivel and tilt the mask in 360 degrees.** To apply a shadow to the mask, choose Effect ⇨ Perspective ⇨ Drop Shadow or Radial Shadow. To apply a bevel to the mask, choose Effect ⇨ Perspective ⇨ Bevel Alpha or Bevel Edges. The controls for the Perspective commands can be adjusted using the Effect Controls panel.

17. **Use the Effect ⇨ Distort ⇨ Bezier Warp command to warp the mask using Beziers.** Use the Beziers and the controls in the Effect Controls panel to adjust the warp.

18. **To invert the mask (reverse the effect of the mask), choose Layer ⇨ Mask ⇨ Inverse.** To bring the mask back to the state it was in before you inverted it, choose Layer ⇨ Mask ⇨ Inverted.

19. **To change how the mask is displayed over the background, choose Layer ⇨ Mask ⇨ Mode.** Choose a mode. By default, the mode is set to Add.

Creating Bezier Masks

The Pen tools used in programs such as Illustrator, Photoshop, and CorelDRAW provide digital artists with the power to draw virtually any shape imaginable. The After Effects Pen tool provides similar power — except that instead of using the Pen tool to create works of art, After Effects users can use the Pen tool to create masks.

Figure 31.12 shows an After Effects Bezier mask project. In the figure, a Bezier mask is applied to a white parrot video clip. In order to isolate the parrot from the background, this example uses a Bezier mask — because using an oval or rectangle obviously wouldn't provide the desired effect. After isolating the parrot from its background by applying the mask, you can add a Photoshop background still image. In Photoshop, to make the background image, you can use the Gradient tool to create a purple, blue, and white gradient. To make the background more interesting, you can apply the Filter ➪ Distort ➪ Pinch command multiple times to the background. In After Effects you can apply effects from the Effect menu to make your backgrounds come alive. To finish the project, you can add text on a path by using the After Effects Effect ➪ Text ➪ Path Text command.

CROSS-REF To use the After Effects Path Text command, you first need to create a new solid by using the Layer ➪ New Solid menu command or a new text layer. For more information on creating and animating text in After Effects, see Chapter 32.

FIGURE 31.12

An After Effects Bezier mask project

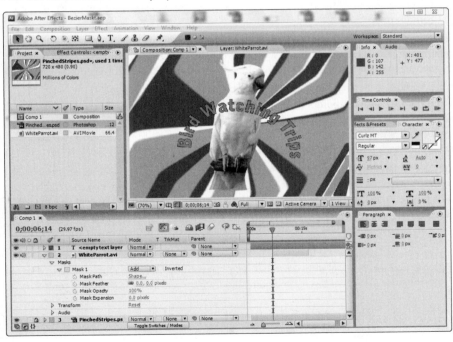

Here's how to create a simple Bezier mask using the After Effects Pen tool:

1. **In After Effects, create a new project by choosing File ➪ New ➪ New Project.**

2. **Choose Composition ➪ New Composition to create a new composition.**

3. **In the New Composition dialog box, specify a frame size.** Click OK.

4. **Choose File ➪ Import ➪ File to import a video clip you want to mask.** In the Import File dialog box, choose a file and then set the Import As menu to Footage. Choose Open to import the selected video clip. The imported video clip appears in the Project panel.

 If you want to use the WhiteParrot.avi video clip shown in Figure 31.12, you can find it in the MoreClips folder on the DVD that accompanies this book.

5. **Drag the imported video clip to the middle of the Composition panel.** The video clip appears in the Composition panel, as well as in the Timeline panel. Notice that the current-time indicator is at the beginning of the clip. Any changes you make to the clip affect only where the current-time indicator is positioned.

6. **Double-click the video clip's name in the Timeline panel to display the video clip in the Layer panel.**

7. **Select the Pen tool in the toolbar.** After you select the Pen tool, you can click the RotoBezier option from the toolbar. The RotoBezier option facilitates making Bezier paths that contain many curves.

8. **Create a path around the image.** Click the edge of the image you want to isolate. Keep clicking the perimeter of the image with the Pen tool to create a path around the image. Be sure not to make too many anchor points, as this makes the path too complex and difficult to edit.

   When the first and last points meet, a tiny circle appears next to the Pen icon. Click the mouse to close the path. As you create a Bezier path in the Layer panel, the effect of the mask appears in the panel. Figure 31.13 shows the parrot without a mask. Figure 31.14 shows the mask path in the Layer panel and the effect of the mask.

   After you create the path around the image, you can edit the path. Use the Selection tool to select and move an anchor point or to delete it. Click and hold the Pen tool in the Tools palette to display the Add Vertex tool, Delete Vertex tool, and Convert Vertex tool. Use the Add Vertex tool to add an anchor point to the path. Use the Delete Vertex tool to delete an anchor point. Use the Convert Vertex tool to convert a curved anchor point to a straight anchor point and vice versa.

 If you find the Pen tool difficult to use, you can start by using the Elliptical Mask tool or Rectangular Mask tool to create a path, and then use the Pen and Selection tools to edit the path.

FIGURE 31.13

The parrot before the mask

FIGURE 31.14

The mask path in the Layer panel and the mask effect

Editing Paths with the Pen Tool

You can edit a path in After Effects. To display the path in the Composition panel, click the video clip in the Timeline panel. To display the path in the Layer panel, double-click the video clip in the Timeline panel. To edit the path, use the Selection tool to select an anchor point and move it, or click a directional line with the Selection tool to change the shape of a curve. You can use the Convert tool, which is found in the same location as the Pen tool, to convert a curve to a corner point, or vice versa. If you need more anchor points, select the Pen + tool and click the path to add a point at that location. To delete a point, click it with the Pen tool.

9. **To see the effects of the mask over a background, choose File ⇨ Import ⇨ File to import a file.** Import either a still image or video clip to use as the background. In the Import File dialog box, locate a file and click Open. The example in Figure 31.12 uses the PinchedStripes.psd file as the background. This file is located in the MoreClips folder in the DVD that accompanies this book.

10. **When the background clip appears in the Project panel, drag it below the clip in the Timeline panel.** To make the background image more interesting, you can apply an effect from the Effect menu. The effect can be adjusted using the Effect Controls panel or in the Timeline panel. The effect can also be animated so that the background moves over time rather than being still. In this example, the background is animated by using the Twirl effect at the beginning and the Mesh Warp effect at the end of the project. Turn to Chapter 32 for more information on using After Effects. To lock the background so that it doesn't move, click the Lock column (next to the triangle icon) in the Timeline panel.

11. **To add text on a path, choose Layer ⇨ New ⇨ Text and then choose Effect ⇨ Text ⇨ Path Text.** In the Path Text dialog box that appears, type some text. Turn to Chapter 32 for more information on working with type and animating it in After Effects.

    Use the Font drop-down menu to choose a font. Click OK to apply the text to your project. Use the Effect Controls panel to edit the path text. To have the text appear around a circle, click the Shape Type drop-down menu in the Effect Controls panel and choose Circle. Notice that when you work with text in After Effects, a new layer is created in the Timeline panel.

NOTE To add horizontal text to your project, click the Horizontal Type tool in the Tools panel. Next, move the cursor to the Composition panel, and then click the mouse button and begin typing. Use the Character panel to change the font and font size. To convert horizontal type into a path outline, select the type with the Selection tool. Then choose Layer ⇨ Create Outlines. The path outline of the text can be edited with the Selection tool. The path outline can also be used as a mask.

12. **To see a preview of your work, move the current-time indicator in the Timeline panel or click the Composition panel and then choose Composition ⇨ Preview ⇨ RAM Preview.** Notice that the mask does not move with the image in the video clip. Proceed to the next section to learn how to animate a mask so that it moves with the image in the video clip.

13. **Save your project in After Effects format by choosing File ⇨ Save.**

Animating a Mask with the Timeline Panel

You can edit a mask's shape, location, feather, and opacity over various time intervals using After Effects' Timeline panel, Composition panel, and Layer panel. Figure 31.15 shows the effects of animating a mask at different points in time. Notice that the mask shape changes as the video progresses.

 Before you begin, you should have a video clip in the Timeline panel. That clip should also have a mask. If not, go back to the previous section to learn how to create a mask.

To use the Timeline panel to edit a mask over time, follow these steps:

1. **Click the triangle next to the video clip's name in the Timeline panel.**

2. **Click the triangle next to the word "Masks" to display the mask.**

3. **Click the triangle next to the mask you want to edit to show the mask options.** The mask options are as follows:

   ▪ **Mask Mode:** The Mask mode appears next to the mask name. By default, the mode is set to Add. (Next to the modes, After Effects provides an area that you can click if you want to invert the mask.)

   ▪ **Mask Path:** This option allows you to set the shape to Rectangle, Oval, or Bezier.

   ▪ **Mask Feather:** This option allows you to apply a horizontal or vertical feather to the edges of a mask.

   ▪ **Mask Opacity:** This option allows you to change the opacity. To make the mask translucent, set the opacity to less than 100 percent.

   ▪ **Mask Expansion:** This option allows you to expand the mask using pixel values.

4. **Move the current-time indicator to the beginning of the clip in the Timeline panel.**

5. **Click the stopwatch icon next to the mask option that you want to animate.** In the example in Figure 31.15, the mask's path is changed so that it follows the parrot as it moves over time. To animate the mask path, click the stopwatch icon next to Mask Path. Notice that a keyframe is created in the Timeline panel. To animate a mask, you need to create keyframes.

FIGURE 31.15

The frames show that the mask shape changes over time.

6. **To create another keyframe, move the current-time indicator to the right just a bit and edit the mask path to follow the shape of the image.** To follow an image the same way as in Figure 31.15, you need to move and edit the mask path in the Composition panel or Layer panel using the Selection tool or Pen tool options.

7. **When you finish editing the mask path in the current time location, move the current-time indicator to the right again.**

8. **Edit the mask shape again.** As you edit the mask shape, notice that another keyframe is created. Continue moving the current-time indicator and editing the mask until you reach the end of the clip in the Timeline panel. You can also edit a mask option from a point other than the beginning. To achieve the same effect as in Figure 31.15, you would begin editing the opacity at the middle of the Timeline.

9. **To see a preview of your work, move the current-time indicator in the Timeline panel.** Alternatively, click the Composition panel and then choose Composition ⇨ Preview ⇨ RAM Preview.

10. **Save your project in After Effects format by choosing File ⇨ Save.** To save your work as a movie, either choose Composition ⇨ Make Movie, or choose File ⇨ Export ⇨ AVI or QuickTime. To export a frame as a file, move the current-time indicator to the frame you want to export, and then choose Composition ⇨ Save Frame As ⇨ File. If you want the frame to appear in Photoshop with layers, choose Composition ⇨ Save Frame As ⇨ Photoshop Layers.

Follow these steps to edit the opacity of a mask:

1. **Move the current-time indicator to the beginning of the clip in the Timeline panel.**

2. **Click the stopwatch icon next to the Opacity option.** Notice that a keyframe is created with the Opacity's default setting of 100 percent.

3. **Move the current-time indicator to the middle of the clip in the Timeline panel.**

4. **Change the mask opacity option by clicking and dragging the Mask Opacity value in the Timeline panel.** Note that you can also use the Mask Opacity command (Layer ⇨ Mask ⇨ Mask Opacity). When the Mask Opacity dialog box appears, type a number and click OK.

5. **Preview the project by choosing Composition ⇨ Preview ⇨ RAM Preview.** When the current-time indicator reaches the keyframe in the middle of the Timeline, the opacity changes to the value you entered in step 4.

6. **Make the opacity (mask option) gradually change from the middle of the clip to the end of the clip.** Move the current-time indicator to the end of the clip. Next, set the desired opacity option.

Importing Masks from Photoshop or Illustrator into After Effects

You can import a black-and-white Photoshop or Illustrator file into After Effects to use as a mask. The Photoshop or Illustrator file can be used to isolate areas in a video clip. You can import a Photoshop or Illustrator shape or path into After Effects to use it as a mask in various ways. One way is to select the path to be used as a mask in Photoshop and Illustrator, and copy it and paste it in After Effects into a video clips Layer panel. Double-click a video clip in the Timeline panel to display a video clip in the Layer panel.

Another way to import a Photoshop or Illustrator path is to use the File ⇨ Import command. You can then drag it over a video clip in the Timeline panel. You can use a Layer Blending mode in the Timeline panel to blend the video clip and the path shape layers together.

Using Photoshop Shapes and Paths as Masks

Here's how to use Photoshop to create a mask in After Effects:

1. **In Photoshop, choose File ⇨ New to create a new file.** In the New dialog box, choose the Video & Film preset. Click OK to create a new document.

   In Photoshop, you can use various tools, such as the Pen tool and the Shape tool, to create a path shape. You can also create a selection with a Selection tool (such as the Lasso tool), and then convert the selection into a path by clicking the Make Work Path command in the Paths palette menu.

   After you create the selection, if you want an opaque mask, fill it with black by choosing Edit ⇨ Fill. In the Fill dialog box, set the Use drop-down menu to Black, the mode to Normal, and the opacity to 100 percent. The Preserve Transparency option should not be selected. Click OK. For a translucent mask, use a medium to light color or gray fill. To deselect the selection, choose Select ⇨ Deselect.

2. **Before using the path shape, set the foreground color in the Toolbox to black.** Click in the Default Foreground and Default Background Color icon at the bottom of the Tools palette to set the foreground to black and the background to white.

3. **Use the Shape tool to create a path shape.** Click the Shape tool in the Tools palette. In the Shapes toolbar, click the Shapes Layer icon. Click the Shapes drop-down menu and select a shape. The example in Figure 31.16 uses the Leaf 5 shape.

4. **Click and drag in the document area to create a shape (as shown in Figure 31.16).**

5. **Choose File ⇨ Save to save the document in Photoshop format.**

6. **Select the shape with the Selection tool.** Choose Edit ⇨ Copy.

FIGURE 31.16

A black-and-white Photoshop path shape can be used as a mask in After Effects.

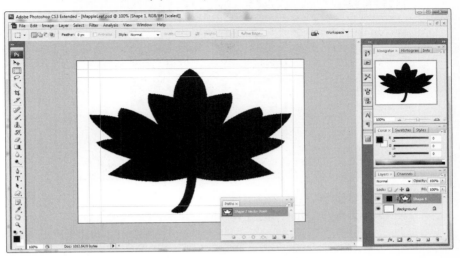

7. **After you create a shape in Photoshop, launch After Effects.** Create a new project by choosing File ⇨ New ⇨ Project, and create a new composition by choosing Composition ⇨ New Composition.

8. **Import the Photoshop or Illustrator file, as well as a video clip, into the project by choosing File ⇨ Import ⇨ Multiple Files.**

ON the DVD This example uses a video clip called Canoeing Rockies, located in the MoreClips folder on the DVD that accompanies this book.

9. **Drag the video clip from the Project panel to the middle of the Composition panel.**

10. **To copy the Photoshop path shape in After Effects, double-click the video clip in the Timeline panel to display the clip in the Layer panel.** Choose Edit ⇨ Paste to paste the Photoshop path shape. The path shape appears as a mask, as shown in Figure 31.17.

ON the DVD You can find the Photoshop MapleLeaf.psd file that is shown in Figure 31.16 in the MoreClips folder.

11. **To import the Photoshop path shape into After Effects, choose File ⇨ Import.** In the dialog box that appears, the Import Kind drop-down menu should be set to Footage. In the Layers Options, choose Merged Layers. Click OK to import the Photoshop file.

12. **Drag the Photoshop path shape from the Project panel to the Timeline panel.** Place it above the video clip in the Timeline panel.

FIGURE 31.17

The effect of a Photoshop path shape (shown in Figure 31.16) pasted into the Layer panel in After Effects as a mask on a video clip

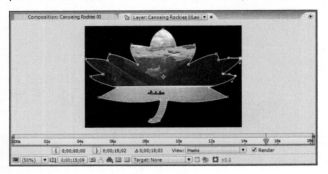

13. **Click the Photoshop path shape in the Timeline panel.** Click the Mode drop-down menu. Choose a mode or choose Layer ⇨ Blending Mode and make a selection. The example in Figure 31.18 sets the blending mode to Lighten.

FIGURE 31.18

The effects of using the Lighten blending mode on the MapleLeaf Photoshop file (shown in Figure 31.16)

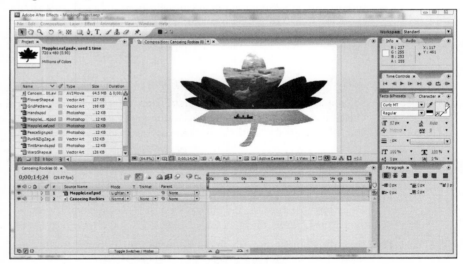

14. **To have the background of the video clip appear in the white area of the mask, reduce the opacity value for the Photoshop path shape layer.** To display the Opacity option, click the sideways triangle next to the Photoshop shape path layer to display the Transform option. Click the sideways triangle to display the Opacity option. Enter **50** for the Opacity value, as shown in Figure 31.19.

FIGURE 31.19

The effects of using the Lighten blending mode on the MapleLeaf Photoshop file with the opacity value set to 50 percent

To see the video clip through a Photoshop mask and add a tint to the video clip (see Figure 31.20), you need to have the Photoshop shape path on a colored background rather than a white background. To do so, you don't need to create a new Photoshop shape path file; you can load the Photoshop shape path file that you created in steps 3 and 4 (see Figure 31.16).

FIGURE 31.20

The results of using the Classic Color Dodge blending mode on the MapleLeaf&Tint Photoshop file

15. **With the Photoshop path onscreen, select the Background layer in the Layers palette.** Select a foreground color. If you want, use the Swatches palette to select a foreground color. This example sets the foreground color to pink. Choose Edit ⇨ Fill. In the Fill dialog box, set the Use drop-down menu to Foreground Color, the Mode drop-down menu to Normal, and the opacity to 100 percent. Click OK to fill the background with the foreground color. Choose File ⇨ Save As. In the Save As dialog box, enter a different name. Click Save to make a copy of the Photoshop file. In After Effects, choose File ⇨ Import to import the Photoshop shape path. Drag above the video clip in the Timeline panel. Use the Classic Color Dodge blending mode. If there is another Photoshop shape path above the video clip, either delete it or click the eye column to hide it.

 The MapleLeaf&Tint.psd file is in the MoreClips folder on the DVD that accompanies this book.

16. **In After Effects, experiment with different modes.** Choose Layer ⇨ Blending Mode ⇨ Normal to remove the blending mode. In Photoshop, create different files with different background colors and use different foreground colors for different shape paths.

    Figure 31.21 shows the results of creating two purple hands with the Shape tool on a blue background (shown in Figure 31.22).

    To achieve this effect in After Effects, you can use the Vivid Light blending mode. The example in Figure 31.23 applies the Stencil Alpha blending mode to the purple hands file. This time you can use a Transparent background for the purple hands, as shown in Figure 31.24. In Figure 31.24, you can create a transparent background by removing the Background layer. To remove the Background layer, double-click the Background layer in the Layers palette to convert it into a regular layer. Then drag it to the trash icon to delete the layer.

FIGURE 31.21

The effects of using the Vivid Light blending mode on the Tint&Hands Photoshop file

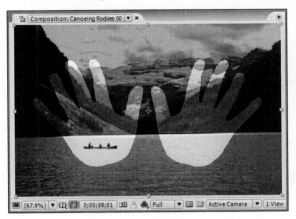

FIGURE 31.22

The Tint&Hands Photoshop file used to create the mask effect shown in Figure 31.21

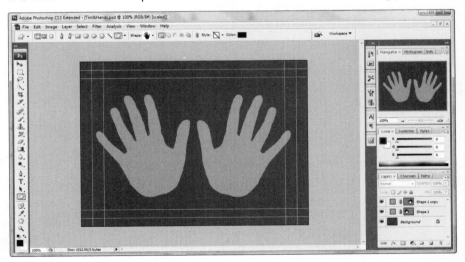

FIGURE 31.23

The effects of using the Stencil Alpha blending mode on a Photoshop path shape file that has a transparent background (shown in Figure 31.24)

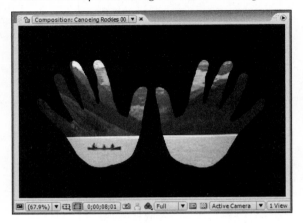

FIGURE 31.24

The Photoshop Hands path shape file with a transparent background (used to create the effect in Figure 31.23)

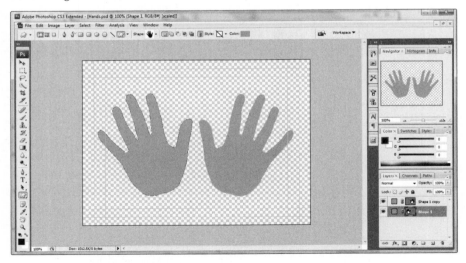

17. In Photoshop, you can also use the Brush tool to create a mask for After Effects. Click the Brush tool. Select a brush size and shape. Pick a color for the foreground and start painting.

Figure 31.25 shows the PeaceSign file that is created in Photoshop using the Brush tool. You can paint the peace sign with lavender on a white background. Figure 31.26 shows the lavender Photoshop peace sign in After Effects using the Classic Color Burn blending mode.

FIGURE 31.25

A peace sign created in Photoshop using the Brush tool

FIGURE 31.26

The Photoshop PeaceSign.psd file using the Classic Color Burn blending mode

 To Import different Photoshop files at the same time, choose File ⇨ Import ⇨ Multiple Files. In the MoreClips folder on the DVD that accompanies this book, there are various Photoshop path shape files that you can use.

18. **Choose File ⇨ Save to save your file in the After Effects project format.** Choose File ⇨ Export ⇨ Premiere Pro Project to export the After Effects project as a Premiere Pro project. To load the After Effects project that has been exported as a Premiere Pro project into Premiere Pro, choose File ⇨ Open in Premiere Pro. Locate the file to open. The After Effects layers from the Timeline appear in Premiere Pro's Project panel. Double-click the After Effects composition icon in the Project panel to have the items appear in the Timeline panel.

 If desired, you can copy a clip from the Project or Timeline panel in After Effects and paste it into either the Project or Timeline panel of Premiere Pro.

Here's how to use a Photoshop file as a track matte in After Effects:

1. **Before you begin, you should have an After Effects project onscreen with a composition.** In the Timeline panel there should be a video clip, and below the video clip there should be a Photoshop mask file. For more interesting results, use a Photoshop shape file with a color for the shape and another one for the background. If you want, you can use the Photoshop Tint&Hands.psd file and the Canoeing Rockies video clip in the MoreClips folder on the DVD that accompanies this book.

2. **In After Effects, click the filename of the mask (the Photoshop file) in the Timeline panel.**

3. **Choose Layer ⇨ Track Matte ⇨ Luma Matte or Luma Matte Inverted.**

4. **Choose Layer ⇨ Track Matte ⇨ No Track Matte to discard the matte effect.**

5. **You can also click the TrackMatte drop-down menu to make a selection.**

Using Illustrator paths as masks

Hardcore Adobe Illustrator users usually prefer to create their masks in Illustrator, which provides more path-editing commands than does After Effects. Fortunately, importing an Illustrator file into After Effects is a simple copy-and-paste operation. Here are the steps:

1. **In Illustrator, choose Edit ⇨ Preferences ⇨ File Handling & Clipboard.** In the Clipboard on Quit section of the Preferences dialog box, the Copy As option should be set to AICB, Preserve Paths. Click OK.

2. **In Illustrator, create a path with the Pen tool, or use the Rectangle, Ellipse, Polygon, or Star tool to create a path.** To create a more unusual shape, you can apply an effect from the Effect menu.

3. **Use the Selection tool to select the path and all of its anchor points, and then choose Edit ⇨ Copy.**

4. **Switch to After Effects.** In After Effects you should have a project onscreen with a composition and a video clip in the Timeline panel. Open the Layer panel for the target layer (the layer with the video clip you want to mask). Double-click a video clip in the Timeline panel to display it in the Layer panel. Choose Edit ⇨ Paste. The Illustrator path appears in After Effects as a mask, as shown in Figure 31.27. This Illustrator path is created by using the Rounded Rectangle tool to create a path filled with black. You can then apply the Effect ⇨ Distort & Transform ⇨ Pucker & Bloat command. In the Pucker & Bloat dialog box, move the slider toward Pucker (the left). To arrive at the shape shown in the figure, apply the Effect ⇨ Distort & Transform ⇨ Zig Zag command.

FIGURE 31.27

The Illustrator Punk&ZigZag path file is pasted into After Effects as a mask.

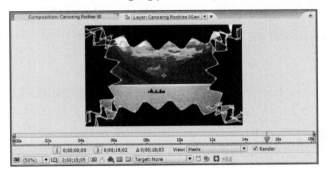

Follow these steps to learn how to import an Illustrator path into After Effects:

1. **In Illustrator, create a new Video & Film document.** In the document, create a shape using the Rectangle, Oval, Star, or Polygon tool. Fill the shape with black. To distort the shape, use the Warp tool. Apply a filter or effect to the shape to create a more interesting shape. Do not rasterize the shape. When you are finished, choose File ⇨ Save. In the Save dialog box, set the Save as Type drop-down menu to Illustrator and click Save.

2. **Import the Illustrator file, as well as a video clip, into the project by choosing File ⇨ Import ⇨ Multiple Files.** On the DVD, there are video clips and Illustrator path shape files that you can use. This example uses the Canoeing Rockies video clip in the MoreClips folder.

3. **Drag the video clip from the Project panel to the middle of the Composition panel.**

4. **Drag the Illustrator file above the video clip in the Timeline panel.**

5. **Click the Illustrator file in the Timeline panel.** Either click the Mode drop-down menu and make a selection, or choose Layer ⇨ Blending Mode and make a selection. The example in Figure 31.28 uses the Stencil Alpha blending mode on the Illustrator shape from Figure 31.27.

FIGURE 31.28

The Illustrator Punk&ZigZag file using the Stencil Alpha blending mode

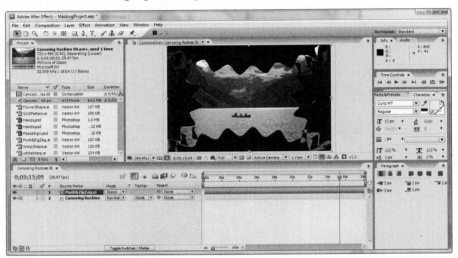

6. **Experiment with different options.** The example in Figure 31.29 uses the Polygon Rectangle tool to create a flower-shaped path filled with black. You can then apply the Effect ➪ Distort & Transform ➪ Pucker & Bloat command. In the Pucker & Bloat dialog box, move the slider toward Bloat (the right) to turn the polygon into a flower shape. In After Effects, apply the Soft Light blending mode.

FIGURE 31.29

The Illustrator FlowerShape file using the Soft Light blending mode

Summary

Although Premiere Pro provides numerous matting effects, it does not enable you to create sophisticated masks or edit masks over time as you can do in After Effects. This chapter covered the following topics:

- After Effects enables you to create oval, rectangular, and Bezier masks.

- In After Effects, you can edit masks in both the Layer and Composition panels using the Pen tool and the Selection tool and by using the commands in the Layer menu.

- After Effects masks can be edited over time using the Timeline panel.

- You can copy and paste either a Photoshop or Illustrator path shape into After Effects to use as a mask.

- An After Effects project can be exported as a Premiere Pro project for use in Premiere Pro.

Chapter 32

Adding Special Effects in Adobe After Effects

lthough Adobe Premiere Pro is packed with powerful video effects, at times you may want to create composite motion or text effects that may not be possible within the confines of Premiere Pro's panels. If your project requires a bit more pizzazz than Premiere Pro can produce, consider using Adobe After Effects.

After Effects can create dozens of effects that aren't possible in Premiere Pro. For example, you can fine-tune a motion path's shape as you would a curve in Adobe Illustrator or Adobe Photoshop. You can also rotate text 360 degrees along a curve over time, and animate in 3-D. After Effects enables you to run multiple clips simultaneously in the video frame — creating a three-ring circus of video effects.

This chapter's goal is not to persuade you to use After Effects instead of Premiere Pro, but to show you how the two programs can work together to create the ultimate video production. Both programs have their strengths, and you can use this to your advantage.

> **NOTE** If you are using the Adobe Creative Suite, you can create a Dynamic link between After Effects and Premiere Pro so that you can take advantage of the strengths of both programs. You can also add a Dynamic link to Adobe Encore DVD. For more information on the Adobe Creative Suite, see www.adobe.com/products/creativesuite/.

How After Effects Works

After Effects combines some of the features of Photoshop and Premiere Pro. To start a project in After Effects, you first create a new project and then create a new *composition*. A composition determines the type of movie you create. In the Composition Settings dialog box, you choose your settings for width, height, and frame rate. Then you import all of the images, sounds, titles, and video clips that you need to create your video production. Like Premiere Pro, After Effects stores all of these imported items in a Project panel. As you need footage items, you drag them from the Project panel into the Timeline panel. Unlike Premiere Pro, the items in the Timeline panel are not stored in video or sound tracks. Video and sound clips don't appear in different tracks; instead, they are organized as layers. In this way, After Effects works like Photoshop.

In both programs, you can also apply transformations (such as scale and rotate), effects, and masks to the layers. However, After Effects enables you to animate the transformation, effects, and masks over time as well as in 3-D; in Photoshop, each layer's properties remain static, unless you animate them using the Animation palette. If you use the Animation palette, you can make animation frames from your layers and output the file as a QuickTime movie.

 For more information on using Photoshop, turn to Chapter 28.

Importing Premiere Pro Projects

You can import an entire Premiere Pro project along with its transitions and effects directly into After Effects to take advantage of the program's powerful features, such as animating transformations and masks over time. Follow these steps to import a Premiere Pro project into After Effects:

1. **In After Effects, create a new project and new composition.** Then choose File ➪ Import ➪ File. The Import File dialog box appears.

2. **Select the Premiere Pro project you want to import.** Click Open. If you created the superimposing projects in Chapter 14, you can select one and import it into After Effects so that you can apply some more interesting effects to it.

3. **In the Import Project dialog box, select a sequence.** Click OK. After Effects imports the Premiere Pro project into the Project panel. Note that titles cannot be imported from Premiere Pro to After Effects, and vice versa.

4. **Double-click the Premiere Pro sequence file that is in the Project panel.** The video and sound tracks now appear in the Composition panel and as layers in the Timeline panel. The first layer in the Timeline panel is the first video or sound track that appears in the Premiere Pro Timeline panel. If you want, you can copy and paste a video clip in the Timeline panel from Premiere Pro to After Effects, and vice versa.

5. **If needed, you can now click a layer and animate it over time, using the Layer ➪ Transform commands or using the Transform options in the Timeline panel.** To reveal the Transform options for a layer, click the triangle next to that layer's name. The Transform options can be animated over time using keyframes — similar to the way Premiere Pro uses keyframes with video effects.

   Effects and masks can be applied to a layer in the Timeline panel and animated over time.

6. **To apply an effect to a layer, first select the layer in the Timeline panel.** Use one of the Effect commands found in the Effect menu or in the Effects & Presets panel. When working with various effects, you should use the Effects workspace. To do so, choose Window ⇨ Workspace ⇨ Effects.

7. **To apply a mask to a layer, select the layer.** Use the Layer ⇨ Mask commands. For more information about working with masks using After Effects, turn to Chapter 31.

> TIP
> You can import a Premiere Pro project into After Effects, and also output your Premiere Pro project as a QuickTime movie or in the AVI movie format. You can then import the movie into After Effects by choosing File ⇨ Import ⇨ File.

Importing and Animating Photoshop Files

To animate a Photoshop file in After Effects, you have two choices: You can create a folder and place all of the Photoshop files in it and import it as a Photoshop Sequence; or you can import a Photoshop file with layers like the one shown in Figure 32.1. When you import a Photoshop file with layers as a composition, a folder is created in the Project panel with the layers inside the folder.

Creating a Photoshop file from within After Effects

You can create a Photoshop file from within After Effects:

1. **Choose File ⇨ New ⇨ Adobe Photoshop File.** When the Save Layered File As dialog box appears, name your file.

2. **Click Save.** The new Photoshop file is loaded into Photoshop, ready for you to work on.

After you make changes to the file, save it so that the changes are updated in After Effects. If you create your new layers in this file, the layers do not show up in the After Effects project unless you import it as a composite file. To do so, follow these steps:

1. **Choose File ⇨ Import ⇨ File.** In the Import File dialog box, locate the Photoshop file with layers.

2. **Click Open.** A dialog box appears.

3. **Set the Import Kind drop-down menu to Composition.** In the Layer Options section, choose Editable Layer Styles.

4. **Click OK.**

5. **Double-click the Photoshop Composition icon in the Project panel to have all of the Photoshop layers appear in the Timeline panel.**

> **NOTE** In Photoshop you can create a 3-D effect using Vanishing Point. For a video tutorial on using Vanishing Point in Photoshop, see `www.adobe.com/designcenter /video_workshop/?id=vid0024`.

A Photoshop file with a vanishing point can be imported into After Effects and animated in 3-D space. In After Effects, choose File ➪ Import ➪ Vanishing Point. Drag the Photoshop vanishing point file from the Project panel to the Timeline panel. Then choose Layer ➪ 3D Layer to work in a 3-D environment.

FIGURE 32.1

The Jewelry Makeover Party file in Photoshop with its layers

Follow these steps to create a Photoshop file with layers and then import it into an After Effects project:

1. **Create a Photoshop file that has layers, as shown in Figure 32.1, and save it in Photoshop format.** Follow these steps to create layers in Photoshop:

   a. **Launch Photoshop.**

   b. **Choose File ➪ Open to load a file into Photoshop to use as a background.**

   c. **To create your own background, choose File ➪ New.** In the New dialog box, set the Preset drop-down menu to Film & Video. Then click OK.

d. **Click the Create New Layer icon in the Layers panel, or choose New Layer from the Layers panel drop-down menu.** To open the Layers panel, choose Window ➪ Layers.

e. **Use the painting tools from the Tools panel and the filters from the Filter menu to create some abstract art to use as the background or to use above the background.** If you prefer, you can copy and paste part of a photograph into the Background layer or on top of the Background layer.

f. **Create an image in the new layer.** You can scan or digitize an image with a digital camera or camcorder. Use one of the Selection tools to select an item in the image, and then copy and paste the digital image into the new layer. Be sure to select only a portion of the image so that you can see the background in the layer below. If you want, you can select and copy one of the files from the MoreClips folder on the DVD that accompanies this book.

g. **Create another new layer.** Keep creating layers until you have all of the layers that you need. If you want, you can also use Photoshop's Horizontal Type tool to create text in a layer.

h. **Choose File ➪ Save to save the file in Photoshop format.**

i. **Quit Photoshop.**

2. **Launch After Effects.**

3. **In After Effects, choose File ➪ New ➪ New Project.** The Project panel appears.

4. **Choose File ➪ Import ➪ File.** The Import File dialog box appears.

5. **Locate the Photoshop layer file that you want to import.** Click Open. In the dialog box that appears (shown in Figure 32.2), set the Import Kind drop-down menu to Composition. In the Layer Options section, choose Editable Layer Styles. Click OK. You can find the Photoshop file (JewelryMakeOverParty.psd) shown in Figure 32.1 on the DVD that accompanies this book.

6. **In the Project panel, a folder and a composition icon appear, as shown in Figure 32.3.**

FIGURE 32.2

After Effects allows you to import a Photoshop file with all of its layers.

FIGURE 32.3

The Jewelry Makeover Party layers shown in After Effects

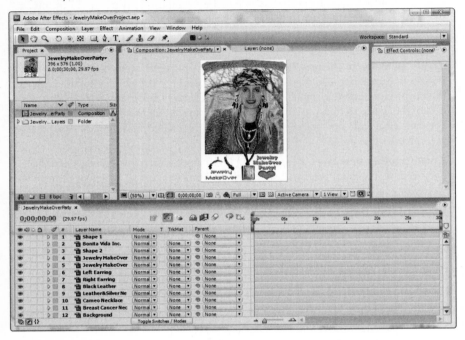

- To see the Photoshop layers in the Project panel, either double-click the folder or click the triangle.

- To view the layers in the Composition panel and Timeline panel, double-click the composition icon, which is above the Photoshop layers folder in the Project panel. Notice that the layers appear in the Composition panel and the Timeline panel. The layers also appear in the Timeline panel in the same order as they did in Photoshop's Layers panel. You don't have to drag each layer to the Timeline panel; After Effects automatically places them there.

- To decrease or increase the view of the Composition panel, first select the panel. Choose Zoom Out or Zoom In from the View menu.

- To have the layers start at different points in time, so that the items progressively appear onscreen, click and drag them to the right in the Timeline. By having the different layers gradually appear onscreen, you create the feeling of a presentation.

TIP To import various Photoshop files as a sequence, create a folder and place the Photoshop files in the folder. Then, in After Effects, choose File ⇨ Import ⇨ Multiple Files. When the Import Multiple Files dialog box appears, click the first Photoshop file of the sequence; then click the Photoshop Sequence option and click Open. Continue to select files, select the Photoshop Sequence option, and click Open until you have selected all of the files. When you are finished, click Done.

After importing a Photoshop file, you can *animate* its layers. When you animate a layer, you do one of three things: transform it (scale, rotate, or change its opacity or position, or both), apply an effect (such as distortion), or apply a mask to the entire layer or just a portion of the layer.

NOTE In Photoshop, you can use the Modes menu at the top of the Layers palette to create composite effects between layers. To display the modes in After Effects, choose a layer in the Timeline panel and click the Mode drop-down menu or choose Layer ⇨ Blending Mode.

Follow these steps to animate Photoshop layers in After Effects:

1. **Click the triangle beside one of the layers in the Timeline panel.** When you expand the layer, the Transform option appears. If you applied Layer Styles (such as a drop shadow) to an item in a layer in Photoshop, a Layer Styles option appears for that layer in the Timeline panel in After Effects. Shapes that you created with the Shape tool in Photoshop have a Masks option. You can also animate the Layer Styles and Masks options.

2. **To display the Transform options, click the triangle next to *Transform*.** Notice that the Anchor Point, Position, Scale, Rotation, and Opacity options are visible. You can animate the layer's anchor point, position, scale, rotation, or opacity.

3. **To animate one of the layer's Transform options (such as position), first move the current-time indicator to the beginning of the clip, or to where you want to start animating.** Click the stopwatch icon in front of the transform that you want to animate (if you are animating the position, you can click the word *Position*). A keyframe is created.

4. **Move the current-time indicator to the right.**

5. **Change the transform (position) of the layer by adjusting the Transform (Position) values in the Timeline panel (you can also change the Position values by moving the layer in the Composition panel).** After you change the Transform values for the layer you are working on, a new keyframe is created. In Figure 32.3, the Opacity is animated so that the different jewelry items gradually appear and disappear.

6. **To continue animating the Transform option (position) of the layer over time, continue moving the current-time indicator to the right.** Adjust the Transform values for the layer you are working on. Another keyframe is created.

7. **To preview your work, choose Composition ⇨ Preview ⇨ RAM Preview.**

8. **To animate a layer using an effect, choose a layer in the Timeline panel.**

9. **Move the current-time indicator to the beginning of the clip.**

10. **Click the Effect menu.** Choose an effect.

11. **Click the Effects triangle in the Timeline panel.** The name of the effect you choose appears onscreen. Click the stopwatch icon next to the effect name to create a keyframe.

12. **Move the current-time indicator to the right.** Then alter the effect in the Effect Controls panel. Notice that another keyframe is created.

13. **Again move the current-time indicator, and alter the effect.** Another keyframe is created.

14. **To preview your work, choose Composition ⇨ Preview ⇨ RAM Preview.**

15. **If you want to add sound to your file, import a sound clip.** Then drag it from the Project panel to the Timeline panel.

16. **When you are finished, choose File ⇨ Save to save your work as an After Effects project.**

To export your work as a Premiere Pro Project, choose File ⇨ Export ⇨ Adobe Premiere Pro Project. Name your project and click Save. After you save your work as a Premiere Pro file, you can open it in Premiere Pro as you would any other Premiere Pro project.

To export your work in either the QuickTime or AVI movie format, choose File ⇨ Export ⇨ QuickTime Movie or AVI. In the settings dialog box that appears, make the necessary adjustments and click OK. In the Save As dialog box, name the file and then click Save to save the file. After you save your work in a movie format, you can import it into a Premiere Pro project as you would any other file.

Importing Photoshop Files with Adjustment Layers

In this section, you learn how to create a Photoshop file with adjustment layers and then import it as a composition file into After Effects. When you import the Photoshop adjustment layer into After Effects as a composition, each adjustment layer is imported, along with the Background layer.

In Photoshop, you can use adjustment layers to change the color of an image in a separate layer from the background. This way, the adjustment layers can be edited or removed without affecting the original image. You can also create adjustment layers in After Effects. (You will learn more about this in the next section.) Follow these steps to create a Photoshop file with adjustment layers:

1. **Launch Photoshop and create a new file, or load a file that already has a background.** If you create a new file, you need to create a background. You can use the Gradient tool, the Paint tools, and the Filter menus to create a background.

2. **Choose Window ⇨ Layers to display the Layers panel.**

3. **Choose Layer ⇨ New Adjustment Layer.** Select a command. This example uses Hue/Saturation. You can also create a new adjustment layer by clicking the Create New Adjustment Layer icon at the bottom of the Layers palette.

4. **Notice that a new adjustment layer appears in the Layers panel, as shown in Figure 32.4.** Create as many adjustment layers as you need.

5. **Choose File ⇨ Save to save your file.** Name your file and save it in Photoshop format.

FIGURE 32.4

A Photoshop file with an adjustment layer

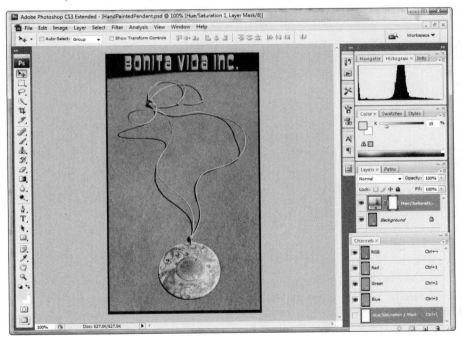

Follow these steps to load a Photoshop file with adjustment layers into After Effects:

1. **Launch After Effects and either create a new project or load a project.**

2. **Choose File ⇨ Import ⇨ File.** In the Import File dialog box, leave the Import As drop-down menu set to Footage. Locate the Photoshop adjustment layer file and click Open. In the dialog box that appears, set the Import Kind drop-down menu to Composition and, in the Layer Options section, click the Editable Layer Styles option. Click OK to import the Photoshop adjustment layer file as a composition.

3. When the Photoshop composition file appears in the Project panel, double-click it. A new composition is created in the Timeline panel with all of the adjustment layers and the Background layer used to create the Photoshop file (shown in Figure 32.5).

FIGURE 32.5

The Photoshop file with an adjustment layer from Figure 32.4 imported into After Effects

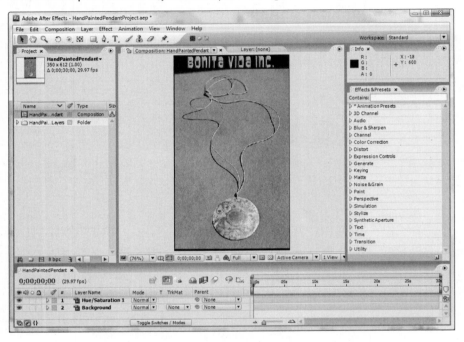

4. If you want to turn off one of the adjustment layers, click the eye icon in the Timeline panel to hide the layer. It is the round circle with an *f* in the middle of it. To turn off an adjustment layer and make the layer appear white, click the Adjustment Layer icon. This icon appears as a circle that is half-white and half-black.

5. Choose Window ➪ Workspace ➪ Effects. The Effect Controls panel appears.

6. Click in one of the adjustment layers in the Timeline panel. Notice that the controls for that adjustment appear in the panel. If you want, you can make adjustments to the controls. When you make changes, you can view them in the Composition panel.

7. If you want, you can import a new background and apply the adjustment layers to the new background. Once you import the new background, move it into the Timeline panel above the old Background layer.

8. Either save your project in After Effects format or export it as a movie or an Adobe Premiere Pro project.

Creating an Adjustment Layer In After Effects

In this section, you use After Effects to create an adjustment layer and apply effects using this layer. These effects affect the layers behind the adjustment layer, but they are not permanent; the adjustment layer can always be deleted. Follow these steps to create an adjustment layer in After Effects:

1. **Launch After Effects and either create a new project or load a project.** If you create a new project, you need to import a file to use as a background.

> **NOTE** In After Effects, you can easily create a Background layer. With a project onscreen, choose Layer ➪ New Solid. In the Solid Settings dialog box, click the color swatch to pick a background color. Click OK to have the solid color layer appear in the Timeline panel. If you want to add an effect to the solid color layer, select an effect from the Effect menu. For a really interesting effect, try Effect ➪ Generate ➪ Fractal.

2. **Drag a file from the Project panel to the Timeline panel to use as a background.**

3. **Choose Layer ➪ New ➪ Adjustment Layer.** An adjustment layer appears above the Background layer in the Timeline panel.

4. **Choose Window ➪ Workspace ➪ Effects.**

5. **Select an effect from the Effects & Presets panel and drag it to the adjustment layer in the Composition panel.** Apply as many effects as you like.

6. **Use the Effect Controls panel to change the effect's settings.**

7. **If you want, you can apply the adjustment layer to another background.** To do so, just drag a clip from the Project panel to the Timeline panel. Then place the clip above the background clip that is already in the Timeline panel.

8. **Either save your project in After Effects format, or export it as a movie or an Adobe Premiere Pro project.**

Importing and Animating Illustrator Files

In this section, you learn how to import an Illustrator file with layers into After Effects and animate it. The following example uses this technique to create a project filled with brush strokes (shown in Figure 32.6). Follow these steps to import an Illustrator file with layers into After Effects:

1. **Using Illustrator CS, create a file with layers, like the one shown in Figure 32.6, and save it in Illustrator format.** Follow these steps:

   a. **Launch Illustrator.**

   b. **Create a new file.**

   c. **In the New dialog box, name the file and set the Preset to Video and Film.** Click OK to create a new Illustrator document.

d. **Choose Window ➪ Layers to open the Layers panel.** Notice that there is one layer. Double-click in the layer's name, and rename it **Background**.

e. **To create a background for the Brushes project, click the Rectangle tool in the Toolbox.** Then make a rectangle inside the safe margins area (as shown in Figure 32.6). Fill the rectangle with a swatch. For a selection of different swatch libraries, choose Window ➪ Swatch Libraries and then make a selection. For the example in Figure 32.6, you can select Window ➪ Swatch Libraries ➪ Pattern ➪ Decorative ➪ Decorative_Classic. Then select the Waves Water Color swatch. You can also add a stroke to the rectangle. For the example in Figure 32.6, you can stroke the rectangle with the Hearts swatch in the Window ➪ Brush Libraries ➪ Decorative ➪ Decorative_Scatter library.

f. **Click the New Layers icon at the bottom of the Layers palette to create a new layer.** Double-click in the layer's name, and rename it **Filmstrip**.

g. **To create brush strokes, select the Brush tool from the Tools palette.** Choose Window ➪ Brush Libraries and select a brush library. Then either click in the document or click and drag to create a small or large stroke. In the example in Figure 32.6, you can use the Window ➪ Brush Libraries ➪ Default Brushes ➪ Video and Film Library and the Pattern Brush 1 swatch to create two filmstrips.

h. **Click the New Layers icon at the bottom of the Layers palette to create another layer.** Double-click in the layer's name, and rename it **Hearts**.

i. **Choose Window ➪ Brush Libraries ➪ Decorative ➪ Decorative Scatter Library.**

j. **In the Decorative_Scatter palette, click the Hearts swatch.**

k. **With the Brush tool selected, click and drag in the artboard area of the document to create a few hearts.**

l. **Continue creating new layers and using the Brush tool to add brush strokes using the swatches in the Decorative_Scatter palette.** You can also use swatches from other brush libraries. Repeat the process until you have at least seven layers with different brush strokes (as shown in Figure 32.6).

m. **Create another layer.** In this layer, use the Brush, Pencil, or Pen tool to create a curved stroke. Using the Path Type tool, create some text on the curve that you created. In the example in Figure 32.6, you can type **Typing on a Brush stroke is lots of fun!** On the curved stroke, you can apply the Banner swatch from the Video and Film library (Window ➪ Brush Libraries ➪ Default Brushes ➪ Video and Film Library).

n. **Choose File ➪ Save to save your file in Illustrator format.**

2. **Launch After Effects, and create a new project.** To import the Illustrator file, choose File ➪ Import ➪ File. In the dialog box that appears, set the Import Kind drop-down menu to Composition and click OK.

Notice that a folder icon and a composition icon appear in the Project panel, as shown in Figure 32.7.

 The Illustrator file (BrushStrokes.ai) shown in Figure 32.6 can be found in the MoreClips folder on the DVD that accompanies this book.

FIGURE 32.6

The Brush Strokes project as shown in Adobe Illustrator

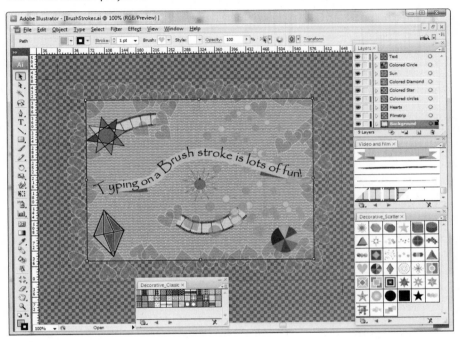

3. **To see the Illustrator layers, either double-click the folder or click the triangle in front of the folder.** To view the layers in the Composition and Timeline panels, double-click the Composition icon in the Project panel. Notice that the layers appear in the Composition panel and the Timeline panel.

4. **To decrease or increase the view of the Composition panel, choose Zoom Out or Zoom In.** The layers also appear in the Timeline panel in the same order as they appeared in Illustrator's Layers panel. You don't have to drag each layer to the Timeline panel — After Effects automatically places them there.

5. **To animate the Illustrator layers, click the triangle of one of the Timeline panel's layers.** You can choose to animate that layer's masks or effects, or to transform the actual layer.

6. **Try animating the brush strokes (shown in Figure 32.7) by rotating, moving, and scaling them, and applying effects over time.**

7. **Choose File ➪ Save to save your work.** Choose File ➪ Export ➪ Adobe Premiere Pro Project to save your work in the Premiere Pro Project format. You can open a Premiere Pro project file in Premiere Pro by choosing File ➪ Open.

FIGURE 32.7

The Brush Strokes project as shown in After Effects

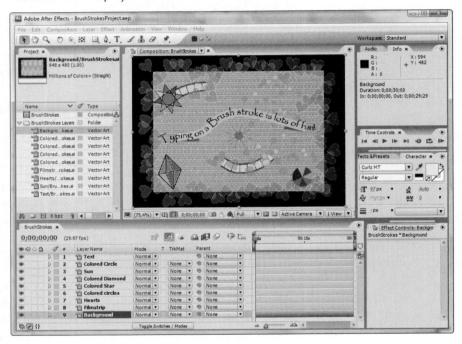

Creating and Animating Type Using After Effects

In an After Effects project with a composition, you can create text either by using the Horizontal Type or Vertical Type tool in the Composition panel, or by choosing Layer ➪ New ➪ Text. You can then enter text with the Type tool in the Text layer in the Composition panel. When you create text with the Type tool, After Effects recognizes the text and automatically creates a Text layer in the Timeline panel.

Follow these steps to create horizontal text and animate it using the After Effects Animate Text command:

 Before you begin, you should have a new After Effects project open, with a composition (choose Composition ⇨ New Composition).

1. **Move the current-time indicator to the position in the Timeline in which you want to apply horizontal text.**

2. **Select the Horizontal Type tool from the Tools panel.** Start typing in the Composition panel. As soon as you add text to the Composition panel, a Text layer appears in the Timeline panel. Use the Character panel to change the font and font size.

3. **Move the current-time indicator to the position in the Timeline in which you want to animate the horizontal text.**

4. **Choose Animation ⇨ Animate Text, or click the word *Animate* (to the right of the Text option) in the Text layer in the Timeline panel.** Then choose the option you want to animate. You can animate the text's position, scale the text, rotate it, or change its color. After you choose an animation option, the Animator option appears in the Timeline panel. Click the stopwatch icon next to the Animator option to create a keyframe.

5. **Move the current-time indicator to the right.** Adjust the Animator option. Another keyframe is created. Repeat this step as many times as you need to.

6. **To animate in 3D space using X, Y, Z coordinates, choose Layer ⇨ 3D Layer.** Notice that X, Y, and Z coordinates appear in the Transform section of the layer. Use the Rotate tool to rotate in 3-D space (X, Y, and Z coordinates). To animate in 3-D space, in the Timeline panel, set keyframes for the X, Y, and Z coordinates.

7. **You can also animate the text in 3-D space by choosing Effect ⇨ Perspective ⇨ CC Sphere.** Use the controls in the Effect Controls panel to adjust the text. The example in Figure 32.8 animates the text by rotating it in the Y axis.

8. **To import a background clip, choose File ⇨ Import ⇨ File to import a file that will work as a background for the path text.** If you import a background file, drag it from the Project panel to the Timeline panel. The background file immediately turns into a layer. In the example in Figure 32.9, you can create the background in After Effects by using the Layer ⇨ New ⇨ Solid command to create a solid-color background in the Timeline panel. You can apply the Effect ⇨ Generate ⇨ 4-Color Gradient, and the Effect ⇨ Distort ⇨ CC Flo Motion commands to the solid-colored background. Then copy and paste the background twice. Apply the Effect ⇨ Perspective ⇨ CC Sphere command to create a sphere, and apply the Effect ⇨ Perspective ⇨ CC Cylinder command to create a cylinder.

FIGURE 32.8

You can animate Text in After Effects in a 3-D environment

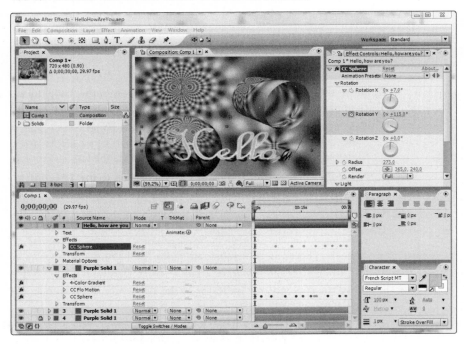

FIGURE 32.9

In After Effects, you can create 3-D shapes from background layers using the Effect ⇨ Perspective ⇨ CC Sphere, and Effect ⇨ Perspective ⇨ CC Cylinder commands.

Using the Effect ➪ Text command, you can choose from three different types of text: Basic Text, Numbers, and Path Text. Choose Effect ➪ Text, and then make a selection. When you select the Basic Text option, you can create horizontal or vertical text. You can also use the Basic Text option to animate one letter of a word at a time. The Numbers option enables you to create numbers. The Path Text option creates text on a path. The following example creates path text. Figure 32.10 shows the panels used to create the Path Type project. You can use the Rotate option, found in the Timeline panel, to animate text around the curve to create the text in this example.

FIGURE 32.10

The panels used to create the Path Type project

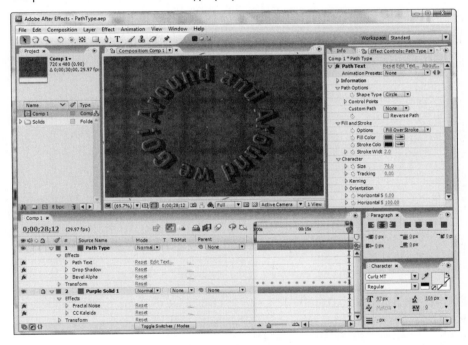

Follow these steps to create and animate path text in After Effects:

1. **Choose File ➪ New ➪ New Project.** The Project panel appears.
2. **Choose Composition ➪ New Composition.** The Composition Settings dialog box appears, as shown in Figure 32.11.
3. **Name your composition.** Choose the width and height that you want to use.
4. **Click OK to create a new composition and display the Timeline panel.**

NOTE If you want to change the settings in the composition, choose Composition ➪ Composition Settings.

5. **To import a background clip, choose File ➪ Import ➪ File to import a file that will work as a background for the path text.** If you import a background file, drag it from the Project panel to the Timeline panel. The background file immediately turns into a layer. To create your own background, you need to create a new solid layer.

The Composition Settings dialog box

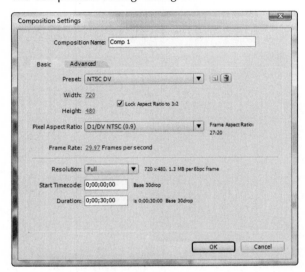

6. **Choose Layer ➪ New ➪ Solid.** When the Solid Settings dialog box appears, as shown in Figure 32.12, type a name for your layer in the Name field. Click the color swatch at the bottom of the dialog box and pick a color. Leave the width and height alone, and click OK to create a new solid. (Usually the width and height are the same as the composition.)

Notice that a new solid layer appears in the Timeline panel. The new solid layer also takes up the entire size of the Composition panel.

7. **To make the solid or background more interesting, you can apply different effects.** The example in Figure 32.10 applies the Effect ➪ Noise & Grain ➪ Fractal Noise command and the Effect ➪ Stylize ➪ Kaleida command to the solid in the Timeline panel.

In the Effect Controls panel, shown in Figure 32.13, set the blending mode for the Fractal Noise effect to Hue. For the Kaleida effect, you can adjust the Scale value and the Rotation controls (found in the Effect Controls panel).

If you don't want to have a static background, you can animate the background over time. To do so, click in front of the solid or Background layer in the Timeline panel to display its controls. In the Effects section, you can animate the effects by moving the current-time indicator and clicking the stopwatch icon next to the effect to make a keyframe. Continue moving and making adjustments to the effect to make keyframes for the effect. The keyframes are what After Effects uses to animate the effect.

FIGURE 32.12

The Solid Settings dialog box

FIGURE 32.13

The Effect Controls panel allows you to adjust the controls of an effect.

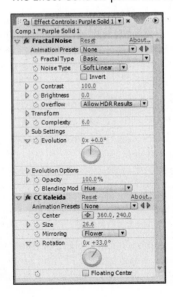

If you don't want to affect the solid or Background layer, you should lock it. Click the Lock column next to the solid or Background layer in the Timeline panel to lock it.

8. **Move the current-time indicator to the position in the Timeline in which you want to apply path text.**

9. **Choose Layer ⇨ New ⇨ Solid to create a new layer for the text from the Effect ⇨ Text command.** When the Solid Settings dialog box appears (shown in Figure 32.12), type **Path Type** in the Name field. Leave the width and height alone, and click OK.

10. **Choose Effect ⇨ Text ⇨ Path Text to create text on a path.**

11. **In the Path Text dialog box, shown in Figure 32.14, select a font.** Enter some text in the text field.

FIGURE 32.14

Type some text in the Path Text dialog box.

12. **Click OK to close the dialog box and view your text on a curve in the Composition panel, as shown in Figure 32.15.** The text appears with round handles. Click the round handles to adjust the curve. The Effect Controls panel, shown in Figure 32.16, appears at the same time as the text on the curve appears in the Composition panel.

 If you can't see the Effect Controls panel for the Path Type layer, you may need to select the Path Type layer in the Timeline panel.

13. **Use the Effect Controls panel to change the size, tracking (letter spacing), fill, and stroke color, or to edit the text you just typed.**

   ▪ To change the size of the text, click and drag the Size slider in the Effect Controls panel.

   ▪ To edit the text, click the words *Edit Text* at the top of the Effect Controls panel, across from the word *Path Text*. When the Path Text dialog box appears, you can edit the text. Click and drag over the letters you want to change.

   ▪ To choose whether you want your text to be filled, stroked, or filled with a stroke surrounding it, click the Options drop-down menu in the Fill and Stroke section. To change the fill or stroke color, click the color swatch next to the words *Fill Color* or

Stroke Color. When the Color dialog box appears, pick a color and click OK. You can also use the Eyedropper tool to change a color. To change the fill or stroke color to the color that you select with the Eyedropper tool, click the Eyedropper tool next to either *Fill Color* or *Stroke Color* and then click a color from the background file. To change the stroke color's width, click the Stroke Width option and type a number.

FIGURE 32.15

The round handles that appear on the curved text allow you to adjust the curve.

FIGURE 32.16

You can use the Effect Controls panel to adjust the text in the composition.

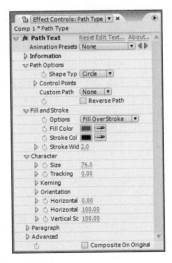

■ Clicking the Shape Type drop-down menu lets you choose whether you want the shape of the text to be on a Bézier curve, circle, loop, or line. Click the circles in the Composition panel to adjust the type path shape.

 If the Effect Controls panel is not onscreen, you can display it by first clicking the layer you want to change and then choosing Effect ⇨ Effect Controls.

14. **Choose Circle from the Shape Type drop-down menu in the Effect Controls panel to have the text appear on a circle.** Click and drag the circle handles (shown in Figure 32.17) to edit the circle. As you edit the circle, you may need to change the font size.

FIGURE 32.17

Move the circle handles to adjust the text on the curve.

15. **To jazz things up a bit, you can apply the Effect ⇨ Perspective ⇨ Drop Shadow, and Effect ⇨ Perspective ⇨ Bevel Alpha commands.** You can adjust the controls for these effects in the Effect Controls panel, shown in Figure 32.18.

16. **To rotate text around a curve and animate it, you can click the triangle next to the Path Type layer in the Timeline panel to display its features.** Click the Transform triangle to display the Rotation option. Then follow these steps:

   a. **Move the current-time indicator to the beginning of the Path Type layer.** Click the stopwatch icon next to the Rotation option (in the Transform options) to create your first keyframe.

   b. **Move the current-time indicator over on the Timeline.** Click the degree amount next to the Rotation option.

   c. **Continue moving the current-time indicator on the Timeline and changing the Rotation degree to create keyframes.** Continue until you have a number of keyframes or until you create a complete rotation.

17. **Choose File ➪ Save to save your work.** To preview your work, choose Composition ➪ Preview ➪ RAM Preview.

18. **To import this project into Premiere Pro, choose File ➪ Export ➪ Adobe Premiere Pro Project.** In the Export As Adobe Premiere Pro dialog box that appears, name the file and click Save to save the file.

FIGURE 32.18

Adding the Drop Shadow and Bevel Alpha effects can make your text dazzle. You can adjust the controls for the Drop Shadow and Bevel Alpha effects in the Effect Controls panel.

Working with Motion Paths

After Effects provides more control over motion effects than Premiere Pro. In After Effects, you can create motion along a path by moving an object along its anchor point. When moving an object along its anchor point, you are essentially using a path similar to Illustrator and Photoshop paths. Figure 32.19 shows a diamond brush stroke that has been animated in After Effects using its anchor point.

 For more information on using the Motion Effect controls in Premiere Pro, refer to Chapter 16.

Animating with anchor points

Follow these steps to animate an object in After Effects using its anchor point:

1. **Choose File ➪ New ➪ New Project to create a new project.** Then choose Composition ➪ New Composition. In the Composition Settings dialog box, set the presets and then click OK. If you prefer, you can choose File ➪ Open to launch an After Effects project.

2. **Choose Window ➪ Workspace ➪ Standard.**

3. **Choose File ➪ Import ➪ File to import a Photoshop or Illustrator object.** If you want, use the BrushStrokes.ai file from the companion DVD's MoreClips folder. When importing the file, select Footage from the Import Kind drop-down menu in the dialog box that appears. Select Choose Layer, and then choose the layer you want to import from the drop-down menu. In this example, you can import the Colored Diamond layer. That way, only the layer you want to work with is imported, instead of all of the layers.

FIGURE 32.19

In After Effects, you can animate a layer by creating a motion path using the anchor point control.

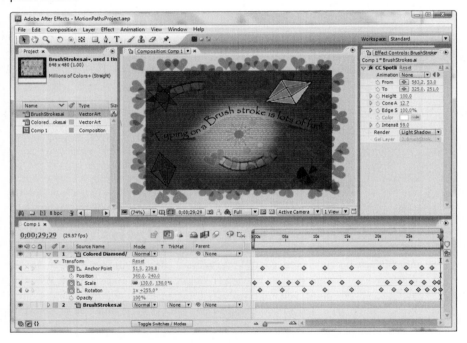

---

4. **Click and drag the imported file from the Project panel to the Timeline panel.** The layer not only appears in the Timeline panel but also in the Composition panel. To change the background color of the Composition panel, choose Composition ➪ Background Color. Click the swatch, pick a color, and then click OK. This example changes the color of the background from black to a vibrant yellow.

5. **Expand the layer by clicking the triangle next to the layer's name in the Timeline panel.**

6. **Click the Transform triangle to display the Transform options.** The Transform options display.

7. **Move the current-time indicator to the Timeline's beginning or to where you want to start animating your object.**

8. **Click the stopwatch icon next to the words** *Anchor Point*.

9. **Double-click the layer in the Timeline panel to display the Layer panel (shown in Figure 32.20).**

10. **In the Layer panel, choose Anchor Point Path from the View drop-down menu.**

11. **Choose View ⇨ Show Grid, and Choose View ⇨ Show Rulers to display a grid and a ruler in the Layer panel where you are working.**

12. **In the Layer panel, click the circle.** Move it to where you want the path to begin.

13. **Move the current-time indicator to a new position in the Timeline.** Move the circle again to start creating the motion path. Continue moving the current-time indicator, and move the circle in succession until you finish creating your motion path. To edit the motion path, you can move the layer keyframe, direction handles, or direction lines.

   Depending upon the path you create, you may want to use the Layer ⇨ Transform ⇨ Auto-Orient Rotation command. In the Auto-Orientation dialog box, choose Orient Along Path and then click OK. The Auto-Orient Rotation command enables you to rotate an object along a path so that the object is facing a different direction.

   To manually adjust the path, use the handles and vector points to control the size and shape of the path's curves.

FIGURE 32.20

In the Layer panel, you can see a motion path being created.

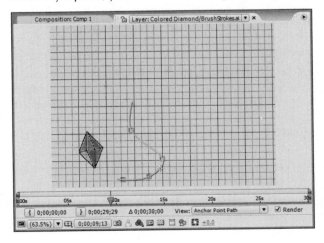

TIP
Animation paths can be saved and reused. In the Timeline panel, select a layer's animation. Then choose Animation ⇨ Save Animation Preset. In the dialog box that appears, name the animation preset and click Save. To apply the animation preset, select a layer in the Timeline panel and choose Animation ⇨ Apply Animation Preset. In the dialog box that appears, select a preset and click Open.

14. **To preview the motion you just created, click the Composition panel.** Then choose one of three commands:

   - Composition ⇨ Preview ⇨ Motion with Trails (fastest)

   - Composition ⇨ Preview ⇨ Wireframe Preview

   - Composition ⇨ Preview ⇨ RAM Preview (slowest)

   To create the effect shown in Figure 32.19, you must also animate the Scale and Rotate options.

15. **Choose File ⇨ Import ⇨ File.** In the Import dialog box, select a file to import to use as a background for your project. In the example in Figure 32.19, you can import the BrushStrokes.ai file. Click Open. If you use the BrushStrokes.ai file, in the dialog box that appears, set the Import Kind drop-down menu to Footage and select the Merged Layers option from the Layer Options section. Then click OK. Click and drag the imported file below the layer in the Timeline panel. To make the Background layer more interesting, you can apply the Effect ⇨ Perspective ⇨ CC Spotlight command.

16. **If you want to keep your work, choose File ⇨ Save to save it in the After Effects format.** Choose File ⇨ Export to export the project in a movie format.

Animating with Sketch a Motion

The Sketch a Motion option enables you to draw your path freehand. Follow these steps to animate using Sketch a Motion:

1. **Choose File ⇨ New ⇨ New Project to create a new project.** Then choose Composition ⇨ New Composition. In the Composition Settings dialog box, set the presets and then click OK. If you prefer, you can choose File ⇨ Open to load an After Effects project.

2. **Choose File ⇨ Import ⇨ File to import a Photoshop or Illustrator object.** If you want, use the BrushStrokes.ai file from the companion DVD's MoreClips folder. When importing the file, select Footage from the Import Kind drop-down menu in the dialog box that appears. Select Layer Options, and then choose the layer you want to import. This example imports the Sun layer so that only the layer you want to work with is imported, instead of all of the layers.

3. **Click and drag the imported file from the Project panel to the Timeline panel.** The layer appears in both the Timeline panel and the Composition panel.

4. **Move the current-time indicator to the Timeline's beginning or to where you want to start animating your object.**

5. **Move the object that you are animating to the place from where you want it to start.**

6. **Choose Window ⇨ Workspace ⇨ Animation to display the animation workspace, including the Motion Sketch panel.**

7. **Click the Start Capture button in the Motion Sketch panel.**

8. **Move the cursor to the Composition panel.**

9. **Press and hold the mouse button while you draw your motion path.** As soon as you let go of the mouse button, After Effects stops creating the motion sketch. The motion sketch is shown in Figure 32.21.

10. **Click the triangle next to the layer that you have selected in the Timeline panel.**

11. **Click the triangle next to the word *Transform*.** Notice that the Motion Sketch command has created keyframes next to the Position section of the Timeline panel. In the example in Figure 32.21, you can copy the keyframes in the Position section and paste them a few times to make the animation longer. To make the sun bigger (as shown in Figure 32.21), you can increase the scale of the Sun layer to 200 percent.

12. **Preview the motion.** Choose the Composition ⇨ Preview ⇨ Motion with Trails command, the Composition ⇨ Preview ⇨ Wireframe Preview command, or the Composition ⇨ Preview ⇨ RAM Preview command.

FIGURE 32.21

The motion sketch appears in the Composition panel. It is created with the Motion Sketch panel.

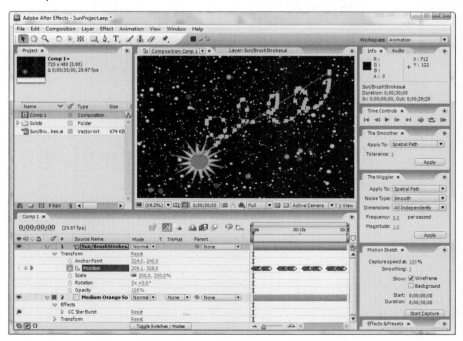

---

13. **Choose File ⇨ Import ⇨ File to import a file to use as the background, or create a background in After Effects.** To create a background in After Effects for your project, as shown in Figure 32.22, choose Layer ⇨ New ⇨ Solid. In the Solid dialog box, click the color swatch to pick a color. This example uses a peach color. Click OK to have the solid-colored background appear as a layer in the Timeline panel. Apply an effect from the Effect menu. The example in Figure 32.22 applies the Effect ⇨ Simulation ⇨ CC Star Burst command.

14. **Choose File ⇨ Save to save your work in After Effects format.** Choose File ⇨ Export to export your After Effects project in a movie format.

FIGURE 32.22

In After Effects, you can create interesting backgrounds by applying an effect to a solid-colored layer.

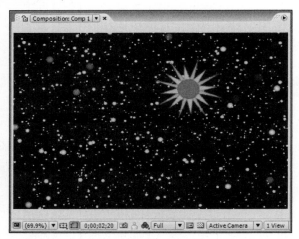

Creating a Composite Video Clip

You can use After Effects to create a *composite video clip*. A composite video clip consists of a few video clips displayed side-by-side on the screen at the same time, as shown in Figure 32.23. To create the Talking Parrots project shown in Figure 32.23, you can place two video clips diagonally across from each other and then add some text next to the two clips. If your project requires it, you can have three or four video clips. The video clips that you use to create a composite clip can be Premiere Pro projects, video captured from your digital camcorder, or even stock video clips.

Follow these steps to create a composite video clip in After Effects:

1. **Choose File ⇨ New ⇨ New Project.**

2. **Choose Composition ➪ New Composition.** The Composition Settings dialog box appears.

3. **In the Composition Settings dialog box, name your composition.** Select the correct frame size for your project's width and height.

4. **Click OK to create the new composition.**

5. **Choose File ➪ Import ➪ Multiple Files.** The Import Multiple Files dialog box appears.

6. **In the Import Multiple Files dialog box, set the Import As option to Footage.**

7. **Select the video clips, and then click Open.** If you want, you can use the clips shown in Figure 32.23 (BlueParrotPlaying.avi and WhiteParrot.avi), which are found in the MoreClips folder on the DVD that accompanies this book. When you have finished importing files, click Done.

8. **Drag the video clips you imported from the Project panel to the Composite panel.**

9. **To scale a video clip in the Timeline panel, click the video clip and display the Transform options.** Click and drag the Scale value to the desired amount. The video clips in Figure 32.23 are scaled to 45 percent.

FIGURE 32.23

The Talking Parrots project is an example of a composite video clip.

10. **If you want your composite to appear as it does in Figure 32.23, place the video clips so that they are diagonally across from each other.** You can also place two clips side-by-side or on top of each other on the left side of the Composition panel, and place text to the right of the video clips. You can also fill the Composite panel video clips and have no text.

11. **If you want your composite to include text, as shown in Figure 32.23, first select the Horizontal Type tool.** Then click the Composition panel, and type some text. Using the Horizontal Type tool in the Composition panel creates a new Text layer. Another way to create a new Text layer is to choose Layer ➪ New ➪ Text, and then use the Type tool to type some text in the new Text layer.

12. **Use the Character panel to change the text size and select a font.**

13. **To add a drop shadow to your text, choose Effect ➪ Perspective ➪ Drop Shadow.**

 In Figure 32.23, there are two Text layers. You can copy the first Text layer in order to make the second Text layer.

14. **To bevel video clips, first select one of the video clips in the Timeline panel.** Then choose Effect ➪ Perspective ➪ Bevel Edges. You may also want to adjust the colors of the video clips; to do so, use the Color Correction effects. This example uses the Levels effect.

15. **To create the background that appears behind the text, as shown in Figure 32.23, you first need to create another solid layer.** Choose Layer ➪ New ➪ Solid. In the Solid Footage Settings dialog box, click the Eyedropper tool and pick a color from one of the video clips. This example chooses red. This is the color that appears in the solid. Leave the other settings as they are. If you want, you can name the solid. Click OK to create the new solid. When the new solid appears in the Timeline panel, it appears in front of the text you just created.

16. **To rearrange the layers in the Timeline panel so that the text appears on top, click and drag the layers up or down.** Figure 32.23 shows the layers in the Timeline panel.

17. **If you want to create a special effect for the background, use one of the commands found in the Effect menu.** This example uses the Effect ➪ Simulate ➪ CC Bubbles command, and the Effect ➪ Simulate ➪ CC Rain command.

18. **To preview your work in RAM, choose Composition ➪ Preview ➪ RAM Preview.**

19. **Choose File ➪ Save to save your work.**

TIP You can save a frame of your After Effects project as a Photoshop file, either with or without layers. Choose Composition ➪ Save Frame As ➪ Photoshop Layers, or Composition ➪ Save Frame As ➪ File.

20. **To export your work as a Premiere Pro project, choose File ➪ Export ➪ Adobe Premiere Pro Project.** In the dialog box that appears, name your file and then click Save. The After Effects file that you save in Adobe Premiere Pro Project format can be opened in Premiere Pro for further editing.

Exporting Movies

To export your movie in a different format, choose Composition ⇨ Make Movie. In the Render Queue panel, click the triangle next to the composition that is being rendered. Next, click Lossless, which is next to the Output Module option. In the Output Module Settings dialog box, click the Format drop-down menu and choose a format. Available format options include Animated GIF, BMP Sequence, Cineon Sequence, ElectricImage IMAGE, FLC/FLI, Filmstrip, IFF Sequence, JPEG Sequence, MP3, MPEG2, MPEG-2DVD, OMF, OpenEXR Sequence, PCX Sequence, PICT Sequence, PNG Sequence, Photoshop Sequence, Pixar Sequence, QuickTime Movie, Radiance Sequence, Real Media, SGI Sequence, TIFF Sequence, TARGA Sequence, Video for Windows, WAV, and Windows Media.

21. **To export your work as a QuickTime movie, choose File ⇨ Export ⇨ QuickTime Movie.** When the Movie Settings dialog box appears, click the Video Settings button to set the compression, color depth, and frames per second. Click the Filter button if you want to apply a filter to your clip. Beware of changing the Size button. You should either leave the size as is, or make it smaller rather than larger. Making your movie size larger causes the clip to become pixilated and blurry.

    You can also adjust sound settings and choose whether you want to stream for the Web. Make the necessary adjustments, and click OK. When the Save As dialog box appears, name your movie and click Save to create a QuickTime movie. After you create a QuickTime movie, you can import it into a Premiere Pro project for further editing.

Summary

Although Adobe Premiere Pro features many video effects, Adobe After Effects provides more motion and compositing effects. This chapter covered these topics:

- You can import a Premiere Pro movie directly into After Effects.
- You can export an After Effects project as an Adobe Premiere Pro project.
- You can animate text on a curve in After Effects.
- You can animate in 3-D space using X, Y, and Z coordinates in After Effects.
- You can open multiple QuickTime movies in After Effects.

Part VII

Appendixes

Appendix A

What's on the DVD

This appendix provides you with information on the contents of the DVD that accompanies this book.

System Requirements

Make sure that your computer meets Adobe Premiere Pro's minimum system requirements listed in this section. If your computer doesn't match up to most of these requirements, you may have a problem using the contents of the DVD.

Windows XP with Service Pack 2 or Windows Vista

- A PC with any of the following:
  - Intel(r) Pentium(r) 4 (2 GHz processor for DV; 3.4 GHz processor for HDV)
  - Intel Centrino(r), Intel Xeon(r) (dual 2.8 GHz processors for HD)
  - Intel Core(tm) Duo (or compatible) processor
  - SSE2-enabled processor required for AMD systems
- 1GB of RAM for DV
- 2GB of RAM for HDV and HD
- 10GB of available hard drive space (additional free space required during installation)

- 1280 x 1024 monitor resolution with a 32-bit video card
- Dedicated 7200 RPM hard drive for DV and HDV
- Striped disk array storage (RAID 0) for HD
- Microsoft DirectX or ASIO compatible sound card
- QuickTime 7 is required to load the QuickTime tutorial files.

Macintosh with Mac OS X v.10.4.9

- Multicore Intel(r) processor
- 1GB of RAM for DV; 2GB of RAM for HDV and HD
- 10GB of available hard drive space (additional free space required during installation)
- Dedicated 7200 RPM hard drive for DV and HDV editing
- Striped disk array storage (RAID 0) for HD
- 1280 x 960 monitor resolution with a 32-bit video card
- Core Audio compatible sound card
- DVD-ROM drive

Using the DVD

To copy the items from the DVD to your hard drive, insert the DVD into your computer's DVD drive. Copy the files that you wish to use by dragging them into a folder on your computer.

What's on the DVD

The following sections provide a summary of materials that you'll find on the DVD.

Tutorial files

The Tutorial Files folder consist of still images, video, and sound clips for following along with the exercises in this book. The still images are in Photoshop, Illustrator, JPEG, TIFF, and PICT file formats. The digital video clips are in AVI or QuickTime file format. Many of the video files used are from Artbeats and FilmDisc, who are providers of royalty-free moving images. The sound files are in WAV format and are from SmartSound, who are providers of royalty-free sound clips. For more information on the royalty-free files, go to www.Artbeats.com, www.Filmdisc.com, and www.Smartsound.com.

The tutorial files are divided into four folders: Artbeats, FilmDisc, SmartSound, and MoreClips. The MoreClips folder contains several completed projects as well as these additional folders: After Effects, America, Illustrator, Photoshop, Premiere, and Video and Sound. Please note that the tutorial files are for instructional purposes only. They are not for commercial use.

PDF files

Each chapter in this book has been converted to a PDF file. You can load the files onto your computer and search for specific topics as you work with Premiere Pro. You need to install a copy of Adobe's Acrobat Reader (also included on this DVD) to view these files.

Troubleshooting

If you have difficulty installing or using any of the materials on the companion DVD, try the following solutions:

- **Turn off any antivirus software that you may have running.** Installers sometimes mimic virus activity and can make your computer incorrectly believe that it is being infected by a virus. (Be sure to turn the antivirus software back on afterward.)
- **Close all running programs.** The more programs you run, the less memory is available to other programs. Installers also typically update files and programs; if you keep other programs running, installation may not work properly.
- **Reference the ReadMe file.** Please refer to the ReadMe file located at the root of the DVD for the latest product information at the time of publication.

If you still have trouble with the DVD, please call the Customer Care phone number: (800) 762-2974. Outside the United States, call (317) 572-3994. You can also contact Customer Service by e-mail at `http://support.wiley.com`. Wiley Publishing, Inc., provides technical support only for installation and other general quality control items; for technical support on the applications themselves, consult the program's vendor or author.

Appendix B

Places to Visit on the Web

You can use the following list of Web resources as a guide to digital video software and hardware manufacturers and distributors. Also included are a variety of resources that should prove valuable to digital video producers.

IN THIS APPENDIX

Software

General resources

Hardware

Stock image, sound, and video clips

Software

www.apple.com

This site offers access to Apple's QuickTime site, as well as useful information about MPEG-4 (www.apple.com/mpeg4).

www.abobe.com

You can check Adobe's site for Premiere upgrades and technical support. The site includes Premiere tutorials, as well as samples from professionals in the digital video field. Be sure to sign up for an e-mail newsletter that provides updates and important Premiere technical information.

www.discreet.com

Find out more about Autodesk Cleaner XL, as well as other programs for editing and creating special effects and animation. To access these products, click on the Media & Entertainment link in the Products menu.

www.mainconcept.com

Produces MPEG encoders and MPEG decoders, DV filters, and CODEC.

www.microsoft.com/windows/windowsmedia

Get updates on the latest Microsoft Windows Media and streaming video products.

www.apple.com/quicktime

Download the latest version of QuickTime or upgrade to QuickTime Pro. The site includes developer and licensing information, as well as links to many sites using QuickTime.

www.realnetworks.com

Find out about RealNetworks audio and video streaming products, and download the latest plug-ins.

www.sorensonmedia.com

Sorenson creates compression software for QuickTime and Flash. You can find out about Sorenson Squeeze and other products at this site.

General Resources

www.adobe.com/support/forums

Here you can find a users-group forum for Adobe products. You can ask questions or scroll through other users' questions and answers.

www.aftra.com

This is the Web site for the American Federation of Television and Radio Artists. Here you can find out about using union talent, find contacts, and catch up on industry news.

www.digitalvideomag.co.uk

This site provides access to Digital Video Magazine and provides news, reviews, and articles on digital video.

www.computeramerica.com

Computer America is a syndicated talk show on computers and technology.

www.creativecow.com

This site provides a forum and news for digital media professionals. This site also includes a Premiere Pro forum.

www.computervideo.net

This site provides news and reviews on computer video editing.

http://forums.digitalmedianet.com

DMN Forums has forums for various products, including Adobe Premiere Pro. On this site, you can also find newsletters that contain information about digital media.

www.dmw.com.au

Digital Media World provides news and information on video, digital imaging, and design.

http://digitalproducer.digitalmedianet.com

This site provides news and tutorials on video editing, special effects, and digital imaging.

www.dv.com

This is the digital video Web magazine, an excellent source of hardware and software information, as well as technical articles. It features news, tutorials, and a buyer's guide. The site enables you to search back issues for product information and technical articles.

www.dvpa.com

This is the Web site for the Digital Video Producers Association. Membership gives you access to thousands of stock clips that are available online for instant download.

www.emedialive.com

This Web site provides news about DVD production and digital video.

www.studiodaily.com/filmandvideo

This site provides news and reviews on film and video technology.

www.ieee.org

This is the Web site for the Institute of Electrical and Electronics Engineers. It contains information on products and services for engineers.

www.pcmag.com

PC Magazine provides news and reviews on PC systems.

www.videomaker.com

On Videomaker magazine's site, you can find articles on video as well as online workshops.

Hardware

www.adstech.com

Check out this site for information on the ADS Pyro video card. Here you can purchase products and download drivers.

www.apple.com

Virtually all new Macs include FireWire ports for transferring digital video directly to desktop or laptop. Purchase a Mac here or find out the latest from Apple's technical support library.

www.aja.com

At this site, you can find information about the Xena PCI card for HD production.

www.boxxtech.com

Boxx makes workstations for HD editing and other graphics-intensive applications.

www.canon.com

At this site, you can find out about Canon DV camcorders, printers, and other products.

www.dell.com

Several Dell computers include digital video cards. Purchase a computer or video board for your computer.

www.hp.com

Find out more about Hewlett-Packard's products, such as desktops, workstations, monitors, projectors, and printers.

www.epson.com

Learn more about Epson's color printers.

www.harman-multimedia.com

Learn more about powered satellite speakers and subwoofers for your computer.

www.jvc.com

Details about JVC professional and consumer video equipment are available at this site.

www.logitech.com

Learn more about Logitech's speakers, Web cameras, mice, trackballs, and other peripherals.

www.matrox.com

Matrox is the creator of video boards and video capture boards (Millennium, Marvel, and so on). Obtain specifications and compatibility information here.

www.nikon.com

At this site, you can find out about Nikon digital cameras and other products.

www.olympus.com

At this site, you can learn more about Olympus's digital cameras.

www.panasonic.com

At this site, you can find out about Panasonic's digital cameras and DVD players.

www.pinnaclesys.com

Find out about technical specifications for Pinnacle's PC video boards, editing systems, and broadcast-quality equipment.

www.shure.com

This site includes information on Shure's audio products, as well as downloadable technical guides.

www.sony.com

Most Sony laptops include i.LINK digital video ports that conform to the IEEE 1394 standard. Find out about the latest Sony computers, monitors, digital camcorders, and professional video equipment.

Stock Image, Sound, and Video Clips

www.artbeats.com

Many of the video clips on the Adobe Premiere Pro CS3 DVD are from Artbeats. Screenshots of these clips appear in different chapters. You can learn more about Artbeats products at this site.

www.filmdisc.com

Many clips on the Adobe Premiere Pro CS3 DVD are from FilmDisc; screenshots of these clips appear in different chapters. You can learn more about FilmDisc products at this site.

www.smartsound.com

Many of the sound clips in this book are from SmartSound. Visit this site to learn more about stock sound clips.

www.gettyimages.com

You can learn more about Getty's video and sound clip products at this site.

Appendix C

The Digital Video Recording Studio

Setting up a small studio to create desktop digital video movies often involves the purchase of a computer, as well as video and sound equipment. For digital video producers, editors, and graphic designers without a technical background, evaluating hardware can be a frustrating and confusing task.

This appendix provides an overview of some of the hardware that you may consider purchasing. The following sections are meant to provide you with a general understanding of the hardware components that you may need to purchase or rent when shooting a video production. For a more thorough analysis of digital video hardware, you can refer to several resources, including Web sites of hardware manufacturers (including www.sel.sony.com, www.canon.com, or www.dell.com), magazine Web sites (www.DV.com), or publishers of books that specialize in DV and file production (www.focalpress.com). Another good resource is your local library. Many video books written over the past 20 years include video shooting, sound, and lighting chapters that are still relevant today. Finally, you may want to investigate television production workshops and classes provided by local colleges and universities.

System Requirements

For most Premiere Pro users, the most important element in their digital studio is their computer. The general rule for running Premiere Pro is to get the fastest system you can afford. Digital video typically consumes 13GB per hour of footage, and so you want a fast system with a lot of storage capacity.

If you're in the market for a video system, you can start by checking preconfigured systems that are designed for video editing. Both Dell and Sony manufacture systems that are configured for video work. For high-definition production, you may want to investigate a Boxx workstation. Boxx (www.boxxtech.com) sells workstations designed for both high-end video and 3-D graphics.

These are the minimum system requirements for Premiere Pro CS3.

Windows XP with Service Pack 2 or Windows Vista

- A PC with any of the following:
  - Intel(r) Pentium(r) 4 (2 GHz processor for DV; 3.4 GHz processor for HDV)
  - Intel Centrino(r), Intel Xeon(r) (dual 2.8 GHz processors for HD)
  - Intel Core(tm) Duo (or compatible) processor
  - SSE2-enabled processor required for AMD systems
- 1GB of RAM for DV
- 2GB of RAM for HDV and HD
- 10GB of available hard drive space (additional free space required during installation)
- 1280 x 1024 monitor resolution with a 32-bit video card
- Dedicated 7200 RPM hard drive for DV and HDV
- Striped disk array storage (RAID 0) for HD
- OHCI compatible IEEE 1394 port for DV and HDV capturing, exporting to tape and to DV devices
- Microsoft DirectX or ASIO compatible sound card
- QuickTime 7 is required to load the QuickTime files.
- DVD-ROM; DVD+R for burning DVD's

Macintosh with Mac OS X v.10.4.9

- Multicore Intel(r) processor
- 1GB of RAM for DV; 2GB of RAM for HDV and HD
- 10GB of available hard drive space (additional free space required during installation)
- Dedicated 7200 RPM hard drive for DV and HDV editing
- Striped disk array storage (RAID 0) for HD
- 1280 x 960 monitor resolution with a 32-bit video card
- Core Audio compatible sound card
- DVD-ROM drive; SuperDrive for burning DVDs

Processing speed

A computer system's central processing unit (CPU) and the speed of its hard drive (or disks) determine its overall speed when working with multimedia projects.

Many users consider the computer's CPU to be the brains of the system. Modern processors, such as the Pentium Xeon, are faster and more sophisticated than the Pentium 4 chips. Chip speed is measured in *megahertz* (MHz)—one million clock cycles per second—where a higher number indicates a faster chip. Thus, a 2.8 MHz chip is faster than a 2.0 MHz chip. As this book goes to press, 3-gigahertz (GHz) processors and higher are the state of the art in processors. Both Intel and AMD have introduced dual- and quad-core processors, which place two or four processors on one chip.

Coprocessors

Two CPUs are better than one. Unlike many computer programs, Premiere Pro takes full advantage of computer systems with two or more processors. If you are working with HD footage, dual processors are required. Preview rendering speeds should be dramatically increased with multiple processors.

NOTE In general, a dual-core processor does not offer the same speed as two processors. Dual-core processors have two processing cores on one chip—somewhat like having two processors in one chip. It's not as fast as two processors because the dual-core processors must share hardware. Here's a simple analogy: it's faster to have two cooks working in two kitchens, than two cooks working in one kitchen.

Hard drive speed

Hard drive speed is generally evaluated by the revolutions per minute, seek speed, and data transfer rate of the drive. Most of the faster hard drives provide a rotational speed of at least 7200 RPM (revolutions per minute). Some high-capacity drives have a rotation speed of 10,000 RPM.

Seek speed essentially measures the time it takes to seek out the section of the hard drive that the computer needs to read or write to. Seek time is measured in milliseconds (ms). Thus, a seek time of 8.5 ms is faster than one of 9.5 ms. A hard drive's transfer rate determines how fast the drive can transfer data. A high-capacity UltraSCSI (Small Computer Systems Interface) drive may be able to support a transfer rate of 320MB per second. The actual sustained transfer rate of the hard drive (how long it takes a hard drive to save data to its platters) is slower. To capture video, Adobe recommends a minimum sustained transfer rate of 3MB per second, and preferably of 6MB per second. Note that the actual video transfer rates are probably about one-half the maximum transfer rates of a hard drive.

If you are capturing video, experts also recommend that you maintain a separate hard drive just for video capture, and that you keep the disk defragmented. If you're interested in finding out more about hard drive storage and hard drive storage rates, go to www.storagereview.com.

IEEE 1394 Cards

Most high-end PCs are now sold with built-in IEEE 1394 cards. The IEEE 1394 standard has been pioneered by Apple Inc., which calls the IEEE 1394 standard FireWire (Sony calls it iLINK). IEEE 1394 ports enable you to copy digitized audio and video from a DV camcorder or DV tape recorder directly to your computer. The actual digitization process takes place in the camera. The IEEE 1394 port enables the transfer of data at high speeds from the camcorder to your computer or from your computer to a hard drive. The top transfer rate for the IEEE 1394/FireWire standard is a blistering 400MB per second. FireWire supports up to 63 connected devices and cables up to 14 feet long.

If your computer does not have an IEEE 1394 port, you may be able to purchase an add-in IEEE 1394 card for $50, and sometimes less. The IEEE 1394 port can also be used to attach a hard drive or CD-ROM recorder. Prices of IEEE 1394/FireWire peripherals have dropped steadily.

Companies such as Pinnacle Systems and Miro sell high-end IEEE 1394 boards, which can cost over $1,000. High-end DV cards usually enable you to export files in MPEG-2 format. MPEG-2 is a high-compression video format that provides extremely high quality output. Most MPEG-2 cards enable you to export your files to DVD-ROM format. A further benefit of high-end cards is that most processing chips are built into the cards and, therefore, can create and render digital effects at high speeds.

Xena HD cards

AJA's Xena HS for SD/HD SDI I/O is a PCI card that provides uncompressed audio and video input and output. For more information and to download manuals for Xena HD cards, see www.aja.com.

Video cards

A third-party video card can speed the display of video effects in real time and often improve image quality. While you're taking a break from your video production work, these cards also speed the processing of 3-D games. Newer, faster GPUs (graphics processing units) are PCI-Express cards, which can deliver high-performance graphics to Pentium-based motherboards. PCI-Express cards are faster than older AGP cards that delivered four times the bandwidth of the PCI bus. PCI-Express cards can transfer data at rates of over 4GB per second. (The PCI, or peripheral component interconnect, is a high-performance system that handles the transfer of data from the CPU to expansion slots. It is standard on most computers.) These cards reduce bottlenecks between the computer's CPU and RAM, providing a very high transfer rate of graphics data.

If you're interested in high-end graphics cards, your best bet is to explore the products offered by NVIDIA and ATI, two of the most prominent graphics card manufacturers. See www.ati.amd.com and www.nvidia.com.

RAID arrays

To help attain extremely high transfer rates, many multimedia producers have installed RAID array systems, in which data is shared among several hard drives. RAID (Redundant Array of Independent Disks) systems can split the data transfer over two or more hard disks in a procedure known as *striping*. Striping is a requirement for HD video editing in Premiere Pro. (RAID arrays that provide basic striping are referred to as RAID 0 or RAID Level 0.) Because the computer can read and write from multiple drives, transfer rates are increased. Many RAID systems use UltraSCSI connections (IDE-RAID systems are also available), which provide faster transfer than standard PC ATA connections or standard SCSI connections.

Peripheral Storage Devices

As you work with digitized video and sound, you consume large amounts of storage space. Where do you store clips and sounds that you no longer need to access directly from your hard drive? One of the most common storage solutions is to use a DLT (digital linear tape) or Super DLT drive. DLT drives can store from several gigabytes of data to over 100GB. For example, Quantum's DLT1 stores 40GB at 3MB per second. Quantum's SDLT 220 can store 110GB at a transfer rate of 11MB per second. (If compression is used, it can store approximately twice is much data.) Apart from using DLT drives as backup drives, you can also use them to master DVDs. Quantum, IBM, Hewlett-Packard, and Dell all sell DLT drives.

For long-term storage, but slower recording and loading, you can use a CD/DVD recorder to record directly onto a CD or a DVD. Most high-end computer models include DVD drives that allow you to record to rewritable DVDs, which can store about 4.7GB on a single disc. CDs store about 650MB.

Analog Capture Boards

Analog capture boards accept an analog video signal and digitize video to a computer's hard drive or other storage device. On the PC, most analog boards are add-in boards that must be purchased separately from the computer system. If you are not shooting video using a DV system, you may consider purchasing an analog board. The three formats used by analog boards are *composite video*, *S-video*, and *component* video.

- **Composite video:** Composite video provides fair- to good-quality capture. In this system, the video brightness and color components are combined into one signal. Most composite boards have three cables: one video and two sound cables. Many of the older DV camcorders that are still on the market enable you to place analog tape in them and transfer data using composite signals. Many VHS tape recorders allow input from composite video.

- **S-video:** S-video provides a higher-quality video signal than composite video because luminance and color are separated into two different signals. Most analog boards that provide S-video also allow composite output. S-video is considered better quality than VHS. Most VHS tape recorders allow input from S-video. (Many DV cameras provide an S-video port to enable you to transfer DV footage to VHS tape decks.)

- **Component video:** Component video provides broadcast-quality video. In component video, two channels handle color and one channel handles luminance. Although composite and S-video boards enable connections to camcorder and consumer tape decks, component boards enable a connection to broadcast-quality Beta SP tape decks.

Digital Video Cameras

With the introduction of HDV cameras, the process of choosing a camcorder has become more complicated. As discussed in Chapter 4, HDV cameras output at 1280 x 720 pixels and 1440 x 1080 pixels, storing data in MPEG-2 format. HDV cameras such as Sony's HDR-FX1 can output progressive scanned video, which provides a more film-like look than traditional interlaced video. (See Chapter 3 for a discussion of the differences between progressive and interlaced video.) Like DV cameras, which output at a resolution of 720 x 480 digitized, HDV cameras record to mini-DV tapes. Both formats allow you to capture video using an IEEE 1394 port. At the time of the publication of this book, many video producers are starting the transition from DV to HDV. However, before you take the leap, keep in mind that HDV camcorders are more expensive than DV camcorders, and you need more RAM and a faster processor to edit HDV footage in Premiere Pro.

Better DV camcorders usually create pictures with more pixels. For example, several Canon Elura models feature a ¼-inch CCD (charge coupler device, which is responsible for converting the image into a signal that can be digitized) that provides over 600,000 pixels. However, some cameras — such as the Canon GL-2 and Sony DCR-VX2100 — provide three CCDs with 410,000 pixels (Canon) and 380,000 pixels (Sony) each, which provides a sharper image. High-end camcorders typically feature three CCDS.

You should also consider accessories. Some cameras enable you to change lenses and have more control when changing exposure and shutter speed. If audio is important, you may want to check whether your camera can connect to a wireless microphone or to an audio mixer. Another consideration is whether you want to be able to use mini-DV cassettes or record directly to DVD.

If you're interested in purchasing a DV or HDV camcorder, start by surveying the Web pages of camcorder manufacturers such as Sony, Canon, and JVC. Look at the features that are listed and compare prices. (Canon's Web site currently allows you to download user manuals, which can help you understand the camera's features.) Usually, the higher the cost, the better the camera and the more features you get. You may also want to view Web sites of DV magazines such as eventdv.net or camcorder-specific Web sites such as www.camcorderinfo.com.

Lenses

Most casual users of video equipment simply purchase a camera and use whatever lens is mounted on the camera. If you work with video equipment often, you should learn more about lenses. Virtually all camcorders sold today include zoom lenses. For example, Canon's XL1S, one of the more expensive pro-consumer cameras on the market, features a 16x zoom. The modifier *16x* indicates that the camera can zoom in to make the focal length 16 times greater. This enables you to alter the built-in focal length of the XL1S from 5.5mm to 88mm. (This lens is interchangeable with other lenses.)

The focal length is from the middle of the lens to the point where an image begins to appear, and is usually measured in millimeters. The focal length indicates exactly what image areas can appear in the lens. If the focal length is low, the viewing area is large; if the focal length is large, the viewing area is correspondingly smaller. Thus, if you focus on a subject with a smaller focal length, such as 10mm (a wide-angle lens), you see more of the subject than at 50mm (telephoto). At 10mm, you may see an image of a person from head to toe; at 50mm, you may only see the person's face, in a close-up.

Many cameras provide digital zooms of up to 50×. Although this provides further zooming capabilities, the picture quality usually isn't as good as optical zooming.

When viewing the specs of high-range cameras, you frequently see the f-stop range. The f-stops control the iris opening of the camera. The lower the f-stop, the greater the amount of light that is allowed in. Higher f-stops allow less light in. Canon's XL1S provides a range from 1.6–16. (You can adjust the shutter speed on this camera, as well.) This enables you to set manual exposure and provides greater control over depth-of-field.

Depth-of-field is typically defined as the area from the nearest point in focus to the farthest point in focus. Having sufficient depth-of-field is especially important if a subject you are shooting is moving. You don't want the subject moving in and out of focus. The focal length of the lens, the distance of the subject from the camera, and the f-stop setting all determine depth-of-field.

Microphones

Although most camcorders feature a built-in microphone, you may want to purchase an external microphone to capture better-quality audio. For sophisticated audio recording, you may want to purchase a mixer that enables you to accept multiple sound inputs and to monitor and set recording levels. Behringer, Shure, Sony, and Soundcraft are among the manufacturers of mixers that are designed for live-event recording.

If you are purchasing a microphone, you want to become familiar with several common audio terms. The first one is *frequency response*, which describes the pickup or sensitivity range of sound for the microphone, from low to high sounds. Sound waves are measured in cycles per second (Hz).

The human ear is sensitive to a range from 20 Hz to 16,000 Hz. A microphone frequency response determines the range of sounds it can record. An expensive studio microphone can have a range from 20 Hz to 20,000 Hz.

Microphones are divided into different categories, according to the inner electronics that control the capture of sound. The primary categories are *condenser*, *dynamic*, and *crystal*.

Condenser microphones are generally used as studio microphones. They are usually expensive, but you get what you pay for. They are sensitive and provide a broad frequency response. Electret condensers are a subcategory of condenser microphones, which can be powered with a small battery. They are good for reproduction of narration. Because these microphones are especially sensitive to heat and humidity, you must be careful both when using and storing them.

Dynamic microphones are often used as external microphones for camcorders. They are inexpensive and usually quite durable. Although the sound quality recorded from dynamic microphones is not excellent, it is generally good enough for most DV taping sessions.

Crystal microphones are the least expensive. They do not record a large frequency range and should generally be avoided.

Another basic audio concept to understand about microphones is that they utilize different pick-up patterns. Microphones can be omnidirectional or unidirectional.

- **Omnidirectional:** These microphones pick up sounds from all directions. If you are not recording in a noisy area and want to capture all sounds from the recording site, you probably want to use an omnidirectional microphone.
- **Unidirectional:** These microphones pick up sound primarily from one direction. If you are recording in a noisy room and want to record someone speaking, a unidirectional microphone can help eliminate background sounds.

To further specify how microphones pick up sounds, microphone manufacturers provide polar graphs showing the response of a microphone. A polar graph is plotted over 360 degrees, with the center of the graph depicting the center of the microphone. The round curves depict the area from which the microphone picks up sound. The graph patterns are described as cardioid and bidirectional.

- **Cardioid:** Pick up sounds primarily from the front of the microphone. They eliminate sounds from the back of the microphone and can pick up some sounds from the sides. If you stand in front of the microphone, most cardioids accept a 30-degree angle range.
- **Bidirectional:** Pick up sounds primarily from the front and back of the microphone.

On a more technical level, microphones are considered either high or low *impedance*. Measured in ohms, impedance is an electrical term indicating resistance in the circuit. Most professional (and thus high-quality) audio/video and studio equipment is low impedance. Low-impedance equipment is often called Low-Z. Less expensive equipment is generally high impedance (called Hi-Z).

Generally, short-cabled microphones are Hi-Z, and long-cabled microphones are Low-Z (15 feet or longer).

As you work with audio, you will also see the terms *balanced* and *unbalanced* to describe audio cabling. Short cables with high-impedance equipment using RCA mini-plugs are using unbalanced lines. Most non-broadcast camcorders provide unbalanced lines. Balanced lines feature XLR and cannon plugs (shielded cables), which eliminate buzzing sounds and other electronic noise. Expensive pro-consumer camcorders, such as the Canon l XL1, provide a connection to a CLR plug for hookup to an audio mixer.

TIP You may also want to visit audio equipment manufacturer Shure's Web site, which includes an education section (`www.shure.com/ProAudio/TechLibrary/ EducationalArticles/index.htm`) which includes technical publications such Audio Systems Guide for Video Production.

Lighting

Lighting is one of the crucial factors that determine video quality. If you are shooting indoors, you should investigate lighting equipment and learn the basics of setting up lights. If you're new to video, you may want to take a basic studio production course or read a book on television lighting. (The Focal press offers a variety of books on this subject.)

If you are primarily going to be shooting interior scenes and you want to produce high-quality video, you should investigate purchasing a lighting kit, along with lighting utilities, such as scrims and barn doors, which can limit and control lights.

Although this appendix is not designed to serve as a lighting guide, to properly light a scene, you typically include a key light and a fill light, with a backlight added to provide more depth. The key light is the main source of illumination. Often, the key light is set at a 45-degree angle between the camera and the subject. The fill light, often placed on the opposite side of the camera from the key light, helps to lighten shadow areas produced by the key light.

If you are setting up lights on location, be wary of blowing out a fuse. A typical U.S. consumer circuit is a 15-amp line and does not handle more than 1800 watts (multiply total amps by voltage to obtain the total watts used: $120 \times 15 = 1800$). It's a good idea to add up all of the watts you are using, including any camera equipment, before you start plugging in electrical equipment. Also remember that other electrical equipment may be using the circuit as well.

Index

SYMBOLS AND NUMERICS

M